Jürgen Strohhecker / Andreas Größler (Hrsg.)

Strategisches und operative

GABLER RESEARCH

Jürgen Strohhecker
Andreas Größler (Hrsg.)

Strategisches und operatives Produktionsmanagement

Empirie und Simulation

Mit einem Geleitwort von
Professor em. Jay W. Forrester

GABLER

RESEARCH

Bibliografische Information der Deutschen Nationalbibliothek
Die Deutsche Nationalbibliothek verzeichnet diese Publikation in der Deutschen Nationalbibliografie; detaillierte bibliografische Daten sind im Internet über <http://dnb.d-nb.de> abrufbar.

1. Auflage 2009

Lektorat: Claudia Jeske | Anita Wilke

Gabler ist Teil der Fachverlagsgruppe Springer Science+Business Media.
www.gabler.de

Umschlaggestaltung: KünkelLopka Medienentwicklung, Heidelberg

Printed in Germany

ISBN 978-3-8349-1766-9

Professor Dr. Dr. h.c. Peter Milling

Preface

It is a pleasure to write a preface to this Festschrift devoted to honoring the many accomplishments of Peter Milling. Peter Milling has been a leader among the second generation of those who have been building the field of system dynamics. Milling was introduced to system dynamics by Professor Gert von Kortzfleisch, who arranged to have Milling come to MIT and work on the "Limits to Growth" project for the Club of Rome. Milling was a co-author of the German edition of *Limits to Growth*.

In his early career in system dynamics, Milling was co-author of the capital sector in *Limits to Growth* as described in the accompanying technical book, *Dynamics of Growth in a Finite World*.

Ever since the early 1970s, Milling has been a leader in the extension of system dynamics, especially in the corporate world. He has published papers in both German and English. His papers have examined difficult frontier issues in management with emphasis on pricing strategies, innovation processes, business simulators, industry cycles, rationality in modeling decision making, adaption to external complexity, and organizational change.

In 2001 Milling received the Forrester Award of the System Dynamics Society for the best paper of the prior five years for his 1996 paper in the *System Dynamics Review*, "Modeling innovation processes for decision support and management simulation".

We look forward to many more years of professional contributions from Peter Milling beyond his 65th birthday.

June 18, 2009 — Jay W. Forrester

Vorwort

Die vorliegende Festschrift ehrt Professor Dr. Dr. h.c. Peter Milling zu seinem 65. Geburtstag.

„Strategisches und operatives Produktionsmanagement – Empirie und Simulation" vereint deutsche und internationale Beiträge, die das weite Feld des Produktionsmanagements thematisieren und dabei im Wesentlichen zwei methodische Ansätze verfolgen: statistische Analysen auf Grundlage großzahliger Befragungen von Industrieunternehmen und modellbasierte Untersuchungen auf Basis des System-Dynamics-Ansatzes. Beide Ansätze haben über Jahrzehnte für die Forschung und Lehre am Industrieseminar der Universität Mannheim, dem der Geehrte vorsteht, eine herausragende Rolle gespielt.

Mehrfach war das Industrieseminar deutscher Kooperationspartner internationaler empirischer Untersuchungen im Produktionsbereich, wie beispielsweise in den „High Performance Manufacturing" und „International Manufacturing Strategy Survey" Projekten. Aus diesen Projekten resultierte eine Vielzahl von relevanten Veröffentlichungen, erfolgreichen Konferenzbeiträgen und hervorragenden Diplom- und Doktorarbeiten. Bereits seit Ende der 1960er Jahre wird System Dynamics als modell- und simulationsbasiertes Paradigma am Industrieseminar in Forschung und Lehre angewendet. Die Erfolgsgeschichte ist in diesem Bereich eher noch eindrucksvoller als die der empirisch-statistischen Forschung: Mit einigem Recht kann man das Industrieseminar der Universität Mannheim als das deutsche und ein europäisches Zentrum systemdynamischer Forschung und Lehre bezeichnen.

Die Beiträge in diesem Sammelband sind in drei Hauptteile gegliedert. Der erste Teil („Ganzheitliche Analysen von Produktionssystemen") enthält fünf Beiträge, die Produktionsunternehmen einer systemischen Betrachtung unterziehen und daraus Erkenntnisse für deren Gestaltung und erfolgreiche Positionierung gewinnen. Im umfangreichen zweiten Teil („Konzepte und Elemente des Produktionsmanagements") finden sich acht Beiträge. Im Gegensatz zum einleitenden Abschnitt des Buches werden in diesen spezielle Aspekte des Produktionsmanagements analysiert und diskutiert. Der letzte Teil des Sammelbands („Methodologische Fragestellungen des Produktionsmanagements") enthält drei Beiträge zu eher allgemeinen Fragen wissenschaftlich fundierter Arbeit in Produktionsunternehmen.

Die Qualität der Beiträge wurde durch ein – für Festschriften eher ungewöhnliches – Begutachtungsverfahren erhöht. Dabei haben teilweise externe Gutachter, teilweise die Autoren eingereichte Beiträge anderer Autoren begutachtet. Die Begutachtung erfolgte fast ausschließlich doppelt-blind. Alle Gutachten waren sehr sorgfältig erstellt und teilweise sehr umfangreich; sie haben mit ihrer konstruktiv formulierten Kritik maßgeblich zur Qualitätssicherung beigetragen. Viele Beiträge haben durch die Einarbeitung der Vorschläge an Relevanz und Stringenz gewonnen. Wir danken den folgenden Damen und Herren für ihre Zeit und Mühe, die sie als Gutachter aufgebracht haben (in alphabetischer Reihenfolge): André Grübner, Jürgen Hasenpusch, Jan Jürging, Florian Kapmeier, Hans Kasperidus, David Lane, Frank Maier, Switbert Miczka, Johannes v. Mikulicz-Radecki, Etiënne Rouwette, Markus Salge, Uwe Schwellbach, Birgitte Snabe, Joachim Stumpfe, Jörn-Henrik Thun, Meike Tilebein.

Auch bei der Finanzierung der Festschrift haben wir vielfältige Unterstützung erhalten. Wir bedanken uns bei den folgenden ehemaligen Doktorandinnen und Doktoranden des Industrieseminars, die unserer nach Abschluss des Begutachtungsverfahrens geäußerten Bitte um Spenden gefolgt sind (in alphabetischer Reihenfolge): Martin Drüke, André Grübner, Jürgen Hasenpusch, Jan Jürging, Martin Liehr, Jens Matz, Christoph Moos, Achim Korten, Birgitte Snabe, Joachim Stumpfe, Jörn-Henrik Thun, Kathrin Türk, Sven Weissmann, Stefan Zickgraf.

Als eine besondere Ehre sehen wir es an, dass Professor em. Jay W. Forrester, der Begründer des System-Dynamics-Ansatzes, sich bereit erklärt hat, ein Geleitwort für diese Festschrift zu erstellen. Ihm sei an dieser Stelle hierfür herzlich gedankt. Frau Jeske von der Gabler | GWV Fachverlage GmbH danken wir für die verlegerische Begleitung des Projekts; Herrn Baier von der SatzReproService GmbH, Jena, für das Layout und die Gestaltung. Herrn Christopher Müller schulden wir Dank für seine Unterstützung beim Korrekturlesen und in organisatorischen Belangen. Bei Frau Iris Scheuermann und bei Frau Gisela Wismann bedanken wir uns herzlich für die Organisation der Veranstaltung zur Überreichung dieser Festschrift.

Als Herausgeber danken wir natürlich ganz besonders den Autoren für die eingesandten Beiträge und ihre Bereitschaft, die konstruktive Kritik der Gutachter aufzunehmen und zur Überarbeitung und Verbesserung ihrer Texte einzusetzen. Mit insgesamt 16 Beiträgen bietet die Festschrift aus Anlass des 65. Geburtstags von Prof. Dr. Dr. h.c. Peter Milling einen guten Überblick über aktuelle Forschungsfragen des strategischen und operativen Produktionsmanagements.

Frankfurt am Main und Nijmegen,
im August 2009

Jürgen Strohhecker und Andreas Größler

Inhaltsverzeichnis

Ganzheitliche Analysen von Produktionssystemen

Resource Coordination and Firm Performance: A System Dynamics View*

John Morecroft

London Business School

Abstract

It is commonly and reasonably assumed that when a firm consistently outperforms rivals there is something special about its strategy that is difficult to replicate. Here I suggest that an explanation of superior strategy can be found in seemingly minor differences among the policies firms use to control and coordinate day-to-day operations. These differences can be brought into sharp focus by using system dynamics in combination with the resource-based view of the firm. An example based on a low cost airline shows that hidden coordination problems can suddenly overwhelm a seemingly successful growth strategy.

Keywords: firm performance, dynamics of strategy, resource based view, operating policy, coordination

1 Introduction

In this paper I describe how system dynamics models provide useful insight into the origins of differential firm performance – a topic of central interest in the strategy field. In an edited volume dedicated to the management of industrial systems one might ask how and why competitive strategy fits in. My argument is that competitive advantage (the ability of a firm to outperform rivals) stems from superior coordination of operations and resources, precisely the coordination issues addressed in modelling studies of industrial systems. To illustrate the complementarity of operations and strategy, the paper is organised as a personal journey. I begin with my doctoral dissertation at MIT on manufacturing and supply chain dynamics that led me to more general work on bounded rationality and cross-functional coordination. From here there is a natural bridge to the strategy area, though it took many years to recognise. Specifically, a combination of system dynamics and the resource-based view of the firm RBV can help to explain anomalies in firms' competitive performance over time. For example why do some firms, despite initial success, subsequently falter and even fail spectacularly. The paper provides a practical example based on the well-known rise and fall of People Express in the highly competitive US airline industry of the mid-1980s. The contribution of RBV and system dynamics to understanding the changing fortunes of the firm is discussed and also critiqued.

---

* Sections 2 and 3 of this paper are excerpts from *Strategic Modelling and Business Dynamics* (Morecroft 2007) and are reproduced with the permission of the publisher John Wiley & Sons Ltd.

2 From the Archives: Manufacturing Dynamics and Information Networks

My doctoral thesis topic arose from an on-the-job discovery that circumstance presented. It was1978 and I was working simultaneously on manufacturing models of Cummins Engine Company and Harley-Davidson Motorcycle Company. When I set-out the ten to fifteen page diagrams of these two models side-by-side, I noticed that the information flows which coordinated multi-stage production in the two factories were arranged in different patterns. Every stage of production in Harley, from final assembly of motorcycles to sub-assemblies and raw materials, was coordinated from a master schedule – a kind of top-down control. There was no such master schedule in Cummins' factory at the time. Stages of production followed local order-point rules. It turned out that Harley-Davidson was using a computer-driven top-down material requirements planning system MRP – which was entirely new to manufacturing firms at the time. My work compared the long-term dynamic performance of these alternative approaches to production planning and control (Morecroft 1979 and 1983). A striking result was that traditional order-point rules outperformed MRP (in terms of operating cost, production stability, inventory availability and lead-time predictability). Only under special and hard-to-achieve factory conditions was MRP superior, despite the cost-savings touted by advocates of MRP. And so my curiosity in information networks and firm performance began.

3 Further Ideas: Bounded Rationality and Behavioural Decisionmaking

My thesis showed that sparse and 'simple' information networks in firms can often deliver business performance that is superior to more complex and sophisticated information networks. Over the next decade this observation led me deeply into the literature of the Carnegie School and Herbert Simon's work on bounded rationality. The idea that the 'structure' of a firm's information feedback network determines the firm's performance and dynamic behaviour is central to system dynamics. The Carnegie literature helped to bring the information network into clear focus and to explain why human decisionmakers, faced with complexity and information overload, prefer sparse information networks. People and organisations are boundedly rational. They cannot gather or process all the information needed to make 'best' (objectively rational) decisions. Whenever people take decisions that lead to action, they selectively filter information sources, disregarding or overlooking many signals while paying attention to only a few. Well-designed policies recognise this human trait, while functional 'stovepipes' are an unfortunate corollary that stem from poor design (or no design at all). In practice bounded rationality leads to departmentalised organisations in which the left-hand quite literally doesn't know (and shouldn't need to know) what the right-hand is doing. Loose coordination among functions, departments or sectors is normal.

Bounded rationality helped me to identify, interpret and better understand information feedback loops in business and social systems. Puzzling dynamics nearly always arise from 'hidden' coordination problems.

3.1 Information Available to Decisionmakers and Bounded Rationality

According to the feedback view of management, information drives the corrective actions of organisations as they seek to build and maintain a balanced set of assets (or resources) needed to compete successfully in their industry secctor. But which information sources, among those available, are actually used by managers? Consider the well-known example of a supply chain comprising retailers, wholesalers, distributors and a factory. What information is most relevant to the factory's production planning? Obviously the factory should take account of distributors' orders because the factory supplies the distributors. The factory should also take account of its own inventory and backlog condition. Yet there is much more information available in the supply chain that, theoretically at least, is relevant to production planning. For example there is customer demand and the amount of downstream inventory and backlog at every stage of the supply chain. But compiling and making sense of all this data is a huge task, beyond the abilities of normally competent people, even in today's information society.

In reality things are much simpler. Factory managers normally pay most attention to tangible information that is available locally such as distributors' orders and factory inventory. The more general point is that decision makers typically use much less information than the total available to them. Moreover the available information is less than is commonly presumed. One way to think about this selection process is to picture operating policy surrounded by information filters, as shown in Figure 1. The figure shows five possible filters. The first and most basic filter stems from people's cognitive limitations or bounded rationality (Simon 1979 and 1982). It doesn't take much information for us to feel overwhelmed and so we pick the signals that seem most relevant and ignore the rest. The torrent of e-mail messages is a daily reminder of our information limits.

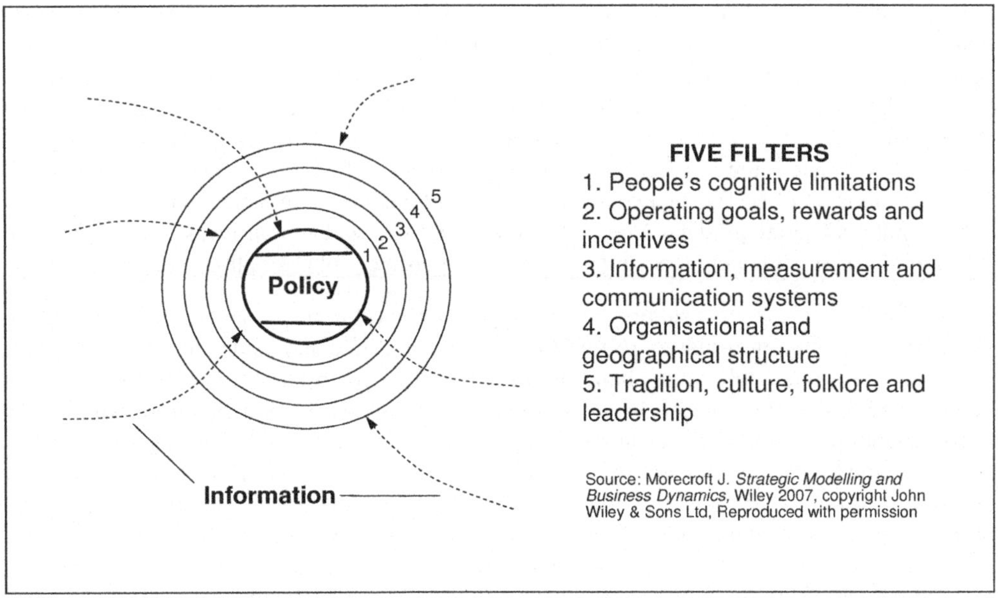

Figure 1: The Policy Function, Information Filters and Bounded Rationality – Behavioural Decisionmaking

The other filters are created by the organisation itself as it parcels out responsibilities across functional areas and departments. In a sense the organisation compensates for individuals' cognitive limitations by placing them in a departmental structure that means they can get on with their own job without worrying about what is happening in every other department. As Simon (1976) and Barnard (1938) originally pointed out, the organisation provides a psychological environment that conditions (sometimes very powerfully) how people act and it is the function of the executive to 'design' this environment so departmental efforts are coordinated. The CEO is a designer with various design tools at his or her disposal (Forrester 1996). Most obvious are operating goals, rewards and incentives (the second filter) that direct people's attention and effort to organisational objectives. Such inducements reduce the complexity of decisionmaking by prescribing what needs to be achieved by different departments. The potential downside is a functional mentality, though this syndrome is not necessarily a problem in a well-designed organisation, it just means people are focussed (and that could be an advantage).

The next filter represents the effect of information, measurement and communication systems on decisionmaking. Undoubtedly computers and the internet have massively boosted the amount of information flowing around and between organisations. Again supply chains are a good example. These days it is possible for factories to hold data on retail orders at point of sale and distributors' inventory for use in production planning. However such data are not necessarily as convenient or trusted as factory shipments and informal demand data gathered from meetings and factory walkabouts.

The fourth filter represents the effect of organisational and geographical structure. Organisations frequently set-up or acquire a new business unit at arms length from the existing business. A good example is the fledgling low-cost airline Go set-up by BA in the 1990s to compete with easyJet and Ryanair in the European short-haul business. Go was deliberately made independent of BA, operating its own planes with its own staff and information systems. The whole point was to design an enterprise that could decide and act in its own right, free from the influence of parent BA. The amount of information flowing between the two organisations was much less than if they were seamlessly merged in a single airline. Another example is the MINI car division of BMW, created as in independent business unit, able to take its own decisions (under corporate guidance) on product development and capital investment in order to develop a new and distinct brand in the highly competitive global small-car market.

The fifth filter is the most subtle and also the most powerful. It captures the attenuating and amplifying effect on information of tradition, culture, folklore and leadership. From a cognitive view these intangible traits shape the psychological environment in which people take decisions and act. They define what the organisation stands for and therefore what really needs attention. Consider for example Google and its co-founders Larry Page and Sergey Brin. Commentators say they are intellectually obsessed with an omniscient and omnipotent algorithm for mining the world's knowledge. This belief is now part of Google's culture, permeating the minds of thousands of employees and helping to coordinate their actions. Another example is MIT with its culture of technological excellence that pervades all departments including the humanities and management, shaping decisions on faculty recruitment, the curriculum and choice of students.

3.2 Nature of Decision Making and the Decision Process

An important conclusion is that the feedback view of organisations incorporates behavioural decisionmaking and assumes bounded rationality (Morecroft 1983, Sterman 1989). This perspective on decisionmaking distinguishes system dynamics sharply from traditional micro-economics in which 'economic man' makes objectively rational decisions, weighing-up all available sources of information to arrive at an optimal (profit maximising) configuration of resources.

Figure 2 captures the essential philosophical stance to decisionmaking in system dynamics. Any operating policy sits amid its filters, bombarded by information originating from all asset stocks in the system. But only a handful of information flows penetrate to the policy core leading to action and stock accumulation.

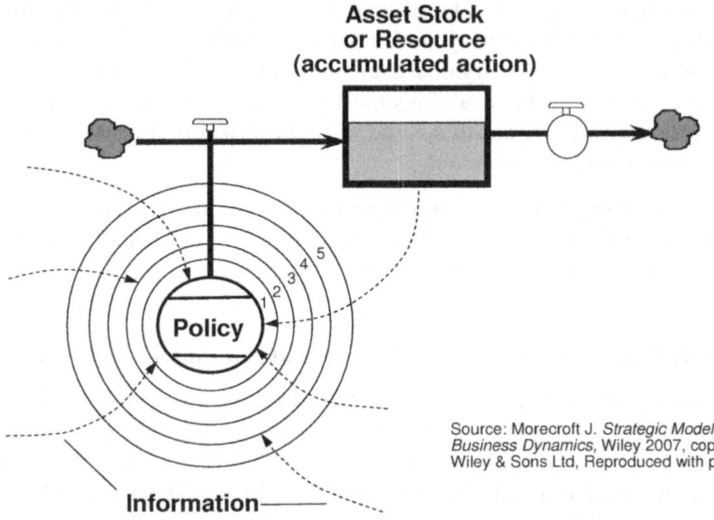

Source: Morecroft J. *Strategic Modelling and Business Dynamics*, Wiley 2007, copyright John Wiley & Sons Ltd, Reproduced with permission

Figure 2: Behavioural Decision Making Leading to Stock Accumulation & Feedback

A corollary is that decisionmaking is conceived as a continuous process for converting varying information flows into signals that determine action (rates of flow). In system dynamics a decision function does not portray a choice among alternatives, as found in a decision tree with its various discrete nodes and branches. Neither is it the familiar logic of 'if-then-else' that applies to individual decisions like whether to take a taxi or catch the bus. The crucial point is that we are viewing decision processes from a distance where discrete choices disappear leaving only broad organisational pressures that shape action.

Notions of rationality and sensemaking continue to be debated and developed in the field. Rationality was the theme of the first European System Dynamics Workshop held in 2003 at Mannheim University and reported in *Systems Research and Behavioral Science* (Lane, Grossler and Milling 2004).

4 Contemporary Research: The Links between Strategy and System Dynamics

In recent years strategy researchers have become increasingly interested in the *dynamic* processes that give rise to performance differences among competing firms. Indeed the editors of a recent special issue in *Management Science* note that "the challenge of fully incorporating dynamics into how we think about strategy is a major one, perhaps the biggest one that the field faces going forward" (Ghemawat and Cassiman 2007).

System dynamics is well positioned to make important contributions to behavioural theories of strategy dynamics. Firms and industries are highly dynamic, complex systems managed by boundedly-rational actors. What better way to understand firms and firm performance than with a 'theory of structure' capturing generic causal relationships and decision making processes that drive the dynamic behaviour of firms and industries over time? Indeed a good example is Peter Milling's paper describing a generic model of innovation management that won the 2001 Jay Wright Forrester Award of the System Dynamics Society (Milling 1996). The modular model of the innovation process reflects the tight relationships between the actions of an innovating firm and competitors' response. The resulting simulator explains how the dynamics of a product life cycle are generated and demonstrates the impact on firm performance of policies for pricing, capacity expansion and quality control.

Here I argue that a combination of system dynamics and contemporary ideas from the strategy field (particularly the resource-based view of the firm RBV) can help to clarify why some firms outperform rivals and why others inadvertently underperform.

4.1 The People Express Case – A Vivid Example of Puzzling Firm Performance

I adopt a well-known business case – the rise and fall of People Express – to demonstrate the complementary use of RBV and system dynamics for understanding firm performance. So my topic, theory building in strategy, is approached in a pragmatic and inductive way by examining, and then reflecting on, the intention and outcome of real-world strategy. The situation is described in a vivid Harvard Business School case study about the airline (Holland and Beer 1990; Whitestone 1983) and further developed in an accompanying business simulator (Sterman 1988). The case and simulator have been widely used in business schools around the world to introduce 'students' of management to the scope, ambition and intellectual challenge of the strategy field. It is one of the few examples of work at the intersection of strategy and system dynamics that is well known in both fields, though it is known primarily as a pedagogical example. In real life People Express grew from obscurity to industry prominence in a period of only five years against powerful rivals. Dramatic growth was followed by equally dramatic demise.

The latent inevitability of the unfolding tragedy has proven attractive to study. In *The Fifth Discipline*, Senge (1990) outlines a feedback 'story' of what happened at People Express that builds on the growth and underinvestment archetype, a kind of performance syndrome that stems from functional interdependencies in a growing business (chapter 8, pages 130–135). At the heart of the story is underinvestment in service capacity as shown in Figure 3. Service capacity, in terms of experienced staff, failed to keep pace with the growth of flights and

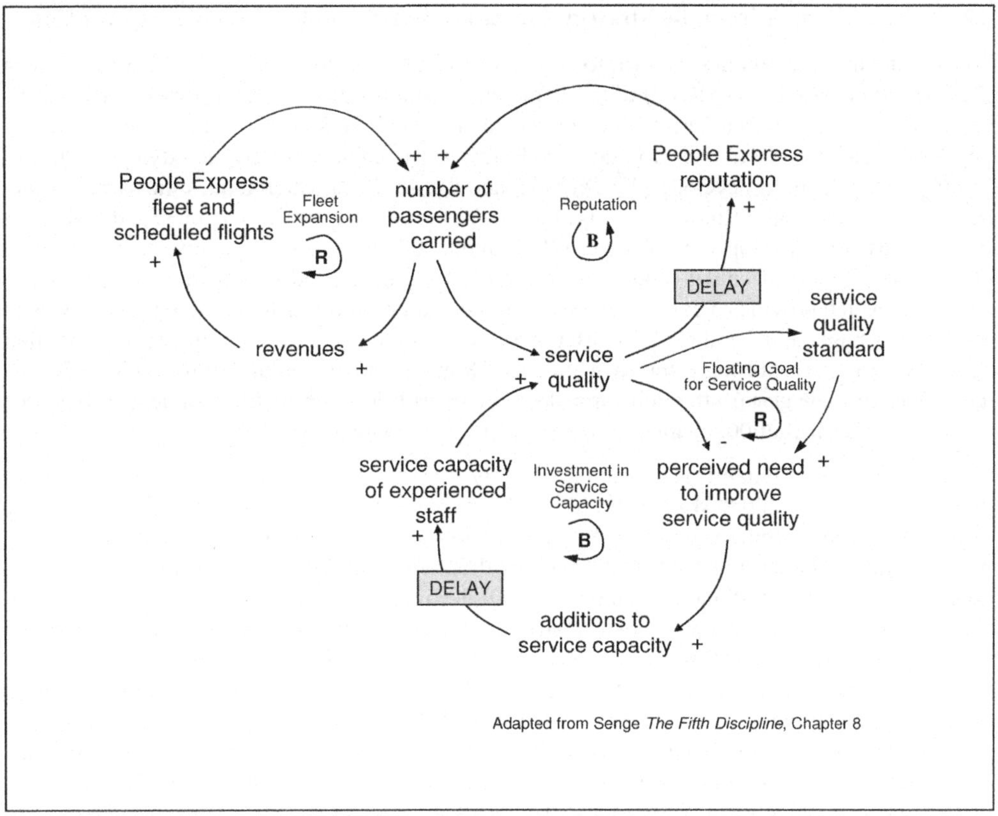

Figure 3: Feedback Loops in Senge's Story of the Rise and Fall of People Express Airlines

passengers and so, ultimately, the service reputation of the business was destroyed. At first glance this argument seems compelling. But it fails to explain why, in real life, a company could have made such a fundamental strategic error without realizing it.

A fundamental proposition (and partial explanation) is that underinvestment in staff was very difficult for managers at People Express to discern at the time the company's spectacular growth was taking place. According to Senge, investment in service capacity was driven by a 'perceived need to improve service quality'. This criterion for investment sounds plausible yet it led to an organization that was chronically short of staff. But why? Senge hints at two reasons (each informed by feedback systems thinking and the chosen archetype): 1. experienced staff (controlled by a balancing loop) did not keep pace with the growth of the fleet (controlled by a powerful reinforcing loop); and 2. implicitly this imbalance was masked by tremendous growth in headcount which did not fully translate into corresponding growth in service capacity. Nevertheless one is left wondering why the company persisted in its aggressive fleet expansion and why in its hiring policy the company did not appreciate that headcount and service capacity are fundamentally different.

4.2 Using Ideas from the Strategy Literature to Interpret the People Express Case

To examine these anomalies we turn to two sets of ideas from the strategy literature.[1] The first is the resource based view (RBV) of the firm which explains differences in firms' performance and competitive position in terms of endowments of critical productive assets or resources (Barney 1991; Foss, Knudsen, and Montgomery 1995). In particular we draw on a dynamic view of resource accumulation developed by Dierickx and Cool (1989) which makes the same distinction between stocks and flows (or levels and rates) as found in system dynamics, and which has been extensively developed in Warren (2002 and 2008) and in doctoral theses by Mollona (1999), Gary (2000), Mandal (2003) and Kunc (2005). The second idea is the notion of dominant logic which provides a cognitive/behavioural explanation for different managerial styles of resource management (Prahalad and Bettis 1986). Senior managers' dominant logic is their belief system or overall logic for firm success. Dominant logic captures information filtering and selective managerial attention typical of real-world decision-making subject to bounded rationality (Sterman 2000, chapter 13; Morecroft 2007, chapter 7).

The first step in a dynamic resource-based study is to classify resources into tangible or intangible (Warren 2002, 2008; Morecroft 2002). The second step is to distinguish resources that are overtly managed or unmanaged. For People Express the relevant information is in the case and it is a matter of modelling judgment which of the many listed resources to include. Obvious tangibles are planes, staff and passengers. Intangibles include service reputation and staff motivation. The classification into overtly managed and unmanaged resources is quite subtle yet vital because it is often drifting and unmonitored resources (invisible at the operating level, and usually intangible) that are the undoing of an otherwise successful strategy of resource accumulation. Figure 4 provides some clues of what to look for in making this managed-unmanaged classification. For a typical managed resource there is usually a clear desired condition or goal. The apparent condition of the resource is readily measurable. As a result the gap that drives corrective action is objective and the managerial feedback control process is purposive and goal-directed. A simple and familiar example would be a production policy that manages factory inventory to a strict goal. If all resources in a firm were managed with such ideal clarity (and if all underlying goals were not only clear but also internally consistent) then an effective resource strategy should emerge. However, in many cases key resources are inadequately managed, or not managed at all. There are many small hints and clues to isolating unmanaged resources in practical situations. Often the resources are intangible or soft, so that it is difficult to discern the apparent resource condition. The desired condition or goal may itself not be clear or appropriate. The resource in development may be invisible. In the case of People Express unmanaged resources include potential passengers, service reputation and staff motivation.

A rough classification of resources in steps 1 and 2 leads to a study of dominant logic in step 3 and a sketch of feedback loops in step 4. This phase of modelling work (spanning conceptual aspects of formulation) reveals the managerial rationale for the firm's continuing resource accumulation strategy. Let's start with the tangible resources at People Express. What is the dominant logic of fleet expansion? Such strategic investment could be governed by funding, market

[1] This interpretation of the People Express Case is an excerpt from my article 'Resource Management Under Dynamic Complexity' (Morecroft 2002). Here I use the example to review the synthesis of strategy concepts and system dynamics and then to critically examine what new insights arise from such a synthesis that are not available from system dynamics alone.

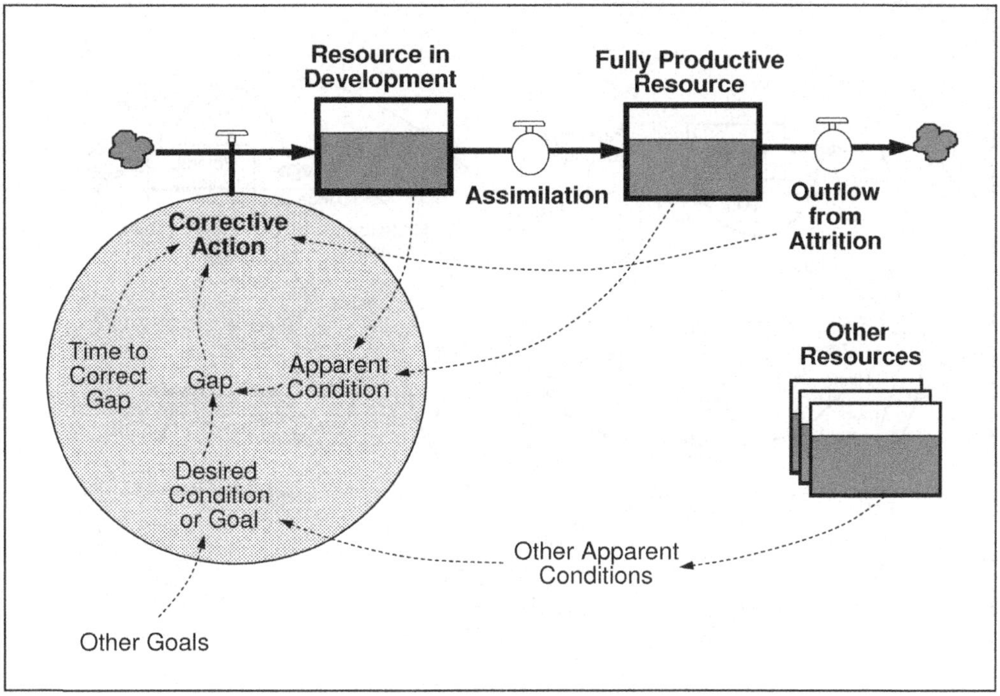

Figure 4: Operating Policy for Resource Management

share goals, return criteria, demand forecasts, or staffing constraints. The dominant logic at People Express however appears to be (reading between the lines of the case and video) CEO Don Burr's ambitious personal growth target, stemming from his vision of industry revolution embodied in the precepts of the company. Clearly such logic is both powerful and persistent. The imposition of Burr's dominant logic leads to reinforcing feedback (R1 in Figure 5, see p. 12) in the resource stock of planes; growth is desirable.

The dominant logic of staff expansion is quite different. From the case one gathers the impression of a Human Resource VP insistent on high-quality recruits, carefully selected by the top management team and trained on the job. The imposition of this dominant logic leads to reinforcing feedback in which the resource stock of experienced staff is the principal determinant of hiring and acts as a constraint on the growth rate (R2 in Figure 5).

The dominant logic of passenger growth is also noteworthy at People Express. Customers are a vital resource stock for all companies. Some companies explicitly manage customers by setting sales targets, tracking customers in databases, and implementing marketing programs to eliminate any gaps relative to goal. Other companies do not actively manage the customer base, but instead allow it to evolve from advertising, word-of-mouth and churn. People Express seems to have adopted an ambitious but essentially unmanaged approach to growth of customers. Deep price discounts coupled with targeted advertising unleashed a powerful word-of mouth effect that caused a very rapid build-up of potential passengers (those fliers willing to try People

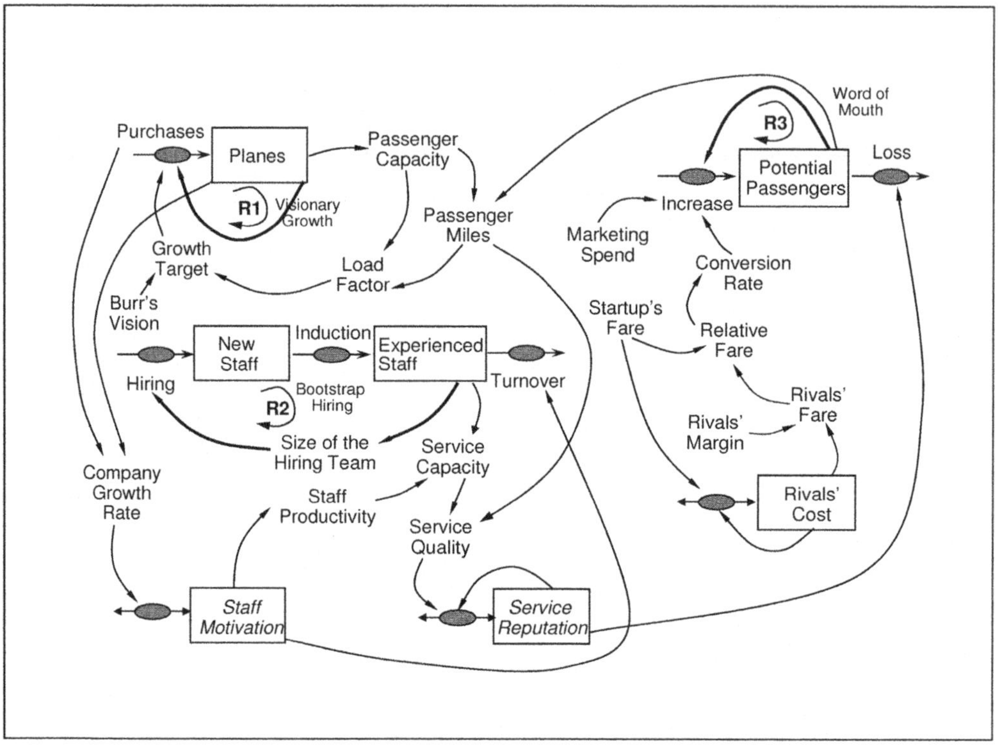

Figure 5: Resources (Asset Stocks) and Feedback Loops in People Express

Express should the opportunity arise). The imposition of this dominant logic embodies reinforcing feedback characteristic of word-of-mouth (R3 in Figure 5).

The resulting tangible resource system contains three reinforcing feedback loops (R1, R2 and R3), each a compelling engine of growth, but each operating independently to produce autonomous expansion of planes, staff and passengers. Partial model simulations in step 5 reveal the power of these growth engines to underpin the kind of spectacular growth achieved by People Express in reality. A summary of the steps in a resource-based investigation is shown in Figure 6.

Step 6 of a dynamic resource-based analysis involves simulation of the full model to investigate the behaviour of the intangibles (service reputation and staff motivation) that explain the demise of People Express and more importantly the invisibility of the company's mounting resource problems. From the case it appears that neither service reputation nor staff motivation is overtly managed. This observation is no surprise when one considers that almost all the requirements for active resource management (in Figure 4) are absent. Operating goals are not clearly defined and the apparent condition of the resource stocks is unknown. It is difficult to read the minds of customers and measure service reputation, or register the emotions of staff to discern motivation. So reputation and motivation just evolve from operating conditions. Motivation responds to a range of dynamic factors such as company growth rate, share price and

1.	Identify, classify and sketch *key* tangible and intangible resources
2.	Distinguish managed from unmanaged resources
3.	Study dominant logic of operating policies
4.	Sketch feedback loops for tangible resources
5.	Run partial model simulations to investigate the behaviour of tangible resources in isolation (under the dominant logic)
6.	Simulate the full model to investigate the behaviour of intangibles and to explain puzzling firm performance over time
....	All steps embedded within an iterative process of model building, simulation and analysis

Figure 6: Summary of the Steps in a Dynamic Resource-Based Investigation

profitability (for visual simplicity only company growth rate is shown in Figure 5). Motivation influences staff productivity which, in combination with experienced staff, determine service capacity.[2] Reputation responds with a time lag to the balance of passenger miles and service capacity.

When the three reinforcing feedback loops driving growth in the firm's tangible resources differ in strength (and it would only be an accident if the gain of all three were identical, since their dominant logic is so different), then problems begin to accumulate in the intangibles. No management action is taken to fix these problems because: 1. the unmanaged intangibles provide only weak signals to the rest of the organization of latent growth stresses; and 2. the powerful dominant logic governing tangibles is insensitive to such weak signals. Indeed the case and video suggest that, according to Don Burr, any problems with employee motivation or customer service reputation were best remedied through further growth.

A full model simulation of People Express' growth strategy reveals the mounting strategic problem. As Figure 7 (see p. 14) shows, service reputation declines steadily for six years between 1980 and 1986 when the airline was growing rapidly. The apparent recovery of reputation in the last two years results from an unintended abundance of staff as disillusioned passengers switch to competing airlines. Motivation, though invisible and beyond direct management, remains both steady and high for the first six years, underpinning People's competitive cost advantage.

But as the customer base saturates and then collapses (as shown in the trajectories for potential passengers and passengers in Figure 8, see p. 15), the excitement and profit-lure of a fast-growth enterprise evaporates. Employees are demoralized. Planes fly half-empty, as reflected in the load factor. The company dies with a configuration of resources both tangible and intangi-

[2] Strictly speaking service capacity depends on experienced and new staff as well as staff productivity. For visual simplicity the link from new staff to service capacity is omitted in Figure 5.

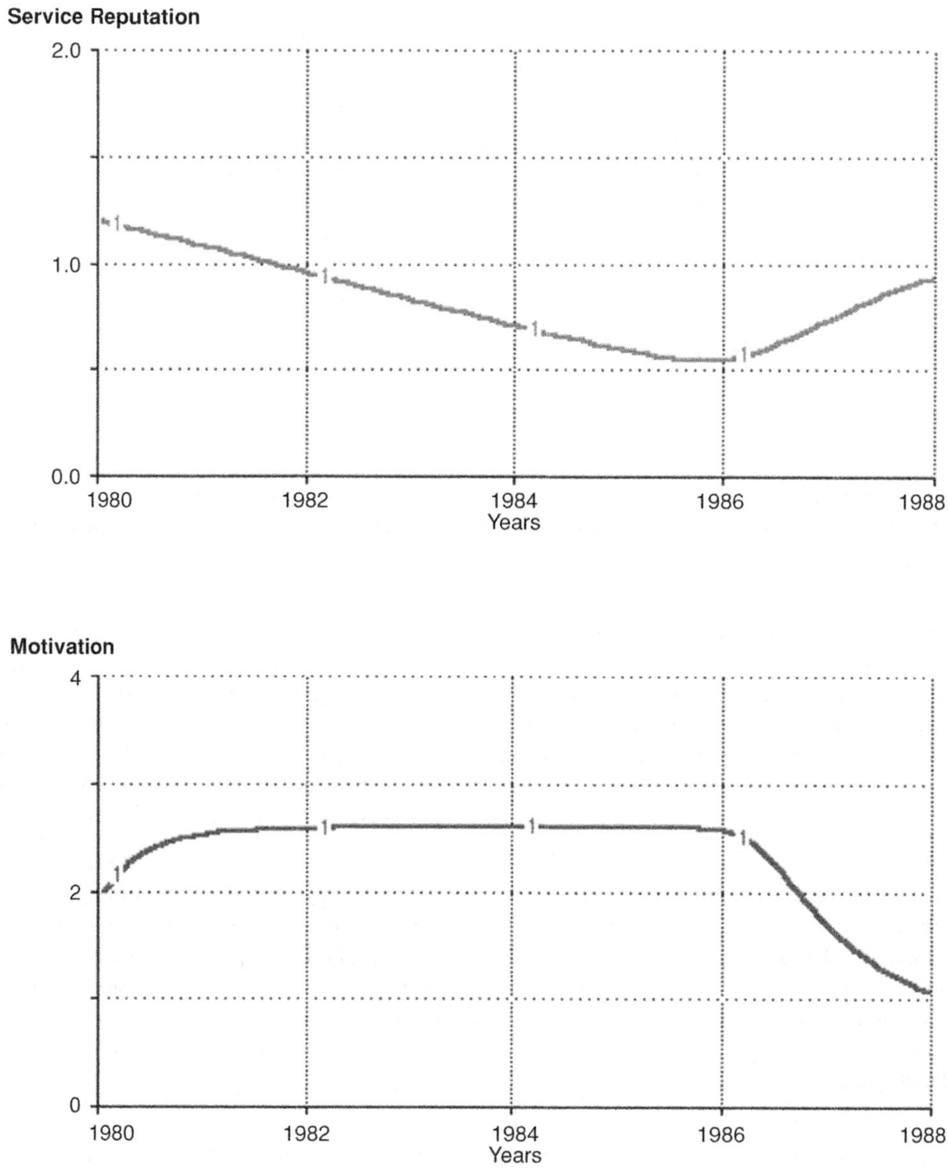

Figure 7: Time Charts for Service Reputation and Staff Motivation

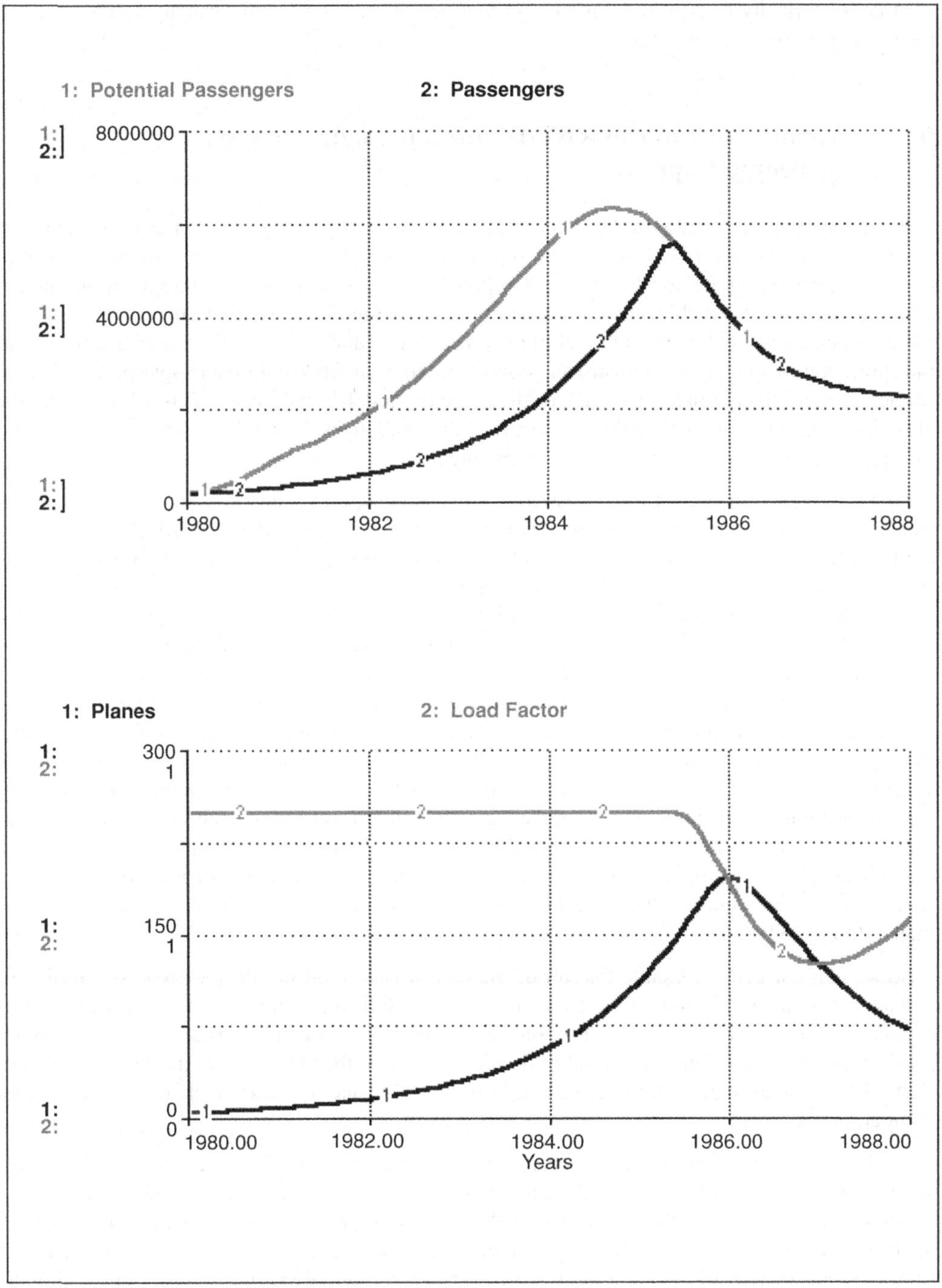

Figure 8: The Rise and Fall of People Express

ble that is markedly inferior to its major competitors. There is no commercially viable route of recovery from this resource trap.

5 What's New in the RBV-Dominant Logic Analysis of People Express?

Scholars and experts in system dynamics may argue there is nothing new in the above analysis of People Express and its failure to sustain growth. Indeed the principal and original contribution to understanding the unfolding drama at People Express came from system dynamics alone and one might therefore think that any later claim of insight is an argument in reverse. In other words, since a system dynamics model of the airline's rise and fall came first, then a subsequent interpretation of this boom-and-bust phenomenon from an RBV-dominant logic point of view cannot be more than icing on the cake of the original model-based theory. This criticism merits close investigation as it goes to the very heart of the challenges facing those who conduct cross-discipline research in system dynamics and strategy.

First we review the facts from a system dynamics viewpoint. The People Express simulator was developed by Sterman in the mid-1980s and first used with students at MIT Sloan in September 1988 as a one-day module in a week-long orientation programme for incoming master's students (this history and more information on the case and model are reported in Graham et al 1994). The simulator constitutes a precisely defined theory of the demise of People Express, with a clear dynamic hypothesis instantiated and quantified in the simulation model. The model-based argument goes beyond Senge's brief account of growth and underinvestment to reveal the feedback effects determining the destiny of People Express. For example the company's equity-based compensation scheme was able to sustain employee motivation during the rapid growth phase, as stock price rose sharply, even though employees were overworked and verging on burnout. The model contains a rich feedback theory of growth and underinvestment, constructed entirely from concepts fundamental to system dynamics analysis including stock accumulation, time delays, information feedback and bounded rationality. Many of these dynamical system concepts are as old as the field itself. For a contemporary overview see the special issue of the *System Dynamics Review* celebrating the 50th anniversary of the field (Sterman, editor 2007).

So we can correctly conclude that all of the creative work on the People Express simulator, and the resulting explanation of the company's rise and fall, was completed without the need for concepts from the strategy field. Chronologically the development and first-use of the People Express simulator overlaps the arrival of dominant logic in the strategy literature (Prahalad and Bettis 1986) and even precedes Dierickx and Cool's 1989 paper on asset stock accumulation and competitive advantage.

So why is it helpful to re-interpret this rich model-based theory with concepts from the mainstream strategy literature? Part of the answer is improved communication with strategy colleagues. System dynamics theories of firm behaviour are more accessible to strategy professionals if couched in strategy-specific jargon such as RBV and dominant logic. Indeed Repenning (2003) argues convincingly that a vital part of 'selling' system dynamics to other professionals is to ground the work in the language and literature of the field one is trying to enter. So 'asset stock accumulation' is a phrase that many RBV strategists understand and corresponds *precisely* to system dynamicists' levels and rates. Similarly, dominant logic is easily recognised by academic strategists and is closely connected to notions of policy and information flow in system dynamics. Dominant logic is another way of saying that top management policies (in key activities such as capital investment, recruitment, pricing and so on) are boundedly rational and that the effect of dominant logic is to focus organisational attention and collective effort on feedback information that coincides with deeply-held beliefs and aspirations of those with the power to act.

But there is more on offer from the strategy literature than palatable phrases. Widely-cited and influential concepts borrowed from academic colleagues often illuminate one's own field in unexpected ways. So although asset stock accumulation is nothing more than levels and rates, the *linkage* of asset stock accumulation to the sustainability of competitive advantage (as Dierickx and Cool originally proposed) bridges the gap from firm-level behaviour to industry-level competition and rivalry. The dynamical puzzle of the rise and fall of People Express becomes transformed into the equally enigmatic puzzle of the apparent overnight switch in the company's competitive advantage (sustained for five years in a highly competitive industry) to competitive disadvantage. This rapid change of fortune can be interpreted as an unexpected shift in the balance of tangible and intangible resources that underpin Burr's radical 'business model' for a low-cost airline. Normally it takes a long time for firms to re-configure their asset stocks (which is Dierickx and Cool's main point about sustainability of competitive advantage and the reason why full-service rivals found it difficult to copy People Express). But sometimes, due to dynamic complexity and causal ambiguity in the feedback processes linking asset stocks, a seemingly superior configuration of asset stocks can prove fragile, as the true condition of 'hidden' intangibles becomes fully apparent. Is this interpretation of events just another way to present growth and underinvestment? I think it is much more than that because the new interpretation explains an important dynamic phenomenon – the collapse of competitive advantage. It is the combination of system dynamics *and* RBV that provides this extra explanatory power.

The distinction of tangible and intangible resources deserves close scrutiny too. The idea that stocks are not restricted to tangibles but also include intangibles such as perceptions, reputation, norms and values goes back a long way in system dynamics – at least to Forrester's (1964) corporate growth model and his widely-cited market growth model (where the delivery delay goal is an intangible stock representing a norm in the organization, Forrester 1968). So RBV, with its broad view of strategically important resources, both tangible and intangible, adds nothing new to system dynamics. But arguably the synthesis of RBV and system dynamics has led to greater clarity in the use of tangibles and intangibles, as evidenced by a complete chapter in Warren's (2002) Competitive Strategy Dynamics devoted to 'the power of intangible resources' and his argument (as a system dynamicist) that even soft factors have a hard face (i.e. they can be quantified and dimensionally specified with a degree of rigour that would surprise most strategy practitioners and scholars).

Our analysis of the rise and fall of People Express also made use of a crucial distinction between managed and unmanaged resources. This idea does not arise directly from the RBV or dominant logic literature but is in fact a central part of information feedback control theory. However, it is (once again) the *synthesis* of RBV, dominant logic and system dynamics that lends power to the analysis. RBV says that resource configurations determine firm performance and competitive advantage. Dominant logic reveals the source of firms' overarching goals – what really matters to management and needs to be achieved by the organisation. And then, as the capstone, control theory and system dynamics say that stock accumulations are managed through stock adjustment. Purposive corrective action, based on the gap between desired and actual system condition, adjusts the stock toward its corresponding goal. From this standard feedback representation of purposive action, there follow two important corollaries about controllability. First, if (for a given resource) there is no clearly defined goal (in the minds of the management team, as expressed in their dominant logic) then there can be no meaningful corrective action. Second, if the condition of a stock cannot be adequately measured or monitored, then again there can be no meaningful corrective action.

RBV neatly overlays and complements this feedback view. If, as RBV says, the overall performance of the firm depends on it maintaining a configuration of resources that confers competitive advantage over rivals, then the functioning and coordination of asset stock adjustment processes in the modelled firm are of central interest in a well-informed dynamic analysis of strategy.

From this synthesis, the competitive significance of intangible resources is made clear. Intangibles like motivation are inherently difficult to monitor. As a result they are often unmanaged and can, as in People Express, drift to extreme values that, after a time delay, are perceived by customers (or other stakeholders) to be totally incompatible with the firm's intended strategy (even though many other resources are 'correctly' configured). To say that such resources are unmanaged is simply to say that they are not subject to timely purposive corrective action and are therefore potentially capable of wreaking havoc with an otherwise successful resource building strategy. In People Express, motivation could not be actively managed, particularly on the downside (even though the firm clearly had ways of boosting the upside motivation of its employees through stock options, job rotation and the sheer excitement of rapid growth). Low and unmanaged motivation translated into service degradation which then fed back through the market to undermine the firm's growth and success.

There is one more point to add about managed and unmanaged resources. For those who take stocks and stock adjustment seriously it may seem that this particular distinction is already captured in the concept of 'overt' and 'implicit' decisions, dating back to the origins of system dynamics in chapter 10 of *Industrial Dynamics* and repeated in Forrester (1994). In this classic archival work, overt decisions are described as the 'conscious decisions made by people as part of management and economic processes'. They involve purposive corrective action predicated on selected information about the goals and current state of the business. By contrast implicit decisions are 'the unavoidable result of the state of the system such as present ability to deliver, depending on the present state of inventories'. Under this special lexicon from *Industrial Dynamics*, both managed resources *and* unmanaged resources belong with overt decisions. Managed resources are easy to categorize in this way: they are simply resources controlled by overt decisions through normal asset stock adjustment. Unmanaged resources are trickier to classify, but there is no doubt they belong with overt rather than implicit decisions. Unmanaged resources reside within faulty (non-functioning or even non-existent) overt decisions, where normal asset stock adjustment fails to happen. The example most familiar to system dynamicists is the stock of 'undiscovered rework' found in project management models (Lyneis and Ford 2007). By definition, undiscovered rework cannot be measured. It is an unobservable state variable and therefore cannot be used as the basis for goal-seeking corrective action, even though such feedback control would be highly beneficial in the elusive quest for on-time and on-budget projects.

In conclusion our review of the conceptual apparatus behind the earlier People Express analysis has shown that it is really the synthesis of system dynamics, RBV and dominant logic that offers something new to would-be strategy modellers, and to scholars and practitioners of strategy. An explanation took shape to explain the rise and fall of People Express. This dynamic resource-based theory provides novel traction on the rapid change in the competitive fortunes of People Express – from highly successful five-year growth wonder (with a seemingly sustainable competitive advantage), to burned-out and bought-out corporate carcass in only six months. Arguably this theory-from-synthesised-concepts is no more insightful, dynamically speaking, than the pure system dynamics theory embedded in Sterman's original People Express Management Flight Simulator. But the conceptual vocabulary is richer. The theory is expressed in terms that are understood by colleagues from the strategy field, and addresses their central concerns about the sustainability of competitive advantage without departing from or diluting the core feedback concepts of system dynamics. These synthesised concepts, when brought to life with simulation, can greatly enhance interpretation of the often-puzzling dynamics of strategy.

Moreover, and this is significant, the 'theory-from-synthesised-concepts' is subtly different from the pure system dynamics theory, even in terms of its main explanatory feedback loops. Recall from Figure 3 the dual reinforcing loops and dual balancing loops in Senge's feedback theory of the rise and fall of People Express. Although this picture is much simplified by comparison with the feedback structure of Sterman's simulator it nevertheless captures the archetypal loops of growth and underinvestment (which are widely used in the field). The key growth-inhibiting structure in Senge's analysis is to be found in the two lower loops which portray investment in service capacity and a floating goal for service capacity. As the service quality goal erodes due to fast growth, management pressure for expansion of service capacity gradually relaxes and inadvertently leads to underinvestment A similarly simplified picture (Figure 5) for the RBV/dominant logic model contains three semi-autonomous reinforcing loops controlling the growth rate of planes, staff and passengers. Due to the company's highly selective and time-consuming recruitment policy the natural growth rate of staff is slower than the growth rate of either planes or passengers, leading (covertly) to staff overload and service degradation that also eventually feeds back to undermine growth of passengers. The same problem of underinvestment in staff happens as in Senge's theory, but for entirely different operational reasons. A more detailed presentation of this alternative model and an accompanying simulator can be found in Morecroft 2007 (CD materials for Chapter 6).

In principle it is possible, in a well-grounded single sample account (or field study), to distinguish which of these two feedback structures best fits the real-world business situation. The resulting simulation model can then be used to generate new testable hypotheses about competitive strategy, growth management and policy design. However the original Harvard case alone is not sufficient for this task of theory selection. Both models are broadly consistent with the limited evidence presented in the case, but they are different and were derived independently by experienced system dynamics modellers. Both model-based theories 'explain' growth and collapse in terms of hidden failure to coordinate investment in planes and seat-miles with growth in service capacity. The essential difference between the two feedback theories lies in the assumed degree of mis-coordination among the functional areas of the firm. The SD-RBV-dominant-logic analysis assumes *extreme* lack of coordination between staff and planes, so that declining-and-*unmanaged* service quality halts new passenger growth, accelerates loss of passengers and leads eventually to the company's demise. The alternative interpretation (characterised in Senge's loops) implies that management is collectively conscious of service quality but fails to implement high standards. The result is a gradual drift to low service quality that again halts new passenger growth, accelerates loss of passengers and leads to demise.

6 The Promise and Challenges Raised by the People Express Example

I have sketched a dynamic resource-based view of the rise and fall of People Express combining system dynamics and two influential sets of ideas from the strategy field: 1. resource accumulation as a way of understanding firms' resource endowments and enduring differences in firms' strategy and performance; and 2. dominant logic guiding firm-specific decision-making as a way of understanding resource management and firm performance. System dynamics is a natural way to unite these ideas as illustrated in Warren 2002, 2008 and in Gary 2005. Stocks and flows portray resource accumulation, while information feedback and policies embody dominant logic and decision-making processes. The stock/flow and policy framework provides a versatile means of visualizing firms' resource systems and formal strategic simulation models enable us to reliably analyse the dynamic consequences arising from the underlying resource management policies. However, there is still some way to go in bridging the gap between this dynamic resource-based view and the mainstream RBV strategy literature. A growing body of contemporary research in this important inter-disciplinary area is reviewed in Gary et al (2008), which describes recent accomplishments and identifies future challenges.

References

Barnard C. (1938): *The Functions of the Executive*. Boston, MA: Harvard University Press.

Barney, J. (1991): Firm Resources and Sustained Competitive Advantage. *Journal of Management* 17(1): 99–120.

Dierickx, I., and K. Cool (1989): Asset Stock Accumulation and Sustainability of Competitive Advantage. *Management Science* 35(12): 1504–1511.

Forrester, J. W. (1961): *Industrial Dynamics*. Cambridge, MA: MIT Press (available from Pegasus Communications, Waltham MA).

Forrester, J. W. (1964): Modelling the Dynamic Processes of Corporate Growth, *Proceedings of the IBM Scientific Symposium on Simulation Models and Gaming*, Thomas J. Watson Research Center, Yorktown Heights, NY, December 1964.

Forrester, J. W. (1968): Market Growth as Influenced by Capital Investment. *Industrial Management Review* (now *Sloan Management Review*) 7(1): 5–17.

Forrester, J. W. (1994): Policies, Decisions and Information Sources for Modeling, Chapter 3 in *Modeling for Learning Organizations* (editors Morecroft and Sterman), Portland OR: Productivity Press.

Forrester, J. W. (1996): The CEO as organization designer. *McKinsey Quarterly Anthologies: Business Dynamics – overcoming the limits to growth*, 98–118, McKinsey & Co, New York.

Foss, N. J., C. Knudsen, and C. A. Montgomery (1995): An Exploration of Common Ground: Integrating Evolutionary and Strategic Theories of the Firm. In: Montgomery, C. A. (ed.): *Resource-Based and Evolutionary Theories of the Firm*, Boston: Kluwer.

Gary, M. S. (2000): *The Dynamics of Resource Sharing in Related Diversification*, London Business School PhD Thesis, June 2000.

Gary, M. S. (2005): Implementation Strategy and Performance Outcomes in Related Diversification. *Strategic Management Journal* 26: 643–664.

Gary, M. S., M. Kunc, J. D. W. Morecroft, and S. F. Rockart (2008): System Dynamics and Strategy. *System Dynamics Review* 24: 407–429.

Ghemawat, P., and B. Cassiman (2007): Introduction to the Special Issue on Strategic Dynamics. *Management Science* 53(4): 529.

Graham, A. K., J. D. W. Morecroft, P. M. Senge and J. D. Sterman (1994): Model-Supported Case Studies for Management Education, Chapter 9 in *Modeling for Learning Organizations* (editors Morecroft and Sterman), Portland OR: Productivity Press.

Holland, P., and M. Beer (1990): People Express Airlines: Rise and Decline. *Harvard Business School* No. 9-490-012.

Kunc, M. H. (2005): *Dynamics of Competitive Industries: A Micro-Behavioural Framework*, London Business School PhD Thesis, May 2005.

Lane, D. C., A. Grossler, and P. M. Milling (2004): Rationality in System Dynamics: Modeling Human and Organizational Decisionmaking. *Systems Research and Behavioral Science* 21: 313–317.

Lyneis, J. M., and D. N. Ford (2007): System dynamics applied to project management: a survey, assessment, and future directions for research. *System Dynamics Review* 23(2/3): 157–189.

Mandal, A. (2003): *The Evolution of Competitive Advantage from the Dynamics and Context of Resources*, London Business School PhD Thesis, September 2003.

Milling, P. M. (1996): Modeling innovation processes for decision support and management simulation. *System Dynamics Review* 12(3): 211–234.

Mollona, E. (1999): *Resource Accumulation Systems, Corporate Competence Evolution and Emergent Strategic Behaviour: A Feedback Approach*, London Business School PhD Thesis, January 1999.

Morecroft, J. D. W. (1979): Influences from Information Technology on Industry Cycles, PhD Thesis, Sloan School of Management, Massachusetts Institute of Technology (available as a pdf document on *The MIT System Dynamics Group Literature Collection*, a DVD published in 2003 by the System Dynamics Society, www.systemdynamics.org)

Morecroft, J. D. W. (1983): A Systems Perspective on Material Requirements Planning. *Decision Sciences* 14(1): 1–17.

Morecroft, J. D. W. (1983): System dynamics: portraying bounded rationality. *Omega* 11(2): 131–142.

Morecroft, J. D. W. (2002): Resource Management under Dynamic Complexity, Chapter 2 in *Systems Perspectives on Resources, Capabilities and Management Processes* (editors Morecroft, Sanchez and Heene), Advanced Series in Management, Oxford: Elsevier Pergamon.

Morecroft, J. D. W. (2007): *Strategic Modelling and Business Dynamics*. Chichester: Wiley.

Prahalad, C. K., and R. A. Bettis (1986): The Dominant Logic: a New Linkage Between Diversity and Performance. *Strategic Management Journal* 7: 485–501.

Repenning, N. P. (2003): Selling system dynamics to (other) social scientists. *System Dynamics Review* 19(4): 303.

Senge, P. M. (1990): *The Fifth Discipline: The Art and practice of the learning organization*. New York: Doubleday Currency.

Simon, H. A. (1976): *Administrative Behavior*. New York: Free Press.

Simon, H. A. (1979): Rational decisionmaking in business organizations. *American Economic Review* 69: 493–513.

Simon, H. A. (1982): *Models of Bounded Rationality*. Cambridge MA: MIT Press.

Sterman, J. D. (1988): *People Express Management Flight Simulator (Application program-feedback system simulation game)*. MIT Sloan System Dynamics Group, Cambridge, MA.

Sterman, J. D. (1989): Misperceptions of feedback in dynamic decisionmaking. *Organizational Behavior and Human Decision Processes* 43(3): 301–335.

Sterman, J. D. (2000): *Business Dynamics: Systems Thinking and Modeling for a Complex World*. McGraw-Hill.

Sterman, J. D. (editor) (2007): *System Dynamics Review* 23(2/3), a special issue celebrating the 50th anniversary of the field.

Warren, K. D. (2002): *Competitive Strategy Dynamics*. Chichester: Wiley.

Warren, K. D. (2008): *Strategic Management Dynamics*. Chichester: Wiley.

Whitestone, D. (1983): People Express (A). *Harvard Business School* No. 9-483-183.

Plädoyer für Langfristorientierung

Markus Schwaninger und Kristjan Ambroz

Institut für Betriebswirtschaft
Universität St. Gallen

Zusammenfassung

Das Spannungsfeld zwischen Kurz- und Langfristorientierung verkörpert den Inbegriff der organisationalen Problematik. Vieles deutet darauf hin, dass in den meisten Unternehmungen die Letztere durch die Erstere dominiert wird. Die Konsequenzen einer dominanten Kurzfristorientierung sind im besten Falle negativ, aber die Fälle resultierender Zerstörungen und Katastrophen sind Legion. Wenige tragfähige Lösungen für den Konflikt zwischen Kurz- versus Langfristigkeit sind entwickelt worden und viele betroffene Menschen haben diesen Zwiespalt zu wenig reflektiert oder sie sind sich desselben nicht hinreichend bewusst. Oft sind es auch Sachzwänge die eine Balance von Kurz- und Langfristorientierung behindern. Ziel dieses Beitrags ist es, diesem Dilemma auf den Grund zu gehen und zu Gestaltungsansätzen zu gelangen, mit denen der Konflikt überwunden wird. Auch der kleinste Fortschritt in diese Richtung wäre hilfreich um die Lebensfähigkeit von Organisationen und die Lebensqualität der in ihnen tätigen Menschen zu erhöhen. Dies gilt für private wie für öffentliche Organisationen. Wir betonen den konzeptuellen Aspekt, unterlegen aber die theoretischen Ausführungen mit einem empirischen Ansatz und Simulationsexperimenten.

Schlagwörter: Langfristorientierung, Modell Systemischer Lenkung, System Dynamics, Modellierung, Simulation

1 Einführung

Wann immer ökonomische und finanzwirtschaftliche Krisen eintreffen und wiederkehren, sind harsche Kritiken an der Kurzfristorientierung der Akteure laut vernehmbar. Im gleichen Zug wird eine Orientierung an langfristigen Zielen und Werten beschworen. Beide Argumente sind im Prinzip richtig. Falsch ist hingegen die Annahme, die nächste Krise wäre vermeidbar. Trotzdem sollten wir die Hoffnung nicht aufgeben, in Zukunft die auf „Kurzsichtigkeit" der Akteure zurückgehenden Krisen zumindest zu entschärfen. Derzeit scheint in Organisationen aller Art insgesamt das Kurzfristdenken die Übermacht gegenüber dem Langfristdenken zu haben (Brown, 2007; Mintzberg, 2007; Mizic, 2007; Krugman, 2001; Berger, Dertouzos et al., 1989). Viel davon mag durch emotionale Faktoren, vornehmlich Gier und Angst, bedingt sein (Mitroff, 2005). Ein ungefähr ebenso starker Einflussfaktor dürfte jedoch das Rationale sein – eine unzureichende Kenntnis der konzeptuellen Grundlagen des Langfristdenkens.

In diesem Beitrag wird zuerst die konzeptuelle Basis für das Langfristdenken eingeführt. In der Folge stellen wir anhand eines Falls aus der Praxis das Dilemma zwischen kurz- und langfristig orientierten Entscheidungen dar. Mit Hilfe eines Simulationsmodells wird sodann anschaulich dargestellt, wie Dilemmata dieser Art gemeistert werden können. Unser Beitrag wird durch Schlussfolgerungen und einen Ausblick abgerundet.

2 Kurzfristige versus langfristige Orientierung – ein konzeptuelles Modell

Das menschliche Denken und Handeln wird maßgeblich durch die ihm zugrunde liegenden Modelle beeinflusst, wenn nicht determiniert. Die dominante Kurzfristorientierung in Unternehmungen hängt aller Wahrscheinlichkeit nach eng mit dem dort vorherrschenden Management-Modell zusammen. Es ist das Modell der doppelten Buchhaltung im Verbund mit der betrieblichen Erfolgsrechnung die weitgehend oder exklusiv auf das Gewinnziel gerichtet ist. Solche Modelle sind zwar seit langem bewährt; die doppelte Buchhaltung geht auf Fra Luca Pacioli (1494) zurück. Sie sind aber, wie andernorts gezeigt wurde (Gälweiler, 2005; Schwaninger, 1989), nicht mehr hinreichend für die Unterstützung eines Managements in unserer Zeit. Konnten in Epochen niedrigen Wachstums und geringer Veränderungsgeschwindigkeit wirtschaftliche Einbrüche in einer Unternehmung durch Kurskorrekturen noch relativ gut abgefedert werden, ist die Situation heute im Normalfall prinzipiell anders: In dem Moment, in welchem sich die ökonomischen Schwierigkeiten manifestieren, ist es bereits zu spät, um mit wirtschaftlich vertretbarem Aufwand erfolgreiche Korrekturen durchzuführen.

Managementmodelle sind unzureichend, wenn sie den Aspekt der Vorsteuerung durch diejenigen Größen vernachlässigen, welche letztlich die Profitabilität und schließlich die Liquidität einer Unternehmung ermöglichen oder behindern. Unter dem evolutionären Druck zunehmender Komplexität und Turbulenz ist eine sophistiziertere Sicht bezüglich der Kriterien kompetenten Managements entstanden. Einer konzeptionellen Innovation haben wir zu verdanken, dass heute neue Managementmodelle vorliegen, deren Potential für einen wirksamen Umgang mit Komplexität wesentlich höher ist als dies bei den traditionellen der Fall ist. In diesen neuen Modellen sind die Kriterien kompetenten Managements im Sinne einer umfassenden organisationalen Intelligenz definiert. Der Gewinn ist dort, um ein Beispiel zu geben, ein Ergebnis von Vorbedingungen, die auf höheren logischen Ebenen geschaffen wurden. Er ist damit nicht ein strategisches Ziel.

In diesem Zusammenhang wurde ein Modell Systemischer Lenkung (MSL) entwickelt (Schwaninger, 1989, 2009). Es wird in abgekürzter Form in seiner Ausprägung für Privatunternehmungen in Abbildung 1 dargestellt.

Das MSL bildet Führung als einen Prozess mit mehreren logischen Ebenen ab – operativ, strategisch und normativ. Eine lebensfähige Unternehmung lenkt sich prinzipiell mit Hilfe der Steuerungsgrößen aller drei Ebenen, wenn auch Widersprüche zwischen diesen auftreten (können).

Wie in Abbildung 1 dargestellt, bestehen zwischen den drei Ebenen Beziehungen. Insbesondere üben die Bezugsgrößen der höheren logischen Ebenen eine Vorsteuerung auf die der nachgelagerten Ebenen aus (Gälweiler, 2005). *Vorsteuerung* heißt, dass in früheren Phasen auf einer höheren logischen Ebene Voraussetzungen geschaffen werden, welche weitgehend determinieren, was an Ergebnissen in späteren Phasen und auf nachgelagerten logischen Ebenen erzielt

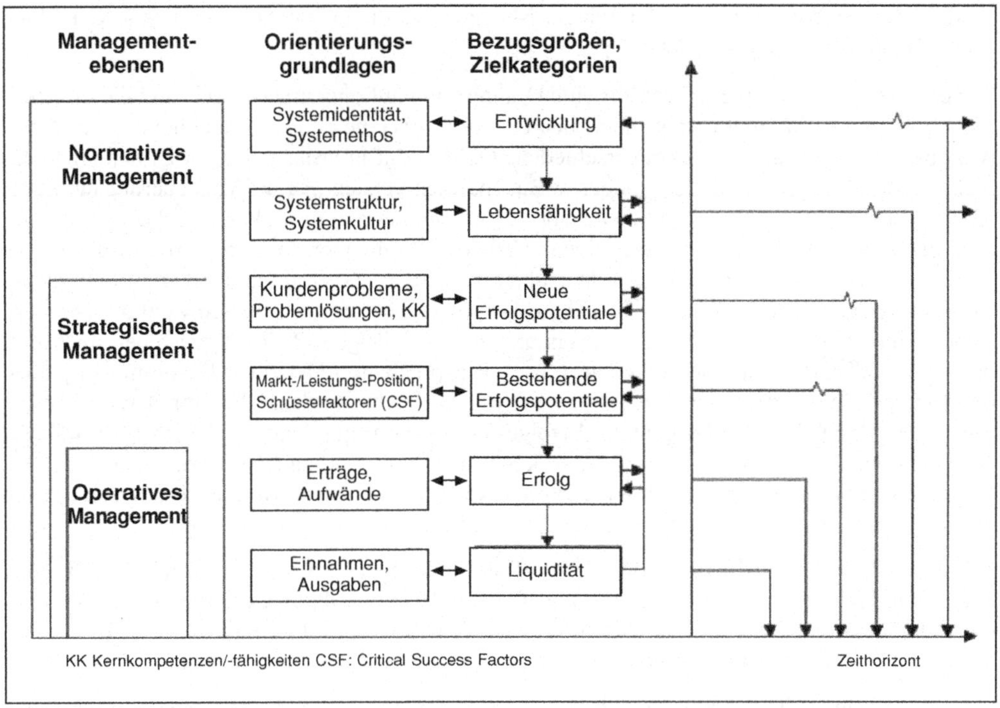

Abbildung 1: Modell Systemischer Lenkung (Version für Privatunternehmungen, leicht gekürzt für didaktische Zwecke; nach Schwaninger 2009)

werden kann[1]. Wenn hier von unterschiedlichen Ebenen der Führung gesprochen wird, sind damit nicht bestimmte Personen oder Organisationseinheiten bezeichnet, sondern drei unterschiedliche Logiken. Jede der drei Ebenen gehorcht einer spezifischen Logik und findet in einer eigenen Sprache ihren Ausdruck. In einer Einpersonenunternehmung muss diese eine Person alle drei Sprachen sprechen und zwischen ihnen unterscheiden können. Ist dies nicht der Fall, ist die Lebensfähigkeit dieser Organisation beeinträchtigt bzw. gefährdet.

Die Aufgaben des Managements sind zwischen den drei logischen Ebenen der Führung wie folgt verteilt:

- Auf *operativer Ebene* geht es um die Schaffung von Nutzen für unterschiedliche Anspruchsgruppen. In Abbildung 1 sind als Beispiel die finanzwirtschaftlichen Größen (insbesondere Erfolg als Determinante des Unternehmenswertes) aufgeführt, welche den Nutzen für die Eigentümer verkörpern. Für andere Stakeholder sind Kundennutzen, sozialer Nutzen und ökologischer Nutzen die einschlägigen Größen.
- Auf *strategischer Ebene* geht es um die Schaffung von Erfolgspotentialen (und im weiteren Sinn Wertpotentialen), welche es ermöglichen, diesen Nutzen zu generieren.

[1] Den Aspekt der Vorsteuerung zwischen operativem und strategischem Management konzeptualisierte als erster Aloys Gälweiler (2005).

- Auf der *normativen Ebene* sind durch das Management die Lebensfähigkeit und Entwicklung der Organisation zu gewährleisten.

Die essentiellen Steuerungsgrößen für eine Organisation auf operativer Ebene sind die Determinanten von Liquidität und Erfolg. Seit Luca Pacioli (1494) die doppelte Buchhaltung einführte, wissen wir, dass es dabei um zwei verschiedene Objekte der Führung geht. Vorher hatte man das nicht gewusst! Für jeden, der die moderne Buchhaltung versteht, ist die Vorsteuerungswirkung, welche der Gewinn auf die Liquidität ausübt, klar. Wenn der Erfolg stark ist, wird dies die Liquidität in der Folge positiv beeinflussen. Dieser Effekt tritt mit einer Zeitverzögerung ein, weil die Zeitkonstanten von Erfolg und Liquidität unterschiedlich sind. Liquidität ist die unmittelbare Konsequenz von Einnahmen und Ausgaben. Der Erfolg hat einen größeren Zeithorizont, weil seine Komponenten – Erträge und Aufwendungen – über längere Perioden entstehen (in Abbildung 1 visualisiert auf der horizontalen Achse). Entsprechend müssen die Bestimmungsgrößen der Liquidität und diejenige des Erfolgs separat verbucht werden. Die Implikation für die Steuerung ist die, dass das Ausmaß des Erfolges ein Frühwarnindikator bezüglich der Liquidität ist. Wenn der Erfolg einmal negativ ist, so kann dies durch vorhandene Reserven oder mittels Krediten kompensiert werden. Mit wiederholten Verlusten jedoch konvergiert das System gegen die Illiquidität, bis der Bankrott unvermeidlich ist. Soweit die operative Ebene.

Darüber hinaus hat sich eine umfassendere Theorie der Steuerungsparameter höherer Ordnung entwickelt. Diese enthüllt wesentlich leistungsfähigere Hebel für die Beeinflussung des Schicksals einer Organisation auf lange Sicht. Die entsprechenden Größen erfüllen eine Vorsteuerfunktion im Verhältnis zu den Steuerungsgrößen der operativen Ebene, welche soeben erläutert wurden.

Vorsteuerung ist die prospektive Schaffung von Voraussetzungen auf höherer logischer Ebene für eine wirksame Lenkung auf nachgelagerten logischen Ebenen des Managements, wie aus Abbildung 1 ersichtlich. Warum erzielen gut geführte Unternehmungen nachhaltige Erfolge auf lange Sicht? Die Antwort ist eine generelle: Unabhängig von einer effizienten Lenkung der Ereignisse von Tag zu Tag verfügen sie über wirksame Lenkungsmechanismen höherer Ordnung, die in einem größeren Zeithorizont operieren.

Auf der strategischen Ebene zielt die Lenkung auf *Erfolgspotentiale* (im weiteren Sinne *Wertpotentiale*), welche dann verfügbar sein müssen, wenn es um die konkrete Wertschöpfung zu Händen von Anspruchsgruppen geht:

- Kundennutzen für die Kunden
- Ein attraktiver Arbeitsplatz und die Honorierung der Mitarbeitenden
- Unternehmenswert für die Eigentümer, etc.

Wesentlich auf der strategischen Ebene ist die Unterscheidung zwischen bestehenden und neuen Erfolgspotentialen. Bestehende Erfolgspotentiale drücken die Erfolgsvoraussetzungen aus, welche sich aus dem Vorhandensein kritischer Erfolgsfaktoren ergeben, z. B. Marktposition, Erfahrung, relative Qualität. In einem noch längeren Zeithorizont allerdings sind diese Faktoren, welche gegenwärtige Stärken ausdrücken, tendenziell nicht ausreichend, um auf Dauer im Geschäft zu bleiben. In einem größeren Zeit- und Sachhorizont geht es deshalb um den Aufbau neuer Erfolgspotentiale, vor allem um die Fähigkeit, Kundenprobleme wirksam zu lösen und neue Problemlösungen (Produkte, Dienstleistungen, Technologien) hervorzubringen. Diese Fähigkeiten sind in von langer Hand aufzubauende Kernkompetenzen eingebettet, die schwer zu fassen sind und möglichst nicht imitierbar sein sollen.

Die Determinanten von Erfolgs- oder Wertpotentialen werden oft als *kritische Erfolgsfaktoren* und *Kernkompetenzen* bezeichnet, mit denen nachhaltige Wettbewerbsvorteile erzielt werden können[2]. Der Gewinn hingegen ist keine strategische Größe. Er ist inhärent kurzfristiger Natur und damit, wie erläutert, der operativen Ebene zuzurechnen. Strategien anhand des Kriteriums *Erfolg* zu entscheiden wäre ein gravierender und gefährlicher Fehler.

Schlussendlich geht es bei der Lenkung auf der Ebene des normativen Managements an erster Stelle um die Stärkung und Erhaltung der *Lebensfähigkeit* der Organisation, das heißt um die Aufrechterhaltung ihrer eigenständigen Existenz und Identität. Es gibt Diagnose- und Gestaltungsmodelle, mit deren Hilfe die Lebensfähigkeit einer Organisation beurteilt werden kann, selbst dann, wenn die Einzelheiten des operativen und des strategischen Bereichs nicht bekannt sind, z. B. das Modell Lebensfähiger Systeme (Beer, 1985). Aber selbst die Fähigkeit zu überleben ist nicht das letzte Ziel einer Organisation. Aus einer systemischen Sicht geht es um eine Lebensfähigkeit, welche das Überleben transzendiert. Deshalb wird in Abbildung 1 *Entwicklung* als eigenständiges höheres Ziel unterschieden. Entwicklung kann eine profunde Transformation implizieren, die so weit gehen kann, dass eine Auflösung der aktuellen Identität und ein Übergang zu einer neuen Identität der Organisation eintritt.

Auf jeder dieser drei logischen Ebenen gilt ein anderes Kriterium organisationaler Fitness oder Intelligenz:

1. Auf operativer Ebene ist es die *Effizienz* mit Aspekten wie Qualität, Produktivität, Profitabilität.
2. Auf strategischer Ebene ist es die *Effektivität*, im Sinne der Wettbewerbs- und Kooperationsfähigkeit.
3. Auf normativer Ebene geht es um die *Legitimität* – die Fähigkeit, die legitimen Ansprüche der Stakeholder zu erfüllen.

Alle drei Kriterien simultan zu erfüllen, ist die Schlüsselaufgabe eines systemischen oder integrativen Managements. In der Tat ist die spezifische Charakteristik derjenigen Organisationen, welche intelligent und wertvoll auf lange Sicht sind, dass sie die drei genannten, interdependenten Kriterien in hohem Maße erfüllen. Sie werden auf eine Art und Weise gelenkt, dass die Lenkungsgrößen aller drei logischen Ebenen simultan unter Kontrolle gehalten werden, trotz der Widersprüche, die zwischen ihnen auftreten. Nur ein solches Modell der mehrstufigen Lenkung kann diese Widersprüche auflösen.

Das konzeptuelle Schema des Modells Systemischer Lenkung ist hilfreich zur Unterstützung des strategischen Diskurses und zur Überwindung von Konflikten im Management. Zudem ist es eine hilfreiche Basis für die Entwicklung von Hilfsmitteln der Entscheidungsunterstützung, wie z. B. Führungskonzepte und Simulationsmodelle.

Im dargestellten Schema nehmen von unten nach oben die Komplexität der Sachverhalte und der Zeithorizont zu. In dieser Abbildung wird der Vorrang der langfristigen Steuerungsgrößen vor den kürzerfristigen ersichtlich. Beispielsweise begünstigen starke Erfolgsvoraussetzungen (strategische Ebene) hohe Erfolge (operative Ebene), wenn sie diese auch nicht garantieren können. Schwache Voraussetzungen für den Erfolg allerdings machen Verluste wahrscheinlich und können sogar dazu führen, dass die Erfolgszone über die Zeit nicht mehr erreichbar ist.

[2] Diese Aspekte sind vor allem in den Beiträgen zur „resource-based view of the firm" ausgearbeitet worden, z. B. Porter 1980, Prahalad & Hamel 1990, Barney 1991, Peteraf 1993.

Dies ist ein zwingendes Argument für eine Langfristorientierung im Management. Wenn der dargestellte Zusammenhang von Führungskräften nicht verstanden wird, sind gravierende Managementfehler kaum vermeidbar. Fast nur das Glück kann in solchen Fällen das Schlimmste von einer Organisation abwenden.

Reicht Langfristorientierung aus für das Gedeihen einer Unternehmung? Wie gesagt, müssen die Steuerungsaufgaben der operativen Ebene gleichermaßen gewährleistet sein.

Diese qualitativen Aussagen haben zweifellos Orientierungswert. Im konkreten Einzelfall kann es aber sehr schwierig sein, auf deren Basis tragfähige Entscheidungen zu treffen. Es sind deshalb Hilfsmittel erforderlich, welche qualitative Erwägungen durch quantitative Beurteilungen stützen. Viele herkömmliche Entscheidungshilfen sind in der Domäne der höheren Managementebenen von geringem Nutzen oder völlig unbrauchbar. Es gilt ja ein solides Verständnis für die dynamische Interaktion der Orientierungsgrößen der unterschiedlichen Ebenen zu gewinnen. Bleiben wir bei der Interaktion der strategischen und der operativen Größen, so sehen wir, dass einfache Spreadsheets oder Optimierungskalküle unzureichend sind. Die Spreadsheets sind nur beschränkt geeignet, Zeitverzögerungen und die sich aus ihnen ergebenden nichtlinearen Verläufe abzubilden. Optimierungen sind entweder statisch oder nur über beschränkte Zeiträume von Nutzen. Geeignet sind hingegen dynamische Simulationsmodelle in denen die Grundstruktur der interagierenden Variablen abgebildet ist und das Verhalten ermittelt wird, welches sich aus deren Interaktion ergibt. In den folgenden Abschnitten wird anhand eines solchen Modells untersucht, ob und wie das Dilemma zwischen kurz- und langfristigen Zielen einer Unternehmung bewältigt werden kann. Zu diesem Zweck soll zunächst der Kontext des Modells geschildert werden.

Es sei bemerkt, dass wir hier von der Ebene des normativen Managements abstrahieren. Auf dieser Ebene geht es um sehr langfristige und sogar zeitlose Sachverhalte. Die entsprechenden Variablen (Ethos, Identität, Vision, Kultur, usw.) sind in hohem Maße qualitativ. Deshalb kommen auf dieser Ebene vornehmlich qualitative Diagnose- und Gestaltungsinstrumente zur Anwendung.

3 Fallstudie

In diesem Kapitel beschreiben wir den praktischen Fall, anhand dessen die Bedeutung der im Vorfeld dargelegten Prinzipien deutlich wird. Gegenstand der Untersuchung ist ein Modellierungsprojekt in einer europäischen Großunternehmung. Um die Anonymität zu wahren, nennen wir sie *Comp*. Wir beginnen mit einer Beschreibung des Unternehmens und der Lage, in der es sich am Anfang des Projektes befand. Danach gehen wir auf die Schlüsselfragen ein, die mit Hilfe des zu entwickelnden Modells beantwortet werden sollten. Das Modell wird später im 4. Kapitel im Einzelnen beschrieben.

Die Fallstudie beleuchtet das Versäumnis, neue Erfolgspotentiale zu entwickeln und seine Folgen für die Unternehmung. Angesichts des langjährigen, kontinuierlichen Wachstums in der gegenständlichen Branche entstand bei den Entscheidungsträgern in der Firma Comp der Eindruck, die souverän beherrschten kritischen Erfolgsfaktoren der Kosteneffizienz und der Marketing-Schlagkraft im Endkundenbereich würden Geschäftswachstum und -erfolg weiterhin und langfristig garantieren. Genau zum Zeitpunkt als bei Comp die größte Sicherheit bezüglich dieser Annahme herrschte, trat eine neue Situation ein: Erstmals wurden Wachstumsgrenzen deutlich sichtbar; die Maxime des ständig wachsenden Marktes brach zusammen. Die zweistellige Marktwachstumsrate sank von einem Jahr zum nächsten auf Null ab, bei markanter Zunahme der Wettbewerbsintensität und drastisch erhöhter Ungewissheit. Der Konkurrenzkampf wurde zum Nullsummenspiel. In einem solchen Umfeld sind substantielle Erfolgspotentiale zwingend nötig für die Selbstbehauptung einer Firma. Allerdings stoßen dabei auch die bestehenden Erfolgspotentiale an Grenzen: Kostenführerschaft ist zwar von Nutzen, aber die Rationalisierungsmöglichkeiten waren im vorliegenden Fall weitgehend erschöpft. Zudem stellte sich heraus, dass auch überlegene Fähigkeiten im Endkundenmarketing zu diesem Zeitpunkt relativ nutzlos waren, weil sie die Wahrscheinlichkeit, dass ein Produkt eines bestimmten Unternehmens gekauft wurde, nicht erhöhten.

Der Fall zeigt einerseits die Unterscheidung zwischen den Ebenen des operativen und strategischen Managements auf, und andererseits zwischen existierenden und neuen Erfolgspotentialen. Die Fokussierung auf bestehende Erfolgspotentiale, die eine hohe Profitabilität in einem wachsenden Markt gewährleistet hatte, erwies sich unter den neuen Marktbedingungen als völlig unzureichend.

Der Fall bezieht sich auf einen Hersteller von Komponenten für Industriegüter, der weltweit zu den fünf führenden Unternehmen auf diesem Gebiet gehört. Diese Komponenten sind sichtbare Bestandteile eines größeren Industriegutes und deren Herstellermarke ist auch klar ersichtlich. Die Komponenten bedienen zwei verschiedene Märkte, nämlich die Industrieguthersteller direkt, für die Erstausrüstung, sowie die Endkunden, die solche Komponenten im Verschleißfall als Ersatzteile verwenden. Je nach Gebrauch ist der Verschleiß unterschiedlich – typisch vergehen zwischen einem und acht Jahren bis zum Ersatz. Im Normalfall wird das Industriegut über seine Lebensdauer hinweg mehrmals mit einem Satz der Komponenten bestückt.

Es gibt nur wenig Möglichkeiten eines „Lock-in" beim Ersatz der Komponenten. Für fast alle der betreffenden Industriegüter gibt es mehrere Komponentenhersteller, deren Produkte fast perfekt substituierbar sind. Dazu können Endverbraucher auch nur selten die Leistungsdifferenz unterschiedlicher Komponenten erkennen. Da die Komponenten aber für den Endverbraucher durch ihre klar gekennzeichneten Markennamen erkennbar sind, hat die ganze Industrie erheblichen Aufwand in das Endverbrauchermarketing investiert, und Marken aufgebaut – ähnlich dem ‚Intel Inside' Prinzip.

Dem Erfolg auf dem Komponentenersatzmarkt gilt in der Branche die höchste Aufmerksamkeit, weil der Ersatzteilmarkt ungefähr zwei Drittel des Gesamtvolumens darstellt, und das Ersatzgeschäft sogar eine noch höhere Quote des Gesamtgewinns einbringt. Im Ersatzgeschäft werden nämlich die Komponenten an die Endverbraucher direkt verkauft. Diese haben im Vergleich zu den Industriegutherstellern, die Komponenten in Stückzahlen von mehreren Millionen einkaufen, eine bedeutend schwächere Verhandlungsposition.

Nun folgt eine detailliertere Beschreibung der Firma Comp, der Probleme, denen sie am Anfang des Projektes gegenüberstand sowie der Ziele des Modellierungsprojektes.

3.1 Untersuchtes Unternehmen

Comp ist seit über einem Jahrhundert ein Lieferant für Industriegüterproduzenten und ist über die Jahre zu einem der größten Anbieter in der Branche herangewachsen. Trotz Diversifizierung im

Lauf der letzten Jahre trägt der ursprüngliche Geschäftszweig der Industriegüterkomponenten noch immer einen bedeutenden Anteil zum Gesamtumsatz und einen Großteil der Gewinne bei.

Im nächsten Unterkapitel stellen wir zuerst die relevanten Produkte dar und erklären die Marktdynamik der letzten Jahre.

3.1.1 Das Produkt

Die beschriebenen Produkte sind essenzielle Komponenten größerer Industriegüter; sie werden hauptsächlich im Endverbrauchermarkt abgesetzt. In einem ersten Schritt werden diese Komponenten an einen Industriegutherstellerverkauft, der sie als Erstausrüstung in seine Produkte einbaut. Die Komponenten werden dann während des Lebenszyklus des Industriegutes in regelmäßigen Zeitabschnitten – je nach Gebrauchsintensität und Einsatzzweck – ersetzt. Die typische Einsatzdauer solcher Komponenten beträgt zirka 15 Monate.

Wenn Ersatzbedarf entsteht, obliegt es dem Endverbraucher, die Komponenten ersetzen zu lassen. Da diese Komponenten als Verschleißteile angesehen werden, besteht keine Art von Garantieleistung, die an die Komponenten gebunden wäre. Sobald der Kunde einen mit der Komponente verbundenen Leistungsabfall bemerkt, oder aber die Komponente nicht mehr den Sicherheitsrichtlinien entspricht, wird ein Ersatz durch befähigtes (gesetzlich autorisiertes) Fachpersonal vorgenommen.[3]

Solche Ersatzaktivitäten werden entweder von einer, dem Industriegutherstellergehörenden autorisierten Wartungsstelle, oder aber von einer unabhängigen Wartungsstelle unternommen. Beide Arten können sowohl Einzelfilialen als auch Kettenbetriebe sein. In beiden Fällen sind die Dimensionen und Leistungsmerkmale der Komponenten vom Industrieguthersteller und der jeweiligen nationalen Gesetzgebung vorgeschrieben. Die Wahl des Endverbrauchers hat zwei Aspekte: welche Marke von Ersatzkomponenten er wählt und von wem er diese Komponenten ersetzen lässt.

Schon lange vermutet die Komponentenindustrie eine Korrelation der zwei Wahlmöglichkeiten, indem manche Ketten von Ersatzstellen ihren Endkunden häufiger Komponenten einer bestimmten Marke empfehlen und diese dadurch beeinflussen würden. Des Weiteren wird vermutet, dass zumindest ein signifikanter Anteil der Endkunden in der Ersatzkomponentenwahl eine klare Markenpräferenz zeigen, was die Wichtigkeit einer Markenwahrnehmung verdeutlicht.

Publizierte Vergleichstests dieser Komponenten weisen auf messbare Leistungsunterschiede zwischen verschiedenen Marken hin, und Marketingkampagnen basieren oft auf solchen Unterschieden. Jedoch werden solche Tests von der Industrie nicht ganz ernst genommen, da dem Endverbraucher (natürlich nicht öffentlich) unterstellt wird, er sei nicht in der Lage, Leistungsunterschiede der unterschiedlichen Produkte in einer bestimmten Preisklasse zu erkennen.

3.1.2 Die Marktlage

Während der letzten 60 Jahre hat sich ein praktisch ununterbrochenes Wachstum im Sektor der Industriegüter, sowie der dazugehörigen Komponenten gezeigt. Dies führte zu einer relativ entspannten Wettbewerbslage, vor allem vor dem Hintergrund, dass die Nachfrage dem Angebot

[3] Die notwendige Ausrüstung, um einen solchen Ersatz durchzuführen, ist wegen der hohen Kosten an spezialisierte Firmen gebunden, d. h. Endkunden sind nur in seltenen Fällen in der Lage, den Ersatz selber durchzuführen.

ständig leicht vorauseilte. Auch als es zu den ersten Nachfrage-Schocks und zu Überkapazitäten im Industriegütersektor kam, führte dies nicht zu einer spürbaren Veränderung im Komponentensektor, weil der Großteil der Nachfrage noch immer aus dem Geschäft mit Ersatzteilen kam, das eine viel geringere Nachfrageelastizität aufwies.

Diese Dynamik hat über lange Zeit dafür gesorgt, dass der Verdrängungswettbewerb in der Komponentenindustrie in Grenzen gehalten wurde. Keiner der etablierten Hersteller hatte die notwendige Kapazität, um andere aus dem Geschäft zu drängen, dazu wies auch keiner die notwendige Zuverlässigkeit auf, um als bevorzugter Partner von einem Industriegüthersteller gewählt zu werden. Zusätzlich war es im Interesse der Industriegüthersteller, mit einer Reihe von Komponentenproduzenten zusammenzuarbeiten, um deren Preise besser unter Druck setzen zu können.

Ein Wachstum im Komponentensektor ist unter solchen Wettbewerbsbedingungen direkt vom Bestandwachstum der Industriegüter abhängig. Um das Wachstumspotenzial der Komponentenbranche zu erhöhen, hat sich die Industrie für ein gemeinsames Lobbying zusammengeschlossen. Ziel war es, gesetzliche Rahmenbedingungen für erweiterte Anwendungen der betreffenden Industriegüter zu schaffen. Zur gleichen Zeit hat die Komponentenindustrie auch eine groß angelegte Aufklärungskampagne für Endkunden gestartet, um das Lobbying auf breiter Basis zu stützen. Beide Initiativen führten dazu, dass die neue Gesetzgebung einen Gebrauch von zwei unterschiedlichen Typen der Komponenten, je nach Anwendung, vorschreibt und dass sich die Endverbraucher im Großen und Ganzen auch daran halten. Im Zuge der geschilderten Initiativen und der Gesetzesänderung änderte sich nämlich auch die Wahrnehmung der Verbraucher, die in der Folge mehrheitlich beide Komponententypen verwendeten.

Die Anzahl der Kunden, die zwei Komponentensätze verwenden, ist insgesamt über die letzten 10 Jahre hinweg – also schon bevor die neue Gesetzgebung in Kraft trat – stark angestiegen. Aufgrund des vermehrten Erstkaufs der zweiten Komponentensätze – sowohl für neue Industriegüter als auch für den bestehenden Bestand – konnte die Komponentenindustrie ein größeres Wachstum verbuchen als der Markt der Industriegüter. Solche Wachstumsraten wurden im Laufe der Zeit von den Herstellern als normal wahrgenommen und flossen in deren Wachstumsvorhersagen ein.

Kurz nachdem das neue Gesetz in Kraft getreten war, fiel der Verkauf der Komponenten rapide ab. Zwar hoffte die Industrie, dieser Rückgang sei nur temporär, jedoch war zum ersten Mal die Einsicht durchgedrungen, dass die bestehenden Geschäftsmodelle von Grund auf untersucht respektive in Frage gestellt werden mussten.

3.2 Probleme zu Beginn des Modellierungsprojektes

Wir wurden ein Jahr nach dem Zusammenbruch des Marktes von Comp beauftragt, ein dynamisches Simulationsmodell zu erstellen. Der Einbruch des Verkaufsvolumens und des dazugehörigen Ertrages galt als ausreichender Grund, um die bestehenden Managementmodelle zu überprüfen und um festzustellen, ob die Simulationen auch in diesem neuen Umfeld eine nützliche Entscheidungshilfe bieten würden.

Die wichtigsten Fragen hierbei waren:

- Wird das langfristige Wachstum dem bisherigen Verlauf folgen, oder könnte es zu einer anhaltenden Stagnation im Markt kommen?

- Kann das Wachstum, sei es für die Gesamtindustrie oder einen spezifischen Hersteller, angekurbelt werden, und wenn ja, wie?
- Welcher Teil des Distributionssystems sollte die größte Unterstützung erhalten, um optimale Resultate zu erzielen?

Im folgenden Abschnitt wird das Modell dargestellt, an Hand dessen diese Fragen bearbeitet wurden.

4 Modellierung

Der Zweck dieses Abschnittes ist es, das Simulationsmodell – ein SD (System Dynamics) – Modell – detailliert zu beschreiben. Die Ergebnisse der Szenarien werden dann im folgenden Abschnitt diskutiert. Das entworfene Modell bildet alle Entscheidungen im Markt von Ersatzkomponenten ab. Um das etablierte Geschäftsmodell in der realen Wirtschaft zu untersuchen, wird ein vollständiges Modell des Geschäftsfeldes von Ersatzkomponenten benötigt. Dieses soll helfen, die Wahrnehmungen verschiedener Entscheidungsträger zu testen und ein einheitliches Bild zu gewinnen, wie das Geschäftsmodell weiterentwickelt und verbessert werden kann.

Der hauptsächliche Datensatz für dieses Modell stammt von einer longitudinalen Verbraucherumfrage (Endverbraucherpanel), die einen Zeitraum von sechs Jahren umfasst. Die Umfrage lieferte über 20.000 Antworten aus Ersatzteilbestellungen sowie zusätzliche Daten von über 5.000 Verbrauchern, die im untersuchten Zeitraum mehr als eine Bestellung getätigt hatten.

Die einzelnen Sektoren des Simulationsmodells werden im Folgenden näher beschrieben.

4.1 Individuelle Modellsektoren

Die Hauptbestandteile des Modells sind eine generelle Bedarfseinschätzung, ein Abschnitt der sich auf die vom Endverbraucher bevorzugten Komponentenmarken bezieht, ein Abschnitt über die Bevorzugung bestimmter Händler durch den Endverbraucher, das Empfehlungsverhalten verschiedener Ersatzteilketten/Händler, und schlussendlich eine Konversionswahrscheinlichkeitsmatrix, welche die Wahrscheinlichkeit eines Produktkaufes in Abhängigkeit von den oben genannten Faktoren aufzeigt. Abbildung 3 (s. S. 36) zeigt in vereinfachter Form den Zusammenhang aller Abschnitte, ausgenommen der gesamten Bedarfsschätzung.

4.1.1 Gesamtbedarfsabschätzung

Der Zweck dieses Modellabschnittes ist es, die zukünftige Größe des Marktes abzuschätzen – besonders um die erste Schlüsselfrage des Unternehmens zu beantworten. Bei einer wenig flexiblen Nachfrage an Ersatzteilen spielt die Quantität der Produkte – weniger der Gesamtumsatz[4] – die entscheidende Rolle.

Historische Daten des Bestands und der Zu- sowie Abflüsse der Industriegüter bildeten die erste Grundlage für die Abschätzung des Basisbedarfs (Gesamtbedarf für Komponenten des

[4] In Zeiten abnehmender Wirtschaftstätigkeit würde sich die Nachfrage hin zu billigeren Marken oder billigeren Produkten einer spezifischen Marke verlagern, anstatt insgesamt abzufallen.

ersten Typs). Der bereits vorhandene Anfangsbestand spielt dabei eine offensichtlich wichtige Rolle – beruht er doch auf einer Berechnung des Ersatzteilbedarfs an besagten Komponenten. Die Flüsse sind von ähnlicher Bedeutung und werden später beschrieben.

Vereinfacht gesagt sollten der gesamte Industriegutbestand und dessen durchschnittliche Abnützung den gesamten Bedarf an Komponenten ergeben. Die Situation wurde in den letzten 15 Jahren komplizierter, als der zweite Komponententyp neu einen großen Teil des „Ersatzteilgeschäftes" ausmachte. Alle Elemente des zweiten Typs werden als Ersatzteilverkäufe bezeichnet, da sie nicht zusammen mit dem eigentlichen Industriegut verkauft werden.

Verkäufe wurden nach Typen getrennt voneinander über den gesamten Zeitraum verfolgt. Jedoch musste eine vorläufige Modellierung vorgenommen werden, um zu ermitteln, welcher Anteil der Komponenten dem ersten Kauf des zweiten Komponententyps zugeordnet werden kann und welcher Anteil auf den Ersatz der verschlissenen Komponenten des zweiten Typs fällt.

Um dies zu ermöglichen, wurde zuerst das Verbrauchsmuster der verschiedenen Endverbrauchergruppen analysiert. Dadurch konnte ermittelt werden, wann die verschiedenen Endverbrauchergruppen den ersten Austauschbedarf anmelden. Wir erreichten dies, indem wir alle Verkäufe des zweiten Typs in drei Kategorien einteilten: den Anteil neuer Industriegüter, für die der zweite Komponententyp erstmals gekauft wurde, den Anteil bereits vorhandener Industriegüter, die mit dem zweiten Komponententyp zum ersten Mal ausgerüstet wurden, um das gesamte Bestandsniveau gemäß der neuen Umrüstquote[5] anzuheben, und schließlich der Ersatzbedarf an Komponenten des zweiten Typs.

Die beiden ersten Teile – welche den ersten Kauf des zweiten Komponententyps umfassen – werden in ein separates Modell des Ersatzmarktes übertragen, um den gesamten zukünftigen Ersatzbedarf zu ermitteln. Das Kalkül erfasste rückwirkend über einen Zeitraum von 10 Jahren und vorausblickend für die nächsten 10 Jahre die Komponenten des zweiten Typs, die bis zu dem Endpunkt 2007 zum ersten Mal gekauft wurden. Die derartig generierten Zahlen wurden dann vom Austauschsektor abgezogen, um den reinen Ersatzbedarf zu ermitteln – derjenigen Endverbraucher, die verschlissene Komponenten des zweiten Typs durch neue ersetzten. Das Wachstum in diesem Markt wurde dann in die Zukunft projiziert.

Die damit erhaltenen Ergebnisse wurden, als Grundlage für die Marktabschätzung, in das Modell eingegeben. In einem späteren Szenario wurden sowohl das Verkaufsvolumen der Industriegüter von der Ausgangslinie[6] als auch der Einfluss des zweiten Komponententyps variiert, um zu erproben, inwiefern die Größe des Komponentenmarktes dadurch beinflusst würde.

Der nächste Abschnitt behandelt die Bekanntheit und Wahrnehmung von verschiedenen Komponentenherstellern.

4.1.2. Wahrnehmung einer Komponentenmarke

Das Markenbewusstsein der Verbraucher und vor allem die Bevorzugung einer bestimmten Marke kann eine entscheidende Rolle für den Marktanteil einer bestimmten Firma spielen. Des-

---

[5] Anteil der Benutzer die beide Arten der Komponenten am Industriegut verwenden.

[6] Die Industrieguthersteller haben ein externes Institut damit beauftragt, Daten zu sammeln und daraus eine Verkaufsprognose des Industriegutverkaufs zu generieren. Diese Verkaufsprognose bezeichnen wir als *Ausgangslinie.*

wegen wurde diese Variable in das Modell eingearbeitet. Die Endverbraucher werden dabei in vier Gruppen eingeteilt: die jeweilige Marke ist unbekannt, diese Marke ist bekannt, Bevorzugung dieser Marke/Markenpräferenz, Bevorzugung einer anderen Marke.

Da jede Bevorzugung die Bekanntheit der Marke voraussetzt, muss eine Marke immer zuerst bekannt sein, bevor eine Bevorzugung dieser oder einer anderen Marke erfolgen kann. Die Flussgrößen gehen dann von Unbekannt zu Bekannt und von dort weiter zur Präferenz, mit einer Möglichkeit des Präferenzwechsels.

Auf dieser Basis lässt sich die Frage beantworten, wie effektiv es ist, einen höheren Bekanntheitsgrad oder Bevorzugung zu erreichen, verglichen mit anderen möglichen Interventionen.

4.1.3 Markenwahrnehmung bei den Vertriebsstellen für Ersatzteile

Dass der Endverbraucher sowohl die Ersatzteilkette als auch die Komponentenherstellerfirma wählt, muss in einer geeigneten Modellstruktur seinen Niederschlag finden. Die dargestellte Struktur unterscheidet zwischen verschiedenen Typen von Ersatzteilhändlern, ob vom Komponentenhersteller kontrolliert oder unabhängig. Zusätzlich wurden „Subscripts" für alle wichtigen Ersatzteilketten, die gemeinsam 95% des Ersatzteilgeschäftes ausmachten, in das Modell integriert[7], die restlichen 5% wurden als eine separate, geblockte Kategorie behandelt.

Endverbraucher wurden den Ersatzteilketten in Abhängigkeit von ihrem letzten Komponentenkauf zugeteilt. Das bedeutet, dass der Komponentenersatzmarkt nach der Größe der Ersatzteilketten gewichtet wurde. Die dazugehörige Formel lautet:

$$N_{(outlet\ brand)} = N_{(overall)} * \textit{Fraction of overall replacement market share}_{(outlet\ brand)},$$

wobei N das Gesamtvolumen des Komponentenersatzmarktes darstellt.

Idealerweise sollte die Modellstruktur erweitert werden, um die Unterteilung zwischen Erstkäufern und wiederkehrenden Kunden zu unterscheiden, aber mangels Daten konnten wir diese zusätzliche Unterscheidung nicht vornehmen. Die Wahrscheinlichkeit, dass ein Kunde zukünftig denselben Händler wieder aufsuchen wird, ist also nicht berücksichtigt.

Nach der Zuteilung der Endverbraucher auf die verfügbaren Ersatzteilhändler muss die Geschäftsbeziehung zwischen Händler und Hersteller des Ersatzteils modelliert werden.

4.1.4 Die Beziehung zwischen Händler und Komponentenhersteller

Die eingangs dargestellten Annahmen sowohl bezüglich des Managements als auch der Händler lassen vermuten, dass die Beziehung zwischen Händlern und Komponentenherstellern eine wichtige Rolle spielt. Um dies zu überprüfen, wurde eine einfache Erstempfehlung der Händler eruiert und modelliert.

Die Komponentenindustrie erstellt eine monatliche ‚Mystery Shopping' Einkaufsstudie, um die Preisgestaltung ähnlicher Produkte verschiedener Ersatzteilhändler zu evaluieren. Gleiches gilt für Empfehlungen, z. B. welche Marke dem Kunden empfohlen wird, der keine spezifische Präferenz äußert. Die Unterhaltung wird aufgezeichnet, wobei monatlich über 100 solcher

[7] Mit anderen Worten wurden die Werte für die unterschiedlichen Ersatzteilketten als Vektoren dargestellt.

Unterhaltungen pro Händler registriert werden. Diese Studie versorgt die Industrie mit einem zuverlässigen Empfehlungsbarometer. Da ein Mitarbeiter im Außendienst einem Endverbraucher bis zu 10 verschiedene Empfehlungen aussprechen kann, stellt sich die erste Frage ob man sich auf die erste Empfehlung beziehen soll oder eher auf das generelle Empfehlungsniveau. Nach vorläufigem Vergleich zwischen erster Empfehlung respektive generellem Empfehlungsniveau[8] mit den aktuellen Verkaufsanteilen von Comp Produkten am Gesamtumsatz des Einzelhändlers wurde eine deutliche Übereinstimmung für beide Arten der Messung mit dem Verkaufsanteil gefunden. Dabei zeigte sich eine bessere Übereinstimmung bei der ersten Empfehlung, wie Abbildung 2 zeigt.

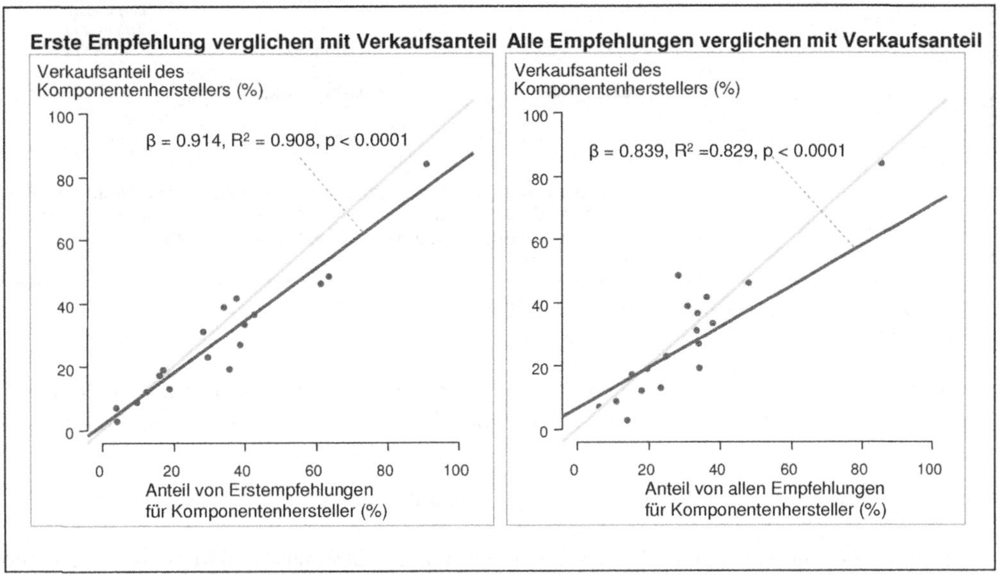

Abbildung 2: Fit des Verkaufsanteils als Funktion erster Empfehlungen (links) und Gesamtempfehlungen (rechts) mit der Regressionsgeraden

Quelle: Klientendaten; eigene Analyse

Um ein ganzheitliches Bild der Branche zu gewinnen, sind weitere Größen erforderlich: Verkaufswahrscheinlichkeit je nach Markenbekanntheit, Präferenz des Kunden und die Empfehlung des Ersatzteilhändlers. Darauf gehen wir im nächsten Abschnitt ein.

4.1.5 Ermittlung der Verkaufswahrscheinlichkeiten

Um das Zusammenspiel der genannten Faktoren zu verstehen und damit das Simulationsmodell zu vervollständigen, wurde ein Baum der Verkaufswahrscheinlichkeiten konstruiert. Das zugrunde liegende Prinzip dabei ist, dass für jede mögliche Kombination von Händlerempfehlung,

[8] *Erste Empfehlung* bedeutet, dass der Ersatzteilhändler an erster Stelle ein Comp-Produkt empfiehlt. Beim *generellen Empfehlungsniveau* werden jeweils von 10 Empfehlungen all jene gezählt, die für die Comp-Produkte ausgesprochen werden.

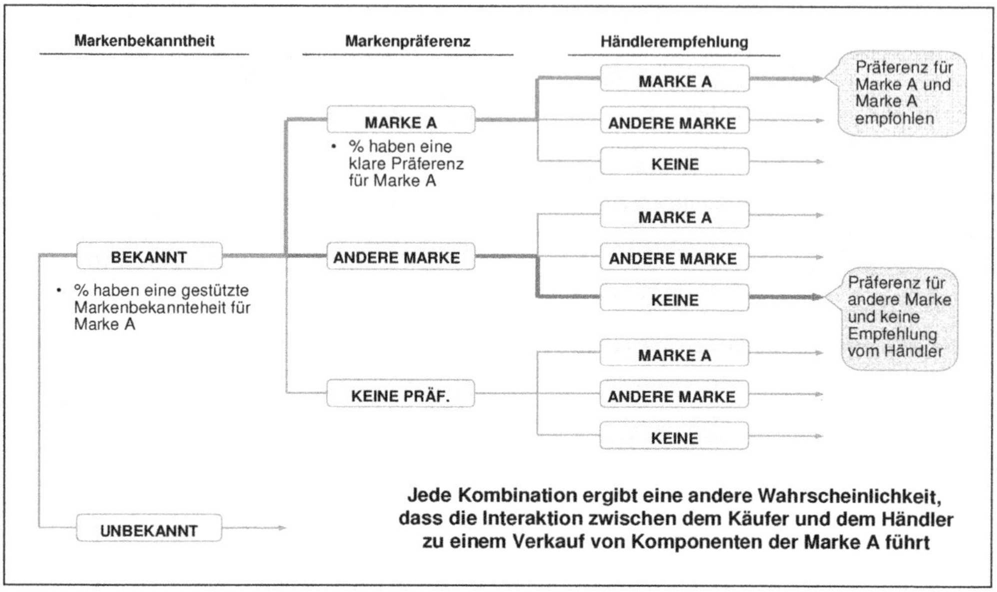

Abbildung 3: Ermittlung der Verkaufswahrscheinlichkeiten – Schema

Bekanntheit beim Endverbraucher und Markenbevorzugung eine Wahrscheinlichkeit für einen Kauf der jeweiligen Marke kalkuliert wird, wie die Abbildung 3 und die unten aufgeführte Formel zeigen:

$$Probability\ of\ purchase_{(brand\ A)} = Brand\ awareness_{(brand\ A)} * Brand\ Preference_{(brand\ A)} * Endorsement\ levels_{(brand\ A)}$$

Nach Beschreibung der Modellsektoren fassen wir nun das Gesamtmodell kurz zusammen und erläutern dessen Einsatzmöglichkeiten.

4.2 Modell – Zusammenfassung

Durch das Simulationsmodell waren wir in der Lage, den bisherigen Ansatz, der auf Endverbrauchermarketing beruht, zu testen, also ob und inwieweit die Firma bei einer Fortsetzung des Status Quo ihre Ziele – dauerhafte Marktführerschaft und kontinuierliches weiteres Ertragswachstum – erreichen würde. Es ermöglichte uns auch, dem Management zu demonstrieren, dass der Erfolg auf der operativen Ebene zukünftig nur durch die Entwicklung von neuen Wertpotentialen aufrecht erhalten werden kann. Das komplette Modell ist in Abbildung 4 konzeptionell dargestellt, entsprechend den in diesem Abschnitt erläuterten Teilen.

4.2.1 Simulationsmöglichkeiten

Es wurde entschieden, ein weitgreifendes Modell des Umfeldes, in dem ein Komponentenhersteller operiert, zu konstruieren. Nur so können die meisten der möglichen Initiativen und Szenarien getestet werden. Obwohl ein derartiges Modell eine viel größere Herausforderung an die

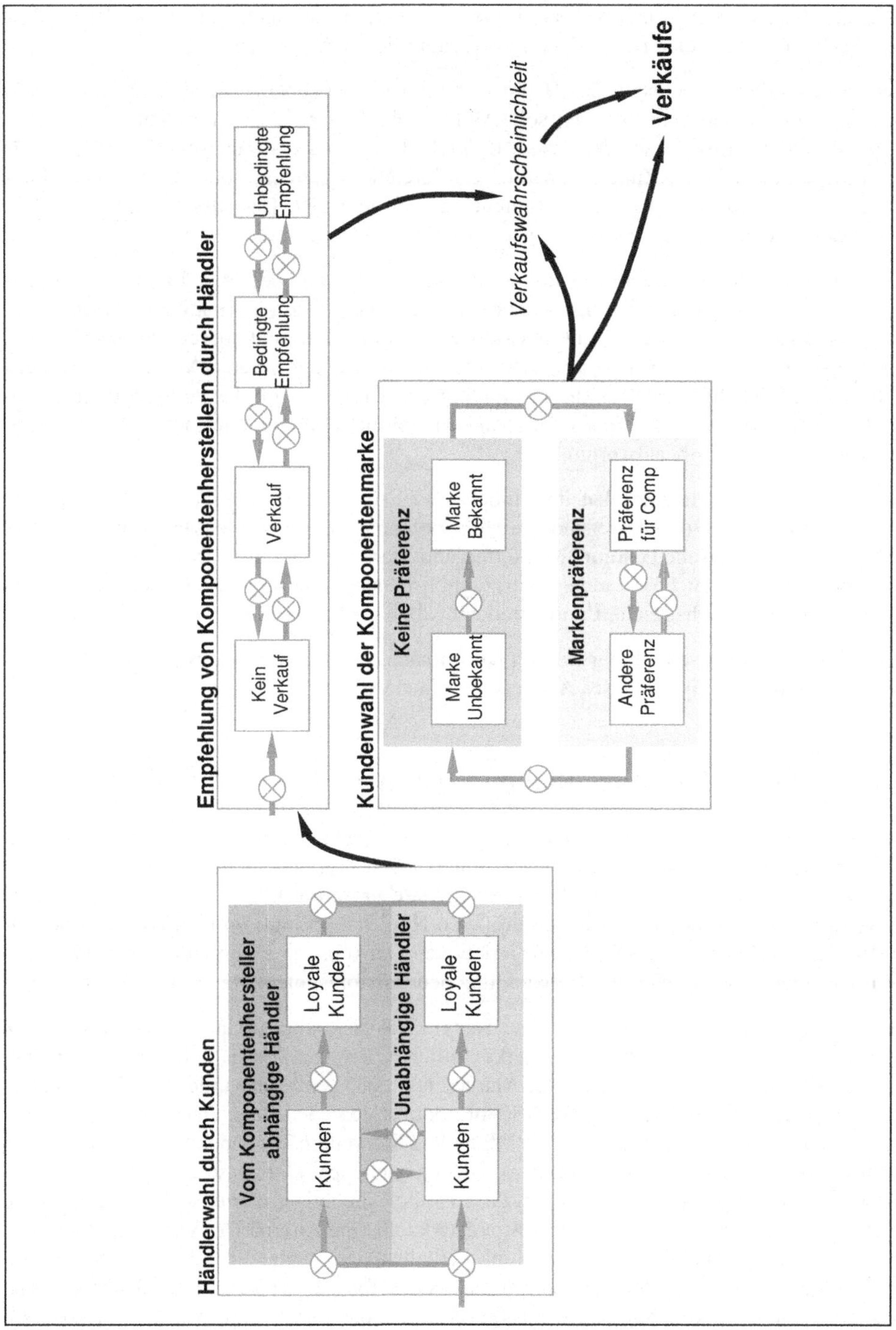

Abbildung 4: Struktur des Simulationsmodells (vereinfacht)

Validierung darstellt, haben uns die erweiterten Simulationsmöglichkeiten sowie die Qualität der zur Verfügung stehenden Daten davon überzeugt, diesen Weg einzuschlagen.

Das Modell erlaubt einerseits die Beantwortung von taktischen Fragen, z. B. auf welche Ersatzteilkette man sich konzentrieren soll. Andererseits können auch grundlegendere Fragen mit dem Modell beantwortet werden, wie z. B. ob die bestehenden strategischen Wertpotentiale ausreichen, um auch in der Zukunft operativ erfolgreich zu bleiben, oder ob eine zusätzliche und frühere Steuerung durch neue Wertpotentiale notwendig ist. Das Modell zeigt auch klar Bereiche auf, in denen diese neuen Erfolgspotentiale zu suchen sind.

Das Simulationsmodell bezieht sich nur auf die strategische und operative Ebene des Modells Systemischer Lenkung und hat keine konkreten Anbindungen zur normativen Managementebene. Eine derartige Anbindung wäre nur schwer quantitativ zu modellieren, da es keine konkreten Schätzungen zum Einfluss der normativen Ebene auf die tieferen Managementebenen gibt. Eine mögliche Diskussion zu diesem Zeitpunkt könnte sein, ob das dauerhafte und weitgehend sogar zeitlose Unternehmensethos Änderungen bei der Strategie indiziert, eine Frage die sich besser qualitativ beantworten lässt.

Die operativen Steuerungsgrößen im Modell sind Erfolg und Liquidität. Auf strategischer Ebene sind im Bereich der bestehenden Erfolgspotentiale Größen wie Marktanteil, relative Qualität, relative technische Position, Marketing und Markenbekanntheit abgebildet. Die neuen Erfolgspotentiale werden unter anderem bezüglich neuer technischer Lösungen, innovativer Kompetenzen im Vertriebsgeschäft und Kundenloyalität repräsentiert.

Nach dieser Modellbeschreibung werden wir im nächsten Abschnitt die Simulationsresultate zeigen, welche die Prinzipien dieses Artikels untermauern.

5 Resultate der Simulation und Implikationen

Mit den Simulationsläufen wurden einerseits Szenarios gerechnet, um existentielle Gefahren für das Unternehmen sowie Verletzbarkeiten zu untersuchen und anderseits mögliche Initiativen ausgelotet, welche die Firma über die nächsten Jahre ergreifen könnte. Gleichzeitig musste abgewogen werden, welche Strategie den größeren Nutzen einbringt: Fortführung des derzeitigen, kurz- und höchstens mittelfristig ausgerichteten Denkens oder eine langfristige Orientierung, insbesondere hinsichtlich der Entwicklung neuer Erfolgspotentiale.

Die Resultate zeigen klar auf, dass eine weitere Fokussierung allein auf die bestehenden Erfolgspotentiale durch Beherrschung herkömmlicher Erfolgsfaktoren wie Produktqualität, technische Effizienz und Schlagkraft des Marketings nicht genügen würde, um die gesetzten Ziele zu erreichen. Die Entwicklung neuer Erfolgspotentiale ließe jedoch eine signifikante Leistungsverbesserung noch immer zu. Die Schaffung von Markenpräferenz beim Endkunden ist ein typisches Beispiel neuer Erfolgspotentiale, von denen noch nicht klar ist, wie sie entwickelt werden können und deren Erhöhung höchstwahrscheinlich nur mit größerer Zeitverzögerung zu erzielen sein wird. Aber es gibt zu dieser Strategie kaum eine Alternative. Vorderhand könnten immerhin Kompetenzen, die das Empfehlungsverhalten der Ersatzteilhändler verändern, entwickelt werden – erheblich schneller und mit praktisch sofortiger Wirkung. Die Firma Comp hat inzwischen auch schon konkrete Schritte vorgesehen, die das Empfehlungsverhalten verbessern könnten. Dadurch wären Ersatzteilhändler stärker an den Komponentenhersteller gebunden und solchen Händlern könnten auch mehrere Endkunden zugeführt werden.[9]

Nun stellt sich die Frage, in welchem Ausmaß die wahrscheinliche Leistung wegen des rückgängigen Komponentenmarktes unter dem Erwartungsniveau liegen wird. Es folgt eine Erläuterung, inwiefern sich die Firmenleistung verbessern muss, um im kleiner werdenden Markt noch immer dasselbe Leistungsniveau zu erbringen. Schlussendlich vergleichen wir, inwiefern sich ein weiterer Fokus auf bestehende Erfolgspotentiale, oder aber die Schaffung neuer Erfolgspotentiale auf den Erfolg des Unternehmens auswirken werden.

5.1 Wahrscheinlicher Leistungseinbruch

Die Erwartung eines weiterhin wachsenden Komponentenmarktes hat sich, wie gezeigt, als nicht zutreffend erwiesen. Der Wechselmarkt, der durch den Erstkauf der zweiten Art von Komponenten entstanden ist, hat das Erwartungsniveau für weiteres Marktwachstum über den wahren Bedarf getrieben, wie in Abbildung 5 ersichtlich ist.

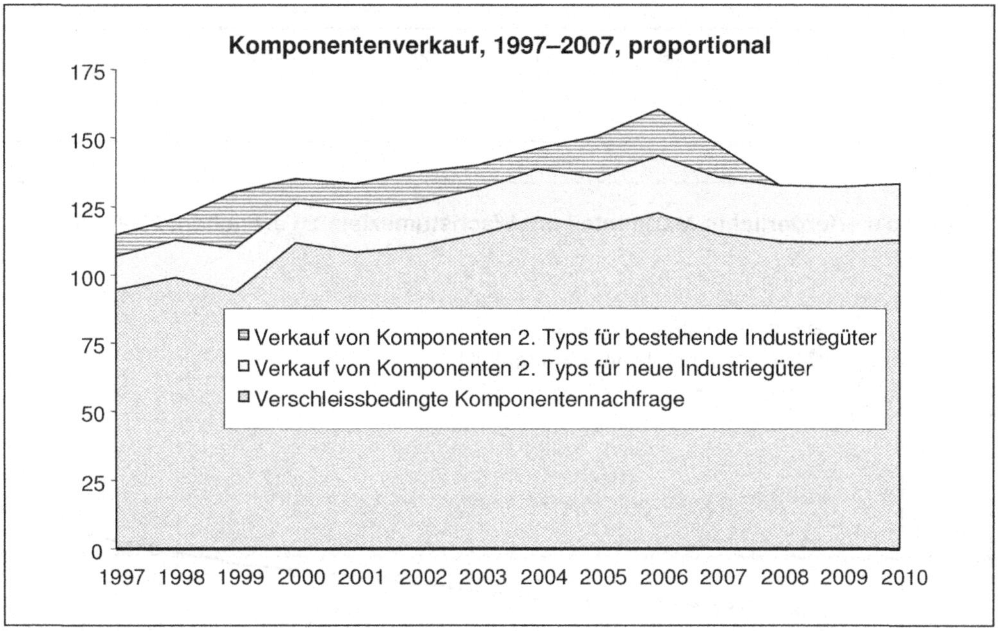

Abbildung 5: Struktur des Marktvolumens

Quelle: Kundendaten; eigene Analyse

Dies hatte zur Folge, dass der Komponentenhersteller die internen Wachstumsziele, ohne verstärkt auf den Verdrängungswettbewerb zu setzen, nicht erreichen könnte, wie in Abbildung 6 (s. S. 40) gezeigt wird.

[9] Dies ist im Prinzip möglich mittels gemeinsamer Marketingaktionen von Hersteller und Händlern sowie loyalitätsbildender Initiativen, mit denen die Kunden stärker an den Händler gebunden werden.

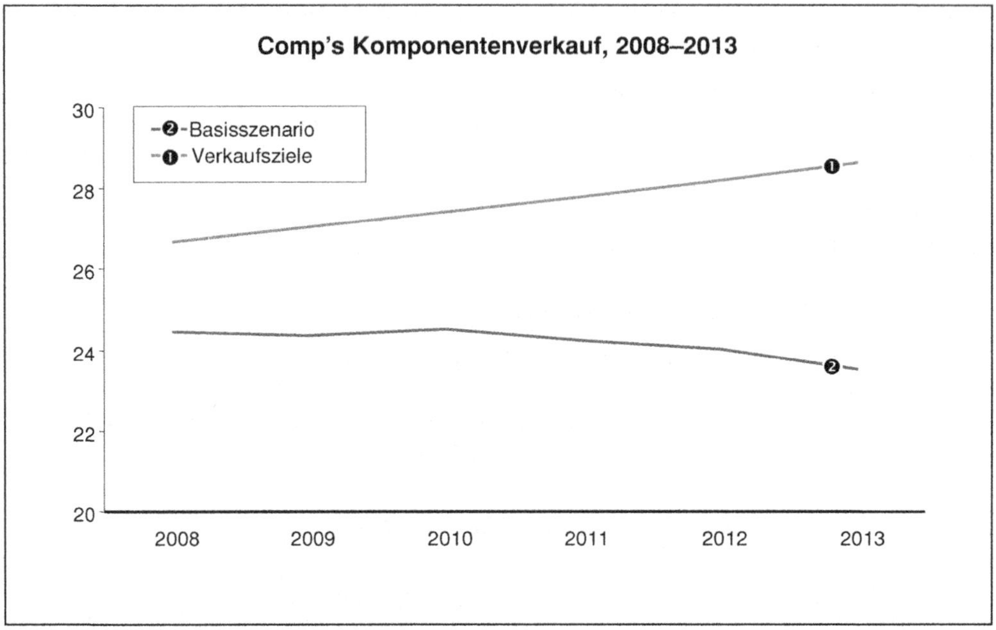

Abbildung 6: Unternehmenserfolg versus Ziele im veränderten Markt sowie für die Zielerreichung erforderliches Marktanteilswachstum

Da dieses Szenario alle Wettbewerber im gleichen Maße treffen würde, ist nicht anzunehmen, dass größere Marktanteile mit bestehenden Methoden im Verdrängungswettbewerb hinzugewonnen werden können. Dies führt uns zum nächsten Abschnitt, in dem wir prüfen werden, wie ein Rückgang der Marktanteile am effizientesten verhindert werden kann: durch bereits existierende Erfolgspotentiale aufgrund von Technik, Marketing und Markenbekanntheit oder durch eine Schaffung neuer Erfolgspotentiale durch die Entwicklung neuer Kompetenzen, die Fortschritte bei Markenpräferenzbildung und Händlerempfehlungsverhalten ermöglichen.

5.2 Leistungsbeitrag von bestehenden und neuen Wertpotentialen

Um zu verstehen, welchen Wert verschiedene Erfolgspotentiale für das Unternehmen generieren können, haben wir zuerst eine elementare ‚Leverage Analysis' durchgeführt. Diese prüft alle möglichen Interventionspunkte auf ihre Effektivität. Nach dieser Analyse wurde ein Managementworkshop durchgeführt, mit der Vorgabe konkrete Initiativen zu gestalten, die auf die Hebelpunkte wirken würden, um zu sehen, mit welcher Verzögerung diese wirken könnten.

Wir gliedern die Hebelpunkte gemäß dem verschiedenen logischen Ebenen im Modell Systemischer Lenkung. Der Erfolg wird sowohl anhand der Kundenzahl als auch des Gewinnes gemessen. Um die Auftraggeberanonymität zu gewährleisten, wurden relative Werte anstatt tatsächlicher Kundenzahlen und Gewinnwerte gewählt.

Die drei wichtigsten Stellhebel, die wir vorstellen werden, sind Wachstum in der Markenbekanntheit bei Endverbrauchern, Markenpräferenz bei Komponenten und die Anzahl der Endverbraucher, die eine spezifische Ersatzteilkette aufsuchen. Kosteneinsparungen und Erhöhung des Empfehlungsverhaltens bei den Ersatzteilketten wurden jedoch vorderhand nicht getestet. Der Grund für ersteres ist, dass das Managementteam keine Initiative zu formulieren vermochte, welche die Kosten signifikant absenken könnten, um durch Kostensenkung mehr Kunden zu gewinnen. Das erhöhte Empfehlungsniveau wurde aus zweierlei Gründen nicht aufgeführt. Erstens ist dessen Effekt ähnlich wie bei einer Gewinnung von zusätzlichen Endkunden bei Händlern mit erhöhtem Empfehlungsverhalten. Zweitens wäre dieses Resultat mit anderen nicht vergleichbar – es ist vorderhand unmöglich den marginalen Beitrag eines zusätzlichen Kunden zu bemessen.

Die Wirkungen der drei Managementhebel, d. h. einer Erhöhung von Markenbekanntheit, Erhöhung von Markenpräferenz und der Anzahl der Kunden, die eine Ersatzteilkette mit hohem Empfehlungsverhalten anpeilen, verdeutlicht die Abbildung 7 (s. S. 42). Die Graphik zeigt den Effekt einer Bewegung von je 1000 Kunden a) aus dem Zustand, in welchem sie die Marke Comp nicht kennen in den Zustand, bei dem ihnen die Marke Comp bekannt ist; b) vom Status der Kunden, die die Marke Comp lediglich kennen hin zum Status in dem sie eine Präferenz für die Marke Comp aufweisen; und c) von Kunden, die einen durchschnittlichen Händler besuchen zu solchen, die zu einem Comp-empfehlenden Händler gehen. Sie zeigt auch klar die Effektivität von bestehenden sowie neuen Wertpotentialen. Auf der linken Seite wird die relative Anzahl zusätzlich verkaufter Komponenten gezeigt, auf der rechten der jeweilige Gewinnbeitrag. Die ersten drei Werte in Abbildung 7 zeigen keinen Unterschied zwischen der relativen Zahl verkaufter Zusatzkomponenten und der relativen Profitabilität, weil angenommen wird, dass diese zusätzlichen markenbewussten/markenaffinen Kunden weiterhin dieselben Ersatzteilketten aufsuchen werden, die dann dasselbe Margenniveau haben werden. In den beiden letzten Fällen ist der Profitabilitätsbeitrag geringer als die Anzahl der zusätzlich verkauften Komponenten. Der Grund hierfür liegt im geringeren Margenniveau der Ersatzteilketten, die von den Kunden frequentiert werden.

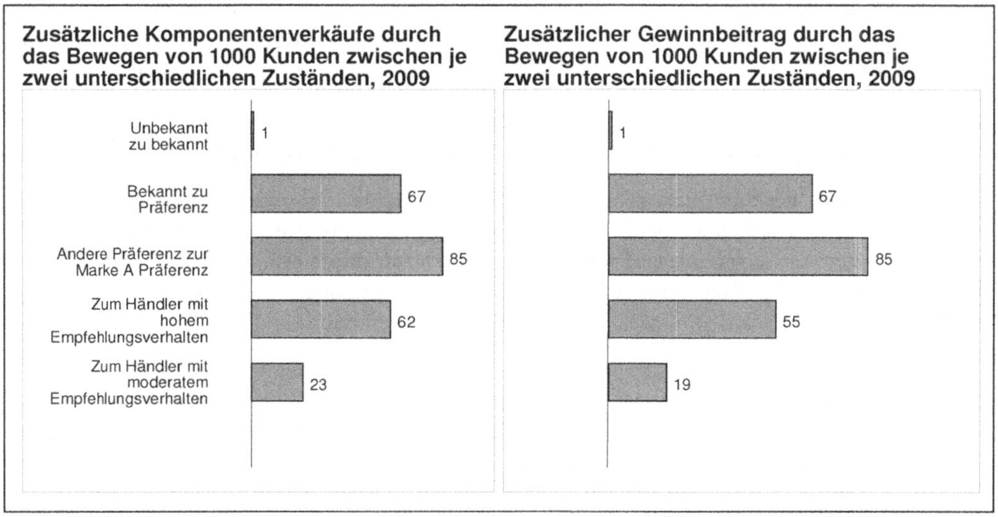

Abbildung 7: Vergleich des Leverage zusätzlichen Verkaufsvolumens auf den Gewinnbeitrag

Die Resultate auf der rechten Seite der Abbildung 7 können auch als Betrag der Geldmittel interpretiert werden, die in eine Initiative einfließen können, ohne dass sie als unprofitabel angesehen wird. Auf dieser Grundlage sind die Resultate eindeutig. Der Ausbau existierender Wertpotenziale, also die Erhöhung der Markenbekanntheit, resultiert in einer nicht signifikanten Erhöhung des Marktwertes. Eine erfolgreiche Initiative, die einen Zuwachs an Markenbekanntheit billiger generieren würde als der dadurch zusätzlich generierte Umsatz, konnte jedoch nicht gefunden werden. Das heißt, dass weitere Investitionen in dieses bestehende Wertpotential zu einer Wertvernichtung führen würden.

Dagegen zeigen beide Interventionen, die auf neuen Wertpotentialen beruhen, beträchtliche Zuwächse an Verkaufsvolumen. Schaffung von Markenpräferenz scheint einen größeren Effekt zu haben, ist aber gleichzeitig auch der weniger verstandene Teil des Geschäfts. Zudem war das Managementteam überzeugt, dass Änderungen in der Markenpräferenz nur nach lang anhaltenden Investitionen erreicht werden können, da schon seit einer längeren Zeit der Markenpräferenzanteil der Komponentenhersteller den jeweiligen Marktanteilen folgen – kein Hersteller hat es bis jetzt geschafft, eine überproportionale Markenpräferenz zu entwickeln. Dies könnte zwei mögliche Gründe haben: Entweder hat bisher kein Komponentenhersteller versucht, sich durch Präferenzgenerierung zu differenzieren, oder aber, der Aufbau von Markenpräferenz ist ein schwieriges und langwieriges Unterfangen. Mit dem heutigen Wissensstand ist es schwer zu beantworten, ob es möglich ist, die Markenpräferenz profitabel zu erhöhen. Klar ist aber, dass der Zusatzwert, der durch eine höhere Markenpräferenz etabliert werden könnte, viel höher ist, als der durch bestehende Wertpotentiale – Markenbekanntheitszuwachs – zu erzielende.

Anders als bei der Markenpräferenz hat das Managementteam konkrete Vorstellungen davon, wie zusätzliche Endverbraucher den Ersatzteilketten mit hohem Empfehlungsverhalten zeitnah vermittelt werden können. Mehrere Interventionen wurden identifiziert, die eine Endkundenloyalität um mindestens 48% innerhalb eines Jahres erhöhen würden. Die Kosten dieser Initiativen sind signifikant niedriger als der Umsatzzuwachs, der dadurch erwirtschaftet wäre, was diesen Ansatz als beste Kurzzeitlösung empfiehlt. Längerfristig müssten dann zusätzliche Fähigkeiten auf dem Gebiet des Ersatzteilketten-Beziehungsmanagements aufgebaut werden. Solche Kompetenzen erscheinen leichter erreichbar als für Wettbewerber, und sie würden einem spezifischen Komponentenhersteller anhaltende Wettbewerbsvorteile verschaffen. Aber schon die ersten Schritte auf diesem Gebiet würden ausreichend Erfolge auf der operativen Ebene generieren, um die weiteren Investitionen auf dem Gebiet finanzieren zu können.

Der Aufbau der langfristig angestrebten, neuen Fähigkeiten wird zweifellos nicht mit einem Mehr derselben Anstrengungen wie bisher erreichbar sein. Er wird zudem Implikationen im organisatorischen Bereich – strukturell und kulturell – haben, auf die wir hier nicht eingehen können.

Soweit die Simulationsergebnisse und ihre Implikationen, die uns zu Diskussion und Schlussfolgerungen führen.

6 Diskussion

Im gegenständlichen Unternehmen floss in der Vergangenheit fast die gesamte Energie in das Kurz- und Mittelfristige. Zum Beispiel war der Fokus des Managements über lange Strecken fast ausschließlich auf Kostensenkungen gerichtet. Zwar waren auch die Faktoren, welche die bestehenden Erfolgspotentiale determinieren, bekannt. Marktanteile, relative Qualität, technologische Position und Schlagkraft des Marketings wurden zwar als wichtig erachtet, aber weniger gezielt gemanagt als Erträge und Aufwendungen. Letztlich war die Erfolgsrechnung den Führungskräften das Maß aller Dinge. Das operative Denken und Handeln dominierte und verdrängte also weitgehend die strategische Orientierung.

Ein langfristig potentiell verhängnisvolles Verhalten zeigte sich darüber hinaus auch innerhalb der strategischen Führung: Hatten bestehende Erfolgspotentiale, wie beschrieben, noch einen gewissen Stellenwert, waren dagegen die neuen Erfolgspotentiale aus der Betrachtung ausgeklammert. Beispielsweise drohte auf lange Sicht eine Konvergenz aller Wettbewerber auf diesem Markt. Alle optimierten ihre Produkte, verwendeten dieselben Technologien, folgten denselben Qualitätsstandards, kämpften um dieselben Absatzkanäle, usw. Sie alle verhielten sich gleich. Es war somit absehbar, dass langfristig jede Differenzierung zu verschwinden drohte – eine gefährliche Entwicklung (Kim & Mauborgne, 2005). Zudem zeichneten sich drastische Änderungen im Handel ab, die leicht zu einer Obsoleszenz des bestehenden Absatzmodus führen könnte. Der „Radarschirm" war aber nicht so eingestellt, dass Entwicklungen dieser Art hätten erkannt werden können.

Comp und die ganze Branche hatten über Jahrzehnte ihre Anstrengungen weitgehend falsch gelenkt. Sie hatten fast ausschließlich in Markenbekanntheit und Technik investiert. Die Firma hatte sich einem „Overengineering" verschrieben, das durch eine von Technikern geprägte Kultur getrieben war – den vorherrschenden Glauben, dass der Erfolg den Produkteigenschaften und technischen Prozessen zuzuschreiben war.

Anhand der Simulationen wurde das Erfordernis einer Neuorientierung klar erkennbar. Zudem wurde dieses Thema mit Hilfe des Modells diskussionsreif. Die Transparenz der modellierten Sachverhalte erleichterte die Kommunikation mit den Führungskräften. Es ist bereits feststellbar, dass sich deren mentale Modelle hin zu einem neuen Verständnis entwickeln. Die neuen Erkenntnisse orientieren zunehmend die Entscheidungen im Unternehmen.

7 Schlussfolgerungen und Ausblick

Wir haben in diesem Beitrag das Dilemma der Führung im Spannungsfeld von kurz- und langfristiger Orientierung dargestellt. Anhand des Simulationsmodells für eine komplexe Unternehmung haben wir versucht, die Tragweite dieser Spannung greifbar zu machen. Dem Ziel dieses Beitrags entsprechend, war es unser Anliegen Wege zu suchen, um das „Problem zu lösen". Es geht aber um ein Dilemma, nicht um ein Problem. Dilemmata aber sind einer Lösung (im engeren Sinn) nicht zugänglich; man kann nur mit ihnen leben. Wir haben anhand des Simulationsmodells gezeigt, wie eine Unternehmung mit dem hier identifizierten Dilemma „besser leben" kann. Es geht in solchen Fällen zunächst darum, alle Einflussfaktoren sorgfältig abzuwägen und die Komplexität anhand von Szenarien auszuloten. Auf dieser Basis kann man dann eine wünschbare Zukunft entwerfen und tragfähige Wege finden, um diese herbeizuführen (Ackoff, 1981). Genau dies wurde im vorliegenden Fall, durch das Ausloten – via Computerexperimente – der Beiträge, die weitere Investitionen in die bestehenden, bzw. neuen Erfolgspotentiale, bringen würden, getan. Das gegenständliche Unternehmen litt zunächst unter der Krankheit der Kurzsichtigkeit. Laufend wurde das Wichtige durch das Unwichtige und der Weitblick durch die Myopie verdrängt. Diese Krankheit war mit der Erstellung des Simulationsmodells zwar noch nicht geheilt. Das Modell wurde aber von einem Kreis maßgebender Führungskräfte begeistert aufgenommen und bald in die Entscheidungsprozesse integriert. Damit sind relativ gute Voraussetzungen geschaffen, dass die Langfristorientierung in dieser Unternehmung auf breiterer Basis Fuß fasst.

Die Einsichten aus diesem Beitrag lassen sich in folgenden Imperativen zusammenfassen:

1. **Steuerungsgrößen und Vorsteuerung verstehen**
   Für eine wirksame Führung sind umfassendere Managementmodelle als die herkömmlichen erforderlich. Es gilt, Orientierungsgrundlagen in einem weiten Sach- und Zeithorizont zu berücksichtigen. Die Lenkungsgrößen aller logischen Ebenen mit den sie verbindenden Vorsteuerungswirkungen müssen abgebildet und verstanden werden.

2. **Vorrang des Langfristigen berücksichtigen**
   Die Erkenntnis, dass das Kurz- und das Langfristige nicht einfach nebeneinander existieren, sondern in einem kausalen Bezug zueinander stehen, ist elementar. Daraus ergibt sich ein prinzipieller Vorrang des Langfristigen (und darüber hinaus des Zeitlosen). Erfolgsvoraussetzungen müssen von langer Hand aufgebaut werden. Nur so können Handlungsspielräume eröffnet werden. Eine Nichtbeachtung dieses Zusammenhangs kann schnell zur Schrumpfung von Potentialen und damit einer Vernichtung von Freiräumen führen.

3. **Bessere Modelle verwenden**
   Zunächst geht es um die konzeptionellen, mentalen Modelle. Die Qualität dieser Modelle ist entscheidend, denn die Resultate eines Managements können nicht besser sein als die ihnen zugrundeliegenden Modelle (Conant & Ashby, 1981), es sei denn durch Zufall. Es geht aber

auch darum, bessere Modelle im Sinne von Führungsinstrumenten zu entwickeln. Dynamische Simulationsmodelle können diesbezüglich enorme Fortschritte bringen. Sie lassen sogar eine Verbindung mit Optimierungsheuristiken zu, wodurch die Kalibrierung von Entscheidungen noch verfeinert werden kann.

4. **Dynamik erfassen**
   Die einem komplexen System inhärente Dynamik kann zwar intuitiv erfasst werden. Um sie besser zu verstehen und daraus Entscheidungen abzuleiten, sind die genannten Simulationsmodelle erforderlich. Damit verlagert sich die Aufmerksamkeit von der Analyse konkreter einzelner Ereignisse hin zu einem tieferen Verständnis der dynamischen Muster in welche diese Ereignisse eingebettet sind sowie der sachlogischen Strukturen, welche diese Muster hervorbringen.
5. **Integrales Systemdesign gewährleisten**
   In einem sich permanent verändernden Umfeld schrumpft die Bedeutung von punktgenau vorgeschriebenen Zielen. Viel wichtiger wird die Frage, welche Art von Entwicklung für eine Organisation wünschbar ist. Es geht darum, einen Korridor zu ermitteln, in dessen Rahmen solche anzustrebenden Entwicklungen möglich sind. Dabei müssen die Handlungsspielräume sorgfältig ausgelotet und die Verletzbarkeiten erkannt werden. Mit *integrales Design* ist hier auch gemeint, dass es nicht genügt, *Policies* im Sinne von Aktivitätenfolgen zu definieren, sondern gleichermaßen und mit diesen in Verbindung, einen adäquaten strukturellen und kulturellen Kontext zu gestalten.

Unter diesen fünf Imperativen haben wir eine Reihe von unseres Erachtens wichtigen heuristischen Prinzipien genannt. Zweifellos gibt es als Ergänzung detailliertere, oft als „strategische Prinzipien" oder auch „metastrategische Prinzipien" bezeichnete Handlungsanleitungen und Gestaltungshilfen. Diese können anderswo nachgelesen werden (Malik, 2008; Pümpin & Pedergnana, 2008; Grossekettler, 1973).

Unser Anliegen mit diesem Beitrag war es, konzeptionelle Grundlagen für die Langfristorientierung in Organisationen aller Art bereitzustellen, durch Förderung einer vermehrt systemischen, integrativen Denkweise. Wird ein solches systemisches Denken gepflegt und in die Praxis umgesetzt, ergibt sich nicht nur eine höhere Intelligenz und Lebensfähigkeit der betreffenden Organisationen. Darüber hinaus wird damit auch tendenziell die Lebensqualität der Führungskräfte und aller in diesen Organisationen tätigen Menschen gefördert.

Literatur

Ackoff, R. L. (1981): *Creating the Corporate Future: Plan of Be Planned for*. New York: Wiley.

Barney, J. (1991): Firm Resources and Sustained Competitive Advantage. *Journal of Management* 17(1): 99–120.

Beer, S. (1985): *Diagnosing the System for Organizations*. Chichester: Wiley.

Berger, S., M. L. Dertouzos, et al. (1989): Toward a New Industrial America. *Scientific American* 260: 21–29.

Brown, P. U. (2007): *Shortsighted Management*. New York Times. November 24, 2007: C 5.

Conant, R. C. and W. R. Ashby (1981): *Every Good Regulator of a System Must Be a Model of that System. Mechanisms of Intelligence: Ross Ashby's Writings on Cybernetics*. R. C. Conant. Seaside, California, Intersystems Publications: 205–214.

Gälweiler, A. (2005): *Strategische Unternehmensführung* (3. Aufl.). Frankfurt a. M. und New York: Campus.

Grossekettler, H. (1973): *Macht, Strategie und Wettbewerb*. Mainz. Dissertation.

Kim, W. C. and R. Mauborgne (2005): *Blue Ocean Strategy: How to Create Uncontested Market Space and Make the Competition Irrelevant*. Boston, MA: Harvard Business School Press.

Krugman, P. (2001): *The New Reality Is Old Economy Shortages*. International Herald Tribune. January 3, 2001: 1.

Malik, F. (2008): *Strategie des Managements komplexer Systeme. Ein Beitrag zur Management-Kybernetik evolutionärer Systeme*. Bern: Haupt.

Mintzberg, H. (2007): Opinion. Productivity Is Killing American Enterprise. *Harvard Business Review* 85(7/8): 25.

Mitroff, I. I. (2005): *Why Some Companies Emerge Stronger and Better from a Crisis: 7 Essential Lessons for Surviving Disaster*. New York: AMACOM.

Mizik, N. J. Robert (2007): Performance: The Cost of Myopic Management. *Harvard Business Review* 85(7/8): 22/24.

Pacioli, L. (1933): *Abhandlung über die Buchhaltung* (Wiederabdruck des Originals von 1494). Stuttgart: Poeschel.

Peteraf, M. A. (1993): The Cornerstones of Competitive Advantage: A Resource-Based View. *Strategic Management Journal* 14: 179–191.

Porter, M. E. (1980): *Competitive Strategies*. New York: Free Press.

Prahalad, C. K. H. G. (1990): The Core Competence of the Corporation. *Harvard Business Review* 68(3): 79–91.

Pümpin, C. und M. Pedergnana (2008): *Strategisches Investment Management: wie Investoren nachhaltige Wertsteigerungen erzielen*. Bern: Haupt.

Schwaninger, M. (1989): *Integrale Unternehmensplanung*. Frankfurt/Main: Campus Verlag.

Schwaninger, M. (2009): *Intelligent Organizations. Powerful Models for Systemic Management* (2. Aufl.). Berlin: Springer.

Komplexität, Flexibilität und Erfolg als Herausforderungen marktorientierter Fertigungsstrategien

Christoph Moos

Freudenberg & Co. KG, Weinheim/Bergstraße

Zusammenfassung

In industriellen Unternehmen wird Fertigungsstrategien ein hohes Potenzial zur Entfaltung der Leistungsfähigkeit des Fertigungsbereiches zugesprochen. Aus Gesamtunternehmenssicht sind sie besonders wirksam, wenn sie im Sinne einer Marktorientierung Wettbewerbsstrategien unterstützen. Fertigungsstrategien sind Ziel- und Maßnahmenbündel zur Umsetzung der Unternehmensstrategie und fungieren somit als Bindeglied zwischen Gesamtunternehmens- und Funktionsebene. Dabei stehen sie vielfältigen Herausforderungen gegenüber.

Planungs-, Entscheidungs- und Handlungssituationen in einem Umfeld, das beispielsweise durch eine zunehmende Fragmentierung der Märkte, das Zusammenwachsen bisher getrennter Technologien oder die Globalisierung gekennzeichnet ist, zeichnen sich durch die Fülle an Parametern, deren Beziehungsgeflecht, die daraus resultierende Eigendynamik und Irreversibilität sowie schwindende Prognostizierbarkeit zukünftiger Zustände aus und lassen sich als komplex beschreiben. Eine wesentliche Grundlage für das Bestehen und das Gedeihen eines Unternehmens ist ferner das frühzeitige Erkennen von Veränderungen in seinem Umfeld und das rechtzeitige Gestalten seines Wettbewerbverhaltens. Zur Lösung dieser zentralen Aufgabe wird Flexibilität häufig als eine bedeutende Eigenschaft von Unternehmen zur Bewältigung komplexer Umweltsituationen betrachtet. Schließlich ist der Erfolg selbst zur Beurteilung marktorientierter Fertigungsstrategien heranzuziehen. Der Beitrag untersucht Komplexität, Flexibilität und Erfolg als Herausforderungen marktorientierter Fertigungsstrategien, die sich konkret mit der Umwelt auseinander setzen, eine proaktive Rolle ausfüllen und die strategische Ausrichtung des Gesamtunternehmens zur Existenzsicherung und Weiterentwicklung unterstützen.

Schlagwörter: Fertigungsstrategie, Marktorientierung, Komplexität, Flexibilität, Erfolg

1 Marktorientierte Fertigungsstrategien zur Unterstützung der Leistungsfähigkeit der Fertigung

Die theoretischen Erkenntnisse und die daraus praktisch resultierenden Handlungsanweisungen der einzelnen Disziplinen der Betriebswirtschaftslehre zielen trotz all ihrer Verschiedenheit in letzter Konsequenz stets auf den Erfolg von Unternehmen ab. Über die Jahrzehnte hinweg haben aufgrund geänderter Rahmenbedingungen und neuer Möglichkeiten Schwerpunktverschiebungen in den praktischen betriebswirtschaftlichen Aufgaben stattgefunden, die nicht nur nach neuen Betrachtungsweisen und Theorien verlangen, sondern auch zu unterschiedlichen

Gewichtungen der in der Vergangenheit gewonnenen Erkenntnisse führen.[1] Sowohl in der Wissenschaft als auch in der betriebswirtschaftlichen Praxis wird dem Konstrukt der Marktorientierung seit den sechziger Jahren ein positiver und vor allem zentraler Einfluss auf den Geschäftserfolg zugeschrieben.[2]

Grundsätzlich leitet sich aus einer marktorientierten Unternehmensführung für das Verhalten von Unternehmen ab, wie sie agieren müssen, um sich von der Konkurrenz positiv abzuheben. Dies zielt auf die langfristige Wettbewerbsfähigkeit und somit auf die Möglichkeit ab, nachhaltig Gewinne erwirtschaften zu können. Es wird eine strategische Wettbewerbsposition innerhalb strategischer Gruppen angestrebt.[3] Aus Sicht des einzelnen Unternehmens gilt es, ausgehend von der Absatzmarktseite, die Wettbewerbspositionen der Wettbewerber und deren Wettbewerbsvorteile in die Analyse der eigenen Stellung am Markt einzubeziehen. Dies schlägt sich auch in der postulierten Rolle von Strategien nieder. „The essence of strategy formulation is coping with competition."[4]

Eine einseitige Ausrichtung unternehmerischer Aktivitäten im Sinne der klassischen Ansätze der Marktorientierung verkannte die Restriktionen und insbesondere die Möglichkeiten, die durch den Einbezug des Fertigungsbereiches in den Strategiebildungsprozess gegeben sind. Jedoch kann nicht geleugnet werden, dass die Entwicklung des strategischen Managements seit der Diskussion marktorientierter Unternehmensführung stark von dieser Perspektive geprägt ist. „Being market orientated is the basis for creating superior value for buyers, the meaning of competitive advantage. Accordingly, being market orientated can never be a negative."[5] Somit liegt der Anknüpfungspunkt für marktorientierte Fertigungsstrategien in der Erkenntnis, dass für industrielle Unternehmen gerade die Verfolgung der Wettbewerbsstrategien im Sinne einer Marktorientierung Unterstützung durch Potenziale im Leistungserstellungsprozess erfahren kann.

Das Erreichen eines umfangreichen Bündels von Effizienzzielen unter vorgebenden Plandaten anderer unternehmerischer Funktionsbereiche war in der Vergangenheit und ist häufig auch gegenwärtig vorrangiges Bemühen des Fertigungsbereiches. Als Vorgaben können beispielsweise die Produktion entsprechender Stückzahlen anhand von Absatzdaten, Investitionen und Desinvestitionen aufgrund finanzieller und steuerlicher Überlegungen oder der Einsatz der Mitarbeiter unter Berücksichtigung der Vorgaben aus dem Personalbereich genannt werden. Aus

---

[1] Für eine Darstellung entsprechender Zyklen von gewonnener Erkenntnis vgl. Gerhard, Thorsten: Moderne Managementkonzepte, Wiesbaden 1997, S. 62–65.

[2] Die Bedeutung der Marktorientierung für den Erfolg von Unternehmen ist anschaulich dargestellt in Fritz, Wolfgang: Marktorientierte Unternehmensführung und Unternehmenserfolg, in: Marketing – Zeitschrift für Forschung und Praxis, Jg. 15 (1993), Nr. 4, S. 237–246. Empirische Studien finden sich bei Kohli, Ajay K. und Bernard J. Jaworski: Market orientation: the construct, research propositions, and managerial implications, in: Journal of Marketing, Vol. 54 (1990), No. 2, S. 1–18, ferner Narver, John C. und Stanley F. Slater: The Effect of a Market Orientation on Business Profitability, in: Journal of Marketing, Vol. 54 (1990), No. 4, S. 20–35.

[3] Dieser Blickwinkel wird auch als „outside-in"-Perspektive bezeichnet. Vgl. dazu Bleicher, Knut: Das Konzept Integriertes Management, 4. Aufl., Frankfurt 1996, S. 91.

[4] Porter, Michael E.: How competitive forces shape strategy, in: Harvard Business Review, Vol. 57 (1979), No. 2, S. 137.

[5] Slater, Stanely F. und John C. Narver: Does Competitive Environment Moderate the Market Orientation – Performance Relationship?, in: Journal of Marketing, Vol. 58, (1994), No. 1, S. 54.

dieser Perspektive heraus scheint die Fertigung nur begrenzt aktiv Einfluss auf die Gestaltung des aktuellen Unternehmensgeschehens und die langfristige Unternehmensentwicklung zu nehmen. Ihr kommt überwiegend die Bedeutung zu, das umzusetzen, was an anderen Stellen im Unternehmen initiiert worden ist.

Die Gefahr der viel zitierten Degradierung des Fertigungsbereiches zu einer Erfüllungsfunktion hängt vom Selbstverständnis der Fertigung ab, in das die Einstellungen und Verhaltensweisen sowohl der Entscheidungsträger als auch der Mitarbeiter einfließen.[6] Ein Denken in Kategorien wie beispielsweise Wettbewerbsvorteile, Verbesserungsmöglichkeiten, unternehmensindividuelle Fähigkeiten oder Stärken und Schwächen ist Ausdruck einer aktiven Rolle, in der sich die Fertigung selbst sieht. Es stellt sich demnach die Frage, wie das Fertigungsmanagement die Leistungsfähigkeit des produzierenden Bereiches sicherstellen kann. Dies darf selbstverständlich keineswegs mit der Reduzierung des Erfolges eines Unternehmens auf den besagten Bereich einhergehen, andernfalls träfe diese Perspektive die oben angeführte Kritik.

Die grundsätzliche Möglichkeit eines jeden Funktionsbereiches, trotz vielfältiger Abhängigkeitsbeziehungen zu anderen Bereichen einen aktiven Einfluss auf das Wesen und die individuelle Prägung eines Unternehmens und somit auf den Erfolg zu nehmen, bedarf eines Rahmenwerkes, das die Gestaltung des entsprechenden Funktionsbereiches leitet. Vor dem Hintergrund der noch anstehenden Diskussion des Unternehmenserfolges ist zunächst davon auszugehen, dass die jeweilige Ausrichtung einer Funktion in den übergeordneten Gesamtunternehmenskontext einzuordnen ist. Die eigene Sicht des Fertigungsbereiches auf sich selbst hat folglich in Einklang mit der Gesamtunternehmensstrategie zu stehen, um den Unternehmenszielen gerecht zu werden. Die Ableitung unternehmensfunktionsbezogener Teilstrategien aus einem übergeordneten Zielbündel führt zu dem Begriff Funktions-, Funktionsbereichs- oder funktionale Strategie. Grundsätzlich haben sie die Konkretisierung der Gesamtunternehmensstrategie zur Aufgabe und bilden dadurch ein Bindeglied zum zugrunde liegenden Funktionsbereich. Sie beinhalten aus der Gesamtunternehmensstrategie abgeleitete Ziele und umschreiben ein Maßnahmenbündel, das sich in Strukturen, geplante und realisierte Prozesse, Entscheidungsfindung und Programme aufspalten lässt.

Für den Fertigungsbereich stellt die Fertigungsstrategie die Verbindung zwischen Gesamtunternehmensperspektive und funktionalem Blickwinkel her. Die Einbettung dieser in den übergeordneten Gesamtunternehmenskontext, wie sie Hill vorschlägt, zeigt Abbildung 1 (s. S. 50).[7]

Die von Hill eingenommene Sichtweise sieht in einer erfolgreichen Fertigungsstrategie die Unterstützung der Unternehmensziele durch den Funktionsbereich der Fertigung, indem die Gegebenheiten im Wettbewerb und die Marktausrichtung Berücksichtigung finden. Dies fordert ebenso Skinner: „When Companies fail to recognize the relationsship between manufacturing decisions and corporate strategy, they may become saddled with seriously noncompetitve production systems which are expensive and time-consuming to change.“[8] Demnach besteht also

---

[6] Vgl. Hayes, Robert H. und Steven C. Wheelwright: Restoring our Competitive Edge. Competing through Manufacturing, New York et al. 1984, S. 41.

[7] Vgl. Hill, Terry J.: Incorporating manufacturing perspectives in corporate strategy, in: Voss, Christopher A.: Manufacturing Strategy, London et al. 1992, S. 9.

[8] Skinner, Wickham: Manufacturing – Missing link in corporate strategy, in Harvard Business Review, Vol. 47 (1969), No. 5/6, S. 136.

Gesamtunternehmenskontext

Unternehmensziele	Marketingstrategie	Kaufentscheidende Merkmale
• Bestandsicherung • Wachstum • Profit • ...	• Marktsegmente • Produktmix • Standardisierungsgrad • ...	• Preis • Qualität • Lieferzeit • ...

Fertigungsstrategie

Prozesse	Infrastruktur
• Prozessalternativen • Prozessabhängigkeiten • Prozesskapazität • ...	• Planungs- / Steuerungssysteme • Organisationsstruktur • Qualitätsmanagement • ...

Abbildung 1: Einbindung der Fertigungsstrategie in den Gesamtunternehmenskontext

nicht nur die Möglichkeit, sondern die Notwendigkeit, Fertigungsstrategien im Strategiebildungsprozess des Unternehmens zu etablieren.[9]

Der strategischen Ausrichtung der Fertigung wird bei dieser neuen Rolle des Bereiches der originären Leistungserstellung große Bedeutung beigemessen. Die Fertigungsleitung muss daher ihre Perspektive aktiv in den Prozess der unternehmensweiten Strategieformulierung einbringen.[10] Wheelwright und Hayes sprechen von einer eigenen Vision, die von der Fertigungsleitung entwickelt und kommuniziert werden muss, um im Fertigungsbereich strategische Potenziale zu fördern.[11] Nicht zuletzt wird daher von einer Fertigungsstrategie gesprochen. Der Begriff hat seit Mitte der siebziger Jahre stark an Bedeutung gewonnen, obwohl eine einheitliche Definition nicht zu existieren scheint. So gehen Mintzberg sowie Hayes und Wheelwright von einem Muster der Entscheidungsprozesse im Fertigungsbereich aus, dessen Konsistenz in

[9] Vgl. Voss, Christopher A.: Manufacturing strategy formulation as a process, in: Voss, Christopher A.: Manufacturing Strategy, London et al. 1992, S. 121f.

[10] Vgl. Gunn, Thomas G.: Manufacturing for Competitive Advantage: Becoming a World-Class Manufacturer, Cambridge (MA) 1987, S. 63, ferner Hill, Terry: Manufacturing Strategy, S. 29.

[11] Vgl. Wheelwright, Steven C. und Robert H. Hayes: Competing Through Manufacturing, in: Montgomery, Cynthia A. und Michael E. Porter: Strategy: Seeking and Securing Competitive Advantage, S. 110f.

einer Fertigungsstrategie resultiert.[12] Schroeder et al. verstehen hingegen unter einer Fertigungsstrategie einen langfristigen Plan oder eine Vision für die Fertigungsfunktion.[13] Gemein ist den im jeweiligen Schwerpunkt unterschiedlichen Auffassungen jedoch im Kern, die Herausbildung einer klaren, an der Leistungsfähigkeit orientierten Strategie unter Berücksichtigung der gesamten Unternehmenskultur anzustreben, um die weitere, zukünftige Entwicklung des Fertigungsbereichs zu unterstützen.[14]

Fertigungsstrategien unterstützen die Leistungsfähigkeit des Fertigungsbereichs. Sie sind Ziel- und Maßnahmenbündel zur Umsetzung der Unternehmensstrategie und fungieren somit als Bindeglied zwischen Gesamtunternehmens- und Funktionsebene. Das Fertigungsmanagement trägt dabei die Verantwortung, Fertigungsstrategien zu formulieren und zu etablieren.

Ein Modell, das hinsichtlich der strategischen Bedeutung der Fertigung in vier Stufen aufgebaut ist und somit Ausdruck ihrer Leistungsfähigkeit ist, geht auf Wheelwright und Hayes zurück und ist in Abbildung 2 dargestellt.[15] Es zeigt nicht nur die zuvor bereits diskutierte Bedeutung einer Gesamtunternehmensperspektive, sondern macht deutlich, dass die Rolle der Fertigung sich nicht auf die Ausräumung von Ineffizienzen oder vergleichbare Performance mit Wettbewerbern beschränken muss.

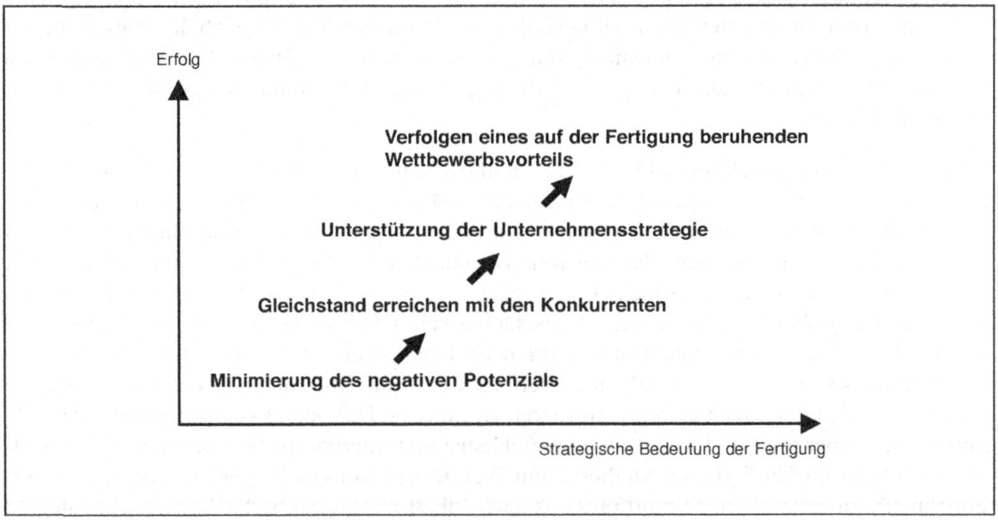

Abbildung 2: Vier Stufen der strategischen Bedeutung der Fertigung

[12] Vgl. Hayes, Robert H. und Steven C. Wheelwright: Restoring Our Competitive Edge, S. 27; Mintzberg, Henry: The Rise and Fall of Strategic Planning, New York et al. 1994, S. 23f.

[13] Vgl. Schroeder, Roger G. et al.: The Content of Manufacturing Strategy: An Empirical Study, in: Journal of Operations Management, Vol. 6, No. 3/4, 1986, S. 405ff.

[14] Vgl. Stumpf, Stephen et al.: Managing Change – Strategic Response, Organizational Realities and Overcoming Resistance, in: Berndt, Ralph (Hrsg.): Total Quality Management als Erfolgsstrategie, Berlin/Heidelberg 1995, S. 77ff.

[15] Vgl. Hayes, Robert H. und Steven C. Wheelwright: Restoring our Competitive Edge. Competing through Manufacturing, New York et al. 1984, S. 100.

Darüber hinaus beschreibt die vierte Stufe, wie Fertigungsstrategien nicht nur monodirektional eine Verbindung von Gesamtunternehmensebene zum Funktionsbereich im Sinne der Umsetzung vorgegebener Ziele herstellen. „We argue … that manufacturing should take a more proactive role in defining the competitive advantage that is to be pursued.“[16] Die Fertigung selbst kann als Quelle für Wettbewerbsvorteile dienen, die im Rahmen des Strategiebildungsprozesses auf Unternehmensebene und im Marketingbereich eine wichtige Rolle spielen können. Eine solche Auffassung geht mit der Verbindung der marktorientierten und der ressourcenorientierten Sichtweise der Unternehmensführung einher.[17]

2 Die Bedeutung von Komplexität, Flexibilität und Erfolg für Fertigungsstrategien

2.1 Komplexität als Aktionsfeld industrieller Unternehmen

Der Begriff einer marktorientierten Fertigungsstrategie wirft die Frage nach ihren Bestimmungsfaktoren auf. Es gilt, neben dem im vorangegangenen Abschnitt bereits erwähnten Erfolgsbezug weitere, wichtige Determinanten zu identifizieren, um beispielsweise sowohl den Abhängigkeitsbeziehungen der involvierten unternehmerischen Funktionsbereiche als auch der vom Markt im Zeitablauf geforderten Anpassungsfähigkeit gerecht werden zu können. Die Bedeutung von Komplexität, Flexibilität und Erfolg für Fertigungsstrategien ist somit Gegenstand der folgenden Ausführungen.

Die Vielfalt der Betrachtungsobjekte, Ziele und Aufgaben in der Betriebswirtschaftslehre, die sich beispielsweise in der Gesamtheit der einzelnen Disziplinen dieser Wissenschaft ausdrückt, spiegelt die Konfrontation von Unternehmen mit dem Phänomen der Komplexität wider. Es handelt sich dabei um eine zunächst wertfreie Begebenheit des Wirtschaftens, die sich im Zuge der Bewertung von und des Entscheidens zwischen Alternativen unter Knappheit von Ressourcen in einer ersten groben Bestimmung mit Vielschichtigkeit, Unüberschaubarkeit und Intransparenz umschreiben lässt.[18] Dementsprechend wird nach einer integrierten Sicht der verschiedenen Unternehmensbereiche, -ziele und -aufgaben verlangt, um Unternehmen unter herrschender Komplexität als Gesamtheit erfolgreich führen zu können. Der betriebswirtschaftlich sinnvolle Umgang mit einer marktinduzierten Komplexitätsherausforderung ist besonders in einem wettbewerbsintensiven Umfeld eine Methode, um Wettbewerbsvorteile gegenüber anderen Marktteilnehmern zu generieren.[19] Somit muss es auch Inhalt marktorientierter Fertigungsstrategien sein, Komplexität entsprechend zu berücksichtigen.

---

[16] Hayes, Robert H. und Steven C. Wheelwright: Restoring our Competitive Edge, S. 41.

[17] Vgl. Thun, Jörn-Henrik: Der markt- und der ressourcenorientierte Ansatz bei der Formulierung der integrierten Fertigungsstrategie, S. 11–18.

[18] So bezeichnet Komplexität für den Soziologen Willke „… den Grad der Vielschichtigkeit, Vernetzung und Folgelastigkeit eines Entscheidungsfeldes“. Willke, Helmut: Systemtheorie, 2. Aufl., Stuttgart 1987, S. 16.

[19] Vgl. Gerwin, Donald: Manufacturing Flexibility: A Strategic Perspective, in: Management Science, Vol. 39 (1993), No. 4, S. 396f.

Komplexität kann allgemein aus einer systemorientierten Perspektive beschrieben werden, die in eine statische sowie in eine dynamische zu unterscheiden ist.[20] Aus objektstrukturbezogener Sicht bestimmt die Anzahl der Systemelemente (Varietät), die Anzahl der Verknüpfungen zwischen den Elementen (Konnektivität) sowie die Art und Unterschiedlichkeit ihrer Relationen (Funktionalität) die Komplexität eines Systems.[21] Diese Dimensionen können unter dem Begriff „Komplexität durch Vielfalt" zusammengefasst werden. Der objektverhaltensorientierte Komplexitätsbegriff betrachtet darüber hinaus Dynamik in einem System. Die Veränderung einer einzelnen Systemgröße bewirkt demzufolge sofortige und unterschiedlich stark ausgeprägte Reaktionen, wie z. B. im Systemverhalten über die Zeit oder einer Veränderung der Systemstruktur.[22] Eine der wesentlichen Ursachen für dynamische Komplexität wird im zeitlichen Auseinanderfallen von Entscheidung und Wirkung in einem System gesehen.[23] Neben den daraus resultierenden Verzögerungen sind die mangelnde Zuordnung von Ursache(n) und Wirkung(en) angesichts zahlreicher, paralleler Entscheidungssituationen in der betriebswirtschaftlichen Praxis für ein zielgerichtetes Handeln hinderlich.

Neben den objektbezogenen Perspektiven gibt der subjekt- bzw. beobachterbezogene Komplexitätsbegriff Aufschluss über das zugrunde liegende Phänomen. So versteht sich Komplexität als „... die Existenz von vielen, voneinander abhängigen Merkmalen in einem Ausschnitt der Realität"[24], wobei die subjektive Betrachtung zum Begriff der Komplexität als einer objektiv messbaren Systemeigenschaft in Widerspruch steht. Dieser Blickwinkel fokussiert die eigene Wahrnehmung der Komplexität seitens des Betrachters und führt zu dem Schluss, dass es die Komplexität schlechthin nicht geben kann. Im Zweifelsfall können objektiv komplexe Sachverhalte durch entsprechende Abstraktion subjektiv als einfach aufgefasst werden. Schließlich lassen sich Unternehmen aus diesen Perspektiven betrachtet als komplexe Systeme beschreiben.

Die bisherigen Ausführungen beschränkten Komplexität auf ein Phänomen, das innerhalb des Systems Unternehmen auftritt. Dieses ist jedoch eingebettet in ein oder mehrere Supersysteme. Unternehmen sehen sich daher in der Interaktion mit der Umwelt Komplexität von außen ausgesetzt, weisen jedoch auch in ihrer Innenwelt Komplexitätsphänomene auf.[25] Beides soll im Folgenden näher erläutert werden.

Unternehmen stehen einem komplexen Gefüge von externen Anforderungen gegenüber, denen sie sich schwer entziehen können. Diese externe Komplexität gliedert sich in folgende

---

[20] Vgl. Schiemenz, Bernd: Komplexität von Produktionssystemen, in: Kern, Werner et al. (Hrsg.): Handwörterbuch der Produktionswirtschaft, 2. Aufl., Stuttgart 1996, Sp. 897.

[21] Vgl. Milling, Peter: Kybernetische Überlegungen beim Entscheiden in komplexen Systemen, in: Milling, Peter (Hrsg.): Entscheiden in komplexen Systemen, Berlin 2002, S. 11 ff.

[22] Zum dynamischen Systemverhalten und den daraus erwachsenden Schwierigkeiten der Steuerung und Vorhersagbarkeit komplexer Systeme, vgl. Milling, Peter: Strategische Planungs- und Kontrollsysteme zur Unterstützung betrieblicher Lernprozesse, S. 11 ff.

[23] Vgl. Sterman, John D.: System Dynamics: Tools for learning in a complex World, in: California Management Review, Jg. 43 (2001), No. 4, S. 10f.

[24] Dörner, Dietrich: Die Logik des Misslingens – Strategisches Denken in komplexen Situationen, Reinbek 1989, S 60.

[25] Vgl. Wildemann, Horst: Komplexität: Vermeiden oder beherrschen lernen, in: Harvard Business Manager, Jg. 21 (1999), Nr. 6, S. 31.

Determinanten der Marktkomplexität:[26] Autonome Individualisierung auf zahlreichen Märkten, wodurch sich die Unternehmen zu einer zunehmenden Fragmentierung der Märkte in immer kleinere Zielgruppen mit sich schnell verändernden Bedürfnissen gezwungen sehen, stellt die Nachfragekomplexität dar. Wettbewerbskomplexität findet Ausdruck in der Erfordernis mehrdimensionaler Wettbewerbsvorteile aufgrund von Globalisierung, Deregulierung, zunehmender Wettbewerbsintensität und -dynamik der Märkte. Neue Technologien und das Zusammenwachsen bisher getrennter Technologien führen zu einer Technologiekomplexität. Darüber hinaus subsummiert die allgemeine Umweltkomplexität das Geflecht rechtlicher Rahmenbedingungen und Vielfalt politischer, gesellschaftlicher und ökonomischer Ansprüche.

In Zusammenhang damit sind Komplexitätstreiber, also komplexitätsfördernde Kräfte, zu beschreiben, die an der Schnittstelle zwischen externer und interner Komplexität anzusiedeln sind.[27] Es handelt sich dabei um einen direkten Ausdruck der Marktkomplexität, wie sie von außen auf Unternehmen trifft, die sich u. a. in den nachfolgenden Phänomenen niederschlägt. Kundenstrukturkomplexität entsteht durch eine hohe Anzahl heterogener Kunden/Kundengruppen mit teilweise geringen Absatzmengen. Ein breites und tiefes Produktprogramm mit hoher Diversifikation und zahlreichen Produktvarianten hat eine entsprechende Programmkomplexität zum Ergebnis. Unter Produktkomplexität sind beispielsweise Produktkonzepte zu fassen, die sich durch eine hohe Anzahl und/oder Verschiedenartigkeit der eingesetzten Rohmaterialien, Teile oder Baugruppen auszeichnen.

Folglich führen die marktbestimmten Komplexitätstreiber in Verbindung mit unternehmenseigenen Anforderungen zu interner Komplexität. Planungs-, Entscheidungs- und Handlungssituationen dieser Art zeichnen sich durch die Fülle an Entscheidungsparametern, deren Beziehungsgeflecht, die daraus resultierende Eigendynamik und Irreversibilität sowie schwindende Prognostizierbarkeit zukünftiger Zustände aus und lassen sich als komplex beschreiben.[28] Im Falle ausgeprägter Komplexität erweist es sich also für Unternehmen als problematisch, vorteilhafte Zustände anzustreben und nachteilige zu verhindern. Unternehmen sehen sich einem Komplexitätsproblem gegenüber.

Die mittelbaren Konsequenzen der Marktkomplexität decken ein Dilemma in Zusammenhang mit der internen Komplexität auf. Die aus markt- und kundenorientierten Zielen resultierenden Strukturen, die sich in den Komplexitätstreibern ausdrücken, führen zu einer komplexen Ausgestaltung der Prozesse, Systeme und Programme, welche im weitesten Sinne nach ressourcenorientierten Aspekten in Hinblick auf das operative Ziel der Produktivität zu organisieren sind. Während auf operativer Ebene die Zielgröße Effizienz im Leistungserstellungsprozess einer der Erfolgsfaktoren ist, um eine Strategie der Kostenführerschaft anstreben zu können, erfährt eine Differenzierungsstrategie ihre konsequente Umsetzung durch eine effektive Marktorientierung.[29] Trotz der Bemühungen um eine ausgewogene Integration dieser beiden grundsätzlichen Wettbewerbsstrategien in Form von Hybridwettbewerbsstrategien scheinen auf operativer Ebe-

[26] Vgl. auch im Folgenden Bliss, Christoph: Management von Komplexität, Wiesbaden 2000, S. 6.

[27] Vgl. Wildemann, Horst: Komplexität, S. 31.

[28] Vgl. auch im Folgenden Bliss, Christoph: Management von Komplexität, S. 3 ff. Vgl. ferner Milling, Peter: Strategische Planungs- und Kontrollsysteme zur Unterstützung betrieblicher Lernprozesse, S. 11.

[29] Vgl. Homburg, Christian und Daniel Daum: Marktorientiertes Kostenmanagement, Frankfurt a. M. 1997, S. 29 f.

ne marktorientierte Ziele auf der einen sowie Produktivität und Effizienz auf der anderen Seite nur bedingt miteinander vereinbar.[30] Es ist das Wesen von marktorientierten Fertigungsstrategien, sich mit solchen Zielkonflikten auseinander zu setzen, indem sie die zugrunde liegende Komplexität berücksichtigen.

Die bisherigen Ausführungen zu Komplexität, insbesondere inwiefern Unternehmen damit konfrontiert sind, decken den Wirkungszusammenhang zwischen den sich scheinbar ausschließenden Alternativen Differenzierungsstrategie und Kostenführerschaft auf. So steht die hohe Varietät des Absatzmarktes beispielsweise im Gegensatz zur geringen Varietät des Leistungserstellungssystems, welches sich im Idealfall dem externen System vollständig, unmittelbar und stetig anpassen sollte. Varietät bezeichnet allgemein die Anzahl möglicher Zustände, die ein System annehmen kann.[31] Beispiele für solche Varietätsasymmetrien sind Nachfrageunsicherheiten, volatile Bedarfsverläufe, Schwankungen im Auftragsmix der Kunden und kürzer werdende Lieferzeiten, denen Unternehmen nur selten gerecht werden. Ziel muss es also sein, externe Varietät zu dämpfen und/oder interne Varietät zu verstärken, um die Systeme auszubalancieren. Ashby bezeichnet dies als „Law of Requisite Variety".[32] Dies impliziert ein Handeln nach dem Prinzip so viel Komplexität wie nötig (möglichst vollständige Erfassung der externen Komplexität), so wenig Komplexität wie möglich (Ziel der Überschaubarkeit im Inneren). Somit ist es Aufgabe der Unternehmensführung, dieses Spannungsverhältnis zum Ausgleich zu bringen.[33] Komplexität gereicht schließlich zum Aktionsfeld industrieller Unternehmen. Ansoff fasst diesen Auftrag wie folgt zusammen: „To assure success and continuity, the speed, subtlety, and complexity of a firm's response must be in tune with the critical success factors and the turbulence level in the environment."[34]

Zum Umgang mit Komplexität bieten sich konkret folgende Möglichkeiten an:[35] Zunächst lässt sich drohende Überkomplexität präventiv durch Komplexitätsvermeidung abwenden. Dabei meint der Begriff der Überkomplexität eine übermäßige Ausrichtung auf die Unternehmensumwelt, die intern nicht gemeistert werden kann. Insbesondere junge Unternehmen und solche in starken Wachstumsphasen sollten bestrebt sein, unbeherrschbare Komplexität frühzeitig zu unterbinden.

Zur Beseitigung bereits bestehender Überkomplexität bietet sich eine Komplexitätsreduktion an. Dies betrifft Unternehmen, die erst nach dem Abschluss von Wachstumsphasen die Komplexitätsproblematik erkennen. Häufig geraten Unternehmen in eine Komplexitätsfalle, indem sie versuchen, Wachstum über Variantenreichtum, Marktsegmentierung und die Besetzung zusätzlicher Nischen zu generieren.[36] Sie verkennen dann die internen Abhängigkeiten in den

---

[30] Vgl. Köster, Oliver: Komplexitätsmanagement in der Industrie, Wiesbaden 1998, S. 28.

[31] Vgl. Milling, Peter: Systemtheoretische Grundlagen zur Planung der Unternehmenspolitik, Berlin 1981, S. 91 ff., ferner Malik, Fredmund (Hrsg.): Strategie des Managements komplexer Systeme, Bern et al. 1996, S. 186.

[32] Ashby, William R.: An Introduction to Cybernetics, New York 1958, S. 202, vgl. ferner Köster, Oliver: Komplexitätsmanagement, S. 34.

[33] Vgl. Malik, Fredmund: Strategie des Managements komplexer Systeme, S. 192–198.

[34] Ansoff, H. Igor: Implementing Strategic Management, Englewood Cliffs et al. 1984, S. 457.

[35] Vgl. im Folgenden Wildemann, Horst: Komplexität, S. 41.

[36] Vgl. Adam, Dietrich: Komplexitätsmanagement, Wiesbaden 1998, S. 5.

Prozessen. Ertragseinbußen, die im Rechnungswesen nicht rechtzeitig oder gar nicht erfasst und zugeordnet werden können, resultieren aus einer solchen Überkomplexität, der bei einer angespannten Finanzsituation der Unternehmen mit weiterer Überkomplexität begegnet wird. Dies zeigt sich in der Flucht in weitere Nischen, der Vernachlässigung des Kerngeschäftes und der Unterschätzung negativer Synergieeffekte.

In einem weiteren Ansatz verspricht eine Komplexitätsbeherrschung die erfolgreiche, steuerbare Ausdehnung interner Varietät zum Abbau der Varietätsasymmetrie.[37] Insbesondere für die Analyse des Beitrags von Fertigungsstrategien zur Marktorientierung ist es von Interesse, solche Unternehmen zu identifizieren, die sich für den Weg der Komplexitätsbeherrschung entscheiden. Ein Vorgehen, das Komplexität im Wesentlichen ignoriert, ist die Komplexitätsakzeptanz. Ursache und Wirkung von betriebswirtschaftlichen Problemstellungen werden als black-box betrachtet und hingenommen, ohne dass eine Auseinandersetzung mit den Zusammenhängen erfolgt.

In der Entscheidung über die richtige Vorgehensweise spielt die Multidimensionalität des Wettbewerbs unter den Konkurrenten eine bedeutsame Rolle.[38] Ausgehend von der Erkenntnis, dass die Realität nicht in vollem Umfang in Unternehmen abgebildet wird und Anforderungen von außen im Unternehmen nicht stets mit adäquaten Maßnahmen begegnet werden kann, sind interne Engpässe zu suchen und zu analysieren, deren Überwindung den größten Fortschritt im Wettbewerb versprechen. Somit kann der Anspruch eines integrierten Komplexitätsmanagements nicht in der vollständigen Lösung der Varietätsasymmetrie begründet sein. Vielmehr gilt es, sich mit ausgewählten Problemen bezüglich der Komplexität zu befassen, die in Unternehmen typischerweise anzutreffen sind und deren Lösung Unternehmen im Wettbewerb zu einer günstigen Position verhelfen.

Für die Analyse marktorientierter Fertigungsstrategien ist es zur Evaluation von Bedeutung, ihren Umgang mit Komplexität zu beleuchten. Es stellt sich die Frage, ob es Unternehmen gelingt, das zuvor erläuterte Dilemma zu überwinden oder dies gar in die Formulierung ihres Zielsystems aufzunehmen. Die jeweilige Umsetzung der Marktorientierung in der Fertigung ist stets auch eine Frage des Umgangs mit Komplexität zwischen den Alternativen Komplexitätsakzeptanz, -vermeidung, -reduktion und -beherrschung.

Darüber hinaus stellt sich die Aufgabe, die Komplexität selbst so zu gestalten, dass eine möglichst passende Abstimmung zwischen marktlichen Anforderungen und unternehmensinterner Flexibilität erfolgt.

2.2 Flexibilität als Wettbewerbsfaktor

Eine wesentliche Grundlage des Erfolges eines Unternehmens ist das frühzeitige Erkennen von Veränderungen in seinem Umfeld und das rechtzeitige Gestalten seines Wettbewerbverhaltens. Zur Lösung dieser zentralen Aufgabe wird Flexibilität häufig als eine bedeutende Eigenschaft von Unternehmen zur Bewältigung komplexer Umweltsituationen betrachtet, um den Fortbestand zu sichern.[39] Flexibilität wird daher die Rolle eines strategischen Erfolgsfaktors zuge-

[37] Vgl. Malik, Fredmund: Strategie des Managements komplexer Systeme, S. 184.

[38] Vgl. Bliss, Christoph: Management von Komplexität, S. 5.

[39] Vgl. Kaluza, Bernd und Thorsten Blecker: Wettbewerbsstrategien – Markt- und ressourcenorientierte Sicht der strategischen Führung. Konzepte – Gestaltungsfelder – Umsetzungen, München 2000, S. 207 f.

schrieben.[40] Im Folgenden wird untersucht, inwieweit Flexibilität für marktorientierte Fertigungsstrategien bedeutsam ist.

Sowohl in der betriebswirtschaftlichen als auch in der ingenieurwissenschaftlichen Literatur werden verschiedene Aspekte der Flexibilität diskutiert. Besonders in den letzten Jahren ist eine enorme Steigerung der Veröffentlichung zu Flexibilität festzustellen.[41] Dabei wird die lange Zeit ausschließlich reaktiv interpretierte Begriffsauffassung, also die Fähigkeit zur Anpassung an Umweltänderungen, um eine proaktive Sichtweise ergänzt.

Neue Organisationskonzepte und technologische Entwicklungen stellen veränderte Rahmenbedingungen dar und erhöhen den Stellenwert der Flexibilität.[42] Konzepte, die die Flexibilität sowie weitere verwandte Eigenschaften der Anpassung und Veränderung von Unternehmen in den Mittelpunkt der Betrachtung stellen, sind erarbeitet worden. In neueren Untersuchungen werden sogar turbulente Umweltbedingungen als Chance gesehen, die es durch Flexibilität zu nutzen gilt.[43] Neue Rahmenbedingungen, das Entstehen innovativer Konzepte zur Steigerung der Anpassungs- und Veränderungsfähigkeit der Unternehmen sowie die erweiterten Interpretationen der Flexibilität zeigen deutlich sowohl die gestiegene Relevanz des Themas für die Unternehmensführung als auch den Bedarf weiterer Forschungsarbeiten auf.

Bedeutende Arbeiten zur Flexibilitätsforschung sind bereits ab Mitte der zwanziger Jahre des vergangenen Jahrhunderts im betriebswirtschaftlichen Schrifttum im deutschsprachigen Raum zu finden.[44] Dabei wurde insbesondere die Anpassung der Unternehmen an Schwankungen des Marktes untersucht und hierfür u. a. auch der Begriff der Elastizität verwendet.[45] In späteren Arbeiten wurde diese enge Fokussierung aufgegeben und die Möglichkeiten der Unternehmen, mit Unsicherheit im Unternehmensumfeld umzugehen, thematisiert. Diese zwar neue, allerdings immer noch vereinfachte Interpretation der Flexibilität ist im Wesentlichen auch heute noch gültig, zumindest stellt es den tragfähigsten Konsens der im Detail sich unterscheidenden Meinungen dar.

Der Begriff der Flexibilität wurde bis zur Mitte des vergangenen Jahrhunderts von vielen Autoren untersucht. Der Fokus dieser Untersuchungen richtete sich auf die Flexibilisierung der Planung, Investitionsentscheidungen unter Unsicherheit, die Analyse der Kostenwirkungen der

---

[40] Vgl. z. B. Meffert, Heribert: Größere Flexibilität als Unternehmenskonzept, in: Zeitschrift für Betriebswirtschaftliche Forschung, Jg. 38 (1985), Nr. 2, S. 121 ff., Eversheim, Walter und Friedrich-Wilhelm Schäfer: Planung des Flexibilitätsbedarfs von Industrieunternehmen, in: Die Betriebswirtschaft, Jg. 40 (1980), Nr. 2, S. 229.

[41] Vgl. Meffert, Heribert und Christoph Burmann: Strategische Flexibilität und Strategiewechsel, in: Häflinger, Gerold E. und Jörg D. Meier: Aktuelle Tendenzen im Innovationsmanagement: Festschrift für Werner Popp zum 65. Geburtstag, Heidelberg 2000, S. 173 ff.

[42] Vgl. Burmann, Christoph: Strategische Flexibilität und Strategiewechsel als Determinanten des Unternehmenswertes, Wiesbaden 2002, S. 110.

[43] Vgl. Meffert, Heribert und Christoph Burmann: Strategische Flexibilität und Strategiewechsel, S. 173.

[44] Einen Überblick gibt beispielsweise Spur, Günther: Evolution der industriellen Produktion, in: Spur, Günther (Hrsg.): Optionen industrieller Produktionssysteme. Forschungsberichte der Interdisziplinären Arbeitsgruppen der Berlin-Brandenburgischen Akademie der Wissenschaften, Bd. 4, Berlin 1997, S. 37.

[45] So stellte beispielsweise Kalveram schon fest: „Elastizität in der Betriebswirtschaft ist der Grad der Anpassungsfähigkeit an die jeweilige Marktlage.“ Kalveram, Wilhelm: Elastizität und Betriebsführung, in: Zeitschrift für Betriebswirtschaft, Jg. 1 (1931), Nr. 8, S. 705.

Flexibilität, die Entwicklung von Anpassungsmaßnahmen an Marktschwankungen und die Untersuchung anpassungsfähiger organisatorischer Abläufe.[46] Dennoch erkannte Massie richtigerweise, dass „Flexibility is one of the concepts that often … receives too little attention in situations which demand its emphasis."[47] Die nächste Häufung an Auseinandersetzungen mit dem Thema Flexibilität ist ab Ende der sechziger Jahre festzustellen. Bedeutsam sind in der deutschen Literatur die Durchsetzung des Begriffs der Flexibilität gegenüber dem der Elastizität sowie die Ausdehnung des Themas über Anpassungen am Absatzmarkt hinaus auf weitere Funktionsbereiche im Unternehmen, was schließlich in der Erkenntnis zur Notwendigkeit einer allgemeinen Flexibilitätstheorie mündet.[48]

Sowohl die damalige als auch die aktuelle Diskussion des Flexibilitätsphänomens zeichnen sich durch eine uneinheitliche Terminologie sowie durch einen fehlenden allgemeingültigen und anerkannten Flexibilitätsbegriff aus.[49] Die trotz des großen Interesses immer noch bestehenden Schwierigkeiten bei der theoretischen Analyse und praktischen Realisierung der Flexibilität sind nicht zuletzt auch auf über 70 Definitionen der Flexibilität in der englischsprachigen Literatur zurückzuführen, wie Untersuchungen zeigen.[50] Dies unterstreicht auch folgende Feststellung: „Flexibility is a complex, multidimensional and hard-to-capture concept. At least 50 different terms for various types of flexibilities can be found in the manufacturing literature."[51]

Eine unreflektierte Übernahme dieser Bedeutung in die betriebswirtschaftliche Terminologie verkannte jedoch die Ursprünge der Wortbedeutung, die sich an der Eigenschaft physischer Objekte, welche beispielsweise nach Formveränderungen ihren ursprünglichen Zustand wieder annehmen können, orientiert. Die Anpassungsfähigkeit von Unternehmen als soziale Systeme ist dabei weniger statisch, sondern eher im Sinne eines evolutorischen Prozesses zu verstehen. Ebenso suggeriert die strenge Übersetzung aus dem Lateinischen, dass Flexibilität eine rein reaktive Eigenschaft von Unternehmen ist, wohingegen die begriffliche Bestimmung im Kontext von Wettbewerbsvorteilen neben der Beherrschung von Risiken durch Anpassung auch die Nutzung von Chancen umfasst. Demnach ist Flexibilität die Eigenschaft eines Systems, proaktive oder reaktive sowie zielgerichtete Änderungen der Systemkonfiguration zu ermöglichen, um die Anforderungen von sich verändernden Umweltbedingungen zu erfüllen und somit Existenz und Gedeihen von Unternehmen zu unterstützen.

---

[46] Vgl. z. B. Tannenbaum, Robert et al.: Leadership and Organization: a behavioral science approach, New York et al. 1961, S. 1 ff., Riebel, Paul: Die Elastizität des Betriebes: eine produktions- und marktwirtschaftliche Untersuchung, Köln et al. 1954.

[47] Massie, Joseph: Flexibility in Management – A Concept in economic decision making, in: Southern Economic Journal, Vol. 24 (1958), S. 447.

[48] Vgl. Jacob, Herbert: Flexibilitätsüberlegungen in der Investitionsrechnung, in: Zeitschrift für Betriebswirtschaft, Jg. 37 (1967), S. 1–34.

[49] Vgl. Reichwald, Ralf und Peter Behrbohm: Flexibilität als Eigenschaft betriebswirtschaftlicher Systeme, in: Zeitschrift für Betriebswirtschaft, Jg. 53 (1983), Nr. 9, S. 831.

[50] Vgl. Shewchuk, John P. and Colin L. Moodie: A Framework and Classification Scheme for Manufacturing Flexibility Types and Measures, in: International Journal of Flexible Manufacturing Systems, Vol. 10 (1998), No. 4, S. 325.

[51] Sethi, Andrea K. und Suresh P. Sethi: Flexibility in manufacturing: A Survey, in: International Journal of Flexible Manufacturing Systems, Vol. 2 (1990), No. 4, S. 289.

Im deutschen Schrifttum wird Flexibilität deshalb nicht nur als bedeutender Wettbewerbsfaktor betrachtet, sondern gar als polymorpher Begriff beurteilt.[52] Die verschiedenen Definitionsversuche stimmen allenfalls insoweit überein, als sie unter Flexibilität eine Fähigkeit zur Anpassung oder Änderung in Bezug auf unterschiedliche Bedingungen verstehen. Entsprechend sieht Upton in der Flexibilität eine Fähigkeit, die nicht zwangsläufig zu Lasten anderer Wettbewerbsfaktoren aufgebaut werden kann: „Flexibility is the ability to change or react with little penalty in time, effort, cost or performance."[53] Im Sinne der Wettbewerbsfaktoren zeichnet sich Flexibilität demnach als eine übergeordnete Größe aus, die mit den anderen Wettbewerbsfaktoren nicht zwangsläufig in Konkurrenz steht, wie es beim Dilemma zwischen Kosten und Qualität beispielsweise der Fall ist. Es ist jedoch kritisch zu hinterfragen, inwieweit Flexibilität tatsächlich losgelöst von, also nicht im Widerspruch zu anderen Wettbewerbsfaktoren erreicht werden kann.

Im Rahmen einer strategischen Ausrichtung der Fertigung bedarf es der Berücksichtigung des Faktors Flexibilität in der Fertigungsstrategie, um den geänderten Herausforderungen gerecht zu werden.[54] Der Wettbewerbsfaktor Flexibilität gewinnt vor dem Hintergrund sich schnell wandelnder und kaum vorhersehbarer Umweltsituationen verstärkt an Bedeutung, wie auch durch Studien belegt ist.[55] Dies ist keineswegs gleichbedeutend mit einer Irrelevanz der zuvor genannten Faktoren, vielmehr lässt sich schlussfolgern, dass Unternehmen von der Fokussierung auf einen oder zwei einzelne(n) Wettbewerbsfaktor(en) immer stärker abrücken und einen ihrer Ausrichtung im Wettbewerb entsprechenden Mix von Faktoren anstreben.[56] Dabei kommt dem Wettbewerbsfaktor Flexibilität eine besondere Rolle zu, denn schließlich bedeutet Anpassung im Zweifelsfall auch, dass Unternehmen in der Lage sein müssen, die Betonung der unterschiedlichen Faktoren je nach Situation verändern zu können. Flexibilität ließe sich demnach gar als ein Metawettbewerbsfaktor beschreiben.

Die Auffassung von Flexibilität im Kontext von Wettbewerbsfaktoren als Fähigkeit zu Veränderung und Anpassung der Komponenten des magischen Dreiecks – Preis/Kosten, Qualität und Zeit – verdeutlicht, dass die im Vorangegangenen beschriebene Komplexität, wie sie das Beziehungsgefüge kennzeichnet, aus dieser Sicht einer Dynamik unterliegt. Somit stellt sich Flexibilität als ein weiterer Bestimmungsfaktor marktorientierter Fertigungsstrategien dar.

2.3 Ansätze der Erfolgsforschung als Basis zur Beurteilung marktorientierter Fertigungsstrategien

In der Betriebswirtschaftslehre ist ein bemerkenswert einseitiges Verständnis des Unternehmenserfolges weit verbreitet. Der Erfolgsbegriff wird vielfach als Nettogröße im Sinne einer wert-

---

[52] Vgl. Mössner, Gerd Ulrich: Planung flexibler Unternehmensstrategien, München 1982, S. 30f.

[53] Upton, David M.: The Management of Manufacturing Flexibility, in: California Management Review, Vol. 36 (1994), No. 2, S. 73.

[54] Vgl. Skinner, Wickham: The Focused Factory, in: Harvard Business Review, Vol. 52 (1974), No. 3/4 S. 113ff.

[55] Vgl. Fiegenbaum, Avi und Aneel Karnani: Output flexibility – A competitive advantage for small Firms, in: Strategic Management Journal, Vol. 12 (1991), No 2, S. 101ff.

[56] Vgl. Slack, Nigel: Flexibility as a manufacturing objective, in: International Journal of Operations and Production Management, Vol. 3 (1983), No. 3, S. 4.

mäßigen Differenz zwischen Ausbringung und Mitteleinsatz bzw. Ertrag und Aufwand verstanden. Diese Differenzgröße wird im positiven Fall als Gewinn und im negativen Fall als Verlust bezeichnet. Der Begriff des Erfolges ist somit unmittelbar aus dem des Gewinns abgeleitet. Dieses traditionelle betriebswirtschaftliche Erfolgsverständnis entspringt einem engen ökonomischen Erfolgskonzept, welches die Komplexität des Erfolgsphänomens verkennt.[57] Unternehmen streben nicht nur Gewinn an, sondern verfolgen vielmehr ein Zielbündel, das neben monetären auch nicht-monetäre Ziele umfasst, etwa in Form eines eigenen Qualitätsanspruchs oder einer positiven Reputation in der Öffentlichkeit.[58] Die in dieser Hinsicht erzielbaren Erfolge eines Unternehmens entziehen sich aber teilweise einer exakten wertmäßigen Erfassung. Ferner sind Beziehungen zwischen den Zielen hinsichtlich Über- und Unterordnung nicht immer zweifelsfrei. Dies erschwert die Vergleichbarkeit zwischen Zielen und deren Erreichung und somit die Bestimmung von Prioritäten. Insbesondere der strategische Erfolg eines Unternehmens ist nicht durch ein Aufwand-Ertrags-Kalkül zu bestimmen.[59] Demzufolge gestaltet sich beispielsweise die Verteilung von Ressourcen, die zur Verfolgung verschiedener, womöglich konfliktärer Ziele einzusetzen sind, naturgemäß problematisch. Diese Problematik wohnt auch marktorientierten Fertigungsstrategien, verstanden als Ziel- und Maßnahmenbündel, im Grundsatz inne.

Konzepte des Wertmanagements versuchen, Erfolg jenseits einer einseitigen Fokussierung auf die klassische Gewinngröße zu erklären, und betonen den Zusammenhang mit Strategien.[60] Doch auch dort stehen überwiegend rein ökonomische Größen im Vordergrund. Es existieren jedoch auch betriebswirtschaftliche Erfolgskonzepte, in denen sich ein erweitertes Erfolgsverständnis äußert. Dieses zeigt sich z. B. in jenen Ansätzen, in denen ökonomische Erfolgsgrößen um vor- oder außerökonomische Erfolgsgrößen ergänzt werden.[61] Der konkrete Inhalt des einzelnen Erfolgsbegriffs hängt eng zusammen mit dem grundlegenden Ansatz der Erfolgsanalyse, auf dem die Überlegungen jeweils aufbauen. Zu diesen Ansätzen der Erfolgsforschung, die sich auf die Ebene der Gesamtorganisation beziehen, zählen u. a. die im Folgenden erläuterten.[62]

Der Logik des Zielansatzes folgend ist das Vorhandensein von Unternehmenszielen, nach denen Unternehmen gesteuert werden, Voraussetzung, um den Unternehmenserfolg bestimmen zu können. Erfolg kann als Grad der Zielerreichung definiert werden.[63] Nach diesem Verständ-

---

[57] Vgl. Albach, Horst: Investitionspolitik erfolgreicher Unternehmen, in: Zeitschrift für Betriebswirtschaft, Jg. 57 (1987), Nr. 7, S. 637.

[58] Vgl. Fritz, Wolfgang et al.: Unternehmensziele in Industrie und Handel, in: Die Betriebswirtschaft, Jg. 4 (1985), Nr. 4, S. 379–383. sowie Fritz, Wolfgang: Unternehmensziele und strategische Unternehmensführung, in: Die Betriebswirtschaft, Jg. 48 (1988), Nr. 5, S. 571 ff.

[59] Vgl. Engelhardt, Werner H. und Bernd Günter: Erfolgsgrößen im internen Rechnungswesen aus der Sicht der Absatzpolitik, in: Domsch, Michael et al. (Hrsg.): Unternehmenserfolg. Planung – Ermittlung – Kontrolle, Wiesbaden 1988, S. 153.

[60] Vgl. Voggenreiter, Dietmar und Martin Jochen: Der kombinierte Einsatz von Wertmanagement und Balanced Scorecard, in: Controlling, Jg. 14 (2002), Nr. 11, S. 615–622.

[61] Zur Einbindung ökonomischen Handelns in Ökologie und Sozialverträglichkeit vgl. Rauschenberger, Reto: Nachhaltiger Shareholder Value, S. 6 ff.

[62] Vgl. Staehle, Wolfgang H.: Management: eine verhaltenswissenschaftliche Perspektive, 5. Aufl., München 1990, S. 411 ff.

[63] Vgl. beispielsweise Grabatin, Günther: Effizienz von Organisationen, Berlin et al. 1981, S. 21.

nis offenbart sich die Komplexität des Strebens vor dem Hintergrund multipler Ziele, eingegrenzt durch sich wandelnde Rahmenbedingungen der externen Umwelt und Gegebenheiten der internen Unternehmenssituation. Diese Komplexität drückt sich dabei in mehreren Komponenten aus.[64] Die Vielfalt unternehmerischer Aufgaben zeigt die Schwierigkeit auf, einer Reihe über-, gleich- und untergeordneter Ziele gleichzeitig nachzukommen, um ein Gesamtoptimum zu erreichen. Dies gestaltet sich umso problematischer, je mehr Ansprüche von außen an Unternehmen herangetragen werden.[65] Darüber hinaus besteht Komplexität hinsichtlich der zunehmenden Vernetzung zwischen den Elementen des Zielsystems. Schließlich tragen die funktionalen, häufig intransparenten Zusammenhänge zwischen den vernetzten Elementen zur Komplexität bei.

Die Abhängigkeiten der Ziele voneinander, sowohl hinsichtlich der Wirkungsweise als auch der Wirkungsrichtung, sind nicht immer eindeutig bestimmbar. Dies zeigen auch die Erklärungsansätze diverser Bereiche der betriebswirtschaftlichen Forschung, die häufig in einem mehrdeutigen Verhältnis zueinander stehen. Entscheidungsträger sind oftmals überfordert, alle im Zielsystem relevanten Elemente simultan und widerspruchsfrei zu berücksichtigen. Nicht zuletzt aus solchen Überlegungen heraus haben sich Bemühungen zur Erforschung einiger weniger grundlegender Erfolgsfaktoren entwickelt. Der Anspruch, allgemeingültige Aussagen für das betriebswirtschaftliche Handeln abzuleiten und wenige, im Idealfall vollkommen beherrschbare Steuerungsgrößen dazu heranzuziehen, findet sich in den verschiedenen Ansätzen der Erfolgsfaktorenforschung.[66]

Eine Erweiterung der Perspektive des Zielansatzes durch die Berücksichtigung vielfältiger Beziehungen im System Unternehmen sowie im Supersystem Unternehmen/Umwelt liefert der Systemansatz. In dieser Sicht ist der Erfolgsbegriff nicht mehr auf die Zielerreichung beschränkt, sondern umfasst eine Beurteilung der Fähigkeit, Ressourcen zu erwerben, interne Systemstabilität zu erhalten und mit der Umwelt zu interagieren.[67] Der Erfolg wird dabei zu einem mehrdimensionalen, abstrakten Konstrukt, das die langfristige Überlebensfähigkeit zum Mittelpunkt hat.[68] Mitunter rückt die Anpassungsfähigkeit an die Unternehmensumwelt, das Supersystem, in den Mittelpunkt der Betrachtung: Folgt man den konzeptionellen Überlegungen der Systemforscher, so besteht das Management und insbesondere das internationale, stra-

---

[64] Zur Komponentenspaltung des Komplexitätsbegriffs vgl. Milling, Peter: Systemtheoretische Grundlagen zur Planung der Unternehmenspolitik, S. 91 ff. sowie die Ausführungen im Vorangegangenen. Ein zusammenfassender Überblick über die Komponenten Varietät, Konnektivität und Funktionalität ist zu finden bei Milling, Peter: Kybernetische Überlegungen beim Entscheiden in komplexen Systemen, S. 2.

[65] Exemplarisch sei die Forderung nach einer Öffentlichkeits- und Gesellschaftsorientierung der Unternehmensführung genannt. Vgl. Ulrich, Hans: Unternehmenspolitik, 2. Aufl., Bern 1987, S. 146f.

[66] Der wichtigste Ansatz verbirgt sich hinter der 1960 initiierten PIMS-Studie. Vgl. Buzzell, Robert D. und Bradley T. Gale: The PIMS principles: linking strategy to performance, New York 1987. Zur Kritik am PIMS-Programm vgl. beispielsweise Nicolai, Alexander und Alfred Kieser: Trotz eklatanter Erfolglosigkeit: Die Erfolgsfaktorenforschung weiter auf Erfolgskurs, in: Die Betriebswirtschaft, Jg. 62 (2002), Nr. 6, S. 579–596.

[67] Vgl Staehle, Wolfgang H.: Management, S. 413. So strebt die Systemforschung danach, Auswirkungen von Entscheidungen u.a. auf Stabilität und Zielerreichung beschreiben zu können. Vgl. Milling, Peter: Systemtheoretische Grundlagen zur Planung der Unternehmenspolitik, S. 15.

[68] Vgl. Bleicher, Knut: Unternehmungsentwicklung und organisatorische Gestaltung, Stuttgart et al. 1979, S. 4.

tegische Management, in der Bewältigung von Komplexität.[69] Diese rührt aus der Interaktion mit der Umwelt aufgrund der Vielzahl von Elementen und Beziehungen sowie der Art ihrer Verknüpfung her.[70]

Dem Interessenpluralistischen Ansatz zufolge sind Unternehmen in dem Maße erfolgreich, in dem es ihnen gelingt, die Interessen möglichst aller Mitglieder der externen Koalition (z. B. Kunden, Lieferanten, Gewerkschaften) und der internen Koalition (z. B. Mitarbeiter, Manager) zufrieden zu stellen.[71] Dieser auch als koalitionstheoretisch bezeichnete Ansatz ist für die Identifikation unternehmensinterner und -externer Einflussfaktoren von großer Bedeutung.

Schließlich beleuchtet der Kontingenzansatz den Erfolgsbegriff aus einer Perspektive, die die Abhängigkeit des Unternehmenserfolges und der Relevanz der einzelnen Erfolgskriterien von der jeweiligen Situation betont, in der sich das Unternehmen befindet. In der Annahme, dass ein einziger, alle Situationen zufriedenstellend gestaltender Weg nicht existiert, wird die jeweilige Ausgangssituation als Grundlage des unternehmerischen Handelns betrachtet. „Es gibt nicht eine generell gültige, optimale Handlungsalternative, sondern mehrere, situationsbezogen angemessene."[72] Demzufolge wird dieser Ansatz auch als situativer Ansatz bezeichnet.[73] Die unternehmensspezifisch unterschiedlichen Einflüsse von Faktoren der Wettbewerbsumwelt, wie sie zur Erläuterung der Entstehungsgeschichte des marktorientierten Unternehmensführungskonzeptes dargestellt wurden, gehen mit den Grundannahmen dieses Ansatzes konform, was den Nutzen des kontingenztheoretischen Ansatzes auch für die marketingwissenschaftliche Forschung belegt.[74] Demnach ist es zum einen ersichtlich, dass es die Marktorientierung schlechthin nicht gibt, sondern dass sie sich nach den jeweiligen externen, aber auch internen Gegebenheiten bemisst. Dies betrifft auch die Wahrnehmung der Marketingfunktion.[75] Hinsichtlich des Erfolgsbegriffs ist für die Evaluation marktorientierter Fertigungsstrategien grundsätzlich festzuhalten, dass sich auch dieser an situativen Bedingungen orientieren muss, obwohl dies objektive, zweifelsfreie Vergleiche möglicherweise einschränkt.

Über die dargestellten Ansätze der Erfolgsforschung hinaus sind weitere Ansätze vorstellbar, die sich aus den vier zuvor aufgeführten ableiten lassen. Trotz diverser Kritikpunkte ist insbesondere dem Zielansatz eine hohe forschungspraktische Relevanz zu attestieren.[76] Dies gilt

---

[69] Perlitz, Manfred et al.: Erfolgsfaktoren im Management von Joint Venture in Osteuropa – Ergebnisse einer empirischen Untersuchung, Mannheim 1996, S. 20.

[70] Zur bidirektionalen Interaktion mit der Umwelt als Beziehungsgefüge vgl. Milling, Peter: Strategische Planungs- und Kontrollsysteme zur Unterstützung betrieblicher Lernprozesse, S. 12.

[71] Vgl. Staehle, Wolfgang H.: Management, S. 415 f.

[72] Staehle, Wolfgang H.: Deutschsprachige situative Ansätze in der Managementlehre, in: Kieser, Alfred (Hrsg.): Organisationstheoretische Ansätze, München 1981, S. 215.

[73] Vgl. Staehle, Wolfgang H.: Management, S. 47–58.

[74] Vgl. u. a. Day, George S. und Robin Wensley: Marketing Theory with a Strategic Orientation, in: Journal of Marketing, Vol. 47 (1983), No. 3, S. 79–89.

[75] Vgl. Ruekert, Robert W. et al.: The Organization of Marketing Activities: A Contingency Theory of Structure and Performance, in: Journal of Marketing, Vol. 49 (1985), No. 4, S. 13–25.

[76] Vgl. zur Kritik am Zielansatz vgl. Bungard, Walter und Gerd Wiendieck: Zur Effizienz von Qualitätszirkeln, in: Bungard, Walter und Gerd Wiendieck (Hrsg.): Qualitätszirkel als Instrument zeitgemäßer Betriebsführung, Landsberg/Lech 1986, S. 288 ff.

umso mehr, als der Zielansatz neben dem Systemansatz nicht selten als die übergeordnete Perspektive der betriebswirtschaftlichen Erfolgsforschung angesehen wird. Da der Zielansatz ferner die Unternehmung in den Mittelpunkt stellt und sich auf die Ebene der Gesamtorganisation beziehen lässt, ist er für die beabsichtigte Analyse marktorientierter Fertigungsstrategien hinsichtlich ihrer Beurteilung von grundsätzlicher Bedeutung. Es ist jedoch zu betonen, dass die Erfolgsanalyse der jeweiligen Fertigungsstrategie neben Komponenten des Zielansatzes Aspekte des Systemansatzes und des Kontingenzansatzes mit einschließt und somit einige Schwächen des traditionellen Zielansatzes einschränkt. Demzufolge ist zwar der Erfolgsbeitrag von marktorientierten Fertigungsstrategien im Sinne des Zielansatzes als Beitrag zur Erreichung von Unternehmenszielen Ausgangspunkt der Beurteilung. Jedoch bleibt festzuhalten, dass zur Erreichung grundlegender Unternehmensziele wie beispielsweise dem der Existenzsicherung Erkenntnisse aus einer systemtheoretischen Perspektive eine wertvollen Beitrag zu leisten vermögen.

Die grundsätzliche Fähigkeit eines Unternehmens als System, sich in einem veränderlichen Supersystem dauerhaft zu etablieren, lässt sich zusätzlich aus einer systemtheoretischen Perspektive betrachten, um Handlungsempfehlungen abzuleiten. Ferner ist es unstrittig, dass der Fertigungsbereich die Ziele und Zielbündel auf Gesamtunternehmensebene in ihrer Umsetzung zu unterstützen zum Inhalt hat. Dabei bietet die Fertigung Potenziale, die den Rahmen der wettbewerbsstrategischen Ausrichtung setzen, um den Unternehmenserfolg zu erzielen.

Eine marktorientierte Sichtweise rückt die marktlichen Anforderungen und Gegebenheiten in das Zentrum der Betrachtung. Aufgabe der Fertigung ist es, situationsspezifisch für bestimmte, unternehmensindividuelle Positionen in den verschiedenen bedienten Märkten Leistungen bereitzustellen. Diese richten sich in ihren Eigenschaften im Sinne des „Strategic Fit" nach den Marktsituationen und den im Wettbewerb verfolgten Prioritäten.[77] Die Betrachtung der Rolle von Fertigungsstrategien aus diesem Blickwinkel veranschaulicht, dass es eine generell überlegene Fertigungsstrategie nicht gibt, sondern situative Faktoren berücksichtigt werden müssen, um erfolgreich zu sein. Somit muss eine Analyse des Erfolges von marktorientierten Fertigungsstrategien auch vor dem Hintergrund des Kontingenzansatzes erfolgen. Eine erfolgreiche marktorientierte Fertigungsstrategie trägt demnach zum Erreichen der Unternehmensziele bei, fördert die Überlebensfähigkeit der Unternehmung als System und weist je nach Position und Situation im Wettbewerb eine adäquate Ausgestaltung auf.

Empirische Untersuchungen des Unternehmenserfolges und des Erfolges verschiedener betriebswirtschaftlicher Maßnahmen bedienen sich bevorzugt finanzieller Erfolgskriterien, unter denen verschiedene Rentabilitätsmaße, wie z. B. der Return on Investment (ROI), nach wie vor eine besonders große Popularität genießen.[78] Andere ökonomische Erfolgskriterien wie beispielsweise Produktqualität, Marktanteil, Mitarbeiterzufriedenheit werden demgegenüber weitaus seltener verwendet oder nehmen in einem hierarchisch gegliederten Zielsystem eine untergeordnete Rolle ein. Die Berücksichtigung außerökonomischer Erfolgsgrößen wie z. B.

[77] Zum Begriff des „Strategic Fit" vgl. Mintzberg, Henry et al.: Strategy Safari – A guided Tour Through the Wilds of Strategic Management, New York 1998, S. 24.

[78] Vgl. Venkatraman, Narasimhan A. und Vidhya Ramanujam: Measurement of Business Performance in Strategy Research: A Comparison of Approaches, in: Academy of Management Review, Vol. 11 (1986), No. 4, S. 803.

des Ansehens in der Öffentlichkeit und dessen langfristiger Anpassungsfähigkeit findet sich nur am Rande.[79] Angesichts der bereits diagnostizierten Einseitigkeit des traditionellen betriebswirtschaftlichen Erfolgsverständnisses überrascht diese Feststellung nicht. Die Einseitigkeit finanzieller Erfolgskriterien in der empirischen Analyse des Unternehmenserfolges erscheint aus mehreren Gründen problematisch. So ist die Aussagefähigkeit der Rentabilitätsmaße deshalb nicht selten eingeschränkt, weil die Berechnung dieser Größen von unternehmensindividuellen und nationalen Unterschieden in der Rechnungslegung beeinflusst wird.[80] Darüber hinaus unterscheiden sich exzellente und weniger exzellente Unternehmen unter dem Aspekt solcher Rentabilitätskriterien vielfach gar nicht signifikant voneinander, wie empirische Studien zeigen.[81] Die Aussagekraft dieser Größen ist somit zwar keineswegs hinfällig, aber eindeutig begrenzt.

Darüber hinaus erscheint es fraglich, ob finanzielle Erfolgskriterien grundsätzlich in der Lage sind, den strategischen Erfolg eines Unternehmens richtig zu erfassen. Unter strategischen Aspekten bedarf es der Berücksichtigung solcher Erfolgsgrößen, welche die Gesamtausrichtung des Unternehmens nach innen und außen widerspiegeln. „Unternehmenserfolg geht dann in eine Erfüllung mehrdimensionaler Unternehmenszielsetzungen über."[82] Er greift damit weit über traditionelle Erfolgsmaßstäbe hinaus.

Die einseitige Betonung finanzieller Erfolgskriterien in den betriebswirtschaftlichen Erfolgsanalysen stellt die Interessen der Anteilseigner bzw. der Kapitalgeber in den Vordergrund und widerspricht somit vordergründig dem interessenpluralistischen Ansatz.[83] Die Interessen anderer Gruppen von Organisationsteilnehmern wie z.B. der Mitarbeiter, der Kunden und der Lieferanten erfahren weitestgehend keine explizite Nennung unter den Kriterien zum Unternehmenserfolg. Doch durch ihre häufig anzutreffende Einbindung in ein Zielsystem ist nicht nur eine indirekte Berücksichtigung gewährleistet. Die Aufdeckung von Wirkungszusammenhängen zwischen finanziellen Zielgrößen und nicht monetären Faktoren, die Identifikation sogenannter Stellhebel sowie die bisweilen anzutreffende Schwierigkeit, Konstrukte einer Operationalisierung zuzuführen, sensibilisieren für das Zusammenspiel solcher Einflussgrößen, deren Wurzeln nicht in der Entstehungsgeschichte des Rechnungswesens liegen.

---

[79] Vgl. Fritz, Wolfgang: Marketing – ein Schlüsselfaktor des Unternehmenserfolges?, S. 94ff.

[80] Dies betrifft sowohl Vergleiche zwischen Unternehmen verschiedener Länder als auch Zeitvergleiche ein und desselben Unternehmens aufgrund von Umstellungen der Rechnungslegungsvorschriften. So sind für Konzernabschlüsse von in der EU börsennotierten Konzernen für Geschäftsjahre, die seit 2005 beginnen, Konzernabschlüsse nach den Regeln der IAS/IFRS aufzustellen. Vgl. Verordnung (EG) Nr. 1606/2002 des Europäischen Parlaments und des Rates, 19. Juli 2002, Amtsblatt der europäischen Gemeinschaften, L 243 vom 11.9.2002, S. 14.

[81] Vgl. Chakravarthy, Bala S.: Measuring Strategic Performance, in: Strategic Management Journal, Vol. 7 (1986), No. 5, S. 442–445.

[82] Engelhardt, Werner H. und Bernd Günter: Erfolgsgrößen im internen Rechnungswesen aus der Sicht der Absatzpolitik, S. 153.

[83] Unterschiede in der Berücksichtigung der Gruppe der Kapitalgeber spiegeln sich in den unterschiedlichen internationalen Rechnungslegungssystemen wider. So wird dem Abschluss nach HGB ein stärkerer Gläubigerschutz attestiert als beispielsweise einer Bilanzierung nach IAS/IFRS bzw. US-GAAP, wonach Eigenkapitalgeber erhöhte Aufmerksamkeit genießen. Vgl. Coenenberg, Adolf G.: Jahresabschluss und Jahresabschlussanalyse, S. 73f.

Von zentraler Bedeutung für die Entwicklung marktorientierter Fertigungsstrategien ist im Lichte des Kontingenzansatzes die Eignung der jeweiligen Fertigungsstrategie zur Unterstützung der jeweiligen Ausprägung der Marktorientierung eines Unternehmens. Dabei orientiert sich die Einschätzung der jeweiligen Situation an Zielbündeln, wie sie zur Erzielung von Wettbewerbsvorteilen am Markt angestrebt werden. Diese Ziele nehmen in den betrachteten Unternehmen mitunter die Rolle von Messgrößen im Sinne des Zielansatzes ein.

3 Anforderungen an die Implementierung marktorientierter Fertigungsstrategien

Komplexität, Flexibilität und Erfolg stellen bedeutsame Determinanten marktorientierter Fertigungsstrategien dar und sind als Herausforderungen marktorientierter Fertigungsstrategien zu betrachten, da sie entscheidenden Einfluss auf deren Effektivität besitzen. Fertigungsstrategien, die diese Größen in keinster Weise berücksichtigen, werden dem Anspruch an eine Fertigungsstrategie grundsätzlich nicht gerecht, denn sie vermögen es nicht, sich konkret mit der Umwelt auseinanderzusetzen oder gar eine proaktive Rolle auszufüllen und die strategische Ausrichtung des Gesamtunternehmens zur Existenzsicherung und Weiterentwicklung zu unterstützen. Die Berücksichtigung von Komplexität, Flexibilität und Erfolg in Fertigungsstrategien mag als Postulat zunächst trivial erscheinen; die Diskussion der Größen zeigte jedoch auf, dass die Ambiguität der Begriffe per se nach zweckadäquaten Definitionen verlangt, um sie im Kontext von Fertigungsstrategien zu thematisieren. In der betriebswirtschaftlichen Praxis zieht dies die Notwendigkeit einer klaren Begriffsbestimmung als Voraussetzung nach sich, um Fertigungsstrategien kommunizieren und somit als Leitlinien einer Akzeptanz unter den Beteiligten zuführen zu können.

Fertigungsstrategien fungieren nicht nur als Bindeglied zwischen Unternehmensführung und Fertigungsbereich. Eine Abstimmung mit Strategien benachbarter Funktionsbereiche ist für die Effektivität im Gesamtunternehmenskontext unabdingbar. Die Betrachtung weiterer unternehmerischer Funktionsbereiche beinhaltet die Gefahr nicht zu lösender Schnittstellenprobleme. Ein Abgleich der Fertigungsstrategien mit anderen Funktionsstrategien kann etwaige Widersprüche zutage fördern. Dieses Vorgehen stellt zwar nicht die Lösung dieser Probleme dar, es bildet aber zumindest eine Grundlage zur Kommunikation unterschiedlicher Denkweisen, die in organisatorischen Einheiten oder auch bereichsübergreifend herrschen.

Im Fertigungsbereich stehen zahlreiche Konzepte und Programme im Sinne des manufacturing proactivity zur Verfügung. Dies bedeutet „taking initiative in improving current circumstances or creating new ones; it involves challenging the status quo rather then adapting to present conditions“.[84] So wird manufacturing proactivity, verstanden als Implementierung fortschrittlicher und vielversprechender Konzepte und Programme im Produktionsmanagement, ein positiver Einfluss auf die Performance sowohl im Fertigungsbereich als auch hinsichtlich finanzieller Kenngrößen auf Gesamtunternehmensebene attestiert.[85]

---

[84] Crant, Michael J.: Proactive Behaviour in Organizations, in: Journal of Management, Vol. 26 (2000), No. 3, S. 436.

[85] Vgl. González-Benito, Javier: A study of the effect of manufacturing proactivity on business performance, in: International Journal of Operations & Production Management, Vol. 25 (2005), No. 3, S. 236.

Unternehmen sind folglich dem Problem ausgesetzt, aus einer Vielzahl von Verbesserungsansätzen zu wählen. In der betriebswirtschaftlichen Praxis zöge ein ungesteuerter Aktionismus neben der Gefahr der Ressourcenbindung und somit der Überlastung der Mitarbeiter die Schwierigkeit der Erfolgskontrolle nach sich. Andererseits illustrieren Fertigungsstrategien den Umfang und die Vernetzung der einbezogenen Elemente. Trotz der Bemühungen der Erfolgsfaktorenforschung, Erfolg aus wenigen Einflussfaktoren heraus zu erklären, ist die unumgängliche Komplexität festzuhalten, die es in marktorientierten Fertigungsstrategien zu berücksichtigen gilt. Aufgabe des Managements im Fertigungsbereich ist es daher, sich mit den Bestandteilen von Fertigungsstrategien in ihrem Zusammenwirken zu beschäftigen. „A complex structure has many masters and none of them can be served exclusively.“[86] Dies birgt allerdings die Gefahr, dass sich Prioritäten und Maßnahmen im Fertigungsbereich durch ihre Vielzahl der Kontrolle entziehen. Folglich gilt es, auf dem Grat zwischen Aktionismus unzähliger Verbesserungsprojekte und der Reduktion auf wenige, allgemeingültige, vermeintliche Erfolgsfaktoren im Unternehmen durch so viel Komplexität wie nötig und so wenig Komplexität wie möglich Balance zu halten.

Literatur

Adam, D. (1998): *Komplexitätsmanagement*, Wiesbaden.

Albach, H. (1987): Investitionspolitik erfolgreicher Unternehmen, in: *Zeitschrift für Betriebswirtschaft*, Jg. 57, Nr. 7, S. 636–661.

Ansoff, H. I. (1984): *Implementing Strategic Management*, Englewood Cliffs et al.

Ashby, W. R. (1958): *An Introduction to Cybernetics*, New York.

Bleicher, K. (1979): *Unternehmungsentwicklung und organisatorische Gestaltung*, Stuttgart et al.

Bleicher, K. (1996): *Das Konzept Integriertes Management, 4. Aufl.*, Frankfurt.

Bliss, C. (2000): *Management von Komplexität*, Wiesbaden.

Bungard, W. und G. Wiendieck (1986): Zur Effizienz von Qualitätszirkeln, in: Bungard, W. und G. Wiendieck (Hrsg.): *Qualitätszirkel als Instrument zeitgemäßer Betriebsführung*, Landsberg/Lech, S. 281–305.

Burmann, C. (2002): *Strategische Flexibilität und Strategiewechsel als Determinanten des Unternehmenswertes*, Wiesbaden.

Buzzell, R. D. und B. T. Gale (1987): *The PIMS principles: linking strategy to performance*, New York.

Chakravarthy, B. S. (1986): Measuring Strategic Performance, in: *Strategic Management Journal*, Vol. 7, No. 5, S. 437–458.

Crant, M. J. (2000): Proactive Behaviour in Organizations, in: *Journal of Management*, Vol. 26, No. 3, S. 435–462.

Day, G. S. und R. Wensley (1983): Marketing Theory with a Strategic Orientation, in: *Journal of Marketing*, Vol. 47, No. 3, S. 79–89.

Dörner, D. (1989): *Die Logik des Misslingens – Strategisches Denken in komplexen Situationen*, Reinbek.

Engelhardt, W. H. und B. Günter (1988): Erfolgsgrößen im internen Rechnungswesen aus der Sicht der Absatzpolitik, in: Domsch, M. et al. (Hrsg.): *Unternehmenserfolg. Planung – Ermittlung – Kontrolle*, Wiesbaden, S. 141–155.

[86] Kelly, Kevin: Out of Control: The New Biology of Machines, Social Systems, and the Economic World. Reading (MA) 1995, S. 470.

Eversheim, W. und F.-W. Schäfer (1980): Planung des Flexibilitätsbedarfs von Industrieunternehmen, in: *Die Betriebswirtschaft*, Jg. 40, Nr. 2, S. 229–248.

Fiegenbaum, A. und A. Karnani (1991): Output flexibility – A competitive advantage for small Firms, in: *Strategic Management Journal*, Vol. 12, No 2, S. 101–114.

Fritz, W. et al. (1985): Unternehmensziele in Industrie und Handel, in: *Die Betriebswirtschaft*, Jg. 45, Nr. 4, S. 375–394.

Fritz, W. (1988): Unternehmensziele und strategische Unternehmensführung, in: *Die Betriebswirtschaft*, Jg. 48, Nr. 5, S. 567–586.

Fritz, W. (1993): Marktorientierte Unternehmensführung und Unternehmenserfolg, in: *Marketing – Zeitschrift für Forschung und Praxis*, Jg. 15, Nr. 4, S. 237–246.

Gerwin, D. (1993): Manufacturing Flexibility: A Strategic Perspective, in: *Management Science*, Vol. 39, No. 4, S. 395–410.

González-Benito, J. (2005): A study of the effect of manufacturing proactivity on business performance, in: *International Journal of Operations & Production Management*, Vol. 25, No. 3, S. 222–241.

Grabatin, G. (1981): *Effizienz von Organisationen*, Berlin et al.

Gunn, T. G. (1987): *Manufacturing for Competitive Advantage: Becoming a World-Class Manufacturer*, Cambrigde (Mass.).

Hayes, R. H. und S. C. Wheelwright (1984): *Restoring our Competitive Edge. Competing through Manufacturing*, New York et al.

Hill, T. (1995): *Manufacturing Strategy – Text and Cases*, Houndmills.

Homburg, C. und D. Daum (1997): *Marktorientiertes Kostenmanagement*, Frankfurt.

Jacob, H. (1967): Flexibilitätsüberlegungen in der Investitionsrechnung, in: *Zeitschrift für Betriebswirtschaft*, Jg. 37, S. 1–34.

Kaluza, B. und T. Blecker (2000): *Wettbewerbsstrategien – Markt- und ressourcenorientierte Sicht der strategischen Führung. Konzepte – Gestaltungsfelder – Umsetzungen*, München.

Kalveram, W. (1931): Elastizität und Betriebsführung, in: *Zeitschrift für Betriebswirtschaft*, Jg. 1, Nr. 8, S. 705–711.

Kelly, K. (1995): *Out of Control: The New Biology of Machines, Social Systems, and the Economic World.* Reading (MA).

Köster, O. (1998): *Komplexitätsmanagement in der Industrie*, Wiesbaden.

Kohli, A. K. und B. J. Jaworski (1990): Market orientation: the construct, research propositions, and managerial implications, in: *Journal of Marketing*, Vol. 54, No. 2, S. 1–18.

Malik, F. (1996): *Strategie des Managements komplexer Systeme*, Bern et al.

Massie, J. (1958): Flexibility in Management – A Concept in economic decision making, in: *Southern Economic Journal*, Vol. 24, S. 447–457.

Meffert, H. (1985): Größere Flexibilität als Unternehmenskonzept, in: *Zeitschrift für Betriebswirtschaftliche Forschung*, Jg. 38, Nr. 2, S. 121–137.

Meffert, H. und C. Burmann (2000): Strategische Flexibilität und Strategiewechsel, in: Häflinger, G. E. und J. D. Meier (Hrsg.): *Aktuelle Tendenzen im Innovationsmanagement: Festschrift für Werner Popp zum 65. Geburtstag*, Heidelberg, S. 173–215.

Milling, P. (1981): *Systemtheoretische Grundlagen zur Planung der Unternehmenspolitik*, Berlin.

Milling, P. (1991): Strategische Planungs- und Kontrollsysteme zur Unterstützung betrieblicher Lernprozesse, in: Milling, P. (Hrsg.): *Systemmanagement und Managementsysteme*, Berlin.

Milling, P. (2002): Kybernetische Überlegungen beim Entscheiden in komplexen Systemen, in: Milling, P. (Hrsg.): *Entscheiden in komplexen Systemen*, Berlin.

Mintzberg, H. (1994): *The Rise and Fall of Strategic Planning*, New York et al.

Mintzberg, H. et al. (1998): *Strategy Safari – A guided Tour Through the Wilds of Strategic Management*, New York.

Mössner, G. U. (1982): *Planung flexibler Unternehmensstrategien*, München.

Narver, J. C. und S. F. Slater (1990): The Effect of a Market Orientation on Business Profitability, in: *Journal of Marketing*, Vol. 54, No. 4, S. 20–35.

Nicolai, A. und A. Kieser (2002): Trotz eklatanter Erfolglosigkeit: Die Erfolgsfaktorenforschung weiter auf Erfolgskurs, in: *Die Betriebswirtschaft*, Jg. 62, Nr. 6, S. 579–596.

Porter, M. E. (1979): How competitive forces shape strategy, in: *Harvard Business Review*, Vol. 57, No. 2, S. 137–145.

Rauschenberger, R. (2002): *Nachhaltiger Shareholder Value*, Bern et al.

Reichwald, R. und P. Behrbohm (1983): Flexibilität als Eigenschaft betriebswirtschaftlicher Systeme, in: *Zeitschrift für Betriebswirtschaft*, Jg. 53, Nr. 9, S. 831–853.

Riebel, P. (1954): *Die Elastizität des Betriebes: eine produktions- und marktwirtschaftliche Untersuchung*, Köln et al.

Ruekert, R. W. et al. (1985): The Organization of Marketing Activities: A Contingency Theory of Structure and Performance, in: *Journal of Marketing*, Vol. 49, No. 4, S. 13–25.

Schiemenz, B. (1996): Komplexität von Produktionssystemen, in: Kern, W. et al. (Hrsg.): *Handwörterbuch der Produktionswirtschaft, 2. Aufl.*, Stuttgart, Sp. 895–904.

Schroeder, R. G. et al. (1986): The Content of Manufacturing Strategy: An Empirical Study, in: *Journal of Operations Management*, Vol. 6, No. 4, S. 405–415.

Sethi, A. K. und S. P. Sethi (1990): Flexibility in manufacturing: A Survey, in: *International Journal of Flexible Manufacturing Systems*, Vol. 2, No. 4, S. 289–328.

Shewchuk, J. P. and C. L. Moodie (1998): A Framework and Classification Scheme for Manufacturing Flexibility Types and Measures, in: *International Journal of Flexible Manufacturing Systems*, Vol. 10, No. 4, S. 325–349.

Skinner, W. (1969): Manufacturing – Missing link in corporate strategy, in: *Harvard Business Review*, Vol. 47, No. 5/6, S. 136–145.

Skinner, W. (1974): The Focused Factory, in: *Harvard Business Review*, Vol. 52, No. 3/4, S. 113–121.

Slack, N. (1983): Flexibility as a manufacturing objective, in: *International Journal of Operations and Production Management*, Vol. 3, No. 3, S. 4–10.

Slater, S. F. und J. C. Narver (1994): Does Competitive Environment Moderate the Market Orientation – Performance Relationship?, in: *Journal of Marketing*, Vol. 58, No. 1, S. 46–55.

Spur, G. (1997): Evolution der industriellen Produktion, in: Spur, G. (Hrsg.): *Optionen industrieller Produktionssysteme. Forschungsberichte der Interdisziplinären Arbeitsgruppen der Berlin-Brandenburgischen Akademie der Wissenschaften*, Bd. 4, Berlin, S. 15–50.

Staehle, W. H. (1981): Deutschsprachige situative Ansätze in der Managementlehre, in: Kieser, A. (Hrsg.): *Organisationstheoretische Ansätze*, München.

Staehle, W. H. (1990): *Management: eine verhaltenswissenschaftliche Perspektive, 5. Aufl.*, München.

Sterman, J. D. (2001): System Dynamics: Tools for learning in a complex World, in: *California Management Review*, Vol. 43, No. 4, S. 8–25.

Stumpf, S. et al. (1995): Managing Change – Strategic Response, Organizational Realities and Overcoming Resistance, in: Berndt, R. (Hrsg.): *Total Quality Management als Erfolgsstrategie*, Berlin/Heidelberg, S. 77–95.

Tannenbaum, R. et al. (1961): *Leadership and organization: a behavioral science approach*, New York et al.

Thun, J.-H. (2004): *Der markt- und der ressourcenorientierte Ansatz bei der Formulierung der integrierten Fertigungsstrategie, Forschungsberichte der Fakultät für Betriebswirtschaftslehre*, Universität Mannheim, Nr. 2004-03, Mannheim.

Ulrich, H. (1987): *Unternehmenspolitik, 2. Aufl.*, Bern.

Upton, D. M. (1994): The Management of Manufacturing Flexibility, in: *California Management Review*, Vol. 36, No. 2, S. 72–89.

Venkatraman, N. A. und V. Ramanujam (1986): Measurement of Business Performance in Strategy Research: A Comparison of Approaches, in: *Academy of Management Review*, Vol. 11, No. 4, S. 801–814.

Verordnung (EG) Nr. 1606/2002 des Europäischen Parlaments und des Rates, 19. Juli 2002, Amtsblatt der europäischen Gemeinschaften, L 243 vom 11.9.2002, S. 1–4.

Voggenreiter, D. und M. Jochen (2002): Der kombinierte Einsatz von Wertmanagement und Balanced Scorecard, in: *Controlling*, Jg. 14, Nr. 11, S. 615–622.

Voss, C. A. (1992): Manufacturing strategy formulation as a process, in: Voss, C. A.: *Manufacturing Strategy*, London et al., S. 121–132.

Wheelwright, S. C. und R. H. Hayes (1991): Competing Through Manufacturing, in: Montgomery, C. A. und M. E. Porter (Hrsg.): *Strategy: Seeking and Securing Competitive Advantage*, Boston (Mass.), S. 89–112.

Wildemann, H. (1999): Komplexität: Vermeiden oder beherrschen lernen, in: *Harvard Business Manager*, Jg. 21, Nr. 6, S. 31–42.

Willke, H. (1987): *Systemtheorie, 2. Aufl.*, Stuttgart.

Implementierungsfelder Organisationalen Lernens in Industriebetrieben

Uwe Schwellbach

Freudenberg Vliesstoffe KG

Zusammenfassung

Organisationales Lernen bildet die Grundlage, um die für die Sicherung des Unternehmenserfolgs ständig erforderliche Neugestaltung und vor allem Anpassung der Geschäftsprozesse und Geschäftsmodelle realisieren zu können. Die Notwendigkeit zur Fähigkeit des Lernens wird durch sich immer schneller verändernde Umfeld- und Umweltbedingungen nochmals untermauert. Ziel des Beitrags ist die Verdeutlichung der Wesentlichkeit der vier Einflussfelder Strategiebildung, Organisationsstruktur/-prozesse, Unternehmenskultur und Human Resource Management. Innerhalb dieser Felder werden Faktoren identifiziert und diskutiert, die Organisationales Lernen direkt oder indirekt fördern. Durch eine bewusste Implementierung und Steuerung dieser Faktoren kann ein Unternehmen demnach maßgeblich und nachhaltig den eigenen Unternehmenserfolg beeinflussen.

Schlagwörter: Organisationales Lernen, Unternehmensstrategie, Organisationsstruktur, Organisationsprozesse, Unternehmenskultur, Human Resource Management

1 Dauerhaftes Bestehen im Wettbewerb durch Organisationales Lernen

Im Verlauf der letzten Jahrzehnte hat sich die Bedeutung traditioneller Produktionsfaktoren enorm verändert. „In this society, knowledge is the primary resource for individuals and for the economy overall. Land, labor, and capital – the economist's traditional factors of production – do not disappear, but they become secondary."[1] Als Katalysator unternehmerischen Wandels dient Organisationales Lernen zum Ausbau des Wissens der Mitarbeiter und der gesamten Unternehmung. Der Wandel zur Wissensgesellschaft kann so u. a. als Auslöser des großen Interesses an Konzepten Organisationalen Lernens gelten. De Geus nennt Unternehmen, die diesen Wandel zur Wissensgesellschaft verinnerlicht haben, „lebende Unternehmen" und konstatiert weiter: „Managers recognize that, unless their companies can accelerate the rate at which they learn, their primary asset will stagnate, and their competitors will outpace them."[2] Die

[1] Drucker, Peter F.: The New Society of Organizations, in: Howard, Robert und Robert D. Haas (Hrsg.): The Learning Imperative: Managing People for Continuous Innovation, S. 3.

[2] De Geus, Arie P.: The Living Company: Habits for survival in a turbulent business environment, S. 16.

Begriffe Wissensmanagement und Organisationales Lernen finden sich oftmals synonym in der Managementliteratur.[3] Wesentlich für die Popularität Organisationalen Lernens sowohl als Untersuchungsgegenstand der Wissenschaft als auch als anwendbares Konzept in der Unternehmenspraxis ist die postulierte Relevanz hinsichtlich der Beschreibung, Erklärung und Gestaltung von zielwirksamen Veränderungen in und von Organisationen.[4] Das Konzept des Organisationalen Lernens wird als eigenständiger organisationstheoretischer Ansatz organisationalen Wandels bezeichnet.[5] Die organisationale Lernfähigkeit wird dadurch zu einem Faktor, der das langfristige Bestehen einer Unternehmung ermöglicht. Diese Sichtweise der Betonung der Fähigkeit zum Wandel setzt sich deutlich von früheren Antworten auf die Frage nach der Existenzsicherung von Unternehmen ab, die oftmals stabile Sicherungspotenziale postulieren und dann in (Norm-)Strategien oder langfristig haltbaren Wettbewerbsvorteilen die anzustrebende Lösung sehen.[6] Das Konzept des Organisationalen Lernens grenzt sich demgegenüber von der Stabilität und dauerhaften Gültigkeit von Problemlösungen ab und macht Veränderungen zur Basis erfolgversprechenden Managements.

Vor dem Hintergrund des ressourcenorientierten Ansatzes wird Organisationalem Lernen in Industriebetrieben eine Schlüsselrolle bei der Entwicklung, der Sicherung und dem Ausbau von Kernkompetenzen zugewiesen.[7] Erst solche Kernkompetenzen oder Kernfähigkeiten erlauben laut diesem Ansatz die Verfolgung einer angestrebten Wettbewerbsstrategie, die wiederum die Marktstellung von Unternehmen determiniert.[8] Für die organisationale Lernfähigkeit ist mit Pettigrew und Whipp festzuhalten, dass „... the most fundamental intangible assets, and those most linkable to competitive performance, are organizational capabilities to learn and change."[9] Auch Milling argumentiert aus einer ressourcenorientierten Perspektive: „Lernen ist ein fundamentales Verhaltensmuster jeglicher Organisation, es findet sich in allen Geschäftsprozessen und ist grundlegende Voraussetzung für die Sicherung der Wettbewerbsfähigkeit."[10]

---

[3] Vgl. überblicksartig zum Begriff und zu Konzepten des Wissensmanagements Amelingmeyer, Jenny: Wissensmanagement: Analyse und Gestaltung der Wissensbasis von Unternehmen, ferner Bullinger, Hans-Jörg, Kai Wörner und Juan Prieto: Wissensmanagement: Modelle und Strategien für die Praxis, in: Bürgel, Hans Dietmar (Hrsg.): Wissensmanagement: Schritte zum intelligenten Unternehmen, S. 22 ff.

[4] Vgl. Probst, Gilbert J.B. und Bettina S.T. Büchel: Organisationales Lernen: Wettbewerbsvorteil der Zukunft, S. 9.

[5] Vgl. Wiegand, Martin: Prozesse Organisationalen Lernens, S. 5.

[6] Vgl. Nagl, Anna: Lernende Organisation: Entwicklungsstand, Perspektiven und Gestaltungsansätze in deutschen Unternehmen – Eine empirische Untersuchung, S. 11 und Porter, Michael E.: Competitive Advantage: Creating and Sustaining Superior Performance.

[7] Siehe Gagnon, Stéphane: Resource-based Competition and the New Operations Strategy, in: International Journal of Operations & Production Management, Vol. 19 (1999), No. 2, S. 135 und Doz, Yves: Managing Core Competency for Corporate Renewal: towards a Managerial Theory of Core Competences, in: Campbell, Andrew und Kathleen Sommers Luchs (Hrsg.): Core Competency-Based Strategy, S. 55 f.

[8] Vgl. Stalk, George Jr., Philip Evans und Lawrence E. Shulman: Competing on Capabilities: The New Rules of Corporate Strategy, in: Howard, Robert und Robert D. Haas (Hrsg.): The Learning Imperative: Managing People for Continuous Innovation, S. 26.

[9] Pettigrew, Andrew M. und Richard Whipp: Strategic Change Capabilities, in: Lorange, Peter et al. (Hrsg.): Implementing Strategic Processes, S. 3.

[10] Milling, Peter: Managementsimulationen im Prozeß des organisationalen Lernens, in: Schwaninger, Markus (Hrsg.): Intelligente Organisationen: Konzepte für turbulente Zeiten auf der Grundlage von Systemtheorie und Kybernetik, S. 462.

Während Organisationales Lernen als gemeinsames Lernen von Organisationsmitgliedern in einem sozialen System interpretiert wird, ermöglicht die lernende Organisation als formales Regelwerk das kontinuierliche Lernen.[11] Lernende Organisationen sind in der Lage, sich in einer rasant verändernden Umwelt durch ihre Anpassungs- und Überlebensfähigkeit zu behaupten, da sie die geforderten Fähigkeiten zur Antizipation von Veränderungen und zur Selbsttransformation besitzen. Ermöglicht wird dies durch die Veränderung des Wissensstandes der Organisationsmitglieder, aber auch des Wissensstandes der gesamten Organisation.[12] „Learning in organizations means the continuous testing of experience, and the transformation of that experience into knowledge – accessible to the whole organization, and relevant to its core purpose."[13] Um die individuellen Lernergebnisse der gesamten Organisation zugänglich zu machen und um eine permanente Erneuerung des vorhandenen Wissens zu vermeiden, bedarf es einer Struktur, die dieses Wissen konserviert und den Individuen zugänglich macht.[14] Eine gedächtnisähnliche Struktur stellt dabei die organisationale Wissensbasis dar, die den Wissensbestand repräsentiert, der einer Organisation zur Verfügung steht.[15] Organisationales Lernen bewirkt somit eine Veränderung der organisationalen Wissensbasis.

Die Fähigkeit einer Unternehmung, sich an veränderte Umweltanforderungen anzupassen, ist schlechthin Grundlage für ihr Überleben. Wie in Abbildung 1 (s. S. 74) dargestellt, bildet das Organisationale Lernen die Voraussetzung, um die für die Sicherung des Unternehmenserfolgs ständig erforderliche Restrukturierung und Anpassung der Geschäftsprozesse realisieren zu können. Hieraus entsteht die Forderung nach der Fähigkeit, „zu lernen, welche dieser Strukturen effektiv und effizient arbeiten, sowie dieses Wissen schnell anzuwenden."[16] Die Gestaltung der Geschäftsprozesse ermöglicht ihrerseits die Effizienz der operativen Ebene. Die Förderung einer solchen Entwicklungs- bzw. Lernfähigkeit gelingt durch die Implementierung interner Mechanismen, die ein Unternehmen befähigen, einen kontinuierlichen Selbsttransformationsprozess zu etablieren und aufrechtzuerhalten. Diese Kompetenz soll langfristig dazu führen, externen und internen Veränderungen proaktiv oder aber mit einer – im Vergleich zum Wettbewerb – nur relativ geringen Reaktionszeit begegnen zu können.[17]

---

[11] Siehe Kluge, Annette und Jan Schilling: Organisationales Lernen und Lernende Organisation: ein Überblick zum Stand von Theorie und Forschung, in: Zeitschrift für Arbeits- und Organisationspsychologie, Jg. 44 (2000), Nr. 4, S. 180.

[12] Zum Zusammenhang von Lernen und Wissen und zu Definitionen von Wissen vgl. Nagl, Anna: Lernende Organisation, S. 46ff.

[13] Ross, Rick et al.: Core Concepts About Learning in Organizations, in: Senge, Peter M. et al. (Hrsg.): The Fifth Discipline Fieldbook: Strategies and Tools for Building a Learning Organization, S. 49.

[14] Vgl. Reuther, Andreas und Andreas Größler: Organisationales Gedächtnis: Konzepte und unterstützende Methoden, Forschungsberichte der Fakultät für Betriebswirtschaftslehre, Universität Mannheim, Nr. 9901, Mannheim 1999, S. 11.

[15] Vgl. Pautzke, Gunnar: Die Evolution der organisatorischen Wissensbasis: Bausteine zu einer Theorie des organisatorischen Lernens, S. 63ff.

[16] Milling, Peter: Organisationales Lernen und seine Unterstützung durch Managementsimulatoren, in: ZfB-Ergänzungsheft, Nr. 3, 1995, S. 94.

[17] Vgl. Reinhardt, Rüdiger: Das Modell Organisationaler Lernfähigkeit und die Gestaltung Lernfähiger Organisationen, S. 18.

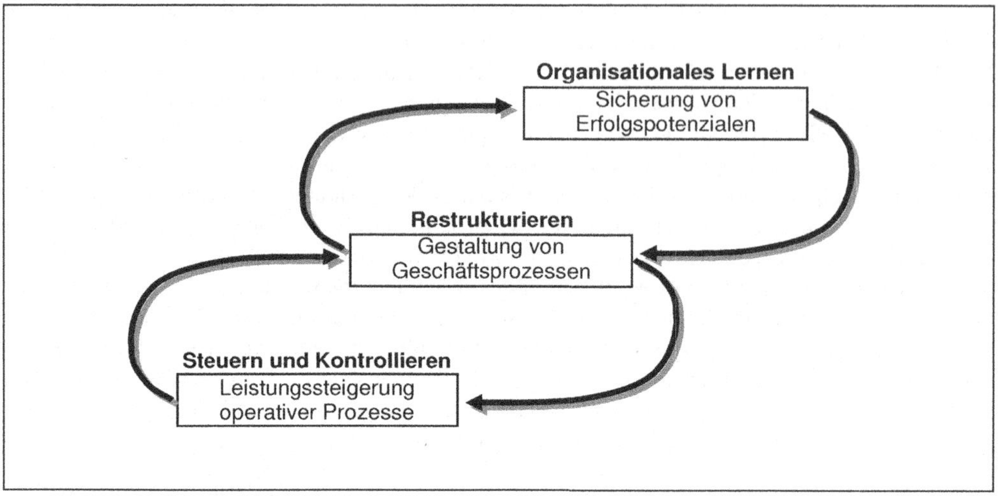

Abbildung 1: Lernen zur Steigerung der Wettbewerbsfähigkeit[18]

Auslöser bzw. Determinanten der Notwendigkeit von Lernprozessen sind bewusst herbeigeführte oder sich evolutionär im Arbeitsalltag ergebende Situationen, die nicht mit bereits vorhandenem Wissen und Verhaltensmustern zufrieden stellend bewältigt werden können. Entsprechend verstärkt sich für Unternehmen die Notwendigkeit zu lernen, wenn sie in einem Umfeld agieren, das sich schnell dergestalt ändert, dass der Unternehmenserfolg nicht mit bisher verfolgten Strategien gesichert werden kann.[19] Insofern gewinnt Lernen nicht nur an Bedeutung für die Entwicklung von Unternehmen, sondern stellt gewissermaßen die Grundlage für ein Bestehen in nicht-stabilen Kontexten dar.

2 Lernfördernde Lenkungsfaktoren in Industriebetrieben

2.1 Strategieformulierung als Lernprozess

In Abhängigkeit des organisatorischen Geltungsbereichs sind Unternehmensstrategien, Geschäftsbereichsstrategien sowie funktionale Strategien zu unterscheiden.[20] Für Industriebetriebe ist dabei die Fertigungsstrategie als funktionale Strategie von besonderer Bedeutung.[21] Als

[18] In Anlehnung an Milling, Peter: Organisationales Lernen und seine Unterstützung durch Managementsimulatoren, S. 95.

[19] Vgl. Gerpott, Torsten J.: Lernprozesse im Zeitwettbewerb, in: Simon, Hermann und Karlheinz Schwuchow (Hrsg.): Management-Lernen und Strategie, S. 67.

[20] Vgl. Welge, Martin K. und Andreas Al-Laham: Strategisches Management, S. 322ff.

[21] Vgl. Hayes, Robert H. und Gary P. Pisano: Manufacturing Strategy: At the Intersection of Two Paradigm Shifts, in: Production and Operations Management, Vol. 5 (1996), No. 1, S. 25ff.

Rahmen für das Organisationale Lernen sind sowohl die Unternehmensstrategie als auch die Fertigungsstrategie und außerdem die Abstimmung zwischen beiden relevant.

Der Strategiebildungsprozess im strategischen Management wird als organisationaler Lern- und Entwicklungsprozess aufgefasst.[22] Dabei wird die Strategiefindung als Lernprozess, der zu einer Überprüfung der „theories-in-use" führt, verstanden.[23] Lernen soll in diesem Zusammenhang nicht als ein Lernen von Eliten verstanden werden.[24] Strategiebildungsprozesse fußen auf der Mitarbeit aller Organisationsmitglieder bis hin zu niedrigen Hierarchiestufen. Die von einer Unternehmung verfolgte Strategie ist stets das Ergebnis des interaktiven Wechselspiels seiner Teile und lässt sich selten ausschließlich auf die Arbeit Einzelner zurückführen.[25] Die Strategie einer Unternehmung resultiert aus einem selbstorganisierenden organisationalen Lernprozess, an dem im Idealfall alle Organisationsmitglieder beteiligt sind. Als Beispiel für ein lernorientiertes Hilfsmittel des strategischen Managements gelten vor allem Unternehmenssimulatoren.[26] Ausgangsbasis für die Strategiefindung in lernenden Organisationen ist die Analyse der internen Stärken und Schwächen, wodurch sich Erfolgspotenziale ableiten lassen. Im Rahmen der Strategieentwicklung entstehen so Informationen entlang der Differenz zwischen Ideen und Wirklichkeit. Diese Informationen werden durch Lernen zu Wissen. Übertragen auf die funktionale Fertigungsstrategie bedeutet dies, dass die *Tragfähigkeit der Fertigungsstrategie* und die Bedeutung, die ihr die Mitarbeiter im Fertigungsbereich beimessen, zu einem lernfördernden Lenkungsfaktor werden.

De Geus beschreibt den strategischen Planungsprozess als institutionellen Lernprozess, „which is the process whereby management teams change their shared mental models of their company, their markets, and their competitors. For this reason, we think of planning as learning and of corporate learning as institutional learning."[27] Aus der strategischen Planung heraus entstehen somit nicht nur neue Ziele oder Strategien, sondern es entsteht auch organisationales Wissen während des Planungsprozesses.[28] Durch diesen Informationsfluss werden vertikal, horizontal und diagonal durch die Organisation sowohl Verständnis und Identifikation geschaffen als auch neue Möglichkeiten gefunden, Wissen auszutauschen. „Der letztendliche Zweck effektiver Planung und Kontrolle in komplexen Systemen liegt nicht in der Anfertigung von Plänen, sondern in der Veränderung der mentalen Modelle der Entscheidungsträger."[29] Die *formale Strategieplanung* fördert unter Ausschluss einer Überformalisierung dadurch das Organisationale Lernen.

---

[22] Vgl. Kremmel, Dietmar: Das Verhältnis zwischen Unternehmensstrategie und Unternehmenskultur unter besonderer Berücksichtigung des organisationalen Lernens, S. 234.

[23] Vgl. Stäbler, Samuel: Die Personalentwicklung der „Lernenden Organisation", S. 214.

[24] Diesen Ansatz verfolgt z. B. Stata. Vgl. Stata, Ray: Organizational Learning, S. 63 ff.

[25] Vgl. Kremmel, Dietmar: Das Verhältnis zwischen Unternehmensstrategie und Unternehmenskultur unter besonderer Berücksichtigung des organisationalen Lernens, S. 260.

[26] Vgl. Größler, Andreas: Entwicklungsprozess und Evaluation von Unternehmenssimulatoren für lernende Unternehmen, S. 37 ff.

[27] De Geus, Arie P.: Planning as Learning, in: Harvard Business Review, Vol. 66 (1988), No. 2, S. 70.

[28] Vgl. Milling, Peter: Strategische Planungs- und Kontrollsysteme zur Unterstützung betrieblicher Lernprozesse, in: Milling, Peter (Hrsg.): Systemmanagement und Managementsysteme, S. 20.

[29] Ebenda S. 31.

Die Kommunikation einer gebildeten Strategie nach vollendetem Planungsprozess kann gewährleisten, dass alle Managementebenen die schwachen Signale von Chancen und Risiken frühzeitig vernehmen, und andererseits, dass „die Vision ‚top-down', Vorschläge und neue Informationen ‚bottom-up' und strategische Interpretationen oder Aktionsideen quer durch die Organisation kommuniziert werden."[30] Eine klare Mission bezeichnet Goh sogar als „strategic building block" einer lernenden Organisation.[31] Ergebnis ist die Förderung von Sprach- und Sozialisationsmustern, so dass in variierenden Situationen keine großen Unterschiede in den Referenzrahmen, Zielorientierungen und Kooperationsnormen auftreten. Genauso können Konflikte auch unter Beteiligung diverser Gruppierungen und unter Einbringung heterogener Sichtweisen einfacher gelöst werden. „Corporate communications should reinforce the messages within the organization, insuring internal and external consistency. (...) Inside the learning organization, managerial and business communication must create a greater sense of connectedness at all levels."[32] Die *Kommunikation der Unternehmensstrategie* bildet somit in Industriebetrieben einen lernfördernden Lenkungsfaktor.

Die *Innovationsorientierung* von Unternehmen umfasst auch die Antizipation neuer Technologien. Sie stellt gerade in Industriebetrieben einen bedeutenden Teil der Unternehmensstrategie dar, da das Innovationsmanagement als Voraussetzung für die Wettbewerbsfähigkeit von Industriebetrieben angesehen wird.[33] „Erforderlich für eine innovative Unternehmung ist kreatives und produktives Lernen, das zur Quelle neuer Technologien und Verfahrensweisen wird."[34] Die Innovationsorientierung dient dabei der Unterstützung Organisationalen Lernens, indem vor dem Hintergrund der geplanten Innovation Bestehendes andauernd überprüft wird. Das Bemühen, bspw. die Potenziale neuer Fertigungstechnologien frühzeitig einzuschätzen, oder das Verfolgen langfristiger Programme, um Fähigkeiten in der Fertigung zu entwickeln, die über dem aktuellen Standard liegen, führen zu organisationalen Lernprozessen und erweitern das organisationale Wissen.

Neben der Aktivierung von bedeutenden Erfolgspotenzialen kommt der *Abstimmung von Fertigungs- und Unternehmensstrategie* eine weitere Rolle zu.[35] Durch das Verfolgen der Konsistenz zwischen den beiden Strategieebenen werden kollektive Sozialisationsprozesse in Gang gesetzt, gemeinsame Werthaltungen sowie Identifikation mit dem Ganzen geschaffen und gleichzeitig die Identifikation mit Geschäftsbereichen oder Subkulturen verringert. Die Mög-

---

[30] Sattelberger, Thomas: Die lernende Organisation im Spannungsfeld von Strategie, Struktur und Kultur, S. 27.

[31] Goh, Swee C.: Toward a Learning Organization: The Strategic Building Blocks, in: S.A.M. Advanced Management Journal, Vol. 63 (1998), No. 2, S. 18.

[32] Barker, Randolph T. und Martin R. Camarata: The role of communication in creating and maintaining a learning organization: Preconditions, indicators, and disciplines, in: The Journal of Business Communication, Vol. 35 (1998), No. 4, S. 463.

[33] Vgl. Maier, Frank: Die Integration wissens- und modellbasierter Konzepte zur Entscheidungsunterstützung im Innovationsmanagement, S. 50ff.

[34] Milling, Peter: Strategische Planungs- und Kontrollsysteme zur Unterstützung betrieblicher Lernprozesse, S. 21.

[35] Vgl. zum Thema Strategiekonsistenz Hasenpusch, Jürgen: Strategiekonsistenz in Geschäftseinheit und Fertigung als Voraussetzung für den Erfolg industrieller Unternehmen: Eine empirische Untersuchung im Rahmen des Projekts „International Manufacturing Strategy Survey", S. 45ff.

lichkeit, dass es zu einem „Throw-it-over-the-wall-Syndrom", dem oberflächlichen Weiterreichen von Problemstellungen einer Abteilung in eine andere, kommt, wird dadurch ebenso beschränkt.[36] Funktionaler Egoismus, der keinen Beitrag zum Organisationalen Lernen leistet, wird begrenzt. Voraussetzung für das Organisationale Lernen ist ein Sinn für die permanente Sicherstellung der internen Konsistenz zwischen Zielen, Strategien, Geschäftsprozessen, Kernkompetenzen und Wissensbeständen.[37]

2.2 Implementierung durch Organisationsstruktur und -prozesse

Meist erfolgt in der deutschsprachigen Literatur eine Untergliederung von Organisationsdimensionen in Aufbau- und Ablauforganisation.[38] Diese Trennung besitzt genauso wie die Trennung von Organisationsstruktur und Organisationsprozessen nur analytischen Charakter und dient der Durchdringung der ganzheitlichen organisatorischen Problemstellung. Durch die Aufbauorganisation wird bestimmt, welche Aufgaben von Menschen und Sachmitteln zu erfüllen sind. Die sich innerhalb des durch die Aufbauorganisation vorgegebenen Rahmens abspielenden Arbeits- und Informationsprozesse werden durch die Ablauforganisation geregelt.

Problemlösungsgruppen als Teil der Aufbauorganisation fördern im Besonderen das Gruppenlernen, dem häufig die Rolle als Bindeglied zwischen individuellem Lernen und Organisationalem Lernen zuteil wird. Ergebnis des Problemlösungsprozesses sind im Sinne der Erweiterung des organisationalen Wissens u. a. Verbesserungen des Fertigungsprozesses.[39] Eine eigenständige Problemlösung durch Mitarbeitergruppen repräsentiert des Weiteren die oft geforderte Selbststeuerung von Gruppen, die als Auslöser Organisationalen Lernens gelten kann. Problemlösungsgruppen stehen auch für die Dezentralisierung der Organisationsstruktur, die als unterstützendes Merkmal für das Organisationale Lernen oft Berücksichtigung findet. Das Denken und Handeln wird somit in die Linientätigkeit reintegriert, indem „think tanks" und Stabsbereiche reduziert werden.[40]

Die *funktionale Integration* geht über eine simple Zusammenarbeit von mehreren Unternehmensfunktionen hinaus. In dem Falle, dass die Mitarbeiter der Marketing- oder der Finanzabteilung Wissen in der Fertigung erworben haben und vice versa, ist eine funktionale Integration gelungen. „Wichtig ist dabei, daß über Informationsnetze die Teileinheiten so miteinander verbunden werden, daß ein organisationales Lernen ermöglicht wird."[41] Durch den Informations-

---

[36] Vgl. Ehrlenspiel, Klaus: Integrierte Produkterstellung: Organisation – Methoden – Hilfsmittel, in: Milberg, Joachim (Hrsg.): Wettbewerbsfaktor Zeit in Produktionsunternehmen: Referate des Münchener Kolloquiums 1991, S. 119.

[37] Vgl. Zahn, Erich: Wissen und Strategie, in: Bürgel, Hans Dietmar (Hrsg.): Wissensmanagement: Schritte zum intelligenten Unternehmen, S. 49.

[38] Vgl. Gaitanides, Michael: Aufbau- und Ablauforganisation, in: Wittmann, Waldemar et al. (Hrsg.): Handwörterbuch der Betriebswirtschaft, Teilband 1, 5. Aufl., Sp. 191.

[39] Vgl. Hayes, Robert H., Steven C. Wheelwright und Kim B. Clark: Dynamic Manufacturing: Creating the Learning Organization, S. 230.

[40] Vgl. Sattelberger, Thomas: Die lernende Organisation im Spannungsfeld von Strategie, Struktur und Kultur, S. 50.

[41] Nagl, Anna: Lernende Organisation, S. 109f.

austausch und das Wissen über das Funktionieren anderer Bereiche im Unternehmen steigt das organisationale Wissen. Strukturelle Barrieren Organisationalen Lernens äußern sich denn auch in unzureichenden Informations- und Kommunikationsbeziehungen.[42] Notwendig sind die Förderung informellen Austausches sowie die Schaffung einer Organisationsstruktur, die Informationsflüsse über abgegrenzte Funktions- bzw. Marktbereiche hinweg ermöglichen. Durch die angestrebte Reflexion komplexer Arbeitsprozesse können Probleme umfassender bearbeitet, Chancen erkannt und Aufgaben ganzheitlicher gelöst werden.

Wird bei der Einführung neuer Verfahren oder Prozesse darauf geachtet, dass die notwendigen organisatorischen Änderungen und die zusätzlich erforderlichen Kompetenzen der Organisationsmitglieder geschaffen werden, impliziert dies die Förderung kontinuierlicher Lern- und Verbesserungsprozesse. Der Faktor *effektive Prozesseinführung* umfasst für die nachfolgenden Analysen bspw. die innerbetriebliche Förderung von Lern- oder Verbesserungsprozessen nach der Inbetriebnahme neuer Anlagen, um das Potenzial einer neuen Fertigungstechnologie voll auszuschöpfen.

Handlungen im Rahmen der *Prozesskontrolle* schließen Soll-Ist-Vergleiche mit ein. Aus der Analyse der Diskrepanz zwischen Soll- und Ist-Zuständen lernt ein Unternehmen. Exakte statistische Methoden garantieren dabei die Reliabilität und Validität der Kontrolle. Anhand des Ergebnisse der Soll-Ist-Vergleiche lassen sich vorhandene Schwachstellen aufzeigen und Verbesserungsmaßnahmen ableiten. Hayes, Wheelwright und Clark postulieren, dass „developing and systematically applying process knowledge is central to building a competitive advantage in manufacturing."[43] Die statistische Prozesskontrolle wird dabei als besonders effektives Mittel angesehen, um neue Einsichten zu gewinnen und zu kommunizieren. Ein verhaltenssteuerndes Controlling gilt damit als Grundlage für ein Informationskonzept zur Prozesssteuerung.[44]

Die *Dokumentation der Fertigungsprozesse* ist vor allem im Sinne des Anpassungslernens eine Determinante Organisationalen Lernens. „Die Dokumentation vermittelt wichtiges Erfahrungswissen für geplante unternehmerische Projekte und Veränderungen. Sie ermöglicht die Konservierung und den Transfer von Lernerfahrungen unabhängig von den einzelnen Organisationsmitgliedern."[45] Ständig aktualisierte, schriftlich fixierte Arbeitsanweisungen können zur Verbesserung des Fertigungsablaufes herangezogen werden. „Ohne eine Messung und Dokumentation der Geschäftsvorgänge ist kein Lern- und Verbesserungsprozeß möglich."[46] Schriftlich fixierte Leitfäden und Arbeitsanweisungen sind ein Paradebeispiel für Routinen in Unternehmen. Routinen wiederum fördern das Organisationale Lernen.[47]

---

[42] Vgl. Stäbler, Samuel: Die Personalentwicklung der „Lernenden Organisation", S. 137.

[43] Hayes, Robert H., Steven C. Wheelwright und Kim B. Clark: Dynamic Manufacturing, S. 228.

[44] Vgl. Grafmüller, Maximilian H.: Prozeßmanagement in der Automobilindustrie: Betriebliche Umsetzung am Beispiel der Volkswagen AG, S. 61.

[45] Kaiser, Karin: Gestaltung lernfördernder Bedingungen in Unternehmen, in: Schatz, Roland (Hrsg.): Netzwerk als Basis der Lernenden Organisation, S. 48.

[46] Riekhof, Hans-Christian: Die Idee des Geschäftsprozesses: Basis der lernenden Organisation, in: Riekhof, Hans-Christian (Hrsg.): Beschleunigung von Geschäftsprozessen: Wettbewerbsvorteile durch Lernfähigkeit, S. 20.

[47] Vgl. Levitt, Barbara und James G. March: Organizational Learning, S. 518ff.

Regelmäßige Kommunikation zwischen verschiedenen Funktionen und Zusammenarbeit bei allen wichtigen Entscheidungen über Abteilungsgrenzen hinweg determiniert das Organisationale Lernen.[48] Die *Koordination durch Kommunikation* führt zu gemeinsamen mentalen Modellen und zu einem Lernen durch geteilte Erfahrungen.[49] Voraussetzung ist die Möglichkeit der Partizipation von möglichst vielen Unternehmensbereichen am Entscheidungsfindungsprozess. Streubel fordert bezüglich der intrasystemischen Koordination eine Kombination aus dem expliziten Gewähren von Freiräumen für Selbstorganisationsprozesse und Plänen zur Koordination, „um die Wahrscheinlichkeit für das Auftreten von Selbstorganisationsprozessen als Prozessen organisationalen Lernens zu erhöhen."[50]

Kontinuierliches *Feedback* in Form einer Rückmeldung über den erreichten Leistungsstand an den Prozessverantwortlichen und die Prozessbeteiligten bildet eine weitere Basis für Lernprozesse.[51] Die meisten Modelle Organisationalen Lernens kommen nicht ohne eine Feedback-Schleife aus, die erst neues Lernen ermöglicht. Michael beschreibt Feedback als „the means by which error is detected and thereby provides the basis for learning how to get from here to there through changes in performance that result in successive reductions in error."[52] Typisch für Industriebetriebe sind Übersichten oder Informationstafeln, die gut zugänglich im Produktionsbereich aushängen, auf denen Informationen über den erreichten Qualitätsstandard, die Häufigkeit der aufgetretenen Fehler, die Produktivität oder die Häufigkeit der Maschinenausfälle zu finden sind. Mittels dieser Informationen bekommen die Organisationsmitglieder Feedback über die Qualität ihrer Tätigkeiten. „Kurze Kommunikationswege und Feedbackschleifen ermöglichen eine effektive Problembearbeitung, die in ihrem Ergebnis zu ganzheitlichen und qualitativ hochwertigen Lösungsszenarien führt."[53]

2.3 Wissensvermehrung durch lernorientierte Unternehmenskulturen

In der Literatur werden die Begriffe Unternehmenskultur und Organisationskultur meist synonym verwandt und auf vielfältige Art und Weise definiert. Die Unternehmenskultur leistet die Vermittlung der Unternehmensidentität, die sich in der Gemeinsamkeit der Werte und in der bewussten Weitergabe dieser Werte ausdrückt.[54] Der Begriff Unternehmenskultur subsumiert nachstehend die von den Mitgliedern einer Organisation gemeinsam geteilten Grundannahmen, Wertvorstellungen und Denkhaltungen, von denen angenommen wird, dass sie deren Handeln beeinflussen.[55] Bea und Haas schlagen zur Förderung des Organisationalen Lernens eine inno-

[48] Vgl. Stäbler, Samuel: Die Personalentwicklung der „Lernenden Organisation", S. 68.

[49] Vgl. Hayes, Robert H., Steven C. Wheelwright und Kim B. Clark: Dynamic Manufacturing, S. 111.

[50] Streubel, Frauke: Organisatorische Gestaltung und Informationsmanagement in der lernenden Unternehmung, S. 227.

[51] Vgl. Riekhof, Hans-Christian: Die Idee des Geschäftsprozesses, S. 16.

[52] Michael, Donald N.: On Learning to Plan & Planning to Learn, S. 265.

[53] Nagl, Anna: Lernende Organisation, S. 111.

[54] Vgl. Krulis-Randa, Jan S.: Einführung in die Unternehmenskultur, in: Lattmann, Charles (Hrsg.): Die Unternehmenskultur: ihre Grundlagen und ihre Bedeutung für die Führung der Unternehmung, S. 6.

[55] Vgl. Stäbler, Samuel: Die Personalentwicklung der „Lernenden Organisation", S. 69f.

vationsorientierte Kultur vor, da diese die Bereitschaft begünstigt, Neues zu wagen: „Eine offene, außenorientierte Unternehmenskultur fördert die Wahrnehmung von Umweltveränderungen und erleichtert die Konfrontation interner Werthaltungen mit andersartigen externen Grundüberzeugungen.“[56] In einer solchen Kultur werden Fehler nicht als Anlass für Sanktionen gewertet, sondern als Quelle besserer Erkenntnis. Eine experimentelle Denkhaltung erleichtert zudem das Erfahrungslernen und das Durchlaufen von „trial-and-error“-Prozessen.[57] Die Kultur eines Unternehmens unterstützt das Organisationale Lernen immer dann, wenn durch die Kultur eine Umgebung für die Organisationsmitglieder entsteht, die das Hinterfragen und Modifizieren von zentralen Normen und Werten erlaubt. „Da Lernen die Notwendigkeit von veränderten Bezugsrahmen und unterschiedlichen Werten und Normen einschließt, stellt Kulturentwicklung einen wesentlichen Weg in Richtung organisationales Lernen dar.“[58]

Eine lernfördernde Unternehmenskultur entsteht durch eine hohe *Identifikation der Mitarbeiter* mit dem Unternehmen. Die Übereinstimmung von Wertvorstellungen von Mitarbeitern und Unternehmen und der Stolz der Mitarbeiter auf ihre Arbeit führen zu gemeinsamen mentalen Modellen, die Organisationales Lernen ermöglichen. Ein starkes emotionales und wertbezogenes Commitment der Organisationsmitglieder zur Organisation lassen eine „Familie“ entstehen, welche die geforderte Lern- und Leistungsbereitschaft erzeugt.[59] Eine solche Unternehmenskultur ist „von großem Vertrauen der Mitarbeiter zu ihrer Organisation geprägt, so daß Veränderungen nicht als Bedrohung, sondern als Chance der persönlichen und organisationalen Entwicklung angesehen werden.“[60] Als Vertrauensaspekt ist auch die Absenz von Angst, Fehler zu begehen und einzugestehen, eine Voraussetzung für Organisationales Lernen.

Die Umsetzung von Verbesserungen beruht zu einem Teil auch auf Vorschlägen von Mitarbeitern. Die Ermutigung der Mitarbeiter, Vorschläge zur Leistungsverbesserung zu machen, soll sich auch darin widerspiegeln, dass die eingereichten Vorschläge ernst genommen werden und die Umsetzung bzw. die Ablehnung den Mitarbeitern erklärt werden. „Mitarbeiter werden ihre Kenntnisse und Fähigkeiten einem Unternehmen nur dann auf Dauer uneingeschränkt zur Verfügung stellen, wenn sie dort auch als wertvolle Träger von Wissen und Können anerkannt und ihre Vorschläge und Ideen entsprechend aufgegriffen und berücksichtigt werden.“[61] Der Auf- und Ausbau eines *Vorschlagswesens* schafft neben den formalen Strukturen einen Kanal für Veränderungsideen und fördert somit kreative Ideen. „Mental models, deeply held images of how the world works, limit us to familiar ways of thinking and acting. (…) As time passes, these models may no longer hold true but may still operate unless an organization has the open-mindedness to question them.“[62] Die Ausprägung des Vorschlagswesens repräsentiert auch die angesprochene Offenheit oder „open-mindedness“ einer Unternehmung.

---

[56] Bea, Franz Xaver und Jürgen Haas: Strategisches Management, S. 409.

[57] Vgl. Nevis, Edwin C., Anthony DiBella und Janet M. Gould: Understanding Organizations as Learning Systems, in: Sloan Management Review, Vol. 37 (1995), No. 2, S. 80.

[58] Probst, Gilbert J. B. und Bettina S. T. Büchel: Organisationales Lernen, S. 140.

[59] Vgl. Würth, Reinhold: Erfolgsgeheimnis Führungskultur: Bilanz eines Unternehmers, S. 314.

[60] Wengelowski, Peter: Entwicklung organisationalen Lernens, S. 213.

[61] Nagl, Anna: Lernende Organisation, S. 126.

[62] Sinkula, James M. und William E. Baker: A Framework for Market-Based Organizational Learning, S. 309.

Neues Wissen aufzubauen ist eine der Hauptaufgaben der lernenden Organisation. Dies erfordert die permanente Hinterfragung des status quo, was wiederum den Organisationsmitgliedern erlaubt, neue Ideen in die Unternehmung einzubringen. „Managers should also be willing to encourage individuals and teams to continuously improve work processes and try new ideas.“[63] Der Begriff der *kontinuierlichen Verbesserung* ist eng mit dem Begriff der Qualität verwoben.[64] Qualität wird als Basis für den durch die kontinuierliche Verbesserung intendierten Wandel – in praktischer und ideologischer Hinsicht – gesehen.[65] Weißmann kommt zu dem Schluss, dass eine Selbstverantwortung der Mitarbeiter für die Verbesserung der Qualität die Basis für eine kontinuierliche Verbesserung auf breiter Basis darstellt.[66] Im Rahmen einer Suche nach immer weiteren Verbesserungen, werden die „theories-in-use“ ständig in Frage gestellt.

Ermutigen Vorgesetzte ihre Mitarbeiter, ihre Ideen und Meinungen offen auszutauschen, intendiert dies eine *Förderung von Gruppenarbeit*. Innerhalb von Gruppengesprächen werden Probleme besprochen und gelöst. Notwendig für das Gruppenlernen sind nicht nur Problemlösungsgruppen oder Gruppenarbeit, sondern auch die Unterstützung durch die Vorgesetzten, indem sie ein Klima schaffen, das Gruppenlernen fördert. Voraussetzung dabei ist allerdings die Vorbildfunktion der Führungskräfte. Die Förderung von Gruppenarbeit entspricht einer Förderung der Mitwirkungskompetenz der einzelnen Mitarbeiter. In diesem Zusammenhang werden von Wunderer drei unternehmerische Schlüsselqualifikationen gefordert.[67] Diese sind die Fähigkeit und Bereitschaft zu strategieorientiertem Problemlösen, effiziente Ideenumsetzung und kooperative Selbstorganisation. Vor allem der Selbstorganisation wird eine große Bedeutung hinsichtlich der Förderung Organisationalen Lernens zugeschrieben.[68] In diesem Verständnis verstehen sich Führungskräfte als Förderer der Mitarbeiter und entwickeln diese in ihren Fähigkeiten, damit eine konsequente Delegation von Aufgaben stattfinden kann.[69]

Die *funktionsübergreifende Präsenz in der Fertigung* beschreibt – in Abgrenzung zur funktionalen Integration – die einseitige Beziehung der Produktion zu anderen Funktionen im Unternehmen. Eine Förderung der Umgebung Organisationalen Lernens setzt so voraus, dass Ingenieure und Fertigungstechniker in der Nähe der Fertigung ihren Arbeitsplatz besetzen, um bei Problemen in der Produktion sofort verfügbar zu sein.[70] Sie stehen im gleichen

[63] Goh, Swee C.: Toward a learning organization, S. 18.

[64] Vgl. Weißmann, Sven: Total Quality Management für Industriebetriebe S. 61.

[65] Vgl. Savolainen, Taina I.: Cycles of Continuous Improvement: Realizing Competitive Advantages through Quality, in: International Journal of Operations & Production Management, Vol. 19 (1999), No. 11, S. 1204.

[66] Vgl. Weißmann, Sven: Total Quality Management für Industriebetriebe, S. 129.

[67] Vgl. Wunderer, Rolf: Mitarbeiter zu Mitunternehmern fördern, in: Kröll, Martin und Herbert Schnauber (Hrsg.): Lernen der Organisation durch Gruppen- und Teamarbeit: Wettbewerbsvorteile durch umfassende Unternehmensplanung, S. 107.

[68] Vgl. Streubel, Frauke: Organisatorische Gestaltung und Informationsmanagement in der lernenden Unternehmung, S. 206f.

[69] Vgl. Wengelowski, Peter: Entwicklung organisationalen Lernens, S. 193.

[70] Vgl. Hayes, Robert H., Steven C. Wheelwright und Kim B. Clark: Dynamic Manufacturing, S. 108f.

engen Kontakt zur Fertigung wie das Management, das Wert auf persönlichen Kontakt zu den Mitarbeitern legt und ebenfalls zur Verfügung steht, falls Probleme in der Produktion eintreten. Nicht nur die räumliche Nähe ergibt die Möglichkeit zur Förderung organisationaler Lernprozesse, sondern auch die Bereitschaft, sich mit Problemen anderer Organisationsmitglieder auseinander zu setzen. In diesem Sinn fördert das Kommunikations- und Informationsmanagement das Organisationale Lernen. „Es ist von existentieller Bedeutung, daß die richtigen Wissensträger zueinander finden und daß die Kommunikation zwischen forschenden und entwickelnden Bereichen einerseits und den anwendenden Unternehmensbereichen andererseits (...) zur Selbstverständlichkeit wird.“[71] Eine neuartige Kombination von explizitem und implizitem Wissen erfordert die Institutionalisierung von Kommunikationsprozessen, die Wissensdiffusion und den Austausch von Know-how sicherstellen oder zumindest wahrscheinlich machen.

2.4 Unterstützung durch das Human Resource Management

Nach Liebel und Oechsler soll HRM im Sinne eines Managementkonzeptes verstanden werden, das die Ressource Mensch als wichtigsten strategischen Erfolgsfaktor einer Unternehmung in den Mittelpunkt stellt.[72] Kennzeichnend für den Ansatz ist die Betrachtung der Organisationsmitglieder als Erfolgsfaktoren, die gemeinsam mit anderen Ressourcen so geführt, motiviert und entwickelt werden, dass dies direkt zum Erreichen von Unternehmenszielen beiträgt.[73] Diese Auffassung wird auch im Operations Management vertreten: „The right management principles, systems, procedures play an essential role, but the capabilities that create a competitive advantage come from people – their skill, discipline, motivation, ability to solve problems, and capacity for learning.“[74] Dieses Potenzial der Mitarbeiter zu entwickeln ist die Hauptaufgabe des HRM im Hinblick auf das Organisationale Lernen. „A major role of the human resource function is to create greater learning potential which is a critical aspect of the learning organization.“[75] Ausgehend von der Forderung nach der Einbeziehung von möglichst allen Organisationsmitgliedern in das Organisationale Lernen ist es erstaunlich, dass in den Veröffentlichungen zu diesem Thema dieser Aspekt fast ausschließlich aus der Sicht der Führungskräfte behandelt wird.[76] Dem einzelnen Mitarbeiter kommt aber eine wesentliche Bedeutung zu, da Organisationales Lernen nur durch das Lernen der Organisationsmitglieder möglich ist. Lernerfolge einer Organisation sind vom individuellen Lernpotenzial ihrer Mitglieder abhängig. Qualifiziertes Personal mit Wissen, Können, Erfahrungen und Kommunikationsfähigkeit stellt einen Ausgangspunkt der lernenden Organisation dar.[77]

---

[71] Sattelberger, Thomas: Die lernende Organisation im Spannungsfeld von Strategie, Struktur und Kultur, S. 43.

[72] Vgl. Liebel, Hermann J. und Walter A. Oechsler: Handbuch Human Resource Management, S. 1.

[73] Vgl. Oechsler, Walter A.: Personal und Arbeit, S. 20.

[74] Hayes, Robert H., Steven C. Wheelwright und Kim B. Clark: Dynamic Manufacturing, S. 242.

[75] Watkins, Karen E. und Victoria J. Marsick: Sculpting the learning organization, S. 160.

[76] Vgl. bspw. Senge, Peter M.: The Fifth Discipline, S. 9 ff.

[77] Vgl. Thun, Jörn-Henrik: Die zeitbasierte Fertigungsstrategie – Methoden zur Leistungssteigerung in Industriebetrieben, S. 93 f.

Der planmäßige und systematische Wechsel von Arbeitsplatz und Arbeitsaufgaben ist unter dem Begriff der *funktionsübergreifenden Personalentwicklung* zu subsumieren.[78] Ein regelmäßiger Wechsel des Einsatzgebietes der Organisationsmitglieder auf allen Hierarchieebenen führt naturgemäß zu einer Erweiterung der Fähigkeiten und wird so zu einem lernfördernden Lenkungsfaktor. „Durch einen geplanten systematischen Arbeitsplatzwechsel kann der Wissenstransfer innerhalb der Organisation gezielt gesteuert werden."[79] Bereichernd für die Kompetenzen der Manager auf höheren Hierarchieebenen ist der Wechsel zwischen verschiedenen Werken einer Unternehmensgruppe. Wenn die für die Produktentwicklung zuständigen Konstrukteure praktische Erfahrung in der Fertigung sammeln können, gilt dies auch als ein lernfördernder Lenkungsfaktor, da in diesem Fall gemeinsame mentale Modelle existieren, auf denen das Organisationale Lernen aufbaut.

Konzepte wie Job enlargement und Job enrichment bewirken eine Steigerung der *Multifunktionalität der Mitarbeiter*.[80] Solche Konzepte umfassen das Erlernen von verschiedenartigen Tätigkeiten, so dass bspw. auch die Vertretung von anderen Mitarbeitern kein Problem darstellt, da die meisten Mitarbeiter über ein sehr breites Wissen verfügen. Basis für eine Arbeitserweiterung und eine Arbeitsbereicherung bilden sowohl das „training-on-the-job" als auch Aus- und Weiterbildungsmaßnahmen. Die genannten Konzepte lassen sich unter dem Begriff des „employee empowerment" subsumieren, der für die Weitergabe von Verantwortung und Entscheidungsautorität vom Management an niedere Hierarchiestufen steht. Je ausgeprägter die Autonomie der Mitarbeiter auf den unteren Hierarchieebenen ist, desto höher ist die Wahrscheinlichkeit für das Auftreten von Selbstorganisationsprozessen als Organisationales Lernen.[81] Die Multifunktionalität der Mitarbeiter wirkt lernfördernd, da die Fähigkeiten und Fertigkeiten von Individuen so genutzt werden, dass sie ohne die Autorität eines Vorgesetzten effektiv arbeiten können. Dieser Selbstorganisationsprozess birgt die Möglichkeit für jedes Organisationsmitglied, selbst zu lernen und bisher benutzte Denkmuster zu hinterfragen.

Einen wichtigen Lenkungsfaktor stellt die *Abstimmung zwischen Fertigung und Personalabteilung* dar. Ein enges Arbeitsverhältnis, das die Güte der Abstimmung zwischen der Fertigung und der Personalabteilung widerspiegelt, äußert sich in einem permanenten Informationsaustausch, der Organisationales Lernen fördert.[82] So ist der Personalabteilung bekannt, welche Kriterien die Fertigung bei der Aus- und Weiterbildung für ihre Mitarbeiter als relevant erachtet. Außerdem wird die Personalauswahl und -entwicklung ebenso wie die Aus- und Weiterbildung genau mit der Fertigung abgestimmt.[83] Eine Abstimmung erfolgt auch bei Änderungen im Fertigungsprozess, der Erstellung einer Stellenbeschreibung oder bei der Gestaltung von Arbeitsplätzen.

---

[78] Vgl. Becker, Manfred: Personalentwicklung: die personalwirtschaftliche Herausforderung der Zukunft, S. 279.

[79] Güldenberg, Stefan: Wissensmanagement und Wissenscontrolling in lernenden Organisationen, S. 289.

[80] Vgl. Oechsler, Walter A.: Personal und Arbeit, S. 343 f.

[81] Vgl. Streubel, Frauke: Organisatorische Gestaltung und Informationsmanagement in der lernenden Unternehmung, S. 218.

[82] Vgl. Schonberger, Richard J.: World Class Manufacturing: The Next Decade: Building power, strength, and value, S. 192 f.

[83] Vgl. Hayes, Robert H., Steven C. Wheelwright und Kim B. Clark: Dynamic Manufacturing, S. 112.

Die *Kriterien der Personalauswahl* in lernenden Organisationen unterstützen organisationale Lernprozesse, indem sie innerhalb des vorgeschalteten Prozesses der Personalauswahl Grundlagen für die Lernfähigkeit der einzelnen Individuen im Unternehmen absichern.[84] So kann ein Kriterium der Mitarbeiterauswahl die Problemlösefähigkeit oder die Bereitschaft und Fähigkeit zur Teamarbeit sein. Eine Auswahl von Mitarbeitern, die potenziell den Fertigungsprozess verbessernde Ideen liefern oder gut in kleinen Gruppen arbeiten können, garantiert, dass die Organisation über genug individuelle Lernkapazität verfügt, um darauf das Organisationale Lernen aufzubauen.

Basierend auf einem adäquaten Beurteilungssystem bewirkt ein *Anreiz- und Entlohnungssystem*, das auf die Ziele des Werkes ausgerichtet ist, eine Unterstützung Organisationalen Lernens, da in einer lernenden Organisation das Lernen zumindest Teil des Zielsystems sein sollte. Die Umgestaltung der Anreiz- und Belohnungssysteme sollte innovative Lösungen von Problemen und kreative Vorschläge honorieren.[85] Eine Balance zwischen monetären und nichtmonetären Anreizen verspricht Erfolg, wenn auch den nicht-monetären Anreizen eine größere Wirkung auf das Organisationalen Lernen zugeschrieben wird: „Nonmonetary rewards are also powerful incentives. Offering employees flexibility in their work practices and implementing other empowerment policies have tremendous benefit to employee esteem and job satisfaction.“[86]

Als besonders wichtiger Teilbereich des Entlohnungssystems gilt die *kompetenzbasierte Entlohnung*. Da sowohl die Erfahrung der Mitarbeiter, die sie durch den Wechsel ihres Arbeitsplatzes erlangen, als auch die Multifunktionalität bedeutende Lenkungsfaktoren darstellen, muss sich dieser Sachverhalt auch in der Entlohnung widerspiegeln. „Die Bezahlung nach Fertigkeiten hat bei den meisten Unternehmen die Nase vorn, weil sie besonders gut mit dem Prinzip der Job rotation und des Über-Kreuz-Lernens harmoniert.“[87] Gefordert wird ein Vergütungssystem, das sich an den Fähigkeiten und dem Wissen der Mitarbeiter orientiert, und das die jeweilige Anzahl an Aufgaben, die ein einzelner Mitarbeiter beherrscht, berücksichtigt.

Komponente des Anreizsystems sollten außerdem *gruppenbasierte Anreize* sein. Das Gruppenlernen gilt als Schnittstelle zwischen individuellem Lernen und dem Organisationalen Lernen. „Participation in a team changes how work is viewed, setting the stage for more important and longer lasting changes in attitude.“[88] Anreize hierfür unterstützen damit direkt das Potenzial des Organisationalen Lernens und können als Lenkungsfaktor klassifiziert werden. So wird die Fähigkeit, mit anderen zusammenzuarbeiten, wesentliche Voraussetzung für eine Beförderung und damit Teil des Personalentwicklungssystems. Anreize sollten allerdings nicht ausschließlich

---

[84] Vgl. Maani, Kambiz: Rapid Team Learning: Lessons from Team New Zealand America's Cup Campaign, in: Organizational Dynamics, Vol. 27 (1999), No. 4, S. 55.

[85] Vgl. Probst, Gilbert J.B. und Bettina S.T. Büchel: Organisationales Lernen, S. 160.

[86] Pegels, C. Carl: Handbook of Strategies and Tools for the Learning Company, S. 4.12.

[87] Byham, William C., Richard S. Wellins und Jeanne M. Wilson: Power-Teams: Spitzenleistungen mit autonomen Arbeitsteams, S. 73. Als Über-Kreuz-Lernen bezeichnen die Autoren die Fähigkeit von Mitgliedern eines Teams, Tätigkeiten aus anderen Teams zu erlernen.

[88] Pegels, C. Carl: Handbook of Strategies and Tools for the Learning Company, S. 6.5.

für Gruppenleistungen vergeben werden, da ansonsten die Leistung des Einzelnen nicht zum Vorschein kommt und somit die Motivation der Mitarbeiter sinkt.[89]

Mit *tätigkeitsbezogenem Training* kann direkt die organisationale Wissensbasis erweitert werden.[90] Dabei stehen insbesondere Konzepte der partizipativen und gruppenorientierten Lerngestaltung im Vordergrund.[91] Eine regelmäßige Aus- und Weiterbildung bezüglich der arbeitsplatzbezogenen Fertigkeiten sichert, unter der Bedingung dass die Mitarbeiter die Verbesserungswürdigkeit von Prozessen verstehen, dass sie die notwendigen Kompetenzen und Fähigkeiten erhalten, um Verbesserungen durchzuführen. Die Trainingsmaßnahmen betreffen nicht nur Mitarbeiter der unteren Hierarchieebenen, sondern ebenso die Führungskräfte eines Unternehmens. Nicht nur im Sinne einer Vorbildfunktion wird auch vom Top-Management eines Unternehmens ein lebenslanges Lernen gefordert.[92] Denn oft fällt es gerade den intelligentesten Mitarbeitern am schwersten, neue Lerninhalte aufzunehmen und in Verbesserungsprozesse umzusetzen.[93]

3 Organisationales Lernen als Grundlage für profitables Wachstum

In seinem Bericht über die Grenzen des Wachstums stellte der Club of Rome 1972 die Gefahren des technisch-wissenschaftlichen Fortschritts und den zunehmenden Verlust menschlicher Kontrolle über diese Wachstumsprozesse dar.[94] Die Autoren wiesen auf die unbegrenzte Lernfähigkeit der Menschen hin und stellten diese als ungenutztes Potenzial zur Lösung dieser Probleme dar. Die Weltwirtschaft steht einer ähnlichen Problematik gegenüber. Die zunehmende Globalisierung und Komplexität des wirtschaftlichen Geschehens, höhere Kundenanforderungen, immer schnellerer Wandel und eine stärkere Marktmacht der in der Wertschöpfungskette vor- und nachgelagerten wirtschaftlichen Einheiten erschweren die Steuerung und Kontrolle von Unternehmen. Genauso wie der Club of Rome weist die betriebswirtschaftliche Literatur auf die Ressource des Lernens und Wissens zur langfristigen Meisterung der neuen Herausforderungen hin. „In an economy where the only certainty is uncertainty, the one sure source of lasting competitive advantage is knowledge."[95] In diesem Sinne bildet organisationales Lernen eine der fundamentalen Grundlagen für unternehmerisches Wachstum – profitables Wachstum.

---

[89] Vgl. Albers Mohrman, Susan, Susan G. Cohen und Allan M. Mohrman: Designing Team-based Organizations: New Forms for Knowledge Work, S. 365f.

[90] Siehe Güldenberg, Stefan: Wissensmanagement und Wissenscontrolling in lernenden Organisationen, S. 283.

[91] Vgl. Probst, Gilbert J. B. und Bettina S. T. Büchel: Organisationales Lernen, S. 156.

[92] Vgl. Simon, Hermann: Management-Lernen als strategische Herausforderung, in: Simon, Hermann und Karlheinz Schwuchow (Hrsg.): Management-Lernen und Strategie, S. 15.

[93] Vgl. Argyris, Chris: Teaching Smart People How to Learn, in: Harvard Business Review, Vol. 69 (1991), No. 3, S. 99ff.

[94] Vgl. Meadows, Dennis et al.: Die Grenzen des Wachstums: Bericht des Club of Rome zur Lage der Menschheit.

[95] Nonaka, Ikujiro: The Knowledge-Creating Company, in: Howard, Robert und Robert D. Haas (Hrsg.): The Learning Imperative: Managing People for Continuous Innovation, S. 41.

Literatur

Albers Mohrman, S., S. G. Cohen und A. M. Mohrman (1995): *Designing Team-based Organizations: New Forms for Knowledge Work*, San Francisco.

Amelingmeyer, J. (2000): *Wissensmanagement: Analyse und Gestaltung der Wissensbasis von Unternehmen*, Wiesbaden.

Argyris, C. (1991): Teaching Smart People How to Learn, in: *Harvard Business Review*, Vol. 69, No. 3, S. 99–109.

Barker, R. T. und M. R. Camarata (1998): The role of communication in creating and maintaining a learning organization: Preconditions, indicators, and disciplines, in: *The Journal of Business Communication*, Vol. 35, No. 4, S. 443–467.

Bea, F. X. und J. Haas (1995): *Strategisches Management*, Stuttgart und Jena.

Becker, M. (1993): *Personalentwicklung: die personalwirtschaftliche Herausforderung der Zukunft*, Bad Homburg.

Bullinger, H.-J., K. Wörner und J. Prieto (1998): Wissensmanagement: Modelle und Strategien für die Praxis, in: Bürgel, H. D. (Hrsg.): *Wissensmanagement: Schritte zum intelligenten Unternehmen*, Berlin et al., S. 21–39.

Bürgel, H. D. (Hrsg.) (1998): *Wissensmanagement: Schritte zum intelligenten Unternehmen*, Berlin et al.

Byham, W. C., R. S. Wellins und J. M. Wilson (1992): *Power-Teams: Spitzenleistungen mit autonomen Arbeitsteams*, Landsberg/Lech.

Campbell, A. und K. Sommers Luchs (Hrsg.) (1997): *Core Competency-Based Strategy*, London und Boston.

Cohen, M. D. und L. S. Sproull (Hrsg.) (1996): *Organizational Learning*, Thousand Oaks.

De Geus, A. P. (1997): *The Living Company: Habits for survival in a turbulent business environment*, Boston/Mass.

De Geus, A. P. (1988): Planning as Learning, in: *Harvard Business Review*, Vol. 66, No. 2, S. 70–74.

Doz, Y. (1997): Managing core competency for corporate renewal: towards a managerial theory of core competences, in: Campbell, A. und K. Sommers Luchs (Hrsg.): *Core Competency-Based Strategy*, London und Boston, S. 53–81.

Drucker, P. F. (1993): The New Society of Organizations, in: Howard, R. und R. D. Haas (Hrsg.): *The Learning Imperative: Managing People for Continuous Innovation*, Boston/Mass., S. 3–17.

Ehrlenspiel, K. (1991): Integrierte Produkterstellung: Organisation – Methoden – Hilfsmittel, in: Milberg, J. (Hrsg.): *Wettbewerbsfaktor Zeit in Produktionsunternehmen: Referate des Münchener Kolloquiums 1991*, München, S. 114–131.

Gagnon, S. (1999): Resource-based competition and the new operations strategy, in: *International Journal of Operations & Production Management*, Vol. 19, No. 2, S. 125–138.

Gaitanides, M. (1993): Aufbau- und Ablauforganisation, in: Wittmann, W. et al. (Hrsg.): *Handwörterbuch der Betriebswirtschaft, Teilband 1, 5. Aufl.*, Stuttgart, S. 190–204.

Gerpott, T. J. (1994): Lernprozesse im Zeitwettbewerb, in: Simon, H. und K. Schwuchow (Hrsg.): *Management-Lernen und Strategie*, Stuttgart, S. 57–77.

Goh, S. C. (1998): Toward a learning organization: The strategic building blocks, in: *S.A.M. Advanced Management Journal*, Vol. 63, No. 2, S. 15–22.

Grafmüller, M. H. (2000): *Prozeßmanagement in der Automobilindustrie: Betriebliche Umsetzung am Beispiel der Volkswagen AG*, Wiesbaden.

Größler, A. (2000): *Entwicklungsprozess und Evaluation von Unternehmenssimulatoren für lernende Unternehmen*, Frankfurt/Main et al.

Güldenberg, S. (1998): *Wissensmanagement und Wissenscontrolling in lernenden Organisationen: Ein systemtheoretischer Ansatz, 2. Aufl.*, Wiesbaden.

Hasenpusch, J. (2001): *Strategiekonsistenz in Geschäftseinheit und Fertigung als Voraussetzung für den Erfolg industrieller Unternehmen: Eine empirische Untersuchung im Rahmen des Projekts „International Manufacturing Strategy Survey"*, Frankfurt/Main et al.

Hayes, R. H. und G. P. Pisano (1996): Manufacturing Strategy: At the Intersection of Two Paradigm Shifts, in: *Production and Operations Management*, Vol. 5, No. 1, S. 25–41.

Hayes, R. H., S. C. Wheelwright und K. B. Clark (1988): *Dynamic Manufacturing: Creating the Learning Organization*, New York und London.

Howard, R. und R. D. Haas (Hrsg.) (1993): *The Learning Imperative: Managing People for Continuous Innovation*, Boston/Mass.

Kaiser, K. (1996): Gestaltung lernfördernder Bedingungen in Unternehmen, in: Schatz, R. (Hrsg.): *Netzwerk als Basis der Lernenden Organisation*, Bonn, S. 43–58.

Kluge, A. und J. Schilling (2000): Organisationales Lernen und Lernende Organisation: ein Überblick zum Stand von Theorie und Forschung, in: *Zeitschrift für Arbeits- und Organisationspsychologie*, Jg. 44, Nr. 4, S. 179–191.

Kremmel, D. (1996): *Das Verhältnis zwischen Unternehmensstrategie und Unternehmenskultur unter besonderer Berücksichtigung des organisationalen Lernens*, Hallstadt.

Kröll, M. und H. Schnauber (Hrsg.) (1997): *Lernen der Organisation durch Gruppen- und Teamarbeit: Wettbewerbsvorteile durch umfassende Unternehmensplanung*, Berlin et al.

Krulis-Randa, J. S. (1990): Einführung in die Unternehmenskultur, in: Lattmann, Charles (Hrsg.): *Die Unternehmenskultur: ihre Grundlagen und ihre Bedeutung für die Führung der Unternehmung*, Heidelberg, S. 1–20.

Lattmann, C. (Hrsg.) (1990): *Die Unternehmenskultur: ihre Grundlagen und ihre Bedeutung für die Führung der Unternehmung*, Heidelberg.

Levitt, B. und J. G. March (1996): Organizational Learning, in: Cohen, M. D. und L. S. Sproull (Hrsg.): *Organizational Learning*, Thousand Oaks, S. 516–540.

Liebel, H. J. und W. A. Oechsler (1994): *Handbuch Human Resource Management*, Wiesbaden.

Lorange, P. et al. (Hrsg.) (1993): *Implementing strategic processes*, Oxford.

Maani, K. (1999): Rapid Team Learning: Lessons from Team New Zealand America's Cup Campaign, in: *Organizational Dynamics*, Vol. 27, No. 4, S. 48–63.

Maier, F. (1995): *Die Integration wissens- und modellbasierter Konzepte zur Entscheidungsunterstützung im Innovationsmanagement*, Berlin.

Meadows, D. et al. (1972): *Die Grenzen des Wachstums: Bericht des Club of Rome zur Lage der Menschheit*, Stuttgart.

Michael, D. N. (1973): *On Learning to Plan & Planning to Learn*, San Francisco et al.

Milberg, J. (Hrsg.) (1991): *Wettbewerbsfaktor Zeit in Produktionsunternehmen: Referate des Münchener Kolloquiums 1991*, München.

Milling, P. (1991): Strategische Planungs- und Kontrollsysteme zur Unterstützung betrieblicher Lernprozesse, in: Milling, P. (Hrsg.): *Systemmanagement und Managementsysteme*, Berlin.

Milling, P. (Hrsg.) (1991): *Systemmanagement und Managementsysteme*, Berlin.

Milling, P. (1995): Organisationales Lernen und seine Unterstützung durch Managementsimulatoren, in: *ZfB-Ergänzungsheft*, Nr. 3, S. 93–112.

Milling, P. (1999): Managementsimulationen im Prozeß des organisationalen Lernens, in: Schwaninger, M. (Hrsg.): *Intelligente Organisationen: Konzepte für turbulente Zeiten auf der Grundlage von Systemtheorie und Kybernetik*, Berlin, S. 461–472.

Nagl, A. (1997): *Lernende Organisation: Entwicklungsstand, Perspektiven und Gestaltungsansätze in deutschen Unternehmen – Eine empirische Untersuchung*, Aachen.

Nevis, E. C., A. DiBella und J. M. Gould (1995): Understanding Organizations as Learning Systems, in: *Sloan Management Review*, Vol. 37, No. 2, S. 73–85.

Nonaka, I. (1993): The Knowledge-Creating Company, in: Howard, R. und R. D. Haas (Hrsg.): *The Learning Imperative: Managing People for Continuous Innovation*, Boston/Mass., S. 41–56.

Oechsler, W. A. (2000): *Personal und Arbeit: Grundlagen des Human Resource Management und der Arbeitgeber-Arbeitnehmer-Beziehungen, 7. Aufl.*, München und Wien.

Pautzke, G. (1989): *Die Evolution der organisatorischen Wissensbasis: Bausteine zu einer Theorie des organisatorischen Lernens*, München.

Pegels, C. C. (1998): *Handbook of Strategies and Tools for the Learning Company*, Portland/Oregon.

Pettigrew, A. M. und R. Whipp (1993): Strategic change capabilities, in: Lorange, P. et al. (Hrsg.): *Implementing strategic processes*, Oxford, S. 3-42.

Porter, M. E. (1998): *Competitive Advantage: Creating and Sustaining Superior Performance*, Reprint Edition, New York.

Probst, G. J. B. und B. S. T. Büchel (1994): *Organisationales Lernen: Wettbewerbsvorteil der Zukunft*, Wiesbaden.

Reinhardt, R. (1993): *Das Modell Organisationaler Lernfähigkeit und die Gestaltung Lernfähiger Organisationen*, Frankfurt/Main et al.

Reuther, A. und A. Größler (1999): *Organisationales Gedächtnis: Konzepte und unterstützende Methoden, Forschungsberichte der Fakultät für Betriebswirtschaftslehre*, Universität Mannheim, Nr. 9901, Mannheim.

Riekhof, H.-C. (1997): Die Idee des Geschäftsprozesses: Basis der lernenden Organisation, in: Riekhof, H.-C. (Hrsg.): *Beschleunigung von Geschäftsprozessen: Wettbewerbsvorteile durch Lernfähigkeit*, Stuttgart, S. 7–28.

Riekhof, H.-C. (Hrsg.) (1997): *Beschleunigung von Geschäftsprozessen: Wettbewerbsvorteile durch Lernfähigkeit*, Stuttgart.

Ross, R. et al. (1994): Core Concepts About Learning in Organizations, in: Senge, P. M. et al. (Hrsg.): *The Fifth Discipline Fieldbook: Strategies and Tools for Building a Learning Organization*, New York et al., S. 48–50.

Sattelberger, T. (1996): Die lernende Organisation im Spannungsfeld von Strategie, Struktur und Kultur, in: Sattelberger, T. (Hrsg.): *Die lernende Organisation: Konzepte für eine neue Qualität der Unternehmensentwicklung, 3. Aufl.*, Wiesbaden, S. 11–55.

Sattelberger, T. (Hrsg.) (1996): *Die lernende Organisation: Konzepte für eine neue Qualität der Unternehmensentwicklung, 3. Aufl.*, Wiesbaden.

Savolainen, T. I. (1999): Cycles of continuous improvement: Realizing competitive advantages through quality, in: *International Journal of Operations & Production Management*, Vol. 19, No. 11, S. 1203–1222.

Schatz, R. (Hrsg.) (1996): *Netzwerk als Basis der Lernenden Organisation*, Bonn.

Schonberger, R. J. (1996): *World Class Manufacturing: The Next Decade: Building power, strength, and value*, New York.

Schwaninger, M. (Hrsg.) (1999): *Intelligente Organisationen: Konzepte für turbulente Zeiten auf der Grundlage von Systemtheorie und Kybernetik*, Berlin.

Senge, P. M. et al. (Hrsg.) (1994): *The Fifth Discipline Fieldbook: Strategies and Tools for Building a Learning Organization*, New York et al.

Senge, P. M. (1990): *The Fifth Discipline: The Art & Practice of The Learning Organization*, New York.

Simon, H. (1994): Management-Lernen als strategische Herausforderung, in: Simon, H. und K. Schwuchow (Hrsg.): *Management-Lernen und Strategie*, Stuttgart, S. 3–18.

Simon, H. und K. Schwuchow (Hrsg.) (1994): *Management-Lernen und Strategie*, Stuttgart.

Sinkula, J. M. und W. E. Baker (1997): A framework for market-based organizational learning: Linking values, knowledge, and behavior, in: *Academy of Marketing Science*, Vol. 25, No. 4, S. 305–318.

Stäbler, S. (1999): *Die Personalentwicklung der „Lernenden Organisation": Konzeptionelle Untersuchung zur Initiierung und Förderung von Lernprozessen*, Berlin.

Stalk, G. Jr., P. Evans und L. E. Shulman (1993): Competing on Capabilities: The New Rules of Corporate Strategy, in: Howard, R. und R. D. Haas (Hrsg.): *The Learning Imperative: Managing People for Continuous Innovation*, Boston/Mass., S. 19–40.

Stata, R. (1989): Organizational Learning: The Key to Management Innovation, in: *Sloan Management Review*, Vol. 30, No. 3, S. 63–74.

Streubel, F. (2000): *Organisatorische Gestaltung und Informationsmanagement in der lernenden Unternehmung: Bausteine eines Managementkonzeptes organisationalen Lernens*, Frankfurt/Main et al.

Thun, J.-H. (2002): *Die zeitbasierte Fertigungsstrategie – Methoden zur Leistungssteigerung in Industriebetrieben*, Wiesbaden.

Watkins, K. E. und V. J. Marsick (1993): *Sculpting the learning organization: Lessons in the art and science of systemic change*, San Francisco.

Weißmann, S. (2001): *Total Quality Management für Industriebetriebe: Praktiken zur Leistungssteigerung*, Wiesbaden.

Welge, M. K. und A. Al-Laham (1999): *Strategisches Management: Grundlagen – Prozess – Implementierung, 2. Aufl.*, Wiesbaden.

Wengelowski, P. (2000): *Entwicklung organisationalen Lernens: Ein Lenkungsmodell*, Wiesbaden.

Wiegand, M. (1996): *Prozesse Organisationalen Lernens*, Wiesbaden.

Wittmann, W. et al. (Hrsg.) (1993): *Handwörterbuch der Betriebswirtschaft, Teilband 1, 5. Aufl.*, Stuttgart.

Wunderer, R. (1997): Mitarbeiter zu Mitunternehmern fördern, in: Kröll, M. und H. Schnauber (Hrsg.): *Lernen der Organisation durch Gruppen- und Teamarbeit: Wettbewerbsvorteile durch umfassende Unternehmensplanung*, Berlin et al., S. 107–130.

Würth, R. (1995): *Erfolgsgeheimnis Führungskultur: Bilanz eines Unternehmers*, Frankfurt und New York.

Zahn, E. (1998): Wissen und Strategie, in: Bürgel, H. D. (Hrsg.): *Wissensmanagement: Schritte zum intelligenten Unternehmen*, Berlin et al., S. 41–52.

Walk the Talk: Implementing Ethical Conduct in Industrial Production Systems

Switbert Miczka[1], *Nicole Zimmermann*[1], *David Andersen*[2] *and George Richardson*[2]

[1] Industrieseminar der Universität Mannheim, Schloss Mannheim

[2] University at Albany, State University of New York, Rockefeller College of Public Affairs and Policy, Albany, USA

Abstract

This paper discusses the effects of an increasing customer need for products with ethical quality. Companies answer this trend either because they hope for growth opportunities or because they are afraid of negative publicity if caught in unfavored activities. The purpose of the present paper is to outline potential reactions and, with focus on the production branch of the firm, the effects of an attempted adjustment of a firm's operations to a demand for more ethical conduct. Based on the qualitative discussion of the phenomenon, a system dynamics model is developed to investigate the market dynamics resulting from the shift in demand. Depending on the level of customer awareness of a product's ethical quality and the companies' attempt to offer only conventional goods in an ethical disguise, different scenarios are analyzed. The importance of well-informed customers for the development of a healthy market for ethical goods is shown delays in adjusting the production structure the major incentive to offer pseudo-ethical goods, and with information being an important regulating mechanism.

Keywords: ethical goods, ethical production, supply chain management, shifting customer demand, system dynamics

1 Ethics as Competitive Factor for Industrial Companies

1.1 The Customers' Need for Ethics

Over the last decades, a stable growth in the demand for goods produced in morally acceptable, humane, and ecologically sustainable – generally spoken: ethical – ways can be observed (Mendelson and Polonsky 1995; Rode, Hogarth, and LeMenestrel 2008). As most consumer products are offered at acceptable prices, as product quality has reached a more than satisfying standard, and as a broad variety of product variants serves all kinds of highly specific customer needs, consumers increasingly care for the ethical quality of the goods surrounding them in everyday life: Organic food neither produced with the extensive use of fertilizers and pesticides, nor emaciating the soil or making use of artificial flavors has become a considerable trend in the food industry (AC Nielsen 2008). Similarly, "animal welfare" is getting more and more attention, e.g. regarding the living conditions of laying hens or the transportation of livestock (Verbeke and Viane 2000; Schröder and McEachern 2004). Clothes and shoes are increasingly scrutinized regarding working conditions, toxic immissions on workers, and the fairness of wages paid by the employers (Harrison and Scorse 2006), and fair trade networks promote fair wages for coffee planters and craftsmen exporting their products to wealthier countries (Hira and Ferrie 2006). These studies underline the significance of a shift in consumer demand towards more ethically produced goods. Consumers increasingly care not only for product characteristics, but also for a product's origin and production and distribution processes behind the actual goods consumed.

Several studies show that the perceived moral obligation of consumers especially in the wealthy nations also translates into behavioral changes. In a laboratory experiment on the general customer interest in social responsible behavior of firms, Becker-Olsen et al. find that 80 percent of their participants expect organizations to behave responsibly, and 52 percent would be likely to boycott a firm in case of socially irresponsible behavior (Becker-Olsen, Cudmore, and Hill 2006: 52). Crane argues that a product's ethical dimension may not be the core characteristic motivating a buying decision, but is becoming more important (Crane 2001: 369). In fact, in an experiment measuring the customers' willingness to pay for fair trade coffee, Pelsmacker et al. find that interest in ethical products – fair trade coffee, in their example – translates into actual sales in spite of higher price, with 27 percent of the participants exhibiting some general interest in fair trade products, and about 10 percent of the probands agreeing on actually paying a premium for such a product (De Pelsmacker, Driesen, and Rayp 2005: 381). And even if consumer interest in the ethical dimension of a product does not immediately translate into a purchasing decision, consumers still like to be confident that the goods they buy do not do social or environmental harm (Roberts 2003: 163). I.e., as the appreciation of ethical conduct becomes more widely spread, a substantial, at the same time fast growing number of consumers considers it as an order-qualifying criterion which has to be fulfilled by a company wanting its products to be competitive. A smaller, yet in many industries still considerable share of the customer base even perceives outstanding ethical conduct as a clearly beneficial, order-winning criterion that may even justify a price premium (Hill 2000: 35–38).

1.2 The Producers' Response

The shift in customer demand may be interpreted as an effect of the satisfaction of basic, general needs, leading to a shift towards a more abstract "higher quality", by trend positively correlating with the wealth of a society. With the traditional competitive dimensions of cost, quality, and time losing their potential for differentiation in many markets (Slack 1983), many industrial producers turn towards this (reasonably) new trend and start serving the customers' need for ethics. In fact, the customers' interest in ethics may be interpreted a result of the industrial companies' long-time strive for exceeding the competitors' performance on the traditional competitive dimensions of cost, quality, and time: Over time, competition has led to the development of production procedures whose negative, initially unrevealed exogenous effects become increasingly discovered and discussed. In the consumers' perception, many practices are perceived to have only little benefit, gained with comparatively strong adverse effects. Some of these practices invented to deliver cheap high-quality consumer products that become severely questioned are, e.g., artificial flavors in food, low wages for coffee planters, and the workers in South-East-Asian "sweatshops" physically and mentally suffering from inhumane working conditions, or the unethical treatment of animals in industrial livestock farming have brought about public discussions and controversies. Means and practices originally intended to achieve advantages in highly competitive consumer markets have apparently been taken to a level that is not unanimously honored any more, but may rather lead to lost sales as soon as alternative goods perceived as being more ethically sound become easily available.

Industrial companies choose different approaches to respond to the consumers' need for ethics. The purpose of the present paper is to outline potential reactions and, with focus on the production branch of the firm, the effects of an attempted adjustment of a firm's operations to a demand for more ethical conduct. In the first section of this paper, alternative reactions are outlined. Second, potential responses demanding changes in the production function and/or the supply chain are discussed. Third, a system dynamics model is used to illustrate the dynamic implications resulting from the market mechanism, delays in the adjustment of the production branch, customer awareness, and the competition between conventional products, pseudo-ethical marketing, and real changes towards ethically sound production procedures.

2 Motivations for Pursuing Ethical Production Procedures

A focus on (more) ethical conduct of the production branch may, in general, be motivated by one or several of the three following considerations: First, ethical production may be assumed to improve the company's market position, giving it a positive edge in the customers' perception against its competitors. This can be seen as a positive motivation, aiming at an "upside opportunity" or order-winning criterion. Second, pursuing ethical manufacturing policies throughout the supply chain may be understood as a means of risk reduction, as negative publicity about a firm's manufacturing practices might harm its corporate or brand image. This can be seen as a "downside protection" or order-qualifying approach, the attempt to reduce the potential of negative reports about manufacturing practices perceived as being unethical. Third, of course, merely altruistic motives may be in place. As honorable as the latter certainly are, lacking the market-link characterizing a firm's behavior in competitive situations they shall not be taken into consideration in this article.

2.1 Ethical Conduct as Downside Protection

There is ample evidence that consumers are increasingly suspicious of ethical and environmental claims (Mendelson and Polonsky 1995; Crane 2001), and examples show that customers may make use of their aggregated buying power and effectively sanction companies whose behavior is not up to the consumers' expectations (Klein, Smith, and John 2004). The most prominent example in this context certainly is the boycott of Shell gas stations as reaction to the attempt to dispose and sink the Brent Spar oil storage buoy in the Atlantic Ocean (Grolin 1998). In a similar vein customers announced to boycott Basic, the German organic groceries dealer, if the German discount retail chain Lidl realized its plan to take a substantial share in Basic. In the months before the takeover attempt, Lidl had been criticized repeatedly for labor conditions, both in its retail stores themselves as well as in some of its suppliers' factories. Basic's customers argued that Lidl represents a lot of what they actually try to avoid when shopping at Basic, and therefore threatened to boycott Basic in case of a takeover. After Basic's major supplier joined the line of criticism, Lidl finally refrained from raising its stake in Basic (Spiegel Online 2008). A lack of ethical compliance apparently limited Lidl's strategic options in this case.

Being perceived as unethical may represent a major threat to a company's image, as well as to its actual sales. A damaged image may lead to harsh short-term reprisals, and cannot be rebuilt easily. Therefore, companies start initiatives to implement ethical codes of conduct to reduce the risk of having undiscovered ethical pitfalls in both their own organization and their supply chain. Peek & Cloppenburg, the German apparel retailer, for example, checks labor conditions and codes of conduct of its about 1,800 first-tier suppliers (Curtis 2006). Yet, the initiative is not actively used for purposes of corporate communication: "To make profit out of corporate ethics is not our objective. We do not use this topic for promotion either. Our main motivation is to maintain our reputation and to live up to our responsibility", Eckhard Spanier says, a Peek & Cloppenburg representative (Curtis 2006).

The downside protection strategy may come into play if a company perceives ethical conduct as a hidden order qualifier: Customers implicitly take for granted that "everything is in order"; yet if they become aware of a company not fulfilling the expected standards, this company may become excluded from competition. Particular product criteria, e.g. a product's ethical integrity, have developed into order-qualifiers without being recognized as such. Only as the customer recognizes the lack of an implicitly assumed criterion it may put a company's market position at risk with only little warning. The probability of such a scenario increases as soon as alternative, similar products are available which can deliver the expected ethical quality. Figure 1 contrast the described downside protection strategy with its counterpart, a behavior aiming at realizing upside opportunities.

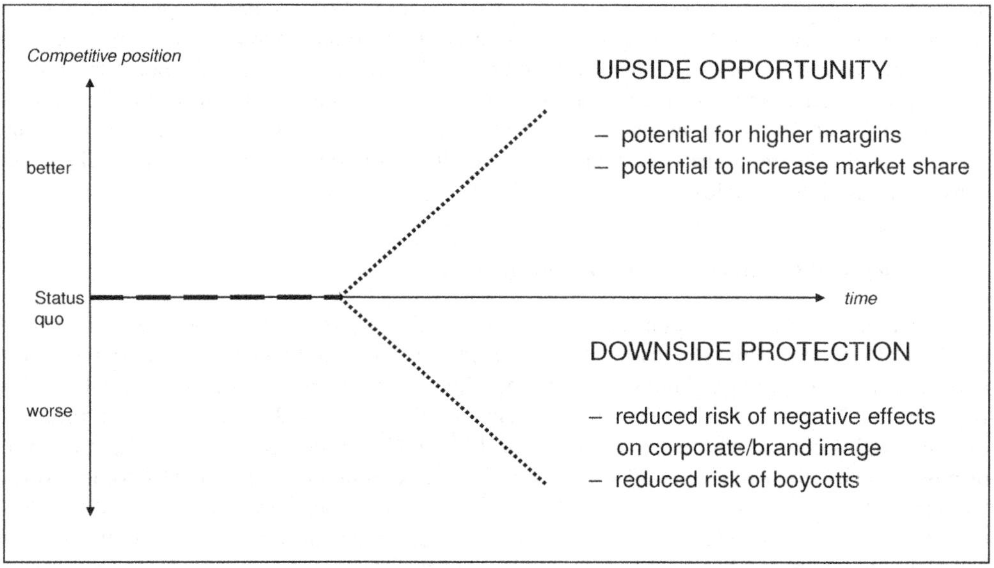

Figure 1: Ethical Conduct to Make Use of Upside Opportunities or for Downside Protection

2.2 Upside Opportunities of Ethical Production

On the other hand, a turn towards ethical production may result from a perception of significant potential for an improvement of the company's market position. With an increasing customer interest in a product's ingredients and production process and considerable premiums being paid for goods exhibiting an ethically sound origin, "ethical quality" may become an attractive way of differentiating products, especially commodities. Fair trade products and organic food are major examples of the potential of such an approach.

Product differentiation aims at an increase of the producer's competitive position – and possibly his gains – by selling similar, but not identical products in competitive markets (Levitt 1980; Sharp and Dawes 2001). Product differentiation, no matter whether it is attempted on the ethical dimension or otherwise, may induce significant changes in the manufacturing function of a company. It can be achieved in four different ways: First, the customers' perception of an existing product can be influenced by marketing the product differently, e.g. by establishing a well-recognized brand name or emotionally loading a product through advertisement. Second, the product characteristics can be altered by introducing new ingredients or product components like, for instance, an innovative motor leading to a reduction of the power consumption of electrical appliances, or using different cocoa beans to get a new taste for a chocolate bar. Third, differences in the end product can be achieved through changes of the production process as it is the case, e.g., for organic production leading to lower pesticide contamination of end products, or the altered processing of (the same) grapes to achieve a particularly tasty or colorful wine. The latter two approaches may result in an actual difference of the product's attributes which can be transported implicitly through the product itself exhibiting different features, as well as explicitly by actively communicating the changes in product quality. But just as much examples can be given where changes in ingredients or the production process cannot be perceived in the end product's attributes. In these cases the altered product composition or product process can

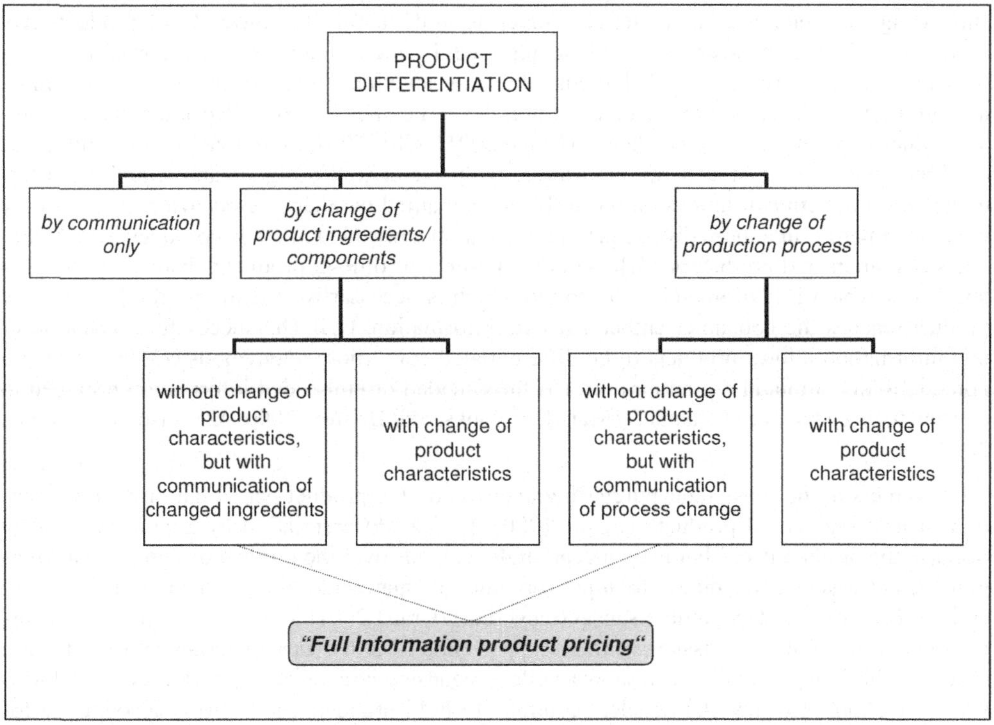

Figure 2: Alternatives for Product Differentiation

be communicated to the customer only by adding information about the change to the end product. An example might be changes in employment policies and wages that do not lead to a different product, but add to the "augmented product" by increasing its ethical quality (Crane 2001: 361–373). Andersen et al. (2008: 3) suggest the term "Full Information Product Pricing" for this particular approach. As Full Information Product Pricing refers to true changes in the product or the production process, it stands in stark contrast to the first approach – differentiation though communication only – which relies on changing the product's perception in the market place without actually varying anything about the product.

Accordingly, communication is an essential element of product differentiation as the customer needs become informed about the advantages of a good. Yet, a perceived need to differentiate combined with large difficulties to change the actual conduct – ingredients or processes – may leave companies tempted to create a more ethical image without actually adjusting their operations accordingly. Communication may be considered a substitute for actual ethical performance to compensate a lack of ethically manufactured offers in a producer's (or retailer's) product portfolio as information asymmetry makes it difficult for the consumer to assess the actual quality of the products (Akerlof 1970), creating incentives to offer low quality "pseudo-ethical" products boosted by an image satisfying the customer's need for ethics. Nevertheless, not backing an image campaign with unquestionably ethical operations can be considered a strategy attempting to exploit an upside opportunity whilst building up a considerable downside risk at the same time: "[E]thical branding might be regarded as particularly problematic, for this requires the firm to ensure that every aspect of the firm's operations […] are in line with, and supporting, the intended brand image. Tinkering with merely the most direct product-level issues is unlikely to be seen as a credible approach by increasingly skeptical consumers. […] Given the intense scrutiny afforded to ethical claims, an ethical brand cannot be seen as simply as a promotional exercise, but rather as a cultural one, i.e. the firm must live and breathe its ethical values and not just espouse them." (Crane 2001: 370). Thus, more than in other initiatives to differentiate a product as being innovative, exclusive or well-designed and reliable, a differentiation on the ethical dimension has to be accompanied by adequate behavior. It is not only the brand image, but a more diverse set of information embedded in ethical products which connects customers and producers: "[I]t is not the number of times a product is handled or the distance over which it is ultimately transported which is necessarily critical, but the fact that the product reaches the consumer embedded with information. […] The successful translation of this information allows products to be differentiated from more anonymous commodities and potentially to command a premium price if the encoded or embedded information provided to consumers is considered valuable." (Marsden, Banks, and Bristow 2000: 425; also cf. Raynolds 2002).

Consumers do not base their purchasing decision on the product per se but on their perception of an "augmented product" (Levitt 1980). Ethical differentiation by augmentation may occur in the product itself, but the concept vitally extends over the product design (e.g. an energy-efficient washing machine), the input (organic raw materials), the production process (e.g. emission control), and even the disposal (recycling) (Crane 2001: 365). As customers hold corporations accountable for issues in their supply chain, i.e. the raw materials and production process, ethical augmentation can show an effect regarding both upside opportunities and downside protection. "[M]any stakeholders continue to hold branded goods firms accountable for issues relating to the production of the raw materials and goods that go into their products, whether or not they own or directly control the production process." (Roberts 2003: 163.) Accordingly – and as the examples of Peek & Cloppenburg and others show – "firms which seek to address ethics as a product or brand issue will need to look not only at their own activities but also those of their parents and subsidiaries, and perhaps more importantly, those of firms throughout the value chain" (Crane 2001: 370). This perception is true even if customers can include only a limited number of attributes into their purchasing decision and will not be able to take into consideration the full supply chain, but rather base it on a subjective aggregate of attributes of product, production processes, and the conduct of supply chain (Crane 2001: 368). Still, this does not give organizations the opportunity to cover their socially or environmentally bad behavior. Examples of inappropriate behavior stand out of the supply chain and most likely may lead to reputational damages and to consumer action like boycotts. Therefore, it can be assumed that simple supply chains are quicker and more successful at implementing ethical initiatives than complex, confusing ones. The implications of this assumption are to be examined with the help of a simulation model later on.

The consumers' interest and their demand for ethically produced items can accumulate to economically relevant dimensions, and induce fundamental changes of the production process as a means of differentiation (Noe and Rebello 1995). In some industries, consumer interests even become institutionalized in groups such as "Food Watch". As the attempt to fulfill the customers' need for ethics with means of communication involves considerable risk, a sincere change of operating procedures is not only the more venerable, but also the strategically more sustainable approach. Yet, it induces significant management challenges.

3 Ethical Conduct – a Target Dimension for Operations Management

"Ethical conduct" in operations – understood as an ecologically and socially sustainable way of producing goods or services – deliberately denies to exploit the full potential for cost-reduction. This potential may exist either due to an imbalance in power that is not exploited to the full extent – e.g. in wage or price negotiations – or because of an unused possibility to exploit elements of the ecosystem that are not protected by the law, e.g. rainforests or soil on private property.[1] Due to the increasing competitive relevance of ethical conduct in many industries – cf. the examples given earlier in this paper – and the necessity of answering the consumers' need for ethics not exclusively by means of communication, ethical conduct can be considered a new target dimension for modern production systems, in addition to cost, quality, time, and flexibility. The following passages examine different aspects of implementing ethical production procedures.

[1] This can be interpreted as paying non-market prices for some of the production factors, or implementation of other technology or policy shifts fundamentally influencing production economies. The term "non-market prices" is meant in contrast to market prices paid in efficient production regimes. From this perspective, market prices do not necessarily represent equilibrium prices equaling marginal costs, but may be higher or lower depending on the distribution of bargaining power. For example, in regions with only few alternatives to coffee growing, buyers may reduce prices almost deliberately as coffee growers do not have any other option for earning money at all besides growing coffee beans and, accordingly, have no bargaining power.

3.1 Ethics and the Complexity of Supply Structures

Up to now, mainly simple production and supply systems in commodity markets have explicitly adopted a systematic approach to improve their operations on the ethical dimension. The majority of contributions addresses labor-intensive production processes as well as industries characterized either by a power imbalance which has led to the exploitation of workers, farmers or other job-holders in a supply chain, or by considerable negative exogenous ecological effects. Roberts, for example, compares three cases in which supply networks introduced ethical codes of conduct into their respective production processes. She finds that certification in the wood products of Do-It-Yourself (DIY) home improvement stores was easy when compared to the pulp and paper industry because DIY items are made of rather few wood components only. Paper product supply chains, in contrast, have much more suppliers and more complicated supply routes compared to DIY. The difference in the complexity of the supply chain leads to a lower level of ethically oriented practices in the paper network. Similarly, in branded confectionary – i.e. the supply chain from cocoa beans to chocolates – the implementation of ethical sourcing is equally difficult as for the paper industry since the upstream supply chain consists of a very large number of small producers. Things are less complex for branded clothes and footwear, and accordingly ethically oriented codes of conduct have become relatively common (Roberts 2003: 164–168). As these examples point out, companies running complex supply chain structures tend to avoid ethical initiatives due to the expected implementation effort, assuming to lack the capabilities to implement them successfully (Bowen et al. 2001: 174). Thus, it can be assumed that the complexity of the supply structure negatively correlates with the implementation of ethical codes of conduct. In an industry characterized by increasing demand for such products, companies might choose to serve customer needs for ethics only by means of communication and pseudo-ethical goods. The actual implementation of changed production processes should be observed only after a considerable amount of time. The implications of this notion are to be examined with the help of a simulation model later on.

3.2 Ethical Production, Costs, and Competitive Pricing

By definition ethically produced goods have a cost disadvantage against conventional products fully exploiting potential for rationalization. Having the price as only differentiating criterion, especially for commodities the efficiency of the supply chain is of major importance, and a deviation from the industry's efficiency standards produces more severe disadvantages than it might be the case for companies selling innovative products and using complex supply chain structures to produce them (Fisher 1997). Yet, taking into account evidence from the literature (and own shopping experience), consumers are willing to pay considerable premiums at the point of sale for a comparatively low nominal difference in, for example, the wages of coffee growers. This phenomenon gives freedom to accept inefficiencies in the supply chain leading to higher costs, but also bears potential for the downstream parts of a supply chain to raise prices beyond the effects of production inefficiencies, skimming the higher willingness to pay for own profit. The development of trust gains importance in this setting (Luna-Reyes et al. 2009). In order to take the argumentation of this paper beyond the qualitative argumentation of the preceding sections, a system dynamics model will be used to investigate the dynamic effects of communication and pseudo-ethical goods as well as the implementation of truly ethical behavior at different levels of customer awareness.

4 A System Dynamics Model of Ethical Conduct in the Production Branch

The previous sections have presented a faceted set of examples for how to master the interaction between the consumers' demand for more ethically produced goods and the different possible responses from industrial companies. Producers of ethical goods compete with those of conventional producers, especially if the latter try to build an ethically appearing image around their product portfolio. In order to investigate the dynamic interplay, a system dynamics model depicting the feedback between demand, communications, and the supply of ethical, conventional, and pseudo-ethical goods – i.e. conventional goods boosted with an ethical image – is used. Previously, Andersen et al have presented a model explicating delays within the production chain and their effect on the supply ratios of ethical (fair trade, in that case) and conventional coffee (Andersen et al. 2008). The here presented paper aims at complementing this work by suggesting a model for analyzing the importance of process adjustments for successful ethical product differentiation. When going from hypotheses to empirical testing, computer simulation can portray the dynamic interplay of cause and effect in different scenarios of ethical manufacturing. It can help to understand the long-term implications of ethically motivated adjustments of industrial operations and the competitive importance of such changes in contrast to communication simply building an ethical image. The system dynamics approach is an adequate method of analysis as the issue under scrutiny is characterized by manifold intertwined feedback mechanisms, and considerable time delays (Forrester 1961; Richardson and Pugh III 1983; Milling 1984; Richardson 1991; Milling 2002). The structure of the simulation model is kept rather generic in order to support the development of abstract insights applicable in very different lines of business. In line with the preceding argumentation of this paper, the boundary of the model is set to encompass the market dynamics resulting from a customer demand for ethical and conventional goods, information about the products' ethical quality, and the supply structures for ethical and conventional goods. For the presented simulation runs examples from the organic produce sector will be used as anchors for illustration. In total, four scenarios will be presented in the course of the analysis.

4.1 Basic Feedback Structures

The simulation model is built around a generic market mechanism for ethical goods: In this core structure, depicted in Figure 3 (see p. 100), the *demand supply ratio* for ethical goods determines the goods' *price*. If, for example, the *demand* rises, it drives up the price, making it more profitable to supply ethical goods and consequently increasing *supply*. This creates the *balancing price supply mechanism for ethical goods*. At the same time a rising price also reduces *demand* again to a small extent, creating a second *balancing price demand mechanism*. The market mechanism for conventional goods has been implemented in a similar, only slightly differing way: The price supply mechanism for conventional goods works in the very same manner. Yet, demand for conventional goods is determined by the difference between a constant total demand and the demand that has been satisfied with ethical products. The two market mechanisms for ethical and conventional goods are related to each other, as it is assumed that a fixed total demand for goods – ethical as well as conventional – exists of which an exogenously determined fraction explicitly wants to buy ethical products. If this specific demand is not served because of a lack of supply or because the price exceeds the customers willingness to pay, customers then buy conventional goods as they are in need of the product (= constant total demand). The unit costs of an ethical product are higher than the ones of a conventional good, due to the deliberately unused potential for increased efficiency described earlier.

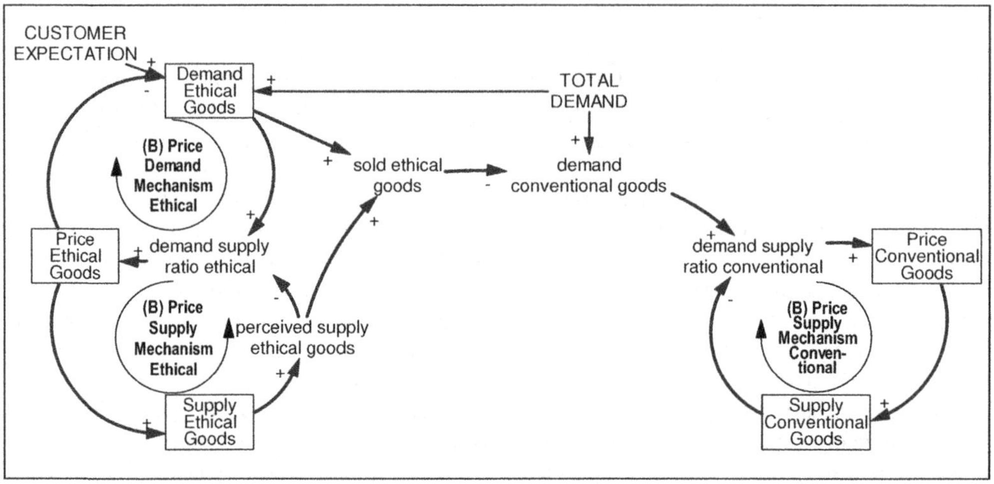

Figure 3: Market Mechanisms for Ethical and Conventional Goods[2]

The mechanism created by the two loops on the left hand side of Figure 3 balances demand and supply with a time delay. Figure 4 shows that this time delay mainly results from a slow *supply adjustment time*, depending on the *complexity* of the supply chain. Supply chain complexity is composed of two different effects: the "member complexity" on the one hand, and an adverse effect of supply chain integration on the other hand. The former effect describes that the more supply rises, the more suppliers are needed, and complexity increases due to the higher coordination effort. Since complexity slows down the further increase of supply, this creates the *balancing loop of SC member complexity*. This mechanism complies with a finding by Roberts according to which the high number of producers in branded confectionary increases complexity and makes it difficult to implement ethical sourcing. Ethics is more easily implemented in the less complex branded clothes sector due to fewer parties in the supply chain (Roberts 2003: 166–168).

Second, at the same time, a *reinforcing effect from supply chain integration* counteracts the balancing mechanism: After a time delay the supply chain is able to integrate and reduce complexity by integrating the material flow and information. As a kind of learning process, the progress of this integration is modeled as depending on cumulative production. This effect conforms to Taylor's finding that the fair trade coffee supply chain shortened due to the commodity chain's organization and the nature of the product (Taylor 2005: 143). Integration affects complexity as well as the number of suppliers. Complexity for ethical as well as for conventional goods depends on the respective nature of the specific supply chain, but the chains' respective causal structures for complexity are the same in both parts of the model.

[2] In the course of the paper, causal loop diagrams are used to exemplify the argumentation. A comprehensive overview of the feedback structure is given in Appendix 1, the stock-flow level is shown in Appendix 2. Boxes in the causal loop diagrams indicate accumulating stocks.

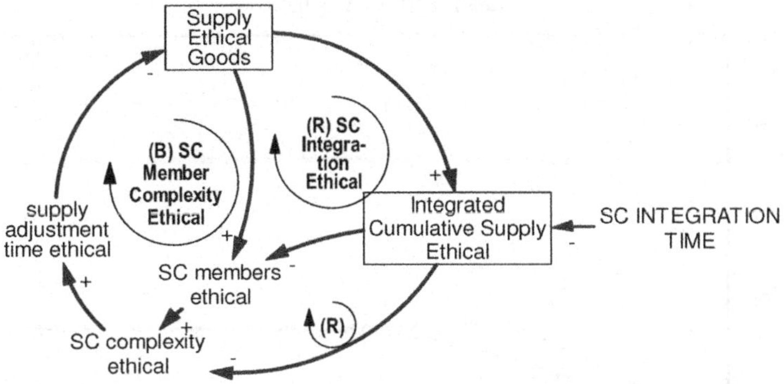

Figure 4: Supply Chain Complexity

Scenario 1: Base Run

Base Run Scenario

In Germany, until few years ago, organic produce was sold in wholesome food stores only. Its introduction to the product portfolio of several discount store chains made it an order qualifier for a growing number of customers. The rising customer demand is the situation that a discount store chain that initially barely carries organic produce faces. The base run thus represents a scenario in which customer demands for ethical products rise from initially 1 percent in the first year by one additional percentage point (i.e. piece of ethical goods) per month during the subsequent two years.[3] The reaction of a discounter which applies a follower strategy is modeled. The rising demand for fair trade coffee or animal welfare in production are alternative examples.

With constant customer demand for ethical products the model is in equilibrium. Due to rising prosperity, concern for health, or frustration about food quality customer expectations for ecologically sustainable goods increases. The results for a company that honestly communicates its products' properties – i.e. it supplies only conventional and truly ethical goods – can be seen in Figure 5 (see p. 102): Triggered by a rising *price for ethical goods* and a correspondingly higher profitability of ethical produce, the company increases its *supply* of this type of product. The balancing price supply mechanism is active. The adjustment time retards the process as a rising supply continuously requires changes in the supply chain. It increases the coordination difficulty and the supply chain complexity, leading to a dominance of the *balancing supply chain member complexity loop*. Over time, the *reinforcing integration mechanism* becomes more important, and the supply chain is able to integrate. Suppliers can provide a greater variety of intermediate goods, and complexity decreases again, also reducing the adjustment time. The system arrives at its new equilibrium.

[3] Parameter values for the four scenarios are recorded in Appendix 2.

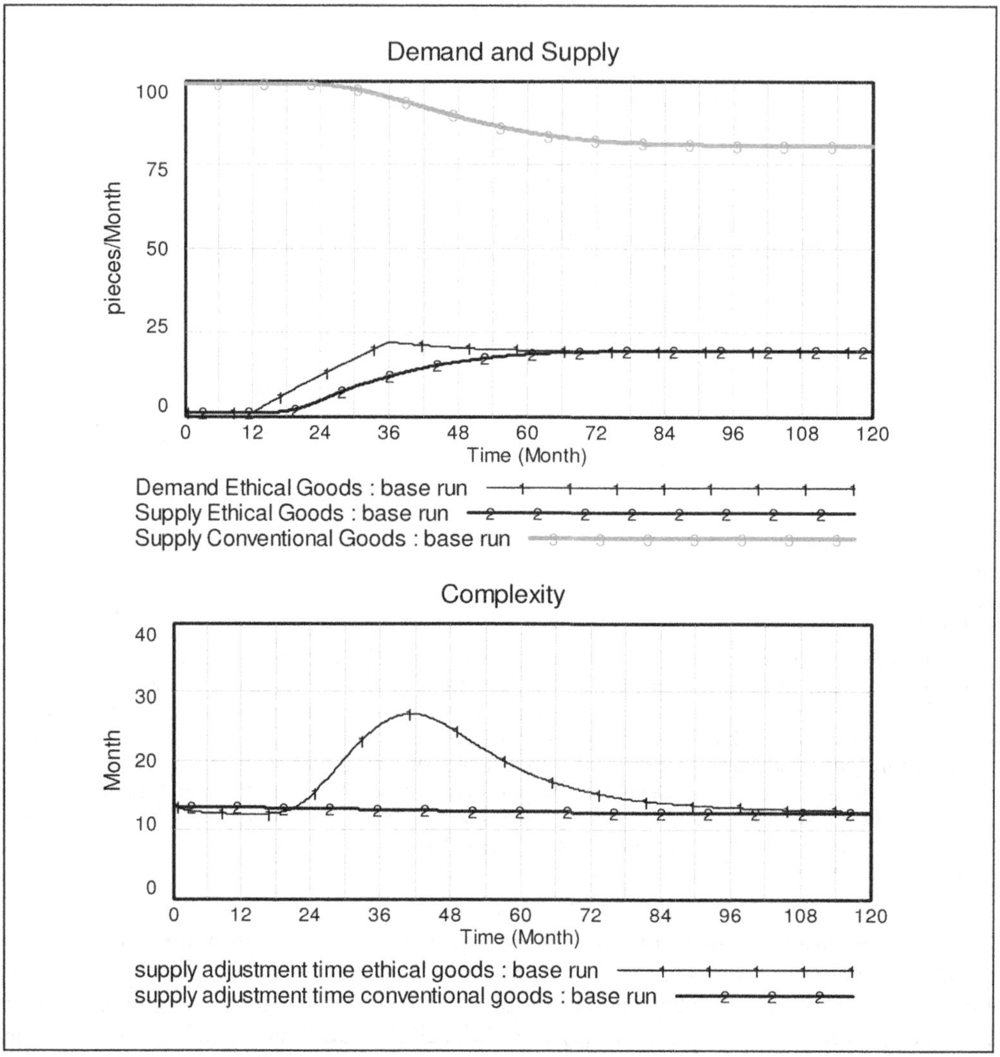

Figure 5: Base Run

On the side of conventional goods, the high number of supplied goods increases complexity, but conventional goods have been supplied for a long time so that the generally larger supply chain is well integrated. As a consequence overall complexity is rather low leading to a relatively constant supply adjustment time for conventional goods.[4]

[4] In an additional test the modeling revealed the importance of supply chain integration for reducing time delays in the increase of ethical supply. A higher cumulated supply and thus higher supply chain integration are able to significantly reduce the supply adjustment time in comparison to the base run, leading to a quicker adaptation to demand.

These results support the notion that there are considerable differences in the implementation of ethical expectations of their customers based on supply chain complexity. While Robert found that the difference in the complexity of the supply chain leads to a lower implementation of ethics, it certainly implies a slower implementation (Roberts 2003: 167). The following scenario will indicate whether it can also induce a lower degree of implementation.

Scenario 2: Competitors Offering Pseudo Goods

Scenario Including Pseudo-Ethical Goods

The second scenario is placed in the same environment. Yet, the producers of conventional goods believe that it will be profitable to sell pseudo-ethical goods which have the properties of conventional goods, but are marketed as being ethically superior. 50 percent of the customer base with an interest in organic produce initially believes this promise.

As corporate scandals show, companies do not necessarily supply clearly distinguishable conventional and purely ethical goods. They may also offer "pseudo-ethical goods", i.e. conventional products and labeled as being ethically superior in relation to other conventional goods. Examples for these pseudo-ethical products are, for instance, food marketed as the output of "controlled farming" that, in fact, does not fulfill the strict legal standards for organic food, or coffee advertised as supporting social initiatives in the growing region, yet paying only very low wages to the coffee planters (Focus Online 2006). It is assumed that the conventional supply chain can switch between conventional and pseudo-ethical goods, as the differences between these two classes of products are the way they are labeled and marketed. The causalities that determine the supply of pseudo goods are modeled as follows base on two feedback mechanisms: In times when demand for ethical goods outweighs supply, pseudo-ethical goods increase the *perceived supply of ethical goods*, causing sales of (presumingly) ethical goods to increase

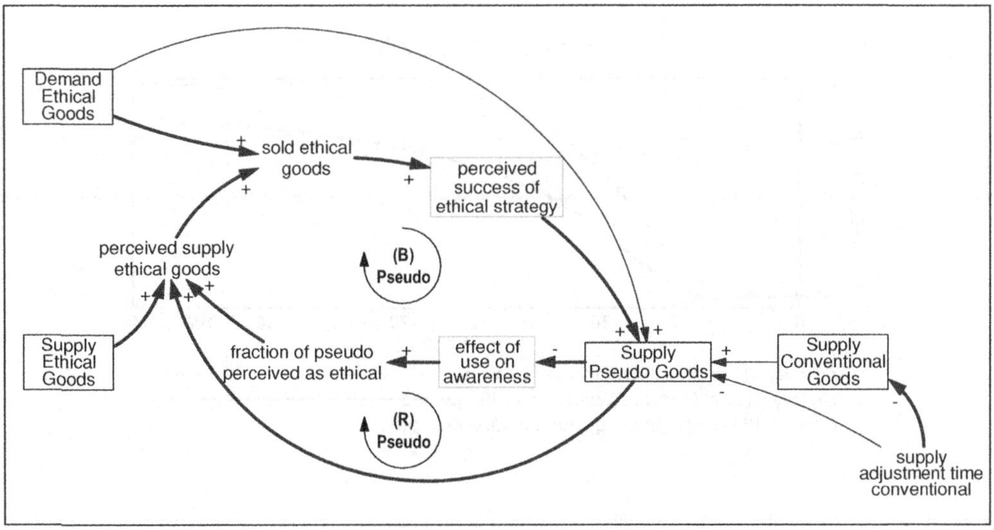

Figure 6: Causal Structure of the Supply Module for Pseudo-Ethical Goods

and making suppliers of the pseudo-ethical believe in their strategy. Yet, a balancing mechanism tarnishes this reinforcing "success story": Customers become more and more aware of the real properties of pseudo goods; the rising customer awareness reduces the *fraction of pseudo goods perceived as being ethical*. As a result, sales of these products slow down, further reducing the success of the current strategy and the supply of pseudo goods.

According to the literature, responsibility initiatives in which the stated objectives and corporate action are not consistent encourage skepticism among customers and do not lead to the intended positive reputation effects (Forehand and Grier 2003; Becker-Olsen, Cudmore, and

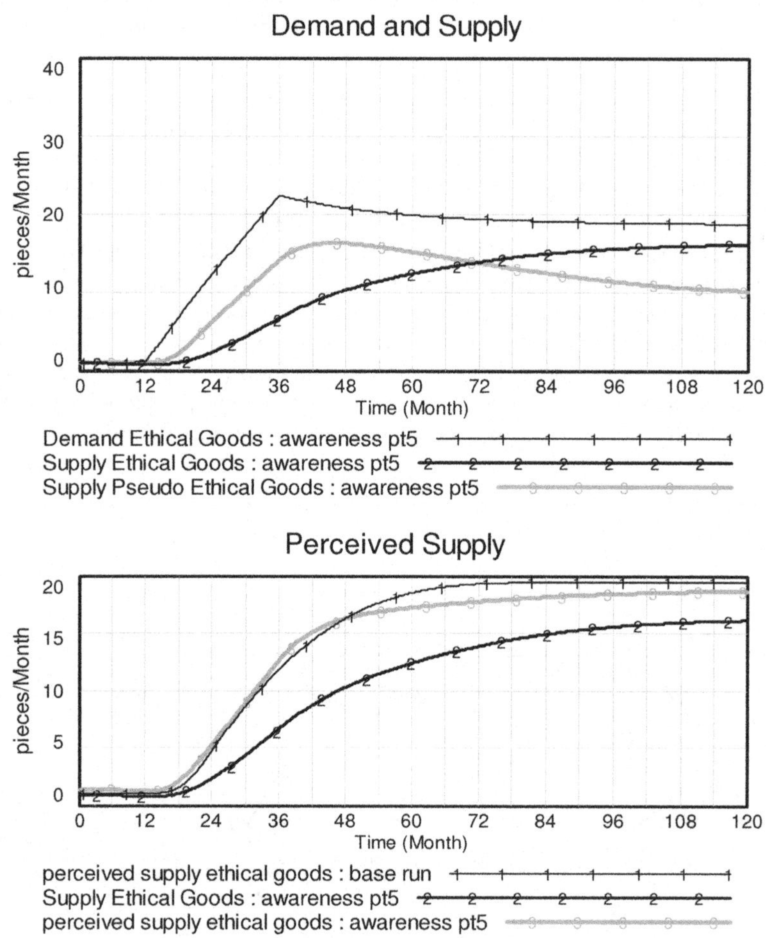

Figure 7: Introducing Pseudo-Ethical Goods

Hill 2006). Assuming a scenario of organic produce in a discount store chain again, the producers of conventional products are now inclined to supply pseudo ethical goods in order to skim the higher willingness to pay of customers demanding ethical products whilst having the low cost basis of conventional production. Initially 50 percent of the customer base is aware of the real properties of the pseudo goods. Customer demand rises as it did in the base run scenario.

The effects on the distribution of supply can be seen in Figure 7. The demand supply inadequacy triggers a strong rise of pseudo-ethical supply. This is the case because pseudo-ethical goods have a cost advantage over truly ethical goods and because of the increasing complexity of the ethical supply chain delaying the shift to organic produce. Over time the ethical supply chain integrates increasingly, and its complexity and adjustment time decrease. But as the peak and decline in the supply of pseudo-ethical goods indicates, the company's reliance on this type of product also gets thwarted by the balancing causal mechanisms described in Figure 6 (see p. 103). While the corporation initially perceives a 100 percent *success of its (un)ethical strategy*, this number slowly adjusts to the real *fraction of pseudo goods perceived as ethical*. Customers using (eating) the product further reduce this fraction, giving even more weight to this balancing process.

The two different effects also become obvious when looking at the lower part of Figure 7. In the case involving pseudo-ethical goods real ethical supply (line 2) is much lower than in the base run (line 1). Until about month 48 the quick *supply of pseudo-ethical goods* nonetheless leads to a higher *perceived supply of ethical goods* (line 3) than in the base run (line 1) where perceived equals real supply. The balancing loops lead to a shift starting in month 48 when due to the diminishing *perceived success of the ethical strategy* the supply of pseudo goods starts to decline. Via the rising price the diminished perceived supply in the pseudo goods scenario then has an effect on demand again. The upper part of Figure 7 shows that demand also adapts downward.

It is thus true that, on the one hand, skepticism and awareness of pseudo goods do not have the intended unrestrictedly positive effects (Forehand and Grier 2003: 352–354; Becker-Olsen, Cudmore, and Hill 2006: 50). However, since customers are not fully aware of the true properties of the products they buy, the corporation can still sell a fair share of its pseudo-ethical supply and does not reduce the production of pseudo-ethical goods to zero. Whether full customer awareness of is able to change this behavior fundamentally will be analyzed in the following.

Scenario 3: Pseudo-Ethical Goods and High Customer Awareness

Scenario Including Pseudo Goods and High Customer Awareness

In the third scenario the conventional producer faces very well-informed customers who are not persuaded by communication easily, but are fully aware of the conventional properties of pseudo-ethical goods.

If none of the customers demanding organic produce or other ethical goods gets persuaded by communication, pseudo-ethical goods are indeed useless. Figure 8 (see p. 106) illustrates that

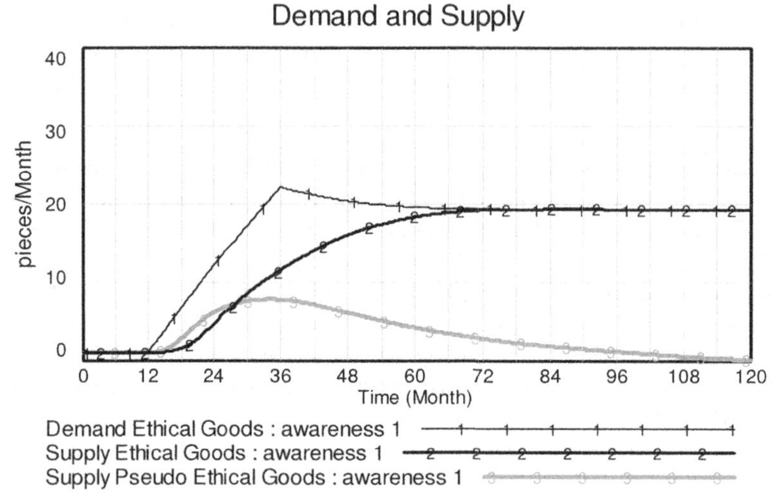

Figure 8: High Customer Awareness

due to the company's original believe in the success of its strategy, it still increases the supply of pseudo-ethical goods in the beginning.

However, the success becomes an illusion quickly so that after less than two years the company starts reducing its supply of pseudo-ethical goods again, finally reaching zero. The supply of truly ethical goods rises and finally meets the slightly decreased demand. A new equilibrium is reached.

Scenario 4: Sudden Increase of Customer Awareness

Scenario with Sudden Awareness Increase

In the last scenario, customers are initially fully unaware that they buy pseudo-ethical products. They fully believe in the producers' communication and labeling. An external information shock about the company's false-faced communication and behavior – e.g. after a leakage to the media – is injected exogenously, enlightening the initially naive customers.

There are many examples when customer awareness has not always been high. Shell's Brent Spar case as well as Lidl's case of buying the organic Basic store chain are examples where awareness suddenly increased. For this reason, the last scenario starts with customers who are fully unaware of the fact that they buy pseudo-organic produce at their local discount store. They trust the producers' communication and labeling completely until they get information about the true nature of the production process underlying the products they buy.

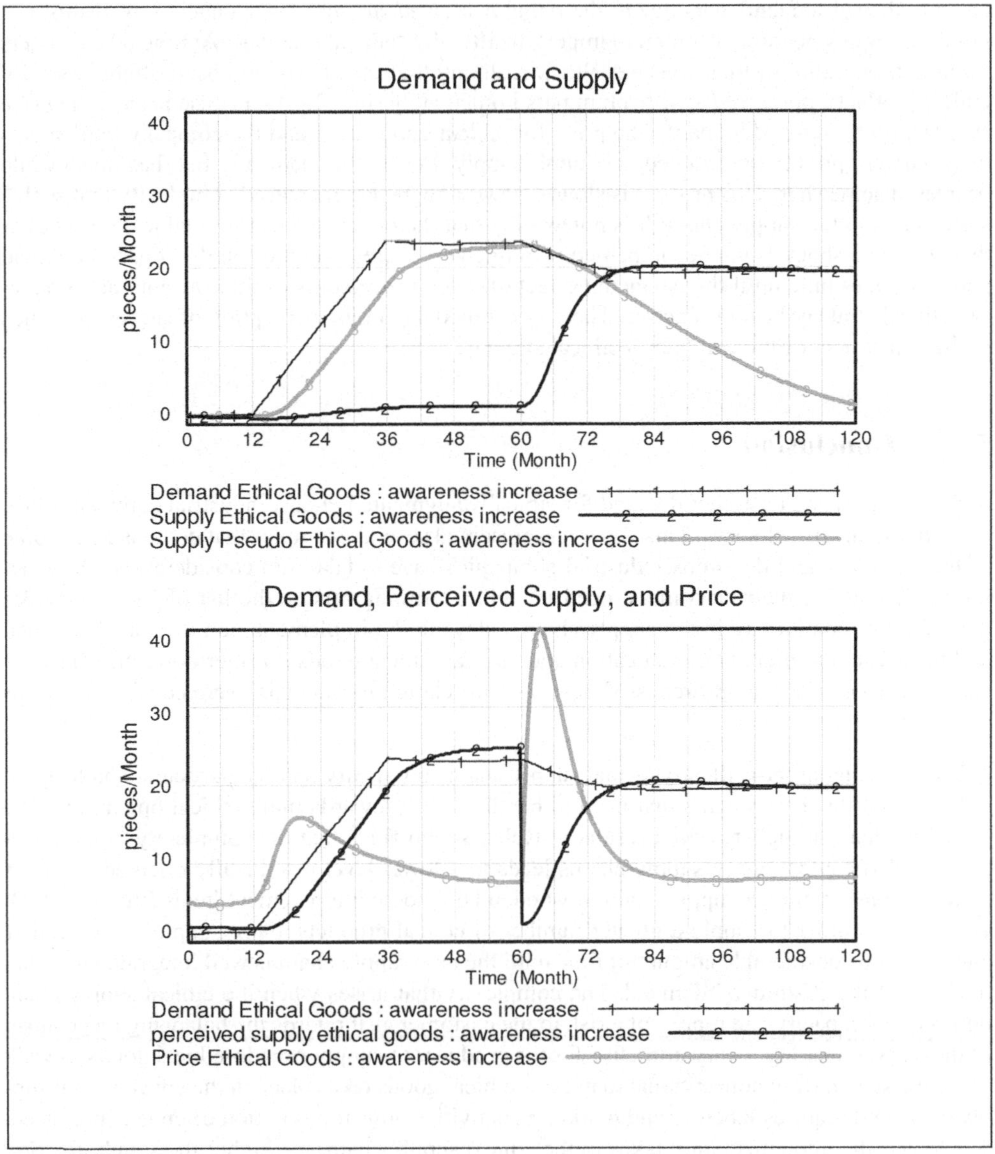

Figure 9: Rise of Customer Awareness

In this case, the pseudo-ethical strategy is initially very successful. As can be seen in the upper part of Figure 9, the system reaches an equilibrium in which the demand for ethical products is almost exclusively served by pseudo-ethical goods (line 3). Demand (line 1) remains at a very high level, it even increases somewhat as supply grows. The price for ethical goods, which is shown in the bottom of Figure 9 (line 3) increases when demand rises after month 12 and falls again in the subsequent years due to the rising *perceived supply*. This balancing mechanism of price and supply becomes even more important after the "ethical scandal": At time 60 customers become fully aware of their mistake. When realizing that they have only been offered pseudo-ethical products, *perceived supply* plummets immediately (line 2). As a consequence, the *price supply loop* becomes dominant: The price for ethical goods rises and the company implements truly ethical production procedures until supply meets the demand that has meanwhile decreased somewhat. This process is slowed down only by the increased complexity that such a shift causes in the supply chain. It is noteworthy that the rather quick rise of ethical goods after the awareness shock is not accompanied by a likewise decrease in the supply of pseudo-ethical goods. It takes time until the balancing effect of *perceived success* of the conventional producer's ethical strategy becomes active. There is a time delay in the perception of success and thus in the adjustment of the company's ethical strategy.

5 Conclusion

In the face of rising customer demand for ethically augmented goods, industrial companies face challenges, but also chances. This paper has presented several examples that demonstrated some of the dilemmas and decisions industrial companies have to take into consideration when facing an increase in their customers' need for ethics. Among others, the list of issues includes the effects of complexity in the supply chain, delays in the implementation of ethical conduct, and the evasion to mere communication and pseudo-ethical goods. Furthermore, the effects of customer awareness and awareness shocks, e.g. in relation to scandals, were considered in this context.

The modeling process illustrates that supply chain complexity poses a particular challenge to industrial production systems that need to handle a shift towards more ethical operations. The modeling thus parallels research results of Roberts who finds that the complexity of the paper and branded confectionary supply chains leads to a lower level of ethically oriented practices than in the less complex supply chain of wooden DIY home improvement items (Roberts 2003: 164–168). In order to supply a greater number of ethical products, more suppliers are needed, and it takes a considerable amount of time until the new supply chain is well integrated to effectively meet the customers' demand. The complexity that arises when the ethical supply chain builds up its capacity can represent a risk to the customer as it retards the balancing mechanism of the market, making it very attractive for the producer to supply pseudo-ethical goods as well. Since the switch from conventional to pseudo-ethical goods takes place in the conventional supply chain and requires labeling and marketing activities only, this solution often gets preferred. The longer the implementation takes in the ethical supply chain, the higher the supply fraction or at least the risk to get pseudo-ethical goods will be.

Depending on the customer characteristics, pseudo-ethical goods may also become a challenge to the supplying company. The risk of increasing customer awareness can turn pseudo-ethical goods into a severe downside risk so that customer awareness becomes an important lever for the success of pseudo ethics. If customers become aware of the company's pseudo-ethical conduct by an information shock, they suddenly refuse buying pseudo-ethical products. It is conceivable that this behavior will result in expensive oversupply and even a loss of reputation that may also impair a producer's further product lines. Nevertheless, if consumers continuously believe in a producer's hypocritical communication, pseudo-goods make an attractive and profitable alternative.

The rising customer expectations just as much represent a real chance for producers and their upstream suppliers. If a company relies on conventional and truly ethical production and refrains from the pseudo-ethical temptation, it can seize the upside opportunity and benefit from the customers' willingness to pay for ethically sound goods. The more successful it is at quickly integrating its new supply chain for this challenge, the quicker the benefits will come. Implementing true ethics in a production network is also a chance for downside protection as it renders customer awareness about the true content of the supply irrelevant and prevents the risks of an ethical scandal.

Depending on the level of customer awareness as well as the company's willingness to supply pseudo-ethical goods, different levels of truly ethical supply can be achieved. Customer awareness and a company's willingness to offer pseudo-ethical supply thus become important policy levers that – if influenced – can determine the fit between customer demands and practiced conduct in industrial production systems. Both the customers by their search for information as well as the company by its more or less ethical orientation have an effect on the dynamic behavior of the system by influencing what the other party supplies or buys. In the real world, the extent to which, for example, companies manufacture products in bad working conditions and to which this emanates the soil depends the company and customer demand for ethics, and also on how informed the customer is and wants to be.

The system dynamics model is able to show the dynamic interplay of customer demand for ethical products, supply chain complexity as well as ethical and pseudo-ethical supply. Sound simulation results give confidence in the hypothesized causal structure, revealing feedback mechanisms, particularly reinforcing and balancing effects in the system. This creates a learning lab and testing device for our assumptions about the system. The model enables managers to build an increased understanding of the effects and side-effects of transformations and the evolution in the ethical products' market.

This testing device being created, various further market settings could now be tested, e.g. involving different producers and production systems that differ in the ease and complexity of implementing ethical production systems. In spite of its quite high level of abstraction and the rather narrow systems border, the model represents a helpful tool for investigating the feedback effects underlying an uprising and very promising trend in consumer markets. Future, extended versions of this basic model should focus on specific aspects that have not been included up to now, such as a more extended representation of consumer trust dynamics as well as the development and effects of information shocks and scandals. A combination with other system dynamics-based research in this field, e.g. the model presented by Andersen et al. (Andersen et al. 2008), may add some more depth to the consideration of production capacity and intra supply chain dynamics. Additionally, the credibility of ethical initiatives in operations might be adversely affected by the complexity of the supply structure, largely due to the customer's perception not to be able to fully oversee the producer's actual behavior. As a consequence, an investigation of trust in relation of a supply chain's complexity and credibility would be a valuable extension of this work.

Appendix 1: Overview of the Causal Structure

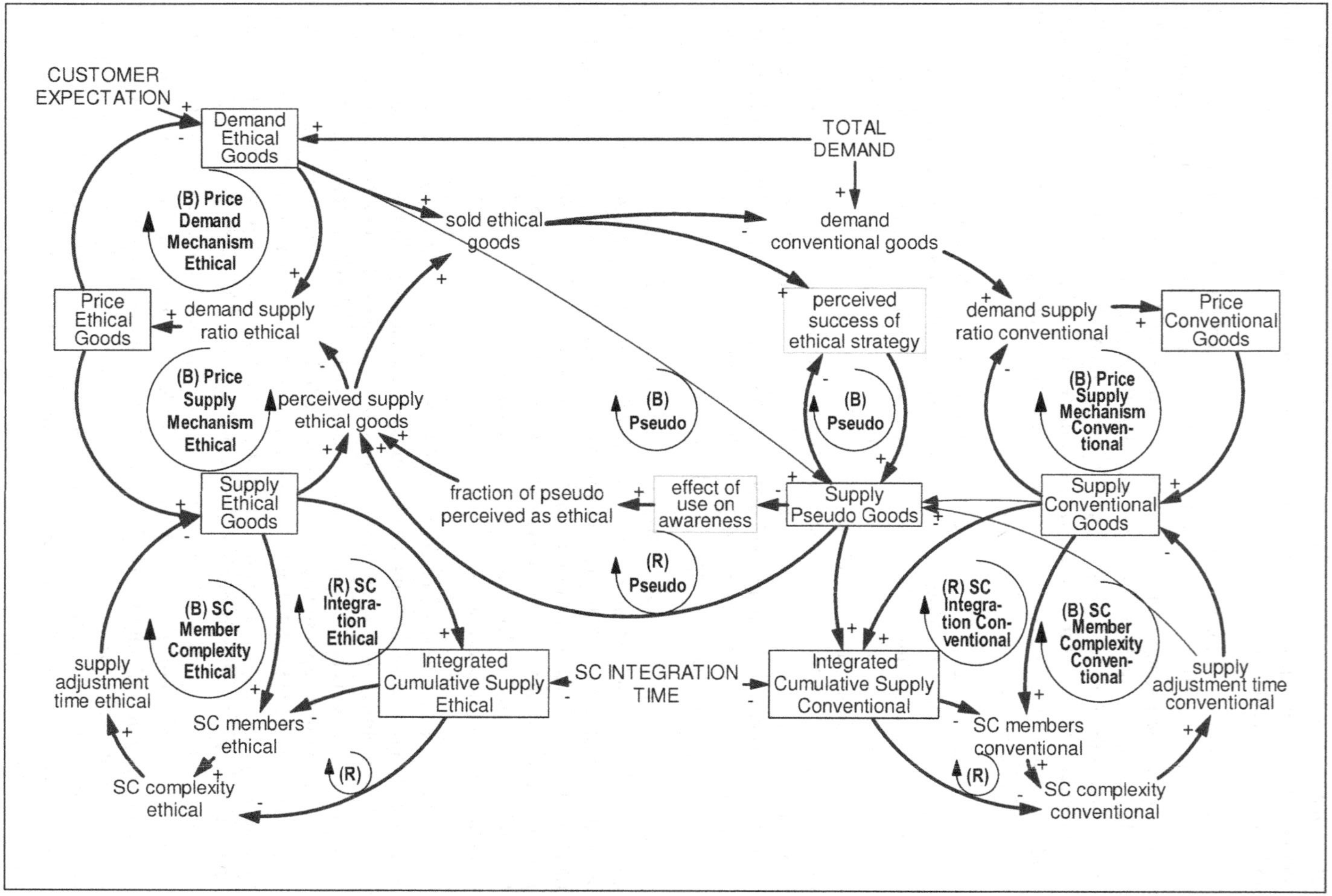

Appendix 2: Overview of the System Dynamics Model

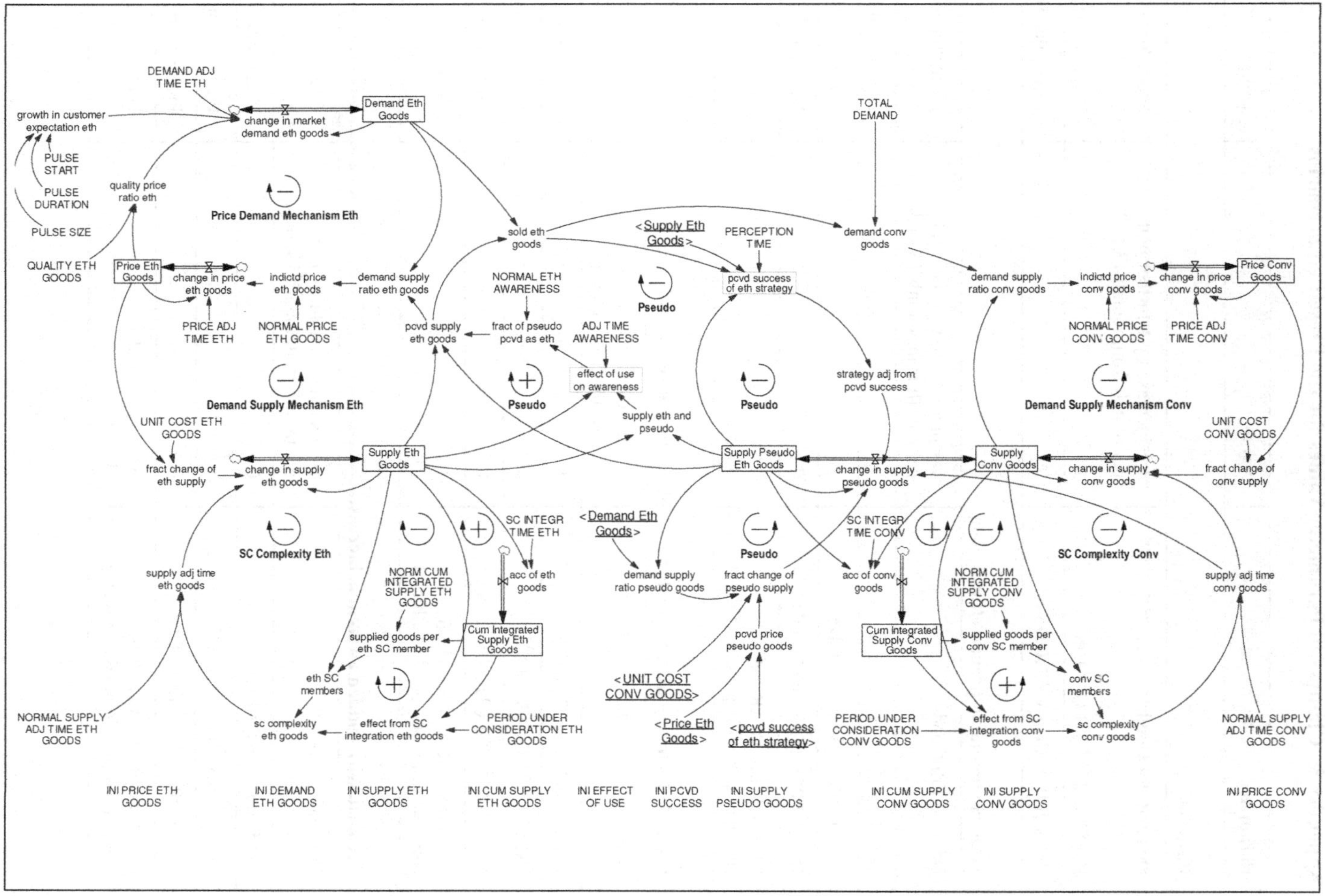

Appendix 3: Changes in Parameter Values for the Presented Scenarios

Parameter	Value	Units
Base run		
Demand Eth Goods	1 + increase by 1 further unit per month from month 13 to 36	Pieces/month
INI SUPPLY ETH GOODS	1	Pieces/month
INI SUPPLY CONV GOODS	99	Pieces/month
Scenario including pseudo ethical good		
Demand Eth Goods	1 + increase by 1 further unit per month from month 13 to 36	Pieces/month
INI SUPPLY ETH GOODS	0.9	Pieces/month
INI SUPPLY CONV GOODS	99	Pieces/month
INI SUPPLY PSEUDO GOODS	0.9	Pieces/month
CUSTOMER AWARENESS (ini fract of pseudo pcvd as ethical)	0.5 (0.5)	Dmnl
Scenario including pseudo goods and high customer awareness		
Demand Eth Goods	1 + increase by 1 further unit per month from month 13 to 36	Pieces/month
INI SUPPLY ETH GOODS	1	Pieces/month
INI SUPPLY CONV GOODS	99	Pieces/month
INI SUPPLY PSEUDO GOODS	0.9	Pieces/month
(CUSTOMER AWARENESS (ini fract of pseudo pcvd as ethical)	1 (0)	Dmnl
Scenario with sudden awareness increase		
Demand Eth Goods	1 + increase by 1 further unit per month from month 13 to 36	Pieces/month
INI SUPPLY ETH GOODS	0.9	Pieces/month
INI SUPPLY CONV GOODS	99	Pieces/month
INI SUPPLY PSEUDO GOODS	0.9	Pieces/month
CUSTOMER AWARENESS (ini fract of pseudo pcvd as ethical)	0 + STEP (1, 60) (1 → 0)	Dmnl

Literature

AC Nielsen (2008): *Bioprodukte bleiben im Trend.* AC Nielsen GmbH, cited 12 Dec 2008. Available from http://de.nielsen.com/news/pr20080211.shtml.

Akerlof, G. A. (1970): The Market for Lemons: Quality Uncertainty and the Market Mechanism. *The Quarterly Journal of Economics* 84(3): 488–500.

Andersen, D. F., L. F. Luna-Reyes, A. Whitmore, J. Zhang and R. Roy (2008): Exploring the Dynamics of Full Information Product Pricing Networks: Fair Trade Coffee in Mexico, in: *26th International Conference of the System Dynamics Society*. Athens: The System Dynamics Society.

Becker-Olsen, K. L., B. A. Cudmore and R. Paul Hill (2006): The impact of perceived corporate social responsibility on consumer behavior. *Journal of Business Research* 59(1): 46–53.

Bowen, F. E., P. D. Cousins, R. C. Lamming and A. C. Faruk (2001): The Role of Supply Management Capabilities in Green Supply. *Production and Operations Management* 10(2): 174–189.

Crane, A. (2001): Unpacking the ethical product. *Journal of Business Ethics* 30(4): 361–373.

Curtis, K. (2008): *Moral messbar machen*, cited 28 Dec 2008. Available from http://www.e-fellows.net/show/detail.php/10278.

De Pelsmacker, P., L. Driesen and G. Rayp (2005): Do Consumers Care about Ethics? Willingness to Pay for Fair-Trade Coffee. *Journal of Consumer Affairs* 39(2): 363–385.

Fisher, M. L. (1997): What is the right supply chain for your product? *Harvard Business Review* 75(2): 105–116.

Focus Online (2008): *Warum Bio? Bio-Siegel für glückliche Kühe*, cited 19 Dec 2008. Available from http://www.focus.de/gesundheit/ernaehrung/gesundessen/lebensmittelskandale/warum-bio_aid_19423.html.

Forehand, M. R. and S. Grier (2003): When Is Honesty the Best Policy? The Effect of Stated Company Intent on Consumer Skepticism. *Journal of Consumer Psychology* 13(3): 349–356.

Forrester, J. W. (1961): *Industrial Dynamics*. Cambridge, MA: M.I.T. Press.

Grolin, J. (1998): Corporate legitimacy in risk society: the case of Brent Spar. *Business Strategy and the Environment* 7(4): 213–222.

Harrison, A. and J. Scorse (2006): Improving the Conditions of Workers? Minimum Wage Legislation and Anti-Sweatshop Activism. *California Management Review* 48(2): 144–160.

Hill, T. (2000): *Manufacturing Strategy*. Boston, MA: Irvin McGraw-Hill.

Hira, A. and J. Ferrie (2006): Fair Trade: Three Key Challenges for Reaching the Mainstream. *Journal of Business Ethics* 63(2): 107–118.

Klein, G. G., N. C. Smith and A. John (2004): Why We Boycott: Consumer Motivations for Boycott Participation. *Journal of Marketing* 68(3): 92–109.

Levitt, T. (1980): Marketing success through differentiation – of anything. *Harvard Business Review* 58(1): 83–91.

Luna-Reyes, L. F., J. Zhang, R. Roy, D. F. Andersen, M. Andersen, J. Arcelus and A. Whitmore (2009): *Information Strategies to Support Full Information Product Pricing: the Role of Trust*. Paper read at 42nd Hawaii International Conference on System Sciences, at Hawaii.

Marsden, T., J. Banks and G. Bristow (2000): Food Supply Chain Approaches: Exploring their Role in Rural Development. *Sociologia Ruralis* 40(4): 424–438.

Mendelson, N. and M. J. Polonsky (1995): Using strategic alliances to develop credible green marketing. *Journal of Consumer Marketing* 12(2): 4–18.

Milling, P. M. (1984): Leitmotive des System-Dynamics-Ansatzes. *Wirtschaftswissenschaftliches Studium* 13: 507–513.

Milling, P. M. (2002): Kybernetische Überlegungen beim Entscheiden in komplexen Systemen, in: Milling, P. M. (ed.): *Entscheiden in komplexen Systemen*. Berlin: Duncker & Humblot, 11–26.

Noe, T. H. and M. J. Rebello (1995): Consumer activism, producer groups, and production standards. *Journal of Economic Behavior & Organization* 27(1): 69–85.

Raynolds, L. T. (2002): Consumer/Producer Links in Fair Trade Coffee Networks. *Sociologia Ruralis* 42(4): 404–424.

Richardson, G. P. (1991): *Feedback Thought in Social Science and Systems Theory*. Waltham, MA: University of Pennsylvania Press.

Richardson, G. P. and A. L. Pugh III. (1983): *Introduction to System Dynamics Modeling with Dynamo*. Cambridge, MA: MIT Press.

Roberts, S. (2003): Supply Chain Specific? Understanding the Patchy Success of Ethical Sourcing Initiatives. *Journal of Business Ethics* 44(2–3): 159–170.

Rode, J., R. M. Hogarth and M. LeMenestrel (2008): Ethical differentiation and market behavior: An experimental approach. *Journal of Economic Behavior & Organization* 66(2): 265–280.

Schröder, M. J. A. and M. G. McEachern (2004): Consumer value conflicts surrounding ethical food purchase decisions: a focus on animal welfare. *International Journal of Consumer Studies* 28(2): 168–177.

Sharp, B. and J. Dawes (2001): What is Differentiation and How Does it Work? *Journal of Marketing Management* 17(7/8): 739–759.

Slack, N. (1983): Flexibility as a Manufacturing Objective. *International Journal of Operations & Production Management* 3(3): 4–13.

Spiegel Online (2008): *Basic stoppt Aktienverkauf an Lidl*, cited 28 Dec 2008. Available from http://www.spiegel.de/wirtschaft/0,1518,503733,00.html.

Taylor, P. L. (2005): In the Market But Not of It: Fair Trade Coffee and Forest Stewardship Council Certification as Market-Based Social Change. *World Development* 33(1): 129–147.

Verbeke, W. A. J. and J. Viane (2000): Ethical Challenges for Livestock Production: Meeting Consumer Concerns about Meat Safety and Animal Welfare. *Journal of Agricultural and Environmental Ethics* 12(2): 141–151.

Konzepte und Elemente des Produktionsmanagements

Innerbetrieblicher Konsens als Indikator industrieller Wettbewerbsfähigkeit

Johannes von Mikulicz-Radecki[1] *und Andreas Hammer*[2]

[1] AXA Liabilities Managers, Paris
[2] Bain & Company, München

Zusammenfassung

In der fertigungsspezifischen Literatur ist in jüngerer Vergangenheit der Ruf laut geworden, einen Wandel im Produktionsmanagement weg von einer zu stark auf technische und technologische Aspekte fokussierten hin zu einer mehr auf den Faktor Mensch zentrierten Fertigungsphilosophie zu vollziehen. Ein wesentliches Erfolgskriterium ist dabei die Einbindung der operativen Basis, sprich der Fertigungsmitarbeiter in die zentralen operativen Entscheidungen im Fertigungsbereich. Idealerweise sollten Entscheidungen getroffen werden, die sowohl im Sinne des Managements als auch der operativen Basis sind. Maßgeblich für Entscheidungen jedweder Art ist die Wahrnehmung des Status quo im eigenen Fertigungsbereich. Divergiert diese Wahrnehmung über Hierarchieebenen hinweg, hat also das Management ein anderes Bild des Fertigungsbereichs als die dort tätigen Fertigungsmitarbeiter, so ist dies zum einen ein Indiz für einen fehlenden innerbetrieblichen Konsens und zum zweiten ein Warnsignal, dass zukünftige Entscheidungen in die falsche Richtung gehen könnten.

Im Mittelpunkt dieses Beitrags stehenden die Fragestellungen, ob ein Konsens in der Praxis tatsächlich vorzufinden ist und ob sich daraus ein Einfluss auf die Leistungsfähigkeit ergibt. Die verwendete Datenbasis geht aus dem multinationalen Forschungsprojekt High Performance Manufacturing hervor, wobei die empirischen Analysen auf der Erhebungsrunde 2004 basieren. Die empirischen Analysen zeigen, dass in Industriebetrieben die operative Basis in Entscheidungen noch zu wenig einbezogen wird; sehr häufig gehen die Wahrnehmungen und Meinungen zwischen Management und operativer Basis auseinander: Dies ist der Fall, obwohl Fertigungsmitarbeiter zumeist über ein valideres und realistischeres Einschätzungsvermögen bezüglich der Situation im eigenen Industriebetrieb verfügen.

Schlagwörter: Produktionsmanagement, Erfolgsfaktoren, Fertigungsmitarbeiter, Innerbetrieblicher Konsens, Informant Bias, MTMM-Analyse

1 Herangehensweise zur Untersuchung des innerbetrieblichen Konsens als Indikator industrieller Wettbewerbsfähigkeit

Der folgende Beitrag widmet sich der über allem stehenden Fragestellung, ob Industriebetriebe, bei denen ein innerbetrieblicher Konsens zwischen den unterschiedlichen Hierarchieebenen vorzufinden ist und somit davon auszugehen ist, dass die getroffenen Entscheidungen im Sinne aller sind, erfolgreicher agieren, was anhand des Erreichungsgrads der klassischen Fertigungsziele Qualität, Kosten und Zeit untersucht wird, als diejenigen, wo Fertigungsmitarbeiter und Management in ihrer Wahrnehmung des Status quo wie auch bezüglich zukünftig zu treffender

Entscheidungen stark divergieren. Entsprechend lautet die zentrale Untersuchungshypothese, im Sinne einer Nullhypothese formuliert:

$H_{0,1}$: *Es besteht kein Zusammenhang zwischen dem innerbetrieblichen Konsens in einem Industriebetrieb und der Erreichung der Fertigungsperformance.*

Um sich dieser zentralen Untersuchungshypothese zu nähern, werden zunächst – nach Darstellung der Untersuchungsbasis sowie einer grundsätzlichen Hinführung zum Thema – weitere Hypothesen aufgestellt und entsprechend verifiziert bzw. falsifiziert. So muss zunächst geklärt werden, ob es einen systematischen Zusammenhang zwischen der hierarchischen Position eines Respondenten und der Wahrnehmung des eigenen Industriebetriebs gibt (unterschieden werden die Hierarchieebenen Fertigungsmitarbeiter, Meister und Funktionsleiter) – die entsprechende Nullhypothese lautet:

$H_{0,2}$: *Es besteht kein Zusammenhang zwischen der hierarchischen Position eines Respondenten und der Wahrnehmung des eigenen Industriebetriebs.*

Durch diese Nullhyothese $H_{0,2}$ soll der Frage nachgegangen werden, ob Fertigungsmitarbeiter ein anderes Bild von ihrem Industriebetrieb, im Konkreten innerhalb der Themenfelder Human Resource Management und Qualitätsmanagement untersucht, haben als ihre Vorgesetzten. Somit können schon erste Aussagen getroffen werden, ob ein innerbetrieblicher Konsens bzw. Nicht-Konsens überhaupt ein reales Problem ist. Anschließend werden die Antworten der Respondenten aus unterschiedlichen Hierarchiestufen validiert; die sogenannte Multitrait-Multimethod-Methode offeriert die Möglichkeit, auf statistischem Wege herauszufinden, welche der untersuchten Fraktionen ein realitätsnahes Bild zeichnen und welche nicht. Bezogen auf die beiden Untersuchungsbereiche Qualitätsmanagement und Human Resource Management sowie die drei untersuchten Fraktionen ergeben sich sechs weitere (Null-)Hypothesen:

$H_{0,3\text{-}1}$: *Fertigungsmitarbeiter können die Qualität und Wirkungsweise des angewandten Human Resource Managements nicht angemessen beurteilen.*

$H_{0,3\text{-}2}$: *Meister können die Qualität und Wirkungsweise des angewandten Human Resource Managements nicht angemessen beurteilen.*

$H_{0,3\text{-}3}$: *Funktionsleiter können die Qualität und Wirkungsweise des angewandten Human Resource Managements nicht angemessen beurteilen.*

$H_{0,4\text{-}1}$: *Fertigungsmitarbeiter können die Qualität und Wirkungsweise des angewandten Qualitätsmanagements nicht angemessen beurteilen.*

$H_{0,4\text{-}2}$: *Meister können die Qualität und Wirkungsweise des angewandten Qualitätsmanagements nicht angemessen beurteilen.*

$H_{0,4\text{-}3}$: *Funktionsleiter können die Qualität und Wirkungsweise des angewandten Qualitätsmanagements nicht angemessen beurteilen.*

Mit Hilfe dieser Hypothesen können schließlich Aussagen getroffen werden, in welchen Bereichen besonders die operative Basis, also die Fertigungsmitarbeiter ein profundes Bild der Realität zeichnen und somit im Idealfall in jegliche Entscheidungen operativer wie strategischer Art einbezogen werden sollten. Schließlich wird der Bogen zurück zur Ausgangsfrage bzgl. erfolgreicheren Agierens bei Existenz eines innerbetrieblichen Konsenses gespannt; hierbei werden alle untersuchten Industriebetriebe gemäß ihrer Performance in den Fertigungszielen Qualität, Kosten und Zeit sowie der Existenz des innerbetrieblichen Konsenses verglichen, um somit diese zentrale Frage und Hypothese zu beantworten.

2 Multiple-Informant-Befragung als Untersuchungsbasis für den innerbetrieblichen Konsens

Durch das multinationale Forschungsprojekt High Performance Manufacturing wird dem häufig in der fertigungsspezifischen Literatur zu vernehmenden Ruf nach einer breit angelegten Studie des Fertigungsbereiches gefolgt, indem es weg von der klassischen Single-Informant-Befragung geht.[1] Zu eng ist zumeist der Fokus vieler solcher Studien ausgerichtet, die durch Befragung nur eines Informanten ein zu kleines Blickfeld eines Industriebetriebes beleuchten.[2] Darüber hinaus ergibt sich die Problematik des Informant Bias, der systematisch verzerrten Wahrnehmung der realen Situation, der ein jedes Individuum abhängig vom eigenen Beurteilungsgrad mal mehr, mal weniger unterliegt.[3] So sei als Exempel zu dieser Problematik der Hochschullehrer genannt, der einen schwindend geringen Informant Bias bei der Frage nach der technischen Ausstattung von Hörsälen aufweist, da er direkter Anwender und Nutzer derselben ist, der aber keineswegs den Zustand der räumlichen Ausstattung eines Hörsaales beurteilen kann, da ihm dieser Einblick zumeist durch ein voll besetztes Auditorium versperrt bleibt. Hier würde sich die Hinzunahme eines weiteren Informanten, nämlich des Studenten, als sinnvoll erweisen, da dieser wiederum das Beurteilungsvermögen für letzteren Sachverhalt besitzt und diesbezüglich eine sehr geringe Verzerrung in der Wahrnehmung aufweist.

Eine solche Form der Befragung wird als Multiple-Informant-Befragung bezeichnet, die sich im Rahmen von High Performance Manufacturing in zwei grundlegenden Richtungen vollzieht. So werden zum einen unterschiedliche Hierarchieebenen zu gewissen Fragestellungen konsultiert.[4] Zieht man noch einmal das gewählte Beispiel zu Rate, so würden sowohl Professor als auch Student zu diversen Sachverhalten bezüglich eines Hörsaales befragt. Um sich nicht der Gefahr einer zu subjektiven Wahrnehmung von einem Mitglied der beiden Fraktionen auszusetzen, wird die Befragung auch innerhalb einer Hierarchieebene auf mehrere Informanten ausgeweitet.[5] Erst so, durch Befragung mehrerer Studenten wie auch Professoren kann der subjektive Einfluss eines Individuums auf ein Minimum gesenkt werden. Eine solche Befragung bedeutet nicht automatisch, dass sich alle Fraktionen schließlich in der finalen Bewertung eines Zustandes wieder finden. Durch Anwendung geeigneter statistischer Methoden kann festgestellt werden, wer als kompetenter Ansprechpartner in gewissen Sachverhalten zu konsultieren ist. So ergeben sich drei potenzielle Auswertungsmöglichkeiten für das gewählte Beispiel: Studenten

---

[1] Vgl. Ketokivi, Mikko und Roger G. Schroeder: Perceptual measures of performance – fact or fiction, in: Journal of Operations Management, Vol. 22 (2004), No. 3, S. 250.

[2] Vgl. Milling, Peter: Wo stehen deutsche Industriebetriebe im internationalen Wettbewerb? –Faktoren, Profile und Analysen des „World Class Manufacturing", Forschungsberichte der Fakultät für Betriebswirtschaftslehre, Universität Mannheim, Nr. 9807, Mannheim 1998, S. 1.

[3] Siehe zum Informant Bias Nisbett, Richard und Lee Ross: Human inference – strategies and shortcomings of social judgement, Englewood Cliffs 1980 und siehe Tversky, Amos und Daniel Kahneman: Judgement and uncertainty – heuristics and biases, in: Science, Vol. 185 (1974), S. 1124ff.

[4] Vgl. Flynn, Barbara B., Roger G. Schroeder, E. James Flynn, Sadao Sakakibara und Kimberley A. Bates: World class manufacturing project – overview and selected results, in: International Journal of Operations & Production Management, Vol. 17 (1997), No. 7, S. 672f.

[5] Vgl. Türk, Kathrin: Informationssysteme in der Produktion und ihre Unterstützung durch Gruppenarbeit zur Steigerung der Wettbewerbsfähigkeit – eine empirische Untersuchung im Rahmen des Projektes World Class Manufacturing, Berlin 1998, S. 28f.

und Professoren erweisen sich beide als kompetent in Fragen zum Zustand des Hörsaales, was grundsätzlich zur Aggregation der beiden Wahrnehmungen zu einer finalen Globalantwort führt. Im zweiten Fall haben entweder die Studenten einen nur geringen Informant Bias, wobei das Antwortverhalten innerhalb der befragten Professorenschaft stark variiert oder der umgekehrte Fall, dass Professoren mehr Einblicke in gewisse Details eines Hörsaals aufweisen, welcher den Studenten verwehrt bleibt und somit zu einer stark verzerrten Wahrnehmung führt. In diesem Fall ist es notwendig, die unvalide Fraktion aus einem Befragungsbereich auszuschließen, also nur die Antwort der Studenten bzw. Professoren zu berücksichtigen. Schließlich muss auch der Fall betrachtet werden, in dem es keiner der beiden Fraktionen gelingt, statistisch valide, also ohne oder nur geringen Informant Bias zu antworten. Zur Gewährleistung einer statistisch validen Datenbasis muss in solchen Fällen auf den befragten Sachverhalt verzichtet werden.

High Performance Manufacturing basiert entsprechend dem Anspruch, ein transversales Bild eines Fertigungsbetriebes zu zeichnen, auf einer Vielzahl von Informanten.[6] Insgesamt werden aus drei Hierarchieebenen Informanten befragt, die in den Ausführungen dieser Arbeit durch die Begrifflichkeiten des Funktionsleiters (FL), des Meisters sowie des Fertigungsmitarbeiters (FM) abgebildet werden sollen. Der Ebene der Funktionsleiter gehören folgende zehn Informanten an: Leiter Controlling (FL_C), Leiter Personal (FL_P), Leiter Informationssysteme (FL_{IT}), Leiter Produktionssteuerung (FL_{PS}), Leiter Materialwirtschaft (FL_M), Leiter Neuproduktentwicklung (FL_{NPE}), Leiter Verfahrenstechnik (FL_V), Leiter des Betriebes (FL_B), Leiter Qualitätssicherung (FL_Q), Leiter Fertigung (FL_F). Aufgrund des einmaligen Vorkommens einer jeden Position in einem Fertigungsbetrieb werden bei fast jeder Frage mindestens zwei oder drei der unterschiedlichen Funktionsleiter befragt, um so den subjektiven Einfluss einzugrenzen.[7] Mit Abnahme der Hierarchieebene wird zunehmend der operative Bereich eines Industriebetriebes betreten. Die den meisten Funktionsleitern offen stehende Vogelperspektive ist diesen Hierarchieebenen immer weniger zugänglich, weswegen man von zunehmend subjektiver Einflussnahme einzelner Individuen ausgeht. Diesem Effekt wird durch Mehrfachbefragung einer Informantenklasse Rechnung getragen. Wenn zu einem Thema befragt, werden immer drei Meister und auf der untersten hierarchischen Ebene, immer zehn Fertigungsmitarbeiter zu Rate gezogen. Je nach Thema kann somit die Anzahl der befragten Individuen zwischen zwei und sechzehn variieren.

Die Themengebiete, denen eine Gesamtzahl von 891 Fragen – aufgeteilt in 81 qualitative und 47 quantitative Fragenkomplexe – zugeordnet sind, wurden zu einem Großteil in den ersten beiden Erhebungsrunden entworfen.[8] Ebenfalls wurde schon in den vorherigen Erhebungsrunden festgelegt, welche Informanten in konkreten Themengebieten zu befragen sind.[9] Historisch

[6] Vgl. Milling, Peter: Wo stehen deutsche Industriebetriebe im internationalen Wettbewerb?, 1998, S. 4.

[7] Gewisse Fragenkomplexe können nur von einem Funktionsleiter beurteilt werden, wie zum Beispiel im Bereich Controlling. Hierbei geht es um Leistungskennzahlen wie Umsatz pro Jahr, Umsatzrendite oder Mitarbeiteranzahl. Bei solchen Themen ist jedoch nicht von einer subjektiven, verzerrten Wahrnehmung auszugehen.

[8] Vgl. Ahmad, Sohel und Roger G. Schroeder: The impact of human resource management practices on operational performance – recognizing country and industry differences, in: Journal of Operations Management, Vol. 21 (2003), No. 1, S. 23.

[9] Siehe Schroeder, Roger G. und Barbara B. Flynn: High performance manufacturing – global perspectives, New York et al. 2000, S. 3 ff.

gesehen war die erste, 1992 nur in den Vereinigten Staaten durchgeführte Projektrunde eine Pilotstudie, die erst 1997 auf ein breiteres, internationales Fundament gestellt wurde. Der damals verwendete Titel World Class Manufacturing, der wegen namensrechtlicher Komplikationen nicht aufrechterhalten werden konnte, wurde in Anlehnung an den von *Hayes* und *Wheelwright* geprägten, gleichnamigen Terminus gewählt.[10] Er stellt die grundlegende Zielsetzung des Projektes dar: die Identifikation erfolgreicher Industriebetriebe, die sich durch ein „... being better than almost every company in your industry in at least one important aspect of manufacturing[.]“[11] charakterisieren lassen. In diesem Zitat finden sich die zwei elementaren Konstanten des Projektes: die untersuchten Industriezweige bzw. Branchen sowie die untersuchten Aspekte in der Fertigung.

Die partizipierenden Industriebetriebe gehören zu den Branchen Automobilbau und Automobilzulieferer, Elektrotechnik und Maschinenbau, wobei als Kriterium für die Verwendbarkeit die Zugehörigkeit zu einem der NACE Codes 29.41, 29.42, 31.1, 31.2 und 34.3 verlangt war.[12] Des Weiteren wurde eine Mindestanzahl von 100 Mitarbeitern pro untersuchte Einheit festgesetzt. Die Akquise erfolgte durch Kontaktaufnahme mit dem Betriebsleiter, dem eine unentgeltliche Teilnahme seines Industriebetriebes angeboten wurde. Als Gegenleistung für die Teilnahme an High Performance Manufacturing erhielten die Teilnehmer detaillierte Feedbacks, in denen ihre Fertigungspraktiken kontextabhängig analysiert wurden. Die Rücklaufquote der Fragebögen betrug etwa 75%, wobei intensiver Telefonkontakt vorausgegangen war.

Um dem Ziel des Projektes zu entsprechen, Erfolgsfaktoren im Produktionsbereich zu erforschen sowie Praktiken zu identifizieren, die sich signifikant auf die Wettbewerbsfähigkeit von industriellen Unternehmen auswirken,[13] bedarf es seit jeher einer sehr breiten Auswahl von Themenkomplexen. Die folgende Abbildung gibt einen Überblick über die untersuchten Bereiche eines Industriebetriebes. Im Vergleich zur im Jahr 1997 durchgeführten Erhebung wurden einige Erweiterungen in den Bereichen IT-Management, Technologiemanagement, Supply Chain Management und Neuproduktentwicklung vorgenommen.

Zur Untersuchung des innerbetrieblichen Konsenses werden die Bereiche Human Resource Management sowie Qualitätsmanagement in Betracht gezogen; Human Resource Management, weil dadurch Maßnahmen abgefragt werden, die Fertigungsmitarbeiter direkt betreffen und

---

[10] Vgl. Hayes, Robert H. und Steven C. Wheelwright: Restoring our competitive edge – competing through manufacturing, New York et al. 1984, S. 375. Vgl. ferner Schonberger, Richard J.: World class manufacturing – the lessons of simplicity applied, New York et al. 1986, S. 2.

[11] Hayes, Robert H., Steven C. Wheelwright und Kim B. Clark: Dynamic manufacturing – creating the learning organization, New York 1988, S. 21.

[12] Die Klassifikation der Wirtschaftzweige (WZ 03) dient dazu, die wirtschaftlichen Tätigkeiten von Unternehmen, Betrieben und anderen statistischen Einheiten in allen amtlichen Statistiken einheitlich zu erfassen. Sie baut auf der durch EU-Verordnungen verbindlich eingeführten statistischen Systematik der Wirtschaftszweige in der Europäischen Union (NACE Rev. 1.1) auf. An der Erarbeitung dieser Klassifikationen waren zahlreiche Wirtschaftsverbände, fachlich zuständige Behörden und andere Institutionen maßgeblich beteiligt. Als Ergebnis ist eine hierarchisch gegliederte Wirtschaftszweigklassifikation mit 17 Abschnitten, 31 Unterabschnitten, 60 Abteilungen, 222 Gruppen und 1041 Unterklassen entstanden, die eine statistische Zuordnung aller wirtschaftlichen Aktivitäten ermöglicht. Siehe Eurostat: Statistical classification of economic activities in the European Community (NACE Revision 1), Luxemburg 2003.

[13] Vgl. Flynn, Barbara B. et al.: World class manufacturing project, 1997, S. 671.

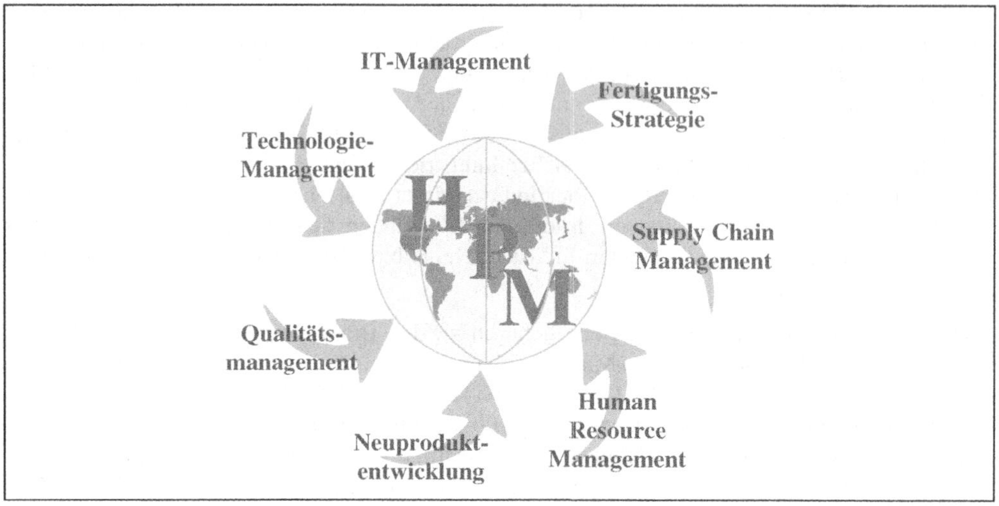

Abbildung 1: Untersuchte Bereiche im Forschungsprojekt High Performance Manufacturing

Qualitätsmanagement, weil die in diesen Themenblöcken abgefragten Maßnahmen eine direkte Umsetzung im Fertigungsbereich bzw. durch die Fertigungsmitarbeiter erfordern. Entscheider, Betroffene bzw. Umsetzer haben in diesen Fragebereichen somit eine „Meinung" und bieten somit die Grundlage zur Untersuchung des innerbetrieblichen Konsenses.

3 Analyse des Potenzials von Fertigungsmitarbeitern

High Performance Manufacturing offeriert eine Vielzahl an Untersuchungsmöglichkeiten, Erfolgsfaktoren im Fertigungsbereich zu ergründen. Besonders das Potenzial der Fertigungsmitarbeiter ist nicht nur anhand der Implementierung von Praktiken wie der Ausbildung zur Multifunktionalität oder der teilautonomen Gruppenarbeit zu bestimmen, es besteht auch die Möglichkeit, das Meinungspotenzial, also das objektive Einschätzungsvermögen bezüglich unterschiedlichster Zustände im Arbeitsalltag, näher zu betrachten. Dieses Einschätzungsvermögen, das infolge immer mehr planerischer und kontrollierender Tätigkeiten stetig zugenommen hat, bleibt von Seiten des Managements vielfach unberücksichtigt, wenn es um operative und strategische Entscheidungen geht.[14] So scheitern Implementierungen innovativer Produktionskonzepte häufig, weil Fertigungsmitarbeiter im Vorfeld schlecht vorbereitet bzw. informiert wurden, aber auch, weil sie bezüglich der Umsetzbarkeit nur unzureichend konsultiert wurden.[15] Die Integration der operativen Basis in Entscheidungsprozesse stellt sich vermehrt als

[14] Vgl. Ruffini, Frans A. J., Harry Boer und Maarten J. van Riemsdijk: Organization design in operations management, in: International Journal of Operations & Production Management, Vol. 20 (2000), No. 7, S. 863.

[15] Vgl. Reger, Rhonda K., Loren T. Gustafson, Samuel D. Demarie und John V. Mullane: Reframing the organization – why implementing total quality is easier said than done, in: Academy of Management Review, Vol. 19 (1994), No. 3, S. 565ff.

Notwendigkeit für industrielle Unternehmen dar. Diese Notwendigkeit wurde im industriellen Kontext erstmalig von *Mintzberg* aufgegriffen, als er strategische Entscheidungen mit der Tätigkeit eines Töpfers verglich. Der Töpfer, der sein Werk in einem langen Prozess formt, muss seine eigenen Fähigkeiten gut genug kennen, um angesichts früherer Erfahrungen und zukünftiger Erwartungen die richtigen Entscheidungen bezüglich des zu bearbeitenden Materials zu treffen.[16] In seinem Gleichnis nehmen die Manager die Rolle des Handwerkers ein und die Strategie die Rolle des zu bearbeitenden Materials. Diese Aussage richtet sich vor allem gegen den Top-down-Ansatz, bei dem eine kleine Gruppe von Führungskräften die Entscheidungen über zukünftiges Handeln trifft, ohne dass dabei ein ausreichender Abgleich mit den zur Verfügung stehenden Ressourcen vollzogen wurde.

Zur Analyse des Meinungspotenzials von Fertigungsmitarbeitern ist es notwendig, sich die projektspezifische Vorgehensweise zur Bildung einer höchst objektiven Antwort bezüglich einer Frage vor Augen zu führen. Pro Frage werden bis zu sechzehn Mitarbeiter, die aus unterschiedlichen Hierarchieebenen stammen, befragt. Im ersten Aggregationsschritt werden, wenn befragt, die zehn Fertigungsmitarbeiter, die drei Meister und eine zwischen eins und drei variierende Anzahl an Funktionsleitern zu jeweils einem repräsentativen Vertreter vereint. Danach werden die so gebildeten repräsentativen Vertreter einer Hierarchieebene interfraktionell zu einer finalen Globalantwort zusammengefasst. Es ist somit ein repräsentatives Bild bezüglich eines bestimmten Sachverhaltes entstanden, dem in der Abbildung 2 durch den Begriff des repräsentativen Mitarbeiters (MA_{REP}) Ausdruck verliehen wird.

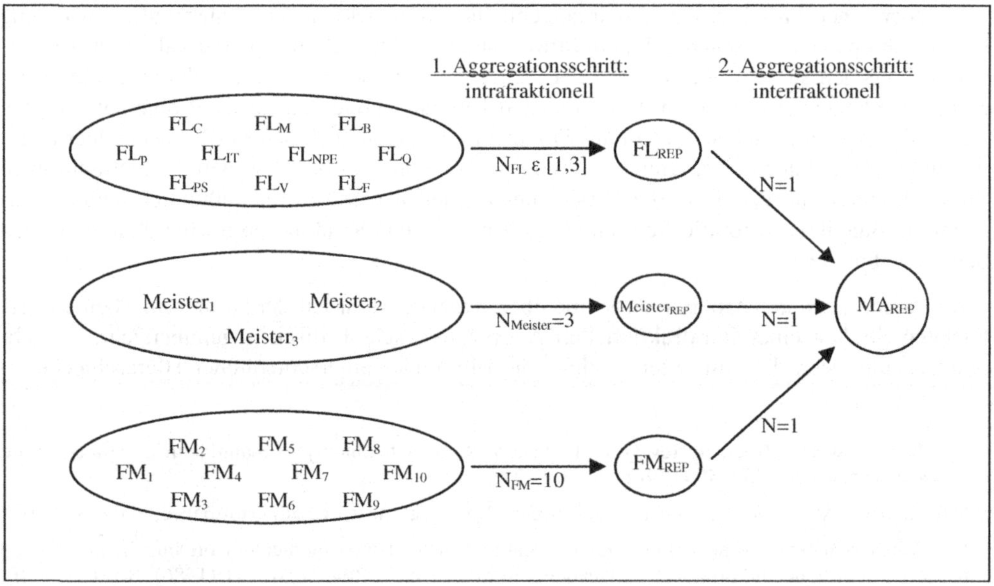

Abbildung 2: Aggregationsschritte von den unterschiedlichen Hierarchieebenen bis hin zum repräsentativen Mitarbeiter

[16] Vgl. Mintzberg, Henry: Crafting strategy, in: Montgomery, Cynthia A. und Michael E. Porter (Hrsg.): Strategy – seeking and securing competitive advantage, Boston 1991, S. 403 ff.

Der erste, als intrafraktionelle Aggregation bezeichnete Schritt ist unumstritten. So zeigen eine Vielzahl wissenschaftlicher Arbeiten, dass durch ein N größer 1 der Informant Bias signifikant abnimmt.[17] In der bisher einzigen, im fertigungsspezifischen Kontext durchgeführten Studie können *Ketokivi* und *Schroeder* zeigen, dass die Befragung mehrerer Individuen einer Hierarchieebene eine signifikant höhere Informationsqualität hervorbringt.[18] Besonders zu erwähnen ist dabei, dass die von den beiden Autoren durchgeführte Analyse auf dem Datensatz der zweiten Erhebungsrunde von High Performance Manufacturing basiert. Es resultierten zum Teil sehr stark ausgeprägte Informant Biases bei Betrachtung einzelner Individuen, die durch Aggregation wesentlich gemindert werden können.[19] Betrachtet wurde dabei nur die oberste Hierarchieebene des Projektes. Beispielsweise wiesen sowohl der Leiter der Fertigung (FL_F) wie auch der Leiter des Betriebes (FL_B) bei Fragen zum Qualitätsmanagement eine starke Wahrnehmungsverzerrung auf. Erst durch Aggregation der beiden Wahrnehmungen näherte man sich dem tatsächlichen Zustand des Qualitätsmanagements.[20]

Der zweite, interfraktionelle Aggregationsschritt ist hingegen kritisch zu beurteilen. Trotz des Fehlens HPM-spezifischer Untersuchungen, die sich mit dem Zusammenhang der hierarchischen Position eines Informanten und dem einhergehenden Informant Bias beschäftigen, muss auf Basis einer Vielzahl von Studien angenommen werden, dass ein solcher zweiter Aggregationsschritt nicht unbedingt sinnvoll ist. So kann *Ernst* zeigen, dass die hierarchische Position eines Informanten einen nachweisbaren Einfluss auf die Wahrnehmung konkreter Sachverhalte ausübt. In der durchgeführten Analyse wurden Informanten unterschiedlicher Hierarchieebenen, im Konkreten Mitglieder des Managements und, auf einer anderen hierarchischen Ebene, Mitglieder einer Projektgruppe zu unterschiedlichen Aspekten der Neuproduktentwicklung befragt. In operativen Fragen gaben die Informanten der Projektgruppe die valideren Antworten, wohingegen strategische Aspekte der Neuproduktentwicklung valider durch die Managementebene beantwortet wurden.[21] Die meisten Untersuchungen zu dieser Problematik finden sich in der psychologischen Forschung. *Kim* und *Lee* untersuchten den Einfluss einzelner Familienmitglieder auf gewisse Kaufentscheidungen des Alltags, wobei zwischen der hierarchischen Stufe Elternteil und der Stufe der Kinder unterschieden wurde.[22] Es stellte sich heraus, dass Mütter infolge ihrer Vermittlerfunktion zwischen Vater und Kind diesen Sachverhalt am besten beurteilen konnten.

Insgesamt ist zu konstatieren, dass eine überwiegende Mehrheit der zu diesem Thema angefertigten Studien einer intrafraktionellen Aggregation sehr kritisch gegenübersteht. Zu sehr unterscheiden sich die Umwelten, welche die Mitglieder unterschiedlicher Hierarchieebenen

---

[17] Vgl. beispielsweise Miller, Jeffrey G. und Aleda V. Roth: A taxonomy of manufacturing strategies, in: Management Science, Vol. 40 (1994), No. 3, S. 288.

[18] Vgl. Ketokivi, Mikko A. und Roger G. Schroeder: Perceptual measures of performance, 2004, S. 249 ff.

[19] Vgl. Venkatraman, N. Venkat und John H. Grant: Construct measurement in organizational strategy research – a critique and proposal, in: Academy of Management Review, Vol. 11 (1986), No. 1, S. 71 ff.

[20] Siehe Ketokivi, Mikko A. und Roger G. Schroeder: Perceptual measures of performance, 2004, S. 258.

[21] Siehe Ernst, Holger: Ursachen des Informant Bias und dessen Auswirkung auf die Validität empirischer betriebswirtschaftlicher Forschung, in: Zeitschrift für Betriebswirtschaft, Jg. 73 (2003), Nr. 12, S. 1261.

[22] Siehe Kim, Chankon und Hanjoon Lee: Development of family triadic measures for children's purchase influence, in: Journal of Marketing Research, Vol. 34 (1997), No. 3, S. 316.

umgeben.[23] Darüber hinaus ist ein elementarer Punkt in der Urteils- und Wahrnehmungsbildung von Individuen gewisser Hierarchieebenen zu suchen. So ergibt sich quasi intuitiv die Vermutung, dass hierarchisch niedrig gestellte Personen nur unzureichende Kenntnis über die von der Organisation verfolgte Strategie haben, wohingegen Managementmitglieder weniger Informationen über operative, projektbezogene Abläufe auf unteren Hierarchieebenen haben.[24]

Zur Analyse des Meinungspotenzials von Fertigungsmitarbeitern muss der bereits dargestellten (Null)Hypothese $H_{0,2}$ nachgegangen werden, wonach (k)ein systematischer Zusammenhang zwischen der Hierarchieebene und der Wahrnehmung des eigenen Industriebetriebes besteht. So haben Fertigungsmitarbeiter einen anderen, zumeist kritischeren Eindruck vom Zustand ihres Industriebetriebes als Funktionsleiter.[25] Zur Klärung der Nullhypothese werden alle Fragen betrachtet, bei denen unter anderem auch Fertigungsmitarbeiter befragt wurden. Insgesamt resultieren 52 Items, die den Bereichen Human Resource Management und Qualitätsmanagement entstammen.

3.1 Beurteilungsvermögen im Bereich Human Resource Management

Im Bereich Human Resource Management wurden Fertigungsmitarbeiter zu insgesamt 26 Sachverhalten befragt, die sich den Fragenkomplexen Dezentralisierung von Entscheidungen, Verbundenheit zum eigenen Unternehmen, Implementierung des betrieblichen Vorschlagswesens, teilautonome Gruppenarbeit und Fähigkeit der Vorgesetzten zuordnen lassen.[26] Pro Fragenkomplex wurden bis zu sieben Fragen gestellt, die quasi gleichen Inhalts sind. Durch die Verwendung von mindestens einem Reverse-Item pro Fragenkomplex, welches den jeweils umgekehrten Sachverhalt wiedergibt, soll die Konsistenz im Antwortverhalten gewährleistet werden.[27]

Eine Besonderheit des untersuchten Bereiches ist, dass alle drei Hierarchieebenen ausnahmslos befragt wurden, also auch die Wahrnehmung der Meister betrachtet werden kann. Meister stehen in der Hierarchie zwischen den beiden anderen Fraktionen; sie verrichten auf der einen Seite direkte Arbeitsaufgaben wie Fertigungsmitarbeiter, haben aber einen größeren Verantwortungsbereich bezüglich indirekter Tätigkeiten. Die durchschnittliche Einschätzung[28] der

---

[23] Vgl. Ireland, R. Duane, Michael A. Hitt, Richard A. Bettis und Deborah A. de Portas: Strategy formulation processes – differences in perceptions of strengths and weaknesses indicators and environmental uncertainty by managerial level, in: Strategic Management Journal, Vol. 8 (1985), No. 5, S. 469 ff.

[24] Vgl. Kiesler, Sara und Lee Sproul: Managerial response to changing environments – perspectives and problem sensing from social cognition, in: Administrative Science Quarterly, Vol. 27 (1982), No. 3, S. 548 ff. und Nisbett, Richard und Lee Ross: Human Inference, 1980, S. 17 f.

[25] Vgl. zum Problem der Method Variance Doty, Harold und William Glick: Common methods bias – does common methods variance really bias results?, in: Organizational Research Methods, Vol. 1 (1998), No. 4, S. 376 f. Vgl. auch zur Inter-Rater-Reliabilität Boyer, Kenneth K. und Rohit Verma: Multiple raters in survey-based operations management research – a review and tutorial, in: Production and Operations Management, Vol. 9 (2000), No. 2, S. 128.

[26] Die verwendeten Fragen sind im Anhang aufgeführt. Vgl. Anhang/Tabelle A-1.

[27] Vgl. Ketokivi, Mikko A. und Roger G. Schroeder: Perceptual measures of performance, 2004, S. 255.

[28] Die Mittelwerte basieren jeweils auf den Items, die einen Fragenkomplex konstituieren. Über diese Items wird der Mittelwert berechnet, um so eine möglichst valide Aussage über die Implementierung eines Konzeptes wie beispielsweise des betrieblichen Vorschlagswesens zu erhalten.

Meister sowie der Fertigungsmitarbeiter (FM) und Funktionsleiter (FL) hinsichtlich der fünf Themenkomplexe sind in nachfolgender Tabelle aufgelistet.[29] Für alle Untersuchungsgruppen werden aggregierte Werte verwendet, so dass jeweils ein repräsentativer Fertigungsmitarbeiter, Meister und Funktionsleiter gegenübergestellt werden.[30]

Tabelle 1: Mittelwertvergleiche im Bereich Human Resource Management

	Human Resource Management I	**1**	**2**	**3**	**Signifikanzniveau**
		Mittelwert FM	Mittelwert Meister	Mittelwert FL	
A	Dezentralisierung von Entscheidungen	4,19	4,69	4,95	12 $p < 0,001$ 13 $p < 0,001$ 23 $p < 0,008$
B	Verbundenheit zum eigenen Unternehmen	4,89	4,97	5,23	12 $p < 0,254$* 13 $p < 0,001$ 23 $p < 0,002$
C	Implementierung des betrieblichen Vorschlagswesens	5,06	5,34	5,47	12 $p < 0,001$ 13 $p < 0,001$ 23 $p < 0,118$*
D	Teilautonome Gruppenarbeit	4,87	5,14	5,27	12 $p < 0,002$ 13 $p < 0,001$ 23 $p < 0,194$*
E	Fähigkeit der Vorgesetzten	4,87	5,29	5,36	12 $p < 0,001$ 13 $p < 0,001$ 23 $p < 0,422$*

*(statistisch nicht signifikante Werte sind mit * gekennzeichnet)*

Die Nullhypothese $H_{0,2}$, wonach kein Zusammenhang zwischen der hierarchischen Position eines Informanten und der Wahrnehmung des eigenen Industriebetriebes besteht, kann auf Basis der sich ergebenden Mittelwerte verworfen werden. Insbesondere bei der Gegenüberstellung von Fertigungsmitarbeitern und Funktionsleitern ergibt sich ein konsistent signifikanter Unterschied. Fertigungsmitarbeiter sehen die Implementierung von mitarbeiterorientierten Maßnahmen wie die Dezentralisierung von Entscheidungen oder die Implementierung des betrieblichen Vorschlagswesens wesentlich weniger vorangeschritten als Funktionsleiter, die häufig für die Implementierung solcher Konzepte verantwortlich sind. Die Wahrnehmungsunterschiede werden noch deutlicher, wenn man den häufig zu beobachtenden Effekt des eingeschränkten Antwortenverhaltens in der Analyse berücksichtigt.[31] So nutzen Respondenten häufig nur die sich

[29] Die Mittelwerte wurden mit Hilfe des T-Tests auf signifikante Unterschiede hin untersucht. In der Tabelle sind in der Spalte „Signifikanzniveau" die Irrtumswahrscheinlichkeiten wiedergegeben, die sich aus den drei Vergleichen ergeben. Vgl. dazu Bortz, Jürgen: Statistik für Sozialwissenschaftler, Berlin 1999, S. 135.

[30] Die dargestellten Mittelwerte sind zum Teil invertiert, so dass alle Werte einheitlich interpretierbar sind. Der Wert 1 steht im Rahmen der verwendeten Likert-Skalen für „trifft überhaupt nicht zu", der Wert 7 für „trifft voll zu".

[31] Vgl. Aaker, David A., Vijay Kumar und George S. Day: Marketing research, 7. Aufl., New York et al. 2001, S. 291 ff.

um den Median befindlichen Ausprägungen einer Likert-Skala und vermeiden die beiden Pole. Dieser Effekt ist auch in den beobachteten Fragenkomplexen aus dem Bereich des Human Resource Managements wieder zu finden, was nachfolgende Abbildung verdeutlicht.

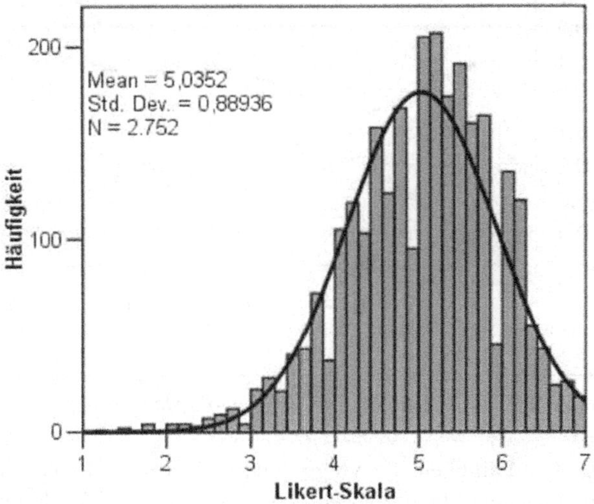

Abbildung 3: Antwortverhalten im Bereich Human Resource Management[32]

Es zeigt sich, dass die Respondenten in einem gewissen Korridor antworten, der den Wert 5 in seiner Mitte trägt. Vor diesem Hintergrund gewinnt ein Unterschied von 0,76 Likert-Skala-Einheiten, wie er sich zwischen Fertigungsmitarbeitern und Funktionsleitern für den Bereich Dezentralisierung von Entscheidungen ergibt, ein noch stärkeres Gewicht.

Die Meister folgen in der Beurteilung der unterschiedlichen Konzepte aus dem Bereich Human Resource Management ihrer hierarchischen Position und sind zwischen den beiden anderen Fraktionen anzusiedeln, wobei eine Tendenz hin zu den Funktionsleitern erkennbar ist. Diese Tendenz manifestiert sich, wenn man die standardisierten Mittelwerte zu Rate zieht (s. Abb. 4, S. 128).[33]

---

[32] Der Stichprobenumfang N basiert auf den fünf betrachteten Skalen aus dem Bereich Human Resource Management. In jeder Skala wurden aus jedem der 189 partizipierenden Fertigungsbetriebe ein repräsentativer Fertigungsmitarbeiter, ein repräsentativer Meister und ein Funktionsleiter betrachtet. Die Tatsache, dass nicht 2835 Antworten berücksichtigt sind, ist auf die Existenz von Missing Values zurückzuführen.

[33] Eine Standardisierung bietet den Vorteil, einer möglichen Verzerrung der Untersuchungsergebnisse durch respondentenspezifische Einflüsse vorzubeugen. Die so genannte z-Transformation der Daten stellt sicher, dass ein hoher Wert unabhängig von der jeweiligen Respondentengruppe auch eine hohe Implementierung eines Konzeptes aus dem Bereich Human Resource Management impliziert. Vgl. Bortz, Jürgen: Statistik für Sozialwissenschaftler, 1999, S. 45f.

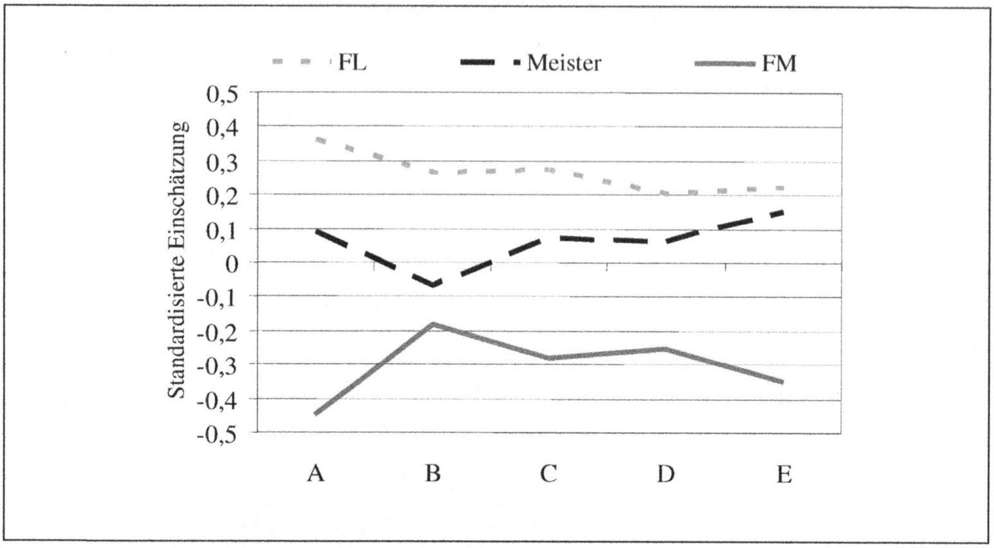

Abbildung 4: Standardisierte Werte im Bereich Human Resource Management

Im Fragenkomplex E – Fähigkeit der Vorgesetzten – vertreten Funktionsleiter und Meister nahezu die gleiche Auffassung: „Ja, die Vorgesetzten verrichten wirklich gute Arbeit. Sie ermutigen die Fertigungsmitarbeiter zum Erfahrungs- und Meinungsaustausch, regen Gruppenarbeit an und tragen zur Problemlösung bei.“[34] Dieser Fragenkomplex verdeutlicht die Problematik der mehrfachen Aggregation zu einem repräsentativen Mitarbeiter eines Industriebetriebes, wie sie bisher häufig praktiziert wurde. Es ist kritisch zu hinterfragen, ob Funktionsleiter und Meister wirklich eine objektive Auffassung bezüglich eines Sachverhaltes vermitteln können, der eigentlich ihre eigene Leistung betrifft. Des Weiteren ist in Frage zu stellen, ob Funktionsleiter, die im Normalfall keine Vorgesetzten mehr über sich haben, eine fundierte Stellungnahme bezüglich eines solchen Sachverhaltes abgeben können. Die einzige Fraktion, die ein wirklich objektives Bild zeichnen kann, ist die der Fertigungsmitarbeiter. Diese Annahme ist jedoch nicht ausreichend, um sich in weiteren Analysen nur auf die Meinung der Fertigungsmitarbeiter zu verlassen. Vielmehr bedarf es zum Test der bereits eingeführten Nullhypothesen $H_{0,3-1}$, $H_{0,3-2}$ und $H_{0,3-3}$ eines Messinstrumentes, welches das Meinungspotenzial von Fertigungsmitarbeitern, Meistern und Funktionsleitern im Bereich Human Resource Mangement unter objektiven Maßstäben evaluiert.

Ein statistisches Instrument, welches objektiven Aufschluss darüber geben kann, welche der drei Fraktionen in spezifischen Fragenkomplexen zu konsultieren ist oder ob an der bewährten Methode der mehrfachen Aggregation zu einem globalen Vertreter festzuhalten ist, stellt die Multitrait-Multimethod (MTMM) Analyse dar.[35] Die MTMM-Analyse zählt zu den Verfahren, durch

[34] Diese Aussage fasst die innerhalb des Fragenkomplexes erfragten Items zusammen.

[35] Die MTMM-Analyse geht auf Campbell und Fiske zurück. Vgl. Campbell, Donald T. und Donald W. Fiske: Convergent and discriminant validation by the multitrait-multimethod matrix, in: Psychological Bulletin, Vol. 56 (1959), No. 2, S. 81–105.

welche die Konstruktvalidität[36] beurteilt werden kann. Der Ablauf der Analyse ist durch die Verwendung von konfirmatorischen und explorativen Faktorenanalysen gekennzeichnet. Durch diese Vorgehensweise wird ergründet, wie sinnvoll die unterschiedlichen Items beantwortet wurden.

Die MTMM-Analyse ermöglicht einen detaillierten Blick auf die Validität eines Konstruktes. Die Validität wird grundsätzlich über die Varianz eines untersuchten Konstruktes bestimmt, die auf drei Quellen zurückzuführen ist: die Trait-, Method- und Error-Varianz. Die fünf Themenkomplexe des Human Resource Managements stellen die Traits dar, die drei befragten Fraktionen die Methods, hinzukommt ein Zufallsfehler, dargestellt durch die Error-Varianz. Im Optimalfall wird die Varianz eines Konstruktes hauptsächlich durch die Trait-Varianz getragen, was bedeutet, dass die zur Konstruktbildung herangezogenen Items sehr hoch korrelieren. Diese Tatsache lässt in einem weiteren Schritt den Schluss zu, dass eine betrachtete Fraktion die konstruktbildenden Fragen sinnvoll, im Sinne von fast identisch beantwortet hat. Die Varianz ist somit auf inhaltliche Aspekte zurückzuführen. Der gegenteilige Fall ist durch eine hohe Method-Varianz gekennzeichnet. Items unterschiedlicher Konstrukte korrelieren stärker als die ein Konstrukt bildenden Items. Innerhalb einer Fraktion bestehen also große Inkonsistenzen bezüglich eines Konstruktes, was wiederum als Indiz herangezogen wird, eine solche Fraktion nicht zu einem solchen Konstrukt zuzulassen. Dieser Effekt entspricht dem bereits in dieser Arbeit erwähnten Informant Bias.[37]

Im ersten Schritt werden nacheinander für jede der drei Fraktionen separate Faktorenanalysen durchgeführt, so dass pro Konstrukt jeweils drei Individualfaktoren resultieren.[38] Als Beispiel sei das Konstrukt „Dezentralisierung von Entscheidungen" genannt. Für jede der drei Fraktionen wird unabhängig voneinander jeweils ein Faktor „Dezentralisierung von Entscheidungen" gebildet. Nur so können die drei Wahrnehmungen des Ausmaßes an Entscheidungsdezentralisierung statistisch valide und reliabel, vor allem aber völlig unabhängig voneinander erfasst werden. So gebildete Individualfaktoren müssen den unterschiedlichen Gütekriterien von explorativer sowie konfirmatorischer Faktorenanalyse Genüge tun.[39] Im Rahmen der explorativen Faktorenanalyse ist vor allem das Cronbachs Alpha[40] zu nennen, für das ein Mindestwert von 0,7 gefordert wird.[41] Darüber hinaus müssen die Faktorladungen den Wert von 0,5 überschreiten, um einen Faktor in

---

[36] Der statistische Begriff Konstrukt kann an Stelle des bisher verwendeten Begriffs Fragenkomplex verwendet werden. Ein Konstrukt gibt einen hinter gewissen Items verborgenen Sachverhalt wieder, die Konstruktvalidität die Güte, mit welcher die Items diesen konstituieren.

[37] Vgl. zu ähnlichen Untersuchungen bezüglich des Antwortverhaltens unterschiedlicher Hierarchieebenen bzw. des Informant Bias Hambrick, Donald C.: Environmental scanning and organizational strategy, in: Strategic Management Journal, Vol. 3 (1982), No. 2, S. 159ff. und vgl. Salancik, Gerald und James R. Meindl: Corporate attributions as strategic illusions of management control, in: Administrative Science Quarterly, Vol. 29 (1984), No. 2, S. 238ff.

[38] Vgl. zur Faktorenanalyse Hartung, Joachim und Bärbel Elpelt: Multivariate Statistik – Lehr- und Handbuch der angewandten Statistik, 4. Aufl., München 1992, S. 505 und vgl. Backhaus, Klaus, Bernd Erichson, Wulff Plinke und Rolf Weiber: Multivariate Analysemethoden – Eine anwendungsbezogene Einführung, 9. Aufl., Berlin et al. 2000, S. 252ff.

[39] Vgl. Homburg, Christian und Anette Giering: Konzeptualisierung und Operationalisierung komplexer Konstrukte – Ein Leitfaden für die Marketingforschung, in: Marketing, Jg. 18 (1997), Nr. 1, S. 5ff.

[40] Vgl. Cronbach, Lee J.: Coefficient alpha and the internal structure of tests, in: Psychometrica, Vol. 16 (1951), No. 3, S. 297ff.

[41] Vgl. Nunnally, Jum C.: Psychometric theory, New York 1978, S. 245 und Brosius, Gerhard und Felix Brosius: SPSS Base System und Professional Statistics, Bonn 1995, S. 825f.

späteren Analysen weiterverwenden zu können.[42] Die konfirmatorische Faktorenanalyse kennzeichnet sich durch eine Vielzahl von Gütekriterien, wobei allgemeiner Konsens darüber besteht, dass der Root Mean Square Error of Approximation (RMSEA) sowie der Goodness of Fit Index (GFI) am relevantesten sind. Für den RMSEA ist ein Maximalwert von 0,05 vorgesehen, der GFI sollte mindestens 0,9 sein. Nur wenn alle zu einem Konstrukt erhobenen Individualfaktoren diesen Gütekriterien entsprechen, ist eine Weiterverwendung in weiteren Schritten der MTMM-Analyse möglich. In nachfolgender Tabelle ist für die unterschiedlichen Konstrukte des Bereiches Human Resource Management dargestellt, ob geforderte Güte erreicht wird und wenn nicht, welcher Aspekt dafür verantwortlich ist.

Tabelle 2: Güte der Konstrukte des Human Resource Managements[43]

Human Resource Management		**Explorative Faktorenanalyse**	**Konfirmatorische Faktorenanalyse**
A	Dezentralisierung von Entscheidungen	ja	nein (RMSEA=0,111)
B	Verbundenheit zum eigenen Unternehmen	ja	ja
C	Implementierung des betrieblichen Vorschlagswesens	ja	ja
D	Teilautonome Gruppenarbeit	ja	ja
E	Fähigkeit der Vorgesetzten	ja	ja

Bis auf „Dezentralisierung von Entscheidungen" können alle anderen Konstrukte in die weitere MTMM-Analyse integriert werden. Die Analyse besteht somit aus vier Traits – Verbundenheit zum eigenen Unternehmen, Implementierung des betrieblichen Vorschlagswesens, Teilautonome Gruppenarbeit und Fähigkeit der Vorgesetzten – und drei Methods: Fertigungsmitarbeiter, Meister und Funktionsleiter.

Im zweiten Schritt der MTMM-Analyse werden die separat voneinander erhobenen Faktoren, die sich als valide und reliabel erwiesen haben, nun in einer gemeinsamen, konfirmatorischen Faktorenanalyse vereint. Neben den resultierenden Gesamtkonstrukten werden innerhalb der Analyse zusätzlich noch drei respondentenspezifische Konstrukte gebildet. So wird beispielsweise ein Faktor Fertigungsmitarbeiter aus den vier unterschiedlichen Individualfaktoren, die auf Basis der Antworten besagter Fraktion gebildet wurden, generiert. Die Gegenüberstellung der themenspezifischen Konstrukte (Traits) mit den respondentenspezifischen Konstrukten (Methods) ermöglicht schließlich die Evaluation der unterschiedlichen Antworten. Die Faktorladungen erweisen sich hierbei als das entscheidende Kriterium. In nachfolgender Abbildung ist die Gesamtanalyse mit den resultierenden Faktorladungen dargestellt. Aus Gründen der Übersichtlichkeit sind darin die in Tabelle 2 verwendeten Deklarationen (B, C, D, E) für die vier verbleibenden Themenkomplexe des Bereiches Human Resource Management verwendet.

[42] Vgl. Backhaus, Klaus et al.: Multivariate Analysemethoden, 2000, S. 264.

[43] Die genauen Werte der Gütekriterien konfirmatorischer und explorativer Faktorenanalyse sind im Anhang/Tabelle A-2 dargestellt.

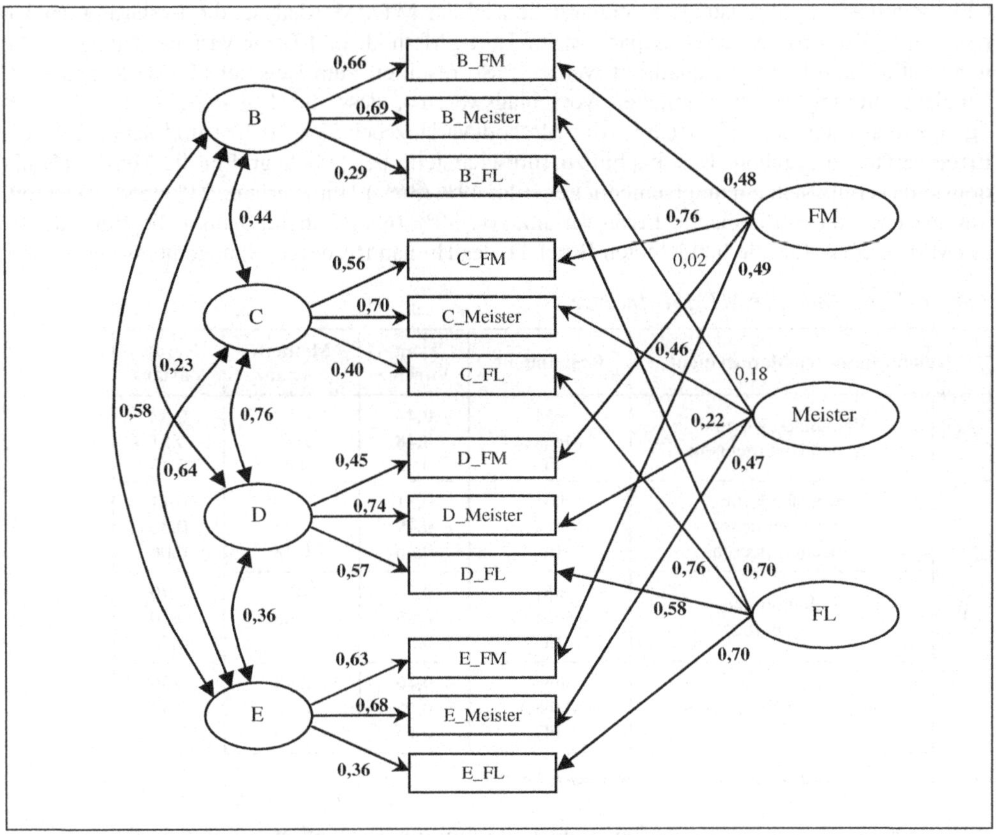

Abbildung 5: Multitrait-Multimethod-Modell (fett gedruckte Faktorladungen sind mit einer Irrtumswahrscheinlichkeit von $p < 0,05$ signifikant)

Das dargestellte Multitrait-Multimethod-Modell ist auf Basis korrelierter Methods und unkorrelierter Traits gebildet.[44] Die geforderten Gütekriterien sind erfüllt: Die Validität ist einerseits durch die konsistente Signifikanz aller Trait-Faktorladungen gegeben, andererseits durch die Tatsache, dass die Interkorrelationen zwischen den vier Traits[45] den Grenzwert 1 unterschreiten.[46] Die Reliabilität ist durch einen RMSEA von 0,04 und durch einen

[44] Die hier vollzogene Art eines MTMM-Modells wird in der englischsprachigen Literatur als CTUM – correlated traits-uncorrelated methods – bezeichnet. Neben dieser existieren noch CTCM (correlated traits-correlated methods) und CU (correlated uniqueness), die jedoch bei gegebener Datenkonstellation zu keinem befriedigenden Ergebnis führen. Vgl. zu den unterschiedlichen Modellen einer MTMM-Analyse Marsh, Herbert W.: Confirmatory factor analysis of multitrait-multimethod data – many problems and a few solutions, in: Applied Psychological Measurement, Vol. 13 (1989), No. 4, S. 356f. Vgl. zu einer in gleicher Form vollzogenen MTMM-Analyse Rindskopf, David M.: Structural equation models – empirical identification, Heywood cases and related problems, in: Sociological Methods and Research, Vol. 13 (1984), No. 1, S. 109–119.

[45] Die Interkorrelationen zwischen den Traits sind auf der linken Seite der Abbildung 5 dargestellt.

[46] Vgl. Bagozzi, Richard P., Youjae Yi und Lynn W. Phillips: Assessing construct validity in organizational research, in: Administrative Science Quarterly, Vol. 36 (1991), No. 3, S. 423ff.

CFI[47] von 0,95 gewährleistet. Das eigentliche Ziel der MTMM-Analyse, die Erklärung der Varianz eines Konstruktes durch Separation in Trait-, Method- und Error-Varianz, wird erreicht, indem alle Faktorladungen quadriert werden.[48] So resultiert zum Beispiel für das Konstrukt C (Implementierung des betrieblichen Vorschlagswesens), dass die Trait-Varianz für die Fertigungsmitarbeiter bei 31% ($0{,}56^2$), die Method-Varianz bei 58% ($0{,}76^2$) und schließlich die Error-Varianz, die sich als Rest bis hin zu 100% darstellt, bei 11% liegt. Für die Meister (Funktionsleiter) ergibt sich ein unterschiedliches Bild: 49% (36%) Trait-Varianz, 21% (58%) Method-Varianz und eine verbleibende Error-Varianz von 30% (6%). Tabelle 3 fasst die Befunde der MTMM-Analyse für alle betrachteten Bereiche des Human Resource Managements zusammen.

Tabelle 3: Befunde der MTMM-Analyse

Human Resource Management		Respondent	Trait-Varianz	Method-Varianz	Error-Varianz
B	Verbundenheit zum eigenen Unternehmen	FM Meister FL	**0,44** **0,48** 0,08	0,23 0,03* 0,49	0,33 0,51 0,43
C	Implementierung des betrieblichen Vorschlagswesens	FM Meister FL	0,31 **0,49** 0,36	0,58 0,21 0,58	0,11 0,30 0,06
D	Teilautonome Gruppenarbeit	FM Meister FL	0,20 **0,55** 0,33	0,01* 0,05 0,34	0,79 0,40 0,33
E	Fähigkeit der Vorgesetzten	FM Meister FL	**0,40** **0,46** 0,13	0,24 0,22 0,49	0,36 0,32 0,38

*(statistisch nicht signifikante Werte sind mit * gekennzeichnet)*

Die Trait-Varianz ist das entscheidende Kriterium zur Evaluation der drei Fraktionen. Gefordert ist ein Wert von mindestens 0,4 (fett gedruckte Werte in Tabelle 3), um einer Fraktion ein fundiertes Urteilsvermögen bezüglich eines der unterschiedlichen Konstrukte des Human Resource Managements ausstellen zu können.[49] Nur so kann sichergestellt werden, dass die Method-Varianz relativ gering ausfällt, durch welche der Informant Bias quantifiziert wird. Insgesamt ergibt sich für Fertigungsmitarbeiter ein Informant Bias von 35%, für Meister ein Wert von 16% und für Funktionsleiter von 48%.[50] Nur bei Meistern liegt die inhaltliche Trait-Varianz mit 50% über dem Methodenfehler, wobei Fertigungsmitarbeiter eine durchschnittliche Method-

[47] Der Comparative Fit Index (CFI) ist das im Rahmen der MTMM-Analyse wichtigste Kriterium der Reliabilität. Der Grenzwert ist bei 0,95 festgesetzt. Vgl. Bentler, Peter M.: Comparative fit indexes in structural models, in: Psychological Bulletin, Vol. 107 (1990), No. 2, S. 241.

[48] Vgl. Doty, Harold und William Glick: Common method bias, 1998, S. 378ff.

[49] Vgl. Kim, Chankon und Hanjoon Lee: Development of family triadic measures for children's purchase influence, 1997, S. 312.

[50] Zur Berechnung des durchschnittlichen Informant Bias werden alle, d.h. signifikante wie nicht signifikante Method-Varianzen einbezogen. Vgl. zu dieser Vorgehensweise Ketokivi, Mikko A. und Roger G. Schroeder: Perceptual measures of performance, 2004, S. 259 und Kim, Chankon und Hanjoon Lee: Development of family triadic measures for children's purchase influence, 1997, S. 316.

Varianz von 34% und Funktionsleiter von 30% aufweisen. Insofern kann konstatiert werden, dass Meister im Mittel die validesten Antworten geben.

Um schließlich die aufgestellten Nullhypothesen $H_{0,3\text{-}1}$, $H_{0,3\text{-}2}$ und $H_{0,3\text{-}3}$ zu validieren, also welche der Fraktionen die Qualität und Wirkungsweise des angewandten Human Resource Managements angemessen beurteilen können und welche nicht, bedarf es einer separaten Betrachtung der vier Bereiche des Human Resource Managements. Im Bereich „Verbundenheit zum eigenen Unternehmen“ erweisen sich Fertigungsmitarbeiter und Meister als beste Respondenten, was nach sich zieht, dass in weiteren Analysen für jedes Item dieses Komplexes ein Mittelwert aus besagten zwei Fraktionen zu bilden wäre.[51] Verbindet man die beiden durchgeführten Analysen, Mittelwertvergleiche und MTMM-Analyse, so ist inhaltlich Folgendes für diesen Fragenkomplex zu konstatieren: Die Funktionsleiter sind im Mittel zwar mehr mit ihrem Industriebetrieb als Meister und Fertigungsmitarbeiter verbunden, jedoch besteht innerhalb der Fraktion der Funktionsleiter eine große Uneinigkeit bezüglich dieses Themas, statistisch erkennbar an einem Informant Bias von 49%. Dieser fällt für Fertigungsmitarbeiter und Meister nur gering aus, so dass deren geringere Verbundenheit zu ihrem Industriebetrieb als statistisch signifikant und für weitere Analyseschritte verwertbar angesehen werden könnte. In den Fragenkomplexen „Implementierung des betrieblichen Vorschlagswesens“ und „Teilautonome Gruppenarbeit“ sind Meister als einzige Fraktion zu nennen, die valide Antworten gibt. Schließlich kann beim Konstrukt „Fähigkeit der Vorgesetzten“ die ursprüngliche Vermutung, Funktionsleiter, die quasi keine Vorgesetzten mehr haben, könnten sich in ihrer Leistung nicht selber beurteilen, verifiziert werden. Tatsächlich sind es die Meister und Fertigungsmitarbeiter, welche die validesten Antworten in diesem Fragenkomplex geben.

Die Nullhypothese $H_{0,2}$, wonach kein Zusammenhang zwischen der hierarchischen Position eines Respondenten und der Wahrnehmung des eigenen Industriebetriebes besteht, kann auf Basis durchgeführter Mittelwertvergleiche sowie einer in vier von fünf Bereichen vollzogenen MTMM-Analyse verworfen werden. Fertigungsmitarbeiter stehen den unterschiedlichen Konzepten des Human Resource Managements und insbesondere der Umsetzung von diesen wesentlich kritischer gegenüber, als dies Funktionsleiter tun. Die Meister folgen in ihrer Wahrnehmung des Human Resource Managements ihrer hierarchischen Position und sind zwischen den beiden anderen Fraktionen einzuordnen. Die kritische Position der Fertigungsmitarbeiter erweist sich zum Teil als realistisch, zum Teil jedoch muss sie als zu kritisch angesehen werden. Den Meistern ist das größte Urteilsvermögen zuzusprechen, sie vermitteln in jedem der betrachteten Bereiche einen realistischen Eindruck vom eigenen Industriebetrieb. Die Nullhypothese $H_{0,3\text{-}2}$ kann entsprechend für die Fraktion der Meister ganzheitlich abgelehnt werden; bei den Fertigungsmitarbeitern ist dies nur für die Bereiche „Verbundenheit zum eigenen Unternehmen“ und „Fähigkeit der Vorgesetzten“ möglich. Funktionsleiter sind die am wenigsten konsistente der drei Fraktionen, was ein durchschnittlicher Informant Bias von 48% zeigt. Die häufig postulierte Hypothese, dass ein Informant Bias insbesondere dann auftritt, wenn Respondenten zu Sachverhalten befragt werden, die im eigenen Verantwortungsbereich liegen, hier die Umsetzung von mitarbeiterorientierten Maßnahmen, erfährt Bestätigung.[52]

---

[51] Die Insignifikanz der Method-Varianz innerhalb dieses Konstruktes ist in der Weise zu interpretieren, dass keine Method-Varianz, also kein Informant Bias vorliegt. Diese Tatsache ändert nichts an der Verwendbarkeit der Antworten der Meister in diesem Konstrukt. Vgl. Doty, Harold und William Glick: Common methods bias, 1998, S. 392f.

[52] Vgl. Ernst, Holger: Ursachen des Informant Bias und dessen Auswirkung auf die Validität empirischer betriebswirtschaftlicher Forschung, 2003, S. 1261.

Abschließend kann für den Bereich Human Resource Management ein sehr geringer Konsens zwischen den unterschiedlichen Hierarchieebenen festgehalten werden. Eine durch mehrfache Aggregation gebildete Globalantwort würde nicht die reale Situation im Industriebetrieb wiedergeben. Respondenten würden Teil einer Globalantwort, ohne ausreichendes Urteilsvermögen zu besitzen oder – wie im Falle der Funktionsleiter – ohne jegliche Befangenheit abgelegt zu haben. Es stellt sich somit als Notwendigkeit für andere Untersuchungen, auch jeden weiteren Fragenkomplex, in dem Fertigungsmitarbeiter involviert sind, auf valides Antwortverhalten zu untersuchen, um somit in weiteren Untersuchungsschritten valide Daten zu gewährleisten.

3.2 Kenntnisstand über das Qualitätsmanagement

Qualitätsmanagement als Teil von High Performance Manufacturing kennzeichnet sich durch 13 Fragenkomplexe mit insgesamt 71 Items, bei denen Fertigungsmitarbeiter und Funktionsleiter durchgängig befragt wurden. In gewissen Aspekten wurde dieses Bild noch durch die Sicht der Meister ergänzt. Im Hinblick auf die im Rahmen dieser Untersuchung intendierte MTMM-Analyse sind nur 5 Fragenkomplexe (26 Items) von Belang, nämlich solche, bei deren Beantwortung Fertigungsmitarbeiter, Meister und Funktionsleiter beteiligt waren. In Tabelle 4 sind die sich für den Bereich Qualitätsmanagement ergebenden Mittelwerte der Fertigungsmitarbeiter (FM), Meister und Funktionsleiter (FL) sowie das Signifikanzniveau aufgelistet.[53]

Tabelle 4: Mittelwertvergleiche im Qualitätsmanagement

Qualitätsmanagement		1	2	3	**Signifikanzniveau**	
		Mittelwert FM	Mittelwert Meister	Mittelwert FL		
A	Sauberkeit und Organisiertheit	5,22	5,53	5,50	12 13 23	p < 0,001 p < 0,004 p < 0,765*
B	Kontinuierliche Weiterentwicklung	5,61	5,59	5,86	12 13 23	p < 0,662* p < 0,001 p < 0,001
C	Fokus Kunde bei Entscheidungen über die Qualität	5,17	5,09	5,24	12 13 23	p < 0,093 p < 0,151* p < 0,006
D	Integration der Kunden in Qualitätsfragen	5,09	5,48	5,56	12 13 23	p < 0,001 p < 0,001 p < 0,279*
E	Kundenzufriedenheit als zentrale Zielgröße bei Qualitätsentscheidungen	5,18	5,34	5,33	12 13 23	p < 0,018 p < 0,050 p < 0,929*

*(statistisch nicht signifikante Werte sind mit * gekennzeichnet)*

Fertigungsmitarbeiter sehen auch im Qualitätsmanagement die Dinge wesentlich weniger vorangeschritten, als dies von Funktionsleiterseite angenommen wird. Mit einer Ausnahme sind die Wahrnehmungsdivergenzen statistisch signifikant, so dass auch im Qualitätsmanagement

[53] Die den 5 Fragenkomplexen zugeordneten Items finden sich im Anhang/Tabelle A-3.

die Nullhypothese $H_{0,2}$ des nicht existenten Zusammenhangs zwischen hierarchischer Position und Wahrnehmung des eigenen Industriebetriebes abgelehnt werden kann.

Die Unterschiede zwischen Fertigungsmitarbeitern und Funktionsleitern erweisen sich als nicht so groß, wie dies noch innerhalb des Bereiches Human Resource Management festgestellt werden konnte. Jedoch ist der Korridor, in dem sich die Antworten innerhalb der Likert-Skala befinden, auch deutlich kleiner, was nachfolgende Abbildung verdeutlicht.

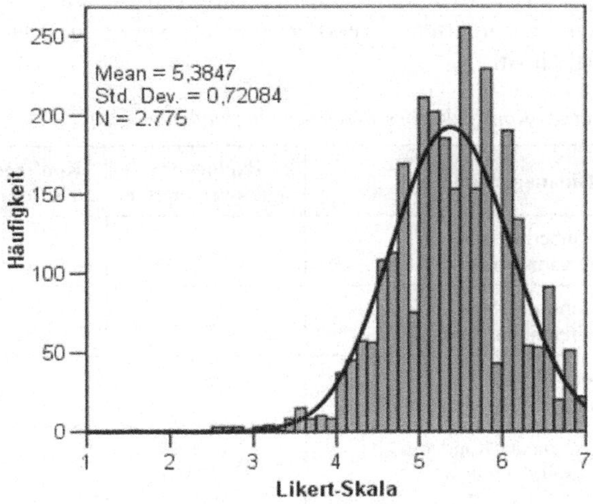

Abbildung 6: Antwortverhalten im Bereich Qualitätsmanagement[54]

Der untere Bereich der Likert-Skala von 1 bis 4 bleibt nahezu ungenutzt, der tatsächliche Antwortbereich bewegt sich zwischen 4 und 7. Eine durchschnittliche Abweichung von 0,24, wie sie zwischen Fertigungsmitarbeitern und Funktionsleitern zu beobachten ist, kann vor dem Hintergrund dieser Relativierung als klare und signifikante Divergenz betrachtet werden.

Die Wahrnehmung der Meister lässt sich nur schwer kategorisieren, da sie auf der einen Seite ihren Industriebetrieb in den Fragenkomplexen „Kontinuierliche Weiterentwicklung" und „Fokus Kunde bei Entscheidungen über die Qualität" noch kritischer als die Fertigungsmitarbeiter wahrnehmen, auf der anderen Seite aber ein äußerst positives Bild zeichnen, wenn es um die Beurteilung der „Sauberkeit und Organisiertheit" des eigenen Industriebetriebes und auch der „Kundenzufriedenheit als zentrale Zielgröße bei Qualitätsentscheidungen" geht. Die Meister stehen also hier nicht entsprechend ihrer hierarchischen Position in der Mitte, sondern schließen sich jeweils einer der beiden anderen Fraktionen in ihrer Beurteilung an. Um schließlich zu klären, welche der befragten Fraktionen in weiteren Analysen zu Rate zu ziehen ist, wird erneut eine MTMM-Analyse durchgeführt; diese Analyse dient ebenfalls der Validierung der an vorangegangener Stelle eingeführten Nullhypothesen $H_{0,4-1}$, $H_{0,4-2}$ und $H_{0,4-3}$ – die Unter-

[54] Der Stichprobenumfang N basiert auf den fünf betrachteten Skalen aus dem Bereich Qualitätsmanagement, zu denen jeweils ein repräsentativer Fertigungsmitarbeiter, ein repräsentativer Meister und ein Funktionsleiter aus jedem der 189 partizipierenden Industriebetriebe befragt wurden.

suchung der Frage, wer die Qualität und Wirkungsweise des angewandten Qualitätsmanagements angemessen beurteilen kann und wer nicht.

Der erste Schritt der MTMM-Analyse verfolgt das Ziel der Skalenoptimierung. Nacheinander werden explorative und konfirmatorische Faktorenanalysen durchgeführt, die unabhängig von der Meßmethode sind, d.h. für jede der drei Fraktionen wird für jeden Fragenkomplex jeweils ein Konstrukt gebildet.[55] Nicht jedes so gebildete Konstrukt kann den unterschiedlichen Gütekriterien genügen, so dass für diese Fragenbereiche kein anschließender Test auf Konstruktvalidität durchgeführt werden kann. Nachfolgende Tabelle zeigt für die fünf betrachteten Fragenkomplexe, ob die geforderten Gütekriterien erfüllt sind und falls nicht, welches Kriterium dafür verantwortlich ist.

Tabelle 5: Güte der diversen Konstrukte des Bereiches Qualitätsmanagement[56]

Qualitätsmanagement		**Explorative Faktorenanalyse**	**Konfirmatorische Faktorenanalyse**
A	Sauberkeit und Organisiertheit	ja	ja
B	Kontinuierliche Weiterentwicklung	ja	ja
C	Fokus Kunde bei Entscheidungen über die Qualität	ja	ja
D	Integration der Kunden in Qualitätsfragen	nein $\alpha = 0{,}420$	ja
E	Kundenzufriedenheit als zentrale Zielgröße bei Qualitätsentscheidungen	ja	ja

Bis auf „Integration der Kunden in Qualitätsfragen" lassen sich alle Fragenkomplexe in den zweiten Schritt der MTMM-Analyse führen. Die Analyse besteht somit aus vier Traits und drei Methods. In nachfolgender Abbildung ist die Gesamtanalyse mit den resultierenden Faktorladungen dargestellt, wobei die in Tabelle 5 verwendeten Deklarationen (A, B, C, E) für die vier verbleibenden Themenkomplexe des Bereiches Qualitätsmanagement verwendet werden.

Das MTMM-Modell ist erneut auf Basis korrelierter Methods und unkorrelierter Traits gebildet. Die Validität ist einerseits durch die konsistente Signifikanz aller Trait-Faktorladungen gegeben, andererseits durch die Tatsache, dass die Interkorrelationen zwischen den vier Traits den Grenzwert 1 unterschreiten. Die Reliabilität ist durch einen RMSEA von 0,04 und durch einen CFI von 0,99 gewährleistet. Die sich ergebenden Trait-, Method- und Error-Varianzen finden sich in Tabelle 6 (s. S. 138).

Der Informant Bias beträgt für Fertigungsmitarbeiter 9%, für Meister 12% und für Funktionsleiter 28%. Bis auf die Fraktion der Fertigungsleiter liegt die inhaltsinduzierte Trait-Varianz über dem Methodenfehler, wobei Fertigungsmitarbeiter im Mittel die validesten Antworten

[55] Vgl. Peterson, Robert A.: A meta-analysis of cronbach's coefficient alpha, in: Journal of Consumer Research, Vol. 21 (1994), No. 2, S. 381 ff.

[56] Die genauen Werte der Gütekriterien finden sich im Anhang/Tabelle A-4.

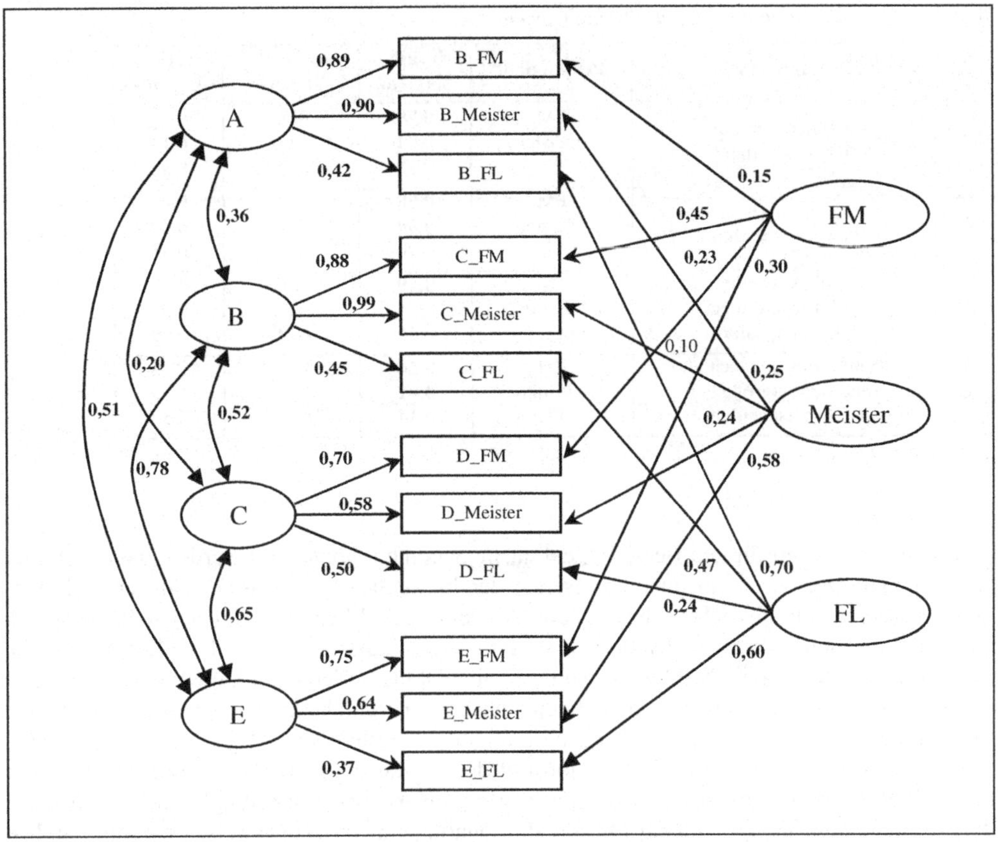

Abbildung 7: MTMM-Analyse für den Bereich Qualitätsmanagement (fett gedruckte Faktorladungen sind mit einer Irrtumswahrscheinlichkeit von p < 0,05 signifikant)

geben.[57] Folgt man dem Grenzwert von 0,4 zur Verwendbarkeit von Respondenten, so sind Fertigungsmitarbeiter in allen untersuchten Konstrukten und Meister mit Ausnahme von „Fokus Kunde bei Entscheidungen über die Qualität" zu konsultieren. Wie schon im Bereich Human Resource Management festgestellt, sind sich Funktionsleiter äußerst uneinig über die tatsächliche Umsetzung der unterschiedlichen Konzepte. Die in diesem Bereich auftretenden hohen Error-Varianzen verdeutlichen darüber hinaus, dass Aspekte wie „Sauberkeit und Organisiertheit" oder „Kontinuierliche Weiterentwicklung" durch die Befragung von Funktionsleitern kaum valide gemessen werden können. Da der Zufallsfehler mit abnehmender Kenntnis des zu beurteilenden Sachverhaltes zunimmt, kann dieser Befund dahingehend interpretiert werden, dass Funktionsleiter womöglich zu weit vom eigentlichen operativen Alltag entfernt sind und somit Wissensdefizite zu Messproblemen führen.[58]

[57] Für Fertigungsmitarbeiter ergibt sich eine durchschnittliche Method-Varianz von 66%, Meister folgen mit 64%, schließlich weisen Funktionsleiter einen Wert von 19% auf.

[58] Vgl. Kumar, Nirmalya, Louis W. Stern und James C. Anderson: Conducting interorganizational research using key informants, in: Academy of Management Journal, Vol. 36 (1993), No. 6, S. 1633ff.

Tabelle 6: Befunde im Bereich Qualitätsmanagement

Qualitätsmanagement		Respondent	Trait-Varianz	Method-Varianz	Error-Varianz
A	Sauberkeit und Organisiertheit	FM	**0,79**	0,02	0,19
		Meister	**0,81**	0,06	0,13
		FL	0,18	0,49	0,33
B	Kontinuierliche Weiterentwicklung	FM	**0,78**	0,20	0,02
		Meister	**0,99**	0,01*	0,00
		FL	0,20	0,22	0,58
C	Fokus Kunde bei Entscheidungen über die Qualität	FM	**0,49**	0,05	0,46
		Meister	0,34	0,06	0,60
		FL	0,25	0,06	0,69
E	Kundenzufriedenheit als zentrale Zielgröße bei Qualitätsentscheidungen	FM	**0,56**	0,09	0,35
		Meister	**0,41**	0,34	0,25
		FL	0,14	0,36	0,50

*(statistisch nicht signifikante Werte sind mit * gekennzeichnet)*

Abschließend kann für den Bereich Qualitätsmanagement konstatiert werden, dass auch hier ein systematischer Zusammenhang zwischen der hierarchischen Position und der Wahrnehmung des eigenen Industriebetriebes besteht (Ablehnung Nullhypothese $H_{0,2}$). Die im Vergleich zu Funktionsleitern kritische Haltung der Fertigungsmitarbeiter kann als valide angesehen werden, wodurch auch die Nullhypothese $H_{0,4\text{-}1}$ abgelehnt werden kann. Funktionsleiter weisen große Uneinigkeit, zum Teil auch ungenügenden Kenntnisstand bezüglich der unterschiedlichen Maßnahmen des Qualitätsmanagements auf (Annahme Nullhypothese $H_{0,4\text{-}3}$). Die Meister sind in diesem Bereich zwar nicht die Fraktion mit den validesten Antworten, erweisen sich aber dennoch als Respondent, dessen Meinung in weiteren Analysen unbedingt einzubeziehen ist; die Nullhypothese $H_{0,4\text{-}2}$, wonach Meister die Qualität und Wirkungsweise des angewandten Qualitätsmanagements nicht angemessen beurteilen können, kann abgelehnt werden.

Die durchgeführten Analysen zeigen, dass Fertigungsmitarbeitern großes Potenzial zugesprochen werden kann. Dieses Potenzial zeigt sich durch eine sehr objektive Wahrnehmung unterschiedlicher Aspekte des eigenen Industriebetriebs. Insbesondere bei der Beurteilung der tatsächlichen Umsetzung diverser produktionswirtschaftlicher Konzepte geben Fertigungsmitarbeiter eine signifikant validere Einschätzung ab, als das höheren Hierarchieebenen angehörende Funktionsleiter tun, bei denen oft eine Tendenz zur Beschönigung der realen Situation zu erkennen ist. Dieses Potenzial im Sinne einer objektiven Wahrnehmung bleibt oft unausgeschöpft, da Industriebetriebe häufig dazu tendieren, in strategischen Entscheidungen die operative Basis auszuschließen.[59] Die Entscheidungsqualität basiert somit auf den Einschätzungen von Personen hoher Hierarchieebenen, die, wie die bisherigen Ausführungen zeigen, nicht unbedingt eine objektive Wahrnehmung besitzen. Ein weiteres Problem, welches aus der Vernachlässigung von Fertigungsmitarbeitern in Entscheidungsprozessen resultiert, ist die bei der Einführung von Produktionskonzepten oft ungenügende Betrachtung des tatsächlichen Leis-

[59] Vgl. dazu Bartlett, Christopher A. und Sumantra Ghoshal: Changing the role of top management – beyond systems to people, in: Harvard Business Review, Vol. 73 (1995), No. 3, S. 140f.

tungsstandes der Fertigungsmitarbeiter, die diese Konzepte umsetzen sollen.[60] Auch hier ist eine Integration von Fertigungsmitarbeitern schon bei der Planung solcher Konzepte sinnvoll, um häufig auftretende Implementierungsprobleme zu vermeiden oder zumindest zu verringern.[61]

Abschließend soll nun der Frage nachgegangen werden bzw. die aufgestellte Nullhypothese $H_{0,1}$ geprüft werden, ob Industriebetriebe, die sich durch hierarchieübergreifenden Konsens kennzeichnen, wo also Fertigungsmitarbeiter und andere Hierarchieebenen eine relativ ähnliche Wahrnehmung aufweisen, auch eine höhere Wettbewerbsfähigkeit kennzeichnet.

4 Untersuchung des Erfolgs bei unterschiedlichen Konsensausprägungen in den untersuchten Industriebetrieben

Die Einteilung in erfolgreiche und weniger erfolgreiche Industriebetriebe wird in Analogie zu einer sehr vergleichbaren, ebenfalls auf Basis des High Performance Manufacturing-Datensatzes durchgeführten Untersuchung vollzogen.[62] Im Rahmen dieser Untersuchung zeigt sich sehr deutlich, dass die 189 untersuchten Fertigungsbetriebe sehr unterschiedlich erfolgreich die Kerngrößen des industriellen Schaffens – Qualität, Kosten und Zeit – erreichen. Auf Basis dieser Einteilung kann nun der durchschnittliche Konsens bzw. Dissens zwischen den drei Fraktionen Fertigungsmitarbeiter, Meister und Funktionsleiter für die Bereiche Human Resource Management und Qualitätsmanagement bestimmt werden und ggfs. auch der Zusammenhang oder Nicht-Zusammenhang zwischen Konsens und Erfolg beobachtet werden (Nullhypothese $H_{0,1}$). Nachfolgende Tabelle 7 (s. S. 140) zeigt für alle drei Fraktionen den Mittelwert bei erfolgreichen (+) und weniger erfolgreichen (–) Industriebetrieben, wobei sich die Signifikanzniveaus auf den intrafraktionellen Unterschied je Themenkomplex beziehen.

Trotz eines überwiegenden Anteils statistisch nicht signifikanter Mittelwertunterschiede ist dennoch ein deutlich größerer Konsens bei den Industriebetrieben vorzufinden, die sich erfolgreich in der Erreichung ihrer Fertigungsziele darstellen. Beim Vergleich der Bandbreite, in welcher sich die drei Wahrnehmungen hinsichtlich eines der fünf Themenkomplexe bewegen, wird dieser Unterschied noch klarer: So bewegen sich die Einschätzungen der drei Fraktionen bei erfolgreichen Industriebetrieben in einer Bandbreite von 0,33 Likert-Skala-Einheiten, wohingegen bei den weniger erfolgreichen ein durchschnittlicher Dissens von 0,58 zu konstatieren ist. Eine weitere Erkenntnis, die bei Betrachtung der Wahrnehmungsunterschiede aller Industriebetriebe auffällt, ist die Tatsache, dass es in erfolgreichen Industriebetrieben hauptsächlich die Fertigungsmitarbeiter sind, die wesentlich positiver die Implementierung der unterschiedlichen Praktiken bewerten als noch auf höchster Aggregationsstufe. Die Funktionsleiter, die immer das

---

[60] Vgl. Zahra, Shaker A. und Sidhartha R. Das: Innovation strategy and financial performance in manufacturing companies – an empirical study, in: Production and Operations Management, Vol. 2 (1993), No. 1, S. 18.

[61] Vgl. Kinnie, Nicholas J. und Roy V. W. Staughton: The problem of implementing manufacturing strategy, in: Storey, John (Hrsg.): New wave manufacturing strategies – organizational and human resource management dimensions, London 1994, S. 50.

[62] Vgl. Mikulicz-Radecki, Johannes von: Die Rolle von Fertigungsmitarbeitern im strategischen Human Resource Management, Mannheim University Press, Mannheim 2006, S. 123 ff.

Tabelle 7: Nach Erfolg und Misserfolg differenzierte Mittelwertvergleiche im Bereich Human Resource Management

Human Resource Management I		Erfolg	1 Mittelwert FM	2 Mittelwert Meister	3 Mittelwert FL	Signifikanzniveau
A	Dezentralisierung von Entscheidungen	+	4,30	4,76	4,98	1^{+-} p < 0,085 2^{+-} p < 0,944 3^{+-} p < 0,799
		-	4,03	4,77	5,03	
B	Verbundenheit zum eigenen Unternehmen	+	5,04	5,10	5,27	1^{+-} p < 0,720 2^{+-} p < 0,251 3^{+-} p < 0,704
		-	4,99	4,95	5,33	
C	Implementierung des betrieblichen Vorschlagswesens	+	5,14	5,14	5,35	1^{+-} p < 0,896 2^{+-} p < 0,001 3^{+-} p < 0,120
		-	5,16	5,61	5,60	
D	Teilautonome Gruppenarbeit	+	5,06	5,14	5,36	1^{+-} p < 0,371 2^{+-} p < 0,189 3^{+-} p < 0,685
		-	4,91	5,36	5,43	
E	Fähigkeit der Vorgesetzten	+	4,94	5,17	5,19	1^{+-} p < 0,964 2^{+-} p < 0,035 3^{+-} p < 0,054
		-	4,93	5,48	5,53	

obere Ende der Bandbreite der drei Einschätzungen konstituieren, verhalten sich unverändert bzw. beurteilen die Situation sogar noch besser. Die Meister, die aus der durchgeführten MTMM-Analyse als Fraktion mit dem fundiertesten Wissen über unterschiedlichste Sachverhalte hervorgingen, stehen entsprechend ihrer hierarchischen Position in der Mitte der beiden anderen Fraktionen, wobei in Abhängigkeit der Themenkomplexe eine Tendenz mal zur Einschätzung der Fertigungsmitarbeiter, mal zur Einschätzung der Funktionsleiter erkennbar ist. Schließlich weisen Meister und Funktionsleiter in weniger erfolgreichen Industriebetrieben teilweise eine sehr hohe Einschätzung auf (Implementierung des betrieblichen Vorschlagswesens/ Fähigkeit der Vorgesetzten). Da diese beiden Themenkomplexe maßgebliche Indikatoren für die so entscheidenden Aspekte des strategischen Human Resource Managements in Industriebetrieben[63], nämlich Kommunikation und Kollektivismus sind, muss die hohe Einschätzung in Anbetracht der ausbleibenden Zielerfüllung als Überschätzung des Ist-Zustandes bewertet werden.

Im Bereich Qualitätsmanagement bestätigen sich die bisher ergründeten Tendenzen: Zum einen ist die durchschnittliche Bandbreite der Wahrnehmungen bei erfolgreichen Industriebetrieben mit 0,15 deutlich kleiner als bei weniger erfolgreichen, wo durchschnittlich 0,38 Likert-Skala-Einheiten zwischen der höchsten und niedrigsten Einschätzung liegen. Zum anderen bewegen sich auch in diesem Themenbereich die Fertigungsmitarbeiter mehr auf die Funktionsleiter zu als dies umgekehrt der Fall ist, woraus hervorgeht, dass die unterschiedlichen

[63] Vgl. Mikulicz-Radecki, Johannes von: Die Rolle von Fertigungsmitarbeitern im strategischen Human Resource Management, Mannheim University Press, Mannheim 2006, S. 138ff.

Aspekte des Qualitätsmanagements nahezu so positiv ausgestaltet sein müssen, wie dies von den Funktionsleitern angenommen wird. Im Gegensatz dazu kennzeichnen sich die Funktionsleiter in weniger erfolgreichen Industriebetrieben durch so positive Einschätzungen, dass angezweifelt werden muss, ob dies die reale Situation wiedergibt, insbesondere wenn man die größtenteils sehr viel kritischere Meinung der Fertigungsmitarbeiter miteinbezieht.

Tabelle 8: Nach Erfolg und Misserfolg differenzierte Mittelwertvergleiche im Qualitätsmanagement

Qualitätsmanagement		**Erfolg**	**1**	**2**	**3**	**Signifikanzniveau**
			Mittelwert FM	Mittelwert Meister	Mittelwert FL	
A	Sauberkeit und Organisiertheit	+	5,51	5,58	5,53	1^{+-} $p < 0,193$ 2^{+-} $p < 0,227$ 3^{+-} $p < 0,632$
		-	5,31	5,75	5,63	
B	Kontinuierliche Weiterentwicklung	+	5,81	5,76	5,92	1^{+-} $p < 0,088$ 2^{+-} $p < 0,056$ 3^{+-} $p < 0,830$
		-	5,63	5,54	5,95	
C	Fokus Kunde bei Entscheidungen über die Qualität	+	5,25	5,18	5,30	1^{+-} $p < 0,839$ 2^{+-} $p < 0,462$ 3^{+-} $p < 0,594$
		-	5,23	5,11	5,37	
D	Integration der Kunden in Qualitätsfragen	+	5,15	5,52	5,44	1^{+-} $p < 0,939$ 2^{+-} $p < 0,805$ 3^{+-} $p < 0,069$
		-	5,14	5,55	5,73	
E	Kundenzufriedenheit als zentrale Zielgröße bei Qualitätsentscheidungen	+	5,42	5,44	5,46	1^{+-} $p < 0,270$ 2^{+-} $p < 0,964$ 3^{+-} $p < 0,504$
		-	5,29	5,43	5,35	

Obwohl auch im Bereich Qualitätsmanagement der intrafraktionelle Vergleich zumeist nicht zu signifikanten Unterschieden in der durchschnittlichen Einschätzung führt, kann dennoch die Hypothese nicht gänzlich verworfen werden, dass erfolgreiches Agieren im Wettbewerb in gewisser Weise auf einen innerbetrieblichen Konsens zurückzuführen ist. Insbesondere die durchschnittlichen Unterschiede in der Bandbreite der Wahrnehmungen zeigen, wie einig bzw. uneinig sich die drei befragten Fraktionen in erfolgreichen bzw. weniger erfolgreichen Industriebetrieben sind und in weiterer Konsequenz, wie gut hierarchieübergreifend kommuniziert und interagiert wird. Besonders die Industriebetriebe, die eine nur unzureichende Zielerreichung kennzeichnet, vermitteln in Anbetracht des festgestellten Dissenses nicht den Eindruck, als würden sich Funktionsleiter häufig und intensiv mit den Fertigungsmitarbeitern über verschiedene Aspekte des eigenen Fertigungsbereiches austauschen.[64] Insofern ist der ausbleibende Erfolg

[64] In einer sehr ähnlichen, konsensorientierten Studie zum strategischen Human Resource Management können Wright und Haggerty vergleichbare Auswirkungen eines innerbetrieblichen Konsenses bzw. Dissenses zeigen. Vgl. Wright, Patrick M. und John J. Haggerty: Missing variables in theories of strategic human resource management – time, cause, and individuals, in: Management Revue, Vol. 16 (2005), No. 2, S. 171 f.

nicht weiter verwunderlich, da einerseits das auf Seiten der Fertigungsmitarbeiter freiliegende Meinungspotenzial weitestgehend ungenutzt bleibt und, in nicht ungehörigem Maße dadurch bedingt, andererseits den getroffenen Entscheidungen eine zumeist unzureichende Einschätzung der höchsten Hierarchieebene zu Grunde liegt.

5 Implikationen für Wissenschaft und Praxis

Die zentralen Implikationen für die industrielle Praxis lassen sich anhand der geprüften Hypothesen dieser Untersuchung darstellen.

Ergebnis 1 *(abgelehnte Nullhypothese $H_{0,2}$):* Es besteht ein Zusammenhang zwischen der hierarchischen Position eines Mitarbeiters und der Wahrnehmung des eigenen Industriebetriebs.

Ergebnis 2 *(teilweise abgelehnte Nullhypothesen $H_{0,3}$ und $H_{0,4}$):* Fertigungsmitarbeiter und Meister, also die operative Basis können die Qualität und Wirkungsweise des angewandten Human Resource Managements und des Qualitätsmanagements angemessen und vor allem deutlich besser als die Managementebene – im Rahmen dieser Untersuchung auf der Ebene der Funktionsleiter untersucht – beurteilen.

Ergebnis 3 *(abgelehnte Nullhypothese $H_{0,1}$):* Es besteht ein Zusammenhang zwischen dem innerbetrieblichen Konsens in einem Industriebetrieb und der Erreichung der Fertigungsperformance.

Diese Ergebnisse, die sich auf die Datenbasis des Forschungsprojektes High Performance Manufacturing stützen, verdeutlichen, dass der in einigen Industriebetrieben schon angestoßene Wandel im Produktionsmanagement, weg von der Technik- und Technologieorientierung hin zur Fokussierung auf den Produktionsfaktor Mensch weiter vorangetrieben werden muss. Insbesondere Fertigungsmitarbeiter haben durch ihre tägliche Arbeit im Fertigungsbereich eine so profunde Kenntnis über die operativen Abläufe und Prozesse, dass sie Schwachstellen und Verbesserungspotenziale sehr schnell und genau erkennen können. Dieses Wissen bleibt bis dato noch relativ häufig ungenutzt in der industriellen Praxis, besonders abzulesen am Ergebnis 3: Diejenigen Industriebetriebe, bei denen ein Konsens vorherrscht, also wo sich die Entscheidungsträger auf die Meinung der Fertigungsmitarbeiter (die gemäß Ergebnis 2 zumeist über die beste Einschätzung bzgl. Qualität und Wirkungsweise von Produktionskonzepten und operativen Maßnahmen verfügen) stützen, sind erfolgreicher als diejenigen Industriebetriebe mit geringem innerbetrieblichen Konsens.

Grundsätzlich sollten Ansätze wie das betriebliche Vorschlagswesen, das seit jeher eine Integration der operativen Basis postuliert, deutlich proaktiver ausgestaltet werden; Mitarbeiter der operativen Basis müssen noch stärker und exponierter in Entscheidungsgremien von Industriebetrieben berufen werden, um dadurch auch sicherzustellen, dass andere, vielleicht bessere Wahrnehmungen des eigenen Industriebetriebs auch Aufnahme in die Entscheidungsprozesse finden.

Schließlich ist aus wissenschaftstheoretischer Perspektive mit besonderem Bezug auf das Produktionsmanagement zu erwähnen, dass eine konsensorientierte Datenbetrachtung, die im fertigungsspezifischen Kontext zumeist völlig vernachlässigt wurde, da häufig die Motivation,

Erfolgsfaktoren mit allen Mitteln zu ergründen, alles andere überragte und somit nur wenig Raum für die offensichtlichen, oft unspektakulären Aspekte einer Datenbasis blieb, zukünftig viel stärker in Betracht gezogen werden sollte. Gerade für die Problemfelder des Fertigungsbereiches, die im Zuge des technischen Fortschritts und dem daraus resultierenden, quasi explodierenden Anforderungsprofil an Fertigungsmitarbeiter eher zu- als abnehmen, offeriert der Vergleich unterschiedlicher Einschätzungen aus unterschiedlicher Perspektive – Fertigungsmitarbeiter, Meister, Funktionsleiter – ein enormes Aufklärungspotenzial. Denn erst durch einen solch innerbetrieblichen Konsens kann das Gleichgewicht geschaffen werden, das die Basis für den Erfolg von Industriebetrieben darstellt.

Literatur

Aaker, D. A., V. Kumar und G. S. Day (2001): *Marketing research*, New York et al.

Ahmad, S. und R. G. Schroeder (2003): The impact of human resource management practices on operational performance – recognizing country and industry differences, in: *Journal of Operations Management*, Vol. 21, No. 1, S. 19–43.

Backhaus, K., B. Erichson, W. Plinke und R. Weiber (2000): *Multivariate Analysemethoden – Eine anwendungsbezogene Einführung, 9. Aufl.*, Berlin et al.

Bagozzi, R. P., Y. Yi und L. W. Phillips (1991): Assessing construct validity in organizational research, in: *Administrative Science Quarterly*, Vol. 36, No. 3, S. 421–458.

Bartlett, C. A. und S. Ghoshal (1995): Changing the role of top management – beyond systems to people, in: *Harvard Business Review*, Vol. 73, No. 3, S. 132–142.

Bentler, P. M. (1990): Comparative fit indexes in structural models, in: *Psychological Bulletin*, Vol. 107, No. 2, S. 238–246.

Bortz, J. (1999): *Statistik für Sozialwissenschaftler*, Berlin.

Boyer, K. K. und R. Verma (2000): Multiple raters in survey-based operations management research – a review and tutorial, in: *Production and Operations Management*, Vol. 9, No. 2, S. 128–140.

Brosius, G. und F. Brosius (1995): *SPSS Base System und Professional Statistics*, Bonn.

Campbell, D. T. und D. W. Fiske (1959): Convergent and discriminant validation by the multitrait-multimethod matrix, in: *Psychological Bulletin*, Vol. 56, No. 2, S. 81–105.

Cronbach, L. J. (1951): Coefficient alpha and the internal structure of tests, in: *Psychometrica*, Vol. 16, No. 3, S. 297–334.

Doty, H. und W. Glick (1998): Common methods bias – does common methods variance really bias results?, in: *Organizational Research Methods*, Vol. 1, No. 4, S. 374–406.

Ernst, H. (2003): Ursachen des Informant Bias und dessen Auswirkung auf die Validität empirischer betriebswirtschaftlicher Forschung, in: *Zeitschrift für Betriebswirtschaft*, Jg. 73, Nr. 12, S. 1249–1276.

Eurostat (2003): *Statistical classification of economic activities in the European Community (NACE Revision 1)*, Luxemburg.

Flynn, B. B., R. G. Schroeder, E. J. Flynn, S. Sakakibara und K. A. Bates (1997): World class manufacturing project – overview and selected results, in: *International Journal of Operations & Production Management*, Vol. 17, No. 7, S. 671–685.

Hambrick, D. C. (1982): Environmental scanning and organizational strategy, in: *Strategic Management Journal*, Vol. 3, No. 2, S. 159–174.

Hartung, J. und B. Elpelt (1992): *Multivariate Statistik – Lehr- und Handbuch der angewandten Statistik, 4. Aufl.*, München.

Hayes, R. H. und S. C. Wheelwright (1984): *Restoring our competitive edge – competing through manufacturing*, New York et al.

Hayes, R. H., S. C. Wheelwright und K. B. Clark (1988): *Dynamic manufacturing – creating the learning organization*, New York.

Homburg, C. und A. Giering (1997): Konzeptualisierung und Operationalisierung komplexer Konstrukte – Ein Leitfaden für die Marketingforschung, in: *Marketing*, Jg. 18, Nr. 1, S. 5–24.

Ireland, R. D., M. A. Hitt, R. A. Bettis und D. A. de Portas (1985): Strategy formulation processes – differences in perceptions of strengths and weaknesses indicators and environmental uncertainty by managerial level, in: *Strategic Management Journal*, Vol. 8, No. 5, S. 469–485.

Ketokivi, M. und R. G. Schroeder (2004): Perceptual measures of performance – fact or fiction, in: *Journal of Operations Management*, Vol. 22, No. 3, S. 247–264.

Kiesler, S. und L. Sproul (1982): Managerial response to changing environments – perspectives and problem sensing from social cognition, in: *Administrative Science Quarterly*, Vol. 27, No. 3, S. 548–570.

Kim, C. und H. Lee (1997): Development of family triadic measures for children's purchase influence, in: *Journal of Marketing Research*, Vol. 34, No. 3, S. 307–321.

Kinnie, N. J. und R. V. W. Staughton (1994): The problem of implementing manufacturing strategy, in: Storey, J. (Hrsg.): *New wave manufacturing strategies – organizational and human resource management dimensions*, London, S. 41–62.

Kumar, N., L. W. Stern und J. C. Anderson (1993): Conducting interorganizational research using key informants, in: *Academy of Management Journal*, Vol. 36, No. 6, S. 1633–1651.

Marsh, H. W. (1989): Confirmatory factor analysis of multitrait-multimethod data – many problems and a few solutions, in: *Applied Psychological Measurement*, Vol. 13, No. 4, S. 335–361.

Mikulicz-Radecki, J. von (2006): *Die Rolle von Fertigungsmitarbeitern im strategischen Human Resource Management*, Mannheim University Press, Mannheim, S. 123 ff.

Miller, J. G. und A. V. Roth (1994): A taxonomy of manufacturing strategies, in: *Management Science*, Vol. 40, No. 3, S. 285–304.

Milling, P (1998): *Wo stehen deutsche Industriebetriebe im internationalen Wettbewerb? – Faktoren, Profile und Analysen des „World Class Manufacturing"*, Forschungsberichte der Fakultät für Betriebswirtschaftslehre, Universität Mannheim, Nr. 9807, Mannheim.

Mintzberg, H. (1991): Crafting strategy, in: Montgomery, C. A. und M. E. Porter (Hrsg.): *Strategy – seeking and securing competitive advantage*, Boston, S. 403–420.

Nisbett, R. und L. Ross (1980): *Human inference – strategies and shortcomings of social judgement*, Englewood Cliffs.

Nunnally, J. C. (1978): *Psychometric theory*, New York.

Peterson, R. A. (1994): A meta-analysis of cronbach's coefficient alpha, in: *Journal of Consumer Research*, Vol. 21, No. 2, S. 381–391.

Porter, M. E. (1980): *Competitive strategy – techniques for analysing industries and competitors*, New York.

Reger, R. K., L. T. Gustafson, S. D. Demarie und J. V. Mullane (1994): Reframing the organization – why implementing total quality is easier said than done, in: *Academy of Management Review*, Vol. 19, No. 3, S. 565–584.

Rindskopf, D. M. (1984): Structural equation models – empirical identification, Heywood cases and related problems, in: *Sociological Methods and Research*, Vol. 13, No. 1, S. 109–119.

Ruffini, F. A. J., H. Boer und M. J. van Riemsdijk (2000): Organization design in operations management, in: *International Journal of Operations & Production Management*, Vol. 20, No. 7, S. 860–879.

Salancik, G. und J. R. Meindl (1984): Corporate attributions as strategic illusions of management control, in: *Administrative Science Quarterly*, Vol. 29, No. 2, S. 238–254.

Schonberger, R. J. (1986): *World class manufacturing – the lessons of simplicity applied*, New York et al.

Schroeder, R. G. und B. B. Flynn (Hrsg.) (2000): *High Performance Manufacturing – Global Perspectives*, New York et al.

Türk, K. (1998): *Informationssysteme in der Produktion und ihre Unterstützung durch Gruppenarbeit zur Steigerung der Wettbewerbsfähigkeit – eine empirische Untersuchung im Rahmen des Projektes World Class Manufacturing*, Berlin.

Tversky, A. und D. Kahneman (1974): Judgement and uncertainty – heuristics and biases, in: *Science*, Vol. 185, S. 1124–1131.

Wright, P. M. und J. J. Haggerty (2005): Missing variables in theories of strategic human resource management – time, cause, and individuals, in: *Management Revue*, Vol. 16, No. 2, S. 164–173.

Venkatraman, N. V. und J. H. Grant (1986): Construct measurement in organizational strategy research – a critique and proposal, in: *Academy of Management Review*, Vol. 11, No. 1, S. 71–87.

Zahra, S. A. und S. R. Das (1993): Innovation strategy and financial performance in manufacturing companies – an empirical study, in: *Production and Operations Management*, Vol. 2, No. 1, S. 15–37.

Anhang

Tabelle A-1: Fragen der Themenkomplexe aus dem Bereich Human Resource Management

Themenkomplex			Fragen
A	Dezentralisierung von Entscheidungen	1	Selbst größere Angelegenheiten müssen keinem Vorgesetzten vor einer endgültigen Entscheidung vorgelegt werden.
		2	Nur wenige Entscheidungen, die ich treffe, bedürfen der Zustimmung meines Vorgesetzten.
		3	Ohne die Zustimmung eines Vorgesetzten können wir hier wenig unternehmen.
		4	Dieser Betrieb ist für solche Mitarbeiter wie geschaffen, die gern selbstständig Entscheidungen treffen.
B	Verbundenheit zum eigenen Unternehmen	1	Ich erzähle meinen Freunden und Bekannten, dass dies ein Unternehmen ist, für das man gerne arbeitet.
		2	Ich würde fast jede Art von Stelle annehmen, nur damit ich weiter für diese Firma arbeiten kann.
		3	Ich finde, dass meine eigenen Wertvorstellungen und die meines Unternehmens sich sehr ähnlich sind.
		4	Ich bin stolz darauf, anderen erzählen zu können, dass ich ein Teil dieses Unternehmens bin.
		5	Durch dieses Unternehmen werde ich dazu angespornt, in meinem Job mein Bestes für die Firma zu tun.
		6	Ich bin sehr glücklich, dass ich mich für dieses Unternehmen entschieden habe und nicht für andere, die ich in meiner Bewerbungsphase auch noch in Betracht gezogen habe.
		7	Für mich ist dies das beste Unternehmen, für das man arbeiten kann.
C	Implementierung des betrieblichen Vorschlags-wesens	1	Das Management nimmt alle Vorschläge zur Produkt- und Prozessverbesserung ernst.
		2	Wir werden ermutigt, Vorschläge zur Leistungsverbesserung des Betriebes zu machen.
		3	Das Management teilt uns mit, warum unsere Vorschläge eingeführt bzw. nicht umgesetzt werden.
		4	Viele nützliche Verbesserungsvorschläge werden in unserem Betrieb umgesetzt.
		5	Man nimmt meine Verbesserungsvorschläge hier nicht ernst.
D	Teilautonome Gruppenarbeit	1	Während einer Sitzung zur Lösung eines Problems versuchen wir, die Meinungen und Ideen aller Teammitglieder zu sammeln, bevor wir eine Entscheidung treffen.
		2	In unserem Betrieb bilden wir Teams, um Probleme zu lösen.
		3	Während der letzten drei Jahre konnten viele Probleme durch kleine Teams gelöst werden.
		4	Durch Teams, die zur Lösung von Problemen eingesetzt werden, konnten die Fertigungsprozesse dieses Betriebes verbessert werden.
		5	Die Mitarbeitergruppen werden ermutigt, ihre Probleme soweit wie möglich selbstständig zu lösen.
		6	In diesem Werk setzen wir nicht sehr oft Teams zur Lösung von Problemen ein.
E	Fähigkeit der Vorgesetzten	1	Die Vorgesetzten ermutigen ihre Mitarbeiter im Team zu arbeiten.
		2	Vorgesetzte ermutigen die Mitarbeiter, ihre Ideen und Meinungen offen auszutauschen.
		3	Unsere Vorgesetzten setzen sich häufig mit ihren Mitarbeitern zu Gruppengesprächen zusammen, in denen sie Probleme ausführlich besprechen.
		4	Unsere Vorgesetzten ermutigen uns selten zusammenzukommen, um Probleme zu lösen.

Tabelle A-2: Gütekennzahlen der methodenspezifischen Faktorenanalysen (Human Resource Management – High Performance Manufacturing 2004)

Themenkomplex		Fraktion	Gütekennzahlen
A	Dezentralisierung von Entscheidungen *(enthalten sind die Items 1,3,4)*	FM	RMSEA = 0,11; CFI = 0,95; GFI = 0,90; AGFI = 0,82; Cronbachs Alpha = 0,75; Erklärte Varianz = 67,40; Eigenwert = 2,0; Faktorladungen: 1. 0,77; 3. 0,86; 4. 0,82
		Meister	RMSEA = 0,11; CFI = 0,95; GFI = 0,90; AGFI = 0,82; Cronbachs Alpha = 0,78; Erklärte Varianz = 69,78; Eigenwert = 2,1; Faktorladungen: 1. 0,84; 3. 0,87; 4. 0,78
		FL	RMSEA = 0,11; CFI = 0,95; GFI = 0,90; AGFI = 0,82; Cronbachs Alpha = 0,82; Erklärte Varianz = 73,86; Eigenwert = 2,2; Faktorladungen: 1. 0,89; 3. 0,87; 4. 0,81
B	Verbundenheit zum eigenen Unternehmen *(enthalten sind die Items 1,3,5)*	FM	RMSEA = 0,01; CFI = 0,99; GFI = 0,97; AGFI = 0,94; Cronbachs Alpha = 0,78; Erklärte Varianz = 69,84; Eigenwert = 2,1; Faktorladungen: 1. 0,82; 3. 0,84; 5. 0,83
		Meister	RMSEA = 0,01; CFI = 0,99; GFI = 0,97; AGFI = 0,94; Cronbachs Alpha = 0,75; Erklärte Varianz = 66,97; Eigenwert = 2,0; Faktorladungen: 1. 0,78; 3. 0,84; 5. 0,83
		FL	RMSEA = 0,01; CFI = 0,99; GFI = 0,97; AGFI = 0,94; Cronbachs Alpha = 0,77; Erklärte Varianz = 69,01; Eigenwert = 2,1; Faktorladungen: 1. 0,85; 3. 0,81; 5. 0,83
C	Implementierung des betrieblichen Vorschlags-wesens *(enthalten sind die Items 1,2,3,4)*	FM	RMSEA = 0,04; CFI = 0,97; GFI = 0,96; AGFI = 0,91; Cronbachs Alpha = 0,86; Erklärte Varianz = 71,95; Eigenwert = 2,8; Faktorladungen: 1. 0,81; 2. 0,87; 3. 0,82; 4. 0,88
		Meister	RMSEA = 0,04; CFI = 0,97; GFI = 0,96; AGFI = 0,91; Cronbachs Alpha = 0,78; Erklärte Varianz = 61,89; Eigenwert = 2,5; Faktorladungen: 1. 0,72; 2. 0,81; 3. 0,78; 4. 0,82
		FL	RMSEA = 0,04; CFI = 0,97; GFI = 0,96; AGFI = 0,91; Cronbachs Alpha = 0,73; Erklärte Varianz = 57,03; Eigenwert = 2,3; Faktorladungen: 1. 0,75; 2. 0,77; 3. 0,68; 4. 0,80
D	Teilautonome Gruppenarbeit *(enthalten sind die Items 2,3,4)*	FM	RMSEA = 0,05; CFI = 0,97; GFI = 0,95; AGFI = 0,90; Cronbachs Alpha = 0,84; Erklärte Varianz = 75,53; Eigenwert = 2,3; Faktorladungen: 2. 0,84; 3. 0,88; 4. 0,87
		Meister	RMSEA = 0,05; CFI = 0,97; GFI = 0,95; AGFI = 0,90; Cronbachs Alpha = 0,80; Erklärte Varianz = 71,54; Eigenwert = 2,2; Faktorladungen: 2. 0,87; 3. 0,83; 4. 0,84
		FL	RMSEA = 0,05; CFI = 0,97; GFI = 0,95; AGFI = 0,90; Cronbachs Alpha = 0,78; Erklärte Varianz = 69,71; Eigenwert = 2,1; Faktorladungen: 2. 0,81; 3. 0,84; 4. 0,85
E	Fähigkeit der Vorgesetzten *(enthalten sind die Items 1,2,3)*	FM	RMSEA = 0,02; CFI = 0,98; GFI = 0,96; AGFI = 0,91; Cronbachs Alpha = 0,75; Erklärte Varianz = 67,93; Eigenwert = 2,0; Faktorladungen: 1. 0,87; 2. 0,86; 3. 0,74
		Meister	RMSEA = 0,02; CFI = 0,98; GFI = 0,96; AGFI = 0,91; Cronbachs Alpha = 0,69; Erklärte Varianz = 64,57; Eigenwert = 1,9; Faktorladungen: 1. 0,86; 2. 0,85; 3. 0,69
		FL	RMSEA = 0,02; CFI = 0,98; GFI = 0,96; AGFI = 0,91; Cronbachs Alpha = 0,71; Erklärte Varianz = 63,25; Eigenwert = 1,9; Faktorladungen: 1. 0,83; 2. 0,80; 3. 0,75

Tabelle A-3: Fragen der Themenkomplexe aus dem Bereich Qualitätsmanagement

Themenkomplex		*	Fragen
A	Sauberkeit und Organisiertheit	1	In unserem Betrieb wird Wert darauf gelegt, dass alle Werkzeuge an ihrem Platz sind.
		2	Wir sind stolz darauf, unser Werk ordentlich und sauber zu halten.
		3	Unser Werk wird jederzeit sauber gehalten.
		4	Mitarbeiter haben häufig Probleme damit, die benötigten Werkzeuge zu finden.
		5	Unser Werk ist chaotisch und schmutzig.
B	Kontinuierliche Weiterentwicklung	1	Wir bemühen uns, alle Produkte und Prozesse kontinuierlich zu verbessern und verfolgen keine periodisch festgelegten Ansätze.
		2	Wenn wir uns nicht ständig verbessern und lernen würden, würde unsere Performance langfristig darunter leiden.
		3	Durch kontinuierliche Verbesserung steigern wir unsere Performance, so dass wir für Wettbewerber schwer angreifbar sind.
		4	Wir sind davon überzeugt, dass Verbesserungen eines Prozesses nie abgeschlossen sind; es können immer noch weitere inkrementale Verbesserungen vorgenommen werden.
		5	Unsere Organisation ist kein statisches Gebilde, sondern verändert sich permanent, um Kundenwünsche besser erfüllen zu können.
C	Fokus Kunde bei Entscheidungen über die Qualität	1	Wir sind überzeugt, dass Kunden ihre Bedürfnisse besser beurteilen können als Produktdesigner.
		2	Wir sind davon überzeugt, dass Unternehmen stets die Initiative ergreifen sollten, um Kundenbedürfnisse frühzeitig zu erkennen.
		3	Wir sind davon überzeugt, dass Kunden ihre Wünsche und Bedürfnisse am besten einschätzen können.
		4	Kundenzufriedenheit ist für die langfristige Performance unserer Organisation wichtig.
		5	Unser Unternehmen erfüllt oder übertrifft die Anforderungen und Erwartungen unserer Kunden.
		6	Ingenieure sind die beste Quelle für Produkt- und Designveränderungen.
D	Integration der Kunden in Qualitätsfragen	1	Wir sind regelmäßig in engem Kontakt zu Kunden.
		2	Unsere Kunden geben uns Rückmeldung über unsere Qualitäts- und Lieferperformance.
		3	Unsere Kunden sind aktiv an unserem Produktdesignprozess beteiligt.
		4	Wir bemühen uns die Bedürfnisse unserer Kunden in hohem Maße zu berücksichtigen.
		5	Wir betrachten regelmäßig die Bedürfnisse unserer Kunden.
E	Kundenzufriedenheit als zentrale Zielgröße bei Qualitäts-entscheidungen	1	Unsere Kunden sind mit unseren Produkten und unserem Service zufrieden.
		2	Unsere Kunden scheinen mit unserer Fähigkeit, schnell auf ihre Probleme reagieren zu können, zufrieden zu sein.
		3	Wir haben eine hohe Anzahl an Wiederkäufern.
		4	Kundenstandards werden von unserem Werk immer erfüllt.
		5	In den letzten drei Jahren hat die Qualität unserer Produkte unsere Kunden zufrieden gestellt.

Tabelle A-4: Gütekennzahlen der methodenspezifischen Faktorenanalysen (Qualitätsmanagement – High Performance Manufacturing 2004)

Themenkomplex		Fraktion	Gütekennzahlen
A	Sauberkeit und Organisiertheit *(enthalten sind die Items 1,4,5)*	FM	RMSEA = 0,03; CFI = 0,98; GFI = 0,96; AGFI = 0,91; Cronbachs Alpha = 0,57; Erklärte Varianz = 54,56; Eigenwert = 1,6; Faktorladungen: 1. 0,76; 4. 0,65; 5. 0,80
		Meister	RMSEA = 0,03; CFI = 0,98; GFI = 0,96; AGFI = 0,91; Cronbachs Alpha = 0,62; Erklärte Varianz = 56,93; Eigenwert = 1,7; Faktorladungen: 1. 0,71; 4. 0,78; 5. 0,77
		FL	RMSEA = 0,03; CFI = 0,98; GFI = 0,96; AGFI = 0,91; Cronbachs Alpha = 0,66; Erklärte Varianz = 59,50; Eigenwert = 1,8; Faktorladungen: 1. 0,75; 4. 0,75; 5. 0,82
B	Kontinuierliche Weiter-entwicklung *(enthalten sind die Items 1,5)*	FM	RMSEA = 0,05; CFI = 0,93; GFI = 0,97; AGFI = 0,90; Cronbachs Alpha = 0,60; Erklärte Varianz = 71,30; Eigenwert = 1,4; Faktorladungen: 1. 0,84; 5. 0,84
		Meister	RMSEA = 0,05; CFI = 0,93; GFI = 0,97; AGFI = 0,90; Cronbachs Alpha = 0,68; Erklärte Varianz = 62,05; Eigenwert = 1,4; Faktorladungen: 1. 0,79; 5. 0,79
		FL	RMSEA = 0,05; CFI = 0,93; GFI = 0,97; AGFI = 0,90; Cronbachs Alpha = 0,60; Erklärte Varianz = 66,92; Eigenwert = 1,4; Faktorladungen: 1. 0,82; 5. 0,82
C	Fokus Kunde bei Entscheidungen über die Qualität *(enthalten sind die Items 1,3)*	FM	RMSEA = 0,03; CFI = 0,99; GFI = 0,98; AGFI = 0,95; Cronbachs Alpha = 0,76; Erklärte Varianz = 80,45; Eigenwert = 1,6; Faktorladungen: 1. 0,90; 3. 0,90
		Meister	RMSEA = 0,03; CFI = 0,99; GFI = 0,98; AGFI = 0,95; Cronbachs Alpha = 0,78; Erklärte Varianz = 82,02; Eigenwert = 1,7; Faktorladungen: 1. 0,90; 3. 0,90
		FL	RMSEA = 0,03; CFI = 0,99; GFI = 0,98; AGFI = 0,95; Cronbachs Alpha = 0,73; Erklärte Varianz = 79,67; Eigenwert = 1,6; Faktorladungen: 1. 0,89; 3. 0,89
D	Integration der Kunden in Qualitätsfragen *(enthalten sind die Items 2,3)*	FM	RMSEA = 0,01; CFI = 1,00; GFI = 0,99; AGFI = 0,96; Cronbachs Alpha = 0,52; Erklärte Varianz = 67,55; Eigenwert = 1,4; Faktorladungen: 2. 0,82; 3. 0,82
		Meister	RMSEA = 0,01; CFI = 1,00; GFI = 0,99; AGFI = 0,96; Cronbachs Alpha = 0,46; Erklärte Varianz = 65,08; Eigenwert = 1,3; Faktorladungen: 2. 0,81; 3. 0,81
		FL	RMSEA = 0,01; CFI = 1,00; GFI = 0,99; AGFI = 0,96; Cronbachs Alpha = 0,42; Erklärte Varianz = 64,30; Eigenwert = 1,3; Faktorladungen: 2. 0,81; 3. 0,81
E	Kundenzu-friedenheit als zentrale Zielgröße bei Qualitäts-entscheidungen *(enthalten sind die Items 1,2,4,5)*	FM	RMSEA = 0,05; CFI = 0,97; GFI = 0,96; AGFI = 0,91; Cronbachs Alpha = 0,87; Erklärte Varianz = 73,12; Eigenwert = 2,9; Faktorladungen: 1. 0,88; 2. 0,80: 4. 0,83; 5. 0,89
		Meister	RMSEA = 0,05; CFI = 0,97; GFI = 0,96; AGFI = 0,91; Cronbachs Alpha = 0,79; Erklärte Varianz = 63,54; Eigenwert = 2,5; Faktorladungen: 1. 0,85; 2. 0,81; 4. 0,72; 5. 0,81
		FL	RMSEA = 0,05; CFI = 0,97; GFI = 0,96; AGFI = 0,91; Cronbachs Alpha = 0,82; Erklärte Varianz = 65,74; Eigenwert = 2,6; Faktorladungen: 1. 0,85; 2. 0,75; 4. 0,81; 5. 0,83

Modellentwicklung und Modellvalidierung in der Praxis der Transaktionsberatung

Achim Korten

Business Modelling Group/KPMG AG

Zusammenfassung

Unternehmenstransaktionen erfolgen häufig in der Erwartung, einen Beitrag zur Steigerung des Unternehmenswertes zu leisten. Mehrere Studien zeigten bereits, dass in zwei Drittel der Transaktionen diese Erwartung nicht erfüllt wird. Erklärungsansätze fokussieren sich regelmäßig auf prozessuale Fragestellungen der Integration von Transaktionsobjekten nach dem Erwerb. Inwieweit bereits die Gestaltung und der Verlauf des Transaktionsprozesses vor dem Erwerb einen Beitrag zur Zielerreichung von Unternehmenstransaktionen leistet, findet in der einschlägigen Forschung wenig Aufmerksamkeit.

Zwischen potenziellem Verkäufer und Kaufinteressenten eines Transaktionsobjektes besteht während des gesamten Transaktionsprozesses ein Informationsungleichgewicht bezüglich der wirtschaftlichen und rechtlichen Situation des Transaktionsgegenstands. Dies gibt es sowohl hinsichtlich der Entwicklung des Transaktionsobjektes in der Vergangenheit als auch bezüglich der Einschätzung der Zukunftsperspektiven, wie sie in der Unternehmensplanung zum Ausdruck kommt.

Aus den objektspezifisch zu berücksichtigenden Aspekten sowie dem wirtschaftlichen und regulatorischen Umfeld ergibt sich die hohe zu bewältigende Komplexität eines Transaktionsprozesses. Auf der Suche nach erfolgreichen Strategien zur Bewältigung dieser Komplexität und Überwindung der Informationsasymmetrien auf Verkäufer- und Käuferseite in einem Transaktionsprozess bietet die einschlägige Forschung bisher wenig Antworten. In vorliegenden Artikel wird ein möglicher Untersuchungsansatz skizziert, um Erklärungsvariablen für die erfolgreiche Gestaltung von Transaktionsprozessen zu finden. Dabei wird auch auf die Möglichkeit eingegangen, die System Dynamics zur Validierung von Unternehmensplanungen bietet.

Schlagwörter: Transaktionsprozess, Erfolgsfaktoren, Systemgrenzen, Informationsungleichgewicht, Unternehmensplanung

1 Transaktionsberatung und System Dynamics

Die Praxis der Transaktionsberatung bietet unterschiedliche Ansatzpunkte für System-Dynamics-basierte Untersuchungen von Transaktionsprozessen. In diesem Artikel werden zwei mögliche Themenstellungen skizziert:

Zum einen geht es um das Thema Informationsungleichgewicht zwischen potenziellem Verkäufer und Käufer: Welche Verhaltensweisen sind seitens eines potenziellen Verkäufers hinsichtlich der Offenlegung von Informationen über das mögliche Transaktionsobjekt vorstellbar?

Demgegenüber steht der Verlauf des Erkenntnisgewinns auf Seiten eines interessierten Käufers – wie kann dieser aussehen? In diesem Artikel wird abstrakt aufgezeigt, dass die Entwicklung der Systemgrenze während Transaktionsprozessen mit ganz unterschiedlicher Dynamik verlaufen kann.[1] Die Identifikation und Analyse von Erklärungsvariablen hierfür stellen Ansatzpunkte für die System-Dynamics-Forschung dar.

Zum anderen wird skizziert, welche aus der System-Dynamics-Forschung bekannten Testverfahren auch in der Transaktionspraxis Anwendung finden; die Betrachtung fokussiert sich auf Planungsmodelle, die regelmäßig Bestandteil von Transaktionen sind. Zunehmend werden die diesen Planungsmodellen zu Grunde liegenden Strukturen ebenso validiert wie die Ergebnisse, die diese Modelle erzeugen. Gerade im Transaktionsgeschäft erwarten finanzierende Institutionen zunehmend mittels Gutachten von unabhängigen Dritten Sicherheit bezüglich der Qualität von Planungsmodellen. Im vorliegenden Artikel soll andiskutiert werden, ob die System-Dynamics-Forschung weitere Testverfahren zur Validierung bietet, die einen Mehrwert für den Adressaten der Modellvalidierung liefern können.[2]

2 Finanzdaten und Perspektiven im Transaktionsprozess

2.1 Finanzielle Grundlagen einer Transaktion

Kapital- und Personengesellschaften sind nach Beendigung eines Geschäftsjahres zur Erstellung eines Jahresabschlusses verpflichtet. Pflichtbestandteile eines Jahresabschlusses sind Bilanz und Gewinn- und Verlustrechnung. In Abhängigkeit der Unternehmensgröße und der anzuwendenden Rechnungslegungsvorschriften kommen Anhang, Lagebericht, Kapitalflussrechnung, Segmentberichterstattung und Eigenkapitalspiegel hinzu. Die Zusammenhänge im externen Rechnungswesen lassen den Vergleich mit geschlossenen Systemen im Sinne des System-Dynamics-Ansatzes zu, da sämtliche notwendigen Erklärungsfaktoren für die historische Entwicklung der Finanzinformationen innerhalb der Systemgrenze erfasst sind.[3] Letztere lässt sich aus den einschlägigen Rechnungslegungsvorschriften ableiten, da sowohl Berichtsbestandteile als auch Berichtsaufbau und wesentliche Gliederungspunkte vorgeschrieben sind.[4]

Bei Unternehmenstransaktionen handelt es sich um die Übertragung von Anteilen an dem Rechtsträger eines Unternehmens („share deal") oder um die Übertragung der Wirtschaftsgüter eines Unternehmens ohne dessen Rechtsträger („asset deal").[5] Im Kontext einer Transaktion werden zwischen den beteiligten Parteien Informationen über das Transaktionsobjekt ausge-

---

[1] Zur Konzeption des Aufbaus von Systemen vgl. Milling, Peter: Leitmotive des System-Dynamics-Ansatzes, in: Wirtschaftswissenschaftliches Studium, 13. Jg., Nr. 10/1984, S. 510.

[2] Die Betrachtungen erfolgen mit Fokus auf finanzielle Aspekte einer Transaktion; wenngleich in Transaktionen oftmals auch nicht-finanzielle Aspekte von Bedeutung sind, werden sie hier außer Acht gelassen. Im Hinblick auf die Themenstellungen erscheint dieser Fokus hinreichend.

[3] Vgl. Milling, Peter: Systemtheoretische Grundlagen zur Planung der Unternehmenspolitik, Berlin 1981, S. 150.

[4] Siehe beispielhaft die §§ 266, 275 HGB, den Deutschen Rechnungslegungsstandard DRS 2 zur Kapitalflussrechnung und den internationalen Rechnungslegungsstandard IAS 1.

[5] Vgl. beispielhaft Holzapfel, Hans-Joachim und Reinhard Pöllath: Unternehmenskauf in Recht und Praxis, 12. Auflage, Köln 2006, S. 109, Tz. 131.

tauscht. Hierzu gehören Informationen über das vergangenheitsorientierte externe Rechnungswesen ebenso wie Unternehmensplanungen. Dies ist insbesondere für Zwecke der Bewertung des Transaktionsobjektes bedeutsam. Dabei stehen häufig die prognostizierten Kapitalflüsse an den künftigen Eigentümer im Vordergrund. Entsprechend sind die im Rahmen einer Transaktion seitens des potenziellen Verkäufers vorgelegten Planungen häufig auf die Darstellung der wesentlichen Erklärungsfaktoren für die in der Zukunft erwarteten Kapitalflüsse reduziert. Auch derartig selektive Planungsrechnungen können als geschlossenes System betrachtet werden; allerdings ist die Systemgrenze gegenüber dem vergangenheitsorientierten externen Berichtswesen enger definiert, da es in einem zukunftsorientierten Planungsmodell weniger erklärungsbedürftige Variablen als in einer vergangenheitsorientierten Berichterstattung gibt.

Transaktionen sind komplexe und dynamische Prozesse; die Komplexität resultiert aus der Vielzahl von miteinander in Beziehung stehenden Aspekten, die bei der Durchführung eines solchen Prozesses von den beteiligten Parteien zu berücksichtigen sind. Hierzu gehören Fragestellungen auf betriebswirtschaftlicher, steuerlicher und juristischer Ebene. Die Dynamik resultiert aus dem sukzessiven Abbau des Informationsungleichgewichts zwischen den an einer Transaktion beteiligten Parteien.[6] Angesichts ihrer Charakteristika stellen Transaktionsprozesse ein interessantes, doch bisher wenig bearbeitetes Forschungsgebiet aus Sicht von System Dynamics dar.[7]

Grundsätzlich lassen sich in einem Transaktionsprozess zwei Perspektiven unterscheiden: die Verkäufer- und die Käufersicht. Gegenstand einer Transaktion sind typischerweise einzelne Vermögensgegenstände, Unternehmens(an)teile oder ganze Unternehmen. Der Verkauf bzw. Kauf erfolgt im Rahmen eines mitunter vielschichtigen und zeitaufwändigen Transaktionsprozesses. Je nach Perspektive unterscheiden sich die zu durchlaufenden Phasen inhaltlich. Nachfolgend werden die einzelnen Phasen zunächst aus Verkäufersicht, anschließend aus Käufersicht umschrieben. Dem schließen sich das Aufzeigen der jeweils wahrnehmbaren Systemgrenzen und die ihnen innewohnende Dynamik im Verlauf des Transaktionsprozesses an.

2.2 Die Verkäufer-Perspektive in einer Transaktion

Abbildung 1 zeigt verallgemeinernd die fünf Phasen eines Transaktionsprozesses aus Verkäufersicht.

Abbildung 1: Phasen des Transaktionsprozesses aus Verkäufersicht

[6] Vgl. Institut der Wirtschaftsprüfer in Deutschland e.V. (Hrsg.): WP Handbuch 2008 Wirtschaftsprüfung, Rechnungslegung, Beratung Band II, Düsseldorf 2007, S. 1079–1080.

[7] Siehe auch Gary, Michael Shayne et al.: System Dynamics and Strategy, Working Paper 2008, available at SSRN.

In der ersten Phase trifft der potenzielle Verkäufer die Entscheidung, einen einzelnen Vermögensgegenstand, Unternehmens(an)teile oder ein ganzes Unternehmen zu verkaufen. Anlass für den Verkauf können ein Strategiewechsel, Liquiditätsprobleme oder andere Gründe sein.

Während der Verkaufsplanung und -vorbereitung (Phase II) werden die Informationen über das Verkaufsobjekt aufbereitet, die der potenzielle Verkäufer möglichen Interessenten im Verlauf des Transaktionsprozesses (sukzessive) bereit stellen möchte. Hierzu gehören beispielsweise Informationen über die Zusammensetzung und Erfahrung des Managements, Organigramme, Handelsregisterauszüge, Gesellschaftsverträge, Informationen aus dem externen Rechnungswesen und Planungsrechnungen. Darüber hinaus legt der Verkäufer seine Verkaufsstrategie fest; dazu gehören die Auswahl von Beratern, die den potenziellen Verkäufer im Prozess begleiten und unterstützen, die Festlegung des Verkaufstyps (öffentliche Ausschreibung oder gezielte Ansprache möglicher Kaufinteressenten), Festlegung der wesentlichen Kriterien für die Auswahl des Käufers (z. B. Höhe des Kaufpreises, Standort- bzw. Arbeitsplatzgarantien) etc.

Verkaufsverhandlungen (Phase III) können ein- oder mehrstufig gestaltet sein; in einem einstufigen Prozess geben potenzielle Käufer ein Kaufangebot ab und der Käufer wird ausgewählt. Ein mehrstufiger Prozess kommt in der Praxis jedoch wesentlich häufiger vor: Interessierte potenzielle Käufer bekommen die Möglichkeit, auf Basis der öffentlich verfügbaren und seitens des Verkäufers bereitgestellten limitierten Informationen ein erstes Angebot abzugeben. Der potenzielle Verkäufer wählt nach definierten Kriterien den Kreis der potenziellen Käufer aus, die im Rahmen einer zweiten Angebotsrunde zusätzliche Informationen über das Verkaufsobjekt erhalten. Die Anzahl der Angebotsrunden wird vom potenziellen Verkäufer häufig vor Beginn des Transaktionsprozesses festgelegt.

Die zusätzlichen Informationen werden in einem sogenannten Datenraum (physisch oder virtuell) bereitgestellt. Darüber hinaus bekommen potenzielle Käufer die Gelegenheit, in schriftlichen oder persönlichen Fragerunden weitere Informationen zu dem Verkaufsobjekt zu erlangen. Auf Basis aller gewonnenen Informationen geben potenzielle Käufer ihr finales und bindendes Angebot ab. Dann obliegt es dem potenziellen Verkäufer, sich für eines der Angebote zu entscheiden.[8]

Nach Auswahl des Käufers werden die Verhandlungen durch Unterschrift eines Kaufvertrages abgeschlossen (Phase IV); dieser enthält unter anderem den vereinbarten Kaufpreis sowie etwaige Kaufpreisanpassungsmechanismen. Hinzu kommen ergänzende Regelungen, beispielsweise Haftungsregelungen, Garantievereinbarungen, Standortgarantien.

In der abschließenden Phase erfolgt die Separierung des verkauften Transaktionsobjektes von der verbleibenden Organisation des Eigentümers (Phase V). Aus Sicht des externen Rechnungswesens sind hier beispielsweise die Zuordnung von Vermögensgegenständen und Schulden, die Abgrenzung der IT-Systeme und die Personalzuordnung bedeutende Themen. Verkäufer und Käufer vereinbaren hierzu meist einen Stichtag, bis zu dem die Separierung durch den Verkäufer abgeschlossen sein soll.

[8] Siehe auch Institut der Wirtschaftsprüfer in Deutschland e. V. (Hrsg.): WP Handbuch 2008 Band II, Düsseldorf 2007, S. 1084–1088. Die Verhandlungsphase wird durch eine Reihe zu treffender Vereinbarungen zwischen dem potenziellen Verkäufer und den Kaufinteressenten begleitet. Hierzu gehören u. a. Vertraulichkeits- und Geheimhaltungsvereinbarungen, Haftungsfreistellungserklärungen, Regelungen zum Ablauf des Transaktionsprozesses, etc.

2.3 Die Käufer-Perspektive in einer Transaktion

In Abbildung 2 sind die fünf Phasen eines Transaktionsprozesses aus Käufersicht dargestellt.

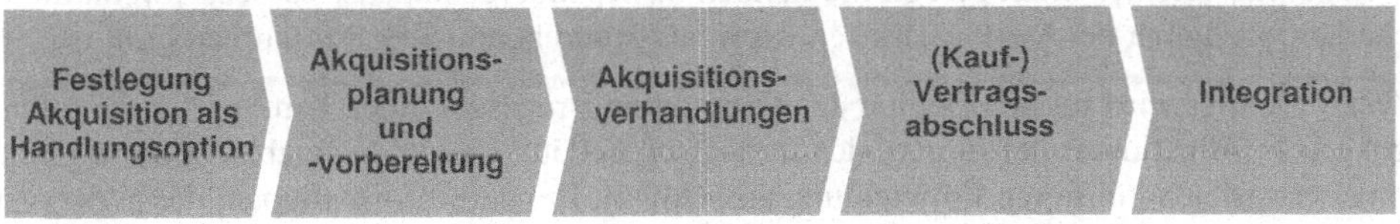

Abbildung 2: Phasen des Transaktionsprozesses aus Käufersicht

Zunächst trifft der Käufer die Entscheidung, mögliche Kaufobjekte zu identifizieren bzw. sein Interesse am Kauf eines bestimmten Transaktionsobjektes zu definieren (Phase I). Gründe hierfür können strategische Interessen wie beispielsweise die Umsetzung einer Wachstumsstrategie sein, die mit Hilfe einer oder mehrerer Akquisitionen realisiert werden soll.

Kaufplanung und -vorbereitung dienen der Informationsgewinnung über mögliche Kaufobjekte bzw. das konkrete Kaufobjekt (Phase II). Hierzu gehören beispielsweise Informationen über die Vermögens-, Finanz- und Ertragslage sowie die Verarbeitung öffentlich zugänglicher Informationen im Rahmen einer indikativen Bewertung des Transaktionsobjektes.

Nach Auswahl des Transaktionsobjektes und bei Verkaufsinteresse bzw. -bereitschaft des Eigentümers des Kaufobjektes treten die Parteien in Verhandlungen ein (Phase III). Der Käufer hat insbesondere Interesse daran, mehr als die öffentlich zugänglichen Informationen über das Transaktionsobjekt zu erhalten. Dies erleichtert dem Kaufinteressenten die Einschätzung der mit dem Erwerb verbundenen Chancen und Risiken. Die Informationssammlung erfolgt insbesondere in den Datenräumen und Fragerunden.

Dem Abschluss des Kaufvertrages (Phase IV) folgt die Integration des Transaktionsobjektes in die Organisationsstruktur des Käufers (Phase V). Dazu gehören beispielsweise die Einbindung in die IT-Landschaft und das Aufsetzen von Berichtsstrukturen und -formaten. Diese Phase beinhaltet auch die Verifizierung der während des Transaktionsprozesses bereitgestellten Informationen.

3 Systemgrenzen im Transaktionsprozess

3.1 Verkäuferseitige Systemgrenzen

Aus Sicht des Verkäufers sind zu Beginn eines Transaktionsprozesses zwei Informationsumfänge zu unterscheiden: die gegenüber einem potenziellen Käufer verdeckten Informationen und die offen gelegten Informationen. Verdeckte Informationen werden einem potenziellen Käufer nicht oder erst im Verlauf des Transaktionsprozesses offen gelegt. Gründe hierfür können in der Unwesentlichkeit der Information für die Transaktion liegen, aber auch in einer strategisch motivierten Informationspolitik gegenüber Kaufinteressenten.

Die verkäuferseitig verfügbaren Informationen enthalten die wesentlichen Erklärungsvariablen für die Entwicklung des Transaktionsobjektes in der Vergangenheit und die erwartete Entwicklung in der Zukunft. Strategisch wesentliche Erklärungsvariablen für die erwartete zukünftige Entwicklung des Transaktionsobjektes werden zu Beginn eines Transaktionsprozesses in der Regel nur selektiv offen gelegt. Sie bleiben insbesondere zunächst verdeckt, wenn die Unsicherheit bezüglich der Realisierbarkeit bspw. aufgrund begrenzter Ressourcen groß ist.[9]

Der Verkäufer wird für den Beginn des Transaktionsprozesses einen Umfang für die offen zu legenden Informationen definieren, der strategisch bedeutsame und sensible Erklärungsfaktoren der erwarteten künftigen Entwicklung ausschließt. Bei den Informationen, die in der ersten Phase eines Transaktionsprozesses bereitgestellt werden, handelt es sich üblicherweise um[10]

- die Jahresabschlüsse der letzten drei Geschäftsjahre;
- Kapitalflussrechnungen der Vergangenheit;
- aus dem externen Rechnungswesen abgeleitete Erfolgskennzahlen;
- Planungsparameter zum operativen Geschäft: Umsatzerlöse, Umsatzkosten, Veränderungen des Netto-Umlaufvermögens;
- Informationen zur Gesellschafterstruktur;
- Organigramm;
- Einschätzung zur Marktsituation und Marktposition des Transaktionsobjektes;
- Leistungsprogramm.

Diese Informationen stehen miteinander in Beziehung; bspw. werden Erfahrungen aus der Vergangenheit zur Herleitung von Planungsannahmen verwendet. Im Sinne des System-Dynamics-Ansatzes können diese Informationen daher auch als System verstanden werden.[11] Dadurch, dass im Rahmen eines Transaktionsprozesses verkäuferseitig Informationen verfügbar sind, die einem potenziellen Käufer zunächst nicht zugänglich gemacht werden, ergibt sich eine Informationsgrenze bzw. Systemgrenze. Erst im Verlauf des Transaktionsprozesses wird diese Systemgrenze zunehmend erweitert. Der Verkäufer legt Informationen offen zu

- dem Anlagevermögen wie beispielsweise verfügbare Kapazitäten, Alter der Vermögensgegenstände und Investitionsplanung;
- den zu einem bestimmten Stichtag bekannten rechtlichen und finanziellen Verpflichtungen (z. B. Haftung gegenüber Dritten, personalbezogene finanzielle Verpflichtungen, steuerliche Situation, Umweltthemen);
- der IT-Architektur des Transaktionsobjektes;
- dem Stand und der Bedeutung von Forschung und Entwicklung im Transaktionsobjekt;
- ausgewählten Erfolgskennzahlen des internen Rechnungswesens (z. B. Kapazitätsauslastung, personalbezogene Kennzahlen wie Fluktuation, Krankheitstand, Aufwand für Fort- und Weiterbildung);
- der Strategie-, Investitions- und Finanzplanung (meist aggregiert).

---

[9] Für einen Vergleich der Ansätze zur Kategorisierung von Ressourcen siehe beispielhaft Korten, Achim: Wirkung kompetenzorientierter Strategien auf den Unternehmenswert, Mannheim/Köln 2001, S. 25f.

[10] Für diese Aufzählung wird unterstellt, dass es sich bei dem Transaktionsobjekt um ein rechtlich selbständiges Unternehmen bzw. Anteile daran handelt („share deal"). Für den Fall des Verkaufes einzelner Vermögensgegenstände und Schulden („asset deal") werden vom Verkäufer teilweise andere Informationen bereitgestellt.

[11] Vgl. Forrester, Jay W.: Grundzüge einer Systemtheorie, deutsche Übersetzung, Wiesbaden, 1972, S. 9.

Außerhalb des offen gelegten Systems sind die Informationen, die (a) für die Transaktion unwesentlich sind, (b) aus Sicht des potenziellen Verkäufers signifikante Risiken für den Erfolg einer Transaktion darstellen (z. B. mögliche künftige Haftungsrisiken, Kenntnisse über einen vorhandenen Investitionsstau) oder (c) Wissen im Sinne eines schutzwürdigen strategischen Vorteils darstellen (z. B. exklusiver Ressourcenzugang, Grundlagenwissen aus der Forschung, besonders effektive und effiziente Fertigungsstrukturen).

Nachfolgende Abbildung veranschaulicht abstrakt sowohl den Unterschied zwischen den verkäuferseitig verfügbaren und den bereitgestellten Informationen als auch die Veränderung des Umfanges der bereitgestellten Informationen. In Phase III wird nur ein Teil der verfügbaren Informationen bereitgestellt; der Inhalt dieser Informationen definiert die Systemgrenze. Im Verlauf des Transaktionsprozesses erhöht sich der Umfang der bereitgestellten Informationen, so dass der Verkäufer in der Regel spätestens in Phase V alle transaktionsrelevanten Informationen bereitstellt, die er bereit ist zur Verfügung zu stellen. Der Umfang der zu dem Transaktionsobjekt verfügbaren Informationen ist erfahrungsgemäß auch am Ende des Transaktionsprozesses größer als der Umfang der verkäuferseitig bereitgestellten Informationen.

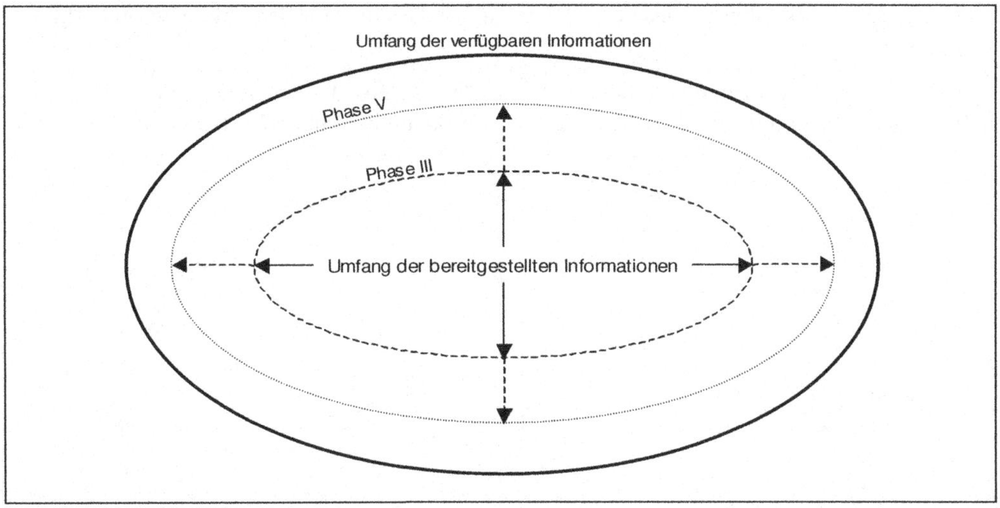

Abbildung 3: Veränderung der verkäuferseitigen Systemgrenze

3.2 Käuferseitige Systemgrenzen

Zu Beginn des Transaktionsprozesses verfügt ein Kaufinteressent zunächst über öffentlich zugängliche Informationen. Im Verlauf des Transaktionsprozesses gewinnt der potenzielle Käufer zusätzliche Erkenntnisse. Umfang und Geschwindigkeit dieses Zugewinns sind insbesondere von der Informationspolitik des potenziellen Verkäufers abhängig.

Darüber hinaus wird sich ein Kaufinteressent aus anderen Informationsquellen Kenntnisse über das Transaktionsobjekt aneignen. Dies dient zum einen dem besseren Verständnis der historischen Entwicklung des Objektes und dessen aktueller wirtschaftlicher Situation. Zum anderen ist dem Kaufinteressenten daran gelegen, eine möglichst gute Einschätzung der Chancen und Risiken der künftigen Entwicklung des Transaktionsobjektes vornehmen zu können. Durch den zunehmenden Erkenntnisgewinn wird die Systemgrenze zunehmend erweitert.

Der Art nach werden Kaufinteressenten in der Praxis in Finanzinvestoren und strategische Investoren unterschieden. Beiden gemeinsam ist das Interesse an der künftigen Ertragskraft des Transaktionsobjektes. Insbesondere für Finanzinvestoren ist dies bedeutsam, um mögliche Leverage-Effekte aus der Refinanzierung der Transaktion bzw. des Transaktionsobjektes einschätzen zu können.[12] Strategische Investoren interessieren neben der erzielbaren Rendite strategische Vorteile hinsichtlich der eigenen Marktposition bzw. der Ausgleich von strategischen Nachteilen im Vergleich zu Wettbewerbern.[13] Angesichts der unterschiedlichen Interessenlage ist bei der Ermittlung käuferseitiger Systemgrenzen die Art des Interessenten bedeutsam.

Während ein Finanzinvestor insbesondere finanzielle Aspekte im Fokus sieht, sind für einen strategischen Investor auch operationale Themen von Bedeutung. Der Nutzen einer Transaktion vermag für einen strategischen Investor in der Realisierung von Synergieeffekten in der Produktion, im Einkauf oder im Verkauf bestehen. Derartige Aspekte sind für den Finanzinvestor nachrangig. Daher ist die käuferseitige Systemgrenze eines strategischen Investors anders als die eines Finanzinvestors. Im Grundsatz ist zu erwarten, dass dies für den gesamten Transaktionsprozess gilt.

In Abbildung 4 ist illustrativ die käuferseitige Veränderung der Erkenntnisse über das Transaktionsobjekt dargestellt. In Phase II basieren die Erkenntnisse über das Transaktionsobjekt im

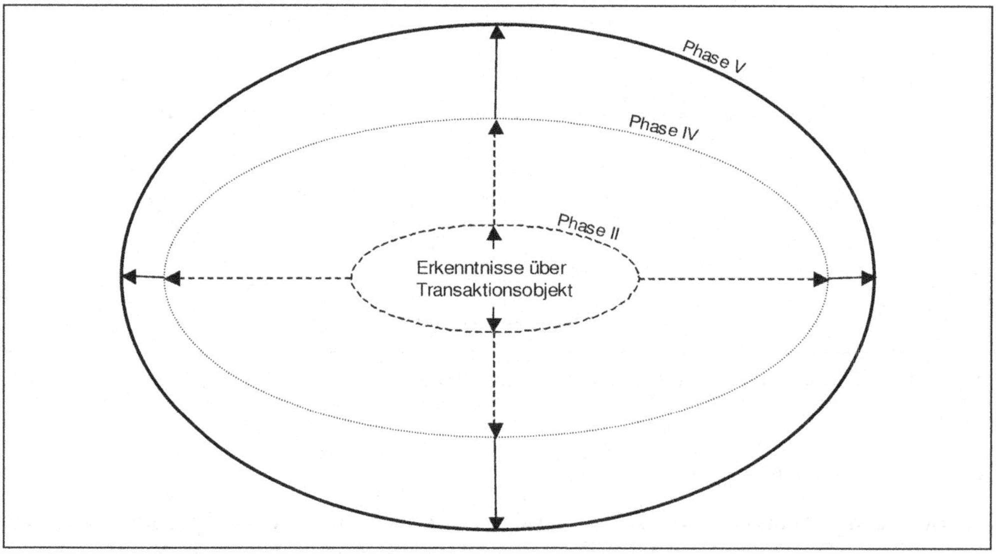

Abbildung 4: Veränderung der käuferseitigen Systemgrenze

[12] Der Leverage-Effekt bezeichnet die Hebelwirkung, die ein Unternehmen mit der Aufnahme von zusätzlichem Fremdkapital zu günstigeren Konditionen erzielt, als die mit diesem Kapital finanzierte Investition an Rendite erbringt.

[13] Beispielsweise eine Ressourcenlücke im strategischen Sinne. Siehe auch Korten, Achim: Wirkung kompetenzorientierter Strategien, S. 29 f.

Wesentlichen auf öffentlich zugänglichen Informationen. In den Phasen III und IV erhöhen sich die Erkenntnisse aufgrund der verkäuferseitig bereitgestellten Informationen. In Phase V werden diese Erkenntnisse weiter gesteigert; es ist sogar vorstellbar, dass die Erkenntnisse über das Transaktionsobjekt auf Seiten des Käufers größer sind als die verkäuferseitig verfügbaren Informationen. Eine Erklärung kann sein, dass der Käufer potenzielle Synergie- und Effizienzsteigerungspotenziale identifiziert hat, die der Verkäufer nicht realisieren kann oder nicht erkannt hat.

3.3 Dynamik der Systemgrenzen

Während eines Transaktionsprozesses kommt es zu Veränderungen in den jeweiligen Systemgrenzen. Potenzielle Käufer analysieren die bereitgestellten Informationen. Sich hieraus ergebende Fragen werden an den potenziellen Verkäufer adressiert. Der Verkäufer entscheidet, welche der Fragen in welchem Umfang beantwortet werden.

Sowohl Verkäufer als auch Käufer definieren nach eigenen Kriterien, welche Informationen bereitgestellt bzw. abgefragt werden. Diese Kriterien stellen die Erklärungsvariablen für die Veränderung der Systemgrenzen dar. Potenzielle Käufer verlieren mitunter das Interesse an einem Transaktionsobjekt aufgrund zögerlicher Informationsbereitstellung durch den Verkäufer. Potenzielle Verkäufer zögern bspw. mit der Bereitstellung von Informationen, wenn sie über die Motive eines potenziellen Käufers verunsichert sind.[14] Informationen werden auch dann nur zögerlich bereitgestellt, wenn Verkäufer befürchten, dass ein potenzieller Käufer in Kenntnis der Informationen das Interesse am Transaktionsobjekt verliert, der Verkäufer jedoch unter Verkaufsdruck steht, oder der erzielbare Verkaufspreis für das Transaktionsobjekt geringer ausfallen könnte.

Diese Überlegungen skizzieren, dass die Dynamik der Systemgrenzen durchaus unterschiedliche Verläufe nehmen kann. Welches die wesentlichen treibenden Einflussgrößen dahinter sind und ob sich generische Strategien des Informationsverhaltens ermitteln lassen, wird mit herkömmlichen wissenschaftlichen Methoden nur schwer zu analysieren sein. Doch gerade an diesem Punkt kann für Forschungszwecke eine Stärke von System Dynamics zum Tragen kommen: Als Allgemeine Strukturtheorie ist System Dynamics in besonderem Maße geeignet, komplexe und nicht-lineare Zusammenhänge wie die innerhalb eines Transaktionsprozesses abzubilden und zu analysieren.[15] Abbildung 5 (s. S. 160) skizziert beispielhaft mögliche Verläufe für die Verschiebung der Systemgrenzen auf Seiten von Verkäufer und Käufer.

An die Untersuchung der Einflussgrößen auf die Dynamik der Systemgrenze gekoppelt ist die Frage, was aus systemischer Sicht überhaupt innerhalb der Systemgrenzen liegen soll, d.h. welches überhaupt die wesentlichen Informationen für einen Transaktionsprozess sind. Insbesondere dann, wenn es um die Frage geht, welche Informationsstrategien im Rahmen eines Transaktionsprozesses unter welcher Zielsetzung erfolgreicher für den potenziellen Verkäufer sein könnten als andere.

[14] Bspw. könnte das Interesse des potenziellen Käufers auf die Gewinnung von wettbewerbsrelevanten Informationen zielen, die dann für eigene Zwecke wie bspw. andere Portfoliogesellschaften oder Transaktionszielobjekte eines Finanzinvestors nutzbringend eingesetzt werden.

[15] Vgl. Forrester, Jay W.: Industrial Dynamics, 4. Auflage, Cambridge 1965, S. 15.

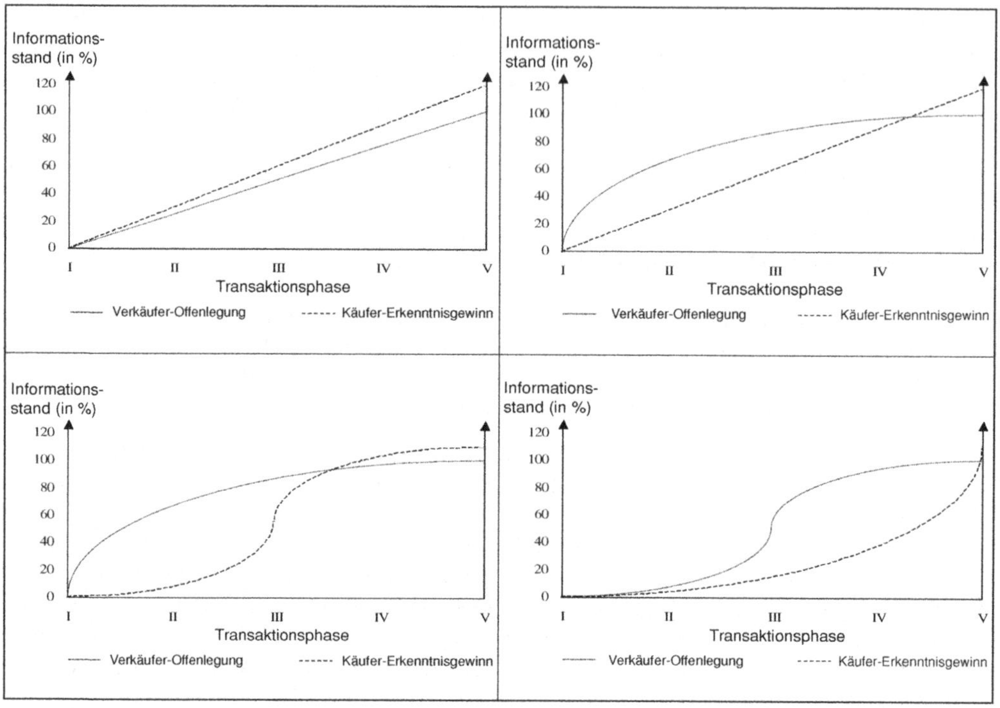

Abbildung 5: Veränderung des Informationsstandes von Käufer und Verkäufer

Bereits im Hinblick auf die Zusammenarbeit des potenziellen Verkäufers mit dem Transaktionsobjekt stellt die Wahl der Informationsstrategie ein Problem dar. Sei es, dass der potenzielle Verkäufer das Management des Transaktionsobjektes über die Verkaufsabsicht nicht informieren möchte. Sei es, dass das Management des Transaktionsobjektes an einem Verkauf an einen fremden Dritten kein Interesse hat.

Denn handelt es sich um eine seitens des Managements des Transaktionsobjektes nicht gewollte Transaktion, werden Informationen bereits gegenüber dem potenziellen Verkäufer zögerlicher offen gelegt als im Fall einer vom Management gewünschten Transaktion. Dies ist beispielsweise zu erwarten, wenn das Management des Transaktionsobjektes einen Management-Buy-out anstrebt, die Muttergesellschaft als Verkäufer jedoch einen fremden Dritten als Käufer bevorzugt. In solch einem Fall definiert zunächst das Management des Transaktionsobjektes die Systemgrenze; diese kann unter den genannten Umständen enger sein als es der potenzielle Verkäufer zur Realisierung seiner angestrebten Informationsstrategie gegenüber potenziellen Käufern erwartet.

Vorstehende Überlegungen deuten an, dass aus Sicht des potenziellen Verkäufers zwei dynamische Prozesse hinsichtlich der Systemgrenzen relevant sein können: Zum einen kann es bereits zwischen dem Transaktionsobjekt und dem potenziellen Verkäufer ein Informationsungleichgewicht geben. Zum anderen bestehen typischerweise Informationsasymmetrien zwischen dem potenziellen Verkäufer eines Transaktionsobjektes und potenziellen Käufern.

Erfahrungen in der Praxis zeigen, dass mitunter monetäre (quantitative) Anreizmechanismen eingesetzt werden, um qualitative Informationsasymmetrien zu reduzieren. System Dynamics bietet Methoden, derartige Zusammenhänge von quantitativen und qualitativen Variablen abbilden und analysieren zu können. Dabei könnten beispielsweise wesentliche Einflussfaktoren und Verzögerungseffekte auf die Systemgrenzen untersucht werden.

Gegenstand von System-Dynamics-basierten Analysen zu Transaktionsprozessen könnte auch sein, welches die Erfolgsfaktoren für einen effizienten Transaktionsprozess hinsichtlich Zeit, Qualität und Kosten sowohl aus Verkäufer- als auch aus Käufersicht darstellen. Zusätzliche Erkenntnisgewinne könnten sich aus der Unterscheidung auf Käuferseite in Finanzinvestor und strategischen Investor ergeben; wie bereits ausgeführt, folgen Finanzinvestoren einem anderen Zielsystem als strategische Investoren.

4 Validierung von Planungsmodellen

Typischerweise werden während eines Transaktionsprozesses von einem potenziellen Verkäufer Informationen zur prognostizierten Ertragskraft des Transaktionsobjektes offen gelegt. Dies geschieht regelmäßig in Form eines Planungsmodells. Idealerweise handelt es sich dabei um integrierte Planungsrechnungen, d. h. dass die Rückkopplungsbeziehungen zwischen Gewinn- und Verlustrechnung, Bilanz und Kapitalflussrechnung strukturell und rechnerisch berücksichtigt sind.

Die Transaktionspraxis zeigt, dass die offen gelegten Planungsmodelle häufig nicht integriert sind; d. h. dass die Auswirkungen von Änderungen in Planungsannahmen nicht durchgängig im Modell gerechnet werden. Es handelt sich dann um statische Modelle, die nicht dahingehend überprüfbar sind, ob die wesentlichen Zusammenhänge in den für das externe Rechnungswesen relevanten Bereichen vollständig oder gar richtig dargestellt sind. Solche Modelle ermöglichen nur sehr eingeschränkte Modelltests; deren Nutzen für strategische Überlegungen seitens eines Kaufinteressenten sind als gering einzuschätzen.

Interessanter für strategische Überlegungen sind integrierte Planungsmodelle. Wie die aktuelle Transaktionspraxis zeigt, steigen diesbezüglich die Ansprüche von Banken in Richtung Investoren. Im Zusammenhang mit der Kreditvergabeentscheidung werden zunehmend integrierte Planungsmodelle verlangt, die überhaupt erst die Abbildung von Zukunftsszenarien und Sensitivitäten ermöglichen. Solche flexiblen und integrierten Planungsmodelle sind sehr viel nützlicher bei der Einschätzung der mit einer Transaktion verbundenen Chancen und Risiken als statische Modelle.

Sofern potenzielle Verkäufer nicht bereits solch ein integriertes Planungsmodell bereitstellen, sind Kaufinteressenten gezwungen, selbst das bereitgestellte statische Planungsmodell in ein flexibles integriertes Planungsmodell zu überführen. In beiden Fällen verlangen Banken zunehmend die Durchsicht des Planungsmodells durch einen unabhängigen Dritten. Bei solchen Modelltests kommen implizit Verfahren zum Einsatz, wie sie aus System Dynamics bekannt sind.

4.1 Validierungen im Transaktionsprozess

Gegenstand von Validierungen in einem Transaktionsprozess sind die bereitgestellten Daten und verfügbaren Informationen über ein Transaktionsobjekt. Bei einer „Due Diligence“ werden diese Daten und Informationen detailliert und systematisch analysiert. Ziele dieser Untersuchungen sind das Aufzeigen der für die potenzielle Transaktion wesentlichen Einflussfaktoren sowie der mit der Akquise des Transaktionsobjektes verbundenen Chancen und Risiken.[16] Die im Rahmen einer „Due Diligence" gewonnenen Erkenntnisse sollen „zur Erhöhung der Qualität der Entscheidungen und Maßnahmen auf betriebswirtschaftlicher, steuerlicher und juristischer Ebene"[17] während des Transaktionsprozesses beitragen.

Dies geschieht nach standardisierten Fragestellungen, jedoch sowohl inhaltlich als auch vom Umfang her individuell auf die Transaktionssituation zugeschnitten. Sämtliche Fragestellungen zielen darauf ab, Chancen und Risiken zu identifizieren, die mit einem Erwerb des Transaktionsobjektes verbunden sind. Damit werden sowohl Fragen einer ressourcen- als auch einer marktorientierten Sicht auf ein Transaktionsobjekt abgedeckt.[18]

Als bedeutendste Fragestellungen für eine „Due Diligence" werden folgende Schwerpunkte unterschieden:[19]

- Finanzielle „Due Diligence": Analyse von vergangenheits- und zukunftsbezogenen Finanzdaten des Transaktionsobjektes (z. B. Jahresabschlüsse, Planungsrechnungen).
- Kommerzielle „Due Diligence": Analyse von Marktumfeld und -stellung, Unternehmensstrategie, Geschäftsmodell.
- Steuerliche „Due Diligence": Analyse der steuerlichen Belange des Transaktionsobjektes und der steuerlichen Gestaltungsoptionen der Transaktion.
- Rechtliche „Due Diligence": Analyse der rechtlichen Rahmenbedingungen wie beispielsweise mögliche Haftungs- und Gewährleistungsansprüche Dritter gegenüber dem Transaktionsobjekt.

Darüber hinaus gibt es „Due Diligence"-Prüfungen zu Einzelthemen wie beispielsweise Umwelt, Personalwesen, Versicherungen, Produktion, Organisation etc. Laut empirischer Untersuchungen sind diese Themen jedoch weniger häufig als die zuvor genannten.[20]

4.2 Validierungsansätze für Planungsmodelle

Planungsmodelle bieten unterschiedliche Ansätze der Validierung. Im Kontext von Transaktionen nennt Prüher-von Au folgende Validierungsschwerpunkte: Neben der Analyse der Modellstrukturen auf ihre Angemessenheit sind dies die analytische Durchsicht der Modellergebnisse auf Plausibilität und insbesondere die Prüfung der rechnerischen Richtigkeit und Integrität des Modells.[21] Optional schlägt er die Prüfung bzw. Plausibilisierung rechnungslegungsbezogener und steuerrechtlicher Planungsannahmen vor.

[16] Vgl. Institut der Wirtschaftsprüfer in Deutschland e.V. (Hrsg.): WP Handbuch 2008 Band II, S. 1079.

[17] Ebenda, S. 1079.

[18] Vgl. Korten, Achim: Wirkung kompetenzorientierter Strategien, S. 4 ff.

[19] Vgl. Institut der Wirtschaftsprüfer in Deutschland e.V. (Hrsg.): WP Handbuch 2008 Band II, S. 1080–1081.

[20] Vgl. Marten, Kai-Uwe und Annette G. Köhler: Due Diligence in Deutschland, in: Der Finanzbetrieb, 1999, 1. Jg., Nr. 11/1999, S. 339.

[21] Vgl. Prüher-von Au, Markus: Beitrag in: Schramm, Margot et al. (Hrsg.): Transaktionshandbuch, Veröffentlichung in Vorbereitung.

Alle diese Prüfungen decken einen Teil der Modelltests ab, die Forrester/Senge für die Prüfung von System-Dynamics-Modellen vorschlagen.[22] Sie unterscheiden mögliche Tests in die Kategorien Modellstruktur, Modellverhalten und Abbildung alternativer Strategien:

- Modellstruktur: Strukturvalidierung, Parametervalidierung, Extremwerttest, Angemessenheit der Systemgrenze, Dimensionstest.
- Modellverhalten: Nachbildung historischen Verhaltens, Vorhersage zukünftigen Verhaltens, Unregelmäßigkeiten, Übertragbarkeit, unerwartete Veränderungen, Extremwerttest, Angemessenheit der Systemgrenze, Verhaltenssensitivität.
- Abbildung alternativer Strategien: Systemverbesserungen, Vorhersage von Verhaltensänderungen, Angemessenheit der Systemgrenze, Alternativensensitivität.

Wie die Praxis zeigt, liegt der Fokus bei der Prüfung der Modellstruktur auf der Struktur- und Parametervalidierung. Insbesondere die als Option von Prüher-von Au erwähnten Prüfungen rechnungslegungsbezogener und steuerrechtlicher Planungsannahmen dienen der Parametervalidierung. Die Durchführbarkeit von Extremwerttests von Planungsmodellen ist dadurch limitiert, dass im Rahmen von Transaktionen nicht immer integrierte Planungsmodelle bereitgestellt werden. Das heißt dass die Interdependenzen von Gewinn- und Verlustrechnung, Bilanz und Kapitalflussrechnung unvollständig im Sinne von nicht automatisiert abgebildet sind.

Dimensionstests sind insbesondere dann erforderlich, wenn Planungsmodelle Treiberstrukturen im Sinne von Preis-Mengen-Gerüsten enthalten. Gegenstand der Dimensionstests sind ggf. Überprüfungen der Umrechnung von Produktionsmengen in Verkaufsmengen. Beispielhaft sei ein Hersteller von chemischen Flüssigkeiten genannt, der seine Produktionsmenge in Litern ermittelt, den Absatz jedoch in Verpackungseinheiten unterschiedlicher Größe (Stück) bemisst. Nur wenn diese Details integriert in der Planung enthalten sind, sind Dimensionstests erforderlich.

Die anderen von Prüher-von Au vorgeschlagenen Schwerpunkte der Validierung sind in Anlehnung an Forrester/Senge der Kategorie der Verhaltenstests zuzuordnen. Sowohl die Plausibilitätsprüfung der Modellergebnisse als auch die Prüfung der rechnerischen Richtigkeit dienen der Feststellbarkeit, ob die Berechnungsalgorithmen dazu geeignet sind, die Ergebnisse der Vergangenheit zu reproduzieren bzw. künftige Ergebnisse rechnerisch richtig zu ermitteln. Planungsmodelle, wie sie in Transaktionssituationen erstellt bzw. verwendet werden, sind nicht dazu bestimmt, zukünftiges Modellverhalten auf Basis endogener Planungsparameter vorherzusagen. Sie dienen vielmehr dazu, zu zeigen, welcher Modellzustand sich ergibt, wenn gewisse Entwicklungen für die Zukunft unterstellt werden; in transaktionsbezogenen Planungsmodellen sind die Planungsparameter exogene Größen im Sinne einer ‚wenn dann'-Bedingung. Es handelt sich nicht um veränderbare Variablen im Sinne einer Anpassungsfähigkeit, um einen angestrebten Modellzustand zu erreichen.

Ein in Transaktionsprozessen mitunter vernachlässigter Verhaltenstest für Planungsmodelle sind Sensitivitätsanalysen. Angesichts der Verwendung von exogenen Planungsparametern stellen Sensitivitätsanalysen jedoch eine nützliche Unterstützung bei der Entwicklung oder Prüfung von transaktionsbezogenen Planungsmodellen dar. Insbesondere im Hinblick auf die angestreb-

[22] Vgl. Forrester, Jay W. und Peter M. Senge: Tests for building confidence in System Dynamics Models, in: Legasto, Augusto A, Forrester, Jay und James M. Lyneis (Hrsg.): System Dynamics, New York 1980, S. 209–228.

te Beurteilung von Chancen und Risiken einer Transaktion können Sensitivitätstests hilfreiche Erkenntnisse liefern.

Die von Forrester/Senge vorgeschlagene Überprüfung der allgemeinen Aussagekraft eines (Planungs-)Modells für vergleichbare Systeme dürfte insbesondere dem potenziellen Käufer möglich sein, der detaillierte Kenntnis oder direkten Zugang zu einem vergleichbaren System hat. Im Falle einer potenziellen Unternehmenstransaktion kann dies eine zukünftige Schwestergesellschaft oder ein Wettbewerber ein. Mitunter kann hierzu auch auf Analysen zu Branchenkennzahlen zurück gegriffen werden.

Die Vorschläge von Prüher-von Au können um Tests von Strategieauswirkungen im Sinne von Forrester/Senge ergänzt werden. In der Transaktionspraxis werden hierunter Szenarioanalysen verstanden. Beobachtungen zeigen, dass im Rahmen von Transaktionen insbesondere Finanzierungsszenarien gerechnet werden. Diese sind regelmäßig erforderlich zur Evaluierung steuerlicher Gestaltungsoptionen und – für den Fall, dass es sich bei dem potenziellen Käufer um einen Finanzinvestor handelt – von Ausstiegsmöglichkeiten bei einem Investment. Strategieauswirkungen, die beispielsweise aus Änderungen in der Produktionsstruktur, den genutzten Vertriebskanälen, der Preispolitik oder Standortverlagerungen resultieren, werden während des Transaktionsprozesses häufig nicht oder nur sehr rudimentär in den Planungsrechnungen als Alternativszenario berücksichtigt. Häufig werden derartige Überlegungen erst nach Abschluss einer Transaktion konkreter analysiert bzw. quantifiziert.

Ergebnis dieser Analysen soll am Ende keine Aussage à la „richtig oder falsch" sein was das Eintreten der Planzahlen betrifft: „Grundsätzlich kann gesagt werden: Ein Modell ist sinnvoll konstruiert und hat sich bewährt, wenn es den ihm gesetzten Zweck erfüllt".[23] Die Durchführung von Tests zur Validierung von transaktionsbezogenen Planungsmodellen zielt auf die Feststellung, ob das Planungsmodell und die darin getroffenen Annahmen transparent und nachvollziehbar sind. Damit implizit verbunden ist eine Bestätigung, ob das Planungsmodell geeignet ist für eine „bessere prospektive Beurteilung von Effektivität und Effizienz möglicher unternehmenspolitischer Maßnahmen".[24] Darüber hinaus ist eine Aussage möglich, ob die Berechnungen in dem Modell (technisch betrachtet) zu richtigen Ergebnissen führen. Aussagen zur inhaltlichen Plausibilität von Planungsannahmen können mittels o. g. Tests nicht getroffen werden.

Es bleibt festzuhalten, dass Forrester/Senge Testverfahren vorschlagen, die ergänzend zu den von Prüher-von Au genannten Verfahren nutzbringend in der Transaktionspraxis eingesetzt werden können. Der Umfang ihres Einsatzes ist an Kosten-Nutzen-Überlegungen zu koppeln.

5 Systemdenken im Transaktionsprozess

Vorstehende Ausführungen skizzieren verschiedene Ansatzpunkte für System-Dynamics-basierte Forschung auf dem Gebiet der Unternehmenstransaktionen. Nicht nur Fragen zu den wesentlichen Einflussgrößen auf die Dynamik von Informations- bzw. Systemgrenzen und die Auswahl von Methoden zur Validierung von Planungsmodellen bieten diese Ansatzpunkte.

[23] Milling, Peter: Systemtheoretische Grundlagen zur Planung der Unternehmenspolitik, S. 168.

[24] Ebenda, S. 179.

Interessant ist auch die Frage, ob sich generische Verhaltensmuster in Transaktionsprozessen ermitteln lassen, die maßgeblich den Erfolg oder Misserfolg von Verkäufer und Käufer in einem Transaktionsprozess beeinflussen. Erfolg bezieht sich in diesem Fall auf den tatsächlichen Abschluss des Verkaufs bzw. den Kauf eines Transaktionsobjektes. Zahlreiche Transaktionen scheitern bereits während des Transaktionsprozesses – z. B. weil ein Verkäufer seine Verkaufsabsicht aufgegeben hat, oder weil ein potenzieller Käufer während des Transaktionsprozesses zu der Auffassung gelangt, das angesichts der bereitgestellten Informationen erkennbar wird, dass die potenzielle Akquisition nicht im erwarteten Maß zur Erreichung der angestrebten Ziele beiträgt.

Die Praxis zeigt Beispiele, bei denen sich eine Akquisition erst nach Abschluss des Transaktionsprozesses als Fehlentscheidung herausstellt. Ursache hierfür können Verkaufs-/Kaufentscheidungen aufgrund zu geringer Informationen sein. Lässt sich mit Hilfe von System-Dynamics-basierten Analysen eine Theorie über die Determinanten des erfolgreichen Abschlusses von Transaktionsprozessen bzw. von Transaktionen im Allgemeinen entwickeln?

Neben systemtheoretisch motivierten Untersuchungen bieten sich empirische Studien an. Darin könnte es z. B. um in der Praxis angewandte Verfahren zur Validierung gehen: Welche Verfahren zur Validierung von Planungsmodellen werden in welcher Häufigkeit angewendet? Gibt es Unterschiede in Abhängigkeit von Branche oder Unternehmensgröße? Zudem könnten Studien interessant sein zu der Frage, inwieweit die Dauer des Transaktionsprozesses und die Qualität der Ergebnisse Relevanz besitzen für die sich dem Vertragsabschluss anschließende Separations- bzw. Integrationsphase. Gleichfalls interessant könnte die Frage sein, inwieweit Verkäufer und/oder Käufer nach einer nicht abgeschlossenen Transaktion die Gründe hierfür untersuchen, welche Gründe identifiziert werden und welche Konsequenzen dies für das eigene Verhalten in nachfolgenden Transaktionen hat.

Der Nutzen, der sich aus dem Tragen der System-Dynamics-Brille bei der Sicht auf dynamische und komplexe Themenstellungen ergibt, ist unbestritten (zumindest in der System-Dynamics-Society). Die Vielfalt der komplexen betriebswirtschaftlichen Fragestellungen, im Kontext derer System Dynamics als ein Lösungsansatz genannt wird, zeigt die Leistungsfähigkeit dieser Theorie bei der Strukturierung und Analyse von Informationen sowie bei dem Bestreben, die Dynamik komplexer Systeme besser verstehen und damit auch effektiver gestalten zu können.[25]

Literatur

Forrester, J. W. (1972): *Grundzüge einer Systemtheorie*, deutsche Übersetzung, Wiesbaden.

Forrester, J. W. (1965): *Industrial Dynamics, 4. Aufl.*, Cambridge.

Forrester, J. W. und P. M. Senge (1980): Tests for building confidence in System Dynamics Models, in: Legasto, A. A., J. Forrester und J. M. Lyneis (Hrsg.): *System Dynamics*, New York, S. 209–228.

Gary, M. S. et al. (2008): *System Dynamics and Strategy*, Working Paper 2008, available at SSRN.

Holzapfel, H.-J. und R. Pöllath (2006): *Unternehmenskauf in Recht und Praxis, 12. Aufl.*, Köln.

[25] Vgl. Milling, Peter: Systemtheoretische Grundlagen zur Planung der Unternehmenspolitik, S. 184.

Institut der Wirtschaftsprüfer in Deutschland e.V. (Hrsg.) (2007): *WP Handbuch 2008 Wirtschaftsprüfung, Rechnungslegung, Beratung Band II*, Düsseldorf.

Institut der Wirtschaftsprüfer in Deutschland e.V. (Hrsg.) (2007): *WP Handbuch 2008 Band II*, Düsseldorf.

Korten, A. (2001): *Wirkung kompetenzorientierter Strategien auf den Unternehmenswert*, Mannheim/Köln.

Marten, K.-U. und A. G. Köhler (1999): Due Diligence in Deutschland, in: *Der Finanzbetrieb*, Jg. 1, Nr. 11, S. 337–348.

Milling, P. (1984): Leitmotive des System-Dynamics-Ansatzes, in: *Wirtschaftswissenschaftliches Studium*, Jg. 13, Nr. 10, S. 507–513.

Milling, P. (1981): *Systemtheoretische Grundlagen zur Planung der Unternehmenspolitik*, Berlin.

Prüher-von Au, M.: Beitrag in: Schramm, M. et al. (Hrsg.): *Transaktionshandbuch*, Veröffentlichung in Vorbereitung.

Fehlteilmanagement als Herausforderung für Industriebetriebe

Jörn-Henrik Thun[1], *Martin Drüke*[2] *und Daniel Hoenig*[1]

[1] Industrieseminar der Universität Mannheim, Mannheim
[2] Logistics Planning & Services John Deere Werke Mannheim, Mannheim

Zusammenfassung

Industriebetriebe sind aufgrund gestiegener Kundenanforderungen gezwungen, an den Kundenbedürfnissen ausgerichtete Produkte bzw. eine große Anzahl verschiedener Produktvarianten anzubieten, woraus die Notwendigkeit, eine hohe Varietät von Teilen zu produzieren, resultiert. Mit dieser Varietät geht ein häufigeres Auftreten von Fehlteilen in industriellen Produktionsprozessen einher, da diesen Entwicklungen eine gestiegene Komplexität bei gleichzeitiger Verschlankung durch den Einsatz von Lean Production in den zugrundeliegenden Prozessen inhärent ist. Ziel des vorliegenden Beitrags ist es, neben der Darstellung der aus dem Auftreten von Fehlteilen resultierenden Herausforderungen für Industriebetriebe Ursprünge von Fehlteilen in modernen Produktionssystemen zu identifizieren. Ebenso werden mögliche Ursachen sowie deren Konsequenzen für industrielle Wertschöpfungsprozesse herausgearbeitet, wobei zwischen internen und externen Ursachen zu differenzieren ist. Darüber hinaus diskutiert der Beitrag Potenziale präventiver und reaktiver Maßnahmen, um so einen konzeptionellen Rahmen für das Fehlteilmanagement zu entwickeln. Basierend auf diesem Rahmen werden Implikationen für ein effektives Fehlteilmanagement abgeleitet.

Schlagwörter: Fehlteile, Produktion, Risikomanagement, Wertschöpfungsprozesse

1 Bedeutung von Fehlteilen in modernen Produktionssystemen

Industrielle Unternehmen sehen sich mit Entwicklungen konfrontiert, die erhöhte Anforderungen an die Fertigung nach sich ziehen. Moderne Produktionssysteme sind demnach häufig durch einen hohen Grad an Komplexität charakterisiert. Um sich von Konkurrenten zu differenzieren, ist es für Industriebetriebe, die in Märkten mit hoher Wettbewerbsintensität agieren, essentiell, stark an den Kundenbedürfnissen ausgerichtete Produkte anzubieten. Gestiegene Kundenanforderungen führen aufgrund der damit einhergehenden Novität und Vielfalt der anzubietenden Erzeugnisse zu einer Zunahme des Spektrums an Produkten.[1] Als Konsequenz resultiert die Notwendigkeit, oftmals auch eine hohe Varietät der Teile zu produzieren, womit ein hoher Komplexitätsgrad in der Fertigung einhergeht. Des Weiteren steigert die Entwicklung zur schlanken Produktion die Komplexität, da damit zwar einerseits die Realisierung signifikanter Effizienzpotenziale verbunden ist, andererseits damit jedoch aufgrund nahezu gänzlich feh-

[1] Vgl. Milling, Peter und Jörn-Henrik Thun: Steigerung der Flexibilität in Produktionsprozessen durch integrative Fertigung, in: Kaluza, Bernd und Thorsten Blecker (Hrsg.): Erfolgsfaktor Flexibilität – Strategien und Konzepte für wandlungsfähige Unternehmen, Berlin 2005, S. 253.

lender Möglichkeiten zur Kompensation von Produktionsstörungen erhebliche Anforderungen an die Zuverlässigkeit der Produktion einhergehen. Eines der Probleme, die in derartigen Produktionssystemen entstehen können, ist das Auftreten von Fehlteilen.

Die Bedeutung eines effektiven Fehlteilmanagements kann anhand eines einfachen Rechenbeispiels illustriert werden: Für die Fertigung eines Produktes seien zehn Komponenten zu verbauen; darüber hinaus wird angenommen, dass jede Komponente mit einer Wahrscheinlichkeit von p = 0,95 verfügbar ist. Dies hätte zur Folge, dass das Produkt nur mit einer Wahrscheinlichkeit von weniger als 60% gefertigt werden kann.[2] Bei komplexeren Produkten wie z. B. im Fahrzeugbau müssen mehrere Tausend Teile verbaut werden.[3] Selbst eine Verfügbarkeit der Teile von 99,99% würde unter Ausschluss von Kompensationsmöglichkeiten implizieren, dass ein Fahrzeug mit 10.000 Teilen nur mit einer Wahrscheinlichkeit von 36,78% gefertigt werden würde.

Risiken von Fehlteilen basieren oftmals auf komplexen Ursache-Wirkungs-Beziehungen. Unternehmen können als komplexe Systeme verstanden werden, in denen unterschiedliche Elemente zusammenwirken; ihr Verhalten ist von vielfältigen Faktoren beeinflusst und kaum exakt vorauszusagen.[4] Die Analyse der Gründe für das Auftreten von Fehlteilen wird darüber hinaus dadurch erschwert, dass die dem System zugrunde liegenden Strukturen häufigen Änderungen unterworfen sind und zusätzliche Abhängigkeiten auftreten.[5]

Gerade im Hinblick auf externe Quellen für Fehlteile ist auf die engere Vernetzung von Wertschöpfungsnetzen hinzuweisen, die zunehmend störanfälliger geworden sind.[6] Diese Störanfälligkeit ist auf die verstärkte Fokussierung auf Kosteneffizienz und auf den Ansatz der Lean Production zurückzuführen. So sind Konzepte wie das Just-in-Time oder Just-in-Sequence in der Automobilindustrie weit verbreitete Konzepte, um das Effizienzstreben umzusetzen.[7] Diese Ansätze reduzieren zum einen die Kapitalbindung und erhöhen somit den Cashflow, zum anderen vermindern sie den Bedarf an Lagerfläche in einem Industriebetrieb. Gleichzeitig konzentrieren sich Manager von Wertschöpfungsnetzen stark auf die Verbesserung der Kosteneffizienz.[8] Durch die Reduktion von Beständen entstehen schlanke Wertschöpfungsnetze, die dadurch jedoch auch störanfälliger werden und so zum Auftreten von Fehlteilen führen: „The leaner and

---

[2] Vgl. Hopp, Wallace J. und Mark L. Spearman: Factory Physics – Foundations of Manufacturing Management, 2. Aufl., Boston et al. 2000, S. 399ff.

[3] Wenn gewährleistet sein soll, dass das Produkt mit einer Wahrscheinlichkeit von 95% gefertigt werden kann, müsste in diesem Beispiel die Verfügbarkeit der Teile bei p = 0,9949 liegen.

[4] Vgl. Milling, Peter: Strategische Planungs- und Kontrollsysteme zur Unterstützung betrieblicher Lernprozesse, in: Milling, Peter (Hrsg.): Systemmanagement und Managementsysteme, Berlin 1991, S. 11.

[5] Vgl. Harland, Christine, Richard C. Lamming und Paul D. Cousins: Developing the concept of supply strategy, in: International Journal of Operations & Production Management, Vol. 19 (1999), No. 7, S. 669.

[6] Vgl. Zsisidin, George A., Gary L. Ragatz und Steven A. Melnyk: The dark side of supply chain management, in: Supply Chain Management Review, Vol. 9 (2005), No. 2, S. 46.

[7] Vgl. Svensson, Göran: Key areas, causes and contingency planning of corporate vulnerability in supply chains, in: International Journal of Physical Distribution & Logistics Management, Vol. 34 (2004), No. 9, S. 732. Vgl. zum Just-in-Time Wildemann, Horst: Das Just-in-Time Konzept – Produktion und Zulieferung auf Abruf, 4. Aufl., München 1995. Vgl. zum Just-in-Sequence Thun, Jörn-Henrik, Martin Drüke und Victor Silveira Camargos: Just in Sequence – Eine Erweiterung des Just in Time durch Sequenzzulieferung, in: Logistik Management, 9. Jg (2007), Nr. 4, S. 34–46.

[8] Vgl. Lee, Hau L.: The Triple-A Supply Chain, in: Harvard Business Review, Vol. 82 (2004), No. 10, S. 102.

more integrated supply chains get, the more likely uncertainties, dynamics and accidents in one link affect the other links in the chain."[9]

Eine weitere Ursache für das vermehrte Auftreten von Fehlteilen ist im Outsourcing einzelner Stufen der Wertschöpfung zu sehen.[10] Die Ausgliederung von Teilen der Produktion an externe Unternehmen resultiert in Abhängigkeiten und einer Komplexitätssteigerung des Wertschöpfungsnetzes, das aufgrund der gestiegenen Zahl an Schnittstellen verwundbarer ist.[11] Auch steigert der Trend zur Globalisierung das Risiko von Fehlteilen, da sich das Wertschöpfungsnetz geografisch ausweitet. „Durch die weltweite Vernetzung können Ereignisse in fernen Ländern und Erdteilen die Wertschöpfungsprozesse in anderen Regionen teilweise erheblich beeinträchtigen."[12] Große geografische Streuung kann z. B. zu erhöhten Transportrisiken, kulturellen Risiken und Wechselkursrisiken führen.[13] So können beispielsweise zollrechtliche Bestimmungen aber auch Sicherheitsbestimmungen erhebliche Verzögerungen in der Supply Chain verursachen, welche in den vergangen Jahren aufgrund des internationalen Terrorismus deutlich zugenommen haben. Ebenso lässt der anhaltende Trend zum Single Sourcing das Risiko des Auftretens von Fehlteilen erhöhen, da zwar Kostensenkungen realisiert werden können, aber aufgrund der verringerten Diversifikation das Risiko auf der Zulieferseite gesteigert wird.[14] Ein plötzliches Ausscheiden oder der Ausfall eines Zulieferers aufgrund von Lieferschwierigkeiten bzw. Qualitätsproblemen kann beim Single Sourcing kaum kompensiert werden. Im Hinblick auf interne Quellen ist als zentraler Aspekt anzumerken, dass die kundenseitig notwendige Produktvielfalt die Wahrscheinlichkeit des Auftretens eines Fehlteils erhöht, da sich durch die Komplexitätssteigerung ebenfalls die Verwundbarkeit steigert.

Die aufgezeigten Entwicklungen machen ein effektives Management von Fehlteilen unabdingbar. Durch die aktive Beeinflussung der oben angeführten Gründe lässt sich einerseits die Eintrittswahrscheinlichkeit für ein Fehlteil verringern, andererseits der durch ein Fehlteil eintretende Schaden mildern.[15] Das Fehlteilmanagement ist in vielen Bereichen der industriellen Fertigung bereits gängige Praxis, in der Wissenschaft hat dieses Thema jedoch lediglich am

---

[9] Norrman, Andreas und Ulf Jansson: Ericsson's proactive supply chain risk management approach after a serious sub-supplier accident, in: International Journal of Physical Distribution & Logistics Management, Vol. 34 (2004), No. 5, S. 434.

[10] Vgl. Jüttner, Uta, Helen Peck und Martin Christopher: Supply Chain Risk Management: Outlining an Agenda for Future Research, in: International Journal of Logistics: Research and Applications, Vol. 6 (2003), No. 4, S. 205.

[11] Vgl. Peck, Helen: Drivers of supply chain vulnerability: an integrated framework, in: International Journal of Physical Distribution & Logistics Management, Vol. 35 (2005), No. 4, S. 214.

[12] Kajüter, Peter: Risk Management in Supply Chains, in: Seuring, Stefan, Martin Müller, Maria Goldbach und Uwe Schneidewind (Hrsg.): Strategy and Organization in Supply Chains, Heidelberg 2003, S. 13.

[13] Vgl. Bernecker, Tobias und Arndt Präuer: Risiken und Risikomanagement in Zuliefernetzwerken, in: Die Unternehmung, Jg. 60 (2006), Nr. 1, S. 31.

[14] Vgl. Zsidisin, George A., Alex Panelli und Rebecca Upton: Purchasing organization involvement in risk assessments, contingency plans, and risk management: an exploratory study, in: Supply Chain Management: An International Journal, Vol. 5 (2000), No. 4, S. 196.

[15] Vgl. Wagner, Stephan M. und Christoph Bode: Empirische Untersuchung von SC-Risiken und SC-Risikomanagement in Deutschland, in: Vahrenkamp, Richard und Christoph Siepermann (Hrsg.): Risikomanagement in Supply Chains, Berlin 2007, S. 67.

Rande eine theoretische Betrachtung erfahren.[16] Dementsprechend nimmt sich dieser Aufsatz diesem Thema an, um eine theoretische Fundierung für das Fehlteilmanagement zu schaffen und so einen Beitrag zu leisten, das existierende Forschungsdefizit auf diesem Gebiet zu verringern. Aus systemischer Perspektive bedeutet Fehlteilmanagement die prozessorientierte Analyse des Materialflusses. Es gilt, den Materialfluss als Transformationsprozess von Input zu Output hinsichtlich potenzieller Fehlteile zu untersuchen. Es sind mögliche Ursachen, deren Konsequenzen und Ansätze zur Behebung aber auch Möglichkeiten zur Vermeidung aufzuzeigen.

Dafür wird im ersten Teil des folgenden Kapitels auf mögliche Ursachen und Ursprünge eingegangen, um aufzuzeigen, wie es einerseits zu Fehlteilen in der Produktion kommt und andererseits wo diese entstehen. Im sich anschließenden Abschnitt werden die aus Fehlteilen resultierenden Konsequenzen für die Produktion behandelt. Den Ausführungen schließt sich eine Betrachtung des Fehlteilmanagements in Industriebetrieben mit den sich anbietenden Instrumenten an, wobei grundlegend zwischen präventiven und reaktiven Varianten unterschieden wird. Eine Diskussion von Implikationen für Industriebetriebe behandelt abschließend die impliziten Auswirkungen und Veränderungen durch ein effektives Fehlteilmanagement.

2 Grundlegende Aspekte von Fehlteilen in der industriellen Fertigung

2.1 Ursachen und Ursprünge von Fehlteilen

Bevor die Ursachen und Ursprünge von Fehlteilen diskutiert werden können, ist es sinnvoll, die Begrifflichkeit zu klären, um so die Eigenschaften eines Fehlteils besser verdeutlichen zu können. Ein Fehlteil liegt dann vor, wenn ein Teil zum zur Produktion benötigten Zeitpunkt nicht in der erforderlichen Qualität am richtigen, d. h. unmittelbaren Verbrauchsort vorhanden ist. Die Analogie zur Definition des Just-in-Time zeigt, dass der Grundgedanke ähnlich ist, nur im Kontext von Fehlteilen vom negativen Fall der Nicht-Existenz eines benötigten Teils ausgegangen wird. Bzgl. der Qualität zeichnet sich ein Fehlteil demnach u. a. durch seine Spezifika aus, d. h. dass es nicht schlichtweg durch ein anderes Alternativteil ersetzt werden kann. Darüber hinaus müssen die an das Teil gestellten Qualitätskriterien wie z. B. das Einhalten von Toleranzgrenzen der Qualitätsspezifikationen erfüllt werden. Hinsichtlich des Ortes ist es notwendig, dass das Teil zur richtigen Zeit am richtigen Ort ist. Auch ein den Qualitätsanforderungen genügendes Teil ist als Fehlteil anzusehen, wenn es nicht für den Einbau am Band verfügbar ist. Anhand dieser Beschreibung zeigt sich, dass die Ursachen von Fehlteilen vielfältig sein können.

Als klassische Ursache eines Fehlteils kann der Fall angesehen werden, wenn von einer im Produktionsprozess vorangelagerten Stufe zu wenig produziert bzw. ein benötigtes Teil nicht gefertigt wurde. Weitere Gründe für ein Fehlteil können Maschinenausfälle bei der vorangelagerten Produktionsstufe sein. Ebenso kann es durch Verschleiß der Maschine zu einer verrin-

[16] Beispielhaft sei hier auf den Beitrag von Lochmahr und Wildemann verwiesen. Vgl. Lochmahr, Andrea und Horst Wildemann: Die Einführung logistischer Konzepte in Theorie und Praxis – Fallbeispiel Kapazitätsmanagement, in: Günthner, W. A. (Hrsg.): Neue Wege in der Automobillogistik, Berlin und Heidelberg 2007, S. 509–524.

gerten Produktionsmenge kommen. Darüber hinaus sind Qualitätsabweichungen möglich, wenn vorgegebene Spezifikationen nicht eingehalten werden. Dies hat ein Fehlteil an der nachgelagerten Produktionsstufe zur Folge, da das Teil in der vorliegenden Form nicht verbaut werden kann. Es kann jedoch auch vorkommen, dass das angelieferte Teil schlichtweg falsch ist, da es sich um ein anderes Teil handelt. Dies kann seine Ursachen bspw. in einer fehlerhaften Produkt- oder Behälterauszeichnung, aber auch im Vertauschen von linken und rechten bzw. geometrisch ähnlichen Teilen haben.

Nachfrageunsicherheit ist eine weitere wichtige Ursache für Fehlteile. Stark schwankende Nachfrage korrespondiert oftmals mit der Notwendigkeit, die Produktionszahlen auf Prognosen zu basieren, welche naturgemäß mit Ungenauigkeiten behaftet sind.[17] Dies wird unterstützt durch die Aussage von Stalk und Hout: „Forecasts are inevitably wrong; by definition they are guesses"[18]. Oftmals wird diesem Problem damit begegnet, dass Sicherheitsbestände aufgebaut werden, so dass Unsicherheit bzgl. der Nachfrage zu höheren Beständen führt, so dass Unsicherheit auch als „mother of inventory" bezeichnet wird.[19] Gestaltet sich der Aufbau von Sicherheitsbeständen als zu kostenintensiv bzw. aufgrund einer zu hohen Variantenvielfalt als nicht praktikabel, kommt es zu Fehlteilen in der Produktion.

Als weitere Ursache für Fehlteile ist der Transport zu nennen. So kann es im Rahmen des Zulieferprozesses via Straßenverkehr zu Verzögerungen durch Staus kommen. Auch können widrige Wetterverhältnisse den Transport behindern. In der Schifffahrt spielt das Wetter z. B. in Form von Sturm oder Eis, in der Luftfahrt bspw. in der Form von Nebel eine bedeutsame Rolle. Ebenso ist ein Ausfall des Transportmittels möglich, so dass das erforderliche Teil in der Produktion nicht rechtzeitig verfügbar ist. Während des Transports kann es auch vorkommen, dass ein Teil beschädigt wird, was im weiteren Verlauf ebenfalls zu Fehlteilen führen kann, da ein qualitativ minderwertiges Teil nicht verbaut werden darf. Der Qualitätsaspekt kann sich auch aufgrund von schlechter Qualität des Rohmaterials bzw. des Vormaterials niederschlagen. Auch können Toleranzabweichungen des Materials oder Bestandskorrekturen beim Zulieferer zu Fehlteilen führen.

Zwar werden Fehlteile häufig erst in der Produktion bemerkt, der Ursprung muss jedoch nicht zwingend in der eigenen Produktion liegen, sondern kann ebenso externen Ursprungs sein, da ein Fehlteil sowohl vom Lieferanten als auch vom eigenen Betrieb verursacht werden kann. Dabei sind die Ursachen des Fehlteils i. d. R. die gleichen, der Ort der Entstehung ist jedoch ein anderer. So können Ursachen wie Maschinenausfälle, Qualitätsprobleme oder Fehlbestände sowohl im eigenen Betrieb als auch beim Lieferanten auftreten. Aus dem Ursprung ergeben sich jedoch unterschiedliche Konsequenzen in der Handhabung, da eine Ursache externen Ursprungs nicht mehr der unmittelbaren Kontrolle des produzierenden Unternehmens unterliegt.

---

[17] Als klassisches Problem bzgl. Nachfrageunsicherheit sei hier auf das sogenannte Newsvendor-Problem verwiesen, das darin besteht, dass ein Zeitungsjunge die Nachfrage nicht genau kennt, jedoch weder auf Umsatz verzichten noch auf nicht verkauften Zeitungen sitzen bleiben will. Vgl. zum Newsvendor-Problem Khouja, Moutaz: The single-period (news-vendor) problem: literature review and suggestions for future research, in: Omega, Vol. 27 (1999), No. 5, S. 537–553.

[18] Stalk, George jr. und Thomas M. Hout: Competing Against Time – How Time-based Competition Is Reshaping Global Market, New York 1990, S. 61 ff.

[19] Vgl. Christopher, Martin: Logistics and Supply Chain Management: Strategies for Reducing Cost and Improving Service, 3. Aufl., London 2004, S. 263.

2.2 Konsequenzen von Fehlteilen

Bei der Betrachtung der Konsequenzen von Fehlteilen ist es zunächst sinnvoll zwischen zwei Arten von Teilen zu unterscheiden, da die negative Auswirkung eines Fehlteils stark davon abhängt, ob es sich um ein sogenanntes Kann-Teil oder Muss-Teil handelt.[20]

Bei Kann-Teilen ist es möglich, die Montage des fehlenden Teils bis zur Verfügbarkeit zu verzögern, so dass ein Montagestillstand vermieden werden kann. Dabei wird das fehlende Teil nachträglich an das bereits komplettierte Produkt montiert. Bei einem Muss-Teil erzwingt die Ausgestaltung des Montageprozesses oder die Produktkonfiguration einen Montagestillstand. Die Möglichkeit der Montage zu einem späteren Zeitpunkt ist hier nicht möglich, so dass Fehlteile, die als Muss-Teile kategorisiert werden, weitreichendere Konsequenzen aufweisen und somit kritischer für die Produktion sind.[21] Weiterhin ergibt sich beim Auftreten von Fehlteilen die Notwendigkeit von Nacharbeit, die oftmals zeitaufwändiger und kostspieliger ist. Hier müssen beispielsweise bereits montierte Elemente des Produkts demontiert werden, um eine nachträgliche Montage des Fehlteils zu ermöglichen.

Ein zweiter wichtiger Aspekt bzgl. der Konsequenzen von Fehlteilen ist die Unterscheidung zwischen internen und externen Konsequenzen. Interne Konsequenzen sind dadurch gekennzeichnet, dass sie sich lediglich innerhalb der Produktion auswirken. Zwar ist das Auftreten von Fehlteilen, deren negative Folgen sich innerhalb der Produktion bemerkbar machen, u. a. mit Nachteilen wie hohen Kosten für Nacharbeit etc. verbunden; im Gegensatz zu Fehlteilen mit externen Konsequenzen sind diese jedoch als weniger schwerwiegend zu bezeichnen. Externe Konsequenzen zeichnen sich dadurch aus, dass die Auswirkung des Auftretens eines Fehlteils nicht innerhalb des Unternehmens kompensiert werden konnte, so dass mitunter Kunden in Form von Wartezeiten, Produktionsstillständen etc. betroffen sein können. Als Konsequenz können hier Konventionalstrafen oder ein Imageverlust resultieren. Die Konsequenzen von Fehlteilen verhalten sich analog zu den Qualitätskosten, die sich neben präventiven Qualitätskosten und Kosten für die Überwachung eines Prozesses in interne und externe Qualitätskosten differenzieren lassen.[22]

3 Maßnahmen des Fehlteilmanagements

3.1 Varianten präventiver und reaktiver Konzeptualisierung

Kern des Fehlteilmanagements stellt die Einleitung von Gegenmaßnahmen zur Risikosteuerung dar. Grundsätzlich lassen sich die Ansätze zum Fehlteilmanagement in zwei Kategorien einteilen, da sie einerseits die Wahrscheinlichkeit des Eintretens eines Fehlteils verringern, anderer-

[20] Eine alternative Benennung für Kann- und Muss-Teil sind die Begriffe baukritisch und nicht baukritische Teile bzw. montagekritisch und nicht montagekritische Teile.

[21] Ein Beispiel für ein Kann-Teil ist ein Außenspiegel eines Automobils, der nachträglich montiert werden kann. Im Gegensatz dazu ist diese Möglichkeit beim Motor nicht gegeben. Dementsprechend handelt es sich in diesem Fall um ein Muss-Teil. Vergleiche zum Unterschied von „Kann"-Teilen und „Muss"-Teilen auch Thun, Jörn-Henrik, Martin Drüke und Victor Silveira Camargos: Just in Sequence – Eine Erweiterung des Just in Time durch Sequenzzulieferung, in: Logistik Management, 9. Jg (2007), Nr. 4, S. 46.

[22] Vgl. zu den Qualitätskosten Juran, Joseph M.: Quality Control Handbook, 2. Aufl., New York, 1962, S. 1 ff. und vgl. Feigenbaum, Armand V.: Total Quality Control, 3. Aufl., New York, 1991, S. 111.

seits die Auswirkungen, die durch das Auftreten eines Fehlteils entstehen, vermindern. Aufgrund dieser zwei grundsätzlichen Herangehensweisen wird im Folgenden zwischen präventiven und reaktiven Maßnahmen unterschieden.[23] Durch präventive Maßnahmen soll das Auftreten eines Fehlteils im Vorhinein verhindert bzw. die Eintrittswahrscheinlichkeit durch proaktive Maßnahmen verringert werden.[24] Im Gegensatz dazu setzen reaktive Maßnahmen, auch wirkungsbezogene Maßnahmen genannt, an den Konsequenzen eines Fehlteils an und versuchen, die negativen Auswirkungen so gering wie möglich zu halten. Auf die Ansätze beider Kategorien soll im Folgenden näher eingegangen werden. Abbildung 1 gibt einen Überblick der verschiedenen Maßnahmen des Fehlteilmanagements.

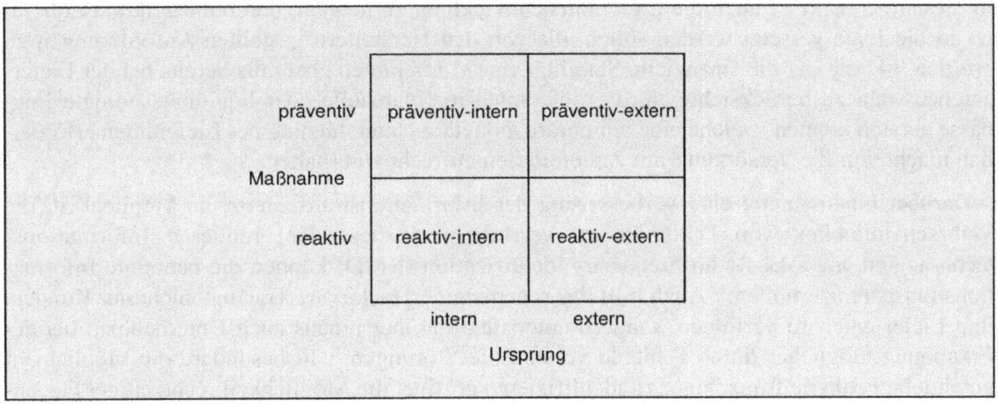

Abbildung 1: Kategorisierung der Maßnahmen zum Fehlteilmanagement

3.2 Präventive Ansätze

Da präventive Ansätze die Wahrscheinlichkeit des Auftretens eines Fehlteils verringern sollen, impliziert dies, dass im Vorhinein mögliche „Phantomfehlteile“ identifiziert und diese durch entsprechende Maßnahmen bestmöglich ausgeschlossen werden. Die präventiven Maßnahmen sollten an den potenziellen Ursachen bzw. Ursprüngen von Fehlteilen ansetzen.

Mitunter besteht die Option, den Eintritt von Fehlteilrisiken überwiegend zu umgehen.[25] Diese Strategie der Risikovermeidung schließt Maßnahmen wie z.B. die Konzentration auf Produkte mit konstanter Nachfrage, das Fernhalten von kritischen Produktions- und Absatzmärkten sowie räumliches Ausweichen von Gebieten mit häufigen Naturkatastrophen etc. mit

[23] Gleißner unterscheidet diesbezüglich zwischen ursachenbezogenen und wirkungsbezogenen Maßnahmen. Vgl. Gleißner, Werner: Analyse und Bewältigung strategischer Risiken, in: Kaiser, Thomas (Hrsg.): Wettbewerbsvorteil Risikomanagement – erfolgreiche Steuerung der Strategie-, Reputations- und operationalen Risiken, Berlin 2007, S. 90.

[24] Vgl. Schimmelpfeng, Katja: Risikomanagement in Industrieunternehmen, in: Götze, Uwe, Klaus Henselmann und Barbara Mikus (Hrsg.): Risikomanagement, Heidelberg 2001, S. 289.

[25] Vgl. Jüttner, Uta, Helen Peck und Martin Christopher: Supply Chain Risk Management: Outlining an Agenda for Future Research, in: International Journal of Logistics: Research and Applications, Vol. 6 (2003), No. 4, S. 206.

ein.[26] Dieses Vorgehen der nahezu gänzlichen Risikovermeidung ist oftmals jedoch schlichtweg nicht möglich oder nicht praktikabel. Dementsprechend sind Wege zu suchen, wie das Risiko des Eintretens eines Fehlteils ökonomisch und praktisch sinnvoll vermindert werden kann.

Durch entsprechende Maßnahmen kann das Risiko zwar nicht gänzlich ausgeschlossen werden, jedoch die Eintrittswahrscheinlichkeit stark gesenkt werden. So besteht eine Möglichkeit, sich bereits bei der Lieferantenauswahl auf einen Zulieferer mit hoher Termintreue, Qualitätszertifizierung und geografischer Nähe zu fokussieren, so dass Fehlteile aufgrund von Lieferengpässen überwiegend vermieden werden können. Ein effektives Lieferantenmanagement stellt dabei eine Grundvoraussetzung dafür dar, Risiken auf der Beschaffungsseite abzubauen.[27] In diesem Kontext ist auch die Lieferantenentwicklung zu nennen, durch die zentrale Zulieferer in die Lage versetzt werden sollen, die von den Herstellern gestellten Anforderungen zu erfüllen.[28] Ferner ist die finanzielle Stabilität eines Lieferanten ebenfalls bereits bei der Lieferantenauswahl zu berücksichtigen, da Lieferanten in finanzielle oder liquiditätsbedingte Engpässe geraten können, welche eine temporäre monetäre Unterstützung des Lieferanten erforderlich macht, um die Versorgung mit Zulieferteilen aufrecht zu erhalten.[29]

Darüber hinaus bietet eine Verbesserung der Informationstransparenz die Möglichkeit, die Wahrscheinlichkeit von Fehlteilen zu verringern. Insbesondere moderne Informationstechnologien wie z.B. Radio Frequency Identification (RFID) können die benötigte Informationstransparenz erhöhen.[30] Auch hilft das sogenannte „Tracking & Tracing“ nicht nur Kunden, ihre Lieferungen zu verfolgen, sondern unterstützt darüber hinaus auch Unternehmen bei der Erkennung möglicher durch Fehlteile verursachte Störungen.[31] Insbesondere die Möglichkeit potentielle Fehlteile frühzeitiger zu identifizieren eröffnet die Möglichkeit rechtzeitiger Gegenmaßnahmen, um das Entstehen von Fehlteilen zu verhindern oder zumindest die negativen Auswirkungen zu vermindern. Allgemein dient eine Verbesserung des Informationsaustausches durch Kooperationen in Wertschöpfungsnetzen einer Vermeidung des Eintretens des sogenannten „Bullwhip“-Effektes und somit auch von Fehlteilen.[32] Zusätzlich sei als Erfolg versprechendes

[26] Vgl. Wagner, Stephan M. und Christoph Bode: Empirische Untersuchung von SC-Risiken und SC-Risikomanagement in Deutschland, in: Vahrenkamp, Richard und Christoph Siepermann (Hrsg.): Risikomanagement in Supply Chains, Berlin 2007, S. 74.

[27] Vgl. Giunipero, Larry C. und Reham Aly Eltantawy: Securing the upstream supply chain: a risk management approach, in: International Journal of Physical Distribution & Logistics Management, Vol. 34 (2004), No. 9, S. 706.

[28] Vgl. Modi, Sachin B. und Vincent A. Mabert: Supplier development: Improving supplier performance through knowledge transfer, in: Journal of Operations Management, Vol. 25 (2007), No. 1, S. 56.

[29] Eine Möglichkeit der monetären Unterstützung stellt beispielsweise der Kauf und die Bereitstellung von Vormaterial für den Lieferanten durch den Kunden dar, wodurch zum einen das finanzielle Risiko für den Kunden begrenzt und zum anderen der Einsatz des Vormaterials zur exklusiven Produktion der benötigten Teile für den Kunden sichergestellt werden kann.

[30] Vgl. Byrne, Patrick M.: RFID: Unlocking high performance in supply chain planning, in: Logistics Management, Vol. 44 (2005), No. 9, S. 29.

[31] Vgl. Sheffi, Yossi und James B. Rice Jr.: A Supply Chain View of the Resilient Enterprise, in: MIT Sloan Management Review, Vol. 47 (2005), No. 1, S. 47.

[32] Vgl. Ouyang, Yanfeng: The effect of information sharing on supply chain stability and the bullwhip effect, in: European Journal of Operational Research, Vol. 182 (2007), No. 3, S. 1117f. Vgl. zum „Bullwhip“-Effekt Lee, Hau L., Padmanabhan, V., Whang, S.: The Bullwhip Effect in Supply Chains. Sloan Management Review, Vol. 38 (1997), No. 3, S. 93–102.

Kooperationskonzept beispielhaft das Konzept des „Vendor Managed Inventory" genannt, bei dem der Zulieferer die Bestandsregelung beim Hersteller übernimmt, so dass auch hier die Wahrscheinlichkeit von Fehlteilen gesenkt wird.[33] Das Vendor-Managed-Inventory-Konzept führt tendenziell zu einer Erhöhung der Bestände, da der Zulieferer Transport- und Produktionslos aufgrund von Transport- und Rüstkostenreduzierungen vereinheitlicht. Die damit einhergehenden Zusatzbestände stellen eine Art von Sicherheitsbeständen dar.

Neben den aufgezeigten Maßnahmen, Fehlteile externen Ursprungs auf proaktive Weise zu vermeiden, existieren auch Ansätze, die zum Ziel haben, die Wahrscheinlichkeit von Fehlteilen innerhalb der eigenen Fertigung des Herstellers zu senken. So können durch Maschinenausfälle verursachte Fehlteile durch Maßnahmen vorbeugender Instandhaltung vermieden werden. Ein Weg, um die Wahrscheinlichkeit von Maschinenausfällen zu senken, ist im Konzept des Total Productive Maintenance zu sehen. Durch eine ganzheitliche Herangehensweise wird beim Total Productive Maintenance versucht, die Gesamtanlageneffektivität durch die Analyse von sechs wesentlichen Verlustquellen zu maximieren.[34] Zentrale Elemente des Konzeptes bestehen in den fünf Säulen: Instandhaltungsprävention, präventive Instandhaltung, autonome Instandhaltung, Training von Mitarbeitern sowie Identifikation und Beseitigung von Schwerpunktproblemen.

Auch ein weiteres umfassendes Konzept des Qualitätsmanagements kann ebenfalls helfen, die Wahrscheinlichkeit von Fehlteilen zu verringern. Die Ansätze des Total Quality Managements dienen dazu, produkt- und prozessseitige Fehler zu vermeiden. So können durch Ansätze wie der statistischen Prozessregelung Abweichungen von der Norm unmittelbar identifiziert, analysiert und behoben werden, so dass Fehlteile von Vornherein ausgeschlossen werden. Weitere Ansätze zur Fehlervermeidung sind die Konzepte des Desing for Manufacturing and Assembly, wobei Produkte und Prozesse bereits bei der Entwicklung so gestaltet werden, dass Fehler möglichst vermieden werden können.[35] Ein neueres, ganzheitliches Konzept zur Vermeidung von Fehlern in Produktionsprozessen und der Verbesserung von Produkten und Prozessen ist der Ansatz des Six Sigma.[36] Beim Six Sigma wird durch kontinuierliches Durchlaufen des sogenannten DMAIC-Zyklusses angestrebt, die Anzahl von Fehlern auf unter 4 dpmo zu verrin-

---

[33] Vgl. Sheffi, Yossi: in: The International Journal of Logistics Management, Vol. 12 (2001), No. 2, S. 5.

[34] Die sechs wesentlichen Verlustquellen sind Verluste durch Anlagenausfälle, Rüst- und Einrichteverluste, Verluste durch Leerlauf und Kurzstillstände, Verluste durch verringerte Taktgeschwindigkeit, Verluste durch Anlaufschwierigkeiten und Qualitätsverluste. Vgl. Al-Radhi, Medhi und Jörg Heuer: Total Productive Maintenance: Konzept, Umsetzung, Erfahrung, München 1995, S. 13. Vgl. zur Gesamtanlageneffektivität Nakajima, Seiichi: Introduction to TPM, Portland 1988, S. 22ff.

[35] Vgl. zum Design for Manufacture and Assembly Ettlie, John E.: Methods That Work for Integrating Design and Manufacturing, in: Ettlie, John E. und Henry W. Stoll (Hrsg.): Managing the Design-Manufacturing Process, New York 1990, S. 53–78; vgl. Boothroyd, Geoffrey und Peter Dewhurst: Product design for manufacture and assembly, in: Manufacturing Engineering, Vol. 100 (1988), No. 4, S. 42–46, vgl. Stoll, Henry: Design for Manufacture: An Overview, in: Applied Mechanics, Vol. 39 (1986), No. 9, S. 1356–1364.

[36] Vgl. Eckes, Georges: The Six Sigma Revolution, How General Electric and Others Turned Process into Profits, New York et al. 2001. Vgl. Harry, M. und Schroeder, Roger G.: The breakthrough management strategy revolutionizing the world's top corporations, New York et al. 2005. Vgl. Pande, P. S., R. P. Neuman und R. R. Cavanagh: The Six Sigma Way: How GE, Motorola, and other top companies are honing their performance, New York 2002.

gern.[37] Darüber hinaus bestehen noch weitere Konzepte zur Qualitätssteigerung wie z. B. das Quality Function Deployment, auf die an dieser Stelle jedoch nicht näher eingegangen werden soll.[38] Trotz der großen Vielfalt an potenziellen Maßnahmen bleibt festzuhalten, dass einerseits das Eintreten von Fehlteilen nie ganz auszuschließen ist und andererseits nicht alle Maßnahmen zwingend praktikabel sein müssen.

3.3 Reaktive Ansätze

Analog zu den präventiven Ansätzen kann auch bei den reaktiven Ansätzen zwischen Maßnahmen, die beim Hersteller in der eigenen Fertigung ansetzen, und externen Maßnahmen unterschieden werden. Ein zentraler Unterschied zu den präventiven Maßnahmen besteht darin, dass sogenannte wirkungsbezogene Steuerungsmaßnahmen nicht beim Risiko an sich ansetzen. Sie haben vielmehr das Ziel, die negativen Konsequenzen, die mit einem Fehlteil einhergehen, zu begrenzen, da das Fehlteil bei dieser Betrachtung de facto aufgetreten ist. Ziel reaktiver Maßnahmen muss es daher sein, zugrundeliegende Prozesse derart zu konfigurieren, dass der durch ein Fehlteil entstehende Schaden minimal bleibt.[39]

Bei der Betrachtung von Fehlteilen externen Ursprungs geht es darum, robuste Wertschöpfungsbeziehungen aufzubauen. Ein dabei zentraler Aspekt ist der Begriff der Elastizität, womit die Fähigkeit beschrieben wird, nach dem Eintreten eines Fehlteils wieder zum ursprünglichen Zustand zurückzukehren oder aber einen neuen, adäquaten Zustand anzunehmen.[40] Eine derartige Elastizität zu erzeugen, kann auf zwei Arten erreicht werden: Zum einen ist es möglich, durch die Generierung von Redundanzen Elastizität zu erzeugen, zum anderen resultiert eine Steigerung der Flexibilität der zugrundeliegenden Prozesse in einer verbesserten Elastizität des Wertschöpfungsnetzes. Maßnahmen beider Ansätze sollen im Folgenden kurz charakterisiert werden.

Die wohl eingängigste Form der Redundanz ist im Aufbau von Sicherheitsbeständen zur Absicherung von Lieferproblemen beim Zulieferer zu sehen.[41] Zwar widersprechen derartige Puffer dem Grundgedanken der Lean Production, jedoch können sie, gezielt eingesetzt, durchaus eine rationale Herangehensweise an die Fehlteilproblematik darstellen.[42] Die Höhe der

---

[37] Vgl. Thun, Jörn-Henrik, Peter M. Milling und Wiebke Roos: Studying Six Sigma – An empirical Analysis of the German Automotive Industry, in: Acur, Nuran, Nesim K. Erkip und Evrim Didem Günes (Hrsg.): Managing Operations in an Expanding Europe, Ankara 2007, S. 2. Das Akronym DMAIC steht für die Anfangsbuchstaben der Begriffe „Define", „Measure", „Analyse", „Improve" und „Control", welche die jeweiligen Phasen des DMAIC-Zyklus darstellen.

[38] Quality Function Deployment beschreibt eine Methode des Qualitätsmanagements, welche eine frühzeitige Integration der Kundenanforderungen in den Produktentwicklungsprozess erreichen und damit eine Äquivalenz von Produkt und Kundenanforderung sicherstellen soll.

[39] Vgl. dazu im Kontext von Wertschöpfungsnetzen Wagner, Stephan M. und Christoph Bode: Empirische Untersuchung von SC-Risiken und SC-Risikomanagement in Deutschland, in: Vahrenkamp, Richard und Christoph Siepermann (Hrsg.): Risikomanagement in Supply Chains, Berlin 2007, S. 70.

[40] Vgl. Christopher, Martin und Helen Peck: Building the Resilient Supply Chain, in: The International Journal of Logistics Management, Vol. 15 (2004), No. 2, S. 2.

[41] Vgl. Sheffi, Yossi und James B. Rice Jr.: A Supply Chain View of the Resilient Enterprise, in: MIT Sloan Management Review, Vol. 47 (2005), No. 1, S. 44.

[42] Solche Sicherheitsbestände werden im Gegensatz zum Just-in-Time auch als „Just-in-Case"-Bestände bezeichnet, da sie eventuelle auftretende Störungen im Materialfluss kompensieren sollen.

Sicherheitsbestände kann sich dabei an Aspekten wie der Güte des Lieferanten hinsichtlich Qualität und Termintreue oder der Distanz zum Zulieferer orientieren. Analoge Redundanzen sind Überkapazitäten in Produktion oder Transport, so dass auf Nachfrageänderungen reagiert werden kann.[43] Zusätzlich zu diesen Redundanzen können auch Maßnahmen wie das Dual Sourcing oder das Multiple Sourcing ergriffen werden, wodurch das Beschaffungsrisiko diversifiziert wird, falls einer der Zulieferer einer bestimmten Komponente ausfallen sollte.[44] Kritisch bei Redundanzen ist jedoch zu sehen, dass diese oftmals mit Effizienzeinbußen verbunden sind. Insbesondere kleinere Betriebe mit geringen Einkaufsvolumina und damit limitierter Verhandlungsmacht gegenüber Zulieferern werden ihre Einkaufsvolumina nicht zwischen mehreren Lieferanten aufteilen und müssen damit höhere Preise akzeptieren. Werden diese Effizienzeinbußen jedoch als Versicherungsprämie gegen den Schaden von Fehlteilen interpretiert, können sie wiederum als rationale Maßnahme angesehen werden.[45]

Neben der Generierung von Redundanzen besteht die Möglichkeit, Maßnahmen zur Steigerung der Flexibilität zu ergreifen, mit denen nicht zwingend Effizienzeinbußen einhergehen.[46] Durch diese Handlungsweisen versetzen sich Unternehmen in die Lage, auf das Eintreten eines Fehlteils schnell zu reagieren, ohne die negativen Konsequenzen, die eigentlich mit einem Fehlteil verbunden sind, in vollem Ausmaß tragen zu müssen. Die erhöhte Elastizität führt in diesem Falle dazu, dass diese kompensiert werden können. Als exemplarische Maßnahmen seien hier die Postponement-Strategie im Sinne einer möglichst späten kundenindividuellen Differenzierung zur Abfederung von Nachfrageänderungen, der Einsatz verschiedenartiger Transportmittel, Alternativrouten und Dienstleister in der Logistik sowie die Konzentration auf lokale Zulieferer im Gegensatz zum Global Sourcing zur schnellen konzertierten Reaktion auf Fehlteile genannt.[47]

Auch stellt die unternehmensübergreifende Kommunikation einen entscheidenden Aspekt bei der Flexibilitätssteigerung dar, da nur durch eine ausreichende Informationstransparenz ein adäquates Reagieren auf Fehlteile möglich ist. Nur wenn der Eintritt eines Fehlteils schnellstmöglich kommuniziert wird, können Unternehmen gemeinsam Gegenmaßnahmen ergreifen und so die negativen Konsequenzen limitieren.[48] Gemeinsame Notfallpläne scheinen ebenfalls eine sinnvolle Maßnahme darzustellen, da so die Elastizität durch eine verbesserte Widerstands-

---

[43] Vgl. Chopra, Sunil und Manmohan S. Sodhi: Managing Risk to Avoid Supply-Chain Breakdown, in: MIT Sloan Management Review, Vol. 46 (2004), No. 1, S. 59.

[44] Vgl. Kleindorfer, Paul R. und Germaine H. Saad: Managing Disruption Risks in Supply Chains, in: Production and Operations Management, Vol. 14 (2005), No. 1, S. 55. Auch hier entstehen Effizienzeinbußen im Sinne von Opportunitätskosten, da Economies of Scales nicht genutzt werden können.

[45] Vgl. Sheffi, Yossi: Supply Chain Management under the Threat of International Terrorism, in: The International Journal of Logistics Management, Vol. 12 (2001), No. 2, S. 2.

[46] Vgl. Sheffi, Yossi und James B. Rice Jr.: A Supply Chain View of the Resilient Enterprise, in: MIT Sloan Management Review, Vol. 47 (2005), No. 1, S. 48.

[47] Vgl. Jüttner, Uta, Helen Peck und Martin Christopher: Supply Chain Risk Management: Outlining an Agenda for Future Research, in: International Journal of Logistics: Research and Applications, Vol. 6 (2003), No. 4, S. 207.

[48] Vgl. beispielhaft für den Fall einer Nachfrageänderung Milling, Peter und Andreas Größler: Simulationsbasierte Analysen von Wertschöpfungsnetzwerken, in: Bellmann, Klaus (Hrsg.): Kooperations- und Netzwerkmanagement, Berlin 2001, S. 66ff.

fähigkeit erhöht wird.[49] Standardisierte Prozesse und Abläufe bei der Entdeckung eines Fehlteils, organisatorische Vollmachten der mit dem Fehlteilmanagement beauftragten Mitarbeiter und die Unterstützung durch das Management sind weitere Maßnahmen zur Erhöhung der Elastizität.

Bei der Betrachtung von reaktiven Maßnahmen zur Elastizitätssteigerung gegen Fehlteile internen Ursprungs kann ebenfalls zwischen Ansätzen zur Generierung von Redundanzen und Ansätzen zur Flexibilitätssteigerung unterschieden werden. Auch in Bezug auf die internen Maßnahmen sind als wohl populärste Maßnahme Sicherheitsbestände zu nennen. Zur Absicherung gegen Fehlteile werden „Überbestände" im Lager gehalten, wobei die Höhe der Sicherheitsbestände von der Wiederbeschaffungszeit bzw. der Möglichkeit zur produktionsinternen Kompensation abhängt.

Bei den internen Maßnahmen zur Flexibilitätssteigerung ist es notwendig, die zugrunde liegenden Prozesse derart zu gestalten, dass die aus Fehlteilen resultierenden negativen Konsequenzen absorbiert werden können, ohne mit Ineffizienzen verbundene Redundanzen aufbauen zu müssen. Ziel reaktiver Maßnahmen zur Flexibilitätssteigerung ist demnach eine Erhöhung der Elastizität ohne Effizienzverlust. Eine Möglichkeit besteht darin, temporär auf das Fehlteil zu verzichten und mit der Montage fortzufahren. Das Fehlteil wird bei entsprechender Verfügbarkeit in späteren Prozessschritten nachmontiert, ohne dass die Produktion unterbrochen werden muss. Diese Vorgehensweise bedingt jedoch, dass es sich bei dem Fehlteil um ein sogenanntes „Kann"-Teil handelt, d. h. eine spätere Montage grundsätzlich möglich ist. Allerdings muss der mit der nachträglichen Montage einhergehende Nacharbeitsaufwand wirtschaftlich sinnvoll sein.

Als weitere reaktive Maßnahme existiert die Möglichkeit, die Produktionsreihenfolge zu ändern. Kann ein Auftrag aufgrund eines Fehlteils nicht wie vorgesehen gefertigt werden und handelt es sich bei dem Fehlteil um ein „Muss"-Teil, kann die Fertigung verzögert werden und der Auftrag wird erst später wieder freigegeben, wenn die Verfügbarkeit aller notwendigen Teile gegeben ist. Auch bei dieser Vorgehensweise sind verschiedene Aspekte zu beachten. So ist es bspw. wichtig, dass keine weiteren Vormontagen angesteuert werden bei denen bereits vormontierte Komponenten oder Module physisch ausgesteuert werden müssten.

Langfristig kann es auch sinnvoll sein, das Produktionsprogramm zu ändern, so dass durch ein Fehlteil betroffene Aufträge vollständig aus dem Produktionsprogramm herausgenommen werden und erst zu einem späteren Zeitpunkt wieder neu eingeplant werden. Kurzfristig besteht eine Möglichkeit darin, die Auftragsreihenfolge bzw. die Sequenz zu ändern und den Auftrag zu einem späteren Zeitpunkt wieder einzuplanen. Dabei muss jedoch gewährleistet sein, dass das Vorziehen von anderen Aufträgen keine neuen Fehlteile bei den vorgezogenen Aufträgen verursacht, da diese nun früher als geplant produziert werden. Diese Maßnahmen sind allerdings nur dann möglich, wenn der zugrunde liegende Produktionsprozess dieses in Anbetracht des gegebenen Flexibilitätsgrades zulässt.[50]

---

[49] In der englischsprachigen Literatur werden hiefür die Begriffe „Business Continuity Planning", „Recovery Planning" oder „Contingency Plans" verwendet. Vgl. z. B. Zsisidin, George A., Gary L. Ragatz und Steven A. Melnyk: The dark side of supply chain management, in: Supply Chain Management Review, Vol. 9 (2005), No. 2, S. 49.

[50] Eine weitere Möglichkeit besteht in der gezielten Beeinflussung der Nachfrage nach bestimmten Produkten, Optionen, Varianten etc. So können beispielsweise von Fehlteilen betroffene Varianten weniger beworben werden oder die Nachfrage wird auf nicht von Fehlteilen betroffene Varianten kanalisiert, indem bspw. preisliche Anreize eingesetzt werden.

Eine weitere reaktive Maßnahme innerhalb der Produktion ist es, höherwertige Optionen zu wählen, d.h. es wird ein qualitativ hochwertigeres Teil anstatt des Fehlteils verbaut, ohne dies dem Kunden zu berechnen. Alternativ können auch Teile von verwandten Baureihen verwendet werden, wenn diese aktuell nicht benötigt werden und gegebenenfalls entsprechend modifizierbar sind. Dafür ist es wiederum in der Regel notwendig, dass das Fehlteil und das Alternativteil eine nahezu identische Geometrie aufweisen. Ferner muss geprüft werden, ob die Verwendung der alternativen Teile oder Optionen keine weiteren Fehlteile für andere Aufträge erzeugt. Falls es sich beim Fehlteil um einen Rohling handelt, kann auch alternatives Rohmaterial verwendet werden. Hierbei ist allerdings zu beachten, dass verschiedene Rohlinge unterschiedliche Stoffeigenschaften wie Härtegrad, Oberflächenstruktur, etc. aufweisen können.

Falls der Engpass bei einer Bearbeitungsmaschine liegt, kann evtl. auch eine alternative Bearbeitungsmethode und damit eine andere Maschine, die keinen Engpass darstellt, verwendet werden. Allerdings können unterschiedliche Bearbeitungsmethoden Auswirkungen auf Kosten, Bearbeitungszeit und Qualität des Produktes haben.

4 Implikationen des Fehlteilmanagements

In diesem Abschnitt wird eine Systematik zur Ableitung der adäquaten Maßnahmenauswahl aufgezeigt, welche sich an einer Kosten/Nutzenbetrachtung in Bezug auf das jeweilige Produktionssystem und das Produktprogramm orientiert. Basierend auf dieser Systematik können Implikationen für das Fehlteilmanagement im Industriebetrieb abgeleitet werden.

Es ist davon auszugehen, dass sich eine simultane Umsetzung aller aufgezeigten Instrumente als zu kostenintensiv und nicht praktikabel erweist, so dass sich Unternehmen für eine Kombination entscheiden müssen. Daher stellt sich die Frage der Vorteilhaftigkeit von einer Kombination im Gegensatz zur ausschließlichen Fokussierung auf eine präventive oder reaktive Maßnahme. Die konkrete Auswahl ist einerseits zwar abhängig von den spezifischen Geschäfts- und Branchenfaktoren sowie von verschiedenen Kosten- und Nutzenaspekten[51], andererseits können gewisse wesentliche Einflussfaktoren identifiziert und grundsätzliche Aussagen zur Maßnahmenauswahl getroffen werden.

Wesentliche Einflussfaktoren auf die Art und die Ausprägung der einzusetzenden Maßnahmen des Fehlteilmanagements sind im Produktprogramm und dem korrespondierenden Produktionssystem zu sehen. Kombinationen dieser beiden Einflussfaktoren werden in der von *Hayes* und *Wheelright* vorgestellten Produkt-Prozess-Matrix aufgezeigt. Das Modell, welches die Produktstruktur der Prozessstruktur gegenüberstellt, liefert Ansätze zur Ausgestaltung der Fertigung, um strategische Zielsetzungen zu verfolgen.[52] In Abbildung 2 ist eine vereinfachte Form der Produkt-Prozess-Matrix illustriert.

Obwohl grundsätzlich jeder Bereich in der Matrix eine mögliche Kombination von Produkt- und Prozessstruktur beschreibt, können einige davon durch rationales Kalkül ausgeschlossen

[51] Vgl. Rice Jr., James B. und Federico Caniato: Building a Secure and Resilient Supply Network, in: Supply Chain Management Review, Vol. 7 (2003), No. 5, S. 26.

[52] Vgl. zur Produkt-Prozess-Matrix Hayes, Robert H. und Steven C. Wheelwright: Link Manufacturing Process and Product Life Cycles, in: Harvard Business Review, Vol . 57 (1979), S. 137.

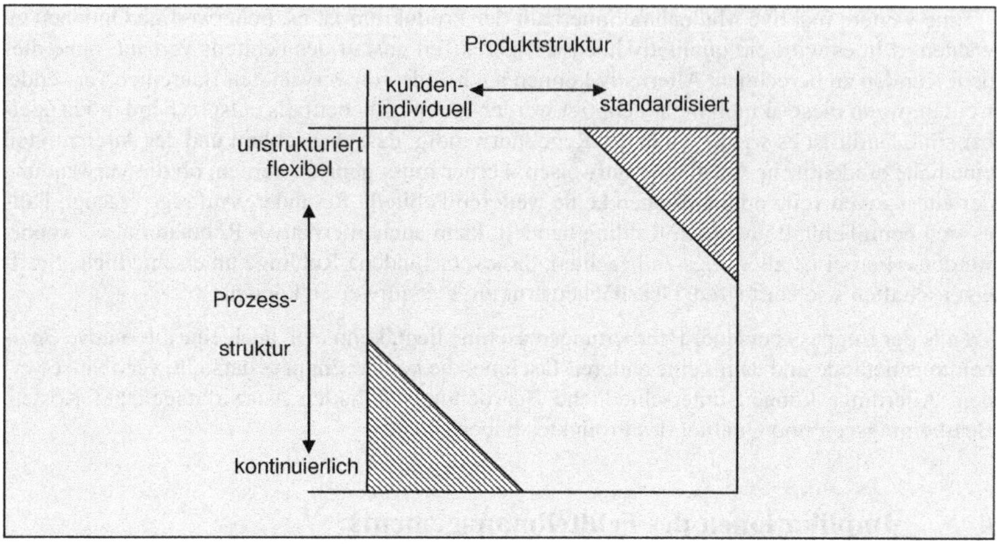

Abbildung 2: Die Produkt-Prozess-Matrix

werden, was durch die Schraffur in obiger Grafik angedeutet wird.[53] So würde eine Produktstruktur, die durch einen hohen Standardisierungsgrad charakterisiert ist, eine kontinuierliche Prozessstruktur implizieren, um sogenannte Skaleneffekte realisieren zu können.[54] Üblicherweise kristallisieren sich im Zeitablauf Konfigurationen heraus, die sich auf der Diagonalen der Matrix befinden, da hier eine Abstimmung der Produktstruktur mit der Prozessstruktur gegeben ist. So erfordert ein an den Kundenbedürfnissen ausgerichtetes Produkt, das demnach einen geringen Standardisierungsgrad aufweist, ein Produktionssystem, welchem die nötige Flexibilität zur Produktion einer Vielzahl von Varianten inhärent ist. Eine mögliche Umsetzungsform eines derartigen Produktionssystems ist die Werkstattfertigung. Für ein Produktionssystem, das Produkte mit hohem Standardisierungsgrad fertigen soll, erscheint es sinnvoll, einen hohen Grad an Kontinuität zur Generierung von Effizienzvorteilen zu realisieren.

Jedes produzierende Unternehmen kann anhand dieser Matrix eingeordnet werden. Es ist davon auszugehen, dass der Grad der Umsetzung des Fehlteilmanagements von der jeweiligen Kombination aus Produkt- und korrespondierender Prozessstruktur determiniert wird. So kann argumentiert werden, dass der erforderliche Implementierungsgrad des Fehlteilmanagements entlang der Diagonalen von oben links nach unten rechts zunimmt. Ursache hierfür ist die abnehmende Kompensationsmöglichkeit bei zunehmend systemischem Charakter des Produktionssystems, weil dieser dazu führt, dass Fehler nur schwer zu beheben sind.

---

[53] Vgl. dazu Thun, Jörn-Henrik und Joachim Stumpfe: Integration von Produkt- und Prozessentwicklung – Zur Problematik von Komplexität und Dynamik bei der Innovation von Produkten und Prozessen, in: Frank Maier (Hrsg.): Komplexität und Dynamik von Systemen – Herausforderungen für die Unternehmensführung, Wiesbaden 2004, S. 162 ff.

[54] Der schraffierte Bereich in der rechten oberen Ecke der Matrix kann demnach als unökonomisch bezeichnet werden.

Aufgrund der geringen Größe des Alternativenraums bei kontinuierlicher Fertigung besteht die Tendenz, dass Fehlteile hier mit schwerwiegenderen Konsequenzen wie z. B. Bandstillständen verbunden sind als dies bei einer flexiblen Prozessstruktur wie der Werkstattfertigung der Fall wäre. Aufgrund der kontinuierlichen Produktion wie z. B. bei der Fließfertigung geht eine Unterbrechung der Fertigung durch das Auftreten eines Fehlteils oftmals mit einem Produktionsausfall einher, da derartige Prozesse tendenziell relativ starr bzw. unflexibel sind. Oftmals sind einzelne Bearbeitungsschritte durch den notwendigen hohen Integrationsgrad technisch fest miteinander gekoppelt, so dass der durch das Auftreten eines Fehlteils verursachte Ausfall einer Bearbeitungsstation nahezu zwangsläufig zu einem Stillstand ganzer Bereiche der Fertigung führt.

Im Gegensatz zum stark systemischen Charakter einer kontinuierlichen Produktion sind die jeweiligen Bearbeitungsstationen diverser Produktionsstufen bei einer Werkstattfertigung entkoppelt, so dass diese zumindest temporär voneinander unabhängig fertigen können. Die Konsequenzen eines Fehlteils sind bei nicht kontinuierlicher Produktion demnach geringer, da negative Auswirkungen tendenziell eher kompensiert werden können.

Je größer der potenzielle Schaden durch das Auftreten eines Fehlteils ist, desto besser ist der Umfang kostenintensiver Maßnahmen zur Vermeidung rational zu begründen. Aufgrund dieser Logik nimmt die Bedeutung des Fehlteilmanagements entlang der Diagonalen zu. Es ist demnach festzuhalten, dass Unternehmen, deren Produktion im rechten unteren Bereich der Matrix positioniert ist, vergleichsweise mehr in Maßnahmen gegen das Auftreten von Fehlteilen investieren sollten. Diese Argumentation behält grundsätzlich auch bei einer unternehmensübergreifenden Betrachtung ihre Gültigkeit. Auch hier sollte das Fehlteilmanagement bei hochgradig integrierten Prozessen, wie es z. B. bei den Konzepten Just-in-Time oder Just-in-Sequence der Fall ist, einen erheblichen Stellenwert einnehmen.

Weiterhin ist es für Unternehmen von besonderer Bedeutung, die für die spezifische Produktion relevanten Ursachen und Ursprünge von Fehlteilen zu identifizieren. Diese sind im Anschluss hinsichtlich ihrer Wahrscheinlichkeit und daraus resultierender Konsequenz zu evaluieren. Somit ergibt sich für jede potenzielle Ursache eines Fehlteils eine Kombination aus Eintrittswahrscheinlichkeit und Konsequenz.

Grundsätzlich ist davon auszugehen, dass je höher eine Konsequenz und deren Wahrscheinlichkeit eingeschätzt wird, desto stärker müssen einzelne Maßnahmen oder eine Kombination verschiedener Maßnahmen implementiert werden. So sollten Unternehmen, die durch eine stark kontinuierliche Produktion geprägt sind, dem Fehlteilmanagement eine erheblich stärkere Rolle beimessen und sich sowohl auf reaktive als auch auf präventive Maßnahmen fokussieren.

Letztlich muss für jede Ursache eine geeignete Maßnahme ausgewählt bzw. eine Maßnahmenkombination definiert werden, welche die Spezifika der Ursache bestmöglich berücksichtigt. Dabei sollten präventive Maßnahmen primär nach Kosten-Nutzen-Aspekten beurteilt werden. Es ist abzuschätzen, zu welchen Kosten die Wahrscheinlichkeit des Auftretens eines Fehlteils reduziert werden kann. Reaktive Maßnahmen sollten überwiegend gemäß ihrer Reaktionsgeschwindigkeit eingeordnet werden. Hier stellt sich die Frage, wie schnell beim Auftreten eines Fehlteils reagiert werden kann, um den auftretenden Schaden bestmöglich in Grenzen halten zu können.

5 Schlussfolgerungen zum Fehlteilmanagement

Eine Pauschalaussage, welche Maßnahme zur Verringerung von Fehlteilen wann eingesetzt werden sollte, ist aufgrund des Einflusses situativer Faktoren nicht möglich bzw. wenig sinnvoll. Jedoch lassen sich aus obiger Betrachtung folgende Tendenzaussagen treffen. So steigt die generelle Bedeutung des Fehlteilmanagements mit zunehmendem Integrationsgrad der Produktionsstruktur. So ist bei einem kontinuierlichen Produktionssystem die Relevanz des Fehlteilmanagements höher als bei einer Produktion mit entkoppelten Produktionsstufen. Ferner nimmt die Vorteilhaftigkeit präventiver Maßnahmen im Gegensatz zu reaktiven Maßnahmen mit der Höhe der Wahrscheinlichkeit eines potenziellen Fehlteils zu. Zusätzlich sollte sich die Auswahl präventiver Maßnahmen primär an den entstehenden Kosten orientieren, wohingegen reaktive Maßnahmen im Lichte der Reaktionsgeschwindigkeit beurteilt werden sollten.

Es ist davon auszugehen, dass die Bedeutung des Fehlteilmanagements in Zukunft weiter zunehmen wird. Dies lässt sich u. a. durch zwei Entwicklungen begründen. Zum einen führt die Tendenz einer stärkeren Kundenorientierung dazu, dass die Variantenzahl innerhalb der Produktion weiter steigt.[55] Zum anderen erhöht ein Effizienzstreben industrieller Unternehmen mit der entsprechenden Entwicklung zur schlanken Produktion die Störanfälligkeit von Prozessen mit der Folge, dass weitestgehend auf Puffer in Produktionsprozessen verzichtet wird.

Literatur

Al-Radhi, M. und J. Heuer (1995): *Total Productive Maintenance: Konzept, Umsetzung, Erfahrung*, München.

Bernecker, T. und A. Präuer (2006): Risiken und Risikomanagement in Zuliefernetzwerken, in: *Die Unternehmung*, Jg. 60, Nr. 1, S. 27–34.

Boothroyd, G. und P. Dewhurst (1988): Product design for manufacture and assembly, in: *Manufacturing Engineering*, Vol. 100, No. 4, S. 42–46.

Byrne, P. M. (2005): RFID: Unlocking high performance in supply chain planning, in: *Logistics Management*, Vol. 44, No. 9, S. 29–30.

Chopra, S. und M. S. Sodhi (2004): Managing Risk to Avoid Supply-Chain Breakdown, in: *MIT Sloan Management Review*, Vol. 46, No. 1, S. 53–62.

Christopher, M. und H. Peck (2004): Building the Resilient Supply Chain, in: *The International Journal of Logistics Management*, Vol. 15, No. 2, S. 1–13.

Christopher, M. (2004): *Logistics and Supply Chain Management: Strategies for Reducing Cost and Improving Service, 3. Aufl.*, London.

Eckes, G. (2001): *The Six Sigma Revolution, How General Electric and Others Turned Process into Profits,* New York et al.

Ettlie, J. E. (1990): Methods That Work for Integrating Design and Manufacturing, in: Ettlie, J. E. und Stoll, H. W. (Hrsg.): *Managing the Design-Manufacturing Process*, New York, S. 53–78.

Feigenbaum, A. V. (1991): *Total Quality Control, 3. Aufl.*, New York, S. 111.

Giunipero, L. C. und R. Aly Eltantawy (2004): Securing the upstream supply chain: a risk management approach, in: *International Journal of Physical Distribution & Logistics Management*, Vol. 34, No. 9, S. 698–713.

[55] Damit geht auch die Problematik einher, dass die Einzigartigkeit von Teilen zunimmt, so dass ein Fehlteil nicht einfach durch ein anderes ersetzt werden kann.

Gleißner, W. (2007): Analyse und Bewältigung strategischer Risiken, in: Kaiser, T. (Hrsg.): *Wettbewerbsvorteil Risikomanagement – erfolgreiche Steuerung der Strategie-, Reputations- und operationalen Risiken*, Berlin, S. 65–96.

Harland, C., R. C. Lamming und P. D. Cousins (1999): Developing the concept of supply strategy, in: *International Journal of Operations & Production Management*, Vol. 19, No. 7, S. 650–673.

Harry, M. und R. G. Schroeder (2005): *The breakthrough management strategy revolutionizing the world's top corporations*, New York et al.

Hayes, R. H. und S. C. Wheelwright (1979): Link Manufacturing Process and Product Life Cycles, in: *Harvard Business Review*, Vol. 57, S. 133–140.

Hopp, W. J. und M. L. Spearman (2000): *Factory Physics – Foundations of Manufacturing Management, 2. Aufl.*, Boston et al.

Juran, J. M. (1962): *Quality Control Handbook, 2. Aufl.*, New York.

Jüttner, U., H. Peck und M. Christopher (2003): Supply Chain Risk Management: Outlining an Agenda for Future Research, in: *International Journal of Logistics: Research and Applications*, Vol. 6, No. 4, S. 197–210.

Kajüter, P. (2003): Risk Management in Supply Chains, in: Seuring, S., M. Müller, M. Goldbach und U. Schneidewind (Hrsg.): *Strategy and Organization in Supply Chains*, Heidelberg, S. 321–336.

Khouja, M. (1999): The single-period (news-vendor) problem: literature review and suggestions for future research, in: *Omega*, Vol. 27, No. 5, S. 537–553.

Kleindorfer, P. R. und G. H. Saad (2005): Managing Disruption Risks in Supply Chains, in: *Production and Operations Management*, Vol. 14, No. 1, S. 53–68.

Lee, H. L., V. Padmanabhan und S. Whang (1997): The Bullwhip Effect in Supply Chains, in: *Sloan Management Review*, Vol. 38, No. 3, S. 93–102.

Lee, H. L. (2004): The Triple-A Supply Chain, in: *Harvard Business Review*, Vol. 82, No. 10, S. 102–112.

Lochmahr, A. und H. Wildemann (2007): Die Einführung logistischer Konzepte in Theorie und Praxis – Fallbeispiel Kapazitätsmanagement, in: Günthner, W. A. (Hrsg.): *Neue Wege in der Automobillogistik*, Berlin und Heidelberg, S. 509–524.

Milling, P. (1991): Strategische Planungs- und Kontrollsysteme zur Unterstützung betrieblicher Lernprozesse, in: Milling, P. (Hrsg.): *Systemmanagement und Managementsysteme*, Berlin, S. 11–31.

Milling, P. und A. Größler (2001): Simulationsbasierte Analysen von Wertschöpfungsnetzwerken, in: Bellmann, K. (Hrsg.): *Kooperations- und Netzwerkmanagement*, Berlin, S. 55–81.

Milling, P. und J.-H. Thun (2005): Steigerung der Flexibilität in Produktionsprozessen durch integrative Fertigung, in: Kaluza, B. und T. Blecker (Hrsg.): *Erfolgsfaktor Flexibilität – Strategien und Konzepte für wandlungsfähige Unternehmen*, Berlin, S. 251–267.

Modi, S. B. und V. A. Mabert (2007): Supplier development: Improving supplier performance through knowledge transfer, in: *Journal of Operations Management*, Vol. 25, No. 1, S. 42–64.

Nakajima, S. (1988): *Introduction to TPM*, Portland.

Norrman, A. und U. Jansson (2004): Ericsson's proactive supply chain risk management approach after a serious sub-supplier accident, in: *International Journal of Physical Distribution & Logistics Management*, Vol. 34, No. 5, S. 434–456.

Ouyang, Y. (2007): The effect of information sharing on supply chain stability and the bullwhip effect, in: *European Journal of Operational Research*, Vol. 182, No. 3, S. 1107–1121.

Pande, P. S., R. P. Neuman und R. R. Cavanagh (2002): *The Six Sigma Way: How GE, Motorola, and other top companies are honing their performance*, New York.

Peck, H. (2005): Drivers of supply chain vulnerability: an integrated framework, in: *International Journal of Physical Distribution & Logistics Management*, Vol. 35, No. 4, S. 210–232.

Rice Jr., J. B. und F. Federico Caniato (2003): Building a Secure and Resilient Supply Network, in: *Supply Chain Management Review*, Vol. 7, No. 5, S. 22–30.

Schimmelpfeng, K. (2001): Risikomanagement in Industrieunternehmen, in: Götze, U., K. Henselmann und B. Mikus (Hrsg.): *Risikomanagement*, Heidelberg, S. 277–297.

Sheffi, Y. und J. B. Rice Jr., (2005): A Supply Chain View of the Resilient Enterprise, in: *Sloan Management Review*, Vol. 47, No. 1, S. 41–48.

Sheffi, Y. (2001): Supply Chain Management under the Threat of International Terrorism, in: *The International Journal of Logistics Management*, Vol. 12, No. 2, S. 1–11.

Stalk, G. jr. und T. M. Hout (1990): *Competing Against Time – How Time-based Competition Is Reshaping Global Market*, New York.

Stoll, H. (1986): Design for Manufacture: An Overview, in: *Applied Mechanics*, Vol. 39, No. 9, S. 1356–1364.

Svensson, G. (2004): Key areas, causes and contingency planning of corporate vulnerability in supply chains, in: *International Journal of Physical Distribution & Logistics Management*, Vol. 34, No. 9, S. 728–748.

Thun, J.-H., M. Drüke und V. Silveira Camargos (2007): Just in Sequence – Eine Erweiterung des Just in Time durch Sequenzzulieferung, in: *Logistik Management*, Jg. 9, Nr. 4, S. 34–46.

Thun, J.-H., P. M. Milling und W. Roos (2007): Studying Six Sigma – An empirical Analysis of the German Automotive Industry, in: Acur, N., N. K. Erkip und E. D. Günes (Hrsg.): *Managing Operations in an Expanding Europe*, Ankara, S. 1–10.

Wagner, S. M. und C. Bode (2007): Empirische Untersuchung von SC-Risiken und SC-Risikomanagement in Deutschland, in: Vahrenkamp, R. und C. Siepermann (Hrsg.): *Risikomanagement in Supply Chains*, Berlin, S. 59–79.

Wildemann, H. (1995): *Das Just-in-Time Konzept – Produktion und Zulieferung auf Abruf, 4. Aufl.*, München.

Zsidisin, G. A., A. Panelli und R. Upton (2000): Purchasing organization involvement in risk assessments, contingency plans, and risk management: an exploratory study, in: *Supply Chain Management: An International Journal*, Vol. 5, No. 4, S. 187–197.

Zsisidin, G. A., G. L. Ragatz und S. A. Melnyk (2005): The dark side of supply chain management, in: *Supply Chain Management Review*, Vol. 9, No. 2, S. 46–52.

Strategische Referenzprofile als Leitmotiv für die Strategieentwicklung industrieller Unternehmen

Jürgen Hasenpusch

Voith Industrial Services, Stuttgart

Zusammenfassung

Die Forderung nach Konsistenz der von der Geschäftseinheit und dem Fertigungsbereich eines Unternehmens verfolgten Strategie ist Ausgangspunkt dieses Beitrags, der auf dem Projekt „International Manufacturing Strategy Survey" basiert. Die Erfolgsbeiträge der Strategiekonfigurationen zeigen, dass die Verfolgung einer konsistenten Strategie zwar Potenzial für unternehmerischen Erfolg birgt, dieser jedoch nicht unabhängig davon ist, welche Strategie gewählt wird. Auf dieser Basis wird ein strategisches Idealprofil ermittelt und gezeigt, inwieweit die Unternehmen der untersuchten Stichprobe mit diesem übereinstimmen und welche Implikationen sich in Abhängigkeit von der Entfernung zum Idealprofil ergeben. Die Untersuchung lässt erkennen, dass ein positiver Effekt auf den Unternehmenserfolg zu verzeichnen ist, wenn Unternehmen dem idealen strategischen Leitbild folgen. Voraussetzung für Definition und wirksame Umsetzung eines strategischen Profils ist jedoch ein grundlegendes strategisches Denken, das alle Ebenen des Unternehmens mit einbezieht. Nur dann kann eine wechselseitige Unterstützung und Integration der verschiedenen Strategieebenen einer Geschäftseinheit verwirklicht werden.

Schlagwörter: Strategisches Management, Strategiebildung, Strategiekonfigurationen, Wettbewerbsstrategie, Fertigungsstrategie

1 Strategiebildung und strategische Konsistenz

Der Prozess der Erstellung und Umsetzung einer Strategie ist für die Unternehmensführung von zentraler Bedeutung. Es ist kaum möglich, eine Organisation übergreifend und sinnvoll zu strukturieren, ohne eine zusammenhängende Vision und eine gemeinsame Richtung zu Grunde zu legen.[1] Ohne klare und konsistente Strategie können Wachstum und Fortschritt nurmehr zufällig und von externen Einflüssen getrieben sein. Die damit verbundene vielfach erhobene Forderung nach strategischer Konsistenz, d. h. der Übereinstimmung und dem sinnvollen Zusammenwirken von Unternehmens- und Funktionsstrategien, entspricht bei produzierenden Betrieben der Integration von Wettbewerbs- und Fertigungsstrategie.[2] Zwar ist, wie Untersu-

---

[1] Vgl. *Kinni*, Theodore B.: Find the Corporate Heartbeat, in: Industry Week, Vol. 243, No. 15, S. 43 ff.

[2] Vgl. *Hinterhuber*, Hans H. und St. A. *Friedrich*: Markt- und ressourcenorientierte Sichtweise zur Steigerung des Unternehmungswertes, in: *Hahn*, Dietger und Bernard *Taylor* (Hrsg.): Strategische Unternehmensplanung, strategische Unternehmensführung: Stand und Entwicklungstendenzen, 8., aktualisierte Auflage, Heidelberg 1999, S. 1000.

chungen zeigen, aus der strengen Strategiekonsistenz im Sinne einer Übereinstimmung von Wettbewerbs- und Fertigungsstrategie nicht bei allen Strategiekonfigurationen eine eindeutige und überragende Erfolgsträchtigkeit im statistischen Sinne abzuleiten; jedoch machen die Ergebnisse hinsichtlich der absoluten Leistungskennzahlen und des Nutzens verschiedener Verbesserungsprogramme sowie die Bedeutung der Geschäftseinheits-Fertigungs-Schnittstelle in konsistenten Strategieumgebungen deutlich, welche Erfolgspotenziale durch die Konsistenz von Wettbewerbs- und Fertigungsstrategie aktiviert werden können.[3]

Die tatsächlichen Charakteristiken des „Mechanismus", der eine gegenseitige Beeinflussung und damit mögliche Angleichung der unterschiedlichen strategischen Ebenen unterstützt, sind noch nicht hinreichend untersucht worden. Zwar wirkt sich die gesteuerte Interaktion verschiedener Unternehmensbereiche im Rahmen eines Innovationsprozesses ebenfalls auf diese Schnittstelle aus; ein expliziter Verweis auf die Zusammenarbeit der verschiedenen strategischen Ebenen bleibt jedoch häufig aus. Ein Hinweis auf die Wichtigkeit der Schnittstelle zwischen Geschäftseinheit und Fertigung findet sich dagegen bei Eisenhardt und Brown. Diese Autoren sehen eine durchlässige Schnittstelle zwischen diesen Ebenen als besonders bedeutsam für Unternehmen in sich schnell verändernden Märkten an.[4]

Die Analyse der Schnittstelle zwischen Geschäftseinheits- und Fertigungsleitung wirft einen weiteren Punkt auf, der im Rahmen der statistischen Analysen, die überwiegend auf einer Zeitpunktbetrachtung basieren, aber nur unzureichend Beachtung findet: die Entwicklung der Strategie als Prozess innerhalb der unternehmensführenden Aktivitäten. Soll der Forderung nach strategischer Konsistenz im *gesamten* Unternehmen nachgekommen werden, so muss hier auch ein Umdenkprozess hinsichtlich der Mitarbeiterführung und -kommunikation auf allen Ebenen der Organisation stattfinden. Im engeren Sinne bedingt dies auch die Einbeziehung aller Funktionsbereiche eines Unternehmens in die Entwicklung der Strategie. Neben einer horizontalen Integration durch die Einbeziehung der Bereiche, die nicht direkt mit der strategischen Lenkung in Verbindung stehen, muss auch die vertikale Integration durch die Einbeziehung der Mitarbeiter in ein umfassendes Strategiekonzept erfolgen.[5]

Mintzberg vergleicht die Entwicklung einer Unternehmensstrategie mit der Tätigkeit eines Töpfers, der sein Werk in einem langsamen Prozess formt.[6] Dieses Bild der *Entwicklung* steht im Gegensatz zur lange populären Allegorie der strategischen *Planung*, bei der der Stereotyp des Lenkungsausschusses, bestehend aus einer Gruppe von Führungskräften, die Aktionspläne für die Zukunft diskutieren und erstellen, bemüht werden kann.[7] Mintzberg kritisiert diese ratio-

---

[3] Vgl. *Hasenpusch*, Jürgen: Strategiekonsistenz in Geschäftseinheit und Fertigung als Voraussetzung für den Erfolg industrieller Unternehmen, Frankfurt et al. 2001, S. 175 ff.

[4] Vgl. *Maier*, Frank: Die Integration wissens- und modellbasierter Konzepte zur Entscheidungsunterstützung im Innovationsmanagement, Berlin 1995, S. 21 sowie *Eisenhardt*, Kathleen M. und Shona L. *Brown*: Time Pacing: Competing in Markets That Won't Stand Still, in: Harvard Business Review, Vol. 86, January–February 1998, S. 62.

[5] Vgl. *Reger*, Rhonda K. et al: Reframing the Organization – Why Implementing Total Quality Is Easier Said than Done, in: Academy of Management Review, Vol. 19, No. 3, 1994, S. 565 ff.

[6] Vgl. *Mintzberg*, Henry: Crafting Strategy, in: *Montgomery*, Cynthia A. und Michael E. *Porter* (Hrsg.): Strategy: Seeking and Securing Competitive Advantage, S. 403 ff.

[7] Vgl. *Ruffini*, Frans A.J., Harry *Boer* und Maarten J. *van Riemsdijk*: Organisation Design in Operations Management, in: International Journal of Operations & Production Management, Vol. 20, No. 7, 2000, S. 863.

nale und systematische „Top-down"-Planung, da möglicherweise zu wenig Abgleich mit den Ressourcen des Unternehmens erfolgt. Die Vorgänge, die zu einer effektiven Strategieimplementierung führen, werden nur unzureichend in Betracht gezogen. Der Töpfer hingegen muss seine eigenen Fähigkeiten gut genug kennen, um angesichts früherer Erfahrungen und zukünftiger Erwartungen die richtigen Aktivitäten für das zu bearbeitende Material zu wählen. Ebenso muss in einer Organisation Klarheit über die Kompetenzen bestehen, auf deren Basis eine strategische Richtung eingeschlagen werden kann. Mintzberg führt seine Metapher weiter, indem er Manager als Handwerker und die Strategie als deren Material sieht, das sie in einem Bearbeitungsprozess „in Form" bringen sollen.[8]

In einem Überblick, sei es im Rahmen einer wissenschaftlichen Arbeit oder einem Zeitungsartikel, ist das Ergebnis eines Strategieprozesses oft leicht erkennbar und verständlich. Dadurch kann eine Strategie möglicherweise auf einzelne Personen und deren Entscheidungen zurückgeführt werden. Werden jedoch Größe und Komplexität einer Organisation in Betracht gezogen, so ist der Ursprung einer Strategie, insbesondere während des Strategieentwicklungsprozesses, nur schwer feststellbar – angesichts zahlloser Managementsitzungen, Diskussionen und Ideen, die angenommen oder auch verworfen werden, ist die Unschärfe unmittelbar einsichtig. Wird vor diesem Hintergrund versucht, ein formales Strategieplanungssystem zu entwerfen und zu implementieren, so ist es nicht verwunderlich, dass strategische Konsistenz in den verschiedenen Unternehmensbereichen so selten verwirklicht wird.[9]

Fraglich ist jedoch häufig, welchem strategischen Idealbild der Strategieprozess folgen soll. Teilweise wird unterstellt, dass das Finden eines solchen Ideals nur durch das Vorhandensein von strategischem *Denken* – im Gegensatz zu bzw. als Voraussetzung der strategischen *Planung* – möglich ist.[10] Beispielhaft wird hier die Führung kleiner und mittlerer Unternehmen angeführt. Selten kann dort über ausreichend Zeit und sonstige (Management-) Ressourcen verfügt werden, um im Rahmen umfangreicher Workshops oder ähnlicher Sitzungen strategische Analysen und Pläne zu entwickeln. Vielmehr muss hier das tägliche Handeln von strategischem Denken durchsetzt und geleitet sein. Die strategische Agenda, die in größeren Unternehmen idealerweise in einen unternehmensweiten und konsistenten Strategieprozess mündet, muss demzufolge das strategische Denken als Basis haben, das eher qualitative als quantitative Elemente berücksichtigt. Dabei wird entwickelt, welche besonderen Stärken, welche „Areas of Excellence" eine Organisation zukünftig aufweisen soll, die notwendig sind, um das Überleben des Unternehmens langfristig zu sichern.[11]

Ausgehend von dieser Notwendigkeit soll im Rahmen dieser Untersuchung ein Referenzprofil für industrielle Betriebe identifiziert werden, das als strategisches Leitbild für Unternehmen aus der Stichprobe der „International Manufacturing Strategy Survey" gelten kann. Dabei wird gezeigt, welche Erfolgsauswirkungen eine Entsprechung der Ausrichtung des Unternehmens mit dem Idealprofil hat und wie sich die Unternehmen der Stichprobe im Verhältnis zu diesem Profil positionieren. Zunächst wird jedoch das Zusammenwirken von Markt- und Ressourcen-

[8] Vgl. *Mintzberg*, Henry: Crafting Strategy, S. 404.

[9] Vgl. *Mintzberg*, Henry: Crafting Strategy, S. 406.

[10] Vgl. *Kinni*, Theodore B.: Find the Corporate Heartbeat, S. 43.

[11] *Service*, Robert W.: The Development of Strategic Intelligence: A Managerial Perspective, in: International Journal of Management, Vol. 23, No. 1, S. 62.

orientierung diskutiert und die Forderung nach strategischer Konsistenz postuliert, die als Basis für eine strukturierte Strategieentwicklung anzusehen ist.

2 Das Spannungsfeld zwischen Wettbewerbsposition und Fertigungskompetenz

Bis vor etwa 15 Jahren galt es als das wesentliche Ziel des Fertigungsbereichs eines Unternehmens, möglichst effizient zu produzieren und dabei den vorgegebenen Qualitätsanforderungen zu entsprechen. Strategische Aspekte tangieren nach dieser Sichtweise die Fertigung erst dann, wenn es um die Umsetzung von Entscheidungen geht, die die Wettbewerbspositionen des Unternehmens gestalten sollen.[12] Das Zusammenwirken und Zusammenpassen von Wettbewerbs- und Fertigungsstrategien spielt hier bestenfalls eine sekundäre Rolle. Die resultierende mangelnde Abstimmung zwischen interner und externer Sicht von Unternehmen und Markt kann Markterfolg und Leistungsfähigkeit von Unternehmen und Fertigung gleichermaßen beeinträchtigen.[13] Ausgangspunkt des vorliegenden Beitrags ist die daraus abzuleitende Forderung nach Konsistenz der von der Geschäftseinheit und dem Fertigungsbereich verfolgten Strategie; es soll auf empirischer Basis untersucht werden, ob die Angleichung der Strategien beider Bereiche Voraussetzung für den Unternehmenserfolg ist.

Die strategischen Gesichtspunkte von Geschäftseinheit und Fertigung finden ihre theoretische Diskussion in verschiedenen Ansätzen, die im Rahmen der Untersuchung gegenübergestellt werden. Die Ausrichtung der Geschäftseinheit ist Gegenstand des marktorientierten Ansatzes, wie er insbesondere von Michael Porter propagiert wurde.[14] Ein wesentlicher Gesichtspunkt in dynamischen und kompetitiven Märkten ist dabei die Positionierung einer Geschäftseinheit, die bei der Diskussion der Begriffe „Markt“ und „Wettbewerb“ zunächst im Fokus steht. Die Wechselwirkungen im Wettbewerb und der Einfluss auf den Unternehmenserfolg, der von Wettbewerbsvorteilen ausgeht, treten hier am deutlichsten hervor. Aufgabe der strategischen Führung ist es daher, bei der Festlegung und Durchsetzung der Unternehmensentwicklung Richtung, Ausmaß, Struktur und Systeme sowie Träger künftiger Entwicklungen festzulegen, um Erfolgspotenziale zu schaffen und zu nutzen.[15] Stehen die marktbezogenen Aspekte im Mittelpunkt der strategischen Steuerung eines Unternehmens, so kann von einer Marktorientierung der Unternehmensführung gesprochen werden.

---

[12] Vgl. *Skinner*, Wickham: Manufacturing in the Corporate Strategy, New York et al. 1978, S. 29; *Hill*, Terry: Manufacturing Strategy – Text and Cases, Houndmills (UK) 1995, S. 30.

[13] Vgl. *Jelinek*, Mariann und Michael C. *Burstein*.: The Production Administrative Structure: A Paradigm for Strategic Fit, in: Academy of Management Review, Vol. 7, No. 2, 1982, S. 242 ff.; *Ward*, Peter T., Deborah J. *Bickford* und G. Keong *Leong*: Configurations of Manufacturing Strategy, Business Strategy, Environment and Structure, in: Journal of Management, Vol. 22, No. 4, 1996, S. 597 ff.; *Stobaugh*, Robert und Piero *Telesio*: Match Manufacturing Policies and Product Strategy, in: Harvard Business Review, Vol. 61, March–April 1983, S. 113 ff.

[14] Vgl. *Porter*, Michael E.: Competitive Strategy – Techniques for Analyzing Industries and Competitors, New York 1980, S. 25 ff.

[15] Vgl. *Hahn*, Dietger: Strategische Unternehmensführung – Grundkonzept, in: *Hahn*, Dietger und Bernard *Taylor* (Hrsg.): Strategische Unternehmensplanung, strategische Unternehmensführung: Stand und Entwicklungstendenzen, 8., aktualisierte Auflage, Heidelberg 1999, S. 31 f.

Die strategische Bedeutung der Fertigung wächst mit der zunehmenden Emanzipation produktionswirtschaftlicher Sachverhalte.[16] Im Nachgang dazu wurde die Fertigungsstrategie – und damit die Akzeptanz der Produktion als strategischer Wettbewerbsfaktor industrieller Unternehmen – erstmals durch Wickham Skinner als Schlüsselelement der Fertigung analysiert. Seit seinem wegweisenden Beitrag aus dem Jahr 1969,[17] in dem er die fehlenden Verbindungen zwischen der Fertigungs- und der Wettbewerbsstrategie deutlich gemacht hat, hat das Interesse am Bereich der Fertigungsstrategie stetig zugenommen. Skinner hatte vorgeschlagen, die grundlegenden Entscheidungen zur Gestaltung eines Fertigungssystems dergestalt auszuführen, dass auf ihrer Basis eine machtvolle Geschäftseinheitsstrategie entwickelt werden kann. Er sah eine Gefahr in isoliert gefällten, nicht zusammenhängenden Entscheidungen, die den Fertigungsbereich eines Unternehmens schwächten und schwer steuerbar machten.[18] Die Lösung von den „Micro-Techniques",[19] die hauptsächlich darauf abzielten, die Fertigungsfunktion Stück für Stück hinsichtlich der Materialfluss-Steuerung, Arbeitsplanung und ähnlicher Aspekte zu verbessern, und die Hinwendung zu einem zusammenhängenden System von strategisch basierten Zielen, auf deren Basis ein Fertigungssystem gestaltet werden sollte, machten Skinners Werk neuartig und revolutionär. Die Fabrik wurde zum Schlüsselelement der Marktstrategie der Geschäftseinheit, womit sie sich von ihrem früheren Status als kapitalintensive und schwierig steuerbare Notwendigkeit lösen sollte.[20] Vermieden werden soll die Situation, dass die Strategie selbst zwar im Bereich der Fertigung umgesetzt wird, sie jedoch oft erst dann offensichtlich wird, wenn die Umsetzung bereits weit fortgeschritten ist.

Aufbauend auf Skinners Ansätzen ist im Bereich des strategischen Managements in den letzten Jahren eine gewisse Verschiebung von der markt- zur ressourcenorientierten Wettbewerbssicht zu verzeichnen gewesen. Die Veränderung des Wettbewerbsparadigmas begann mit Hinweisen Wernerfelts darauf, dass der Erfolg eines Unternehmens hauptsächlich durch die Stärke seiner Ressourcen und nicht nur durch seine Marktposition erklärt werden kann.[21] Eine weitere Verbreitung erfuhr das Konzept des ressourcenbasierten Wettbewerbs durch Prahalad und Hamel, die für die Verbindung zwischen den Kernkompetenzen einer Unternehmung und deren Wettbewerbsstärke explizit eintraten.[22] Diese Kompetenzen werden als Grundlage des gemeinsamen Lernens in einer Organisation gesehen, gleichsam als Koordinationsfunktion verschiedener Produktionsfähigkeiten und unterschiedlicher technologischer Richtungen.[23] Die Abstim-

[16] Vgl. *Hoitsch*, Hans-Jörg und Bülent *Akin*: Geschichte der Produktionswirtschaft, in: Wirtschaftwissenschaftliches Studium, Heft 2, 1998, S. 56f.

[17] Vgl. *Skinner*, Wickham: Manufacturing: the Missing Link in Corporate Strategy, in: Havard Business Review, Vol. 47, May-June 1969, S. 136ff.

[18] Vgl. *Skinner*, Wickham: Manufacturing Strategy on the „S" Curve, in: Production and Operations Management, Vol. 5, No. 1, 1996, S. 5.

[19] *Skinner*, Wickham: Manufacturing Strategy on the „S" Curve, S. 5.

[20] Vgl. *Skinner*, Wickham: Manufacturing Strategy on the „S" Curve, S. 6.

[21] Vgl. *Wernerfelt*, Birger: A Resource-Based View of the Firm, in: Strategic Management Journal, Vol. 5, 1984, S. 172.

[22] Vgl. *Prahald*, C.K. und Gary *Hamel*: The Core Competence of the Corporation, in: Harvard Business Review, May–June 1990, S. 80.

[23] Ebd.

mung von Wettbewerbs- und Fertigungsstrategie findet damit besondere Beachtung, die insbesondere der Verschiedenartigkeit der strategischen und funktionalen Gesichtspunkte der Fertigungs- und Unternehmensstrategie Rechnung trägt.

Die veränderten Anforderungen und Aktivitäten haben das Bewusstsein für die Notwendigkeit von Fertigungsstrategien und -zielen geschärft, die die Wettbewerbsstrategie sinnvoll ergänzen und unterstützen.[24] Nach wie vor besteht jedoch auch in diesen Konstellationen die Gefahr, dass das Bestreben des Managements, bessere Leistungen im Fertigungsbereich zu erbringen, die Grenzen der strategischen Steuerung überschreitet und die Fertigung wieder zum Erfüllungsgehilfen des Marketings degradiert.[25] Ein bedeutsamer Punkt in diesem Zusammenhang ist, dass eine leistungsfähige Fertigung – wie jeder andere wertvolle Kompetenzbereich eines Unternehmens – sorgfältig, systematisch und zweckgerichtet entwickelt werden muss, wenn sie als Basis eines Wettbewerbsvorteils wirken soll.[26] Dies bedeutet, dass sie sowohl hinsichtlich ihrer Aufgaben, als auch der Mittel, die für deren Erfüllung zur Verfügung stehen, aktiv in die zu unterstützenden Produktstrategien integriert werden muss.[27]

3 Integration und Konsistenz von Geschäftseinheits- und Fertigungsstrategie

3.1 Unternehmensstrategien im Lichte von Markt- und Ressourcenorientierung

Die Verbindung von interner Kompetenz und Marktorientierung zieht weitreichende Konsequenzen hinsichtlich der strategischen Steuerung und damit der strukturellen Gestaltung, insbesondere der Fertigung, nach sich. Die sich daraus ergebende Forderung nach einer Verbindung zwischen Wettbewerbsstrategie und Fertigungsstrategie und -struktur ist nicht neu. Bereits Chandler hat darüber publiziert und insbesondere den Begriff des „Fit", der Angleichung von organisatorischen Strukturen und Umweltbedingungen, geprägt.[28]

Die Rolle der Fertigung hinsichtlich der Wettbewerbsstärke einer Unternehmung wurde von Hayes und Wheelwright systematisiert. Sie wiesen in ihrem Stufenmodell darauf hin, dass eine nur reaktiv ausgerichtete Fertigung, deren primäres Ziel es ist, mit der Konkurrenz Schritt zu halten, kein besonderes Potenzial für Wettbewerbsvorteile besitzt.[29] Eine Abkehr von dieser reaktiven Sicht bedingt eine Fertigung, die der Wettbewerbsstrategie zunächst bedeutende Unterstützung angedeihen lässt und in der höchsten Stufe des Modells die Quelle bzw. Basis des Wettbewerbsvorteils des Unternehmens ist.

[24] Vgl. *Skinner*, Wickham: Manufacturing – the Missing Link in Corporate Strategy, S. 141.

[25] Vgl. *Stobaugh*, Robert und Piero *Telesio*: Match Manufacturing Policies and Product Strategy, S. 113.

[26] Vgl. *Hayes*, Robert H. und David M. *Upton*: Operations-Based Strategy, in: California Management Review, Vol. 40, No. 4, 1998, S. 22.

[27] Vgl. *Stobaugh*, Robert und Piero *Telesio*: Match Manufacturing Policies and Product Strategy, S. 113.

[28] Vgl. *Chandler*, Alfred D.: Strategy and Structure: Chapters in the History of the Industrial Enterprise, Cambrigde (MA) 1962.

[29] Vgl. *Hayes*, Robert H. und Steven C. *Wheelwright*: Restoring Our Competitive Edge: Competing Through Manufacturing, New York et al. 1984, S. 396. Diese Unternehmen befinden sich in den Stufen 1 und 2.

Insgesamt kann in der Entsprechung von Wettbewerbs- und Fertigungsstrategie von einem der grundlegenden Probleme der strategischen Planung und Entwicklung gesprochen werden: Zwar wird in der Literatur von der strategischen Planung als dem „Bemühen um eine optimale Allokation von Ressourcen"[30] gesprochen, jedoch scheint sich in der Praxis oftmals zu zeigen, dass gerade die Umsetzung der detaillierten Strategiepläne, d.h. Aufbau und Allokation der Ressourcen, das eigentliche Problem darstellen. Die mangelnde Abstimmung von interner und externer Sicht von Unternehmung und Markt scheint demgemäß Markterfolg und Leistungsfähigkeit von Unternehmen und Fertigung gleichermaßen zu beeinträchtigen.[31]

Die Interaktion von Variablen der Fertigungs- und Wettbewerbsstrategie wurde in fallbasierten und empirischen Untersuchungen betriebswirtschaftlicher Erfolgsfaktoren bereits in verschiedener Weise diskutiert. Das Zusammenspiel von Fertigungsstrategien und Umweltvariablen bildete den Schwerpunkt der „Manufacturing Futures Survey", einer Studie, innerhalb der beispielsweise die Eigenschaft der Flexibilität in besonderem Maße untersucht wurde.[32] Die Verbindung zwischen Geschäftseinheitsstrategien und Fertigungsstrukturen erhielt in anderen Studien besondere Aufmerksamkeit. Eine unterstützende Kombination der Strategien und Strukturen zeigte positive Effekte auf den Erfolg einer Unternehmung.[33] Eine Reihe weiterer empirischer Hinweise hinsichtlich eines positiven Zusammenhangs mit verschiedenen Erfolgsgrößen konnte gesammelt werden, wobei sich hier Vorteile durch eine Konsistenz von Fertigungs- und Marketingstrategien ergaben. Angesichts dieser Anerkennung der Bedeutung des strategischen „Fit" wurde die Beziehung zwischen Geschäftseinheits- und Fertigungsstrategie bereits in Teilen dokumentiert. Studien geben ebenso statistischen Nachweis darüber, wie sich technologische und fertigungsstrategische Ziele und Strukturen mit der Wettbewerbsstrategie – und letztlich mit dem Erfolg des Unternehmens – verbinden lassen.[34] Trotz des vielfach gezeigten Potenzials der konsistenten strategischen Ausrichtung eines Fertigungsbetriebs scheint die Praxis dieses Konzept jedoch noch nicht hinreichend akzeptiert zu haben. Eine Reihe empirischer Untersuchungen geben Hinweise darauf, dass die Konsistenz der gewählten Strategien in Geschäftseinheit und Fertigung nicht immer in ausreichendem Maße gegeben ist.[35]

---

[30] *Welge*, Martin K. und Andreas *Al-Laham*: Strategisches Management: Grundlagen – Prozeß – Implementierung, 2., vollst. überarb. u. erw. Aufl., Wiesbaden 1999, S. 10.

[31] Vgl. *Welge*, Martin K. und Andreas *Al-Laham*: Strategisches Management, S. 11.

[32] Vgl. *De Meyer*, Arnoud et al.: Flexibility: The Next Competitive Battle – The Manufacturing Futures Survey, in: Strategic Management Journal, Vol. 10, 1989, S. 135–144.

[33] Vgl. *Jelinek*, Mariann und Michael C. *Burstein*.: The Production Administrative Structure, S. 242 ff.; *Ward*, Peter T., Deborah J. *Bickford* und G. Keong *Leong*: Configurations of Manufacturing Strategy, Business Strategy, Environment and Structure, S. 597 ff. Eine fallbasierte Diskussion des strategischen „Fit" findet sich bei Stobaugh und Telesio am Beispiel von Deere & Company sowie Warwick Electronics. Vgl. *Stobaugh*, Robert und Piero *Telesio*: Match Manufacturing Policies and Product Strategy, S. 113 ff.

[34] Vgl. *Zahra*, Shaker A. und Jeffrey G. *Covin*: Business Strategy, Technology Policy and Firm Performance, in: Strategic Management Journal, Vol. 14., No. 6, 1993, S. 462 ff.

[35] Vgl. *Venkatraman*, N. und John E. *Prescott*: Environment-Strategy Coalignment: An Empirical Test of its Performance Implications, in: Strategic Management Journal, Vol. 11, 1990, S. 15; *Nath*, Deepika und N. *Sudharshan*: Measuring Strategy Coherence Through Patterns of Strategic Choices, in: Strategic Management Journal, Vol. 15, 1994, S. 53 f.; *Milling*, Peter und Jürgen *Hasenpusch*: Zielrelationen in Geschäftseinheit und Fertigung, in: Forschungsberichte der Fakultät für Betriebswirtschaftslehre der Universität Mannheim, Nr. 9903, Mannheim 1999.

Die Analysen im Rahmen dieses Beitrags werden auf der Basis einer empirischen Studie, des „International Manufacturing Strategy Survey“ (IMSS), durchgeführt.[36] Die IMSS-Datenbank erlaubt die Untersuchung von Fertigungsstrategien in einem internationalen Rahmen, wobei zentrale Bereiche der Untersuchung die Strategien und Marktziele der Geschäftseinheiten sowie deren Umsetzung in Fertigungsziele sind. Zusätzlich wurden Informationen über die daraus resultierenden Fertigungspraktiken und die Bereiche der Fertigung, in denen heute und zukünftig Verbesserungsprogramme realisiert und geplant werden, gesammelt.

3.2 Konfigurationen aus Geschäftseinheits- und Fertigungsstrategie

Grundlage der folgenden Analyse ist die Identifikation der Wettbewerbs- und Fertigungsziele der Geschäftseinheiten der Stichprobe und deren Verdichtung zu Oberzielen. Der erste Schritt ist dabei die Identifikation der Ziele, die die Geschäftseinheiten im Wettbewerbsumfeld verfolgen. Die Stärken, die hier aufgebaut werden sollen, sind im Markt transparent und stellen für die Kunden den kaufentscheidenden Faktor dar.[37] Die den Befragten vorgelegten Ziele lassen sich gleichsam als strategische Stoßrichtungen im Sinne des angestrebten Tätigkeitsfelds einer Geschäftseinheit bezeichnen. Die Ziele betreffen die Schnittstelle zwischen Unternehmensressourcen und Unternehmensumwelt, an deren Verbindung die übergreifende Strategie der Geschäftseinheit entsteht.[38] Die Dimensionen dieser strategischen Ziele wurden bereits mehrfach im Bereich der Erfolgsfaktorforschung verwendet und haben sich als stabil erwiesen.[39]

Die sieben bei der IMSS-Untersuchung abgefragten Wettbewerbsziele werden zunächst mit Hilfe einer explorativen Faktorenanalyse zu vier Skalen verdichtet, um die Komplexität der Analyse zu verringern. Die explorative Faktoranalyse ist ein geeignetes Instrument, um unbekannte Strukturen aufzudecken. Im vorliegenden Fall können damit einzelne Ziele, die von den Geschäftseinheiten gemeinsam verfolgt werden, kombiniert werden, ohne dass vorher entsprechende Hypothesen über diesen Zusammenhang generiert wurden. Die Zusammenfassung erfolgt im Sinne einer besseren Anschaulichkeit, wobei der Datenumfang durch die Faktorenanalyse ohne größeren Informationsverlust reduziert wird.[40] Für die Anwendung der Faktorenanalyse spricht außerdem, dass das Hypothesensystem, das in dieser Arbeit überprüft wird, eher aggregierte Dimensionen als einzelne Variablen reflektiert.[41] Die vier resultierenden Strategiedimensionen der Geschäftseinheit sind „Produkt/Innovation“, „Zeit“, „Preis“ und „Qualität“;

[36] Zum IMSS-Projekt vgl. *Lindberg*, Per, Christopher A. *Voss* und Kathryn L. *Blackmon*: International Manufacturing Strategies: Context, Content, and Change, Boston (MA) 1997, S. 3f.

[37] Vgl. *Aspesi*, Claudio und Dev *Vardhan*: Brilliant Strategy, But Can You Execute?, in: The McKinsey Quarterly, No. 1, 1999, S. 89.

[38] Vgl. *Verdin*, Paul und Peter *Williamson*: Successful Strategy: Stargazing or Self-Examination?, in: European Management Journal, Vol. 12, No. 1, 1994, S. 10.

[39] Vgl. *Nieschlag*, Robert, Erwin *Dichtl* und Hans *Hörschgen*: Marketing, 18., durchges. Auflage, Berlin 1997, S. 114ff. Für eine detaillierte Diskussion der Zieldimensionen vgl. *De Meyer*, Arnoud et al.: Flexibility: The Next Competitive Battle, S. 138ff.

[40] Vgl. *Bortz*, Jürgen: Statistik für Sozialwissenschaftler, 5., vollst. überarb. u. aktual. Aufl., Berlin et al. 1999, S. 474.

[41] Vgl. zu dieser Problematik auch *Miller*, Danny: Strategy Making and Structure: Analysis and Implications For Performance, in: Academy of Management Journal, Vol. 30, No. 1, 1987, S. 17.

ihre Zusammensetzung, die anhand der Faktorladungen illustriert wird, sowie die Werte der Reliabilitätsanalyse nach Cronbach (Cronbachs Alpha) sind in Tabelle 1 dargestellt.[42] Die Faktorladungen geben die Korrelation zwischen den Ausgangsvariablen und dem resultierenden Faktor, hier also dem verdichteten Ziel, an.

Tabelle 1: Dimensionen der Geschäftseinheitsstrategien im IMSS-Projekt

Faktor	Items	Faktorladung	Cronbachs Alpha
Produkt/ Innovation	Breite Produktpalette Große Anzahl neuentwickelter Produkte	0,873 0,838	0,668
Zeit	Schnelle Lieferung Termintreue	0,820 0,809	0,554
Preis	Niedriger Preis	0,985	–
Qualität	Fertigungsqualität Überlegenes Produktdesign	0,823 0,822	0,597

Die Vorgehensweise der Zielidentifikation in der Fertigung wird analog der Operationalisierung der Geschäftseinheitsziele im vorigen Abschnitt durchgeführt. Den Befragten wurde eine Liste von insgesamt elf Fertigungszielen vorgelegt, die als Taxone für die Facetten der Fertigungsstrategien fungieren. Die vorgelegten Ziele bilden die Entsprechung der nach außen gerichteten Wettbewerbsziele auf der Geschäftseinheitsebene. Die Skalen repräsentieren die Bedeutung der Ziele für die betriebliche Leistungsfähigkeit, hinsichtlich derer das Fertigungssystem besondere Stärken besitzen soll. Die elf abgefragten Fertigungsziele werden mit Hilfe einer explorativen Faktorenanalyse zu vier zusammengefassten Skalen verdichtet, deren Benennung analog der Geschäftseinheitsebene erfolgt. Die vier resultierenden Strategiedimensionen der Fertigung und ihre Faktorladungen sowie die Reliabilitätsmaße nach Cronbach sind in Tabelle 2 (s. S. 194) dargestellt.[43]

Anschließend werden auf Basis der Stichprobe mit Hilfe zweier Clusteranalysen jeweils auf Geschäftseinheits- und Fertigungsebene drei Strategietypen bzw. -gruppen identifiziert, nämlich Unternehmen, die (i) einer vermehrten Qualitätsorientierung folgen, (ii) Zeitwettbewerber sowie (iii) Innovations- bzw. Preiswettbewerber. Die Interpretation der drei strategischen

[42] Vgl. dazu *Backhaus*, Klaus et al.: Multivariate Analysemethoden: eine anwendungsorientierte Einführung, 8., verb. Aufl., Berlin et al. 1996, S. 209. Auf die Darstellung weiterer Reliabilitätsgrößen dieser und der folgenden Faktoranalysen wird hier verzichtet. Die interne Konsistenz der Faktoren wird zunächst mit einer Reliabilitätsanalyse nach Cronbach überprüft. Jeder der Faktoren erreicht einen Wert für Cronbachs Alpha, der die untere Akzeptanzschwelle, die bei 0,5 bis 0,6 liegt, zumindest erreicht oder übersteigt. Weitere Hinweise auf die Verlässlichkeit der Ergebnisse der Faktoranalyse gibt das Kaiser-Meyer-Ohlkin-Kriterium, das mit KMK = 0,634 einen noch ausreichenden Wert annimmt. Die Anti-Image-Matrix gibt einen Hinweis auf den Grund dieses niedrigen Wertes: Das „Measure-Of-Sampling-Adequacy“, das für jede Variable berechnet wird, weist für die Variable Preis einen mit MSA = 0,480 sehr niedrigen Wert aus. Letztlich übersteigen jedoch alle Faktorladungen die geforderte Schwelle von 0,5. Aufgrund dessen und der inhaltlichen Bedeutung des Zieles der Preisführerschaft sowie der insgesamt zufriedenstellenden Reliabilität des Faktorenmodells wird diese Dimension jedoch in der Analyse belassen.

[43] Weitere Ergebnisse bezüglich der Faktorenanalyse sind beim Autor erhältlich.

Tabelle 2: Dimensionen der Fertigungsstrategien im IMSS-Projekt

Faktor	Items	Faktorladung	Cronbachs Alpha
Produkt/ Innovation	Anzahl neuentwickelter Produkte Entwicklungsgeschwindigkeit Produktvielfalt	0,882 0,819	0,756
Zeit	Vorlaufzeit Auslieferung Vorlaufzeit Beschaffung Durchlaufzeit	0,811 0,749 0,647	0,724
Kosteneffizienz	Fertigungsstückkosten Material- und Gemeinkosten Produktivität	0,842 0,767 0,696	0,674
Qualität/ Liefertreue	Fertigungsqualität Termingerechte Lieferung	0,811 0,692	0,501

Gruppen, die entsprechend ihrer Zielgewichtungen „Qualität/Zuverlässigkeit", „Zeit" und „Innovation/Preis"[44] genannt werden, basiert zunächst auf den Unterschieden der Clustermittelwerte, deren Signifikanz auch im statistischen Sinne besteht.[45] Als hinreichende Interpretationskriterien sind die Gewichtung der Ziele im Clustervergleich und die relative Rangfolge der Bedeutung einzelner Ziele innerhalb der Cluster heranzuziehen.[46] Dadurch lassen sich die strategischen Inhalte der einzelnen Typen bestimmen. Die Clusteranalysen resultieren sowohl auf der Wettbewerbs- als auch auf der Fertigungsebene in gleichartigen Strategietypen; beispielhaft sind in Abbildung 1 die Profile der fertigungsstrategischen Typen FQ, FZ und FI dargestellt.[47]

---

[44] Die Kombination der Innovations- und Preisziele in einem strategischen Typ mag zunächst überraschen; allerdings ist dieser Strategietyp auch in einer anderen Untersuchung, ebenfalls identifiziert worden (vgl. dazu Vgl. *Milling*, Peter M., Frank H. *Maier* und Daoud *Mansury*: Impact of Manufacturing Strategy on Plant Performance – Insights from the International Research Project: World Class Manufacturing, in: Bartezzaghi, Emilio et al. (Hrsg.): Managing Operations Networks, Padova 1999, S. 578.) Diese Ziele sind nicht etwa als unvereinbar oder konkurrierend, sondern als zwei Quellen von Wettbewerbsvorteilen anzusehen, hinsichtlich derer eine Geschäftseinheit hohe oder niedrigere Anstrengungen unternehmen kann. Das Erreichen eines günstigen Angebotspreises wird für diese Unternehmen auch im Falle größerer Innovativität gelten, da das niedrige Preisniveau in vielen Märkten als „conditio sine qua non" angesehen werden kann. Die Anwendung einer „Skimming"-Strategie der Preisabschöpfung scheint hier nicht möglich zu sein. Zusätzlich besteht bei einer hohen Innovationsdichte stets die Gefahr, dass die Kostensituation des Unternehmens durch die beständigen anspruchsvollen Neuerungen außer Kontrolle gerät. Daher ist es für innovative Unternehmen gleichsam von größter Bedeutung, anspruchsvolle Preisziele zu setzen. Die Priorisierung der niedrigen Preise mag daher auch in der zurückliegenden Leistung der Geschäftseinheit auf diesem Gebiet liegen, die wesentlichen Einfluss auf die Zielhierarchie nehmen kann.

[45] Die Ergebnisse des dabei verwendeten F-Tests ergaben signifikante Unterschiede hinsichtlich aller Strategie-Dimensionen. Vgl. dazu Hasenpusch, Jürgen: Strategiekonsistenz in Geschäftseinheit und Fertigung als Voraussetzung für den Erfolg industrieller Unternehmen, S. 85 ff.

[46] Diese Vorgehensweise wird von Miller und Roth vorgeschlagen. Vgl. *Miller*, Jeffrey G. und Aleda V. *Roth*: A Taxonomy of Manufacturing Strategies, in: Management Science, Vol. 40, No. 3, 1994, S. 290.

[47] Die Bezeichnungen ergeben sich aus den inhaltlichen Schwerpunkten der Cluster, wobei FQ für Qualitätsorientierung in der Fertigung, FZ für Zeitorientierung und FI für Innovations- und Kostenorientierung steht.

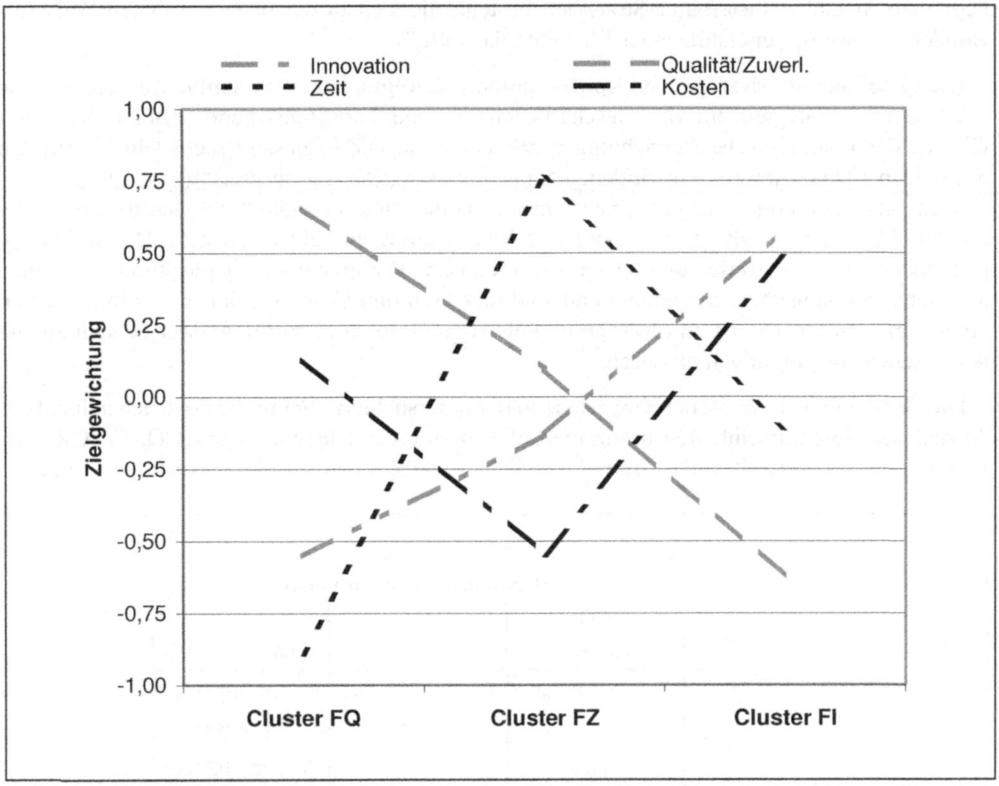

Abbildung 1: Inhaltliche Profile der fertigungsstrategischen Typen

Die Cluster werden in einem nächsten Schritt zu neun strategischen Konfigurationen kombiniert, die aus den entsprechenden Gruppen der Wettbewerbs- sowie der Fertigungsstrategie bestehen (siehe Abbildung 2, die numerischen Werte geben die Anzahl der Unternehmen an, die die jeweilige Strategie wählen). Der Konfigurationsansatz wurde gewählt, da er ein systematisches, detailliertes und ganzheitliches Abbild der zugrundeliegenden Daten gewährt, ohne jedoch einzelnen Teilen des Modells zunächst kausale Attribute zuzuweisen.[48] In dieser Hinsicht wird anderen Autoren gefolgt, dass eine übergeordnete Konsistenz die einzelnen strategischen und strukturellen Dimensionen in gewisser Weise ordnet, ohne anzunehmen, dass diese Ordnung aufgrund einer bestimmten Dimension entstehen muss.[49] Die ermittelten Konfigurationen setzen sich daher aus systematischen Konstellationen gegenseitig mehr oder minder unterstützender Elemente zusammen. Für die Wahl des Konfigurationsansatzes spricht weiterhin das Argument, dass davon auszugehen ist, dass in einer bestimmten Unternehmensumwelt nur eine

[48] Vgl. *Ward*, Peter T., Deborah J. *Bickford* und G. Keong *Leong*: Configurations of Manufacturing Strategy, Business Strategy, Environment and Structure, S. 602.

[49] Vgl. *Miller*, Danny und Henry *Mintzberg*: The Case for Configuration, in: *Miller*, Danny und Peter H. *Friesen* (Hrsg.): Organizations: A Quantum View, Englewood Cliffs (NJ) 1984, S. 10ff.

begrenzte Anzahl realisierbarer Strategien besteht, die sich in der oben erwähnten Weise als Bündel gegenseitig unterstützender Elemente darstellt.[50]

Die Erstellung der strategischen Konfigurationen erfolgt nach einem einfachen Schema: Die Analyse der Strategien auf der Geschäftseinheits- und Fertigungsebene ergibt jeweils drei Cluster, deren strategische Ausrichtung vergleichbar ist. Die insgesamt sechs Cluster mit den auf beiden Ebenen jeweils vorhandenen Strategietypen „Innovation/Preis" (bzw. „Innovation/ Kosten" als Fertigungsstrategie), „Zeit" und „Qualität/Zuverlässigkeit" können untereinander kombiniert werden, wodurch insgesamt eine Matrix mit neun Feldern entsteht. Die drei Gruppen, bei denen wettbewerbs- und fertigungsstrategische Komponenten übereinstimmen, werden als strategisch konsistent bezeichnet und sind hier grau hinterlegt. Von ihnen – zumindest von einem Teil von ihnen – ist zu erwarten und als Hypothese zu überprüfen, dass sie sich als die überlegenen Ausprägungen erweisen.

Die Verbreitung strategischer Konsistenz in der untersuchten Stichprobe lässt sich anhand der Anzahl der Geschäftseinheiten bestimmen, die in eine der Kategorien FQ:GQ, FZ:GZ oder FI:GI fallen.[51] Die zweitgrößte Gruppe von 53 Geschäftseinheiten (18,0%) verfolgt die konsis-

Fertigungsstrategie \ Geschäftseinheitsstrategie	GQ Qualität	GZ Zeit	GI Innovation/Preis
FI Innovation/Kosten	Innovation/Kosten FI:GQ (22) Qualität	Innovation/Kosten FI:GZ (16) Zeit	Innovation/Kosten FI:GI (64) Innovation/Preis
FZ Zeit	Zeit FZ:GQ (4) Qualität	Zeit FZ:GZ (53) Zeit	Zeit FZ:GI (53) Innovation/Preis
FQ Qualität	Qualität FQ:GQ (23) Qualität	Qualität FQ:GZ (35) Zeit	Qualität FQ:GI (25) Innovation/Preis

Abbildung 2: Matrix der strategischen Konfigurationen

[50] Die Argumentation folgt *Miller*, Danny: Configurations of Strategy and Structure: Towards a Synthesis, in: Strategic Management Journal, Vol. 7, 1986, S. 236f.

[51] Hierbei gibt der erste Teil der Bezeichnung der strategischen Konfiguration die Fertigungsstrategie und der zweite Teil die Geschäftseinheitsstrategie wieder, wobei als Trennungszeichen ein Doppelpunkt verwendet wird. D. h. die hier angeführte Strategie FI:GI umfasst als fertigungsstrategische Komponente die Strategie „Innovation/Kosten" und als wettbewerbsstrategische Komponente die Strategie „Innovation/Preis". Dieses Schema wird auch bei allen weiteren Strategiekonfigurationen verwendet.

tente Zeitstrategie FZ: GZ; die konsistente Qualitätsstrategie FQ: GQ wird nur von 23 Geschäftseinheiten (7,8 %) gewählt. Insgesamt fallen 140 Geschäftseinheiten in die Kategorie der strategischen Konsistenz, was 47,4 % der gesamten Stichprobe entspricht.

4 Strategieentwicklung und strategisches Leitbild

4.1 Ein Referenzprofil strategisch konsistenter Ausrichtung

Die Analyse der vorliegenden Stichprobe zeigt, dass in den wenigsten Fällen nur eine einzelne strategische Dimension verfolgt wird; in der Regel wählen die Geschäftseinheiten sowohl hinsichtlich ihrer Wettbewerbs- als auch ihrer Fertigungsstrategie eine Kombination verschiedener Ziele. Es ist daher zu klären, welches Zielmuster mit signifikant größerem Erfolg verbunden ist als andere Zielkonstellationen. Die Analyse der einzelnen Dimensionen des strategischen „Fit" aus den vorigen Abschnitten wird damit weitergeführt und auf die Kombination mehrerer „Fits" ausgeweitet.

In diesem Beitrag soll nun eine Referenzkombination strategischer Ziele gefunden werden, die sich hinsichtlich der Umsatzrendite signifikant von anderen Kombinationen im positiven Sinn unterscheidet. Diese kann dann Grundlage einer strategischen Agenda für Unternehmen der entsprechenden Industrien werden. Dabei bietet sich die Nutzung eines Profils an, das aus der Zielkombination besonders erfolgreicher Geschäftseinheiten ermittelt wird. Im weiteren kann dann für jede Geschäftseinheit der Stichprobe die Distanz zu diesem „Idealprofil" gemessen werden. In dieser Perspektive der Musteranalyse („Pattern Analysis") wird als „Fit" also der Grad der Entsprechung mit diesem Profil angesehen.[52]

Die Vorgehensweise bei dieser Profilanalyse sieht vor, dass zunächst ein möglichst „ideales", d.h. mit einer signifikant besseren Performance verbundenes Profil der strategischen Konsistenz identifiziert wird. Daraus ergibt sich, dass die Entsprechung einer Geschäftseinheit mit diesem multidimensionalen Profil positiv mit den gewählten Erfolgsgrößen verbunden sein wird. Im umgekehrten Sinne repräsentiert eine Abweichung von diesem Erfolgsmuster eine Schwäche in der konsistenten strategischen Ausrichtung der Geschäftseinheit, die wiederum in einer verringerten Leistungsfähigkeit resultiert.

Die Dimensionen des Profils für die IMSS-Stichprobe ergeben sich aus den in den vorigen Abschnitten diskutierten Konsistenz-Variablen. Diese Variablen geben jeweils das Ausmaß der Übereinstimmung der Prioritäten in Geschäftseinheit und Fertigung an. Die Dimensionen der Kosten, Innovativität, Zuverlässigkeit und Zeit sind isoliert betrachtet in unterschiedlicher Weise mit der Umsatzrendite als Erfolgsgröße verbunden.

Die Erstellung des Profils kann auf zwei Arten erfolgen. Die theoretische Erzeugung eines Idealprofils verlangt die Spezifikation eines bestimmten Ausmaßes an Priorisierung der einzelnen Konsistenz-Variablen, die hinsichtlich des Erfolgs der Geschäftseinheit besonders vorteilhaft sind. Während dieses Konzept intuitiv schlüssig wirkt, ist die tatsächliche Bestimmung der

[52] Vgl. zur Methodik der Muster- und Profilanalyse *Venkatraman*, N.: The Concept of Fit in Strategy Research: Toward Verbal and Statistical Correspondence, in: Academy of Management Review, Vol. 14, No. 3, 1989, S. 433f.

Werte für die einzelnen Dimensionen äußerst schwierig.[53] Alternativ ist daher eine empirische Basis heranzuziehen, anhand derer – unter Zuhilfenahme eines Kalibrierungssamples – ein besonders erfolgreiches Profil ermittelt werden kann.

In der vorliegenden Untersuchung werden die beteiligten Unternehmen der Stichprobe anhand ihrer Umsatzrendite in fünf Pentile eingeteilt.[54] Die Umsatzrendite wird hier wiederum als letztlich entscheidendes Maß für den Fortbestand einer Unternehmung gewählt. Vor allen anderen Kriterien, die für die Erfolgsmessung denkbar sind, stellt sie den hauptsächlichen Indikator für den Unternehmenserfolg dar. Die Kalibrierungsgruppe, anhand derer Werte das Musterprofil erstellt wird, umfasst das obere Pentil und damit 20% der gesamten Stichprobe. Für diese Geschäftseinheiten werden die Mittelwerte der einzelnen Strategiedimensionen berechnet und auf das Intervall [0;1] normiert. Die dargestellten Werte geben die Zielgewichtungen an, die von den erfolgreichsten Geschäftseinheiten der Stichprobe den jeweiligen Strategiedimensionen durchschnittlich zugewiesen werden. Diese Priorisierungen der Ziele sind in Abbildung 3 ersichtlich. Der höchste Wert für die Innovativität gibt die stärkste Bedeutung dieses Ziels im oberen Pentil der Umsatzrendite wieder; die geringste Bedeutung wird der Kosten- bzw. Preisführerschaft beigemessen. Das Ziel der Zuverlässigkeit ist nahezu eben so stark gewichtet wie das der Innovativität.

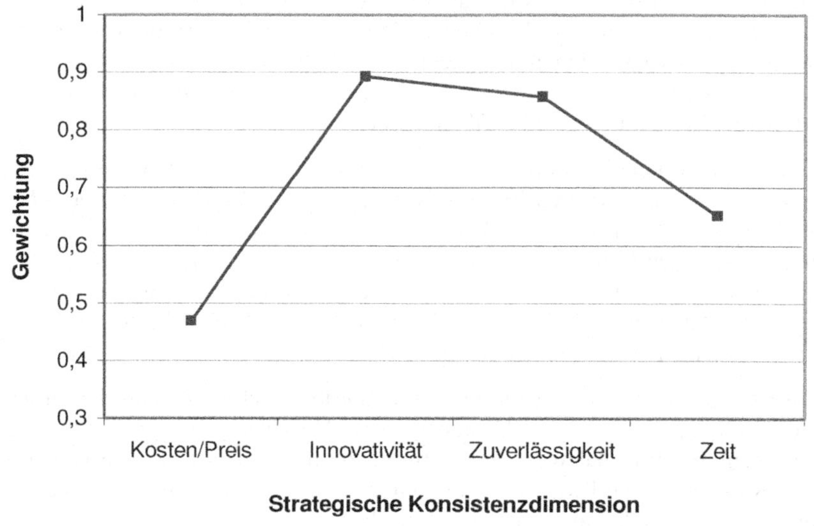

Abbildung 3: Referenzprofil der strategischen Gewichtungen im oberen Pentil

[53] Während beispielsweise Porter eine konzeptuelle Basis für die Identifikation idealer Strategien für bestimmte Umweltkonstellationen entwickelt hat, erscheint die Umsetzung seiner verbalen Aussagen in numerische Werte nicht befriedigend machbar. Vgl. *Porter*, Michael E.: Competitive Strategy, S. 191 ff.

[54] Die Pentile sind ein Spezialfall der Quantile. Als Quantile werden Merkmalswerte bezeichnet, durch die Gesamtheiten in gleich große Teile zerlegt werden. Die Pentile zerlegen die Gesamtheiten in fünf Teile; jeder Teil umfasst damit 20% der Gesamtheit. Vgl. *Bourier*, Günther: Beschreibende Statistik, S. 77.

Neben der grundsätzlichen Erstellung des Idealprofils sind zwei weitere wesentliche Gesichtspunkte zu beachten.[55] Zum einen müssen die einzelnen Dimensionen des Profils mit einer Gewichtung versehen werden; zum anderen ist ein grundlegender Test durchzuführen, um die Aussagefähigkeit und Signifikanz des Profils zu überprüfen.

Die Gewichtung der einzelnen strategischen Dimensionen soll die relative Bedeutung für die entsprechende Basisgröße – hier die Umsatzrendite – widerspiegeln. Ein ungewichtetes Schema trägt der Vielschichtigkeit strategischer Ziele und deren unterschiedlicher Bedeutung für Erfolg und Misserfolg nicht ausreichend Rechnung. Daher ist eine Gewichtung vorzunehmen, deren Parameter in dieser Analyse auf Grundlage einer Regressionsanalyse gewonnen werden, die den Zusammenhang zwischen den einzelnen Konsistenz-Dimensionen und der Umsatzrendite in zufriedenstellender Weise zeigt.[56] Für die Profilanalyse sind die standardisierten Beta-Koeffizienten des Regressionsmodells heranzuziehen, die in Tabelle 3 nochmals abgebildet sind. Sie stellen gleichzeitig die Gewichtungsparameter für das Profilmodell dar. Dabei ist darauf hinzuweisen, dass hier auch die insgesamt nicht signifikant erklärenden Variablen „Innovativität“ und „Zuverlässigkeit“ verwendet werden, da sie in unterschiedlichen Pentilen verschiedene Erklärungsgehalte besitzen. Für das Gewichtungsschema werden die Absolutbeträge der standardisierten Beta-Koeffizienten verwendet.

Tabelle 3: Gewichtungsparameter strategischer Ziele im Idealprofil

Dimension	**Gewichtung**
Innovativität	0,154
Zeit	0,353
Kosten/Preis	0,540
Zuverlässigkeit	0,245

Tabelle 3 zeigt, dass die Gewichtungsparameter den im Musterprofil zugewiesenen Bedeutungen weitgehend entgegenstehen. Der höchste Wert für das strategische Ziel „Innovativität“ geht mit der niedrigsten Gewichtung – und damit dem geringsten Zusammenhang mit der Umsatzrendite im Regressionsmodell – einher. Im Gegensatz dazu gibt der hohe Beta-Koeffizient für das Ziel „Kosten- und Preisführerschaft“ eine starke (negative) Bedeutung für die Höhe der Umsatzrendite an.[57] Dieser Umstand verleiht der Notwendigkeit der Gewichtung der einzelnen Ziele zusätzliche Bedeutung.

Als letzter Schritt ist die Aussagefähigkeit des Profilmodells zu überprüfen. Die Übereinstimmung der strategischen Ausrichtung jedes Unternehmens in der Stichprobe mit dem dargestell-

---

[55] Vgl. *Venkatraman*, N.: The Concept of Fit in Strategy Research, S. 434 f.

[56] Für eine ausführliche Vorstellung und Diskussion der Analyse vgl. Hasenpusch, Jürgen: Strategiekonsistenz in Geschäftseinheit und Fertigung als Voraussetzung für den Erfolg industrieller Unternehmen, S. 193 ff.

[57] Eine starke Betonung der Kosten- und Preisführerschaft geht mit einer niedrigen Umsatzrendite einher. Vgl. dazu *Milling*, Peter und Jürgen *Hasenpusch*: Strategiekonsistenz in Geschäftseinheit und Fertigung – Angleichung der Strategien als Voraussetzung für den Erfolg industrieller Unternehmen?, in: *Lingnau*, Volker und Hans *Schmitz*: Aktuelle Aspekte des Controllings, Festschrift für Hans-Jörg Hoitsch, Heidelberg 2002, S. 155.

ten Referenzprofil wird mit Hilfe einer Maßzahl operationalisiert. Diese Maßzahl ist hier die mit den Werten aus Tabelle 3 gewichtete euklidische Distanz, die sich als Quadratwurzel der Summe der gewichteten quadrierten Differenzen zwischen den Werten für die Geschäftseinheit und den Werten des Idealprofils berechnet. Dieses Ähnlichkeitsmaß gibt die Abweichung der strategischen Ausrichtung eines Unternehmens vom Idealprofil an und nimmt höhere Werte für eine geringere Ähnlichkeit an. Es muss eine signifikant höhere Vorhersagequalität hinsichtlich der Umsatzrendite haben als eine Abweichung von einem zufällig ermittelten strategischen Profil; nur dann ist der Validitätsanspruch als erfüllt anzusehen.[58] In der vorliegenden Analyse wird daher die folgende Hypothese überprüft:

$H_{1,1}$: *Größere Übereinstimmung mit dem Idealprofil führt zu einer höheren Umsatzrendite.*

Diese Hypothese wird mittels einer einfachen linearen Regressionsanalyse überprüft, bei der die Umsatzrendite als abhängige und das Ähnlichkeitsmaß als unabhängige Variable gewählt wird. Die Gütemaße der Regression sind in Tabelle 4 dargestellt.

Tabelle 4: Gütemaße der Regression des Ähnlichkeitsmaßes über die Umsatzrendite[59]

R	R^2	Korrigiertes R^2	Residual Std.fehler	Durbin-Watson-Koeffizient
0,397	0,158	0,129	0,080	1,734

Das Bestimmtheitsmaß $R^2 = 15{,}8\%$ wird wegen $p < 0{,}05$ als signifikant verschieden von Null gedeutet.[60] Damit kann die Hypothese angenommen werden; die entgegengerichtete Nullhypothese der Unabhängigkeit wird verworfen. Mit Hilfe dieser einfachen linearen Regression kann ein signifikanter Teil der Variabilität der Umsatzrendite in Höhe von 15,8% aus dem gewichteten Ähnlichkeitsmaß erklärt werden. Es kann davon ausgegangen werden, dass eine höhere Übereinstimmung der strategischen Ausrichtung mit dem Idealprofil mit einer höheren Umsatzrendite einhergeht.

Die Prüfung der Residuen auf die Prämisse der Normalverteilung und Autokorrelation ergibt zunächst keine optischen Anhaltspunkte für die Vermutung von Prämissenverletzungen. Der Durbin-Watson-Test resultiert in einem Koeffizienten von $d = 1{,}734$. Dies deutet tendenziell auf eine positive Autokorrelation der Residuen (1. Ordnung) hin. Da der Koeffizient jedoch außerhalb der Grenzwerte ($d_u^- = 1{,}37$ und $d_o^+ = 1{,}50$) liegt, die sich aufgrund der Durbin-Watson-Tabelle im zweiseitigen Test ergeben, gibt es nicht genügend Grund zu der Annahme, dass Autokorrelation besteht. Damit stellt die Autokorrelation hier kein bedeutendes Problem dar.[61]

Die Interpretation des identifizierten Referenzprofils stützt sich auf mehrere Beobachtungen: Der gezeigte negative Zusammenhang zwischen der Fokussierung auf niedrige Kosten bzw.

---

[58] Vgl. *Venkatraman*, N.: The Concept of Fit in Strategy Research, S. 435.

[59] Bei der einfachen linearen Regression entspricht der standardisierte Beta-Koeffizient dem linearen Korrelationskoeffizienten R und wird daher hier nicht ausgewiesen.

[60] Auf die Erläuterung weiterer Einzelheiten der Analyse wird hier verzichtet. Sie sind beim Autor erhältlich.

[61] Vgl. *Backhaus*, Klaus et al: Multivariate Analysemethoden, S. 42 ff.

Preise und dem finanziellen Erfolg der Geschäftseinheit spiegelt sich in der niedrigen Gewichtung dieses Ziels durch die erfolgreichen Unternehmen wider. Es ist anzunehmen, dass diese Unternehmen bereits eine Kostensituation erreicht haben, die eine Betonung dieses Ziel nicht weiter erfordert. Eine andere Möglichkeit ist, dass Produkte angeboten werden, deren bestimmte Eigenschaften höhere Preise rechtfertigen, wodurch niedrigste Kosten – wenigstens kurzfristig – nachrangig werden.

Die Ziele „Innovativität" und „Zeitwettbewerb" werden wesentlich stärker betont; ihr Zusammenhang mit der Umsatzrendite ist jedoch gespalten. Dem negativen Zusammenhang zwischen einer zeitorientierten Strategie und der Umsatzrendite steht eine starke Betonung zeitorientierter Ziele durch die erfolgreichen Unternehmen entgegen. Daher ist anzunehmen, dass im Zusammenspiel mit anderen Zielen eine gute Zeitperformance zum finanziellen Erfolg beitragen kann, während eine exklusive Verfolgung dieser Zeitziele ohne ein unterstützendes komplementäres Ziel eher als nachteilig anzusehen ist. Bezüglich der Breite der Produktpalette und dem Anteil neuentwickelter Produkte kann keine generelle Aussage getroffen werden, da diese Strategiedimension zwar eine sehr hohe Gewichtung von Seiten der erfolgreichen Unternehmen genießt, ihr Zusammenhang mit der Umsatzrendite jedoch statistisch nicht signifikant ist. Daraus ist zu schließen, dass erfolgreiche Unternehmen zwar auf eine aktuelle Produktpalette achten, diese jedoch nicht hinreichend zur Erklärung ihres Erfolgs beitragen kann.

Hinsichtlich der Betonung von Qualität und Liefertreue, die hier unter dem Begriff „Zuverlässigkeit" subsumiert werden, lässt sich eine mittlere Gewichtung und eine ebenso mittlere Bedeutung für den Erfolg beobachten. Ein möglicher Schluss kann sein, dass hohe Leistungen im operativen Bereich zwar eine gewisse Bedingung für erfolgreiches Agieren am Markt sind – und einen dezidierten Erfolgsbeitrag leisten – aber als alleiniger Differenzierungsfaktor nicht ausreichend sein können. Produkt- und Fertigungsqualität sowie Liefertreue erscheinen demgemäß als Standard im erfolgreichen Pentil der IMSS-Stichprobe. Aus diesem Grund wird diesen Kriterien zwar eine starke Bedeutung zugewiesen, die jedoch nicht an vorderster Stelle rangiert.

Die Analyse des Idealprofils der erfolgreichsten 20% der Geschäftseinheiten der Stichprobe ergibt insgesamt ein differenziertes Bild. Zwar entspricht die geringe Gewichtung der Kostenkriterien durch die Geschäftseinheiten ihren mangelnden Erfolgspotenzialen, jedoch ist gerade die im Zusammenspiel mit den anderen Dimensionen am stärksten gewichtete Strategiedimension „Innovativität" einzeln betrachtet nicht statistisch signifikant mit dem finanziellen Erfolg verbunden. Hier sei auf die komplementäre Wirkung gemischter Zielkonstellationen verwiesen, die sich an anderer Stelle als erfolgversprechend gezeigt hat.[62]

4.2 Übereinstimmung der strategischen Konfigurationen mit dem Referenzprofil

Das in den vorigen Abschnitten entwickelte und untersuchte Referenzprofil ist ein Konstrukt, das sich als Durchschnitt der strategischen Ausrichtungen der erfolgreichsten 20% der Stichprobe ergeben hat. Dieses Profil besteht aus strategisch unterschiedlich positionierten Geschäftseinheiten und ist daher im realen Geschehen nicht unbedingt erreichbar. Die Verbindung zwischen der analytisch erzeugten „Idealstrategie" und der unternehmerischen Praxis soll daher

---

[62] Vgl. *Hasenpusch*, Jürgen: Strategiekonsistenz in Geschäftseinheit und Fertigung als Voraussetzung für den Erfolg industrieller Unternehmen, S. 175ff.

im Folgenden gebildet werden. Gegenstand der nachstehenden Untersuchung ist, inwieweit sich die in Abschnitt D gebildeten strategischen Konfigurationen hinsichtlich des Abstandes vom Referenzprofil bzw. der zugrundeliegenden strategischen Konsistenz-Dimensionen unterscheiden.

Zunächst wird die Frage überprüft, ob die einzelnen Konfigurationen in unterschiedlicher Entfernung vom strategischen Referenzprofil positioniert sind. Dazu wird die folgende Hypothese überprüft:

$H_{I,2}$: Die Entfernungen der strategischen Konfiguration vom Idealprofil sind nicht gleich.

Die Hypothesenprüfung erfolgt mittels einer einfaktoriellen Varianzanalyse. Dabei kann die Hypothese nicht bestätigt werden, da eine Irrtumswahrscheinlichkeit von $p > 0{,}05$ vorliegt. Es ist also davon auszugehen, dass zwischen den Konfigurationen keine signifikanten Unterschiede hinsichtlich des Abstands vom theoretischen Idealprofil bestehen. Das Idealprofil scheint damit nicht in hinreichend genauer Weise einer einzelnen strategischen Konfiguration zu entsprechen. Es ergibt sich mithin als Mischung der beobachteten Strategien innerhalb der Stichprobe.

Die nicht ausreichende Signifikanz der Ähnlichkeitsunterschiede macht eine detaillierte Betrachtung der vier Konsistenz-Dimensionen notwendig, die dem Idealprofil zugrunde liegen. Zunächst wird daher geprüft, ob sich die neun strategischen Konfigurationen hinsichtlich ihrer Ausprägungen strategischer Konsistenz unterscheiden. Dazu wird für jede der Konsistenz-Dimensionen eine univariate Varianzanalyse zur Prüfung der folgenden Hypothese durchgeführt:

$H_{I,3-6}$: Die Ausprägungen der Konsistenz-Dimension in den unterschiedlichen strategischen Konfigurationen unterscheiden sich.[63]

Für alle vier Dimensionen kann die Ungleichheitshypothese auf hoch signifikantem Niveau akzeptiert werden ($p < 0{,}001$). Damit ist davon auszugehen, dass hinsichtlich der Ausprägungen der Dimensionen strategischer Konsistenz zwischen den Konfigurationen signifikante Unterschiede bestehen. Diese sind in Abbildung 4 grafisch dargestellt, wobei hier ein Wert von Null eine vollkommene Übereinstimmung mit der im Rahmen des Referenzprofils ermittelten Zielgewichtung angibt.

Die Abbildung zeigt deutlich, dass sich alle Konfigurationen unterschiedlich stark vom Referenzprofil unterscheiden. Bezüglich der drei Konfigurationen, deren fertigungsstrategische Komponente qualitätsorientiert ist (Konfigurationen FQ:GQ, FQ:GZ und FQ:GI) kann festgestellt werden, dass hier hinsichtlich der Konsistenz-Dimension „Zuverlässigkeit“ eine sehr gute Übereinstimmung mit dem Idealprofil vorliegt, was bei zwei der wettbewerbsstrategisch qualitätsorientierten Strategien (FZ:GQ und FI:GQ) nicht der Fall ist. Auch die konsistenten Konfigurationen sind – wenn das Ähnlichkeitsmaß zugrundegelegt wird – in der Gesamtheit der Konsistenz-Dimensionen nur in einigen Aspekten besser an das empirische Idealprofil angepasst. Eine deutliche Übereinstimmung von Strategietypen mit dem Idealprofil ist beispielsweise bei der konsistenten Innovationsstrategie FI:GI zu beobachten, die hinsichtlich der Dimen-

[63] Dabei gilt Hypothese $H_{1,3}$ für die Dimension „Innovation“, $H_{1,4}$ für „Zeit“, $H_{1,5}$ für „Kosten“ und $H_{1,6}$ für „Zuverlässigkeit“.

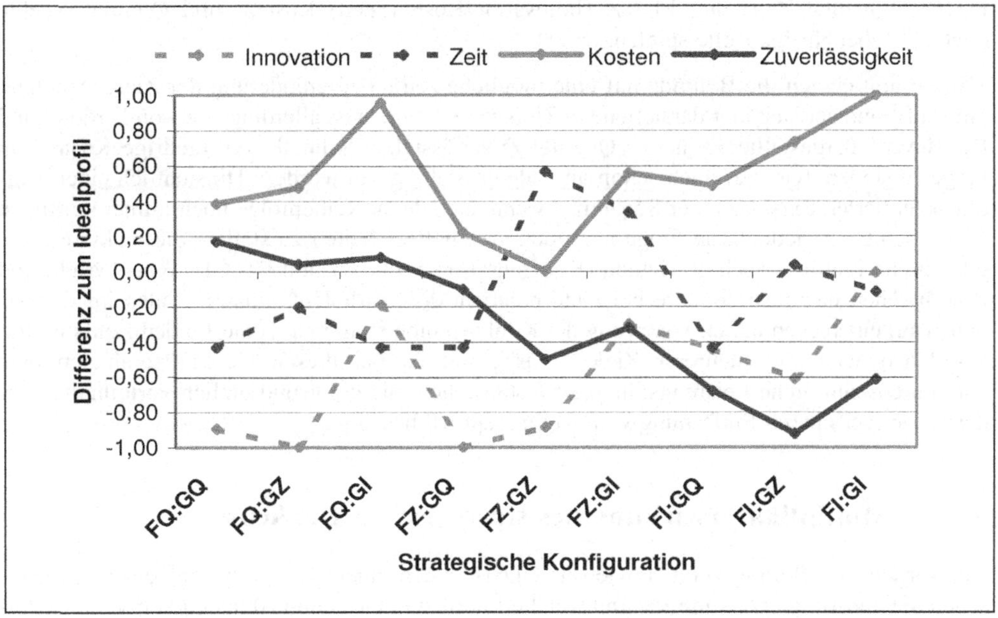

Abbildung 4: Abstand der Konsistenzprofile der strategischen Konfigurationen vom Referenzprofil

sionen „Innovation“ und „Zeit“ relativ exakt dem Idealprofil entspricht, dem entgegen aber eine starke Überbetonung der Dimension „Kosten“ und eine Vernachlässigung der Dimension „Zuverlässigkeit“ steht. Die konsistente Zeitstrategie FZ:GZ erweist sich hinsichtlich der Kostenkonsistenz dem Idealprofil entsprechend, weist jedoch hinsichtlich der Zeitdimension eine deutlich stärkere Gewichtung auf.

Bei keiner der vorliegenden strategischen Konfigurationen ist gegenüber dem Idealprofil eine Überbetonung der Dimension „Innovativität“ zu beobachten. Dementgegen übergewichten von neun Strategietypen acht die Dimension „Kosten“. Dies ist insofern zu hinterfragen, als sich bei der Untersuchung des Erfolgsbeitrags der einzelnen Konsistenz-Dimensionen die Dimension „Kosten“ als signifikant negativ mit der Umsatzrendite korreliert herausstellt.[64]

Die Verbindung der Abstände vom Referenzprofil mit der Gesamtleistungsfähigkeit zeigt Vorteile für die Konfigurationen, die die Konsistenz-Dimension „Kosten“ gegenüber dem Idealprofil übergewichten.[65] Im Falle der Konfigurationen FI:GZ (Innovation/Kosten:Zeit), FZ:GZ (konsistente Zeitstrategie) und FI:GI (konsistente Innovationsstrategie) ist gleichzeitig eine starke Untergewichtung der Dimension „Zuverlässigkeit“ zu verzeichnen. Darüber hinaus zeigt sich, dass die Strategie FZ:GZ im Gegensatz zu den anderen zeitorientierten Strategiekonfigurationen eine nahezu ausschließliche Zeitfokussierung aufweist, während bei den Strategien

[64] Vgl. dazu *Hasenpusch*, Jürgen: Strategiekonsistenz in Geschäftseinheit und Fertigung als Voraussetzung für den Erfolg industrieller Unternehmen, S. 189ff.

[65] Vgl. *Hasenpusch*, Jürgen: Strategiekonsistenz in Geschäftseinheit und Fertigung als Voraussetzung für den Erfolg industrieller Unternehmen, S. 175ff.

FQ:GZ (Qualität:Zeit) und FI:GZ (Innovation/Kosten:Zeit) Kosten- und Qualitätsaspekte noch eine ebenbürtige Rolle spielen.

Insgesamt deuten die Befunde auf eine mögliche zeitliche Veränderung der Zielgewichtung hin. Aufgrund der sich hier darstellenden Zielkonstellationen ist allerdings die von Ferdows und De Meyer[66] dargestellte Sequenz „Qualität-Zuverlässigkeit-Schnelligkeit-niedrige Kosten" in Frage zu stellen, wie dies auch schon an anderer Stelle getan wurde.[67] Hinsichtlich einer weithin akzeptierten Existenz einer Sequenz – wenn auch deren Reihenfolge noch immer strittig zu sein scheint – ist jedoch die Frage nach den Geschäftseinheiten zu stellen, die mehrere Ziele überdurchschnittlich hoch gewichten (Konfigurationen FQ:GI und FZ:GI). Wheelwright und Bowen sehen hier insbesondere bei Unternehmen, die „aufholen" müssen – also im wesentlichen auf einen eventuellen Vorsprung der Konkurrenten reagieren – eine Tendenz zur simultanen Übergewichtung mehrerer Ziele.[68] Insgesamt ist bei diesen Geschäftseinheiten eine unterdurchschnittliche Leistungsfähigkeit festzustellen, die die grundsätzlich vorteilhafte Tendenz einer geringeren Entfernung vom Referenzprofil bestätigt.

5 Multiplikatorwirkung des strategischen Denkens

Der vorliegende Beitrag zeigt, inwieweit Unternehmen einer Stichprobe mit einem strategischen Idealprofil übereinstimmen und welche Implikationen sich in Abhängigkeit von der Entfernung zu diesem Idealprofil ergeben. Die Untersuchung lässt erkennen, dass ein positiver Effekt erkennbar ist, wenn Unternehmen einem strategischen Leitbild folgen, das verschiedene Stärken vereint. Damit folgen die hier diskutierten Ergebnisse im weitesten Sinne einer strategischen Schule der Differenzierung, wie sie beispielsweise von Jones und Butler vertreten wird.[69] Voraussetzung für die Definition eines strategischen Profils und dessen Implementierung ist jedoch das eingangs erwähnte strategische Denken. Es mag in kleineren Unternehmen genügen, dass die Unternehmensführung strategisch „denkt", in größeren Organisationen ist es jedoch unerlässlich, dass die Strukturen mit strategischem Denken förmlich durchwirkt sind, da die Umsetzung einer gewählten Strategie ansonsten verwässert, die ursprünglich formulierte Strategie gleichsam unkenntlich wird.

Das Beispiel der – bei den Unternehmen der Stichprobe erfolgreichen – Innovationsstrategie und der damit zu verbindenden Maßnahmen ist ein Beleg dafür, dass eine konsistente Ausge-

[66] Vgl. *Ferdows*, Kasra und Arnoud *De Meyer*: Lasting Improvements in Manufacturing Performance, S. 174.

[67] Während Qualität sich auch in einer Untersuchung auf Basis der hier verwendeten Stichprobe als Basis der Fertigungsziele und -kompetenzen herausgestellt hat (vgl. Fußnote 62), ist die weitere Folge noch umstritten. Vgl. dazu *Da Silveira*, G. und F.S. *Fogliatto*: Competitive Priorities in Manufacturing: An Empirical Analysis of the Cumulative Model, in: *Van Dierdonck*, Roland und Ann *Vereecke* (Hrsg.): Operations Management, S. 143. Auch hier wurde die Sequenz dergestalt verändert, dass niedrige Kosten wesentlich früher an Priorität gewinnen.

[68] Vgl. *Wheelwright*, Steven C. und Kent H. *Bowen*: The Challenge of Manufacturing Advantage, 1996, S. 61.

[69] Vgl. *Jones*, Gareth R. und John E. *Butler*: Cost, Revenue and Business-level Strategy, in: Academy of Management Review, Vol. 13, No. 2, 1988, S. 202ff.

staltung von Zielen und Mitteln Voraussetzungen für langfristig erfolgreiches Handeln schafft.[70] Die Multiplikatorwirkung des strategischen Denkens und der strategischen Konsistenz setzt sich in weiteren funktionalen und strategischen Bereichen der Organisation fort. Die Schnittstelle zwischen Geschäftseinheit und Fertigung deutet auf die Notwendigkeit einer weiteren Operationalisierung von Koordinationsmechanismen zur Erzielung strategischer Konsistenz hin.[71] Dies kann beispielsweise im Rahmen eines strategischen Produktionscontrollings geschehen, mit dessen Hilfe strategische Aspekte der Fertigung besser identifiziert und entwickelt werden könnten. Ebenso wie personalpolitische Maßnahmen nicht eine rein funktionale Basis haben dürfen, sind andere Konzepte wie die im Rahmen dieser Arbeit diskutierten Verbesserungsprogramme in unternehmensweiter Form zu entwickeln und zu implementieren. Nur dann kann eine wechselseitige Unterstützung und Integration der verschiedenen Strategieebenen einer Geschäftseinheit verwirklicht und die Umsetzung der gewählten Strategie erreicht werden.

Literatur

Aspesi, C. und D. Vardhan (1999): Brilliant Strategy, But Can You Execute?, in: *The McKinsey Quarterly*, No. 1, S. 89–99.

Backhaus, K. et al. (1996): *Multivariate Analysemethoden: eine anwendungsorientierte Einführung, 8., verb. Aufl.*, Berlin et al.

Bartezzaghi, E. et al. (Hrsg.) (1999): *Managing Operations Networks*, Venice.

Bortz, J. (1999): *Statistik für Sozialwissenschaftler, 5., vollst. überarb. u. aktual. Aufl.*, Berlin et al.

Chandler, A. D. (1962): *Strategy and Structure: Chapters in the History of the Industrial Enterprise*, Cambridge (MA).

Da Silveira, G. und F. S. Fogliatto (2000): Competitive Priorities in Manufacturing: An Empirical Analysis of the Cumulative Model, in: Van Dierdonck, R. und A. Vereecke (Hrsg.): *Operations Management: Crossing Borders and Boundaries: The Changing Role of Operations*, Ghent, S. 139–146.

De Meyer, A. et al. (1989): Flexibility: The Next Competitive Battle – The Manufacturing Futures Survey, in: *Strategic Management Journal*, Vol. 10, S. 135–144.

Dierdonck, R. van und A. Vereecke (Hrsg.) (2000): *Crossing Borders and Boundaries: The Changing Role of Operations*, Ghent.

Eisenhardt, K. M. und S. L. Brown (1998): Time Pacing: Competing in Markets That Won't Stand Still, in: *Harvard Business Review*, Vol. 86, January–February, S. 62.

Ferdows, K. und A. De Meyer (1990): Lasting Improvements in Manufacturing Performance: In Search of a New Theory, in: *Journal of Operations Management*, Vol. 9, No. 2, S. 168–184.

Hahn, D. und B. Taylor (Hrsg.) (1999): *Strategische Unternehmensplanung, strategische Unternehmensführung, 8., aktualisierte Aufl.*, Heidelberg.

---

[70] Vgl. dazu auch: *Harveston*, Paula D., Ben E. *Kedia* und John D. *Francis*: Strategic Consistency in diverse Environments: Revisiting the Diversification-Performance Relationship, in: Academy of Management Proceedings, 1997, S. 175 ff.

[71] Vgl. *Milling*, Peter und Jürgen *Hasenpusch*: Innovation Strategies and the Business-Manufacturing Interface, in: *Dierdonck*, Roland van und Ann Vereecke (Hrsg.): Crossing Borders and Boundaries: The Changing Role of Operations, Ghent 2000, S. 242 ff.

Hahn, D. (1999): Strategische Unternehmensführung – Grundkonzept, in: Hahn, D. und B. Taylor (Hrsg.): *Strategische Unternehmensplanung, strategische Unternehmensführung: Stand und Entwicklungstendenzen, 8., aktualisierte Aufl.*, Heidelberg, S. 28–50.

Harveston, P. D., B. E. Kedia und J. D. Francis (1997): Strategic Consistency in diverse Environments: Revisiting the Diversification-Performance Relationship, in: *Academy of Management Proceedings*, S. 175–179.

Hasenpusch, J. (2001): *Strategiekonsistenz in Geschäftseinheit und Fertigung als Voraussetzung für den Erfolg industrieller Unternehmen*, Frankfurt et al.

Hayes, R. H. und D. M. Upton (1998): Operations-Based Strategy, in: *California Management Review*, Vol. 40, No. 4, S. 8–25.

Hayes, R. H. und S. C. Wheelwright (1984): *Restoring Our Competitive Edge: Competing Through Manufacturing*, New York et al.

Hinterhuber, H. H. und St. A. Friedrich (1999): Markt- und ressourcenorientierte Sichtweise zur Steigerung des Unternehmungswertes, in: Hahn, D. und B. Taylor (Hrsg.): *Strategische Unternehmensplanung, strategische Unternehmensführung, 8., aktualisierte Aufl.*, Heidelberg, S. 988–1016.

Hoitsch, H.-J. und B. Akin (1998): Geschichte der Produktionswirtschaft, in: *Wirtschaftwissenschaftliches Studium*, Heft 2, S. 54–59.

Jelinek, M. und M. C. Burstein (1982): The Production Administrative Structure: A Paradigm For Strategic Fit, in: *Academy of Management Review*, Vol. 7, No. 2, S. 242–252.

Jones, G. R. und J. E. Butler (1988): Cost, Revenue and Business-level Strategy, in: *Academy of Management Review*, Vol. 13, No. 2, S. 202–213.

Kinni, T. B.: Find the Corporate Heartbeat, in: *Industry Week*, Vol. 243, No. 15, S. 43ff.

Lindberg, P., C. A. Voss und K. L. Blackmon (1997): *International Manufacturing Strategies: Context, Content, and Change*, Boston (MA).

Lingnau, V. und H. Schmitz (2002): *Aktuelle Aspekte des Controllings*, Festschrift für Hans-Jörg Hoitsch, Heidelberg.

Maier, F. H. (1995): *Die Integration wissens- und modellbasierter Konzepte zur Entscheidungsunterstützung im Innovationsmanagement*, Berlin.

Miller, D. und H. Mintzberg (1984): The Case for Configuration, in: Miller, D. und P. H. Friesen (Hrsg.): *Organizations: A Quantum View*, Englewood Cliffs (NJ), S. 10–30.

Miller, D. und P. H. Friesen (Hrsg.) (1984): *Organizations: A Quantum View*, Englewood Cliffs (NJ).

Miller, D. (1986): Configurations of Strategy and Structure: Towards a Synthesis, in: *Strategic Management Journal*, Vol. 7, S. 233–249.

Miller, D. (1987): Strategy Making and Structure: Analysis and Implications for Performance, in: *Academy of Management Review*, Vol. 30, No. 1, S. 732.

Miller, J. G. und A. V. Roth (1994): A Taxonomy of Manufacturing Strategies, in: *Management Science*, Vol. 40, No. 3, S. 285–304.

Milling, P. und J. Hasenpusch (2000): Innovation Strategies and the Business-Manufacturing Interface, in: Dierdonck, R. van und A. Vereecke (Hrsg.): *Crossing Borders and Boundaries: The Changing Role of Operations*, Ghent, S. 423–430.

Milling, P. und J. Hasenpusch (2002): Strategiekonsistenz in Geschäftseinheit und Fertigung – Angleichung der Strategien als Voraussetzung für den Erfolg industrieller Unternehmen?, in: Lingnau, V. und H. Schmitz: *Aktuelle Aspekte des Controllings*, Festschrift für Hans-Jörg Hoitsch, Heidelberg, S. 143–164.

Milling, P. und J. Hasenpusch (1999): Zielrelationen in Geschäftseinheit und Fertigung, in: *Forschungsberichte der Fakultät für Betriebswirtschaftslehre der Universität Mannheim*, Nr. 9903, Mannheim.

Milling, P. M., F. H. Maier und D. Mansury (1999): Impact of Manufacturing Strategy on Plant Performance – Insights from the International Research Project: World Class Manufacturing, in: Bartezzaghi, E. et al. (Hrsg.): *Managing Operations Networks*, Padova, S. 578.

Mintzberg, H. (1991): Crafting Strategy, in: Montgomery, C. A. und M. E. Porter (Hrsg.): *Strategy: Seeking and Securing Competitive Advantage*, Boston, S. 403–420.

Nath, D. und N. Sudharshan (1994): Measuring Strategy Coherence Through Patterns of Strategic Choices, in: *Strategic Management Journal*, Vol. 15, S. 43–61.

Nieschlag, R., E. Dichtl und H. Hörschgen (1997): *Marketing, 18., durchges. Aufl.*, Berlin.

Porter, M. E. (1980): *Competitive Strategy – Techniques for Analyzing Industries and Competitors*, New York.

Prahalad, C. K. und G. Hamel (1990): The Core Competence of the Corporation, in: *Harvard Business Review*, Vol. 68, May–June, S. 79–91.

Reger, R. K., L. T. Gustafson, S. M. Demarie und J. V. Mullane (1994): Reframing the Organization – Why Implementing Total Quality Is Easier Said than Done, in: *Academy of Management Review*, Vol. 19, No. 3, S. 565–584.

Ruffini, F. A. J., H. Boer und M. J. van Riemsdijk (2000): Organisation Design in Operations Management, in: *International Journal of Operations & Production Management*, Vol. 20, No. 7, S. 860–879.

Service, R. W. (2006): The Development of Strategic Intelligence: A Managerial Perspective, in: *International Journal of Management*, Vol. 23, No. 1, S. 61–77.

Simon, H. (1998): *Die heimlichen Gewinner – Hidden Champions. Die Erfolgsstrategien unbekannter Weltmarktführer*, Frankfurt/New York.

Skinner, W. (1969): Manufacturing – the Missing Link in Corporate Strategy, in: *Harvard Business Review*, Vol. 47, May–June, S. 136–145.

Skinner, W. (1996): Manufacturing Strategy on the „S" Curve, in: *Production and Operations Management*, Vol. 5, No. 1, S. 3–15.

Stobaugh, R. und P. Telesio (1983): Match Manufacturing Policies and Product Strategy, in: *Harvard Business Review*, Vol. 61, No. 2, S. 113–120.

Venkatraman, N. und J. E. Prescott (1990): Environment-Strategy Coalignment: An Empirical Test of Its Performance Implications, in: *Strategic Management Journal*, Vol. 11, S. 1–23.

Venkatraman, N. (1989): The Concept of Fit in Strategy Research: Toward Verbal and Statistical Correspondence, in: *Academy of Management Review*, Vol. 14, No. 3, S. 423–444.

Verdin, P. und P. Williamson (1994): Successful Strategy: Stargazing or Self-Examination?, in: *European Management Journal*, Vol. 12, No. 1, S. 10–19.

Ward, P. T., D. J. Bickford und G. K. Leong (1996): Configurations of Manufacturing Strategy, Business Strategy, Environment and Structure, in: *Journal of Management*, Vol. 22, No. 4, S. 597–626.

Welge, M. K. und A. Al-Laham (1999): *Strategisches Management: Grundlagen – Prozeß – Implementierung, 2., vollst. überarb. u. erw. Aufl.*, Wiesbaden.

Wernerfelt, B. (1984): A Resource-Based View of the Firm, in: *Strategic Management Journal*, Vol. 5, S. 171–180.

Wheelwright, S. C. und K. H. Bowen (1996): The Challenge of Manufacturing Advantage, in: *Production and Operations Management*, Vol. 5, No. 1, S. 59–77.

Wohlgemuth, A. (1989): Dem Unternehmenserfolg auf der Spur: Die klippenreiche Suche nach Erfolgsfaktoren, in: *Die Unternehmung*, Jg. 43, Nr. 2, S. 89–110.

Zahra, S. A. und J. G. Covin (1993): Business Strategy, Technology Policy and Firm Performance, in: *Strategic Management Journal*, Vol. 14, No. 6, S. 451–478.

Theory of Constraints and System Dynamics for Decision Making in Operations Management

Andreas Größler

Radboud University Nijmegen
Institute for Management Research

Abstract

The major constraint in most companies is not physical but related to managerial policy and decision-making. The main objective of this theoretical and literature-based article is the presentation of examples showing how deficient managerial decision-making in operations management can be. Supporting indications are gathered from different fields of science, for instance, decision science, psychology, sociology, and biology. Examples of apparently deficient decision-making in production contexts are given. It is shown how the 'theory of constraints' and the broader field of system dynamics offers concepts and methods to mitigate some issues of poor decision-making. Further, the relationship between the 'theory of constraints' and system dynamics is discussed.

Keywords: theory of constraints, system dynamics, operations management, decision-making, complexity

In today's complex and dynamic world of business, the major constraint on companies does not seem to be physical any longer: in many cases, it is not a shortage in supply, a too small workforce, or capacity restrictions of machinery that are the basic bottlenecks of manufacturing or service enterprises. The ability of management on any hierarchical level to formulate sound policies and to make effective decisions has a substantial influence on success or failure of a firm. In other words, the primary constraint in most organisations has become policy/decision-making related (Goldratt, 1990a). The constraint is managerial, not material.

This proposition leads to an important implication: from different fields of science it is known that policy/decision-making is affected by virtually unavoidable biases, in particular stemming from biological, psychological, and social characteristics of individual or organisational decision makers.[1] Frequently, these influences generate decisions and outcomes that are far from optimal and are not at all in accordance to what 'conventional' economic theory suggests concerning utility maximisation. Today's operations management therefore has to address deficiencies of managerial decision-making as a focal point of its interest.

[1] Although it is acknowledged that crafting policies might be an even more important task for management than making single decisions (Forrester, 1961), in the rest of the paper these two activities are subsumed under the more common term 'decision-making'. Indeed, crafting a policy might be interpreted as deciding about a rule to follow in the future.

The paper is structured as follows. The first section elaborates the basic assumption that the capability to make appropriate decisions is the primary constraint in business firms. In the following section, basic sources of deficient decisions and their results are discussed. How the 'theory of constraints' (ToC) can help overcoming some presumably negative consequences of deficient decision-making is discussed in the third section. The paper ends with an investigation of the intersection of the 'theory of constraints' and system dynamics.

1 Characteristics of Decision Makers as Constraints in Manufacturing Systems

Starting with Gutenberg's (1951) seminal book about the foundations of business administration, four factors have been identified that are supposed to be the basic input of any production system: materials ('repetitive factor'), machinery ('potential factor'), workforce doing operative work ('human factor'), and *directing activity* (of course, mainly also done by people but in a different role than in the human factor). The first three are also called *elementary* input factors; they are combined in order to achieve an efficient way to produce an outcome. The amount to which they are utilised in this combination process is described with the help of production functions. In the production theory literature one can find various different forms of production functions. Elementary factors are supposed to be relatively easy to quantify and calculate (Fandel, 1991).

However, this is not the case for *directing activity*, which is responsible for the combination process of the elementary factors. In other words, the *directing activity* symbolises the function of management that plans, organises, controls, and structures the production process. Although Gutenberg and his successors emphasise the importance of the *directing activity*, most of the time it is only indirectly treated after stating its existence: while efficient combinations of elementary factors are discussed in great depth and length, the *directing activity* is addressed only insofar as the discussion of factor combinations is meant to support management in fulfilling its task of establishing useful production functions and production environments. In which way the *directing activity* tries to achieve its goal is not discussed; if and how it can be included into production functions like the rest of the input factors does not find particular treatment in the literature about production and operations management. Even though there is plenty of literature about management in general, there is no production theory that addresses the *directing activity* in the same way in which the elementary factors are included.

The reason for this neglect is threefold. Firstly, at the time production theory had its origin, management was a relatively well-structured task – at least compared to the uncertainty and complexity management faces today (some often cited reasons why this has happened are: globalisation, substantial intra-industry competition, substitution between industries and products, an abundance of data about almost everything, demands for transparency from capital markets, changed expectations of employees, customers, and stake holders, etc.). Secondly, the *directing activity* and its influence on production outcome are much more difficult to define and to quantify than the elementary factors. Thus, the reason for the reluctance to include 'softer' factors into production theory might also be an educational one: until today the realm of production and operations is dominated by managers with a quantitative, 'hard-facts' background, which are presumably not willing to accept qualitative, soft variables in the concepts and methods they use. Thirdly, production theory follows the micro-economic approach of absolute rational decision-making with utility maximising actors (von Neumann and Morgenstern, 1944). From this point of view, the *directing activity* does not really need special attention because its task is completely determined by rationality and therefore rather simple: it just has to employ the most efficient production function which production theory suggests. However, the simplicity vanishes when one considers that knowledge about production functions in real organisations is typically incomplete and fuzzy (Nelson and Winter, 1982).

The history of the 'theory of constrains' (ToC)[2] shows a development from dealing with 'hard' issue to also addressing 'soft' factors (Rahman, 1998). In the beginning, capacity backlogs and machinery or workforce constraints were the major issues of consideration. To a great deal, ToC was understood as an algorithmic method to smooth the technical process of production. This interpretation was partly induced by the success and publicity of methods like 'optimized production timetables' (Goldratt, 1980). However, the concept has evolved. As many authors including Goldratt (1988) emphasise in more recent writings, its focus has changed from a sheer quantitative and technical approach to also include qualitative aspects of production and general management (an overview of application areas can be found in Rahman, 1998, and Kim et al., 2008). With Rahman it can be stated that 'the main constraint in most organizations may not be physical but managerial-policy related' (1998: 336). An important role in this transition from algorithmic method to managerial concept plays the so-called 'thinking process', which is nowadays accepted as the probably most influential part of the whole 'theory of constraints' (Noreen et al., 1995). Broadly speaking, the 'thinking process' provides a toolbox of methods for problem solving and decision-making (Goldratt, 1994).

Without describing the 'thinking process' in further detail at this point, already the wording makes clear that cognitive characteristics of decision subjects become crucial in production. Decision subjects constitute the *directing activity* in Gutenberg's terms. It is the management as an individual or a group that decides on how production is conducted and which policies are employed in operations. However, other than production theory suggests, the task of the *directing activity* does not simply consist of picking an appropriate combination of elementary factors. The reason for this is that formulating a production function in reality often is not as simple as theory suggests. Furthermore, outcomes, prerequisites, and side effects of different production functions can hardly be estimated. Therefore, the decision subjects' abilities and their shortcomings have the most profound impact on the performance of the firm. Cognitive characteristics drift into the centre as the main constraint of production and therefore need special attention, for instance in the 'theory of constraints'.

Cognitive prepositions of decision makers must be seen interlinked with features of the decision situation and the environment of the production process in their effects on decision-making (Simon, 1959). Specifically, the increasing complexity of the competitive arena influences whether decision-making behaviour shows positive or negative results for the operative system. This complexity is caused by various sources, for example legal and governmental actions, social norms and pressures, geographically extended areas of competition (Größler et al., 2006).

---

[2] With some justification one can have doubts whether the 'theory of constraints' really is a *theory* or rather a concept and/or set of methods. However, since it is the usual name, in this paper it is named 'theory of constraints'.

As research in many scientific areas has demonstrated, human decision-making is only partly able to deal with complexity (Rabin, 1998). Systematic errors can be observed. If a concept for production management acknowledges the limited abilities of its agents it therefore fulfils an old request of Simon and other authors of the 'behavioural economics' school (Simon, 1959). Their claim is an integration of empirically-based evidence about human decision-making into economic theory. With the help of concepts like the 'theory of constraints', behaviourally-based operations management can better explain reality in organisations and help to overcome restrictions of human decision-making.

2 A Review of Deficient Decision-Making in Complex Environments

Deficiencies in decision-making mainly occur in complex, not in simple decision-making environments. Complex situations can abstractly be characterised by three distinct aspects: (1) a large number of objects that are (2) linked to each other, where (3) there are many types of functional relations between the objects (Milling, 2002). Furthermore, sometimes detail and dynamic complexity (Sterman, 2000), or behavioural and dynamic complexity (Roth and Senge, 1996) are differentiated. However, what constitutes a 'complex situation' is subjective within a certain range: what is an easy decision to make for an expert might be impossible to comprehend for a novice (Strohhecker, 1998). Nevertheless, there seems to be a certain limit of complexity beyond that even the most skilled expert cannot act fully rationally.[3] It is the major assumption of this paper that many decisions in production and operations management lie beyond this complexity border and, thus, production is a complex setting affecting decision-making. Therefore, it is assumed that the creation and the behaviour of a production system (as well as of the firms as a whole) are determined by the limited rational action of its members (March and Simon, 1993). Decisions in operations management are determined by the interplay of complexity with physiological, psychological, and social characteristics of humans (Sterman, 1994).

In the rest of this section, these three characteristics are discussed in more detail. Examples are given, how limitations of decision subjects might affect decision-making in manufacturing. It has to be noted, however, that the borders between physiological, psychological, and social limitations to decision-making are fuzzy and that the following classification therefore is arbitrary to a certain degree.

2.1 Physiological Restrictions of Humans

Several barriers exist that limit the amount and quality of data that can be perceived and processed by humans. These limitations are built in the interlinked system of perceptive organs and the nervous system including the human brain. For instance, humans can only hear sound in the frequency range from 20 Hz to 20 kHz, and see light within a range of wavelengths between 400 to about 700 nm (Zimbardo, 1992). Although these issues block us from an enormous amount of data regarding the current situation, they do not play a vital role in the context

[3] This complexity border might have to do with a limitation of the working memory of the human brain (Klingberg, 2008).

discussed in this paper, i.e. in managerial decision-making. Nevertheless, they might be important for operative and manual work at the shop floor, for instance when considering the trade-off between speed and accuracy of perceptions (Viale, 1992; Thun et al., 2007).

Restrictions of the information processing speed and the storage capacity (of the working memory), which are imposed on individuals by biological characteristics of the brain (Simon, 1978), have bigger influences on decision-making. For instance, due to time restrictions it is often not possible to mentally simulate the results of all alternatives in a decision situation (besides the effect that people often even then do not consider all alternatives when they have the resources to do so; Brehmer and Dörner, 1993). In the same way, not all variables connected to a decision situation can be handled in working memory at the same time; necessarily, some factors are not considered in most decision-making contexts (Miller, 1956; Süß, 1996).

In manufacturing many situations can be thought of that are potentially hampered by these limitations of decision makers, for instance:

- people deciding about order sequencing cannot take into account all possible sequences and find the optimal solution;
- the effects of a machine break down can often not be overseen because there are plenty of side effects;
- the switch to another production technology cannot be fully comprehended because – again – not all effects can be calculated and not all influencing variables can be considered.

Many of these problems can be mitigated with the help of computers applying both, algorithmic procedures and simulation analyses (Pidd, 2004). However, also the promising combination of intuitive human brains and powerful processing of computers (Milling, 1991) often comes to limits when outcomes are uncertain, decision variables are not considered, or their usage is affected by political processes inside the organisation. Some of these issues are discussed in the following two sub-sections.

2.2 Psychological Characteristics of Humans

Another group of decision-making deficiencies is related to psychological characteristics of humans. In contrast to the limitations discussed in the previous section, these are not simply physiologically determined. Thus, they can – at least in principle – be overcome when decision makers are aware of these flaws, for instance with the help of special trainings (Milling, 1995).

Generally, and also when observing a decision situation, humans show a behaviour called 'selective perception' (Hogarth, 1987). This means that not every sensation that reaches the perceptive organs is actually perceived, even when the 'hardware' in form of nerves and brain could handle more data. The reasons for this issue are manifold. For instance, the attention of humans usually cannot be directed at many things simultaneously; if an individual's attention is occupied by something, it might not pay attention to something else, anyway how important this other thing objectively is (Broadbent, 1958). The limited amount of attention leads to an overemphasising of the current, most accessible line of thinking in individuals (Dörner, 1996; 'recency bias' and 'proximity bias'). Another reason for 'selective perception' is symbolised by the saying 'you can only see, what you know'. In general, the beliefs, expectations and assumptions possessed by a human being determine what can be perceived (Sterman, 1994).

Again, it is possible to list some examples of how these limitations might influence decision-making in a manufacturing context:

- being too much occupied with shortening cycle times might prevent seeing that machinery urgently needs maintenance;
- when deciding about the purchasing of new machinery one might oversee that worker motivation is decreasing;
- if production does not know about the demands of the final customers they might not see small differences in final products, for instance in colouring.

Another form of psychological deficiency concerning decision-making is named 'illusion of control' (Langer, 1975). The term describes the behaviour of humans to appear competent, no matter how complicated the situation in reality is. In other words, people try to be perceived as being fully in control of the situation, although this might objectively not be the case (Dörner, 1996). More generally, it can be stated that humans want to maintain their self concept (Steele, 1988).

An example from manufacturing is quality problems in a production line. Although the production manager might not know at all why these quality issues occur or how they can be fixed, the manager pretends to be in control of the situation: giving commands, inducing action, letting people measure something, letting people maintain machinery, reorganize workflows, etc. In this way, the production manager tries to prove to himself as well as to others that the situation can be mastered. As can be seen from the last statement, 'illusion of control' leads to deficient decision-making which is related to the fact that decision makers do not act in isolation but in connection with other people.

2.3 Social Behaviour of Humans

Managerial decisions are (nearly) always made in social situations. One can distinguish two meanings of this statement: firstly, decisions are made by groups, and, secondly, even the individual, seemingly independent decision maker is influenced by the social setting of a decision situation. One category of deficiencies occurring when groups make decisions is called 'group think', which means that the group arrives at a decision prematurely (Janis, 1982). But also in the case of an individual's decision, deficiencies can occur, for instance, because a decision maker is watched by others, consulted by others, has a superior (to whom must be reported to), has inferiors (which want to be informed and led), etc. All in all, there exist influences from various stakeholders that the decision maker has to take into account (Boudon, 1992); hierarchical and power structures in organisations influence how decisions are being made.

Again, it is not very demanding to think of examples from manufacturing:

- when deciding about a shop floor layout, after a very short discussion the production team arrives at a decision being exactly equal to the CEO's idea (who does not know a lot about the basics of production);
- a production manager avoids to conduct preventive maintenance because this might look to superiors as if the workforce would be underutilised normally;
- the purchase of an efficient machinery is delayed because it affects the current quarter figures, which would undermine the manager's (current) success record.

The literature about 'group think' and effective communication in organisations offer some remedies for these socially related deficiencies of decision-making. However, it might be crucial to accept that human decision-making can never be separated from its social context.

3 Supporting Managerial Decision-Making Based on the 'Theory of Constraints'

In the section above some methods to support managerial decision-making were already briefly discussed. This section will focus on the question, to what extent the 'theory of constraints' (ToC) offers starting points to improve managerial decision-making. Before that, however, it should be noted that human decision-making is – in general – quite successful and sensible, particularly in the light of the many potential deficiencies that were described above (March, 1978). Throughout the history of mankind and by education of each individual, humans have acquired a set of strategies and heuristics that in many occasions are reasonable to employ, when a decision has to be made (Gigerenzer and Todd, 2000). However, as research shows there seem to be situations were these otherwise useful methods of the mind are prone to systematic errors (Dörner, 1996). Such situations are identified above as being complex like, for instance, decision-making in production and operations management.

The 'theory of constraints' can help to mitigate the potential problems of deficient decision-making in two ways: on a conceptual level and on a methodological level. Conceptually, the 'theory of constraints' makes clear that there *are* constraints in every production process that represent opportunities for improvement (Rahman, 1998). Thus, the 'theory of constraints' guides thinking, through providing ideas and by stating facts about production processes. Methodologically, ToC offers methods and instruments in order to control this process and to think about it more efficiently.

A brief review of the most fundamental step-like approach to improve a production system according to the 'theory of constraints' gives further indication supporting this argument (Goldratt, 1990b):

1. Identify constraints in the system (there is at least one in any system). These constraints determine the performance of the system.
2. Determine how to exploit/eliminate the constraints in order to improve system's performance.
3. All resources should be subordinated to Step 2.
4. Do all things necessary to improve system's performance by elevating/eliminating the constraints.
5. If a constraint has been broken or a new one appears go back to Step 1 and start again.[4]

This simple five step procedure of the 'theory of constraints' can support decision makers in all three areas of deficiency discussed above:

[4] There are also other approaches to deal with constraints. One could argue that – in order to become really world-class in something – a firm has to concentrate on the few things it can best and improve them further; all other functions (where presumably the constraints lie) should be outsourced (also in this reduced set of core functions one activity is the constraint, which could be improved – at least in theory).

- Physiology: The concentration on the constraints of a production system helps to avoid an overload of the working memory. Issues that are not primarily responsible for the performance of the manufacturing system are faded out of consideration.
- Psychology: The attention of the responsible decision maker is drawn to key factors for success, which lie in removing constraints that limit system's performance. It becomes more difficult to concentrate on less important issues. When knowing that there must be constraints one might also get the chance to observe and identify these issues. Furthermore, the 'illusion of control' effect is lessened because the theory acknowledges that there are constraints in any production process, no matter how perfectly it is managed. Thus, the decision maker can maintain a self image of being in control of the situation.
- Social behaviour: The statement that there is a constraint in every manufacturing system helps to actually tackle the problem because nobody is to blame for the general existence and occurrence of constraints. (However there might be somebody responsible for a specific constraint.) The process of group decision-making becomes structured because – at least – the problem is clearly defined by the constraints for anyone in the decision group.

Besides the general approach of the 'theory of constraints' as described in the five steps above, particularly the so called 'thinking process' can help to mitigate potential fallacies of decision-making (Kim et al., 2008; Goldratt, 1994). The 'thinking process' was created as a reaction to the fact that managerial decision-making constraints gained importance in comparison to physical shop floor constraints (Rahman, 1998). The methods comprised in the 'thinking process' are supposed to support management in deciding about necessary change (induced by constraints). In particular, it should help regarding the following issues: (1) deciding what to change, (2) deciding what to change to, and (3) deciding how to change. For this end, five forms of cause-and-effect diagrams are described: 'current reality trees', 'evaporative clouds', 'future reality trees', 'prerequisite trees', and 'transition trees'. With the help of these instruments (or a subset of the instruments), problems can be identified and practical solutions to these problems can be found and implemented.

Cause-and-effect diagrams help to diminish issues from all three areas of potentially deficient decision-making: load on the working memory is reduced; attention can be directed to the causes of problems, not the symptoms; mental models of decision makers become 'explicit' and are therefore easier to change; criticism can focus on issues, not on people.

4 The 'Theory of Constraints' and System Dynamics

In this section, the relationship between ToC and system dynamics (SD; Forrester, 1961; Sterman, 2000) is discussed. It is shown that ToC is based on a well-known principle from system dynamics and that it uses methods which are similar to ones that are applied in system dynamics studies. In other words, the intersection of ideas and methods between ToC and SD is substantial. Indeed, various authors have reported on possibilities to combine the 'theory of constraints' with system dynamics (e.g., Balderstone, 1999; Davies et al., 2004; Cox et al., 2005; Mabin et al., 2006) or compared the two approaches in their effectiveness for problem-solving (Musa et al., 2005).

The notion that a constraint exists in every production system is in accordance to the 'limits to growth' archetype as identified in system dynamics: there is always a limitation to indefinite growth of a system (Meadows et al., 1972; Meadows et al., 1974). Also, the recommendations are similar: "Don't push on the reinforcing (growth) process, remove (or weaken) the source of limitation." (Senge 1990, 380) Dettmer (1997) emphasises this systemic approach of the 'theory of constraints'.

Like system dynamics, the 'theory of constraints' proposes that there are many advantages of using formalized ways to diagram production systems (in the 'theory of constraints': the thinking process; in system dynamics: causal loop diagrams and level/rate diagrams):

- hypotheses about causal linkages can be stated in a formalised, but easy to understand way;
- mental models of individuals and groups can easily be elicited;
- they offer the possibility to evaluate, discuss and criticise assumptions that underlie decisions;
- because of the necessary simplification inherent in all modelling approaches discussions can focus on the relevant issues.

Although the usefulness of ToC's cause-and-effect diagrams is not doubted, there are some additions from system dynamics. Among others, Senge (1990) emphasises feedback as a structural element that most decisional situations comprise and which fundamentally determines the behaviour of a system. However, the identification of feedback loops is still not a common task in many cause-and-effect diagram techniques, for instance in the 'thinking process'. In contrast to that, ToC's cause-and-effect diagrams put more emphasis on the implementation of solutions and on the consideration of power structures within organisations, two areas sometimes identified as problematic within SD (Größler, 2007; van der Smagt, 2006; Snabe and Größler, 2006). Potential fallacies of cause-and-effect diagrams in general are discussed in Richardson (1986).

As system dynamics, ToC does not promise an optimal solution but a satisfying and reasonable one. With the help it provides for overcoming deficiencies of human decision-making, the 'theory of constraints' has its foundation in the observation of real world situations. Thus, like system dynamics it does not pose many assumptions on the nature of its agents but accepts individual and organisational shortcomings (Größler, 2004). Although it is not aiming for optimality, the 'theory of constraints' is nevertheless able to offer some prescriptive guidelines and to help practitioners in complex decision situations, similar as SD does.

5 Summary

In this article, it has been shown that decision-making in operations management is prone to systematic failures because operations is a complex environment. The 'theory of constraints' as well as system dynamics offer ways to mitigate or to prevent some of these failures. ToC and SD have a substantial overlap of common goals, concepts, and methods.

In the broader operations management context, the three main challenges that can be derived from the findings in this paper are:

1. that the concept of limited rational decision-making should find its way into standard operations strategies and procedures,
2. that managerial policy and decision-making should be supported by organisational and technical means to mitigate presumably negative effects of cognitive biases, and
3. that both, the 'theory of constraints' and system dynamics should concentrate on and extend their competence in providing means to handle limitations of managerial decision-making.

References

Balderstone, S. J. (1999): Increasing user confidence in system dynamics models through use of an established set of logic rules to enhance Forrester and Senge's validation tests. *Proceedings of the 17th International System Dynamics Conference and 5th Australian and New Zealand Systems Conference.* Wellington, New Zealand.

Baron, J. (1994): *Thinking and Deciding*. Cambridge, MA: Cambridge University Press.

Boudon, R. (1992): Subjective rationality and the explanation of social behaviour. In: Simon, H. A., M. Egidi, R. Marris and R. Viale (eds.): *Economics, Bounded Rationality and the Cognitive Revolution,* Aldershot: Edward Elgar. 123–147.

Brehmer, B. and D. Dörner (1993): Experiments with computer-simulated microworlds: escaping both the narrow straits of the laboratory and the deep blue sea of the field study. *Computers in Human Behavior* 9: 171–184.

Broadbent, D. (1958): *Perception and Communication.* London: Pergamon Press.

Cox, J. F., V. J. Mabin and J. Davies (2005): A Case of Personal Productivity: Illustrating Methodological Developments in TOC. *Human Systems Management* 24(1): 39–65.

Davies, J., V. J. Mabin and J. F. Cox (2004): The Theory of Constraints and System Dynamics: a Suitable Case for Multi-Methodology. *Proceedings of the System Dynamics International Conference*. Oxford, UK.

Dettmer, H.W. (1997): *Goldratt's Theory of Constraints: A Systems Approach to Continuous Improvement.* Milwaukee: ASQC.

Dörner, D. (1996): *The Logic of Failure.* New York: Metropolitan Books/Henry Holt.

Fandel, G. (1991): *Theory of Production and Cost.* Heidelberg: Springer.

Forrester, J.W. (1961): *Industrial Dynamics.* Cambridge, MA: MIT Press.

Gigerenzer, G. and P. M. Todd (2000): *Simple Heuristics that Make Us Smart.* Oxford: Oxford University Press.

Goldratt, E. (1980): Optimized production timetable: beyond MRP: something better is finally here. *APICS 23rd Annual International Conference Proceedings.*

Goldratt, E. (1988): Computerized shop floor scheduling. *International Journal of Production Research* 26(3): 443–455.

Goldratt, E. (1990a): *What is This Thing Called Theory of Constraints and How Should it be Implemented.* New York: North River Press.

Goldratt, E. (1990b): *The Haystack Syndrome – Sifting Information Out of The Data Ocean.* Great Barrington: North River Press.

Goldratt, E. (1994): *It's Not Luck.* Aldershot: Gower.

Größler, A. (2004): A Content and Process View on Bounded Rationality in System Dynamics. *Systems Research & Behavioral Science* 21(4): 319–330.

Größler, A. (2007): System Dynamics Projects That Failed to Make an Impact. *System Dynamics Review* 23(4): 437–452.

Größler, A., A. Grübner and P. M. Milling (2006): Organisational Adaptation Processes to External Complexity. *International Journal of Operations and Production Management* 26(3): 254–281.

Gutenberg, E. (1951): *Grundlagen der Betriebswirtschaftslehre, Band 1, Die Produktion.* Berlin: Springer.

Hogarth, R. (1987): *Judgement and Choice* (2. ed.). Chichester: John Wiley.

Janis, I. L. (1982): *Groupthink: Psychological Studies of Policy Decisions and Fiascos* (2. ed.). Boston, MA: Houghton Mifflin.

Kim, S., V. J. Mabin and J. Davies (2008): The Theory of Constraints Thinking Processes: Retrospect and Prospect. *International Journal of Operations and Production Management* 28(2): 155–184.

Klingberg, T. (2008): *Multitasking.* München: Beck.

Langer, E. J. (1975): The illusion of control. *Journal of Personality and Social Psychology* 32: 311–328.

Mabin, V. J., J. Davies and J. Cox (2006): Using the Theory of Constraints Thinking Processes to Complement System Dynamics Causal Loop Diagrams in Developing Fundamental Solution. *International Transactions in Operational Research* 13(1): 33–57.

March, J. G. (1978): Bounded rationality, ambiguity, and the engineering of choice. *Bell Journal of Economics* 9: 587–608.

March, J. G. and H. A. Simon (1993): *Organizations* (2. ed.). Cambridge, MA: Blackwell.

Meadows, D. L., D. H. Meadows, P. M. Milling and E. O. K. Zahn (1972): *Die Grenzen des Wachstums – Bericht des Club of Rome zur Lage der Menschheit.* Stuttgart: Deutsche Verlags-Anstalt.

Meadows, D. L. et al. (1974): *Dynamics of Growth in a Finite World.* Cambridge, MA: Wright-Allen.

Miller, G. A. (1956): The magical number seven plus or minus two: some limits of our capacity for processing information. *Psychological Review* 63(2): 81–97.

Milling, P. M. (1991): Strategische Planungs- und Kontrollsysteme zur Unterstützung betrieblicher Lernprozesse. In Milling, P. M. (ed.): *Systemmanagement und Managementsysteme.* Berlin: Duncker & Humblot, 11–31.

Milling, P. M. (1995): Organisationales Lernen und seine Unterstützung durch Managementsimulatoren. *Zeitschrift für Betriebswirtschaft* Ergänzungsheft 3: Lernende Unternehmen: 93–112.

Milling, P. M. (2002): Understanding and Managing Innovation Processes. *System Dynamics Review* 18(1): 73–86.

Musa, P. F., V. C. Edmondson and G. Munchus (2005): Analyses of Information Students' Applications of Two Holistic Problem Solving Methodologies. *Journal of Information Systems Education* 16(4): 391–408.

Nelson, R. R. and S. G. Winter (1982): *An Evolutionary Theory of Economic Change.* Cambridge, MA: Harvard University Press.

Neumann, J. von and O. Morgenstern (1944): *Theory of Games and Economic Behavior.* Princeton, NJ: Princeton University Press.

Noreen, E., D. Smith and J. Mackey (1995): *The Theory of Constraints and Its Implications for Management Accounting.* Great Barrington: North River Press.

Pidd, M. (2004): *Computer Simulation in Management Science* (5. ed.). Chichester: John Wiley.

Rabin, M. (1998): Psychology and Economics. *Journal of Economic Literature* 36: 11–46.

Rahman, S. (1998): Theory of constraints – A review of the philosophy and its application. *International Journal of Operations and Production Management* 18(4): 336–355.

Richardson, G. (1986): Problems with causal loop diagrams. *System Dynamics Review* 2(2): 158–170.

Roth, G. L. and P. M. Senge (1996): From Theory to Practice: Research Territory, Processes and Structure at an Organisational Learning Centre. *Journal of Organisational Change Management* 9(1): 92–106.

Senge, P. M. (1990): *The Fifth Discipline – The Art and Practice of The Learning Organization.* New York: Currency Doubleday.

Simon, H. A. (1959): Theories of Decision-Making in Economics and Behavioral Science. *American Economic Review* 49(3): 253–283.

Simon, H. A. (1978): On how to decide what to do. *The Bell Journal of Economics* 9(2): 494–507.

van der Smagt, T. (2006): Causation and Constitution in System Dynamics: Modelling a Socially Constructed World. *Systems Research and Behavioral Science* 23(4): 513–524.

Snabe, B. and A. Größler (2006): System Dynamics Modelling for Strategy Implementation – Concept and Case Study. *Systems Research & Behavioral Science* 23(4): 467–481.

Steele, C. M. (1988): The psychology of self-affirmation: sustaining the integrity of the self. In: Berkowitz, L. (ed.): *Advances in Experimental Social Psychology,* New York, NY: Academic Press, 261–302.

Sterman, J. D. (1994): Learning in and about complex systems. *System Dynamics Review* 10(2–3): 291–330.

Sterman, J. D. (2000): *Business Dynamics*. Boston, MA: Irwin McGraw-Hill.

Strohhecker, J. (1998): *System- und objektorientierte Simulation betriebswirtschaftlicher Entscheidungen.* Berlin: Duncker & Humblot.

Süß, H.-M. (1996): *Intelligenz, Wissen und Problemlösen.* Göttingen: Hogrefe.

Thun, J.-H., A. Größler and S. Miczka (2007): The Impact of the Demographic Transition on Manufacturing: Effects of an Ageing Workforce in German Industrial Firms. *Journal of Manufacturing Technology Management* 18(8): 985–999.

Viale, R. (1992): Cognitve constraints of economic rationality. In Simon, H. A., M. Egidi, R. Marris and R. Viale (eds.): *Economics, Bounded Rationality and the Cognitive Revolution,* Aldershot: Edward Elgar, 174–193.

Zimbardo, P. G. (1992): *Psychology and Life* (13. ed.). Glenview: Scott & Foresman.

Messung von Flexibilität in der Produktion

Klaus Bellmann, Frank Himpel und Andreas Böhm

Johannes Gutenberg-Universität, Mainz

Zusammenfassung

Als zentraler Lösungsansatz zum Umgang mit komplexen und dynamischen Unternehmensumwelten rückt das Konstrukt der produktionswirtschaftlichen Flexibilität in den Mittelpunkt strategisch-taktischer Gestaltung sowie operativer Optimierung. Aufgrund der weit reichenden Bedeutung der Flexibilität für die leistungswirtschaftliche Performanz von Produktionssystemen beschäftigen sich sowohl betriebswirtschaftliche als auch ingenieurwissenschaftliche Zugänge mit Ansätzen zur Beschreibung, Interpretation, Konzeptualisierung und Messung unterschiedlicher Erscheinungsformen von Flexibilität in der Produktion. Dies betrifft insbesondere Käufermärkte. Dabei ist in den vergangenen Jahrzehnten in der wissenschaftlichen Rezeption jedoch kein einheitliches Begriffsbild und kein kohärentes Konstruktverständnis zur Flexibilität emergiert.

Die Diskussion über Flexibilitätsarten und ihre Interdependenzen soll verdeutlichen, dass der Flexibilitätsbegriff aus sehr unterschiedlichen Perspektiven betrachtet werden kann und muss. Da Flexibilität keinen Selbstzweck darstellt, sondern als ein Mittel zur Erreichung von Systemzielen dient, ist es konsequent, dass eine Vielzahl von Zugängen zur Messung von Flexibilität existiert. Bei der Konzeptualisierung von Modellen zur Messung von Flexibilität in der Produktion ist es deshalb unumgänglich, Flexibilitätspotenziale im Kontext mit Flexibilitätsbedarfen situationsbezogen zu analysieren. Eine umfassende Literaturanalyse bildet die Grundlage zur Untersuchung von 19 Modellen zur Flexibilitätsmessung mit dem Ziel, zunächst eine Klassifikation der Messmodelle vorzunehmen und nachfolgend deren Eignung hinsichtlich praktischer Anwendbarkeit zur Messung von Flexibilität in der Produktion zu bewerten.

Schlagwörter: Flexibilität, Flexibilitätsarten, Flexibilitätspotential, Produktion, Flexibilitätsmessung, Ursache-Wirkungs-Beziehungen

1 Systemorientierter Bezugsrahmen

Die Hervorbringung von kundenindividuellen Leistungsangeboten für Nachfrager in ausdifferenzierten und hinsichtlich ihrer Produktanforderungen mitunter ausgesprochen veränderlichen Käufermärkten ist aus produktionswirtschaftlicher Sicht als komplexes Gestaltungsproblem interpretierbar. Als zentraler Lösungsansatz zum Umgang mit diesen komplexen Unternehmensumwelten rückt das Konstrukt der produktionswirtschaftlichen Flexibilität in den Mittelpunkt strategisch-taktischer Gestaltung sowie operativer Optimierung. Aufgrund der weit reichenden Bedeutung der Flexibilität für die leistungswirtschaftliche Performanz von Produktionssystemen beschäftigen sich sowohl betriebswirtschaftliche als auch ingenieurwissenschaftliche Zugänge mit einer Vielzahl an Ansätzen zur Beschreibung, Interpretation, Konzeptualisierung und Messung unterschiedlicher Erscheinungsformen von Flexibilität in der Produktion.[1] Dabei ist in den vergangenen Jahrzehnten jedoch kein einheitliches Begriffsbild und kein kohärentes Konstruktverständnis zur Flexibilität emergiert.

Bei vertiefter Betrachtung der wissenschaftlichen Diskussion zur Flexibilität im deutschsprachigen Raum fällt auf, dass der Intensivierungsgrad der Auseinandersetzung mit diesem Konstrukt gekoppelt ist an die allgemeine wirtschaftliche Entwicklung: Der Ausbruch der Weltwirtschaftskrise im Jahr 1929 führte im deutschsprachigen Raum zunächst zur Einführung von Flexibilitätskonzepten. Dabei wurde auf die Flexibilität ein eher reaktiver Charakter attribuiert, d. h., (produktionswirtschaftliche) Flexibilität schien erforderlich, um auf die Nachfrageschwankungen in den Märkten verbessert reagieren zu können und die Ausrichtung der Leistungserstellungspotenziale auf diese Veränderungen verbessert anzupassen. Diesem reaktiven Charakter wurde in den 1950er Jahren eine aktive Attribuierung beigezogen: Der allgemeine Wirtschaftsaufschwung nach dem 2. Weltkrieg fokussierte die Diskussion zur Flexibilität auf die Potenziale zur verbesserten Nutzung sich bietender Marktchancen. Flexibilität war von da an sowohl als reaktiv-adaptives wie auch als proaktiv-potenzialorientiertes Konstrukt konzeptualisiert.[2] Im Zuge der folgenden wirtschaftlichen Entwicklung verfeinerten sich die Ansätze und Zugänge zur Beschreibung, Erklärung und Messung von Flexibilität in beiden Sichten weiter aus. Im Zuge der Ölkrise in den 1980er und 1990er Jahren wurde dabei vor allem der strategische Stellenwert von Flexibilität betont.[3] Während bis dahin aus produktionswirtschaftlicher Sicht allein Entscheidungen zur Kapazitätsgestaltung strategischen Charakter aufwiesen, wurde die Flexibilität hiernach gleichsam als strategische Aktionsvariable aufgenommen. Der aus heutiger Sicht durchaus klassisch anmutende Diskurs über „Kapazität versus Flexibilität" unterstellt dabei noch ein antinomisches Verhältnis beider Gestaltungsfelder.[4]

Flexibilität wird in seinem etymologischen Ursprung auf die Eigenschaften biegsam, anpassungsfähig und geschmeidig zurückgeführt. In produktionswirtschaftlicher Konkretisierung bezieht sich der Begriff auf die Fähigkeit eines Produktionssystems, Produkte und Leistungen in einer Vielzahl mengen- und artverschiedener Konkretisierungen unter dem Einfluss von unterschiedlichen externen und internen Einflüssen ausbringen zu können. Dabei sind die Begriffe Flexibilität und Elastizität seit Jahrzehnten häufig Gegenstand betriebswirtschaftlicher Betrachtungen und werden oftmals sogar gleichgesetzt. Beide Begriffe dürfen inhaltlich jedoch nicht notwendigerweise synonym verwendet werden: Elastizität bezieht sich im Kern auf ein deterministisches Konzept und dient als Indikator zum Aufzeigen der Ursache-Wirkungs-Kopplung zwischen einer relativen Änderung einer unabhängigen Größe auf die relative Änderung einer abhängigen Größe. Im Rahmen der Anpassung an exogen oder endogen induzierte Einwirkungen spielt die Anpassungsfähigkeit eines (Produktions-)Systems eine bedeutsame Rolle.

[1] Für einen Überblick siehe De Toni, A.; Tonchia, S.: Manufacturing flexibility. A literature review.

[2] Zur Ausprägung des aktiv-potenzialorientierten Zugangs siehe Dormayer, H.J.: Konjunkturelle Früherkennung und Flexibilität im Produktionssystem.

[3] Siehe weiterführend Voigt, K.-I.: Zeit und Zeitgeist in der Betriebswirtschaftslehre, dargestellt am Beispiel der betriebswirtschaftlichen Flexibilitätsdiskussion, S. 596 f.; zum strategischen Stellenwert der Flexibilität siehe Gerwin, D.: Manufacturing flexibility. A strategic perspective.

[4] Vgl. Kaluza, B.: Rahmenentscheidungen zu Kapazität und Flexibilität produktionswirtschaftlicher Systeme, S. 51 f.

In systemorientierter Interpretation stellen Unternehmen sozio-techno-ökonomische Systeme dar, die sich ihrerseits aus einem Gefüge von Teilsystemen konstituieren. Die Beziehungen zwischen den Systemelementen innerhalb und zwischen den einzelnen Teilsystemen werden durch eine Systemgrenze kontextualisiert und auf das betrachtete System attribuiert. Die Anpassungsfähigkeit eines Produktionsbereichs an exogene Einflüsse ist einerseits aktiv darauf ausgerichtet, unter Berücksichtigung der Gestaltungsalternativen optimale Wege zur Anpassung zu finden. Andererseits fokussiert diese Fähigkeit auch darauf, negative Auswirkungen einer Anpassungsmaßnahme nach Möglichkeit so niedrig wie möglich zu halten, somit Risiken zu begrenzen oder zu vermeiden. Damit ein Produktionssystem hinreichend geeignet zwischen Adaption und Risikobegrenzung abwägen kann, sind Handlungsspielräume erforderlich. Derartige Handlungsspielräume sind für die Aufrechterhaltung der (Produktions-)Flexibilität konstitutiv.

Während der Handlungsspielraum das mehrdimensionale Volumen des Flexibilitätspotenzials verkörpert, richtet sich die Handlungsgeschwindigkeit in erster Linie auf die Schnelligkeit, mit der auf Einflüsse reagiert werden kann: Hierzu gehören neben der reinen Beobachtungszeit auch die Aktionszeit und die Wirkzeit, also in summe die Zeitspanne von der Realisierung einer Handlungsnotwendigkeit bis zum Eintreten eines Effekts. Je komplexer ein System ausgestaltet ist, und je diffuser die Ursache-Wirkungs-(Ursache-)Beziehungen auf Sicht der Entscheidungsträger interpretierbar sind, desto schwieriger und unpräziser wird die Kalibrierung des Handlungsprozesses bei der Nutzung der Handlungsspielräume. Im produktionswirtschaftlichen Kontext vollzieht sich diese Prozesskalibrierung im Spannungsfeld von Effektivität und Effizienz der Produktion: Der Aufbau von (Produktions-)Potenzialen ist kontextualisiert durch die Effizienz der Nutzung von flexibilitätsorientierten Handlungsspielräumen. Demgegenüber lassen sich (Produktions-)Potenziale hinreichend geeignet nutzen, wenn Handlungsspielräume und -geschwindigkeiten in permanenter Entsprechung des Wechselspiels zwischen outside/in-orientierter Produktentwicklung und inside/out-orientiertem Ressourcenaufbau ausgebaut werden.

Im produktionswirtschaftlichen Zusammenhang interessiert neben der Öffnung des Handlungsraums und der Konzeptualisierung der damit verbundenen Gestaltungsalternativen zum Aufbau und zur subsequenten Nutzung von Flexibilitätspotenzialen insbesondere auch die Messung der betriebsindividuell anliegenden Flexibilität, z. B. im Rahmen von Entscheidungen zur Produktionsoptimierung. Ein derartiges Konstrukt entzieht sich jedoch einer unmittelbaren, direkten Messung. Es ist – analog den in anderen betriebswirtschaftlichen Disziplinen im Forschungsfokus stehenden Konstrukten (so z. B. die Kundenzufriedenheit im Marketing) – nur indirekt, also anhand von Operationalisierungen, messbar. Eine derartige Operationalisierung versteht sich als eine Variante der Ausdifferenzierung des Flexibilitätskonstrukts mit Blick auf quantitativ erfassbare Artefakte. Dabei wird das an sich mehrdimensionale Konstrukt der Flexibilität in Anlehnung an die konkret gewählte Operationalisierungsvariante in ein ein- bzw. zweidimensionales Messartefakt überführt und in diesem Sinnzusammenhang für Entscheidungen zum Produktionssystem geeignet aufbereitet.

Mit diesem Vorgehen sind aus methodischer Sicht sowohl Vor- als und Nachteile verbunden: Wenngleich ein Nachteil der Dimensionsreduzierung des Flexibilitätskonstrukts zu einem Verlust an Aussagekraft in der Messebene führt, da nicht mehr sämtliche qualitative und quantitative Wirkungsfaktoren berücksichtigt sind, stehen diesem Nachteil zwei Vorteile gegenüber. Durch die Reduzierung auf ein niedrigdimensioniertes Messartefakt lassen sich anhand von komparativ-statischen Kennzahlenvergleichen für (operative) Anpassungsentscheidungen im

Zeitablauf gegenüber rein intuitiven Entscheidungen verbesserte Aussagen über die Wirksamkeit von Anpassungen ableiten. Darüber hinaus dient die Messung der Flexibilität in einem übergeordneten Zusammenhang auch der verbesserten Führung des unternehmensbezogenen Gesamtsystems, z. B. im Wechselspiel der Analyse von mehreren Kennzahlen aus unterschiedlichen Funktionsbereichen (intraorganisationale Flexibilität) bzw. über Wertschöpfungspartner hinweg (interorganisationale Flexibilität). Voraussetzung für eine – die „innere Vielschichtigkeit" des Flexibilitätskonstrukts nicht zu stark beschneidende – Operationalisierung ist dabei jedoch die genaue Beschreibung der produktionswirtschaftlichen Flexibilität.

Analog einer Typologisierung lassen sich dabei unterschiedliche Artefakte fokussieren, die für eine hinreichend genaue Beschreibung geeignet erscheinen. Typischerweise wird zunächst auf das Aggregationsniveau in der Systembetrachtung abgehoben und die Systemgrenze des Entscheidungsbezugs definiert: Die Flexibilität eines technischen Aggregats (Teilsystem) wird durch seine inhärenten Flexibilitätspotenziale bestimmt, wohingegen die Flexibilität eines gesamten Produktionsbereichs auf dem Leistungsvermögen seiner Teilsysteme beruht.

Der Flexibilitätsbedarf eines (Teil-)Systems wird aus Sicht einer marktorientierten Unternehmensführung regelmäßig durch Beschaffungs- und Absatzmarktcharakteristika kontextualisiert. Die Handlungsspielräume in Bezug auf die Umweltkomplexität sind dabei ausgesprochen schwierig zu gestalten, da die dynamischen Komponenten der Systemumwelt nur bedingt antizipierbar sind. So sind im Grundsatz aktive Maßnahmen zur Flexibilitätsgestaltung zweckmäßig, andererseits aber oftmals nur reaktiv umzusetzen. Die Flexibilitätsbedarfe schlagen dabei auf drei Ebenen an: Kurzfristige Schwankungen in den Umweltbedingungen erfordern operative (Teil-)Systemanpassungen. In diese Kategorie können sowohl unternehmensexterne wie auch -interne Faktoren gehören, so z. B. Nachfrageveränderungen, Ausfall von Maschinenkapazität oder Krankheitsstände in der Belegschaft. Einflüsse, die nicht mehr operativ kompensiert werden können, schlagen auf die nächst höhere Ebene, die Unternehmensebene, durch. Hiervon wird im Prinzip der Entwicklungsverlauf des bestehenden Geschäfts berührt, z. B. durch die erforderliche Neueinführung von Produkten. Auf der strukturellen Ebene erwachsen Flexibilitätsbedarfe durch fundamentale Modifikationen, z. B. durch einen grundständigen technologischen Wandel.

Analog der Charakterisierung von Systemen als kompliziert oder komplex in Abhängigkeit von der Zeitveränderlichkeit der anliegenden Ursache-Wirkungs-(Ursache-)Beziehungen konkretisiert sich die Flexibilität als statisch, wenn die Veränderungen, die durch einen Anpassungsvorgang entstehen, von vornherein absehbar und prognostizierbar sind. Statische Flexibilität ist damit in ihrem Kern auf ein deterministisches Konzept zurückführbar. Wenn die mit der Anpassung einhergehenden Veränderungen demgegenüber nur bedingt erfassbar bzw. nur diffus prognostizierbar sind, erwachsen stochastische Charakteristika einer dynamischen Flexibilität. Im Rahmen der Anpassung gilt die Flexibilitätsreichweite als Spektrum zur Abbildung der grundsätzlich vorhandenen, unterschiedlichen Flexibilitätspotenziale. Demgegenüber sagt die Rückmeldung etwas darüber aus, in welchem Umfang sich ein System innerhalb dieser Reichweite konkret angepasst hat.[5] Um einen Eindruck von der Fristigkeit derartiger Anpassungsvorgänge zu erhalten, werden typischerweise kurz-, mittel- und langfristige Anpassungen

[5] Vgl. Slack, N.: The flexibility of manufacturing systems, S. 39.

unterschieden.[6] In ihrem Kern rekurriert die Zeitabhängigkeit auf die durch die Handlungsgeschwindigkeit beeinflusste Zeitspanne einer Anpassung. Die Konzeptualisierung einer Operationalisierung zur Messung von Flexibilität im produktionswirtschaftlichen Kontext vollzieht sich in Anlehnung an diese Durchmusterung in einem Spannungsfeld, welches durch das Aggregationsniveau (System vs. Teilsystem), die Ausbaufähigkeit der Potenziale (Bestand vs. Entwicklung) und ihren Zeitbezug (statisch vs. dynamisch) gekennzeichnet ist, wobei die Konstitution des Systems art- und volumenbezogen (Zustand vs. Reichweite) sowie zeitorientiert (kurzfristig vs. langfristig) beschrieben werden kann.

2 Zugänge zur Konzeptualisierung von Flexibilität

Zur Operationalisierung zum Zwecke einer Messbarmachung werden in der Forschung verschiedene Dimensionen herangezogen, um die Potenziale beschreibend zu typisieren. In der Literatur wird insbesondere häufig auf die Reichweite abgehoben, um die Anzahl der Freiheitsgrade bzw. die Bandbreite der Flexibilitätspotenziale, die bei gegebenem Systemzustand realisiert werden kann, zu operationalisieren. Dabei spielt nicht nur die Anzahl unterschiedlicher Anpassungsmöglichkeiten eine Rolle, sondern auch die inhaltlich-qualitative Verschiedenartigkeit der einzelnen Optionen.[7] Die Beschreibungsdimensionen „Bandbreite der Reichweite" sowie „Heterogenität der Reichweite" heben auf diese beiden Aspekte ab.[8] Die Dimension „Mobilität" wird in diesem Kontext häufig herangezogen, um eine Aussage über den Veränderungsaufwand zu erhalten. Der Veränderungsaufwand entsteht, um von einem Systemzustand in einen anderen zu gelangen. Sofern der Veränderungsaufwand, ausgedrückt durch die Mobilität, niedrig ist, besteht ein größerer Spielraum hinsichtlich weiterer Flexibilitätspotenziale (und umgekehrt).[9] Die langfristige Performanz des Flexibilitätspotenzials nach der Anpassung, also die tatsächlich erreichte Flexibilität, wird als „Uniformität" in der Literatur rezipiert.[10] Diese Dimension beschreibt die Beständigkeit des Outputs bei einer gegebenen Flexibilitätsbandbreite.[11] Zur Bewertung der Uniformität wird auf Aspekte der Effizienz, der Produktivität, der Qualität sowie diverser Prozessparameter rekurriert. Um die Flexibilitätspotenziale aufzubauen und langfristig zu sichern, erwachsen einem Unternehmen entsprechende Wertverzehre, die sich anhand von „Potenzialaufwendungen" beschreiben lassen.[12]

Die Maßnahmen zum Ausbau, zur Aufrechterhaltung und zur Nutzung von Flexibilitätspotenzialen finden ihren Niederschlag in (Zweck-)Aufwendungen, die gleichsam als (Grund-) Kosten interpretierbar sind. Analog von Kosten-Nutzen-Abwägungen sind diese Kosten den

[6] Vgl. Parker, R. P.; Wirth, A.: Manufacturing flexibility. Measures and relationships, S. 430f.

[7] Vgl. Koste, L. L.; Malhotra, M. K.: A theoretical framework for analyzing the dimensions of manufacturing flexibility, S. 78.

[8] Vgl. Koste, L. L.; Malhotra, M. K.; Sharma, S.: Measuring dimensions of manufacturing flexibility, S. 172.

[9] Vgl. Upton, D.-M.: The management of manufacturing flexibility, S. 80. Nach diesem Verständnis können z. B. Rüstaufwendungen als Anhaltspunkte dienen.

[10] Vgl. Kosta, L. L.; Malhotra, M. K.: Framework, a. a. O., S. 79.

[11] Eine weniger flexible Produktionsanlage weist z. B. eine qualitative und/oder quantitative höhere Unbeständigkeit der Ausbringung auf als eine im Vergleich dazu flexiblere Anlage.

[12] Vgl. Slack, N.: Flexibility as a manufacturing objective, S. 7.

durch die Anpassungsmaßnahmen realisierten (zusätzlichen) Erlösen i. S. e. Deckungsbeitragsrechnung beizuziehen und abzugleichen.[13] Neben den Grundkosten für den Aufbau und die Aufrechterhaltung von Flexibilität im Produktionssystem fallen darüber hinaus Opportunitätskosten an: Diese lassen sich interpretieren als Kosten von Inflexibilität. Aufbau und Änderungen von Anpassungspotenzialen schlagen sich in entsprechenden Aufbaukosten nieder.[14] Die laufende Pflege dieser Potenziale manifestiert sich in entsprechenden Vorhaltungskosten.[15] Beispiele hierfür sind höhere Fixkosten durch Erweiterung von technischen Anlagen oder höhere Personalkosten. Die Vorhaltungskosten lassen sich als „Versicherungsprämie“ interpretieren: Durch das Vorhandensein eines vorsorglichen Anpassungspotenzials i. S. e. Leistungs- bzw. Kapazitätsüberschusses fallen (Vorhaltungs-)Kosten an, die dem erwerbswirtschaftlichen Ziel der Gewinnmaximierung durchaus zuwiderlaufen. In der Kostenrechnung schlagen sich diese ungenutzten Potenziale bspw. als Leerkosten nieder. Werden diese Potenziale nachfolgend jedoch deckungsbeitragsgenerierend genutzt (z. B. durch Produktneueinführungen), alimentieren diese Potenziale das Primat der Gewinnmaximierung. Kapazität und Flexibilität stehen damit nicht per se in einem Spannungsverhältnis, sondern nur im Fall von (kurzfristig) ungenutzten Kapazitätsreserven. Sofern ein Produktionssystem weiterführend nicht über situativ, unternehmensbezogen bzw. strukturell erforderliche Potenziale verfügt, entstehen Opportunitätskosten,[16] die sich z. B. durch Kosten für entstehenden Terminverzug operationalisieren lassen. Aus diesem Grund sollte die Flexibilität nicht grenzenlos angehoben werden, da durch die damit einhergehende (Steuerungs-)Komplexität Handlungsineffizienzen entstehen, die sich den Kosten für Inflexibilität (Handlungsunfähigkeit auf Grund von Übersichts- und Durchgriffsmangel sowie Handlungsunmöglichkeit auf Grund von Potenzialmangel) beiziehen lassen.

Die unterschiedlichen Potenzialarten diffundieren aus phänomenologischer Sicht in korrespondierende Kostenarten der Flexibilität, aus systemorientierter Sicht stellen sie die Elemente des konzeptualisierten Operationalisierungszugangs dar. Zwischen diesen Messartefakten bestehen aus abstrakter Sicht Querverbindungen, die gleichsam als Relationen des Bewertungssystems zur quantitativen Abbildung der Flexibilität interpretierbar sind. Die unterschiedlichen Arten der Flexibilität bilden sich in entsprechenden Potenzialobjekten ab. Dazu zählen aus produktionswirtschaftlicher Sicht insbesondere die *Maschinenflexibilität*, die *Humanflexibilität* und die *Routingflexibilität*. Die Maschinenflexibilität bezieht sich auf Potenziale, die aus der Fertigungssteuerung erwachsen, wobei die Bandbreite der Einsatzmöglichkeiten einer Maschine den unterschiedlichen Arbeitsabläufen entspricht, die bewerkstelligt werden können. Gleichsam wird auch auf die Unterschiedlichkeit dieser Arbeitsabläufe abgehoben. Rüstzeiten sowie Rüstkosten und Produktionsausfallkosten dienen zur Erfassung der Mobilität. Änderungen in der Maschinenleistung können bspw. auf Änderungen in der Arbeitsablaufszeit begründet sein und beschreiben die Uniformität. Übertragen auf menschliche Arbeit werden im Rahmen der

---

[13] Siehe ausführlicher Voigt, K.-I.; Wildemann, H.: Quantifizierung der Flexibilität im Rahmen wertschöpfungspartnerschaftlicher Zusammenarbeit, S. 123 f.

[14] Vgl. Fischer, T. M.: Kostenmanagement strategischer Erfolgsfaktoren. Instrumente zur operativen Steuerung der strategischen Schlüsselfaktoren Qualität, Flexibilität und Schnelligkeit, S. 165 ff.

[15] Vgl. Frischke, S.: Simulationsbasierte Entscheidungsunterstützung bei der Gestaltung flexibler Produktionsbereiche auf taktischer Ebene, S. 14.

[16] Vgl. Horstmann, J.: Operationalisierung der Unternehmensflexibilität. Entwicklung einer umwelt- und unternehmensbezogenen Flexibilitätsanalyse, S. 219.

Humanflexibilität Anzahl und Unterschiedlichkeit der von einem Mitarbeiter im Produktionsbereich durchführbaren Arbeitsverrichtungen erfasst. Die Routingflexibilität repräsentiert die Fähigkeit eines Systems, ein Produkt in unterschiedlichen Maschinenfolgen herzustellen. Volumenflexibilität ist gegeben, wenn ein Produktionssystem auch bei unterschiedlichen Ausbringungsmengen innerhalb seiner Kapazität wirtschaftlich produzieren kann.

Mit Blick auf die *Materialflexibilität* werden Versorgungspotenziale durch die Anzahl unterschiedlicher Materialflusspfade zwischen einzelnen Fertigungsbereichen sowie durch die Heterogenität der Materialien, die das System transportieren kann, beschrieben. Die *Durchlaufflexibilität* fokussiert auf die unterschiedlichen Fertigungswege, die ein Werkstück – bzw. mehrere Werkstücke – bei einem vorgegebenen Arbeitsprozess in einem Fertigungssystem durchlaufen können. Je vielseitiger die einzelnen Produktionsoptionen sind, desto komplexer und kapitalintensiver gestaltet sich dabei das System. Die Konstanz des Produktionsprozesses spiegelt hierbei die Qualitätsunterschiede, welche durch die verschiedenen Produktionswege entstehen können. Im Unterschied zur Durchlaufflexibilität setzt die *Arbeitsablaufflexibilität* bei den unterschiedlichen Abläufen für Arbeitsprozesse an, um ein Werkstück herzustellen. Je höher dabei die Arbeitsablaufflexibilität eines Fertigungssystems, desto effizienter lässt sich das Produktionsvolumen durch ausgewogene Auslastung aussteuern. Die Bandbreite definiert sich analog der Durchlaufflexibilität, wobei die Rangreihung der Kombinationsmöglichkeiten in einem Prozess die Heterogenität indiziert. Allerdings kann es bei hoher Heterogenität zu abweichenden Kostenstrukturen sowie zu Qualitätsschwankungen kommen. Aus produktionswirtschaftlicher Sicht beschreibt die *Erweiterungsflexibilität*, inwieweit sich ein Fertigungssystem durch eine Steigerung der Maschinenanzahl ausdehnen lässt oder nicht. Im Unterschied zu den bislang angeführten Potenzialarten bezieht sich die Erweiterungsflexibilität nicht auf bestehende Ressourcen des Fertigungssystems.[17] Die Anzahl der möglichen Erweiterungsalternativen ist beschränkt durch die Aufnahmefähigkeit des Systems. Dabei spielt der organisatorische Aufbau in Anlehnung an entsprechend geeignete Aufgabenanalyse und -synthese eine wesentliche Rolle. Die *Absatzflexibilität* resp. *Marktflexibilität* beruht auf gegenwärtigen und zukünftigen Absatzpotenzialen und beschreibt den Kapazitätsausweitungsprozess anhand eines aggregierten Outputniveaus entlang definierter Produktlinien. Entscheidend ist dabei das Leistungsvermögen aller bestehenden Komponenten des Fertigungssystems. Die Mobilität des Prozesses spiegelt die zeitliche Anpassung wider, während die Uniformität auf die Vielfalt von Fertigungskosten und Qualitätsmerkmalen rekurriert. Je weniger die durchschnittlichen Grenzkosten auf die Gesamtkostensituation bei einer Variation des Outputniveaus durchschlagen, desto flexibler ist das betrachtete System.

In die *Programmflexibilität* fließen verschiedene Flexibilitätsmaße ein: Die *Produktflexibilität*, auch als *Produktmixflexibilität* bezeichnet, verkörpert die Fähigkeit eines Produktionssystems, verschiedene Produkte oder Produkte in unterschiedlichen Zusammenstellungen zu fertigen. Die *Prozessflexibilität* hebt auf das Produktionsprogramm ab. Genauer wird hier die Veränderung einer Produktlinie bei gegebener Kapazität und Faktorausstattung subsumiert. Insofern ist diese Art der Flexibilität als Charakteristik der Anlagenausstattung zu interpretieren, einerseits bezogen auf die Anzahl der Produkte im Produktionsprogramm, andererseits fokussiert auf die unterschiedlichen Arten der hervorbringbaren Produkte ohne Umrüstung der

[17] Vgl. Tempelmeier, H.; Kuhn, H.: Flexible manufacturing systems. Decision support for design and operation, S. 16.

Maschinen. Mit Blick auf die *Produktinnovationsflexibilität* gilt ein Produkt als Innovation, wenn seine funktionellen Eigenschaften sich von denen der vorhergehenden Produkte, die von derselben Maschine hergestellt wurden, unterscheiden. Die Anzahl sowie die Originalität der neu entwickelten Produkte spiegeln die Tragfähigkeit des Flexibilitätspotenzials wider. Sofern nicht ein Produkt neu entwickelt, sondern nur modifiziert, wird rezipiert die Literatur dies als *Produktmodifikationsflexibilität*. Hinsichtlich der Beschreibungsdimensionen gelten dieselben Zugänge wie bei der Produktinnovationsflexibilität.

Mit Blick auf die Relationen und die Durchmusterung der angeführten produktionswirtschaftlichen Flexibilitätsarten gilt,[18] dass die Flexibilitäten hinsichtlich von Produktmix, Produktinnovation, Produktmodifikation, Absatz, Erweiterung und Prozess auf der Ebene von Fertigungssystemen anschlagen. Sie sind phänomenologisch zwar die übergeordneten, inhaltlich aber die abhängigen Flexibilitätspotenziale des Produktionsbereichs. Die Maschinenflexibilität, Humanflexibilität, Routingflexibilität, Materialflexibilität, Durchlaufflexibilität und Arbeitsablaufflexibilität schlagen demgegenüber auf der nachgeordneten Ebene der Betriebsmittel an. Sie repräsentieren die unabhängigen Flexibilitätspotenziale: So können Produktinnovationen abhängig sein von den eingesetzten Maschinen und den eingesetzten Mitarbeitern – dies gilt aber nicht umgekehrt. Mit Blick auf das konkrete Produktionsprogramm, die konkret anliegende Faktorausstattung und die gegebenen Marktbedingungen lässt sich ein Aussagesystem konzeptualisieren, welches einen konkreten Messzugang zur vorhandenen Anpassungsfähigkeit ermöglicht.

Die vorstehende Diskussion soll verdeutlichen, dass der Flexibilitätsbegriff aus sehr unterschiedlichen Perspektiven betrachtet werden kann, so dass jeweils ein bestimmter Aspekt, in diesem Sinn eine Teilflexibilität, angesprochen wird. In der betriebswirtschaftlichen Literatur sind in Untersuchungen bis zu 50 verschiedene Flexibilitätsbegriffe bzw. Flexibilitätsarten identifiziert worden.[19] Doch verwenden viele Autoren größtenteils nur unterschiedliche Bezeichnungen, um die gleiche Teilflexibilität zu benennen, so dass, folgt man Sethi u. Sethi, prinzipiell im Grunde 11 verschiedene Flexibilitätsarten bestimmt werden können (s. Abbildung 1).

Andere Autoren unterscheiden hingegen zwischen *Bestandsflexibilität* (bei gegebenem Betriebsmittelbestand eines Systems) und *Entwicklungsflexibilität* (Möglichkeit der Weiterentwicklung des Systems)[20] oder kategorisieren Flexibilität in die drei Ausprägungen *quantitative Flexibilität* (Anpassung an unterschiedliche Ausbringungsmengen), *qualitative Flexibilität* (Anpassung an unterschiedliche Aufgaben) und *zeitliche Flexibilität* (benötigte Zeitspanne für die Anpassung).[21]

---

[18] Siehe zur Interpretation von Kennzahlen als Elemente eines Messzugangs sowie dazugehöriger Relationen einführend Oke, A.: A framework for analyzing manufacturing flexibility.

[19] Vgl. Meffert, H.: Größere Flexibilität als Unternehmenskonzept, S. 121; Sethi, A. K.; Sethi, S. P.: Flexibility in Manufacturing: A Survey, S. 296ff.; siehe ergänzend ebenfalls die Ansätze von Sethi, A. K.; Sethi, S. P.: Flexibility in Manufacturing: A Survey, Vokurka, R. J.; O'Leary-Kelly, S. W.: A review on empirical research on manufacturing flexibility, Upton, D.: Process range in manufacturing: an empirical study of flexibility.

[20] Vgl. Jacob, H.: Flexibilität und ihre Bedeutung für die Betriebspolitik, S. 17ff.

[21] Vgl. Wildemann, H.: Investitionsplanung und Wirtschaftlichkeitsrechnung für flexible Fertigungssysteme (FFS), S. 4ff.

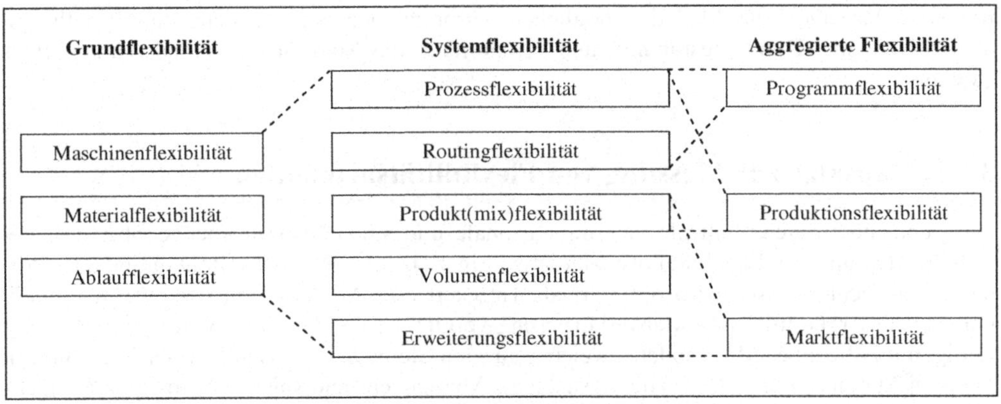

Abbildung 1: Flexibilitätsarten und ihre Beziehungen nach Sethi und Sethi

Quelle: Eigene Darstellung in Anlehnung an Sethi, A. K.; Sethi, S. P.: Flexibility in Manufacturing: A Survey, S. 297.

Da Flexibilität keinen Selbstzweck sondern ein Mittel zur Erreichung der Systemziele darstellt, ist es nötig, das Verhältnis von Flexibilitätspotenzial und Flexibilitätsbedarf zu klären. Ein Flexibilitätspotenzial kann nur dann unter wirtschaftlichen Gesichtspunkten vorteilhaft sein, wenn der entsprechende Flexibilitätsbedarf gegenübersteht. Mit anderen Worten, es muss die im System zu schaffende Flexibilität auf mögliche oder für möglich gehaltene Veränderungen der Systemumwelt (die Flexibilitätsbedarfe) abgestimmt werden. Reichwald und Behrbohm entwickeln dazu eine Klassifikation, um verschiedene Flexibilitätspotenziale und -bedarfe zu unterscheiden (z. B. nach Ursprung, Informationsbasis, Wirkungsweise, Objekt etc.).[22]

Neben dem Begriff der Flexibilität findet sich in der Literatur auch noch eine Anzahl verwandter Begriffe, deren grundlegende Bedeutung aber von der der Flexibilität abweicht. So beschreibt Elastizität[23] im Allgemeinen die relative Änderung einer abhängigen Variablen bei Veränderung der Basisvariablen, Robustheit[24] die Unempfindlichkeit eines Systems gegenüber Veränderungen in der Systemumwelt (idealerweise ohne dass eine Anpassungsreaktion notwendig wird), Agilität[25], ein primär in der US-amerikanischen Literatur zu findender Begriff, als Fähigkeit einer Unternehmung, in einer sich entwickelnden Umgebung gewinnbringend operieren zu können, Wandlungsfähigkeit,[26] die Fähigkeit eines Systems, Strukturen kurzfristig anpassen und langfristig weiterentwickeln zu können, Anpassungsfähigkeit,[27] die Fähigkeit eines Systems, sich an Veränderungen der Systemumwelt anpassen zu können (nur reaktiv, nicht

[22] Vgl. Reichwald, R.; Behrbohm, P.: Flexibilität als Eigenschaft produktionswirtschaftlicher Systeme, S. 842 ff.

[23] Vgl. Horváth, P.; Mayer, R.: Produktionswirtschaftliche Flexibilität, S. 69.

[24] Vgl. Meier-Barthold, D.: Flexibilität in der Material-Logistik, S. 18 f.

[25] Vgl. Goldman, S. L. et al.: Agil im Wettbewerb. Die Strategie der virtuellen Organisation zum Nutzen des Kunden, S. 3.

[26] Vgl. Dohms, R.: Methodik zur Bewertung und Gestaltung wandlungsfähiger, dezentraler Produktionsstrukturen, S. 8.

[27] Vgl. Damisch, P. N.: Wertorientiertes Flexibilitätsmanagement durch den Realoptionsansatz, S. 44 f.

proaktiv), Varietät,[28] das Maß der möglichen Ausprägungen eines Systems (als Handlungsalternativen eines Handlungsraumes) und Variabilität,[29] das Maß für die Veränderbarkeit eines Systems.

3 Ansätze zur Messung von Flexibilitätsartefakten

Aufgrund ihrer Eigenschaft als mehrdimensionale und situationsbezogenen Größe, gestaltet sich die Messung von Flexibilität weitaus schwieriger als die von Kosten, Rentabilität oder Produktivität. Denn Messen wird definiert als Tätigkeit oder Vorgang, mit der eine quantitativ unbekannte Größe mit einer Maßverkörperung verglichen und bewertet wird.[30] Die Messung erfolgt mit Hilfe eines Messmodells, welches aus den Elementen Messgröße (hier: Flexibilität), Messobjekt (hier: z. B. eine Fertigungsanlage), Messgegenstand (hier: z. B. messbare Eigenschaft der Fertigungsanlage), Messwerte (Resultate des Messvorgangs) besteht.[31] So muss zur Messung von Flexibilität eine geeignete Eigenschaft bestimmt werden, die eine quantitative Abbildung erlaubt. Damit ein solches Messmodell den Ansprüchen einer verlässlichen Messung entsprechen kann (d. h. ein hohes Flexibilitätspotenzial soll auch als ein solches und nicht als ein niedriges gemessen werden), sind Anforderungen an das Messmodell zu stellen. Dazu können bspw. Objektorientierung, Multidimensionalität, Trennung der Messung von der Bewertung, Rationalität etc. gezählt werden. Die in Abbildung 2 chronologisch zum Publikationsdatum aufgeführten 19 Modelle zur Flexibilitätsmessung sind das Ergebnis einer umfassenden Literaturanalyse mit dem Ziel, eine Klassifikation der Messmodelle vorzunehmen und deren Eignung zu würdigen.

Modell von ...	**misst die ...**
Marschak/ Nelson	*Flexibilität von Entscheidungen* über die Teilmengenbeziehung der Mengen der nach der Anfangsentscheidung noch bestehenden Handlungsmöglichkeiten.[32]
Gupta/ Rosenhead	*Flexibilität einer Entscheidungsfolge* über das Verhältnis der Anzahl der erreichbaren „akzeptablen Endzustände“ zu der Gesamtzahl der „akzeptablen Endzustände“.[33]
Jacob	*Bestandsflexibilitätsmaßzahl* sowie *Entwicklungsflexibilitätsmaßzahl* als Quotienten des Gewinns bei optimaler Anpassung bei „prophetischem Wissen“ und dem Gewinn bei optimaler Anpassung entsprechend einer Entscheidung, jeweils vermindert um den Gewinn bei Nicht-Anpassung.[34]

Abbildung 2: Analyse von Flexibilitätsmodellen *(Fortsetzung auf S. 231)*

[28] Vgl. Hillmer, H.-J.: Planung der Unternehmensflexibilität. Eine allgemeine theoretische Konzeption und deren Anwendung zur Bewältigung strategischer Flexibilitätsprobleme, S. 22 f.

[29] Vgl. Eversheim, W.; Schaefer, F.-W.: Planung des Flexibilitätsbedarfs von Industrieunternehmen, S. 231.

[30] Vgl. Richter, W.: Gegenstand der Messtechnik, S. 27.

[31] Vgl. Richter, W.: Messtechnische Disziplinen, Aufgaben und Ziele, S. 29 f.

[32] Vgl. Marschak, T.; Nelson, R.: Flexibility, Uncertainty, and Economic Theory, S. 42 ff.; zitiert nach Pibernik, R.: Flexibilitätsplanung in Wertschöpfungsnetzwerken, S. 98 f.

[33] Vgl. Gupta, S. K.; Rosenhead, J.: Robustness in Sequential Investment Decisions, S. B18 ff.

[34] Vgl. Jacob, H.: Unsicherheit und Flexibilität. Zur Theorie der Planung bei Unsicherheit, S. 322 ff.

Modell von ...	misst die ...
Mahlmann	*Flexibilität einer Entscheidung* sowie *Flexibilität eines Planungsprozesses*. Flexibilität des Planungsprozesses wird bestimmt über die Menge der Planrevisionszeitpunkte und Flexibilität der Entscheidung über die Anzahl von Entscheidungsmöglichkeiten, die über die Menge an Entscheidungsmöglichkeiten einer optimalen Strategie hinaus bestehen.[35]
Hanssmann	*Flexibilität einer Strategie* über den Gesamterfolg, der damit erreicht wird. Dazu wird ein Quotient aus Gesamterfolg der Strategie und Gesamterfolg bei optimaler Anpassung, jeweils vermindert um den Gesamterfolg bei Inflexibilität, gebildet.[36]
Eversheim/ Schaefer	*Flexibilität als Kapazität eines Produktionssystems.* Flexibilität wird als quantitative oder qualitative Überkapazität verstanden. Dementsprechend soll das Kapazitätsangebot auf die Kapazitätsnachfrage abgestimmt werden.[37]
Lasserre/ Roubellat	*Flexibilität einer Entscheidung* über das Volumen des bestehenden Handlungsraumes. Die Nebenbedingungen einer zu wählenden Zielfunktion (z. B. Minimierung der Lagerkosten) bilden dabei die Beschränkungen des Handlungsraumes. Zur Berechnung des Volumens wird ein von Lasserre aufgestelltes und bewährtes Theorem verwendet.[38]
Kumar	*Flexibilität eines Fertigungssystems* über die Anzahl der Wahlmöglichkeiten im System (z. B. Anzahl der Aggregate oder Routen) und die „Verfügbarkeit" der jeweiligen Wahlmöglichkeiten. Zur Berechnung zieht der Autor ein Entropiemaß aus der Thermodynamik bzw. Informationstheorie.[39]
Pauli	*Flexibilität über Kennzahlen.* So steht bspw. das Verhältnis von Anzahl wirtschaftlicher Absatzregionen zur gesamten Anzahl von Absatzregionen für die statische örtliche Leistungsflexibilität.[40]
Wolf	*Flexibilität als Kapazität eines Produktionssystems*, die in Matrizen beschrieben wird. Wenn die Kapazitätsnachfrage größer als das Kapazitätsangebot ist, besteht eine „Kapazitätslückenmatrix". Interpretiert als Flexibilitätslücken, ist ein System um so flexibler, desto mehr Flexibilitätslücken gedeckt werden können.[41]
Mandelbaum/ Buzacott	*Flexibilität einer Entscheidung* über die Mächtigkeit der Menge der Folgeaktionen. D. h., je mehr Handlungsoptionen eine Entscheidung ermöglicht, desto flexibler ist sie.[42]

Abbildung 2: Fortsetzung *(Fortsetzung auf S. 232)*

[35] Vgl. Mahlmann, K.: Anpassung und Anpassungsfähigkeit der betrieblichen Planung, S. 124 ff.

[36] Vgl. Hanssmann, F.: Einführung in die Systemforschung. Methodik der modellgestützten Entscheidungsvorbereitung, S. 228 ff.

[37] Vgl. Eversheim, W.; Schaefer, F.-W.: Planung des Flexibilitätsbedarfs von Industrieunternehmen, S. 229 ff.

[38] Vgl. Lasserre, J. B.; Roubellat, F.: Measuring Decision Flexibility in Production Planning, S. 447 ff.; zitiert nach Meier-Barthold, D.: Flexibilität in der Material-Logistik, S. 31 ff.

[39] Vgl. Kumar, V.: Entropic Measures of Manufacturing Flexibility, S. 957 ff.

[40] Vgl. Pauli, J.: So wird Ihr Unternehmen flexibel. Leitlinien und Maßnahmen, S. 87 ff.

[41] Vgl. Wolf, J.: Investitionsplanung zur Flexibilisierung der Produktion, S. 25 ff.

[42] Vgl. Mandelbaum, M.; Buzacott, J.: Flexibility and Decision Making, S. 17 ff.

Modell von …	misst die …
Schneeweiß/ Kühn	*Flexibilität einer Aktionenfolge* über ein Verrichtungsmaß. Das Verrichtungsmaß gibt an, welche Systemzielwirkung eine Aktionenfolge besitzt, z. B. im Bezug auf Kosten, Gewinn etc. Die Flexibilität einer Aktionenfolge wird berechnet als Quotient aus dem Verrichtungsmaß der Aktionsfolge und dem Verrichtungsmaß einer optimalen Aktionsfolge bei Sicherheit über zukünftige Zustände, jeweils vermindert um das Verrichtungsmaß einer Aktionsfolge, die keine Anpassung vorsieht.[43]
Ost	*Flexibilität von Maschinen* über Kennzahlen, die für einen Teilflexibilitätenkatalog bestimmt werden. Durch die Zuteilung eines Wahrheitsgrades im Rahmen einer fuzzy logic-Berechnung erstellt der Autor eine Hierarchie von Flexibilitätsbedarfen für die Teilflexibilitäten.[44]
Chen/Chung	*Flexibilität Flexibler Fertigungssysteme* (FFS) über Kennzahlen in Form von Bearbeitungsflexibilität und Routenflexibilität. Die Maßzahl für Bearbeitungsflexibilität ist der Quotient aus Anzahl der durch ein FFS durchführbaren Aufgaben und Gesamtanzahl aller Aufgaben eines Produktionssystems, Routenflexibilität der Quotient aus der Summe aller möglichen Wege der Werkstücke durch ein FFS und Menge aller Werkstücke.[45]
Meier-Barthold	*Flexibilität von Problemlösungsverfahren* über die Menge zulässiger Entscheidungsfolgen als diskretes Flexibilitätsmaß bzw. das Volumen der Menge zulässiger Entscheidungsfolgen als kontinuierliches Flexibilitätsmaß. Dazu bildet er den Quotient aus Mächtigkeit der Menge zulässiger Entscheidungsfolgen eines Problemlösungsverfahrens und Mächtigkeit der Menge der zulässigen Entscheidungsfolgen eines „best case" bzw. den Quotient aus Volumen der Menge zulässiger Entscheidungsfolgen eines Problemlösungsverfahrens und Volumen der Menge der zulässigen Entscheidungsfolgen eines „best case".[46]
Nagel	*Flexibilität eines Produktionssystems* über Flexibilitätskosten, die durch Ressourcenmehrbedarfe entstehen. Um diese Mehrbedarfe ermitteln zu können, nutzt die Autorin den System Dynamics-Ansatz zur Erfassung des gesamten Ressourceneinsatzes und -bedarfes.[47]
Corsten/ Gössinger	*Flexibilität eines Produktionssystems für Dienstleistungen* über die Berechnung der Volumina, die durch die Mengen an „lösbaren Problemen" und „akzeptablen Problemlösungen" bestimmt sind. Beide Mengen sind jeweils durch die Entscheidung über das Produktionssystem festgelegt.[48]

Abbildung 2: Fortsetzung *(Fortsetzung auf S. 233)*

[43] Vgl. Schneeweiß, C.; Kühn, M.: Zur Definition und gegenseitigen Abgrenzung der Begriffe Flexibilität, Elastizität und Robustheit, S. 380 ff.

[44] Ost, S.: Entwicklung eines Verfahrens zur differenzierten Flexibilitätsanalyse und -bewertung, S. 39 ff.

[45] Vgl. Chen, I. J.; Chung, C.-H.: An Examination of Flexibility Measurements and Performance of Flexible Manufacturing Systems, S. 379 ff.

[46] Vgl. Meier-Barthold, D.: Flexibilität in der Material-Logistik, S. 51 ff.

[47] Vgl. Nagel, M.: Flexibilitätsmanagement. Ein systemdynamischer Ansatz zur quantitativen Bewertung von Produktionsflexibilität, S. 37 ff.

[48] Vgl. Corsten, H.; Gössinger, R.: Output-Flexibilität in der Dienstleistungsproduktion. Eine produktionstheoretische Analyse, S. 39 ff.

Modell von ...	misst die ...
Mirschel	*Flexibilität von Produktionssystemen mit Kennzahlen.* Zur Operationalisierung von Flexibilitätspotenzialen unterscheidet der Autor Teilflexibilitäten auf drei Ebenen und nutzt bspw. Kapazitätsdifferenzen zwischen minimaler und maximaler Kapazität eines Aggregates als Messgrößen.[49]
Realoptions-bewertungs-modelle	*Flexibilität von Realoptionen.* Analog Finanzoptionen erlauben es Realoptionen eine zukünftige Wahl zwischen zwei Zuständen (z. B. Erweiterung oder Nicht-Erweiterung der Kapazität einer Anlage zu treffen, was als eine Form der Flexibilität interpretiert wird. Instrumente zur Finanzoptionspreisbewertung können dementsprechend genutzt werden, um die Flexibilität von Realoptionen zu messen.[50]

Abbildung 2: Fortsetzung

Bei einem Vergleich der vorgestellten Modelle zur Messung von Flexibilität sind vorrangig drei Konzepte zu erkennen, auf denen die Modelle aufbauen. Es sind dies indikatorbasierte Modelle, auf potentiellen Entscheidungen basierende Modelle und auf ökonomischen Zielkriterien basierende Modelle. Daneben sind noch kapazitätsorientierte Ansätze zur Flexibilitätsmessung sowie Konzepte aus der Thermodynamik bzw. Informationstheorie (Entropie) und der Optionspreistheorie aufzuzählen (vgl. Abbildung 3).

Klassifikationsmerkmal	Modellansatz von ...
Indikatoren	Pauli, Ost, Chen/Chung, Mirschel
Entscheidungsoptionen	Marschak/Nelson, Gupta/Rosenhead, Mahlmann, Lesserre/Roubellat, Mandelbaum/Buzacott, Meier-Barthold, Corsten/Gössinger
Ökonomische Zielkriterien	Jacob, Hannsmann, Schneeweiß/Kühn, Nagel
Kapazitätsmaße	Eversheim/Schaefer, Wolf
Entropie	Humar
Realoptionsbewertung	Diverse Autoren

Abbildung 3: Klassifikation der Messmodelle

Indikatorbasierten Messmodellen ist gemeinsam, dass sie Flexibilität mit Hilfe von Kennzahlen messen. Die Flexibilität eines (Produktions-)Systems soll dabei durch Indikatoren abgebildet werden. Dabei ist unter einem Indikator ein empirisch beobachtbarer Tatbestand zu verstehen, der die Quantifizierung eines physikalisch nicht messbaren Konstrukts (in diesem Fall Flexibilität) ermöglicht. Beispiele dafür sind die Anzahl ausführbarer Aufgaben auf einer Anlage, die Anzahl ersetzender Aggregate in einem Produktionssystem oder die Dauer der Rüstzeit einer Maschine.

[49] Vgl. Mirschel, S.: Messung und Bewertung von Produktionsflexibilitätspotentialen in geschlossenen und offenen Entscheidungsfeldern, S. 104 ff.

[50] Vgl. Trigeorgis, L.: A Real-Options Application in Natural-Resource Investments; Bengtsson, J.; Olhager, J.: Valuation of Product-Mix Flexibility using Real Options; Damisch, P. N.: Wertorientiertes Flexibilitätsmanagement durch den Realoptionsansatz.

Messmodelle, die auf potentiellen Entscheidungen basieren, haben dagegen als gemeinsame Annahme, dass die Menge an Handlungsoptionen, die nach einer Anfangsentscheidung noch durchführbar sind, die zu messende Flexibilität eines Systems darstellt. Dazu stellen die verschiedenen Modelle auf unterschiedliche Aspekte dieser Menge ab, bspw. auf die Teilmengenbeziehungen zwischen zwei Mengen von Handlungsmöglichkeiten oder den Vergleich der Mächtigkeit der Mengen von Handlungsmöglichkeiten.

Auf ökonomischen Zielkriterien basierende Messmodelle messen Flexibilität hingegen, indem die Zielwirkung, die durch unterschiedliche Flexibilitätspotenziale bedingt werden, betrachtet wird. So führt eine spezifische Handlungsfolge zu dem Wert einer Zielfunktion, der, ins Verhältnis gesetzt zu einem Optimalwert und normiert über einen Mindestwert, eine Aussage über das Flexibilitätspotenzial dieser Handlungsfolge ermöglicht. Die Zielfunktion kann dabei ein monetäres Ziel aber auch andere betriebswirtschaftliche Ziele abbilden.

Eine gewisse Besonderheit innerhalb der auf ökonomische Kriterien fokussierenden Ansätze stellt der Ansatz von Nagel dar, der den Aufbau der Ressourcenbedarfsstruktur eines Produktionssystems mittels eines Simulationsmodells abbildet (System Dynamics-Ansatz). Die daran anschließend mögliche Identifizierung von Mehrbedarfen und schließlich von Mehrbedarfskosten wird als Flexibilitätskosten interpretiert, die verglichen werden können.

Kapazitätsorientierte Messmodelle greifen auf Kapazitätsmaße zur Messung von Flexibilität in Produktionssystemen zurück. Flexibilität wird dabei als durch quantitative und/oder qualitative Überkapazität darstellbar begriffen. In dem Maße wie das Kapazitätsangebot der Kapazitätsnachfrage entspricht, entspreche das Flexibilitätsangebot der Flexibilitätsnachfrage.

Das auf einem Entropiemaß aufbauende Messmodell soll die Flexibilität eines Produktionssystems durch die Anwendung des Entropiemaßes auf Parameterwerte des Systems messen. Dabei wird das ursprünglich aus der Thermodynamik stammende und später in der Informationstheorie angewandte Maß zur Berechnung des Flexibilitätsmaßes eingesetzt.

Messung von Flexibilität mit Modellen der Realoptionsbewertung verwenden Instrumente und Methoden aus dem finanzwirtschaftlichen Bereich der Optionspreistheorie. Finanz- als auch Realoptionen werden als eine Form von Flexibilität betrachtet, da sie zu einem zukünftigen Zeitpunkt eine Auswahlentscheidung zulassen. Die Berechnung des Wertes einer solchen Option ermöglicht dann einen Vergleich bezüglich der Flexibilität.

4 Bewertung der Ansätze zur Messung von Flexibilität

Obwohl alle vorgestellten Modelle zur Messung von Flexibilität in der Produktion entwickelt worden sind, ist ihre Eignung dazu bzw. die Güte ihrer Ergebnisse unterschiedlich zu bewerten. Um eine möglichst objektive Betrachtung der Modelle sicherzustellen, sind diese an der Erfüllung von mehreren Anforderungen an ein Messmodell zu bewerten. Entsprechend der in der Untersuchung verwendeten Definition von Flexibilität sind dies:

- Orientierung an realen Flexibilitätsträgern,
- Beachtung von Teilflexibilitäten,
- Ausrichtung auf zukünftige Veränderungen,
- Berücksichtigung einer stochastischen Umwelt,
- Annahme rationaler Aktivitäten,
- Betrachtung mehrerer Perioden.

Neben diesen Kriterien sollten in die Bewertung der Modelle generell auch weitere einfließen, wie bspw. die Anwendungsfreundlichkeit, der benötigte Aufwand an Ressourcen, der auch die Kosten der Anwendung bestimmt, oder die Ebene der Ergebnisverwertung (strategische, taktische und/oder operative Ebene). Diese erweiternde Betrachtung scheitert jedoch an fehlender praktischer Anwendung und Erfahrung.

Manche der sechs Anforderungen werden durch das Konzept und die Prämissen, die dem jeweiligen Modell zugrunde liegen, erfüllt bzw. ausgeschlossen, andere sind am Modell selbst zu hinterfragen. Abbildung 4 zeigt das Ergebnis der Bewertungsanalyse synoptisch auf. Die untersuchten Modelle werden im Folgenden, entsprechend ihrer Zugehörigkeit zu den eingeteilten Klassen, bezüglich ihrer Eignung zur Flexibilitätsmessung in der Produktion bewertet.[51]

	Anforderungen an Messmodelle					
Messmodell von ...	Orientierung an realen Flexibilitätsträgern	Beachtung von Teilflexibilitäten	Ausrichtung auf zukünftige Veränderungen	Berücksichtigung einer stochastischen Umwelt	Annahme rationaler Aktivitäten	Betrachtung mehrerer Perioden
Pauli	✓	✓				(✓)
Ost	✓	✓				(✓)
Chen/Chung	✓	(✓)				(✓)
Mirschel	✓	✓	✓			(✓)
Marschak/Neson		(✓)	✓	✓	(✓)	
Gupta/Rosenhead		✓	✓		✓	
Mahlmann		(✓)	✓		✓	✓
Lasserre/Roubellat	✓	✓	✓	✓		✓
Mandelbaum/ Buzacott		✓	✓	✓		
Meier-Barthold	(✓)	(✓)	✓	✓		✓
Corsten/Gössinger			✓	✓		
Jacob	✓	✓	✓		✓	✓
Hanssmann	✓	✓	✓		✓	✓
Schneeweiß/Kühn	✓	✓	✓	✓	✓	✓
Eversheim/ Schaefer	✓	✓	✓		✓	
Wolf	✓	✓	✓	✓		(✓)
Kumar	✓	✓				
Nagel	✓		✓	✓	✓	
Realoptionen	✓	✓	✓		✓	✓

Abbildung 4: Ergebnis der Überprüfung der Messmodelle auf Erfüllung der Anforderungen

[51] Vgl. hierzu Mirschel, S.: Messung und Bewertung, S. 101 ff. und S. 179 ff.; Schlüchtermann, J.: Planung, S. 122 ff.

Die auf Indikatoren basierenden Messmodelle haben den Vorteil, dass sie Flexibilität an in der Realität vorkommenden Eigenschaften messen. Dies können z. B. die Anzahl unterschiedlicher Werkzeuge in einem Werkzeugwechselmagazin einer Fertigungsanlage, die Dauer der Umstellung eines Aggregates zwischen verschiedenen Aufgaben oder die maximale zusätzliche Anzahl an Paletten in einem Transportsystem sein. Ein Nachteil dieses Konzeptes liegt aber darin, dass die gemessene Flexibilität unabhängig von möglichen Veränderungen betrachtet wird. Eine Abstimmung von Flexibilitätsbedarf und Flexibilitätsangebot ist nicht vorgesehen.

Modelle, die Flexibilität auf der Grundlage potentieller Entscheidungsmöglichkeiten messen, sind in dieser Hinsicht schon besser dazu geeignet, solche zielgerichteten Flexibilitätspotenziale zu erfassen, da die Menge der Entscheidungsmöglichkeiten immer in Abhängigkeit von der relevanten Veränderung zu bestimmen ist. Trotzdem zeigt auch dieser Ansatz eine bedeutende Schwäche: Es wird nicht zwischen den möglichen Optionen hinsichtlich ihrer Zielwirksamkeit differenziert. Eine Aktion, die dem Systemziel u. U. sogar entgegenwirken kann, wird als gleich bedeutend für das Flexibilitätspotenzial angesehen wie eine Aktion, die das Erreichen des Systemziels unterstützt. Zudem kann es eine nicht zu unterschätzende Aufgabe sein, eine abstrakte Menge von Entscheidungsmöglichkeiten für eine praxisnahe Anwendung umzusetzen.

Die Messmodelle, die auf ökonomischen Zielkriterien basieren, sind als allgemein am aussagekräftigsten zu bezeichnen. Dabei gehen sie über eine reine Flexibilitätsmessung hinaus und bieten eine Bewertung von Flexibilitätspotenzialen an. Grundlage dieser Bewertung sind Zielfunktionen, die meist monetär formuliert werden, aber auch in anderer Form vorliegen können (z. B. als Qualitätsmaß bei Schneeweiß/Kühn).

Kapazitätsorientierte Messmodelle eignen sich aufgrund ihres Ansatzes, Flexibilität über Kapazitätsmaße zu messen, prinzipiell für den Einsatz in der Praxis, da Kapazitätsmaße relativ einfach zu bestimmen sind. Jedoch ist zu beachten, inwieweit vorhandene Kapazitätskennzahlen genutzt werden können; die zusätzliche Bestimmung von weiteren Kapazitätskennzahlen kann den Aufwand für die Messung erheblich erhöhen.

Das Messmodell von Kumar, welches auf einem Entropiemaß basiert, ist eher als theoretisch zu bezeichnen. Eine praxisnahe Anwendung erscheint wenig wahrscheinlich. Gleichermaßen ist das Modell von Nagel, welches auf dem System Dynamics-Ansatz aufbaut, zu bewerten. Sicher ein interessanter Ansatz, aber die Durchführbarkeit und damit auch ein Nutzen in der praktischen Anwendung sind nicht zu erfassen.

Die realoptionsbasierten Messmodelle bieten die Möglichkeit, den Wert einer als Form von Flexibilität verstandenen Realoption zu bestimmen. Damit wird aber auch schon der Nachteil dieses Ansatzes erkenntlich: Es wird eine Bewertung anstelle einer Messung vorgenommen, so dass Aussagen über das Ausmaß von Flexibilität nicht möglich sind.

In Theorie und Praxis herrscht weitgehend Übereinstimmung dahingehend, dass eine Abstimmung zwischen Unternehmensstrategie und Flexibilität in der Produktion das Geschäftsergebnis positiv beeinflusst. Trotz vieler empirischer Untersuchungen in Fallstudien wird ein kausalanalytischer Zusammenhang jedoch nicht greifbar. Dies ist verständlich angesichts der mit Flexibilität in der Produktion verbundenen dimensionalen Vielfalt des Begriffs, die sich in zahlreichen Definitionen, Auflistungen von Bestimmungs- und Wirkungsfaktoren sowie hierarchischen Strukturierungsansätzen sehr unterschiedlicher Art niederschlägt. Aufgrund des offenen Bedingungs- und Wirkungsfelds sowie dem Mangel an Methoden zur Messung und Bewertung komplexer Flexibilitätseffekte besteht deshalb auch im Einzelfall keine Einigkeit über das „Wie“.[52]

Das Thema der Flexibilität wird auch zukünftig in der Praxis und subsequent im Rahmen betriebswirtschaftlicher Forschung von Bedeutung sein. Eine wesentliche Herausforderung ist die Entwicklung einer umfassenden Flexibilitätstheorie, welche die Einzelansätze zu einem ganzheitlichen Theoriegebäude integriert. Ein zweiter wichtiger Ansatzpunkt ist die Erforschung von Interdependenzen zwischen Flexibilität und weiteren produktionswirtschaftlichen Artefakten, wie bspw. sein. Produktivität, Kosten oder Qualität. Einige durchaus attraktive Ansätze zur Messung von Flexibilität scheitern letztlich daran, dass eine Anwendung im realen Umfeld, wenn auch nicht unmöglich, jedoch mit (zu) großem Aufwand verbunden ist. Aus diesem Grunde sollte auch die Ausrichtung auf praxisnah anwendbare Messmodelle vorangetrieben werden.

Literatur

Bengtsson, J. und J. Olhager (2002): Valuation of Product-Mix Flexibility using Real Options, in: *International Journal of Production Economics*, Vol. 78, S. 13–28.

Chen, I. J. und C.-H. Chung (1996): An Examination of Flexibility Measurements and Performance of Flexible Manufacturing Systems, in: *International Journal of Production Research*, Vol. 34, Nr. 2, S. 379–394.

Corsten, H. und R. Gössinger (2006): Output-Flexibilität in der Dienstleistungsproduktion. Eine produktionstheoretische Analyse, in: *Zeitschrift für Betriebswirtschaft*, Jg. 76, Nr. 1, S. 29–53.

Damisch, P. N. (2001): *Wertorientiertes Flexibilitätsmanagement durch den Realoptionsansatz*, Wiesbaden 2002, zugl. Diss. Technische Universität Dresden.

De Toni, A. und S. Tonchia (1998): Manufacturing flexibility. A literature review, in: *International Journal of Production Research*, Vol. 36, No. 6, S. 1587–1617.

Dohms, R. (2001): *Methodik zur Bewertung und Gestaltung wandlungsfähiger, dezentraler Produktionsstrukturen*, Aachen, zugl. Diss. Technische Hochschule Aachen 2000.

Dormayer, H. J. (1986): *Konjunkturelle Früherkennung und Flexibilität im Produktionssystem*, München.

Eversheim, W. und F.-W. Schaefer (1980): Planung des Flexibilitätsbedarfs von Industrieunternehmen, in: *Die Betriebswirtschaft (DBW)*, 40. Jg. Nr. 2, S. 229–248.

Eversheim, W. (1992): Produktionssysteme, flexible, in: Frese, E. (Hrsg.): *Handwörterbuch der Organisation, 3., völlig neu gestaltete Aufl.*, Stuttgart, Sp. 2058–2066.

Fischer, T. M. (1993): *Kostenmanagement strategischer Erfolgsfaktoren. Instrumente zur operativen Steuerung der strategischen Schlüsselfaktoren Qualität, Flexibilität und Schnelligkeit*, München.

Frischke, S. (2006): *Simulationsbasierte Entscheidungsunterstützung bei der Gestaltung flexibler Produktionsbereiche auf taktischer Ebene*, Cottbus.

Gerwin, D. (1993): Manufacturing flexibility. A strategic perspective, in: *Management Science*, Vol. 39, No. 4, S. 395–410.

Goldman, S. L. et al. (1996): *Agil im Wettbewerb. Die Strategie der virtuellen Organisation zum Nutzen des Kunden* [Agile Competitors and Virtual Organizations. Strategies for Enriching the Customers, Söffing, R. (Übers.)], Berlin-Heidelberg-New York.

[52] Siehe bspw. Koste, L. L.; Malhotra, M. K.: A perspective on research opportunities in manufacturing flexibility, in; Decision Line, July 1999 Volume 30(4), S. 5–8.

Gupta, S. K. und J. Rosenhead (1968): Robustness in Sequential Investment Decisions, in: *Management Science*, Vol. 15, No. 2, S. B18–B29.

Hanssmann, F. (1993): *Einführung in die Systemforschung. Methodik der modellgestützten Entscheidungsvorbereitung, 4., unwesentlich veränderte Aufl.*, München.

Hillmer, H.-J. (1987): *Planung der Unternehmensflexibilität. Eine allgemeine theoretische Konzeption und deren Anwendung zur Bewältigung strategischer Flexibilitätsprobleme*, Frankfurt am Main-Bern-New York, zugl. Diss. Universität Osnabrück 1986.

Horstmann, J. (2007): *Operationalisierung der Unternehmensflexibilität. Entwicklung einer umwelt- und unternehmensbezogenen Flexibilitätsanalyse*, Wiesbaden.

Horváth, P. und R. Mayer (1986): Produktionswirtschaftliche Flexibilität, in: *Wirtschaftswissenschaftliches Studium*, Jg. 15, Nr. 1, S. 69–76.

Jacob, H. (1974): Unsicherheit und Flexibilität. Zur Theorie der Planung bei Unsicherheit, in: *Zeitschrift für Betriebswirtschaft*, Jg. 44, S. 299–326, 403–448, 505–526.

Jacob, H. (1989): Flexibilität und ihre Bedeutung für die Betriebspolitik, in: Adam, D. et al. (Hrsg.): *Integration und Flexibilität. Eine Herausforderung für die Allgemeine Betriebswirtschaftslehre*, 51. Wissenschaftliche Jahrestagung des Verbandes der Hochschullehrer für Betriebswirtschaftslehre e.V. 1989 in Münster, Wiesbaden, S. 15–60.

Janssen, H. (1997): *Flexibilitätsmanagement. Theoretische Fundierung und Gestaltungsmöglichkeiten in strategischer Perspektive*, Stuttgart, zugl. Diss. Universität München 1997.

Kaluza, B. (1993): Flexibilität, betriebliche, in: Wittmann, W. et al. (Hrsg.): *Handwörterbuch der Betriebswirtschaft. Teilband 1 A–H, 5., völlig neu gestaltete Aufl.*, Stuttgart, Sp. 1173–1184.

Kaluza, B. (1994): Rahmenentscheidungen zu Kapazität und Flexibilität produktionswirtschaftlicher Systeme, in: Corsten, H. (Hrsg.): *Handbuch Produktionsmanagement*, Wiesbaden, S. 51–72.

Kern, W. (1979): Produktionswirtschaft, in: Kern, W. (Hrsg.): *Handwörterbuch der Produktionswirtschaft*, Stuttgart, Sp. 1647–1659.

Koste, L. L. und M. K. Malhotra (1999): A theoretical framework for analyzing the dimensions of manufacturing flexibility, in: *Journal of Operations Management*, Vol. 18, No. 1, S. 75–93.

Koste, L. L. und M. K. Malhotra (1999): A perspective on research opportunities in manufacturing flexibility, in: *Decision Line*, Vol. 30, No. 4, S. 5–8.

Koste, L. L., M. K. Malhotra und S. Sharma (2004): Measuring dimensions of manufacturing flexibility, in: *Journal of Operations Management*, Vol. 22, No. 4, S. 171–196.

Krahnen, J.-P., R. H. Schmidt und E. Terberger (1989): Der ökonomische Wert von Bindung und Flexibilität, in: Hax, H., W. Kern und H.-W. Schröder (Hrsg.): *Zeitaspekte in betriebswirtschaftlicher Theorie und Praxis*, 50. Wissenschaftliche Jahrestagung des Verbandes der Hochschullehrer für Betriebswirtschaft e. V. Köln, 24.–28. Mai 1988, Stuttgart: Poeschel.

Kumar, V. (1987): Entropic Measures of Manufacturing Flexibility, in: *International Journal of Production Research*, Vol. 25, No. 7, S. 957–966.

Lasserre, J. B. und F. Roubellat (1985): Measuring Decision Flexibility in Production Planning, in: *IEEE Transactions on Automatic Control* (AC-30), S. 447–452.

Mandelbaum, M. und J. Buzacott (1990): Flexibility and Decision Making, in: *European Journal of Operational Research*, Vol. 44, S. 17–27.

Mahlmann, K. (1976): *Anpassung und Anpassungsfähigkeit der betrieblichen Planung*, o. O., zugl. Diss Universität Göttingen 1976.

Marschak, T. und R. Nelson,(1962): Flexibility, Uncertainty, and Economic Theory, in: *Metroeconomica*, Vol. 14, S. 42–58.

Meffert, H. (1985): Größere Flexibilität als Unternehmungskonzept, in: *Zeitschrift für Betriebswirtschaftliche Forschung*, Jg. 37, S. 121–137.

Meier-Barthold, D. (1999): *Flexibilität in der Material-Logistik*, Wiesbaden, zugl. Diss. Universität Magdeburg 1998.

Mirschel, S. (2007): *Messung und Bewertung von Produktionsflexibilitätspotentialen in geschlossenen und offenen Entscheidungsfeldern*, Berlin, zugl. Diss. Universität Greifswald 2006.

Nagel, M. (2003): *Flexibilitätsmanagement. Ein systemdynamischer Ansatz zur quantitativen Bewertung von Produktionsflexibilität*, Wiesbaden, zugl. Diss. Universität Eichstätt-Ingolstadt 2002.

o.V. (1997): *Brockhaus. Die Enzyklopädie in vierundzwanzig Bänden, 7. Bd. EW-FRIS, 20., überarbeitete und aktualisierte Aufl.*, Leipzig-Mannheim.

Oke, A. (2005): A framework for analyzing manufacturing flexibility, in: *International Journal of Operations & Production Management*, Vol. 25, No. 10, S. 973–996.

Ost, S. (1993): *Entwicklung eines Verfahrens zur differenzierten Flexibilitätsanalyse und -bewertung*, o. O., zugl. Diss. Technische Universität Hamburg-Harburg 1993.

Parker, R. P. und A. Wirth (1999): Manufacturing flexibility. Measures and relationships, in: *European Journal of Operational Research*, Vol. 118, No. 3, S. 429–449.

Pauli, J. (1987): *So wird Ihr Unternehmen flexibel. Leitlinien und Massnahmen*, Zürich.

Pibernik, R. (2001): *Flexibilitätsplanung in Wertschöpfungsnetzwerken*, Wiesbaden, zugl. Diss. Universität Frankfurt am Main 2001.

Reichwald, R. und P. Behrbohm (1983): Flexibilität als Eigenschaft produktionswirtschaftlicher Systeme, in: *Zeitschrift für Betriebswirtschaft*, Jg. 53, S. 831–853.

Richter, W. (2007): Gegenstand der Messtechnik, in: Hoffmann, J. (Hrsg.): *Handbuch der Messtechnik, 3., neu bearbeitete Aufl.*, München, S. 27.

Richter, W. (2007): Messtechnische Disziplinen, Aufgaben und Ziele, in: Hoffmann, J. (Hrsg.): *Handbuch der Messtechnik, 3., neu bearbeitete Aufl.*, München, S. 28–31.

Schlüchtermann, J. (1996): *Planung in zeitlich offenen Entscheidungsfeldern*, Wiesbaden, zugl. Habil.-Schr. Universität Saarbrücken 1995.

Schneeweiß, C. und M. Kühn (1990): Zur Definition und gegenseitigen Abgrenzung der Begriffe Flexibilität, Elastizität und Robustheit, in: *Zeitschrift für betriebswirtschaftliche Forschung*, Jg. 42, Nr. 5, S. 378–395.

Sethi, A. K. und S. P. Sethi (1990): Flexibility in Manufacturing: A Survey, in: *The International Journal of Flexible Manufacturing Systems*, Vol. 2, S. 289–328.

Slack, N. (1983): Flexibility as a manufacturing objective, in: *Journal of Operations & Production Management*, Vol. 3, No. 3, S. 4–13.

Slack, N. (1987): The flexibility of manufacturing systems, in: *International Journal of Operations & Production Management*, Vol. 7, No. 4, S. 35–45.

Steven, M. (2007): *Handbuch Produktion. Theorie – Management – Logistik – Controlling*, Stuttgart: W. Kohlhammer.

Tempelmeier, H. und H. Kuhn (1993): *Flexible manufacturing systems. Decision support for design and operation*, New York.

Thielen, C. A. L. (1993): *Management der Flexibilität, Integriertes Anforderungskonzept für eine flexible Gestaltung der Unternehmung*, o. O., zugl. Diss. Hochschule St. Gallen 1993.

Trigeorgis, L. (1990): A Real-Options Application in Natural-Resource Investments, in: *Advances in Futures and Options Research*, Vol. 4, S. 153–164.

Upton, D.-M. (1994): The management of manufacturing flexibility, in: *California Management Review*, Vol. 36, S. 72–89.

Upton, D. (1997): Process range in manufacturing: an empirical study of flexibility, in: *Management Science*, Vol. 43, No. 8, S. 1079–1092.

Voigt, K.-I. (2007): Zeit und Zeitgeist in der Betriebswirtschaftslehre, dargestellt am Beispiel der betriebswirtschaftlichen Flexibilitätsdiskussion, in: *Zeitschrift für Betriebswirtschaft,* Jg. 77, Nr. 6, S. 595–613.

Voigt, K.-I. und H. Wildemann (2007): Quantifizierung der Flexibilität im Rahmen wertschöpfungspartnerschaftlicher Zusammenarbeit, in: Günther, W. A.: *Neue Wege der Automobillogistik*, Berlin/Heidelberg, S. 123–136.

Vokurka, R. J. und S. W. O'Leary-Kelly (2000): A review on empirical research on manufacturing flexibility, in: *Journal of Operations Management,* No. 18, S. 485–501.

Weber, H.-J. (1979): Produktionstechnik und -verfahren, in: Kern, W. (Hrsg.): *Handwörterbuch der Produktionswirtschaft*, Stuttgart, Sp. 1604–1619.

Wildemann, H. (1987): *Investitionsplanung und Wirtschaftlichkeitsrechnung für flexible Fertigungssysteme (FFS)*, Stuttgart.

Wolf, J. (1989): *Investitionsplanung zur Flexibilisierung der Produktion*, Wiesbaden, zugl. Diss. Technische Hochschule Darmstadt 1989.

Logistische Netzwerke im Bereich der Sekundärrohstofflogistik

Dieter Specht und Dirk Braunisch

Brandenburgische Technische Universität Cottbus
Lehrstuhl für Produktionswirtschaft

Zusammenfassung

Der vorliegende Beitrag thematisiert die logistische Netzwerkbildung im Bereich der rückfühenden Logistik. Die Sekundärrohstofflogistik beinhaltet die Planung, Steuerung und Kontrolle der Rückführung sowie der Aufarbeitung und Aufbereitung von Altprodukten und Reststoffen. Im Ergebnis entstehen sekundäre Materialien, die für den Wiedereinsatz in den Produktionsprozess vorgesehen sind. Altprodukte und Reststoffe weisen keine gleich bleibende Qualität auf und fallen in unregelmäßigen und unvorhersehbaren Abständen an. Dies kann nachteilige Auswirkungen auf die Teilbereiche der Sekundärrohstofflogistik zur Folge haben. Um auf die Unregelmäßigkeit und Unvorhersehbarkeit dieser Materialflüsse zu reagieren, ist eine kooperative Arbeit im Verbund erforderlich.

Schlagwörter: Reverse Logistics, Sekundärrohstofflogistik, Netzwerke, Logistiknetzwerk, Netzwerkbildung

1 Einleitung

Als Folge der ungewissen Entwicklung der Rohstoffpreise gewinnt ein effizienter Umgang mit Material an Bedeutung. Handlungsoptionen liegen in der Suche nach alternativen Bezugsquellen, in einem wirkungsvolleren Energie- und Materialeinsatz und in der Verwendung hochwertiger Sekundärrohstoffe.

Sekundärrohstoffe lassen sich mittels Recycling oder durch „Urban Mining“[1] gewinnen. Ausgangsprodukte dafür sind Rückstände[2] aus den Bereichen Produktion, Distribution und Konsumtion. Diese müssen gesammelt, sortiert und einem Unternehmen der Aufarbeitung oder Aufbereitung zugeführt werden. Anschließend stehen sekundäre Materialien für den Wiedereinsatz zur Verfügung. Die Sekundärrohstofflogistik erhält die Aufgabe, diese auftretenden Mengenströme zu planen, zu koordinieren, durchzuführen und zu kontrollieren.

Eine große Herausforderung für die Sekundärrohstofflogistik in der nahen Zukunft wird die fehlende Konstanz der Rückstandsströme sein. Altprodukte und Reststoffe fallen nicht in

---

[1] Das Konzept des Urban Mining betont das „Abbauen“ und die Nutzung von Zivilisationsabfällen.

[2] „Unerwünschte oder unvermeidbare Nebenwirkung von Produktion und Konsum“, Gabler Wirtschaftslexikon 2004, S. 2572.

Massenströmen und in gleich bleibender Qualität an, so wie es die produzierende Industrie von den Primärrohstoffen gewohnt ist. Zudem sind die Rückflüsse aus dem Bereich der Konsumtion nur schwer vorherzusehen.[3]

Um auf die Unregelmäßigkeit und Unvorhersehbarkeit dieser Materialflüsse zu reagieren, ist eine intensive und kooperative Zusammenarbeit der beteiligten Akteure im Netzwerk anzustreben.[4]

Der vorliegende Beitrag betrachtet zunächst kurz Trends und Entwicklungen in der rückführenden Logistik. Anschließend werden die Netzwerktheorie im Zusammenhang mit Logistiknetzwerken und die Sekundärrohstofflogistik näher beleuchtet. Als Ergebnis sollen Vorschläge zu möglichen Handlungsalternativen für die Akteure von Netzwerken im Bereich der Sekundärrohstofflogistik aufgezeigt werden.

2 Trends und Entwicklungen

Ein gestiegenes Interesse an der Wiederverwendung von Rohstoffen und Materialien hat in den letzten Jahren zu einer Sensibilisierung für die rückführende Logistik geführt. Zudem steht der Gedanke der Reduzierung von Rückständen und Reststoffen in Industrienationen stark im Vordergrund.[5]

Bereits in den frühen 70er Jahren wurde dieser Trend durch Studien erkannt. In den weiteren Jahren hat sich die Thematik der nachhaltigen Entwicklung in der Wissenschaft, Wirtschaft und Gesellschaft weit verbreitet und etabliert. Begriffe wie Recycling, Wiederverwendung oder Remanufacturing sind zu gewohnten Bezeichnungen geworden. Die Unternehmen sind zusätzlich durch den Wettbewerb und strategische Entscheidungen anderer Unternehmen angetrieben worden, sich mit Aktivitäten der Rückführung auseinanderzusetzen. Im Ergebnis führte dies zu einem allgemeingültigen Verständnis der Wiedergewinnung und des Wiedereinsatzes von Materialien.[6]

Diese Entwicklung ist auch geprägt durch gesetzliche Vorgaben wie die des Kreislaufwirtschafts- und Abfallgesetz (KrW/AbfG) in Deutschland. Dieses fördert und fordert die Schonung natürlicher Ressourcen und die Nutzung sekundärer Rohstoffe.[7]

Diese Forderungen zielen darauf ab, Produkte zukünftig verwertbarer zu gestalten, die Lieferketten zu schließen und eine nachhaltige Entwicklung zu gewährleisten.[8]

---

[3] Vgl. Clausen/Nickel 2007a, S. 26.

[4] Vgl. Steven et. al. 2003a, S. 646.

[5] Vgl. Fleischmann et al. 2000, p. 653.

[6] Vgl. de Brito/Dekker 2002, S. 1.

[7] Vgl. KrW/AbfG § 1, S. 3 und § 4 (3), S. 6 sowie Guide Jr. 2000, p. 468.

[8] Vgl. Atasu et al. 2008, p. 1732 und Guide Jr. 2000, p. 467–468.

3 Grundlagen der Netzwerkforschung

Das folgende Kapitel beschreibt die Grundlagen für die Bildung von Netzwerken. Ausgehend von der Netzwerktheorie werden Netzwerktypen vorgestellt. Abschnitt 3.3 widmet sich der Koordination, die ein wichtiger Bestandteil für die Arbeit im Netzwerk ist. In Abschnitt 3.4 wird die Bildung von Logistiknetzwerken erläutert. Zum Schluss des Kapitels wird das Netzwerkmanagement als Erfolgskriterium für die Netzwerkbildung hervorgehoben.

3.1 Netzwerktheorie

Die Netzwerktheorie beschreibt Grundelemente für die Entstehung und Funktionsweise von Unternehmens- aber auch von Logistiknetzwerken. Die Netzwerktheorie betrachtet Unternehmensnetzwerke als eine Organisationsform und bietet ein Beschreibungsmodell für die Gestaltung von Netzwerkunternehmen.[9]

Unternehmensnetzwerke konstituieren eine Zusammenarbeit von Unternehmen mit einer bestimmten Zielstellung. Eine Definition die diesen Terminus exakter erfasst und in der Literatur vielfach Verwendung findet, stammt von Sydow. „Ein Unternehmensnetzwerk stellt eine auf die Realisierung von Wettbewerbsvorteilen zielende Organisationsform ökonomischer Aktivitäten dar, die sich durch komplex-reziproke, eher kooperative denn kompetitive und relativ stabile Beziehungen zwischen rechtlich selbständigen, wirtschaftlich zumeist unabhängigen Unternehmungen auszeichnet."[10]

Kleine und mittlere Unternehmen können Wettbewerbsvorteile aufgrund der zunehmend globalisierten Märkte und Komplexität der Produkte nur schwer erreichen. Ihnen fehlt zumeist das nötige Know-how, Innovationsfähigkeit, Finanzkraft oder die globale Präsenz. Ein Ausweg aus dieser Situation ist die Konzentration auf die jeweiligen Kompetenzfelder der Unternehmen. Die Kompetenzen sind in einem Netzwerk derart zusammenzuführen, dass im Ergebnis in kooperativer Zusammenarbeit eine sinnvolle und ganzheitliche Leistungserstellung möglich ist. Die Unternehmen nehmen im Netzwerk somit die Funktion wahr, die sie gegenüber den anderen Unternehmen am besten beherrschen. Netzwerke bieten damit die Möglichkeit als wettbewerbsfähige Einheit aufzutreten.[11]

3.2 Netzwerktypologisierung

In der Literatur ist eine Vielzahl an Netzwerktypen zu finden. Die Typenbildung erfolgt in Abhängigkeit vom zur Typologisierung herangezogenen Merkmal. Corsten definiert beispielsweise

- Netzwerkzusammenstellung,
- Koordinationsrichtung,
- Kooperationsrichtung sowie
- Stärke und Dauer der Wirkung

[9] Vgl. Butz/Straube 2008, S. 68 und Sydow 1992, S. 224 ff.

[10] Wittig 2005, S. 26–27 und Sydow 1992, S. 79.

[11] Vgl. Wildemann 1996, S. 18–19 und Butz/Straube 2008, S. 70.

als mögliche Merkmale zur Bildung von Netzwerktypen.[12] Wittig hingegen legt für die Charakterisierung von Merkmalen oben genannte Definition zugrunde und grenzt folgende Dimensionen ab:

- Rechtliche Selbständigkeit und gewisse wirtschaftliche Abhängigkeit,
- Kooperative Beziehungen,
- Erzielung von Wettbewerbsvorteilen.[13]

Die gedankliche Verknüpfung der verschiedenen Merkmalsausprägungen lässt unterschiedliche Netzwerktypen entstehen. Eine in der Literatur oft anzutreffende, idealtypische Typologisierung ist eine Unterscheidung in Strategische, Operative und Regionale Netzwerke sowie Virtuelle Unternehmen.[14] Diese Differenzierung ist jedoch mit anderen Möglichkeiten der Netzwerktypisierung nicht überschneidungsfrei. Zudem kann derselbe Netzwerktyp unterschiedliche Merkmalsausprägungen aufweisen. So kann beispielsweise ein strategisches Netzwerk stark oder weniger stark hierarchisch organisiert sein. Zudem kann das häufig in strategischen Netzwerken vorkommende fokale Unternehmen auch in anderen Netzwerktypen die Wertschöpfung koordinieren. Tabelle 1 soll einen Überblick über Typisierungsmöglichkeiten geben.

Tabelle 1: Typologisierungsmöglichkeiten interorganisationaler Netzwerke

Netzwerktyp	**Bestimmung über bzw. Synonyme**
industrielle Netzwerke – Dienstleistungsnetzwerke	Sektorenzugehörigkeit der meisten Unternehmungen
Beschaffungs-, Produktions-, Marketing-, Logistiknetzwerke	betriebliche Funktionen, die im Netzwerk kooperativ erfüllt werden
Konzerninterne – konzernübergreifende Netzwerke	Konzernzugehörigkeit der meisten Unternehmen
Vertikale – horizontale Netzwerke	Stellung der Unternehmen in der Wertschöpfungskette
Stabile – dynamische Netzwerke	Stabilität der Mitgliedschaft bzw. der Netzwerkakteure
Hierarchische – heterarchische Netzwerke	Steuerungsform nach der Form der Führung
Formale – informale Netzwerke	Formalität bzw. Sichtbarkeit des Netzwerkes
Offene – geschlossene Netzwerke	Möglichkeit des Eintritts bzw. Austritts
Einfache – komplexe Netzwerke	Zahl der Netzwerkakteure, Dichte des Netzwerks, Komplexitätsgrad des Beziehungsgeflechts
Innovationsnetzwerke – Routinenetzwerke	Netzwerkzweck in Hinblick auf Innovationsgrad
Soziale – ökonomische Netzwerke	dominanter Zweck der Netzwerkmitgliedschaft
Zentrierte – dezentrierte Netzwerke	Grad der Polyzentrizität

Quelle: Eigene Darstellung in Anlehnung an Sydow 2003, S. 299

[12] Vgl. Corsten 2001, S. 5–7; siehe zu Netzwerktypologisierung auch Axelsson 1992, S. 242 ff.; Miles/Snow 1986, S. 64 ff. oder Stengel 1999, S. 136 ff.

[13] Vgl. Wittig 2005, S. 28.

[14] Vgl. Corsten 2001, S. 5–7 und Wittig 2005, S. 30.

Typische Netzwerkformen, die in der Praxis häufig auftreten, sind interne, stabile oder dynamische Netzwerke. Interne Netzwerke existieren auf Geschäftsbereichsebene innerhalb eines Unternehmens und dienen der Verbesserung der Innovations- und Leistungsfähigkeit. In Stabilen Netzwerken tragen die beteiligten Unternehmen jeweils die verschiedenen erforderlichen Ressourcen zur Leistungserstellung bei. Durch die partielle Auslagerung von Teilprozessen kann die Flexibilität der Wertschöpfungskette im Netzwerk erhöht werden. Dynamische Netzwerke sind gekennzeichnet durch ein führendes Unternehmen, welches als Steuerungsinstanz und Koordinator agiert. Das Unternehmen verfügt über wenig ausgeprägte Ressourcen. Stattdessen identifiziert und kombiniert es die Ressourcen und Kernkompetenzen der Netzwerkpartner für die Erstellung einer neuen Marktleistung.[15]

3.3 Koordinationstheorie

Die Koordination im Netzwerk nimmt in der betriebswirtschaftlichen Literatur eine zentrale Rolle ein.[16] Die Koordinationstheorie identifiziert und beschreibt Koordinationsprobleme und stellt für deren Lösung Mechanismen bereit.[17]

Bei der Koordination handelt es sich „um eine wechselseitige Abstimmung einzelner Aktivitäten in einem arbeitsteiligen System auf ein übergeordnetes Gesamtziel"[18]. Arbeitsteilung in einem Netzwerk verursacht Abhängigkeiten zwischen den beteiligten Akteuren. Diese Abhängigkeiten müssen gesteuert und aufeinander abgestimmt werden. Die Koordinationstheorie stellt für diesen Umgang mit Abhängigkeiten Lösungsregeln zur Verfügung. Dies ist immer dann notwendig, wenn mindestens zwei Bereiche die gleichen Ressourcen, Produktionsmittel oder bestimmte Zwischenprodukte benötigen.[19]

Der Koordination obliegt die Aufgabe, „die durch Zerlegung einer Gesamtaufgabe entstandenen Teilaufgaben den unterschiedlichen Aufgabenträgern zuzuordnen und aufeinander abzustimmen"[20]. Darüber hinaus sind spezifizierend die vertikale Koordination und die horizontale Koordination zu unterscheiden. Bei der vertikalen Koordination bilden übergeordnete Entscheidungen den Rahmen für nachgeordnete Entscheidungen. Die Voraussetzung dafür ist eine festgelegte Strukturierung der unterschiedlichen hierarchischen Ebenen im System. Bei der horizontalen Koordination findet eine Abstimmung zwischen den Abteilungen auf derselben hierarchischen Ebene statt. Dafür ist eine entsprechende Segmentierung notwendig.[21]

Die Logistik ist in vielen Netzwerken die verantwortliche Leistungseinheit für die Koordination. Sie sorgt dafür, „dass sich die richtige Ressource [...] zum richtigen Zeitpunkt [...] am

[15] Vgl. Butz/Straube 2008, S. 68–69.

[16] Vgl. Corsten 2001, S. 11; siehe zu Koordinationsforschung auch Benkenstein 1987, S. 16ff.; Frese 1989, Sp. 913ff. oder Kirsch/Meffert 1970, S. 20ff.

[17] Vgl. Butz/Straube 2008, S. 69.

[18] Corsten 2001, S. 11.

[19] Vgl. Butz/Straube 2008, S. 69.

[20] Corsten 2001, S. 11–12.

[21] Vgl. Corsten 2001, S. 12.

richtigen Ort befindet [...] und somit zum Konsum zur Verfügung steht“[22]. In diesem Zusammenhang ist der Begriff der Logistiknetzwerke formuliert worden.

3.4 Logistiknetzwerke

„Die Hauptaufgabe von Logistiknetzwerken liegt in der überbetrieblichen Organisation und Gestaltung von Waren- und Informationsflüssen entlang der gesamten Wertschöpfungskette zwischen verschiedenen Standorten eines Unternehmensnetzwerks zum Zweck einer gemeinsamen kostenoptimalen Leistungserstellung.“[23] Die Logistik kann als Kooperationsmechanismus angesehen werden.

Der Denkansatz des Logistiknetzwerks beruht auf dem Konzept der Flussorientierung und dem Systemdenken in Netzwerken. Dabei werden alle Material- und Informationsflüsse von den Quellen über alle Zwischenknoten bis hin zu den Senken ganzheitlich und integrativ betrachtet.[24]

In Logistiknetzwerken ist die Optimierung des Gesamtsystems hinsichtlich logistischer Ziele wie etwa die Verringerung der Durchlaufzeiten, Einhaltung niedriger Bestände, hohe Lieferfähigkeit und Termintreue sowie geringer Steuerungsaufwand der Materialflüsse von Bedeutung. Aufgrund der Komplexität der Materialflüsse im Netzwerk, müssen die Logistikziele in einer umfassenden und konsequenten Art und Weise umgesetzt werden, um eine Optimierung des Gesamtsystems zu erreichen. Die Flexibilität und Transparenz sowie die Versorgungs- und Lieferservices sollen über die gesamte Wertschöpfungskette hinweg erhöht werden. Die Logistikkosten können im Netzwerk reduziert werden.[25]

In Abhängigkeit von unternehmensinternen und -externen Betrachtungsperspektiven lassen sich Logistiknetzwerke in *Intralog-*, *Extralog-* und *Interlog-Netze* unterscheiden.

- *Intralog-Netze* sind innerbetriebliche Logistiknetzwerke innerhalb einzelner Betriebsstätten eines Unternehmens.
- *Extralog-Netze* sind außerbetriebliche Logistiknetze zwischen den Betriebsstätten der Unternehmen.
- *Interlog-Netze* sind die Logistiknetze aller Unternehmen und Wirtschaftsteilnehmer.

Logistiknetzwerke sind Systeme, die aus Teil- und Subsystemen mit verschiedenen Funktionen bestehen. Das *Interlog-Netz* setzt sich aus den Logistiknetzwerken der einzelnen Unternehmen zusammen. Die Logistiknetzwerke der Einzelunternehmen setzen sich wiederum aus den Intralog- und Extralog-Netzen zusammen. Subsysteme des *Intralog-Netzes* sind beispielsweise die Lager-, Transport- oder Kommissioniersysteme. Teilsysteme des *Extralog-Netzes* sind die Beschaffungs-, Distributions- oder Entsorgungssysteme der Unternehmen (Tabelle 2).[26]

[22] Butz/Straube 2008, S. 69; vgl. auch Malone 1999.

[23] Butz/Straube, 2008, S. 71.

[24] Vgl. Vahrenkamp/Mattfeld 2007, S. 5 und Butz/Straube 2008, S. 71.

[25] Vgl. Butz/Straube 2008, S. 71.

[26] Vgl. Gudehus 2005, S. 568.

Tabelle 2: Merkmale der Logistiknetzwerke

	Intralog	Extralog	Interlog
Merkmale			
Abgrenzung	Innerbetriebliches Logistiknetzwerk einer Betriebsstätte	Außerbetriebliches Logistiknetzwerk eines Unternehmens	Unternehmensübergreifende Logistiknetzwerke mit vielen Teilnehmern
Betriebsstandorte	einer	mehrere	viele
Vernetzung	gering	mittel	hoch
Logistikketten	innerbetrieblich	zwischenbetrieblich	überbetrieblich
Quellen	Wareneingang Produktionsstellen	Lieferanten andere Betriebsstätten	Unternehmen Haushalte
Senken	Verbrauchstellen Warenausgang	Kunden andere Betriebsstätten	Unternehmen Haushalte
Teilsysteme	Maschinensysteme Lagersysteme Kommissioniersysteme Förder- und Transport-systeme	Beschaffungssysteme Distributionssysteme Entsorgungssysteme Intramodale Transport-systeme	Intralog-Systeme Extralog-Systeme Verkehrssysteme Speditionssysteme
Betreiber			
Betriebsstätten	Unternehmen	Dienstleister	Dienstleister
Betriebsmittel	Unternehmen/ Dienstleister	Unternehmen/ Dienstleister	Dienstleister
Trassennetz	Unternehmen	Verkehrsbetriebe/Staat	Verkehrsbetriebe/Staat
Transportmittel	Unternehmen/ Dienstleister	Unternehmen/ Dienstleister	Dienstleister
Unternehmen:	Industrie- und Handelsunternehmen		
Dienstleister:	Logistikdienstleister, Speditionen, Umschlagbetrieb usw.		
Verkehrsbetriebe:	Eisenbahnen, Schifffahrtsgesellschaften, Luftfahrtgesellschaften		
Haushalte:	Privathaushalte, Gastronomie, Verwaltungen, Krankenhäuser u. a.		

Quelle: Gudehus 2005, S. 568

Die Vernetzung in Logistiknetzwerken ermöglicht eine Integration der Informationsflüsse unabhängig von den Materialflüssen zwischen den beteiligten Akteuren. Störungen oder Bedarfsschwankungen im Bereich der Materialflüsse werden in der Regel über Bestandsaufbau und -abbau abgefangen. Eine Integration der Informationsflüsse soll dieses Bestandsmanagement zum Bewegungsmanagement entwickeln. Die Materialien werden im Fluss gehalten. Störungen oder Bedarfsschwankungen werden durch eine Beschleunigung oder Verzögerung der Materialflüsse abgefangen. Die Vorratshaltung kann reduziert und die Lagerbestände abgebaut werden. Dies kann zum einen zu einer Minimierung der Kosten führen. Zum anderen werden zusätzliche Potentiale freigesetzt, die sich in Konzepten wie Just-in-Time/Just-in-Sequence, Vendor/Buyer/Co-Managed Inventory, Continuous/Automatic Replenishment oder in Transshipment und Cross-Docking Lösungen wiederfinden.[27]

[27] Vgl. Wittig 2005, S. 6 und Heiserich 2002, S. 230.

3.5 Netzwerkmanagement

Eine große Zahl beteiligter Akteure und Materialflüsse in den Netzwerken erschwert die zielgerechte Umsetzung logistischer Kenngrößen. In der Praxis ist zu erkennen, dass sich Unternehmen an mehreren Netzwerken beteiligen. Diese Komplexität erfordert eine effektive Koordination. Die Voraussetzung dafür schafft ein aktives Netzwerkmanagement, ein wesentliches Erfolgskriterium in Logistiknetzwerken.

In der Literatur existiert keine einheitliche Definition für das Netzwerkmanagement. Die Charakterisierung des Netzwerkmanagements erfolgt in der Regel über die Umschreibung der Netzwerkziele und die notwendigen Aufgabengebiete.[28] Als Beispiel sind folgende Definitionen genannt.

- „Netzwerkmanagement umfasst den Aufbau und die Entwicklung von Netzwerkstrukturen und -beziehungen sowie deren Koordination im Hinblick auf Netzwerkziele. Es beinhaltet all diejenigen Aufgaben, die zur Gestaltung der Zusammenarbeit der Mitglieder über ihren gesamten Kooperationszyklus erforderlich sind.“[29]
- „Netzwerkmanagement (im funktionalen Sinne) bezeichnet die kooperationsweite Gestaltung und Koordination aller zwischenbetrieblichen Abhängigkeitsbeziehungen in sachlicher, zeitlicher und sozialer Dimension, die zur Erreichung des gemeinsamen Kooperationszwecks unterhalten werden.“[30]

Wie die genannten Definitionen zeigen, wird das Netzwerkmanagement als ein Komplex von Aufgaben verstanden. Es werden wichtige Aufgabenfelder unterschieden, die vor Beginn einer Zusammenarbeit und während des Netzbetriebs auszuführen sind.

Die Tätigkeit des Netzwerkmanagements beginnt mit dem Aufbau der Netzwerkstruktur und der interorganisationalen Beziehungen. Dafür sind geeignete Netzwerkpartner, die Standorte und die Netzwerkform zu wählen. Die Infrastruktur eines Netzwerkes ist sowohl in organisatorischer und technischer als auch in personeller Hinsicht zu gestalten. Des Weiteren sind die Strukturen und Abläufe im Netzwerk zu planen und festzulegen.

Nach der Konfiguration des Netzwerks sind die Abläufe und Aktivitäten während des Netzwerkbetriebs zu steuern und zu kontrollieren. Ein wesentlicher Aspekt liegt in der Pflege und Erhaltung der Netzwerkstruktur, der Beziehungen im Netzwerk und deren synergienutzende Koordination. Mit Hilfe von Simulations- und Modellierungsmechanismen können die Netzwerkprozesse optimiert werden.[31]

4 Netzwerkbildung in der Sekundärrohstofflogistik

In Kapitel 4 wird die Logistik für die Sekundärrohstoffe betrachtet. Es wird geklärt, was Sekundärrohstoffe sind und wie diese gewonnen werden. Abschnitt 4.3 behandelt die Bildung von

[28] Vgl. Kaczmarek et. al. 2004, S. 4.

[29] Beck 1998, S. 11.

[30] Wohlgemuth 2002, S. 42.

[31] Vgl. Butz/Straube 2008, S. 72 und Kaczmarek et. al. 2004, S. 5.

Logistiknetzwerken im Bereich der Sekundärrohstofflogistik. Die Eigenschaften dieser Netzwerke und die Motive für eine Netzwerkgründung werden erläutert, eine Netzwerktypologisierung und eine Netzwerkmodellierung beschrieben und Beispiele von Netzwerken in der Sekundärrohstofflogistik vorgestellt.

4.1 Sekundärrohstoffe

„Sekundärrohstoffe entstehen durch die Aufbereitung von Abfällen und Reststoffen, aus denen die als Rohstoffe nutzbaren Elemente extrahiert und wieder in den Produktionsprozess eingefügt werden.“[32] Für die Gewinnung von Sekundärrohstoffen existieren vorrangig zwei Methoden. Dies ist zum einen das Recycling und zum anderen das Konzept des Urban Mining. Beide werden nachfolgend kurz vorgestellt.

Recycling

Recycling ist ein Prozess des Aufarbeitens und Aufbereitens von Abfällen bei dem Sekundärrohstoffe entstehen. Die Durchführung von Recyclingmaßnahmen erhöht die Ressourceneffizienz und reduziert das Beschaffungsvolumen von Primärrohstoffen für die Produktion. Vier strategische Richtungen sind beim Recycling zu erkennen.

- Wiederverwendung: wiederholte Nutzung des aufgearbeiteten Wertstoffs im gleichen Einsatzbereich, z. B. Pfandflaschen, Mehrwegverpackungen.
- Weiterverwendung: wiederholte Nutzung des aufgearbeiteten Wertstoffs in einem neuen Einsatzbereich, z. B. Autoreifen für Sicherungsmaßnahmen.
- Wiederverwertung: Rückführung des aufbereiteten Wertstoffs in den gleichen Produktionsprozess, z. B. Altglas-, Altpapierrecycling.
- Weiterverwertung: Rückführung des aufbereiteten Wertstoffs in einen neuen Produktionsprozess, z. B. Schrott zu Stahl.[33]

Urban Mining

Sekundärrohstoffe können auch durch „Urban Mining“ gewonnen werden. Der Begriff Urban Mining beschreibt „die Gewinnung von Sekundärrohstoffen aus Zivilisationsabfällen und Produktionsreststoffen“.[34] In urbanen Abfällen steckt ein hohes Rohstoffpotential, so ist beispielsweise der Goldanteil in gebrauchten Toner-Kartuschen höher als in dem Material, welches in Südafrika zur Goldgewinnung abgebaut wird. In Baurestabfällen steckt ebenfalls ein mitunter höherer Anteil an Kupfer als in dem Erz, welches aus Kupferbergwerken stammt. Des Weiteren stellt Elektronikschrott mit seinem Stoffgemisch aus Aluminium, Platin, Kupfer, Gold und vielen weiteren Stoffen eine vielfältige Rohstoffquelle dar.[35]

---

[32] Bardt 2006, S. 4.

[33] Vgl. Werner 2008, S. 177; vgl. hierzu auch Thierry et al. 1995, p. 120 und pp. 125–126.

[34] Clausen et. al. 2007b, S. 229.

[35] Vgl. Clausen et. al. 2007b, S. 229.

Das Urban Mining ist derzeit ein Forschungsthema. Dieses sieht in städtischen Abfällen aufgrund des hohen Energiegehalts und der darin enthaltenen Chemikalien und Metalle eine reiche Rohstoffquelle. Ein Beispiel ist die Entwicklung von Methoden zur Rückgewinnung von Rohstoffen aus der Asche und Schlacke der Restmüllverbrennung. Bei der klassischen Müll- bzw. Restmüllverbrennung bleiben circa 25 bis 30 Gewichtsprozent des Abfalls als Schlacke, so genannte Müllverbrennungsschlacken übrig, die auf Deponien gelagert werden. Es werden chemische und mechanische Verfahren erprobt, um aus den Schlacken Kupfer, Edelstahl, Aluminium oder Eisen zu gewinnen.[36]

Die Gewinnung von Sekundärrohstoffen aus Abfällen ist jedoch in vielen Fällen noch nicht wirtschaftlich sinnvoll, da die Kosten für die Gewinnung im Verhältnis zu den Marktpreisen für Primärrohstoffe nicht konkurrenzfähig sind. Abfälle die nicht stofflich genutzt und wieder aufbereitet werden können, werden auch als Sekundärbrennstoffe zur Energieerzeugung eingesetzt und stellen somit ein Substitut für die fossilen Brennstoffe Erdöl und Kohle dar.[37]

4.2 Sekundärrohstofflogistik

In Zukunft könnte aufgrund zunehmender Rohstoffverknappung die Entwicklung dahin gehen, dass die genutzte Menge an Sekundärrohstoffen steigen wird. Es ist auch möglich, dass sich für weitere Rohstoffarten Ersatzbedarf ergibt. Für die Planung, Steuerung, Kontrolle und Optimierung dieser auftretenden Stoffströme werden logistische Systeme benötigt. Zentrale Aufgabe ist, die Netzwerke mit den beteiligten Akteuren der Sekundärrohstoffwirtschaft auszugestalten und zu steuern.[38]

Um geeignete Modelle für diese Logistik zu entwickeln und zu optimieren, soll dieses Subsystem näher betrachtet und definitorisch eingegrenzt werden.

In der Literatur haben sich für diese rückführende Logistik verschiedene Begriffe herausgebildet wie beispielsweise Entsorgungslogistik, Ressourcenlogistik oder Reverse Logistics. Die Definition des letztgenannten Konzepts der Reverse Logistics trifft die Thematik dieser Ausarbeitungen.

Das Konzept und erste Beschreibungen von Reverse Logistics stammen aus dem Jahre 1981 und thematisieren die Umkehrung der Materialflüsse.[39] Reverse Logistics „umfasst den Prozess der effektiven und effizienten Planung, Implementierung und Steuerung von eingehenden sekundären Stoffströmen, deren Lagerung und die damit verknüpften Informationsflüsse, die entgegengesetzt der traditionellen Richtung einer Versorgungskette fließen, mit der Absicht, den Stoffkreislauf zu schließen und deren Wert zu erhalten, zu steigern oder eine […] angemessene Entsorgung zu gewährleisten.“[40] Diese Definition ist grundlegend für die in diesem Beitrag besprochene Logistik. Um den speziellen Aspekt der Sekundärrohstoffe zu unterstreichen, wird jedoch der Begriff Sekundärrohstofflogistik verwendet.

[36] Vgl. Kugler 2008.

[37] Vgl. Clausen/Nikel 2007a, S. 25.

[38] Vgl. Clausen/Nikel 2007a, S. 25–26.

[39] Vgl. Lambert/Stock 1981, S. 19 und Wutz 2008, S. 5.

[40] Wutz 2008, S. 8; weitere Definitionen zu Reverse Logistics in de Brito/Dekker 2002, S. 2–4.

Logistische Objekte

Sekundärrohstoffe werden aus Abfällen und Reststoffen, so genannten Rückständen[41], mittels geeigneter Aufarbeitungs- und Aufbereitungsprozesse gewonnen. Rückstände stellen die logistischen Objekte im Aufarbeitungs- und Aufbereitungsprozess dar.

In jedem Herstellungsprozess fallen Produktionsrückstände in stofflicher oder energetischer Form an. Stoffliche Produktionsrückstände sind beispielsweise Materialrückstände in Form von Verschnitten oder Spänen. Beim Verfehlen vorher festgelegter Qualitätsforderungen können nicht mehr verwendete Ausschüsse als Rückstände entstehen. Des Weiteren können durch Instandhaltungs- und Reparaturmaßnahmen ausgetauschte Teile anfallen, die für den produktiven Einsatz nicht mehr zu verwenden sind.

Im Bereich der Distribution können stoffliche Distributionsrückstände anfallen. Einwegverpackungen aber auch Mehrwegverpackungen sind nach ihrer Funktionserfüllung derartige Rückstände. Transportbehälter wie Paletten oder Gitterboxen sind nach ihrer Lebensdauer ebenfalls als Rückstand zu betrachten. Falsches oder fehlerhaft geliefertes Material sowie nicht benötigtes Material bei Überlieferungen können Rückstände im Distributionsprozess darstellen. Weiterhin sind zurückgerufene oder am Markt nicht mehr nachgefragte Produkte als Objekte für die Sekundärrohstofflogistik anzusehen.

In der Konsumphase sind gleichermaßen stoffliche Rückstände anzutreffen. Einerseits handelt es sich dabei um Ver- und Gebrauchsgüter. Güter die nach ihrer Anwendung verbraucht oder nach Ablauf ihrer Nutzungsdauer nicht mehr funktionsfähig sind und keinen Nutzen mehr generieren können, fallen als Rückstände an. Andererseits können ähnlich wie in der Produktion durch Wartungs- und Reparaturmaßnahmen an Konsumgütern ausgetauschte Teile als Rückstände auftreten.[42]

Logistische Aktivitäten

Die folgende, in Anlehnung an Wildemann und Wutz entwickelte Abbildung 1 (s. S. 252), veranschaulicht die Einbindung der Sekundärrohstofflogistik in die Unternehmenslogistik. Wildemann hat die Bedeutung der logistischen Aktivitäten zur Rückführung von Rückständen in den Stoffkreislauf in einer Delphi-Studie nachgewiesen.[43] Die betrachteten Aktivitäten befinden sich im unteren Teil der Abbildung.

Die Redistributionslogistik ist das Bindeglied zwischen dem Entstehungsort der Rückstände und der Bereitstellung für die anschließende Aufarbeitungs- und Aufbereitungslogistik. Ein notwendiger Prozess im Rahmen dieser Logistik ist die Sammlung der Rückstände an definierten Übergabeorten. Die erfassten Rückstandsmengen sind anschließend in Rückstandsfraktionen zu sortieren. Für die zeitliche Überbrückung zwischen Anfall und Verwendung sowie zum Ausgleich der mengenmäßigen Schwankung von Angebot und Nachfrage von Rückständen wird eine Lagerhaltung benötigt. Des Weiteren sind Transportprozesse zu den Nachfrage- bzw.

---

41 „Unerwünschte oder unvermeidbare Nebenwirkung von Produktion und Konsum", Gabler Wirtschaftslexikon 2004, S. 2572.

42 Vgl. Wutz 2008, S. 15–18 und Dutz 1996, S. 19–22; vgl. hierzu auch de Brito/Dekker 2002, S. 10–12.

43 Vgl. Wildemann 1997, S. 47–69.

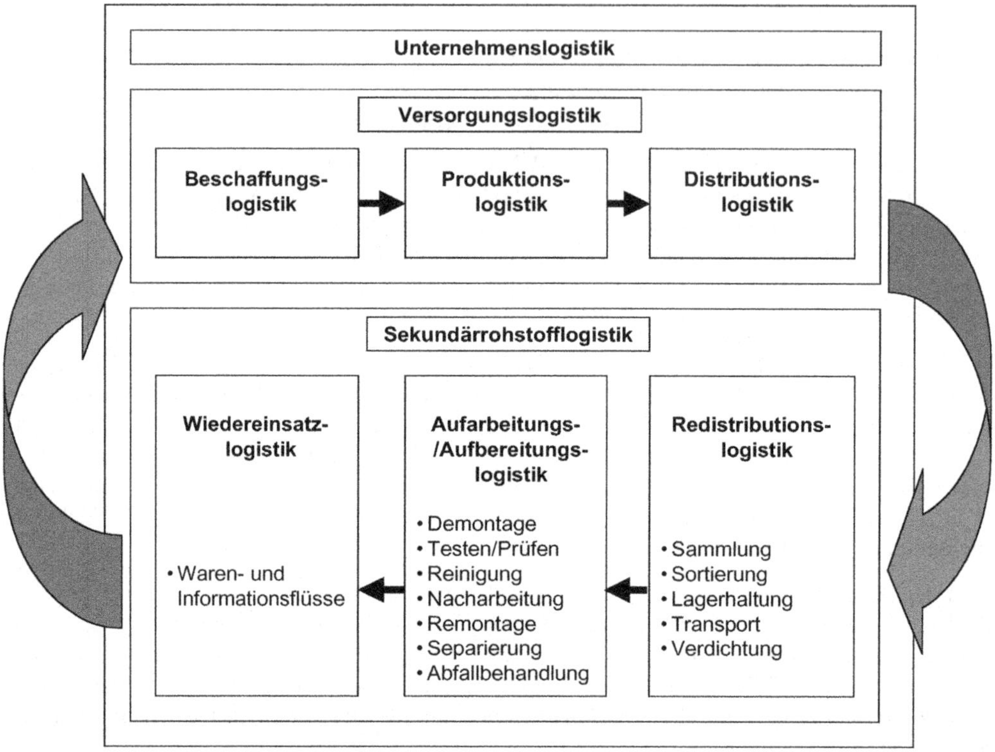

Abbildung 1: Subsysteme der Unternehmenslogistik

Quelle: Eigene Darstellung in Anlehnung an Wildemann 1997, S. 48 und Wutz 2008, S. 26[44]

Bedarfsorten der Rückstände erforderlich. In bestimmten Fällen können auch Verdichtungsprozesse zur besseren Auslastung der Transportkapazitäten zum Einsatz kommen.[45]

Die Aufarbeitungs- und Aufbereitungslogistik dient der Planung, Steuerung und Durchführung von Aufarbeitungs- und Aufbereitungsprozessen. Diese werden bei der Verwendung und Verwertung von Produkten und Stoffen eingesetzt und dienen im speziellen dem Recycling.[46] Zu Beginn kann bei komplexen Rückständen oder Produkten eine Demontage in die Einzelteile oder ein Ausbau von Einzelteilen notwendig sein. Dabei entstehen mindestens zwei neue Elemente. Die Materialflüsse beim Demontageprozess haben ein Input-Output-Verhältnis von 1:N mit (N = 2, …, n). Für die Wertermittlung und die Überprüfung des qualitativen Zustands der Rückstände sind Test- oder Prüfprozesse durchzuführen. Damit verschmutzte oder korro-

[44] Vgl. hierzu auch de Brito/Dekker 2002, S. 15–16.

[45] Vgl. Wutz 2008, S. 26–29; vgl. hierzu auch Pohlen/Farris 1992, S. 38; Stölzle 1993, S. 224; Rudolph 1999, S. 57–58; Steven et al. 2003, S. 645 und Pfohl 2004, S. 245.

[46] Vgl. Wutz 2008, S. 13; vgl. hierzu auch Steinhilper/Hudelmaier 1993, S. 17; Liesegang/Pischon 1996, Sp. 1793–1794; Schneider 1999, S. 23; Spengler 1994, S. 11–12 und Heeg et al. 1994, S. 23.

dierte Rückstände überhaupt getestet oder geprüft und einer weiteren Verwendung zugeführt werden können, sind Reinigungsarbeiten zu verrichten. Wird der Rückfluss von Rückständen auf Produktebene betrachtet, so sind bei Nutzungsschäden, insbesondere bei Bauteilen und Produkten, Nacharbeiten notwendig. Diese zielen darauf ab, sowohl funktionale technische als auch optische Mängel für eine Wieder- oder Weiterverwendung zu beheben. Remontageprozesse kommen zum Einsatz, wenn alte und neue Bauteile zu neuen Produkten oder Modulen zusammengefügt werden sollen.

Im Bereich der Aufbereitung sind Separierungs- und Abfallbehandlungsprozesse anzutreffen. Die Separierung ist wie die Demontage ein Trennungsprozess, der jedoch durch zerstörende Maßnahmen erfolgt. Im Anschluss können bei der Separierung nur Rückstandsfraktionen gebildet werden. Eine genaue Trennung in die einzelnen Elemente ist aufgrund des zerstörenden Charakters nicht möglich. In Abfallbehandlungsprozessen werden schadstoffbelastete Rückstände einer Schadstoffentfrachtung unterzogen. Dabei können chemische, physikalische oder biologische Verfahren zum Einsatz kommen.

In Abhängigkeit vom jeweiligen Zustand müssen die Rückstände nicht alle genannten Prozesse der Rückführungs-, Aufarbeitungs- und Aufbereitungslogistik durchlaufen, manche dagegen mehrmals.[47]

Im Bereich der Wiedereinsatzlogistik sind Prozesse des Material- und Informationsflusses zu den Wiedereinsatzbetrieben durchzuführen. Diese führen die gewonnenen Sekundärrohstoffe einem neuerlichen Gebrauch zu.[48]

Logistische Akteure

Für die logistischen Teilprozesse der Rückführung, Aufarbeitung und Aufbereitung sowie des Wiedereinsatzes können ein oder mehrere Akteure zum Einsatz kommen. In diesem Beitrag werden Lieferanten, Dienstleister und Händler als beteiligte Akteure angenommen. Weiterhin sind Original Equipment Manufacturer (OEM) und Konsumenten Akteure im Rahmen der Sekundärrohstofflogistik.

Die Lieferanten können sowohl als Quelle als auch als Senke agieren. In der Funktion der Quelle sind sie Produzenten von Stoffen und Bauteilen und stellen diese für die Fertigung und Montage bereit. In der Funktion der Senke kaufen sie einerseits Sekundärrohstoffe, -produkte oder -bauteile auf oder nehmen sie zurück und verwenden sie wieder. Andererseits bearbeiten und bereiten sie Rückstände zur Gewinnung von Recyclaten selbständig auf.

Die Aufarbeitungs- und Aufbereitungsprozesse können aber auch von Dienstleistern übernommen werden. Häufig führen diese noch weitere logistische Tätigkeiten der Rückführung[49] oder des Wiedereinsatzes aus.

---

[47] Vgl. Wutz 2008, S. 29–33.; vgl. auch Spengler 1994, S. 14–15; Rudolph 1999, S. 63–67; Adam 1998, S. 14; Dyckhoff 2003, S. 93; Guide 2000, S. 468; Steinhilper/Hudelmaier 1993, S. 206; Souren 1996, S. 27–28 und Guide/Jayaraman 2000, S. 3787–3788.

[48] Vgl. Wildemann 1997, S. 48–49; vgl. zu Logistischen Aktivitäten auch de Brito/Dekker 2002, S. 12–14.

[49] Wie z.B. Sammlung, Sortierung, Lagerhaltung, Transport etc., vgl. Wutz 2008, S. 28; vgl. zu Dienstleistern auch Flapper et al. 2005, S. 13.

Die Händler[50] als Bindeglied zwischen OEM und Konsumenten nehmen neben Vertriebs- auch Rücknahmeaufgaben wahr. Sie agieren dabei als Empfänger von Altprodukten, Garantierückläufen oder umzutauschenden Waren. Makler übernehmen häufig die Vermittlerposition bei Angeboten und Nachfragen nach Rückständen.

Die OEM müssen ihre hergestellten und vertriebenen Produkte, vor allem Altprodukte, im Zuge der erweiterten Produktverantwortung zurücknehmen und einer Verwertung oder Verwendung zuführen. Des Weiteren sind sie gehalten, bereits in der Produktgestaltungsphase auf demontage- und recyclinggerechte Konstruktion zu achten.

Die Konsumenten nehmen in der Sekundärrohstofflogistik eine zentrale Rolle ein. Sie bestimmen durch ihr Konsumverhalten die Art der Altprodukte, durch ihr Gebrauchsverhalten den Zustand und durch ihr Rückgabeverhalten die Mengen sowie den Zeitpunkt der Rückgabe. Die Aufarbeitungs- und Aufbereitungsprozesse werden dadurch stark beeinflusst.[51]

4.3 Logistiknetzwerke in der Sekundärrohstofflogistik

Die Literatur belegt, dass die Bildung von Unternehmensnetzwerken vorwiegend in der Beschaffungs-, Produktions- und Distributionslogistik Anwendung gefunden hat. Für die rückführende und im Besonderen für die spezielle Logistik der Sekundärrohstoffe sind ebenfalls logistische Netzwerkstrukturen notwendig, um Rückstände zu sammeln, zu den Unternehmen der Aufarbeitung oder Aufbereitung zu transportieren und die gewonnenen Rohstoffe für den Wiedereinsatz bereitzustellen.[52] Für diese Aufgaben sind drei Teilsysteme des Netzwerkes erforderlich. Das sind die Rückstandssammel-Systeme (Redistribution), die Aufarbeitungs- und Aufbereitungs-Systeme sowie die Sekundärrohstoffhändler-Systeme (Wiedereinsatz). Abbildung 2 verdeutlicht diese netzwerkartigen Strukturen.

Die Netzwerkstruktur ist gekennzeichnet durch einen konvergenten Materialstrom im Bereich der Redistribution sowie durch einen divergierenden Materialstrom im Bereich des Wiedereinsatzes der sekundären Materialien. Die Sekundärrohstofflogistik verfügt über einen zweiseitigen Marktfokus. Das sind zum einen der Beschaffungsmarkt von Rückständen und zum anderen der Nachfragemarkt nach Sekundärrohstoffen.

Die dargestellte Netzwerkstruktur weist exemplarischen Charakter auf und wird in den weiteren Ausführungen konkretisiert. Netzwerke im Bereich der Sekundärrohstofflogistik sind nicht identisch und unterscheiden sich hinsichtlich der beteiligten Akteure, der Verantwortlichkeiten, des Zentralisationsgrades und der Anzahl der Netzwerkebenen.[53] Des Weiteren sind Netzwerke innerhalb der Subsysteme Redistribution, Aufarbeitung und Aufbereitung sowie Wiedereinsatz und systemübergreifende Netzwerke zu differenzieren.[54] Die Netzwerke können dabei unabhängig voneinander oder interdisziplinär agieren.

---

[50] Groß- und Einzelhändler, Importeure, Makler, vgl. Wutz 2008, S. 35.

[51] Vgl. Wutz 2008, S. 33–35; vgl. zu Logistischen Akteuren auch de Brito/Dekker 2002, S. 12ff.; de Brito/Dekker 2004, S. 19; Fleischmann 2001, S. 19 und Carter/Ellram 1998, S. 90.

[52] Vgl. Martens 2007, S. 54 und Fleischmann et. al. 2004, S. 65; vgl. hierzu auch Fleischmann et al. 2000, S. 657–659 und Blackburn et al. 2004, S. 7–8.

[53] Vgl. Fleischmann et. al. 2004, S. 67–69.

[54] Vgl. Martens 2007, S. 55.

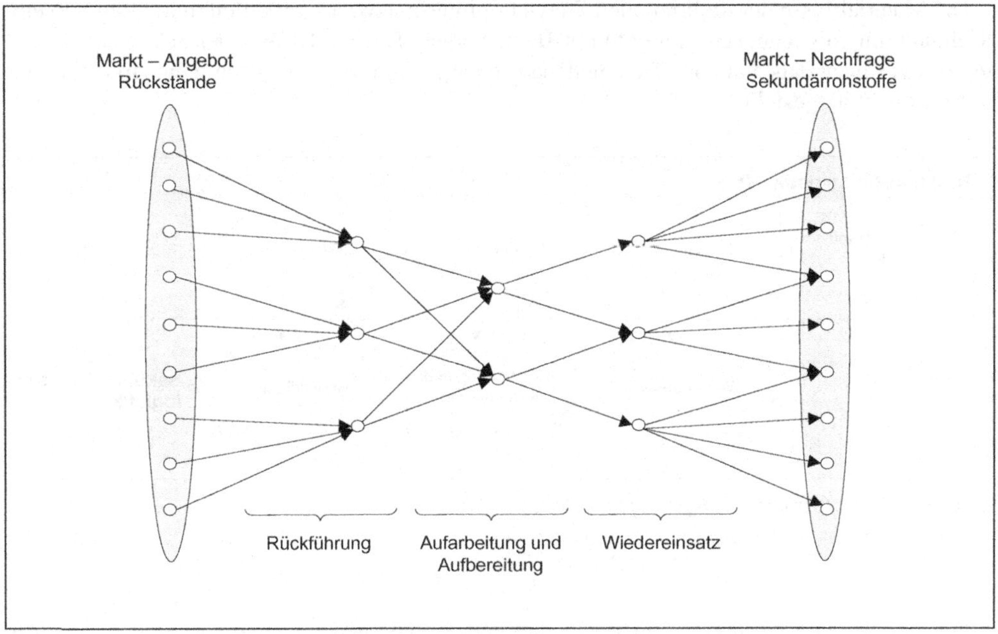

Abbildung 2: Materialflüsse im Netzwerk

Quelle: Eigene Darstellung in Anlehnung an Fleischmann et. al. 2004, S. 68

Zunächst werden besondere Eigenschaften von Netzwerken im Bereich der Sekundärrohstofflogistik betrachtet.[55]

4.3.1 Netzwerkeigenschaften

Die Netzwerkstrukturen im Bereich der vorwärtsgerichteten und der rückwärtsgerichteten Logistik zeigen in einem Vergleich Übereinstimmung. In einzelnen Punkten bestehen jedoch Differenzen.

Bei beiden Lieferketten ist der Umfang der Nachfrage unbekannt. Bei der Sekundärrohstofflogistik befindet sich eine zusätzliche Ungewissheit auf der Beschaffungsseite. Rückstände fallen nicht in Massenströmen und in gleich bleibender Qualität an. Der Zeitpunkt des Rückflusses ist unbekannt und nicht beeinflussbar. Eine große Herausforderung liegt in einer wirksamen Abgleichung des Angebotes an Rückständen und der Nachfrage nach Sekundärrohstoffen.[56] Mit Hilfe der Netzwerke im Bereich der Sekundärrohstofflogistik sollen die Materialflüsse unter Berücksichtigung der Unsicherheiten und Unregelmäßigkeiten stabilisiert werden.

[55] Vgl. zu Reverse Logistics Netzwerken auch Guide Jr. 2000, S. 475 und Fleischmann et al. 2000, S. 654–657.

[56] Vgl. Guide Jr. 2000, S. 472–473; vgl. hierzu auch Fleischmann et al. 2000, S. 658–659 und Thierry et al. 1995, S. 116–117.

Die Materialflüsse der traditionellen Wertschöpfungsnetzwerke verlaufen in der Regel in eine Richtung mit vorgegebenen Input-Output-Beziehungen. Die Stoffströme der Sekundärrohstofflogistik verfügen dagegen über verschiedene Eingangs- und Ausgangsströme, wie in Abbildung 3 vereinfacht dargestellt.

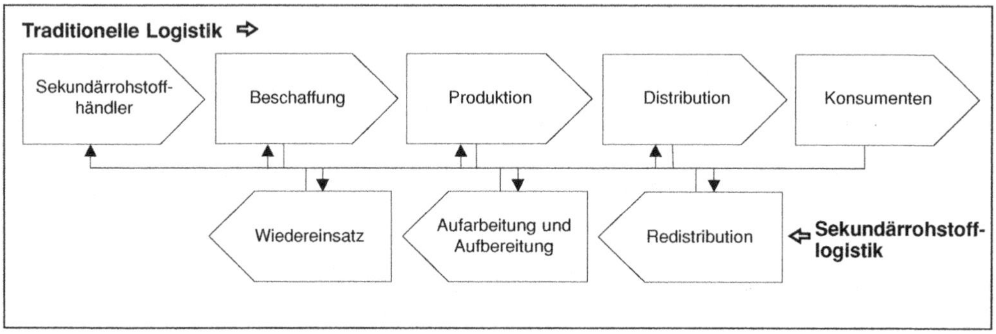

Abbildung 3: Stoffströme und Input-Output-Beziehungen

Quelle: Eigene Darstellung in Anlehnung an Steven 2003b, S. 164

Die beiden Materialflüsse beinhalten Synergiepotentiale und tragen zur Erzielung von Skaleneffekten bei. So können beispielsweise Aktivitäten der vorwärts- und rückwärtsgerichteten Logistik in denselben Betriebsstätten durchgeführt werden, wobei eine Senkung der Gemeinkosten möglich ist. Des Weiteren können die Aktivitäten zur Sammlung von Rückständen mit denen der Distribution integriert werden. Dies kann helfen, die Anzahl an Leerfahrten zu reduzieren.[57]

4.3.2 *Motive für eine Netzwerkgründung*

Die Hauptmotivation zur Gründung von Unternehmensnetzwerken liegt in der „Erzielung einer Kooperationsrente in den Bereichen der Zusammenarbeit".[58] Die Kooperationsrente bezeichnet dabei einen Vorteil, der durch kooperative Zusammenarbeit erreicht werden kann. Dieser Vorteil kann unterschiedliche Formen annehmen. So können beispielsweise Kosten reduziert, Skalenerträge erzielt und der monetäre Unternehmenserfolg allgemein erhöht werden. Die Arbeit im Netzwerk gewährt Zugang zu Ressourcen oder Kompetenzen, über welche die Unternehmen nicht selbst verfügen. Durch die komplementäre und gemeinsame Leistungserstellung im Verbund mit anderen Unternehmen ist die Generierung von Wettbewerbsvorteilen möglich.[59]

Mögliche Kooperationsbereiche in der Sekundärrohstofflogistik liegen in den Subsystemen *Redistribution*, *Aufarbeitung und Aufbereitung* sowie *Wiedereinsatz*. Darüber hinaus ist eine Zusammenarbeit in prozessübergreifenden Netzwerken denkbar.

---

[57] Vgl. Fleischmann et. al. 2004, S. 69–70 und Steven 2003b, S. 164.

[58] Martens 2007, S. 55.

[59] Vgl. Martens 2007, S. 41–54.

Im Bereich der *Redistribution* entstehen logistische Kosten für den Transport der Rückstände. Diese Kosten sind möglichst gering zu halten. Ist die räumliche Rückstandsstruktur jedoch sehr großflächig mit einer Vielzahl an Rückstandsquellen, kann ein einzelnes Unternehmen diesen Rückstandsraum möglicherweise nicht kostenoptimal bedienen. Eine Transportkooperation, beispielsweise in Form eines Hub-and-Spoke-Systems, könnte in diesem Bereich zu einem besseren Ergebnis führen. Netzwerke im Bereich der Redistribution bieten sich bereits dort an, wo die Rückstandsquellen ebenfalls netzwerkartig organisiert sind.[60]

Die Hauptaufgabe der *Aufarbeitung und Aufbereitung* ist die Gewinnung von Sekundärrohstoffen. Die Qualität der Sekundärrohstoffe trägt einen hohen Anteil zu einer Generierung hoher Umsätze in der Absatzphase bei. Die Erfolgsfaktoren dafür sind zum einen ein hoher Reinheitsgrad der sekundären Materialien und zum anderen eine hohe Anlagenauslastung zur Erzielung geringer Stückkosten. Die Qualität der Sekundärrohstoffe kann durch eine höhere Anzahl an Aufarbeitungs- und Aufbereitungsstandorten verbessert werden. Wenn durch die Netzwerkbildung mehr Aufarbeitung- und Aufbereitungsoptionen zur Verfügung stehen, kann damit die Qualität der sekundären Materialien erhöht werden. Diese Möglichkeit der Vernetzung ist jedoch nur gerechtfertigt, wenn der logistische Mehraufwand für den Qualitätsgewinn durch höhere Absatzpreise mindestens ausgeglichen wird.

Eine Zusammenarbeit im Netzwerk in diesem Bereich ist erforderlich, wenn mit zunehmender Komplexität der Rückstände eine effiziente Aufarbeitung und Aufbereitung in einem einzelnen Betrieb nicht sichergestellt werden kann. Die Aufarbeitungs- und Aufbereitungsprozesse sind entsprechend der Kompetenzen in den verschiedenen Betrieben des Netzwerkes durchzuführen.

Eine ungleiche Verteilung der Rückstandsmengen innerhalb eines Netzwerkes kann zu einer Minderauslastung der Anlagen in den einzelnen Betrieben führen. Dadurch können die Stückkosten in den betroffenen Betrieben nicht verringert werden. Ist das der Fall, kann eine Netzwerkstruktur im Bereich der Aufarbeitung und Aufbereitung eine gleichmäßige Verteilung der Rückstandsmengen herbeiführen.[61]

Im Bereich des *Wiedereinsatzes* entstehen wie bei der Redistribution logistische Kosten für den Transport der Sekundärrohstoffe zu den produzierenden Unternehmen. Eine Netzwerkstruktur bietet sich an, wenn der Absatzraum von einem einzelnen Logistikunternehmen nicht kostenoptimal bedient werden kann. Die kooperative Planung im Netzwerk kann in dem Fall zu einer Reduktion der Logistikkosten beitragen.[62]

Nach der separaten Betrachtung des Kooperationspotentials innerhalb der einzelnen Prozesse der Sekundärrohstofflogistik, wird im Folgenden die systemübergreifende Zusammenarbeit betrachtet. Prozessübergreifende Netzwerke agieren branchenübergreifend und schließen auch Netzwerke der Güter versorgenden und Rohstoff verbrauchenden Unternehmen mit ein. Eine Voraussetzung für den wirtschaftlichen Betrieb dieser Netzwerke ist die Anbindung möglichst vieler Rückstandsquellen (Handel, Industrie) an die Senken des Netzwerks. Für die angeschlossenen Betriebe wird zum einen die gesicherte und transparente Abnahme der Rückstände

---

[60] Vgl. Martens 2007, S. 55–56 und S. 177; siehe zu Hub-and-Spoke-Systemen Arnold et al. 2002, A1–17 und Krampe/Lucke 1993, S. 95.

[61] Vgl. Martens 2007, S. 56–57 und S. 182–183.

[62] Vgl. Martens 2007, S. 57; vgl. zu logistischen Kosten Bilitewski et al. 1994, S. 61.

gewahrt. Zum anderen wird für die produzierende Industrie der Rohstoffnachschub gewährleistet. Die Betriebe der Sekundärrohstofflogistik können dadurch Größeneffekte erzielen. Für die prozessübergreifende Weitergabe und Nutzung dieser Skalenerträge ist eine enge Zusammenarbeit im Verbund notwendig. Gegenüber den quantitativen Vorteilen erzeugt die Netzwerkbildung eine Reihe qualitativer Vorteile. Ein regelmäßiger Informationsaustausch im gesamten Netzwerk kann zu einer Erhöhung der Marktanpassungsfähigkeit, der Flexibilität und der Innovationsfähigkeit beitragen. Durch abgestimmtes Verhalten[63] können die kooperierenden Unternehmen die Branchenstruktur beeinflussen und somit die Marktposition und die Marktmacht des Netzwerks verbessern. Die strategischen Netzwerkziele sind damit besser durchsetzbar. Des Weiteren besteht die Möglichkeit zu gemeinsamer Forschungs- und Entwicklungsarbeit hinsichtlich demontagegerechter und recyclingfähiger Produktkonstruktionen. Diese sollen einen effizienten Materialfluss in den späteren Produktlebensphasen ermöglichen. Die folgende Tabelle 3 fasst die Auswirkungen der Netzwerkbildung in den einzelnen Subsystemen der Sekundärrohstofflogistik und im Gesamtsystemverbund zusammen.[64]

Tabelle 3: Maßnahmen und Auswirkungen der Netzwerkbildung auf die Unternehmensziele

Bereich	**Kooperative Maßnahmen**	**Auswirkungen auf Unternehmensziele**
Redistribution	Logistische Optimierung	Kostensenkung
	Input-Mengenbündelung	Kostensenkung
	Vergrößerung des Marktraumes	Höhere Wettbewerbsfähigkeit
Verwertung	Kombination von Anlagen	Kapazitätssteigerung
	Steigerung der Verwertungsoptionen	Höhere Absatzpreise
Wiedereinsatz	Logistische Optimierung	Kostensenkung
	Output-Mengenbündelung	Marktmachtsteigerung
	Vergrößerung des Absatzmarktes	Preiserhöhung
System-übergreifend	Sicherung von Mengen	Kostensenkung
	Abgestimmtes Verhalten	Markmachtsteigerung
	Informationsaustausch	Verbesserte Innovationsfähigkeit, Marktflexibilität, gemeinsame FuE

Quelle: Martens 2007, S. 58

4.3.3 Netzwerktypologisierung

In den nächsten Ausführungen soll eine kurze Typologisierung der Netzwerke im Bereich der Sekundärrohstofflogistik vorgenommen werden.

Wie bereits oben genannt, existiert eine Vielzahl unterschiedlicher Netzwerktypen. Bei einer Typologisierung anhand der Wertschöpfungsstufe lassen sich *horizontale*, *vertikale* und *laterale* Netzwerke unterscheiden.

63 Zum Beispiel in Form von Lobbyismus, Interessenvertretungen, gemeinsame Marktpräsenz. Martens 2007, S. 58.

64 Vgl. Martens 2007, S. 57–58; vgl. auch zur besseren Durchsetzung strategischer Ziele Walther 2005, S. 72.

In *horizontalen* Netzwerken erfolgt eine Kooperation zwischen Unternehmen auf derselben Wertschöpfungsstufe, wie es zum Beispiel in reinen Redistributions- oder Verwertungsnetzwerken der Fall ist. In *vertikalen* Netzwerken arbeiten Unternehmen der Sekundärrohstofflogistik aus verschiedenen vor- oder nachgelagerten Wertschöpfungsstufen zusammen. In *lateralen* Netzwerken kooperieren Unternehmen verschiedener Branchen und Wertschöpfungsstufen. Es sind auch Unternehmen integriert, die nicht der Branche der Sekundärrohstofflogistik angehören.

Eine weitere Form der Typologisierung basiert auf dem Modell des Supply Chain Managements. Dabei wird die traditionelle Supply Chain um Funktionen wie die Rücknahme von Rückständen und die Rückführung sekundärer Materialien in das Produktionsnetz ergänzt. Dadurch entstehen geschlossene Regelkreisläufe, die in der Literatur als Closed-loop Supply Chain bezeichnet werden.[65]

4.3.4 Netzwerkmodellierung im Bereich der Sekundärrohstofflogistik

Für die Unterstützung einer Entscheidung zur kooperativen Zusammenarbeit wird ein Grundmodell eines Netzwerkes der Sekundärrohstofflogistik entworfen.

Der Modelltyp, die Modellelemente und die Modellprozesse sollen bestimmt werden. Für die Darstellung der Mengenströme zwischen den räumlich getrennten Quellen und Senken eines Sekundärrohstofflogistiknetzwerks über die Zwischenstationen ist der Typ eines graphenbasierten Transportmodells geeignet. Das Ziel dieser Modellierung ist die Verteilung der Mengenströme zwischen den Quellen und den Senken zu minimalen Transportkosten.[66]

Die grundlegenden Elemente des Modells sind die Anfallstellen der Rückstände und die Nachfrager auf den Sekundärrohstoffmärkten. Sie stellen die Netzwerkquellen und Netzwerksenken dar. Das Modell ist um weitere Elemente, welche die Besonderheiten eines Sekundärrohstofflogistiknetzwerks widerspiegeln, zu erweitern. Die Sammel- und Zwischenlager (Logistiklager) sowie die Aufarbeitungs- und Aufbereitungsbetriebe sind Zwischenelemente des Netzwerks. In diesem Fall wird der Aspekt der Entsorgung integriert, welcher in den vorherigen Ausführungen vernachlässigt worden ist. Dies basiert auf der Annahme, dass die Rückstände nicht vollständig verwertet werden können. Daher sind Deponien als weitere Netzwerkelemente zu definieren und haben die Funktion einer Netzwerksenke.

Die Kanten in diesem Modell bilden die logistischen Prozesse Redistribution, Zwischentransporte und Wiedereinsatz ab. Die Knoten stellen dagegen die nicht-logistischen Prozesse dar, die ortsgebunden durchgeführt werden. Diese sind zum einen die Quellen und Senken des Netzwerks und zum anderen die dazwischen liegenden Knotentypen Lager sowie Aufarbeitungs- und Aufbereitungsbetrieb.

Die Abbildung der realen Sachverhalte in einem Modell erfordert eine Reduktion der Ausgangsdaten auf entscheidungsrelevante Faktoren. Dazu werden im Folgenden Annahmen festgelegt, die als Rahmenbedingungen für die Modellierung betrachtet werden.

---

[65] Vgl. Martens 2007, S. 59–60; vgl. zu Netzwerktypologisierung auch Schwinn 1993, S. 197 und Balling 1998, S. 41ff., vgl. zu Closed-Loop-Netzwerken Flapper et al. 2005, S. 4.

[66] Vgl. zu Minimierung der Transportkosten Arnold et al. 2002, A2–11f.

Der Materialfluss beginnt bei den Anfallstellen, deren Knoten die Netzwerkquellen darstellen. Sie sind in einem Hol- oder Bring-System[67] integriert und überführen die Rückstände in das Netzwerk. In der Realität existiert eine Vielzahl von Anfallstellen wie beispielsweise öffentliche Sammelstellen, Sammelcontainer, Annahmestellen oder Wertstoffhöfe. *Annahme 1* der Modellierung begrenzt die Zahl zentraler Anfallstellen auf eine endliche Zahl, die als Sammelstationen von Rückständen dienen. Des Weiteren erfolgt die Rückgabe der Rückstände nach dem Bring-System. Die Anbieter von Rückständen sind für den Transport selbst verantwortlich. Den Anfallstellen entstehen keine Sammelkosten.

Die Rückstände können im Anschluss von den Anfallstellen zu den Logistiklagern transportiert werden. In diesen werden sie gesammelt, sortiert, zu Transporteinheiten zusammengefasst, auf Transportmittel umgeschlagen oder eingelagert. In der *Annahme 2* findet das Prinzip „Verwertung vor Beseitigung" Anwendung.[68] Das bedeutet, dass alle Rückstände entweder direkt von den Anfallstellen oder von den Logistiklagern den Aufarbeitungs- und Aufbereitungsbetrieben zugeführt werden. Die Rückstände müssen mindestens einen Verwertungsprozess durchlaufen. Eine Umgehung der Aufarbeitungs- und Aufbereitungsbetriebe ist nicht möglich.

Annahme 3 definiert den Verwertungsprozess. Alle Rückstände werden in den Aufarbeitungs- und Aufbereitungsbetrieben verwertet. Die Verwertung ist abhängig von den vorhandenen Verwertungstechnologien, von der Verwertungsfähigkeit[69] der Rückstände und vom Verwertungsaufwand.[70] Es werden zwei Arten der Verwertung unterschieden: die durchlaufende Verwertung und die analytische Verwertung. Bei der durchlaufenden Verwertung erfolgt keine Zerlegung der Rückstände. Sie können nach erfolgter Aufarbeitung direkt wieder als Sekundärrohstoff verwendet werden. Das Input-Output-Verhältnis der Materialströme beträgt 1:1.[71] Bei der analytischen Verwertung werden die Rückstände in mehrere Komponenten zerlegt. Dies können aufbereitete Sekundärrohstoffe oder nicht verwertbare Reststoffe zur Deponierung sein. Das Stoffstromverhältnis beträgt in diesem Fall 1:N mit (N = 2, …, n).

Die Netzwerksenken in der Modellierung sind die Absatzmärkte für Sekundärrohstoffe und die Deponien. Die Materialversorgung der Senken wird in *Annahme 4* betrachtet. Diese werden ausschließlich mit den Output-Materialströmen der Aufarbeitungs- und Aufbereitungsbetriebe versorgt. Die Absatzmärkte erhalten die aufgearbeiteten und aufbereiteten Sekundärrohstoffe. Die nicht verwertbaren Reststoffe gelangen hingegen zu den Deponien.

Die folgende Abbildung 4 veranschaulicht die Netzwerkmodellierung unter Berücksichtigung der getroffenen Annahmen.

In der Abbildung sind die Beziehungen der Netzwerkelemente durch einen gerichteten Graphen dargestellt. Die Pfeile mit einem Start- und Zielknoten beschreiben eine logistische Verbindung. Die kurzen Pfeile zeigen mögliche Outputströme zu verschiedenen Zielknoten.[72]

---

[67] Vgl. zu Bring-Systemen und Hol-Systemen Ivisic 2002, S. 183.

[68] Vgl. KrW/AbfG § 5 (2), S. 6.

[69] Verwertungsfähigkeit oder Verwertungspotential bedeutet, dass nicht alle Rückstände vollständig verwertet werden können. In der Regel nimmt die Verwertungsfähigkeit einen Wert x ($0 \leq x \leq 1$) ein.

[70] Ein hohes Verwertungspotential kann nur mit der entsprechenden Verwertungstechnologie und mit hohem Verwertungsaufwand erreicht werden.

[71] Vgl. Kap. 4.1 S. 14.

[72] Vgl. Martens 2007, S. 141–151.

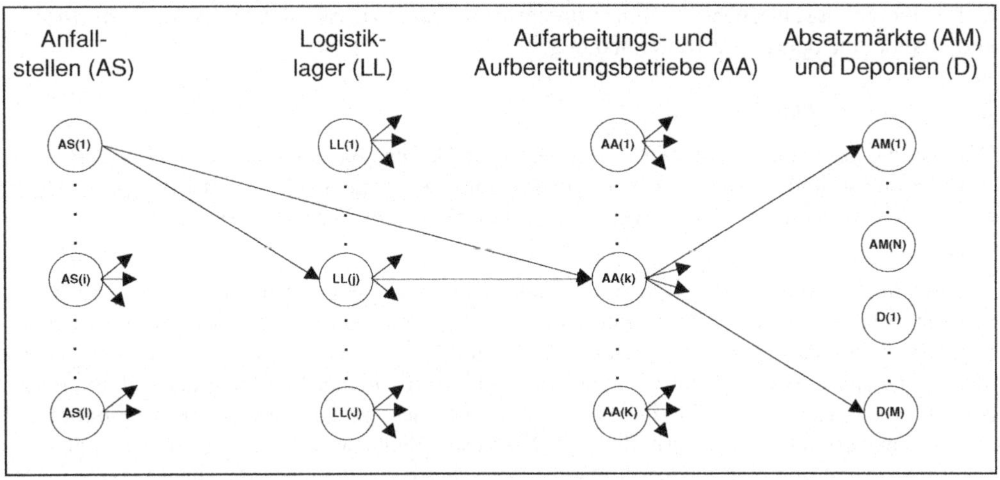

Abbildung 4: Darstellung eines Netzwerkgrundmodells

Quelle: Eigene Darstellung in Anlehnung an Martens 2007, S. 152

4.3.5 *Beispiele von Netzwerken*

Im Folgenden werden als Ergebnis einer erfolgreichen Netzwerkmodellierung drei spezifische Netzwerkformen beispielhaft vorgestellt, die im Bereich der Sekundärrohstofflogistik Anwendung finden können.

Regionale Netzwerke

In einem regionalen Netzwerk sind die Logistik-Dienstleister der Redistribution und des Wiedereinsatzes sowie die Unternehmen der Aufarbeitung und Aufbereitung einer Region organisiert. Das Netzwerk agiert in einem räumlich begrenzten Gebiet als Komplettanbieter der Sekundärrohstofflogistik. Die einzelnen Unternehmen des Netzwerks verfügen über begrenzte Ressourcen. Diese sind durch Bündelung optimal zu nutzen. Aufgrund des vorhandenen Auftragspotentials und geeigneter Netzwerkpartner ist die Zusammenarbeit nur in Ballungsgebieten zweckmäßig. Die Steuerung übernimmt ein Gremium der beteiligten Unternehmen. Dieses vergibt die einzelnen Aufträge und ist in der Lage, die Netzwerkkapazitäten optimal auszulasten.

Die Prozesse der Rückführung, der Aufarbeitung und Aufbereitung sowie der Redistribution führen zu weiteren Verkehrsströmen. Sie belasten das Verkehrssystem in Ballungsgebieten zusätzlich. Das regionale Netzwerk trägt einen erheblichen Teil dazu bei, dieses durch eine optimierte Standort- und Tourenplanung zu entlasten. Mithilfe von kombinierten Wiedereinsatz- und Redistributionsprozessen können weitere Verkehrsströme verhindert werden. Die informatorische Kopplung der Aufarbeitungs- und Aufbereitungsunternehmen mit den Logistik-Dienstleistern führt zu einer frühzeitigen Information über die Mengen und Anlieferzeitpunkte von Rückständen. Dadurch ist eine genauere Planung der Aufarbeitungs- und Aufbereitungsprozesse möglich. Auf der Seite des Wiedereinsatzes bietet die Kooperation mit den Aufarbeitungs-

und Aufbereitungsunternehmen frühzeitige Informationen zu vorhandenen Sekundärrohstoffen und erlaubt eine optimierte Tourenplanung.[73]

Virtuelle Unternehmen

Die Qualität der Sekundärrohstoffe kann, wie oben bereits genannt, durch eine hohe Anzahl an Aufarbeitungs- und Aufbereitungsoptionen verbessert werden. Die qualitativ hochwertigen Materialien ermöglichen höhere Absatzpreise und können zu einer Steigerung der Gewinne beitragen.

Große Aufarbeitungs- und Aufbereitungsunternehmen können sich zu einem Virtuellen Unternehmen (VU) auf nationaler oder internationaler Ebene zusammenschließen. Sie übernehmen zugleich die Steuerung des Netzwerks. Die Integration und informatorische Anbindung vieler kleiner und spezialisierter Unternehmen in das VU führt zu einer Erhöhung der Aufarbeitungs- und Aufbereitungsoptionen. Die integrierten Unternehmen erzielen durch die Konzentration auf ihre spezialisierten Prozesse Lerneffekte.[74] Diese ermöglichen den Unternehmen eine Erhöhung der Produktivität und eine Verbesserung der Wirtschaftlichkeit.[75] Die einzelnen Aufarbeitungs- und Aufbereitungsprozesse werden elektronisch erfasst und in einer Datenbank abgespeichert. Der Zugriff auf die zentrale Datenbank durch das Steuerungsgremium ermöglicht eine Kombination der spezialisierten Prozesse. Die qualitativen Eigenschaften der erzeugten Sekundärrohstoffe können durch die Zusammenführung der Prozesse verbessert werden. Zudem können die Ressourcen und Kapazitäten im VU wirtschaftlich und optimal genutzt werden.[76]

Strategische Netzwerke

Ein strategisches Netzwerk kann aus den Logistik-Dienstleistern der Redistribution und des Wiedereinsatzes, den Aufarbeitungs- und Aufbereitungsunternehmen sowie Unternehmen anderer Branchen bestehen. In diesem Beispiel ist ein Wartungsunternehmen aus Industrie und Handel integriert. Das Ziel dieser Zusammenarbeit ist die Nutzung von Synergien, die sich aus der Symbiose von Wartung, Redistribution, Aufarbeitung und Aufbereitung sowie des Wiedereinsatzes ergeben. Das Strategische Netzwerk agiert als Systemdienstleister auf nationaler oder internationaler Ebene. Die Aufgaben der Steuerung übernimmt eine unabhängige Organisation aus den beteiligten Unternehmen. Ein wesentlicher Vorteil für das Netzwerk wird in der frühzeitigen Übermittlung von Planungsinformationen der beteiligten Unternehmen an das Steuerungsgremium erreicht. Diese werden an zentraler Stelle aufbereitet und bereitgehalten.

Die Informationen der Wartungsunternehmen über den Standort, Zustand und Art der Rückstände ermöglichen den Logistik-Dienstleistern eine Optimierung der Redistribution. Sie können kurzfristig auf Kundenaufträge reagieren, Bündelungseffekte stärker nutzen und ihre Tourenplanung besser gestalten. Des Weiteren können die Anforderungen der Aufarbeitungs- und Aufbereitungsunternehmen in der Planung und Durchführung der Redistribution größere Berücksichtigung finden. Die Unternehmen der Aufarbeitung und Aufbereitung nutzen die ver-

[73] Vgl. Frille 1998, S. 18–19.

[74] Vgl. Frille 1998, S. 19.

[75] Vgl. Laarmann 2005, S. 110.

[76] Vgl. Frille 1998, S. 19.

fügbaren Informationen für die Losgrößenplanung ihrer Prozesse. Die informatorische Kooperation versetzt die Logistik-Dienstleister des Wiedereinsatzes ebenfalls in die Lage, ihre Tourenplanung zu optimieren.

Die Voraussetzung für die genauen Planungen und Optimierungen ist die Aktualität der Daten entlang der gesamten Logistikkette. Die Gewährleistung der Aktualität erhöht die Auslastung und die Wirtschaftlichkeit des Strategischen Netzwerks.[77]

5 Zusammenfassung

Es wurde gezeigt, dass die Sekundärrohstofflogistik aufgrund der veränderten Rohstoffversorgung an Bedeutung gewinnt. Der Trend geht zur Ergänzung der Primärrohstoffe durch sekundäre Materialien. Eine große Herausforderung der Sekundärrohstofflogistik ist die Beherrschung der Unregelmäßigkeit und Unvorhersehbarkeit der Rückstandsflüsse, die durch kooperative Zusammenarbeit im Netzwerk bewältigt werden muss.

Ausgangspunkt des Beitrags ist die Netzwerktheorie. Sie bildet die theoretische Grundlage für die Entstehung von Unternehmens- und Logistiknetzwerken. Der Aufbau, die Entwicklung und die effektive Koordination in Netzwerkstrukturen werden durch ein aktives Netzwerkmanagement begleitet.

Die Sekundärrohstoffe und die zugehörige Logistik werden definiert. Unternehmens- und Logistiknetzwerke existieren vorwiegend in der traditionellen Logistik. Erforderlich sind Netzwerke auch in der Sekundärrohstofflogistik. Die Modellierung eines Logistiknetzwerks im Bereich der Sekundärrohstofflogistik wurde durchgeführt. Beispiele von Netzwerkformen veranschaulichen die praktische Anwendbarkeit.

Literatur

Adam, D. (1989): *Produktions-Management*, Wiesbaden.

Arnold, D., H. Isermann, A. Kuhn und H. Tempelmeier (Hrsg.) (2002): *Handbuch Logistik*, Berlin Heidelberg.

Atasu, A., M. Sarvary and L. N. van Wassenhove (2008): Remanufacturing as a Marketing Strategy, in: *Management Science*, Vol. 54, No. 10, S. 1731–1746.

Axelsson, B. (1992): Network research – future issues, in: Axelsson, B. (Hrsg.) and G. Easton: *Industrial networks. A new view of reality*, London/New York 1992, S. 237–251.

Balling, R. (1998): *Kooperation: Strategische Allianzen, Netzwerke, Joint Ventures und andere Organisationsformen zwischenbetrieblicher Zusammenarbeit in Theorie und Praxis*, Frankfurt/Main.

Bardt, H. (2006): Die gesamtwirtschaftliche Bedeutung von Sekundärrohstoffen, in: *IW-Trends – Vierteljahresschrift zur empirischen Wirtschaftsforschung aus dem Institut der deutschen Wirtschaft Köln*, Jg. 33, 2006, Nr. 3, Köln.

Beck, T. C. (1998): *Kosteneffiziente Netzwerkkooperation: Optimierung komplexer Partnerschaften zwischen Unternehmen*, Wiesbaden.

[77] Vgl. Frille 1998, S. 19–20.

Benkenstein, M. (1987): *F&E und Marketing. Eine Untersuchung zur Leistungsfähigkeit von Koordinationskonzeptionen bei Innovationsentscheidungen*, Wiesbaden.

Bilitewski, B., G. Härdtle und K. Marek (1994): *Abfallwirtschaft: Eine Einführung*, Berlin Heidelberg.

Blackburn, J. D., V. D. R. Guide Jr., G. C. Souza and L. N. van Wassenhove (2004): Reverse Supply Chains for Commercial Returns, in: *California Management Review*, Vol. 46, No. 2, S. 6–22.

Butz, C. und F. Straube (2008): Entstehung und Implementierung von Innovationen in der Produktionslogistik, in: Nyhuis, P. (Hrsg.): *Beiträge zu einer Theorie der Logistik*, Berlin Heidelberg, S. 67–84.

Carter, C. R. and L. M. Ellram (1998): Reverse logistics – A review of the literature and framework for future investigation, in: *Journal of Business Logistics*, Vol. 19, No. 1, S. 85–102.

Clausen, U. und A. Nikel (2007a): Ressourcenlogistik – Neue Chancen in Zeiten knapper Rohstoffe, in: *Jahrbuch Logistik 2007*, free beratung Gesellschaft für Kommunikation im Marketing mbH, Korschenbroich, S. 24–27.

Clausen, U., P. Meyer, A. Nikel und H. Paschlau (2007b): Von der Abfall- zur Ressourcenlogistik, in: *Müll und Abfall*, Jg. 5, S. 228–236.

Corsten, H. (2001): *Unternehmungsnetzwerke – Formen unternehmungsübergreifender Zusammenarbeit*, München.

de Brito, M. P. and R. Dekker (2002): *Reverse Logistics – a framework*. Econometric Institute Report EI 2002-38, clrb.com.br/publicacoes/academico_framework.pdf, abgerufen am 09.04.2009.

de Brito, M. P. and R. Dekker (2004): A framework for reverse logistics, in: Dekker, R., M. Fleischmann, K. Inderfurth, K. and L. N. van Wassenhove (Hrsg.): *Reverse logistics – Quantitative models for closed-loop supply chains*, Berlin Heidelberg.

Dutz, E. (1996): *Die Logistik der Produktverwertung*, München.

Dyckhoff, H. (2003): *Grundzüge der Produktionswirtschaft*, Berlin Heidelberg.

Flapper, S. D. P., J. A. E. E. van Nunen and L. N. van Wassenhove (2005): Introduction, in: Flapper, S. D. P., J. A. E. E. van Nunen and L. N. van Wassenhove (Hrsg.): *Managing Closed-Loop Supply Chains*, Berlin Heidelberg, S. 3–18.

Fleischmann, M. (2001): *Quantitative models for reverse logistics*, Berlin Heidelberg.

Fleischmann, M., and H. R. Krikke, R. Dekker and S. D. P. Flapper (2000): A characterisation of logistics networks for product recovery, in: *Omega*, Vol. 28, S. 653–666.

Fleischmann, M., J. M. Bloemhof-Ruwaard, P. Beullenes and R. Dekker (2004): Reverse Logistics Network Design, in: Dekker, R., M. Fleischmann, K. Inderfurth and L. N. van Wassenhove: *Reverse Logistics*, Berlin Heidelberg, S. 65–94.

Frese, E. (1989): Koordinationskonzepte, in: Szyperski, N. (Hrsg.): *Handwörterbuch der Planung*, Stuttgart, Sp. 913–923.

Frille, O. (1998): Potentiale von Netzwerken in der Kreislaufwirtschaft, in: *Entsorgungspraxis*, Jg. 16, Nr. 12, S. 16–20.

Gabler Wirtschaftslexikon (2004): *K–R*, Wiesbaden.

Gudehus, T. (2005): *Logistik – Grundlagen, Strategien, Anwendungen*, Berlin Heidelberg.

Guide Jr., V. D. R. (2000): Production planning and control for remanufacturing: Industry practice and research needs, in: *Journal of Operations Management*, Vol. 18, No. 4, S. 467–483.

Guide Jr., V. D. R. and V. Jayaraman (2000): Product acquisition management – Current industry practice and a proposed framework, in: *International Journal of Production Research*, Vol. 38, No. 16, S. 3779–3800.

Heeg, F.-J., M. Veismann and M. Schnatmeyer (1994): Recycling-Management, in: *UmweltWirtschaftsForum*, Jg. 2, Nr. 4, S. 23–30.

Heiserich, O.-E. (2002): *Logistik – Eine praxisorientierte Einführung*, Wiesbaden.

Ivisic, R.-A. (2002): *Management kreislauforientierter Entsorgungskonzepte: Erfolgsfaktoren und Gestaltungsinstrumente*, Bern.

Kaczmarek, M., A. Sonnek und F. Stüllenberg (2004): Das Management von Unternehmensnetzwerken – Aufgabenfelder und industrielle Unterstützung, in: Gericke, J., M. Kaczmarek, S. Neweling, A. Schulze im Hove, A. Sonnek und F. Stüllenberg: *Management von Unternehmensnetzwerken*, Hamburg, S. 1–24.

Kirsch, W. und H. Meffert (1970): *Organisationstheorien und Betriebswirtschaftslehre*, Wiesbaden.

Krampe, H. und H.-J. Lucke (1993): *Grundlagen der Logistik: Einführung in Theorie und Praxis*, München.

Kugler, M. (2008): Wissenschaft: Der Schatz aus dem Restmüll, in: *„Die Presse"*, Print-Ausgabe, 19.03.2008.

Laarmann, A. (2005): *Lerneffekte in der Produktion*, Wiesbaden.

Lambert, D. M. and J. R. Stock (1981): *Strategic Physical Distribution Management*, Homewood, IL.

Liesegang, D. G. and A. Pischon (1996): Recycling und Downcycling, in: Kern, W., H.-H. Schröder und J. Weber (Hrsg.): *Handwörterbuch der Produktionswirtschaft*, Stuttgart, Sp. 1788–1798.

Malone, T. W. (1999): Tools for inventing Organizations – Towards a handbook of organisational processes. *Management Science*, Vol. 45, No. 3, www.ccs.mit.edu/21/mgtsci.

Martens, H. (2007): *Planung und Steuerung von Produktion und Recycling in kreislaufwirtschaftlich ausgeprägten Unternehmensnetzwerken*, Hamburg.

Miles, R. E. and C. C. Snow (1986): Network Organizations. New Concept for New Forms, in: *California Management Review*, Vol. 28, No. 3, S. 62–73.

Pfohl, H.-C. (2004): *Logistiksysteme – Betriebswirtschaftliche Grundlagen*, Berlin Heidelberg.

Pohlen, T. L. and M. T. Farris (1992): Reverse logistics in plastics Recycling, in: *International Journal of Physical Distribution & Logistics Management*, Vol. 22, No. 7, S. 35–47.

Rudolph, A. (1999): *Altproduktentsorgung aus betriebswirtschaftlicher Sicht*, Heidelberg.

Schneider, B. (1999): *Recycling-Informationssysteme – Integration von Produktion und Recycling*, Wiesbaden.

Schwinn, R. (1993): *Betriebswirtschaftslehre*, München Wien.

Souren, R. (1996): *Theorie betrieblicher Reduktion – Grundlagen, Modellierung und Optimierungsansätze stofflicher Entsorgungsprozesse*, Heidelberg.

Spengler, T. (1994): *Industrielle Demontage- und Recyclingkonzepte – Betriebswirtschaftliche Planungsmodelle zur ökonomisch effizienten Umsetzung abfallrechtlicher Rücknahme und Verwertungspflichten*, Berlin.

Steinhilper, R. und U. Hudelmaier (1993): *Erfolgreiches Produktrecycling zur erneuten Verwendung oder Verwertung – Ein Leitfaden für Unternehmen*, Eschborn.

Stengel, R. v. (1999): *Gestaltung von Wertschöpfungsnetzwerken*, Wiesbaden.

Steven, M., S. Tengler und R. Krüger (2003a): Reverse Logistics (I), in: *Das Wirtschaftsstudium*, Jg. 32, Nr. 5, S. 643–647.

Steven, M. (2003b): Networks in Reverse Logistics, in: Dyckhoff, H., R. Lackes and J. Reese: *Supply Chain Management and Reverse Logistics*, Berlin Heidelberg, S. 163–180.

Stölzle, W. (1993): *Umweltschutz und Entsorgungslogistik – Theoretische Grundlagen mit ersten empirischen Ergebnissen zur innerbetrieblichen Entsorgung*, Berlin.

Sydow, J. (1992): *Strategische Netzwerke – Evolution und Organisation*, Wiesbaden.

Sydow, J. (2003): Management von Netzwerkorganisationen – Zum Stand der Forschung, in: Sydow, J. (Hrsg.): *Management von Netzwerkorganisationen*, Wiesbaden, S. 293–354.

Thierry, M., M. Salomon, J. van Nunen and L. N. van Wassenhove (1995): Strategic Issues in Product Recovery Management, in: *California Management Review*, Vol. 37, No. 2, S. 114–135.

Vahrenkamp, R. and D. C. Mattfeld (2007): *Logistiknetzwerke: Modelle für Standortwahl und Tourenplanung*, Berlin Heidelberg.

Walther, G. (2005): *Recycling von Elektro- und Elektronik-Altgeräten: Strategische Planung von Stoffstrom-Netzen für kleine und mittelständische Unternehmen*, Wiesbaden.

Werner, H. (2008): *Supply Chain Management: Grundlagen, Strategien, Instrumente und Controlling, 3. Aufl.*, Wiesbaden.

Wildemann, H. (1996): Management von Produktions- und Zuliefernetzwerken, in: Wildemann, H. (Hrsg.): *Produktions- und Zuliefernetzwerke*, Tagungsband zur Sitzung der wissenschaftlichen Kommission Produktionswirtschaft im September 1995 in München, München, S. 13–45.

Wildemann, H. (1997): *Trends in der Distributions- und Entsorgungslogistik, Ergebnisse einer Delphi-Studie*, München.

Wittig, A. (2005): *Management von Unternehmensnetzwerken*, Wiesbaden.

Wohlgemuth, O. (2002): *Management netzwerkartiger Kooperationen: Instrumente für die unternehmensübergreifende Steuerung*, Wiesbaden.

Wutz, A. (2008): *Das Produktalterungsmodell und deterministische Losgrößenmodelle im Rahmen von Reverse Logistics*, Hamburg.

Gesetze

Kreislaufwirtschafts- und Abfallgesetz (KrW/AbfG) vom 27. September 1994, zuletzt geändert durch Artikel 2 des Gesetzes vom 19. Juli 2007.

Improving Operations Management by Synthesizing Participant Knowledge and System Data

Etiënne A. J. A. Rouwette and Jac A. M. Vennix

Methodology Department
Faculty of Management
Radboud University Nijmegen

Abstract

With the advent of Enterprise Resource Planning (ERP) systems such as SAP and Oracle, availability of data is no longer the bottleneck to decision making in many organizations. Instead the reverse seems to apply more frequently. Integrated organization-wide computer systems overwhelm managers with data to such an extent that it becomes difficult to assess its relevance for managing operations. A number of methodologies attempt to help management to distill meaning from large amounts of data, such as the Balanced Scorecard, discrete event simulation, qualitative modeling approaches and system dynamics. These methodologies enable managers to identify multiple performance indicators and determine tradeoffs between effects of proposed improvements. Implementation of improvements however entails small or large scale organizational change. Methodologies are commonly used in an expert mode, which makes them prone to many of the potential traps of change management, such as lack of commitment. The approaches can often only be used by experienced consultants. Indeed the literature shows many cases in which ERP systems are not used to their full extent, even though expert consultants supervise implementation months or years after the initial roll-out. Alternative methodologies that enable problem owners to identify problems and combine knowledge and system data in solving these are available. Group model building, which combines system dynamics and active involvement of problem owners, may circumvent the traps to which expert methods are prone. In this chapter we explore three projects in which master students with limited experience used group model building to model and improve operations management. We address the context in which the projects were carried out and the process of client participation and model construction. We describe effects in terms of end products, quality of solutions, results as judged by the clients (such as commitment and implementation) and outcomes of system changes. Our contribution to the literature on ERP systems is a definition of the necessary conditions that need to be in place, in order for group model building to succeed in improving operations management. Our contribution to the group model building literature is a clarification of where the standard process of participative modeling needs to be adapted when used in operations management.

Keywords: ERP systems, user involvement, group model building, system dynamics, operations management, information systems

1 Motivation

Decision making in organizations and in operations management in particular, increasingly profits from integrated information systems across the entire organization. Several benefits are expected to result from implementing these Enterprise Resource Planning (ERP) systems. Integration of business processes and integration of key business and management processes is assumed to lead to a central overview of organizational affairs. Access to enterprise-wide data which provides information-sharing across business processes contributes to coordination and monitoring of performance in real time (Benders, Batenburg, & Van der Blonk, 2006). However, these expected benefits are not always realized as implementation of ERP systems is often incomplete. In this sense ERP systems are not unlike other information systems. According to the Standish Group (2003), ICT projects repeatedly fail to deliver: 15% of projects lead to no result, another 50% are too expensive, too late and/or produce outcomes of low quality and only 35% are successful on all relevant criteria. Several studies are conducted about success and failure of ERP projects (Davenport, 1998; Fahy, 2002; Hall, 2002; Trunick, 1999). Trunick (1999) for example estimates that 40% of ERP projects are only partly completed and 20% are a total failure. The reasons for this lack of implementation and ways to change this situation have been studied for a number of years now.

The literature cites human factors as the main reason for implementation failure. In an overview of implementation research, Muscatello and Parente (2006) find that many authors see user related issues, and not the technology itself, as the main causes of failure. Changing over to an ERP system is more than starting to use a new technology. ERP providers maintain that their systems capture the best business practices. An ERP system is thus also a new 'way of doing business' (Mabert, Soni, & Venkataramanan, 2003), which may threaten the existing power positions of individuals in the organization. ERP systems are an innovation (Benders et al., 2006) and organizational adoption can be slow or incomplete. The most common reason for failure of ERP projects is that end users are not willing to adopt the new system (Nah, Tan, & The, 2004). ERP providers offer support methods to facilitate implementation of their specific systems (Benders et al., 2006: 199). SAP has developed ASAP (Accelerated SAP) to facilitate implementation of SAP R/3. Oracle has developed FastTrack. The focus of these support methods is on standardizing the implementation trajectory and project management. These methods operate on the premise that the organization will have to adapt to the system, instead of vice versa. In essence approaches such as ASAP and FastTrack are expert based. Amoako-Gyampah (2007) cites evidence that user-focused approaches, such as communication and training programs, increase the use of ERP. A more fundamental way of focusing on the user, user involvement in system development, is potentially even more effective in increasing system use. However, there is a clear tension between implementing best industry practice and involving users in system development.

While changing the way of doing business is perhaps an effect of ERP systems that is not always expected by their users, systems also offer a challenge to organizations exactly because of their intended use. ERP systems present and integrate enterprise-wide data. In doing so, they may overwhelm users and make it difficult to separate important from unimportant facts. A client in one of the projects described in this paper formulated this as: *'I am up to my knees in data and I have no idea on the structure behind it'*. Several methodologies are available to provide and analyze this structure. A generic approach such as the Balanced Scorecard (Kaplan & Norton, 1996, 2004) facilitates the identification of performance indicators. Other methodologies offer a structure in the form of a simulation model or (qualitative) map of the enterprise. Banker and Kaufmann (2004) discuss the use of discrete event and continuous simulation approaches to information systems development. While these methodologies are commonly used in an expert mode, a number of facilitated modeling approaches are used for information systems development as well. Examples are Soft Systems Methodology (Checkland & Holwell,

1998; Checkland & Poulter, 2006) and cognitive mapping (Ackermann & Eden, 2005). A general discussion on the use of causal mapping for information systems development is given by Hodgkinson and Clarkson (2005). These facilitated modeling approaches clearly surface the opinions of users. They do not directly support contrasting opinions with system data.

In summary, implementation and deducting sensible process improvements from large amounts of data are recurring problems in ERP system use. Approaches developed to tackle the first problem are offered by system providers. These methodologies facilitate implementation by focusing on project management rather than on user involvement in system design. The second problem is addressed by approaches such as the Balanced Scorecard and simulation. These methodologies are expert based. Facilitated modeling approaches are available but do not allow for combining problem owners' opinions with system data. This in effect means that we are loosing out on one of the main strengths of ERP systems. It seems there is room for a methodology that combines user involvement with simulation. Group model building, based on system dynamics, is one of these methodologies. System dynamics originated in the 1950s as industrial dynamics (Forrester, 1958) and has been applied to operations management since. Recently, Milling (1996; Milling, 2002) reviewed its use in innovation processes. Größler, Thun and Milling (2008) propose to use system dynamics as a general theory for operations management. Client involvement has been a topic of interest in system dynamics modeling since the 1970s (e.g. Roberts, 1973). A couple of approaches for involving clients have been developed and used in practice (for an overview, see Andersen, Vennix, Richardson, & Rouwette, 2007). In this paper we use group model building as a general term for system dynamics modeling in cooperation with clients. Group model building has much in common with other participatory modeling approaches, particularly in operational research. Facilitated modeling methods in operational research are commonly called Problem Structuring Methods (PSMs). Practitioners from the system dynamics and PSM fields have frequently compared their approaches, borrowed from each other's techniques or discussed their methodological assumptions (see for example the papers at the 1994 International System Dynamics Conference; the special issue of System Dynamics Review on group model building; Howick, Ackermann, & Andersen, 2006; Lane, 1994).

Group model building enables user involvement and the integration of problem owners' opinions with system data. In this paper we focus on the contribution group model building may have in ERP system implementation. Are the expected benefits of group model building realized in an ERP context? Does the generic procedure for group model building need to be adapted in this context? We use three master thesis projects as cases to provide an exploratory answer to these questions. The remainder of this paper is structured as follows. The next section describes our approach to case analysis. An existing framework for reviewing group model building cases, based on a study by Rouwette, Vennix and Van Mullekom (2002) will be used to distill the essential elements of our cases. Following this framework, we then describe the context, process and outcome of the three applications of group model building. We end by listing our conclusions on benefits and process adaptations of group model building in an ERP context.

2 Approach to Case Analysis

Rouwette et al. (2002) have conducted a meta-analysis of 107 cases of client involvement in system dynamics modeling. Following Pawson and Tilley (1997), they argue that modeling interventions may have different impacts because the context in which they are used is subtly different, or because modeling techniques are not exactly similar from one context to another. For instance, a modeling intervention might take place in a politically sensitive situation, in which some participants have "hidden" agendas and use the project to advance their own interests. As a result, participants might not reveal all relevant information. Another intervention might focus on an issue in which all participants share an interest and data are readily available. In the first example, an initial simulation model might be built but validation may be incomplete due to a lack of client interest and data availability. In the second case, available data allow the model to be validated and used to test policy options against a variety of scenarios. Clearly the context and process (or mechanism) shape the projects' results in both cases. Pawson and Tilley (1997) argue that a realistic accumulation of evaluation studies boils down to discovering which combinations of mechanism and context lead to which outcomes. Hence the second goal of this paper: to produce meaningful and potentially robust patterns of interventions, contexts and outcomes. Rouwette et al. (2002) propose to focus analysis of group model building cases on the following central elements:

Context
- Background: authors, title, source, date of publication
- Organization: profit, sector, name and size organization, location, consultant
- Problem: motive, research question and type, importance, implementation expected

Mechanism
- Intervention: techniques used, type of model, phases of modeling and participation, number and functions of participants, sources of information, software and other materials, time span of project

Outcome
- Impact: research design, data collection method, subjects, researchers, time span, way of feedback (report and presentation), outcome variables

We add the following factors to the list of elements proposed above. With regard to context, we also include the type of ERP system in the case. With regard to mechanism, our second research question calls for a comparison to the generic modeling approach. A generic process for modeling is available in the form of Hines' approach (Otto & Struben, 2004). Hines' approach includes the following steps:

- Diagnose the problem: gather and cluster problem variables, visualize problem by drawing the reference mode of behavior.
- Visualize model structure in a causal diagram, using the problem variables.
- Identify accumulations in the system, to form the stocks in the model.
- Construct the computer model. In this step most work is done by the modelers, with client participation limited to providing data such as numerical values and details of the work processes relevant to the problem at hand. Model structure and behavior is then explained to the client. Discussions with the client then lead to a series of model iterations, increasing confidence of the client in model calibration and validity.
- Simulate policies to test proposed interventions in the problem.

In our discussion of the process, we will compare the steps and techniques used in the cases to Hines' generic approach.

With regard to outcomes we look at a number of intended results of group model building in particular. By bringing the parties involved in the problem together and facilitating a joint modeling effort with these parties, group model building is expected to create a more shared view on the problem and on actions available to improve the situation (Andersen et al., 2007; Richardson & Andersen, 1995; Vennix, 1996; Vennix, Akkermans, & Rouwette, 1996). The system dynamics model created in this joint effort aims to explain problematic behavior by capturing the essential structure of the problem. Thus group model building aims for two sets of outcomes. The first are outcomes related to participants' direct involvement in modeling:

- improved quality of communication,
- mental model change or insight,
- consensus and
- commitment with regard to proposed actions in the problem.

These goals are important not only because they guarantee a high quality input for modeling but more so because each decision maker is thought to have a degree of discretion in implementing options: commitment of those involved in the problem is instrumental in implementing conclusions of the modeling effort. The second set of outcomes concerns the technical goals of modeling. The model should be technically correct in the sense that it passes a set of validation tests (e.g. Forrester & Senge, 1980). Simulations with the model should point to high leverage points for steering problematic behavior in the right direction, and these high leverage points should logically connect to proposed options in the real world.

In the following, we describe three cases in which ERP users were involved in system dynamics modeling using this framework.

3 Context

Context factors for the three cases are listed in the Table 1 (see p. 272) below. The cases are described in three master theses (Ewalts, 2005; Goedhart, 2002; Venderbosch, 2007) available from Radboud University Nijmegen, The Netherlands. The third case is also reported in a conference paper (Deenen, 2007a) and master thesis from Delft University (Deenen, 2007b).

The three modeling cases take place in profit organizations in the production sector. All organizations are divisions of multinationals based in the Netherlands. The information systems in the three cases were SAP and Hyperion (a financial planning system), SAP and Mercia (a forecasting program) and the SAP PM module, respectively. The consultants in all cases were master students with limited experience in system dynamics and group model building, coached by supervisors from Radboud University (and from Delft University in the third case). In the research by Rouwette et al. (2002), research questions were coded as explorative, descriptive, explanatory and/or prescriptive. In line with most system dynamics modeling efforts, the research questions that prompted the projects contained an explanatory and prescriptive part. In the first case, the research problem concerns the sales and operating planning process of Vinamul Polymers Europe. The financial forecast is critical for completion of the management review but frequently finalized behind schedule. The goal of the modeling project is to integrate available system information with judgments by staff for constructing the financial forecast. The second case, at Akzo Nobel, concerns logistical performance. The performance on indica-

Table 1: Context Factors

	Goedhart (2002)	Ewalts (2005)	Venderbosch (2007)
Organization name	Vinamul Polymers (National Starch and Chemical Company)	Akzo Nobel Decorative Coatings Europe	ONEgas (NAM/Shell)
Organization type	Profit, chemics	Profit, chemics	Profit, oil and gas
Organization size	Parent company 10,000 employees in 38 countries, case site Geleen 140 employees	Parent company 64,000 employees in 80 countries, case site Darwen 650 employees	Parent company 104,000 employees in 110 countries, case site Assen 2,500 employees
ERP	SAP, Hyperion	SAP, Mercia	SAP PM module
Consultant	Author	Author	Author and second master student
Problem and research question	How can judgmental and quantitative elements be integrated in a forecast?	How can logistic performance be explained and improved?	How can corrective maintenance performance be explained and optimized?
Problem type	Explanatory/prescriptive	Explanatory/prescriptive	Explanatory/prescriptive
Problem importance	Project initiated by client	Project initiated by client	Project initiated by client Importance high (pretest and posttest)

tors such as service level, inventory level, costs and replenishments lead-time is lower than desired. The previous quote on the need for structure started off the modeling project in the third case. ONEgas had been using a SAP module supporting the corrective maintenance process for several years, but was not able to identify levers for improving performance.

In all cases the project was initiated by the client organization, indicating that the problem was felt to be important and clients expected results that could be implemented in their organization. In the third case participants filled out a pretest and posttest questionnaire. In both the pretest and posttest subjects were asked to rate the importance of the issue to their organization and to them individually. All mean scores are significantly higher than neutral, indicating that the problem is important in the eyes of the participants.

Important similarities between case contexts are the following. In all projects a crucial phase of the firms' operations is modeled. Clients feel the issues are important. Modeling and session facilitation is done by master students with limited experience.

4 Mechanism

The central part of the mechanism or process description by Rouwette et al. (2002) is how the client was involved in the different phases of modeling. Andersen and Richardson have coined the term 'scripts' to refer to specific techniques of involving clients (1997; Luna-Reyes et al., 2006). Scripts are specific parts of modeling sessions in which the consultant and participants interact, usually taking 15 minutes or less. An example of a script that can be used in the phase of problem definition, is eliciting reference modes. Employing this script means that the consultants first asks the group to identify the time horizon of interest for this problem. Second, the group is invited to think of important 'dynamic success measures' that should be or are the focus of management attention. The group then draws the graph over time of the success measure over the specified time horizon. If the same success measure is depicted differently by different group members, this can be the focus of a discussion. Conclusions from the discussion and the completed graphs are used as a basis for the model in the remainder of the project. In addition to scripts (techniques used), the mechanism is also described by listing the type and size of the model, participants involved, sources of information used, software and time span of the project. The following Table 2 summarizes the mechanism elements in the three modeling cases.

Table 2: Mechanism Factors

	Goedhart (2002)	Ewalts (2005)	Venderbosch (2007)
Techniques used	Sessions, CLDs, formalization in spreadsheet	Interviews, CLD, sessions, parameter estimation, s&f, formalization, workbooks	Interviews, sessions, NGT, s&f, scenarios, workbooks
Type of model	Quantitative	Quantitative	Quantitative
Model size	Large: top level view 33 variables, structure repeated for 29 customers	Large: top level view 45variables, structure repeated for three categories of products	Large: top level view 45 variables, structure repeated for seven categories of priorities
Phases of modeling and participation	All Researcher responsible for formalization, validation, testing	All Researcher responsible for formalization, validation, testing	All Participants involved in all phases
Number and functions of participants	Per session 2 participants: financial manager and accountant, production managers in small sessions, senior management in presentations	On each site 6 or 7 managers: demand, product, logistic, supply chain, distribution, production leader and production planner	Per session 5 to 13 managers maintenance
Sources of information	Participants, database	Participants, database	Participants, database
Software and other materials	Vensim (CLD), Excel	Vensim	Dynaplan, Powersim
Time span of project	May–Oct 2002	Feb–August 2005	March–Sept 2007

4.1 Mechanism Case 1: Vinamul

The process followed in case 1 is shown in the following Figure 1.

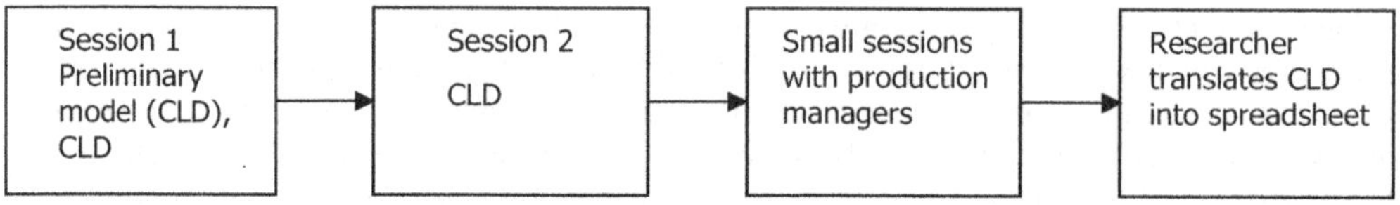

Figure 1: Process Followed in Case 1

In the first case, two sessions were used to construct the model. The first session involved the financial manager and an accountant. The session started by a presentation of a small preliminary model constructed by the consultant. The model consisted of variables explaining trading profit. In the session a causal loop diagram (CLD) was constructed, describing the different elements of the financial forecasting process. Participants identified a specific model variable, raw material container costs, as a very volatile factor and thus difficult to model. In the second session the same persons participated. Most important for explaining trading profit was volume sold and gross sales. The final model organizes the variables in a hierarchy, starting from trading profit, the main categories of revenue and costs and lower levels of increasing detail. This model was checked and adapted on the basis of discussions with production managers. The causal loop diagram was then translated into a formal model in the form of an Excel spreadsheet, using data from the financial system. Excel was chosen to formalize the model as data were available in spreadsheet format, Excel was used in financial planning in this company and financial managers and senior management were familiar with the tool. The top level view of the final model contains 33 variables. The structure is repeated for 29 key customers and simulates two years ahead in time on a monthly basis. The final model and recommendations were captured in a report and a presentation to senior management. The total project took about six months.

4.2 Mechanism Case 2: Akzo Nobel

The process followed in case 2 is shown in the following Figure 2.

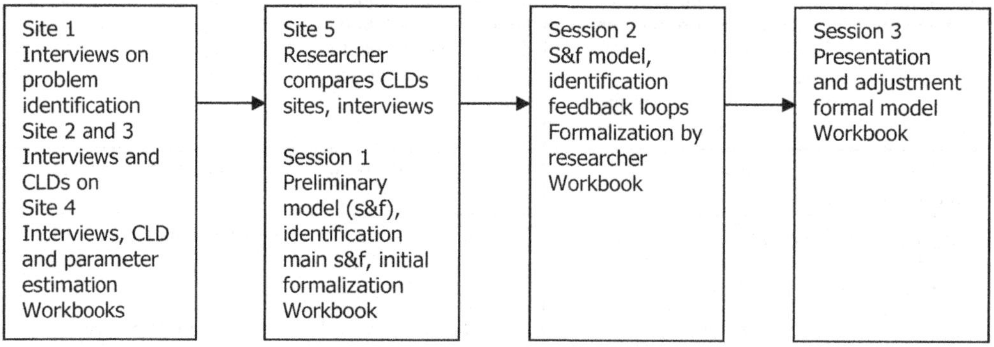

Figure 2: Process Followed in Case 2

In the second case the project started by visiting four different production sites of the client company. The modeler spent one week at each site. During the first visit (Cologne), production managers were interviewed to identify the central problem. The following visits (Adrian, Sege and Groot Ammers) were again used to interview production managers. Interviewees then constructed causal loop diagrams in two sessions at each site. In the last of the four site visits, data were gathered for initial parameter estimation. The formal model was constructed on a fifth site (Darwen). Before the modeling sessions in Darwen, the researcher compared the qualitative models constructed at the different sites and interviewed participants. The first modeling session started with the presentation of a preliminary stocks and flows (S&F) model which included the company's key performance indicators for the logistic process. During the session the main stocks and flows in the model were identified. At the end of the session participants spent some time on gathering data for formalizing the model. Results of this and subsequent sessions were reported back in the form of a workbook. The second session addressed the feedback loops in the model. After the session the researcher formalized the model. In the third and final meeting this model was presented and adjusted on the basis of participants' comments. The top level view of the final model contains 45 variables. Each plant produces a large variety of paints and its inventory contains thousands of stock keeping units. These products were thus categorized into three different product types and the model structure was repeated for each. The time horizon for the model was two years, run on a daily basis. The final model and recommendations were captured in a report and presented to senior management. The total project took about seven months.

4.3 Mechanism Case 3: ONEgas

The process followed in case 3 is shown in the following Figure 3.

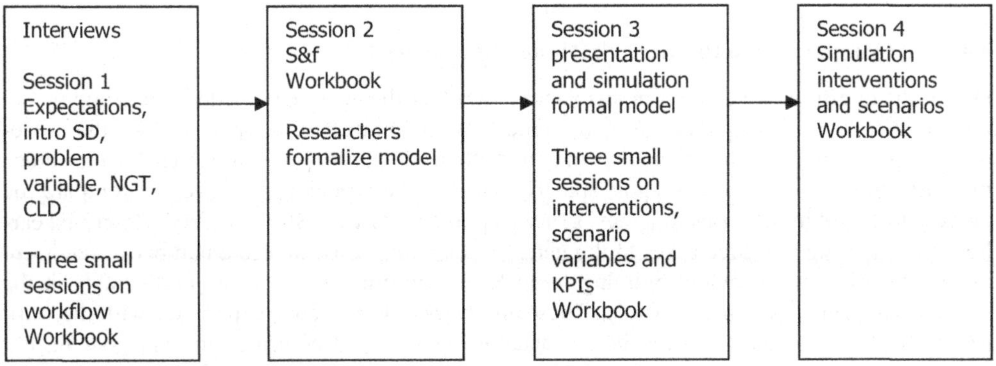

Figure 3: Process Followed in Case 3

In the third case the project started by a round of interviews. The first session addressed participants' expectations of the process followed by a short introduction of system dynamics. The participants, 13 in total, then identified the central problem variable. Nominal Group Technique (individual notation of ideas on paper, followed by bringing ideas to the board in a round robin fashion) was used to identify model variables. No preliminary model was used, although the researcher feels that this would have been useful to speed up the process. In the session a small causal loop diagram model was constructed. The initial problem variable, compliance (finishing maintenance projects before a set deadline) proved to be too distant from factors in the work process. Participants referred to a basic flow model of the work process, constructed in an earlier project. The group decided to use this model as a starting point and the focus shifted to identifying the subsequent phases in the work process and factors influencing these. Modelers and participants agreed that the specialized knowledge on the workflow would be most easily accessed in sessions with experts instead of in plenary sessions. In three sessions, two to three experts on the workflow elaborated the initial model. Similar to the Akzo Nobel case, results of this and subsequent sessions were reported back in the form of a workbook. In the second plenary session 10 managers participated. Participants created an integrated stocks and flows model on the basis of the previous models. The researchers then used data from the SAP system to quantify the model. In SAP maintenance projects were subdivided into seven different priorities, and this structure was followed in the model. The next session was planned after the first simulation results were available. The third session took place around the time of a production shutdown and only five people participated. In this meeting the formal model was presented and simulation results shown. The participants agreed that the model captured the essence of the maintenance process. They wanted to proceed to use the model to test policy interventions in different scenarios. Three additional sessions in small groups helped in identifying interventions, scenario variables and key performance indicators. The fourth and final session presented conclusions and ways of improving the maintenance process. The top level view of the final model contains 45 variables. The structure is repeated for seven types of maintenance projects and simulates three years on a monthly basis. The final model and recommendations were captured in a report and a presentation to management. The total project took about seven months.

4.4 Comparison to the Generic Modeling Process

One of the questions we address in this paper is whether the generic procedure for group model building needs to be adapted in an ERP context. As the notion of 'scripts' implies, the procedure for constructing system dynamics models with participants is very versatile. A wide choice of techniques is available to support specific parts of the modeling process. We compare the process followed in the cases to Hines' generic approach (Otto & Struben, 2004) described earlier. In comparing the three cases to the generic modeling steps, we see a number of recurrent themes in using group model building in an ERP environment. First, the participants in the sessions are primarily content experts. These are the people that have experience with the work process to be modeled. Final results are usually reported and presented to management, but senior managers are not present in the sessions. A management flight simulator, as used in the third case, is a way of engaging senior management that transfers insights in a time-efficient manner.

Second, only in the last case no preliminary model was used. Subsequently it proved difficult to find a central problem variable and focus for the model: compliance was proposed but proved too distant from daily work operations. Only after a basic flow model of the work process was identified to which participants were already familiar, did the modeling process take up speed. Vennix (1996) points out several advantages and disadvantages of using a preliminary model.

Its use accelerates the modeling process as it focuses the initial discussion, avoiding time spent on finding the central relevant problem variable. An inexperienced facilitator will find it easier to guide these model-based discussions than to facilitate wide-ranging deliberations on what should be the focus of the model or even the project. A possible disadvantage of using a preliminary model is loss of ownership over modeling outcomes, as participants have not created the complete model themselves. However, the advantages seem to outweigh the disadvantages in this context. Models in an ERP context focus on a work process and participants usually are familiar with basic work flow diagrams. A preliminary model that captures the basic work flow in system dynamics terms is thus a logical starting point for a modeling project.

A third point is the type of model used. Although the phases in a workflow closely correspond to a stocks and flows model, initial models are in the form of causal diagrams in the first and third case. In the first case, the goal is to explain and predict trading profit, by specifying underlying components in more and more detail. Here causal relations are central and separating accumulations from flows might not have added much benefit in this case. In the third case the change to a stocks and flows model was made immediately after the first session as the work process became central to the modeling effort. A general conclusion is that when a work process is concerned, using a stocks and flows model seems most beneficial as it clearly shows different work phases. A related issue is that all cases start by using a qualitative model. Richardson (2006) provides guidelines on how to use formal preliminary models. Since in all cases data are available, using a formal model as a starting point is possible. This may speed up the modeling process further.

A fourth issue is client participation in model formalization. In Hines' approach the modeler has the lead here and checks results in sessions with participants. In the three cases, small groups were frequently used to conceptualize and find data on specific model parts. Participants also help the modeler in obtaining access to ERP data. Another striking point is that the similarity of model output to ERP data is an important face validity check for participants. Nevertheless, similarity to ERP data does not mean similarity to real life work processes. Frequently participants' experience and knowledge were needed to explain unexpected data in the ERP system. In this way participants' opinions and system data are clearly complementary.

Fifth, in all projects a model with relatively limited feedback complexity is created, but multiple units are captured in the structure (29 customers, three product categories, seven priorities, respectively). This is in line with Rouwette and Hoppenbrouwers' (2008) observation that system dynamics models are high in feedback complexity, while information systems models are high in detail complexity.

Finally, the first project seems to be different in comparison to the generic modeling process and both other cases. In the Vinamul case, the first session focuses on the system rather than the problem. The model does not contain feedback, which makes it possible to capture the formal model in Excel. Since this is a package participants are experienced with, this makes the model transparent and user friendly. According to Goedhart (2002: 44), the model *'should have the same structure as output of the forecasting model, for the ease of use, ease of interpretation and ease of implementation to forecasters, users and senior management'*. Although group model building elements are used in the first case, the resulting formal model cannot be described as a system dynamics model as it does not contain feedback or accumulations.

5 Outcome

In the foregoing we identified two sets of intended outcomes of group model building. Benefits of participating in modeling are thought to be an increase in quality of communication, insight, consensus and commitment. Technical goals of modeling include a valid model and identification of steering points to improve the problematic situation. In addition to intended benefits of modeling, Rouwette et al. (2002) look at how evidence on outcomes is gathered by coding research design, data collection method, subjects, researchers, time span and feedback to the client. The following Table 3 lists the outcome variables for the three cases. Note that the number of subjects in the evaluation may be lower than the total number of participants.

Table 3: Outcome Factors

	Goedhart (2002)	**Ewalts (2005)**	**Venderbosch (2007)**
Research design	Case study	Case study	One group pretest posttest
Data collection method	Session observations, participatory observation, interviews	Post questionnaires, session observation	Pre and post questionnaires, session observation
Subjects	2 managers	12 managers	12 managers
Researchers	Consultant	Consultant	Consultant
Time span	Project	Project	Project
Feedback to client	Report, presentation	Report, presentation	Report, presentation, MFS
Outcome variables	Learning, commitment, responsibility for continued use	CICC Comparison to regular meetings Elements GMB Efficiency and success	A, SN, PBC, I: PBC and I change CICC Comparison to regular meetings Elements GMB Efficiency and success

The first case uses a case study design to determine impact of the modeling project. The researcher gathers data by working in the client organization for the duration of the project, conducts interviews and observes sessions. The researcher is the same person as the modeler and the two managers involved in the sessions are the research subjects. The research is limited to the project (no measurements before or after the project are done). The feedback to the client consists of a report and a presentation. The master thesis (Goedhart, 2002: 53) contains conclusions on learning by subjects in the modeling project, commitment to results and expected continued use of the model: *'The implementation of the forecasting model is, because the involvement of users in the model building process, relatively easy. The finance department is aware of the model structure and functions.'*

'The finance department is responsible for the total forecasting model. They fully control and own the forecasting model.'

The second project also uses a case study design. The researcher is the same person as the modeler and 12 managers involved in the sessions are the research subjects. The research is limited to the project. The feedback to the client consists of a report and a presentation. Data are gathered using project observations as well as a posttest questionnaire on impacts of the project. The questionnaire is based on work by Vennix and colleagues and described by Vennix and Rouwette (2000) and contains questions on communication, mental model change or insight, consensus, commitment (CICC), a comparison of the group model building (GMB) sessions to regular meetings, the contribution of elements of modeling (for instance the facilitator or group discussion), project efficiency and success. Similar to the cases reported by Vennix and Rouwette (2000), results are in line with expectations.

The third project uses a one group pretest posttest design. Again, the researcher is the same person as the modeler and 12 managers involved in the sessions are the research subjects. The research is limited to the project (pretest and posttest are administered immediately before and after the project). The feedback to the client consists of a report, presentation and a management flight simulator. Data are gathered using project observations as well as a pretest and posttest questionnaire. The questionnaire consists of the CICC questionnaire described above and items based on work by Rouwette (2003). Rouwette proposes to conceptualize the impact of modeling, by focusing on the relation of modeling to changes in participants' behavior. Ajzen (2001) sees intentions as the immediate antecedent of behavior. Intentions (I) are in turn explained by attitudes toward behavior (A), subjective norms (SN) and perceived behavioral control (PBC). A similar conceptual model is used to explain user acceptance of ERP systems (Amoako-Gyampah, 2007; Nah et al., 2004). In the case on ONEgas, only intentions and perceived behavioral control are found to change over the course of the modeling interventions. Results of the CICC questionnaire are in line with expectations.

We can conclude that group model building in these cases indeed seems to have contributed to improved quality of communication, insight, consensus and commitment with regard to proposed actions in the problem. In the third case, where more specific measures were used, the project results in change in perceived behavioral control and intentions. Learning effects are illustrated by the fact that while all projects started out by focusing on one key performance indicator, important additional indicators were identified over the course of the modeling project identified. In this sense participants' problem view has broadened. The quality of the model is high judged in the eyes of participants.

6 Conclusions

We started this paper with a description of methodologies for fostering client involvement in ERP system implementation and deduction of interventions from large amounts of system data. Methodologies include approaches developed by ERP providers, the Balanced Scorecard, simulation and qualitative mapping. We identified group model building as a possible candidate for combining client involvement and identification of system improvements. We focused on two questions in particular: First, are the expected benefits of group model building realized in an ERP context? Second, does the generic procedure for group model building need to be adapted in this context?

With regard to outcomes, group model building in an ERP setting seems to result in positive effects such as learning, improved communication, consensus and commitment. The quality of the model is high judged in the eyes of participants. A limitation of this study is that actual implementation in the client organizations, and whether or not expected improvements in work processes were realized, are not considered. On the basis of three cases, we identified five points in which the generic group model building approach is adapted in an ERP context:

1. Participants in the sessions are primarily content experts. Senior management is typically informed about the modeling outcomes via a report or presentation. A management flight simulator may be used to transfer insights to senior management in a time-efficient and engaging manner.
2. A preliminary model that captures the basic work flow in system dynamics terms is a logical starting point for an ERP modeling project.
3. A stocks and flows model corresponds most closely to participants' conceptualization of a work flow. A formal preliminary model may speed up the modeling process.
4. Similarity of model output to ERP data is an important face validity check for participants.
5. Projects tend to result in models of relatively limited feedback complexity but high detail complexity.

Our contribution to the literature on Enterprise Resource Planning is the description of a methodology for ERP system implementation and deduction of interventions from ERP data. We describe the essential elements of such a methodology by outlining context, process and outcome of three cases. Our contribution to the group model building literature is a clarification of where the standard process of participative modeling needs to be adapted when used in ERP systems modeling.

Further research may focus on two issues: how modeling of workflows is impacted by different organizational settings and on the extent of client involvement in group model building. Other organizational settings may include workflows in nonprofit settings and/ or multiple organization settings. Checking of tax forms is an example of a complicated work process managed by a single government organization. The criminal justice chain is a workflow involving police, public prosecution, judges and prison administration (Rouwette & Vennix, submitted). Experiences so far suggest that the organizational setting does not have a large impact on the modeling process. Nevertheless, it is conceivable that implementation of conclusions is more difficult – in a nonprofit setting because multiple goals are operational, and in a multi-organizational setting because actors are more independent from one another. This issue deserves to be explored further. The second issue concerns whether group model building is in essence not another way of adapting the organization to the proposed system. Methods developed by ERP providers, such as Accelerated SAP, operate on the premise that the organization will have to adapt to the system. Is the use of group model building really different in this respect, since it focuses on improvement of the existing work flow? Snabe and Größler (2006) report on a facilitated modeling project in which the strategic goal is already set. Participants are invited to identify the way in which these preset goals may be reached. How does this setting influence participants' expectations and evaluations of the modeling project? A comparison of cases in which decision are open to cases in which goals are (partially) set may shed more light on this question.

References

Ackermann, F., and C. Eden (2005): Using causal mapping to support Information Systems development: some considerations. In: Narayanan, V. und D. Armstrong (eds.): *Causal mapping for research in Information Technology*, Hershey, PA: Idea Group Publishing, 263–283.

Ajzen, I. (2001): Nature and operation of attitudes. *Annu. Rev. Psychol.* 52: 27–58.

Amoako-Gyampah, K. (2007): Perceived usefulness, user involvement and behavioural intention: an empirical study of ERP implementation. *Computers in Human Behaviour* 23: 1232–1248.

Andersen, D., and G. Richardson (1997): Scripts for group model building. *Syst. Dyn. Rev.* 13: 107–129.

Andersen, D. F., J. A. M. Vennix, G. P. Richardson and E. A. J. A. Rouwette (2007): Group model building: problem structuring, policy simulation and decision support. *J. Oper. Res. Soc.* 58(5): 691–694.

Banker, R., and R. Kaufmann (2004): The evolution of research on information systems. A fiftieth year survey of the literature in Management Science. *Manage. Sci.* 50(3): 281–298.

Benders, J., R. Batenburg and H. van der Blonk (2006): Sticking to standards; technical and other isomorphic pressures in deploying ERP-systerns. *Information & Management* 43(2): 194–203.

Checkland, P., and S. Holwell (1998): *Information, systems and information systems*. Chichester: Wiley.

Checkland, P., and J. Poulter (2006): *Learning for action. A short definitive account of Soft Systems Methodology and its use for practitioners, teachers and students*. Chichester: Wiley.

Davenport, T. H. (1998): Putting the enterprise into the enterprise system. *Harvard Business Review* 76(4): 121–131.

Deenen, R. E. M. (2007a): *Maintenance performance improvement with system dynamics: a corrective maintenance showcase*. Paper presented at the ISDC, Athens, Greece.

Deenen, R. E. M. (2007b): *Performance improvement of a corrective maintenance process. A showcase of a system dynamics approach*. TU Delft, Delft.

Ewalts, D. (2005): *Painting by numbers*. Radboud University Nijmegen, Nijmegen.

Fahy, M. (2002): *Enterprise Resource Planning Systems*. London.

Forrester, J. (1958): Industrial dynamics. A major breakthrough for decision makers. *Harvard Business Review* (July–August): 37–66.

Forrester, J., and P. Senge (1980): Tests for building confidence in system dynamics models. *TIMS Studies in the Management Sciences* 14: 209–228.

Goedhart, K. (2002): *Bringing judgement into a forecasting model.* Radboud University Nijmegen, Nijmegen.

Größler, A., J. H. Thun and P. M. Milling (2008): System dynamics as a structural theory in operations management. *Production and operations management* 17(3): 373–384.

Hall, R. (2002): Enterprise resource planning systems and organizational change: transforming work organization? *Strategic Change* 11: 263–270.

Hodgkinson, G., and G. Clarkson (2005): What have we learned from almost 30 years of research on causal mapping? Methodological lessons and choices for the Information Systems and Information Technology communities. In: Narayanan, V. and D. Armstrong (eds.): *Causal mapping for research in Information Technology,* Hershey, PA: Idea Group Publishing, 46–80.

Howick, S., F. Ackermann and D. Andersen (2006): Linking event thinking with structural thinking: methods to improve client value in projects. *Syst. Dyn. Rev.* 22(2): 113–140.

Kaplan, R. S., and D. P. Norton (1996): *The balanced scorecard: translating strategy into action*. Boston, MA: Harvard Business School Press.

Kaplan, R. S., and D. P. Norton (2004): *Strategy maps: converting intangible assets into tangible outcomes*. Boston, MA: Harvard Business School Press.

Lane, D. C. (1994): With a little help from our friends. How system dynamics and soft OR can learn from each other. *Syst. Dyn. Rev.* 10(2/3): 101–134.

Luna-Reyes, L., I. Martinez-Moyano, T. Pardo, A. Cresswell, D. Andersen and G. Richardson (2006): Anatomy of a group model-building intervention: building dynamic theory from case study research. *Syst. Dyn. Rev.* 22(4): 291–320.

Mabert, V. A., A. Soni and M. A. Venkataramanan (2003): Enterprise resource planning: managing the implementation process. *Eur. J. Oper. Res.* 146(2): 302–314.

Milling, P. M. (1996): Modeling innovation processes for decision support and management simulation. *Syst. Dyn. Rev.* 12(3): 211–234.

Milling, P. M. (2002): Understanding and managing innovation processes. *Syst. Dyn. Rev.* 18(1): 73–86.

Muscatello, R., and D. H. Parente (2006): Enterprise Resource Planning (ERP): A Postimplementation Cross-Case Analysis. *Information Resource Management Journal* 19(3): 61–80.

Nah, F., Tan, X., and S. H. The (2004): An Empirical Investigation on End-Users' Acceptance of Enterprise Systems. *Information Resource Management Journal* 17(3): 32–53.

Otto, P., and J. Struben (2004): Gloucester fishery: insights from a group modeling intervention. *Syst. Dyn. Rev.* 20(4): 287–312.

Pawson, R., and N. Tilley (1997): *Realistic evaluation*. London: Sage.

Richardson, G. (2006): *Concept models*. Paper presented at the International Conference of the System Dynamics Society, Nijmegen, The Netherlands.

Richardson, G., and D. Andersen (1995): Teamwork in group model building. *Syst. Dyn. Rev.* 11(2): 113–137.

Roberts, E. (1973): Strategies for effective implementation of complex corporate models. *TIMS-ORSA Interfaces* 8(1, part 1): 26–33.

Rouwette, E. A. J. A. (2003): *Group model building as mutual persuasion*. Nijmegen: Wolf Legal Publishers.

Rouwette, E. A. J. A., and Hoppenbrouwers, S. (2008): *Collaborative systems modeling and group model building: a useful combination?* Paper presented at the System Dynamics Conference Athens.

Rouwette, E. A. J. A., and J. A. M. Vennix (submitted): Modeling crime control in the Netherlands: insights on process. *Eur. J. Oper. Res.*

Rouwette, E. A. J. A., J. A. M. Vennix and T. van Mullekom (2002): Group model building effectiveness. A review of assessment studies. *Syst. Dyn. Rev.* 18(1): 5–45.

Snabe, B., and A. Größler (2006): System dynamics modelling for strategy implementation – Case study and issues. *Syst. Res. Behav. Sci.* 23(4): 467–481.

The Standish Group, T. S. (2003): *Chaos Chronicles Version 3.0*. West Yarmouth, MA.

Trunick, P. (1999): ERP: Promise or pipe dream? *Transportation and Distribution* 40(1): 23–26.

Venderbosch, T. (2007): *Using Group Model Building to optimize the maintenance process in an ERP environment at ONEgas*. Radboud University Nijmegen, Nijmegen.

Vennix, J. (1996): *Group model building. Facilitating team learning using system dynamics*. Chichester: Wiley.

Vennix, J. A. M., H. A. Akkermans and E. A. J. A. Rouwette (1996): Group model building to facilitate organisational change. An exploratory study. *Syst. Dyn. Rev.* 12(1): 39–58.

Vennix, J. A. M., and E. A. J. A. Rouwette (2000): *Group model building. What does the client think of it now?* Paper presented at the International System Dynamics Conference, Bergen, Norway.

Methodologische Fragestellungen des Produktionsmanagements

A Pilot Study for Testing the Effect of Stock and Flow Thinking on Stock and Flow Management Performance

Jürgen Strohhecker

Frankfurt School of Finance and Management, Frankfurt am Main

Abstract

The stock and flow management (SFM) problem is of high relevance for a broad range of decision makers in society, business, and personal affairs. Although in some areas highly sophisticated models and control concepts have been developed, the phenomena of excess stock and shortages are omnipresent. One recent explanation for these observations is offered by a stream of research, which finds evidence for widespread and persistent deficits in stock-flow thinking (SFT) capabilities even among well-educated adults. Building on this explanation, an attempt is made to test the hypothesis that the better people understand accumulation, the higher will be their performance in SFM tasks. However, the results of a small sample pilot study indicate falsification. Therefore, Ackerman's PPIK theory is introduced and used to formulate an elaborate causal model, which could be tested in future research.

Keywords: Accumulation, Bathtub Dynamics, Dynamic decision making, Intelligence, Stocks and flows, Stock-flow failure, System Dynamics

1 Introduction – The Stock and Flow Management Problem

Stock and flow management is of high relevance for a broad range of decision makers in society, business, and personal affairs: A Secretary of Finance, for example, has to manage tax inflows and public expenditure outflows which accumulate in the national debt or asset stock. Purchasing managers have to decide when to order which quantities so that both stock-outs and inventory costs are minimized. In terms of an everyday application, each human being is obliged to manage both the intake and burning of calories to maintain a healthy weight. Anecdotal evidence of poor SFM performance is omnipresent in everyday life. TV series increasingly portray unlucky fellow human beings who have accumulated such a high amount of debt by overusing credit cards or consumer credits that they will never ever be able to pay off their pile of debt. Finally, the financial crisis of 2008 and 2009 shows that even bank managers struggle to keep their banks' liquidity in balance when capital markets are disrupted and the economic environment radically changes.

Inventory management is another well investigated field with ample examples of poor SFM performance. For example, it happens regularly that one goes to a supermarket in order to replenish the refrigerator at home only to find the milk shelf empty. As surveys show, out-of-stock products rank indeed high in the top list of customer annoyances (2008a; 2008b). Severe stock-out or parts shortage phenomena are even reported in the news – for example, Bosch's delivery problems of diesel-fuel injection pumps, which caused production stops at Mercedes, BMW, Audi, and Opel (Milne, 2005), or Apple's iPhone shortage (Hansell, 2008). Such shortages can severely damage earnings and raise costs.

Excess inventories are, however, just as bad as stock-outs. Large inventories increase the working capital and the inventory risk. When goods perish before they can be sold at the regular price – either literally in the sense of food spoiling or figuratively in the sense that products could go out of fashion – shareholder value is obviously destroyed (e.g., Foster, 2004). In the worst-case-scenario of extreme excess inventory coinciding with decreasing demand, a company's financial solvency is endangered and bankruptcy will be the consequence.

For complex systems, dynamic decision making research has accumulated evidence of SFM failures by conducting a broad range of decision making experiments. (e.g., Ackerman & Kanfer, 1993; Brehmer, 1995; Diehl & Sterman, 1995; Kleinmuntz, 1985; Reichert & Dörner, 1988). This work suggests that human beings have severe difficulties understanding and managing systems which are dynamically complex, that is, which are characterized by feedback, time delays, nonlinearities, and accumulation. Sterman's (1989a; 1989b) pioneering behavioural supply chain research that made use of the Beer Game (Senge, 1990) as an experimental setting shows that the subjects' inventory management performance suffers systematically from the use of inappropriate anchoring heuristics and misperceptions of time lags. Croson and Donohue (2003; 2006) build on this research by confirming that low – albeit improved – supply chain performance still exists when participants are aware of the underlying demand distribution or point of sales data. Bloomfield, Gino, and Kulp (2007) find lamentable results even in a single echelon supply chain experiment, where inter-echelon coordination problems are absent. In summary, prior work suggests that dynamic decision making tasks, regardless whether complex or "simple", represent real challenges for human beings.

Moreover, recent work has revealed that a large fraction of highly educated people is unable to infer the behaviour of even the most simple stock-flow-systems consisting of only one stock, one inflow, and one outflow (Booth Sweeney & Sterman, 2000). As no feedback, no time delays, or nonlinearities were incorporated in those simplistic systems, they cannot be characterized as dynamically complex. Nevertheless, the average understanding of these systems' dynamic is lamentable. The subjects showed a rather poor performance in a variety of paper-and-pencil tasks involving such systems, which supports the conclusion that human beings indeed have a poor understanding of accumulation. Subsequent studies by Ossimitz (2002), Sterman and Booth Sweeney (2002; 2007), Cronin and Gonzales (2007) corroborate the hypothesis that poor SFT is a persistent phenomenon, comparable to the deep-rooted problems people have in probabilistic judgements and decision making (Hastie & Dawes, 2001; Kahneman & Tversky, 1972).

This research attempts to contribute to both research streams outlined above by linking them with the hypothesis that SFT capabilities causally affect SFM performance. This hypothesis is put to the test by making two observations in a laboratory setting. The first observation setting uses a collection of three stock and flow tasks that were used in prior studies for assessing SFT ability. The second setting employs a dynamic, yet simple inventory management game with stochastic demand, a four period lead time, and costs for ordering, inventory keeping, and stock outs. The performance is assessed by subtracting the cumulated costs from two benchmarks derived from applying two optimized order-quantity order-point (Q, r) rules. A pilot study is conducted to test the research design. The results of this pilot indicate that the hypothesis in its simple, one-dimensional form has to be rejected and replaced by a more elaborate cause-and-effect model.

The paper continues in Section 2 with a description of the hypothesis to be tested and the research method used. Section 3 describes how the SFT ability is measured and outlines the results. Section 4 provides details on the inventory management task and the assessment of the subjects' performance. Section 5 presents the results of the hypothesis test, and Section 6 introduces an advanced causal model derived from Ackerman's PPIK theory. The paper concludes with a discussion of limitations and contributions of this research and outlines directions for further research.

2 Hypothesis and Research Method

Prior work has revealed that people perform rather badly in both rather complex (Croson et al., 2003, 2006; Sterman, 1989a, b) and rather simple SFM tasks (Bloomfield et al., 2007). In searching for the simplest dynamic task that people can cope with, Sterman and others developed paper-and-pencil tasks based upon the simplest system possible with one inflow, one stock, and one outflow, with no feedback, time delays, and non-linearity, and found that even well educated subjects still struggle with the understanding of stocks and flows (Booth Sweeney et al., 2000; Cronin, Gonzalez, & Sterman, 2009; Ossimitz, 2002; Sterman, 2002). Cronin et al. (2009) find that poor SFT performance persists regardless of whether the data are displayed in line graphs, bar graphs, tables, or text; poor performance is robust to changes in the cover story that frames the task and provides a specific context, for example the management of a stock of cash or the amount of water in a bathtub; it is also robust to situations that involve discrete entities or continuously varying quantities; even reducing the task complexity by decreasing the number of data points presented does not increase SFT performance. SFT capabilities obviously suffer from important and pervasive shortcomings in human reasoning. A high percentage of people seriously misunderstands "the basic principles of accumulation" (Cronin et al., 2009).

Whereas the reasoning of Sterman (2002), Cronin et al. (2009) and others is plausible, that is, that poor SFM performance is related to poor stock flow understanding, as far as I know, this hypothesis has not yet been put to the test. The objective of this research is to contribute to the literature by formulating and testing the following hypothesis:

> *Hypothesis 1: The better people understand stocks and flows, the better they perform in managing a stock and flow system.*

For testing this hypothesis, a non-experimental research design with two observations and no treatment was deemed appropriate (Trochim & Donnelly, 2007). First, SFT performance was observed by using research instruments and methods, which have already been applied in prior work. A SFT test was compiled using three rather simple paper-and-pencil tasks. Second, SFM performance was observed by employing a simple inventory management game. The subjects had to place orders for one single product stored in one single inventory with no interconnectedness to other inventories. The orders led to an inflow of products to the inventory after a lead time of four weeks. The outflow was determined by stochastic demand; excess demand was lost.

The game was run over 25 periods. The objective was to minimize cumulated costs, which consisted of inventory, ordering, and stock-out costs.

To trial the research design outlined above, a pilot study was conducted. Two classes of a specialization course in operations management with 11 and 19 undergraduate students in their last semester were used as a research site. By the time the tests were carried out, the students should have had a solid knowledge in business administration and quantitative methods. They also had attended two prior courses in operations management; their knowledge in inventory control, however, was basic. The SFT test and the inventory management game were carried out in the very first session of the supply chain management module at the end of September 2008. The game was played first and took about 60 minutes. After a 15 minute break, the SFT test was done second. The participants were to spend up to 30 minutes on that test and, when completed, were allowed to leave. The average time spent was approximately 15 minutes. No incentive was offered, which possibly reduced the participants' motivation and effort. Yet, the effects of financial incentives in experiments have been found to be ambiguous (Camerer & Hogarth, 1999). Instead, the subjects were openly asked to do their best, because the results would be used anonymously in a research project. In the end, 26 students participated, 22 men and 4 women.

3 Difficulties in Understanding Accumulation Confirmed

For assessing the SFT ability, three relatively simple paper-and-pencil tasks were compiled that had already been used in prior studies in an identical or very similar form (Cronin et al., 2007; Cronin et al., 2009; Kainz & Ossimitz, 2002; Ossimitz, 2002; Sterman, 2002). Each task was designed to measure the subjects' understanding of stocks and flows and their ability to infer their behaviour over time. The type of the tasks ranged from sketching behaviour over time patterns, reading and interpretation of line graphs to multiple choice questions.

The first task is referred to as rainwater tank (RWT) task. It was taken from Kainz and Ossimitz (2002). The instructions were as follows: "A rainwater tank with a capacity of 100 litres is empty at noon. At exactly 2 PM, rain sets in and the water from the gutter flows into the tank at a rate of 25 l/hr until midnight. The tank has no drain; it simply fills up until the water spills over. The spill over is seen as outflow." The task was threefold: The subjects were asked to sketch in a behaviour-over-time chart, which was provided as template, (1) the inflow of rain water in the tank, (2) the outflow spilling over the tank, and (3) the stock of water in the tank.

The correct solution to this task is provided in Figure 1. Both inflow and outflow step up instantaneously at 2 PM and 6 PM respectively. In-between 2 PM and 6 PM, the water level in the tank rises at the constant rate of 25 litres per hour. After four hours of constant inflow, the volume of water in the tank has accumulated to 100 l, which exhausts the tank's filling capacity. From 6 PM onwards, water spills over at a constant rate of 25 litres per hour.

As Table 1 shows, the performance in the RWT task was poor. Only five out of 26 students completed all three tasks accurately. While almost everybody succeeded in correctly sketching the behaviour over time of the stock, less than 1/3 charted the inflow and outflow graphs properly. While some of the participants erroneously the same time pattern for the inflow as for the

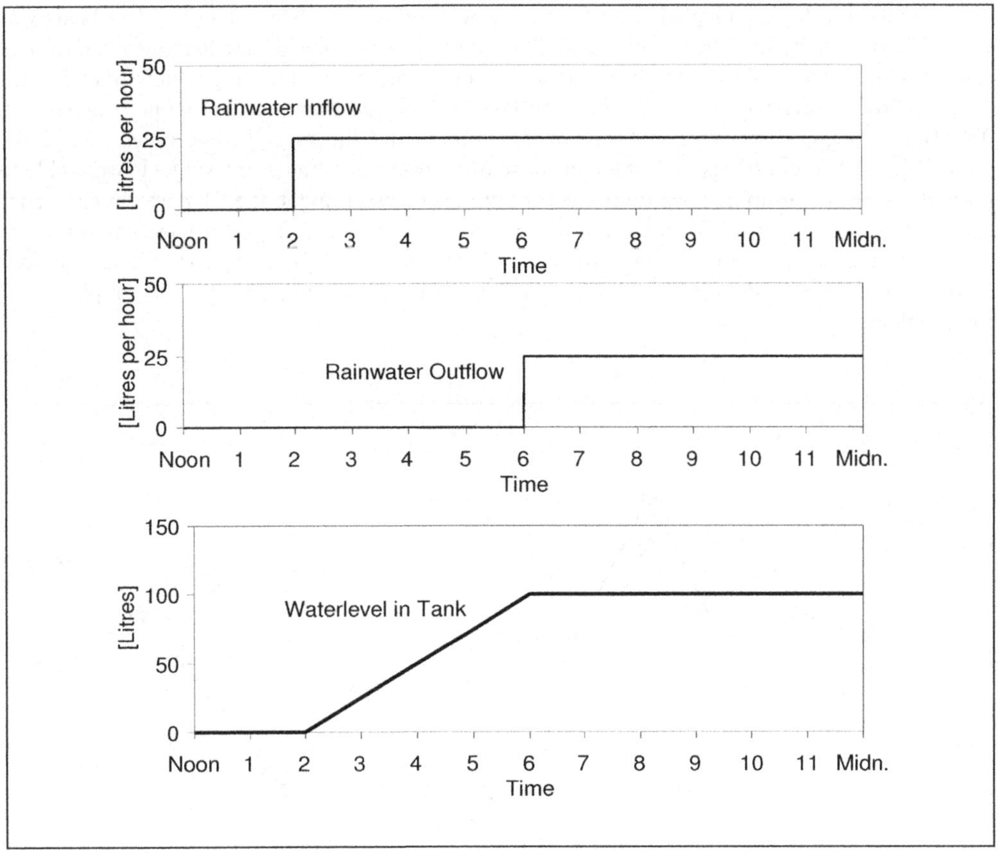

Figure 1: Correct Solution to the RWT Task

stock, others got the instantaneous step up at 2 PM wrong. Those graphs showed an inflow of zero for 2 PM and then an upward ramping line, which became flat at 25 litres per hour for 3 PM till 12 PM. Not surprisingly, the same ramp-up error could be observed for the outflow. Sometimes, subjects drew a straight line for the outflow ramping up from 0 litres per hour at 6 PM to 150 litres per hour at 12 PM. When compared to the results of Kainz and Ossimitz (2002), this study finds somewhat less disastrous results. Specifically, it is noticeable that all but two students got the time pattern for the stock correct.

Table 1: Percentages of Correct Answers in the RWT Task

	RWT 1	RWT 2	RWT 3	All 3 Tasks	N
This study	30.8%	30.8%	92.3%	19.2%	26
Kainz Ossimitz 2002	na	na	47%	3%	64

The second task was adapted from Cronin et al. (2009). While the identical data basis was used, the cover story was slightly changed. Instead of persons entering and leaving a department store, Figure 2 was said to show the number of people entering and leaving a bank branch. This task is therefore referred to as bank branch (BB) task. The questions asked remained unchanged. The first two questions were: "During which minute did the most people enter (leave) the store?" These two questions served the purpose of identifying whether the subjects were able to correctly read line graphs. They do not contribute to the assessment of SFT performance; consequently, these two questions are not included in the aggregate SFT performance measure. As Table 2 indicates, the results do not differ much for the two tasks BB1 and BB2 among the four studies listed. Very high percentages of correct answers suggest that reading line graphs is not the problem.

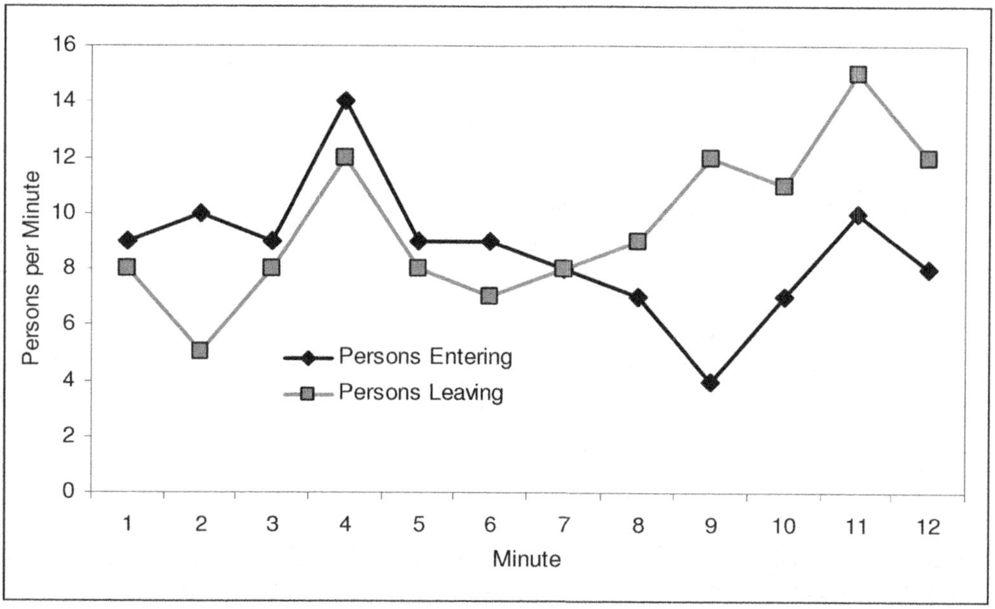

Figure 2: Bank Branch Task

Table 2: Percentages of Correct Answers in the Bank Branch Task (or Comparable Ones)

	BB1	BB2	BB3	BB4	BB3 & 4	All 4	N
This study	88.5%	92.3%	30.8%	42.3%	19.2%	15.4%	26
Cronin et al. 2009	94%	87%	52%	41%	na	na	63
Sterman 2002	94%	94%	42%	30%	na	na	172
Ossimitz 2002	na	94%	24%	na	na	na	154

In obvious contrast to this, the high percentages of wrong answers to questions three (BB3) and four (BB4) reflect the erroneous understanding of stocks and flows. Question BB3 was as follows: "During which minute were the most people in the bank branch?", while BB4 asked "During which minute were the fewest people in the store?"

The determination when the most people were in the branch does not require any calculation, although it would, of course, be possible to find the correct answer by extracting the data points from the line graph, subtracting the number of persons leaving from the number of persons entering per minute, and cumulating the net flow over the time span of twelve minutes. The correct answers can be found more easily and more quickly if one recognizes that the number in the branch accumulates the flow of people entering less the flow of people leaving, and if one understands that a stock rises when its inflow exceeds its outflow and falls when outflow exceeds inflow. Since until minute 7 the number entering always exceeds the number leaving, the stock of people in the branch grows. From minute 8 onwards, the outflow is bigger than the inflow, and therefore the number of persons lingering in the bank branch falls. The most people are in the branch when the inflow curve crosses the outflow line, which happens to be in minute 7. As in the other studies reported in Table 2, answers were considered correct if they were within ± 1 of the correct response, that is, minute 6, 7, or 8. The fact that still less than one third of the subjects in my pilot study managed to provide an accurate answer (and less than 50% in the other studies) can be regarded as strong evidence of stock-flow thinking failure.

Again, no calculation is required to find the correct answer for BB4. Based on the reasoning portrayed above, one knows that the number of people in the branch rises through minute 7 and falls thereafter. Consequently, the fewest persons are in the bank branch either at the beginning or at the end. Determining which is the case requires an assessment whether the area between the rate of entering and rate of leaving up to minute 7 is greater or smaller than the area between the two curves from minute 8 on. As the second area is, in fact, twice as large as the first area, it is not really difficult to deduce minute 12 as the correct response – if one ever reaches that level of reasoning.

In the studies by Sterman (2002) and Ossimitz (2002), a more complex version of the task was used. Instead of 24 data points, line graphs over 30 minutes were shown, which amounts to 60 data points. However, Cronin et al. (2009) tested the hypothesis that performance would improve in simpler versions of the task with fewer data points and rejected it. When comparing the results for BB3 and BB4 provided in Table 2, the fact must be noted that in this study subjects performed better in BB4 than in BB3, while Cronin et al. (2009) and Sterman (2002) reported a reverse order. Because of the rather small target population in my study, the disparity in performance results observed is probably statistically not significant.

The third and last task intended to test whether the subjects were aware of the difference between the net flow "budget deficit" and the stock "national debt". It is referred to as budget deficit (BD) problem. No graphical presentation of information was given or required in this task. Instead, it consisted of six multiple choice questions, which had to be answered by checking one of four possible answers. The instructions were as follows: "In Taka Tuka land, the amount by which the annual federal expenses exceed the annual federal income, is defined as budget deficit. In 2006, the budget deficit was 60 billion thaler; a year later it was 40 billion thaler." The subjects were given six statements, which are, along with the correct answer, shown in Figure 3 (see p. 292). As an answer, the participants had to check one of the options "correct", "wrong", "not answerable", and "don't know".

		Correct	Wrong	Not answer-able	Don't know
BD1	In 2007 20 Billion thaler of public debt have been paid back.	☐	☒	☐	☐
BD2	The minister of finance could reduce the public debt from 2006 to 2007 by a third.	☐	☒	☐	☐
BD3	If the minister of finance is able to reduce the federal budget deficit to zero thaler, (a balanced budget), then Taka Tuka land is free from debt.	☐	☒	☐	☐
BD4	The national debt in Taka Tuka land grew both in 2006 and in 2007.	☒	☐	☐	☐
BD5	If the minister of finance is able to reduce the budget deficit permanently to zero thaler (a balanced budget) and there was no budget surplus in the past, then public debt has reached its highest level.	☒	☐	☐	☐
BD6	A decreasing budget deficit automatically implies a decrease in public debt.	☐	☒	☐	☐

Figure 3: BD Task and Correct Solution

To find the correct solution, one has to see the "budget deficit" as net inflow into the stock "national debt". Such a simple system with one inflow to one stock can only show three possible behaviour modes over time: First, as long as the inflow is positive, the stock is increasing; second, when the inflow is zero, the stock is staying constant, and third, only if the inflow is negative can the stock fall. While – according to the instructions – the net inflow "budget deficit" to the stock "national debt" is decreasing from 60 to 40 billion thaler, the stock itself is still increasing. Consequently, the statements BD1 and BD2 are wrong. By the end of 2007, national debt amounts to 100 billion plus the unknown opening stock in 2006. If the finance minister were able to achieve a balanced budget, for example, in 2008, the net flow would be zero, and national debt would stay constant at 100 billion. It never ever could be zero itself, which means that BD3 is wrong, too. Assuming that there was never a budget surplus in the past, the reduction of the budget deficit to zero would indeed keep the national debt at its highest level; BD5 is therefore correct. Because of a positive budget deficit for both 2006 and 2007, the stock is increasing in both years; BD4 is correct, too.

Once more, the subjects' performance is poor. Table 3 compares this study's results to the outcomes reported by Ossimitz (2002). Except for BD1, I find consistently higher percentages of

Table 3: Percentages of Correct Answers in the BD Task

	BD1	BD2	BD3	BD4	BD5	BD6	All 6	N
This study	53.8%	50.0%	69.2%	61.5%	46.2%	96.2%	23.1%	26
Ossimitz 2002	68%	36%	62%	44%	17%	42%	na	154

correct answers. In particular, BD5 and BD6 stand out with a performance more than twice as high as in Ossimitz's study. Nevertheless, only about 50% of correct answers in response to the rather simple stock and flow problems BD1, BD2, and BD5 constitute a fairly devastating result.

Overall SFT performance was poor. Only one person out of 26 was able to find the correct solution to all eleven tasks. One subject got only one answer right. On average, about 55% of the answers given were correct. This study corroborates the findings of previous work (Booth Sweeney et al., 2000; Cronin et al., 2007; Cronin et al., 2009; Kainz et al., 2002; Ossimitz, 2002; Sterman, 2002; Sterman et al., 2002, 2007). Once more, it demonstrates a profound and notable shortcoming in human reasoning: The inability of even smart and well-educated people to understand the dynamic relationships between stocks and flows, that is, the process how flows into and out of a stock accumulate over time. Cronin et al. (2009) demonstrate that poor SFT performance persists regardless of the cover story, the display format of the data, and the quantity of information provided. They reveal that learning is slow when tasks can be done repeatedly and outcome feedback is provided. Moreover, they show that modest incentives do not improve performance. This last finding matches my own experience. In a written exam for the master level, I included the same bank branch task. As this exam was graded, students should have had a sufficient incentive to do as best as they could. However, the outcome did not differ much from the results shown in Table 2. Out of 18 students, only 9 (50%) got BB3 and only 7 (38%) got BB4 right.

In dynamic decision making and system dynamics literature it is hypothesized that effective decisions in dynamic settings require decision makers to understand accumulation (Cronin et al., 2009; Dörner, 1996; Pala & Vennix, 2005; Sterman, 2002). Consequently, if SFT performance is as poor as this and various other studies show, decision making performance is expected to be extremely deficient, too. The next section outlines how decision making performance in a dynamic inventory management task is determined. The subsequent chapter then analyses whether SFM performance and SFT performance is correlated to test the hypothesis outlined above.

4 An Inventory Management Game for Determining SFM Performance

Inventory management games were developed many years ago and used as educational instruments in practice and academia for many years (e.g., Renshaw & Heuston, 1957). They have also been used as research laboratories (e.g., Barlas & Özevin, 2004; Sterman, 1989a, b). The inventory management game utilized in this study to measure judgemental decision making performance is regularly played in operations management courses at both Bachelor and MBA levels.[2] By "practicing" inventory management, students get a realistic impression of the challenges and possible strategies in inventory control problems. To facilitate learning, detail complexity of the task is kept as simple as possible; the same holds true for dynamic complexity.

[2] I am grateful to Prof. Dr. Rainer Sibbel, who brought the game to my attention and helped me to run it myself.

Feedback and non-linearities are not included. This limited complexity also qualifies the game to serve as a measuring device for SFM performance in this study. According to the game's cover story, participants act as inventory expeditors in a retail company. They are responsible for one single product, for example, a flat screen television set. Aware of all relevant costs and the lead time, their only decision is when to reorder how many items so that total costs are minimized. The game is run over a time span of 25 weeks, and therefore participants have to make 25 decisions.

To make the game realistic and minimize the chance that smart participants base their decisions on optimal solutions derived from simple standard inventory management models, a more advanced task with a lead time of four weeks and inventory as well as ordering and stock-out costs is chosen. Inventory costs amount to 2 € per item per week; one order is said to cost 100 €, and stock-out costs per item stand at 70 €. By setting demand for the product randomly beyond the players' control, the possibility of calculating the optimal strategy is eliminated. The players have indeed to rely on their judgement – potentially enhanced by some simple additional calculations.

Demand is determined using a set of playing cards. The number of cards included is shown in Table 4. Additionally, each card reveals the assigned demand; if, for example, in week 8 an ace is drawn, the demand for that week is one item. If a card showing a king is drawn, two additional cards are taken, and the demand for all non-king cards is added up. If once more a king card is unveiled, two additional cards are taken again. If two king cards are put on the table, four more cards are drawn. In all cases, the demand is derived by adding up the figures.

Table 4: Playing Cards Used in the Inventory Game

	King	**Joker**	**Ace**	**2**	**3**	**4**	**5**	**6**	**7**	**8**	**9**	**10**
Number of cards	3	1	1	2	4	6	8	8	8	8	5	3
Demand	see Figure 4	0	1	2	3	4	5	6	7	8	9	10

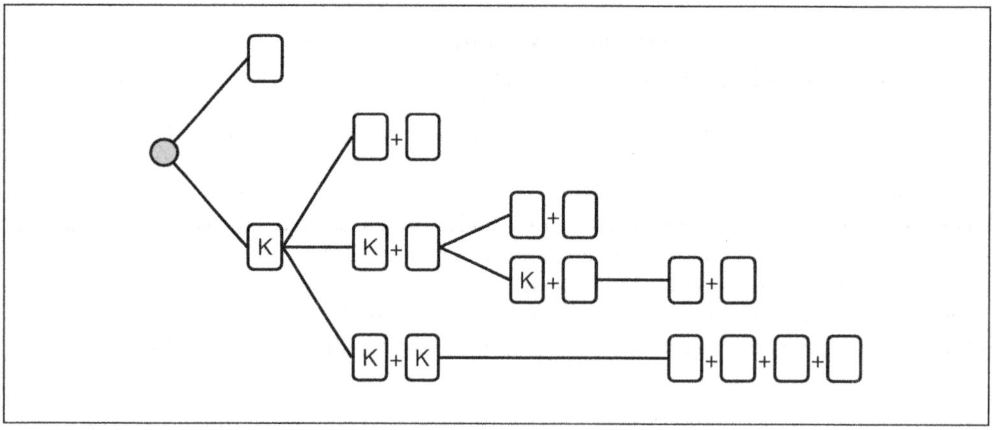

Figure 4: Drawing Algorithm Used in the Inventory Game

By using the set of cards shown in Table 4 and the rather complex algorithm illustrated in Figure 4, determining the probability density function is not straightforward. While it is obvious that minimum demand per week is zero and maximum demand is 39, working out the exact frequency distribution would be impossible in the approximately 15 minute time span, which is provided to develop a procurement policy. Consequently, the participants are forced to rely on their judgements and – depending on the decision rule they choose – on proximate calculations. If necessary, for example, they could approximate the expected demand by ignoring the king playing cards and the complicated drawing algorithm associated with them. This would result in an expected demand of 5.375 items per week.

The game is thoroughly introduced: Participants receive both a verbal briefing and written instructions, which outline the setting, the task, and the objective. A protocol sheet is handed over to the participants. The sheet is blank except for the initial inventory of 40 for week one. Participants receive explanations how to fill in and calculate the cells. Two or three rows are completed as an exercise to ensure as best as possible that the participants do not make mistakes. The game is run in two steps per week. First, demand is determined using the set of playing cards. Second, each player calculates inventory, sales, closing inventory, and shortages. The decision on the order quantity for that week is made and recorded both in column I and – four weeks later – in column D. Finalising step two, inventory, ordering, and shortage costs per week are calculated and entered. When week 25 is finished, the participants add up all costs and calculate total costs. The results are exchanged and discussed in class.

After class, each subject's decision series is transferred to a spreadsheet, which automatically recalculates all measures and cost outcomes. In one case, errors that could not be corrected were discovered; this case had to be eliminated, which resulted in a reduced N of 25.

While the widespread evaluation of decision quality based on outcomes can be criticised (e.g., Davern, Mantena, & Stohr, 2008; Keren & Bruin, 2003), the same laboratory situation for all participants allows to control for factors otherwise beyond control, such as topicality and comparability of information. Following Sterman (1989a; 1989b), Süß (1996), and many others, this study therefore uses the following outcome performance measures: inventory, ordering, stock-out, and total costs. Inherent in the game's design is that increasing the order quantity also increases inventory costs, yet decreases stock-out costs. More frequent orders increase ordering costs but decrease inventory costs. Consequently, total costs can be seen as a balanced measure for decision quality in the inventory game and is therefore used as measure for inventory management performance. While absolute cost figures could be used to rank the participants of one game session, they neither allow for drawing a comparison between two games based on different demand scenarios nor for making a judgment about the inventory management quality in general. For these reasons, the outcome of an optimized standard (Q, r) inventory control policy[3] is calculated as benchmark. As this benchmark is just used to make participants' results comparable, no attempt is made to find the overall optimal policy. From an educational perspective, the (Q, r) policy has the advantage that it is rather simple and easily understood by the participants. They readily agree to this benchmark policy and accept its outcome as a point of reference.

[3] When the inventory position falls below r, an order for Q is placed.

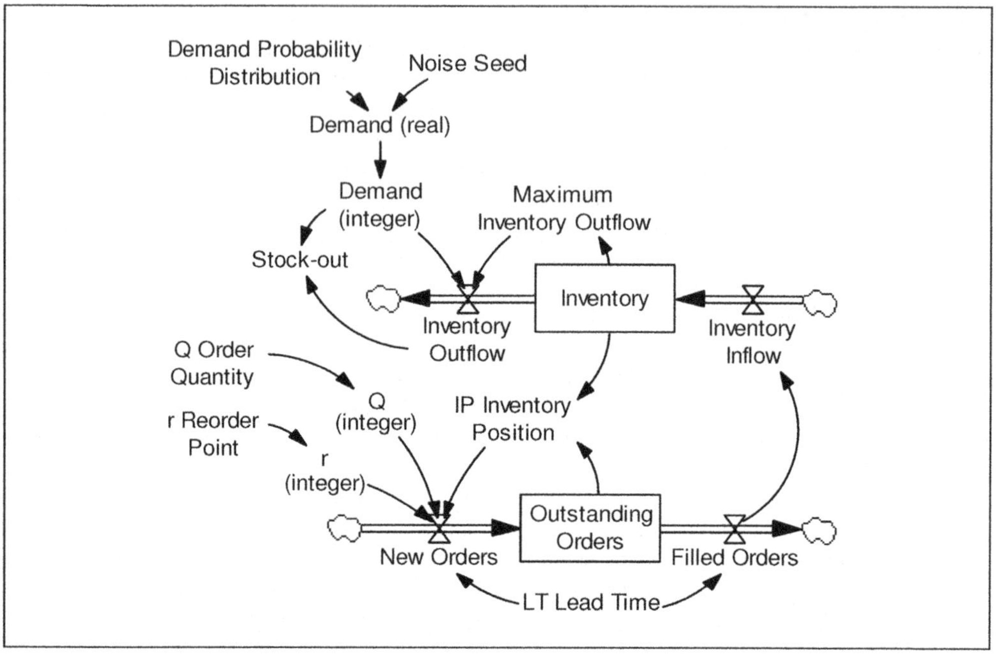

Figure 5: Stock and Flow Structure of the Inventory Game Simulation Model

The optimal order quantity Q and reorder point r for the given demand probability distribution are determined using a simulation model of the game (see Figure 5) and the Powell optimization procedure built into the software package Vensim. Minimizing expected total costs over 500 different time series of random demand is used as objective function. Q and r are set as parameters, which are to be optimized. The Powell search is restarted 10 times and results in an optimal reorder point r of 35 and an optimal order quantity Q of 28. Expected total costs are 1,973 €, minimum costs amount to 1,616 €, while maximum costs result in 3,978 €.

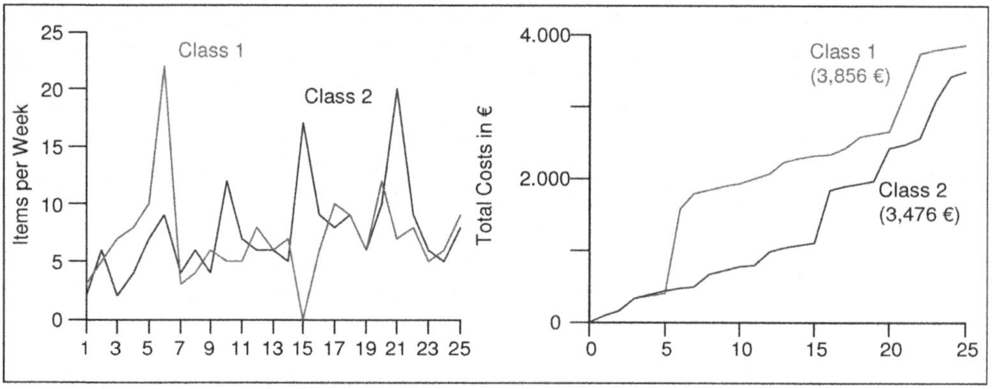

Figure 6: Outcome of the (28, 35) Benchmark Policy

As the inventory game was played in two different classes, two different demand patterns were generated (see Figure 6, left side). Both demand time series are characterized by at least two outliers resulting in total costs close to the maximum value. Benchmark costs of 3,856 € for class 1 and 3,476 € for class 2 show that the (28, 35) order policy does result in total costs nearly double the expected value (1,973 €). While most participants should be able to outperform the (28, 35) policy, this is no objection to using these cost figures as benchmarks.

The inventory management performance (IMP) measure is calculated by subtracting the total costs achieved by the participants from the benchmark total costs. For example, a participant in class 1, who obtained total costs of 2,828 €, is assigned 3,856 € – 2,828 € = 1,028 €, which can be interpreted as over-achievement. Therefore, the higher the IMP score the better the performance in IM. Negative values express under-achievement, that is, the participant's performance is below the results of the benchmark policy. As the inventory management game is used as one example of a stock and flow management task, SFM performance is set equal to IMP.

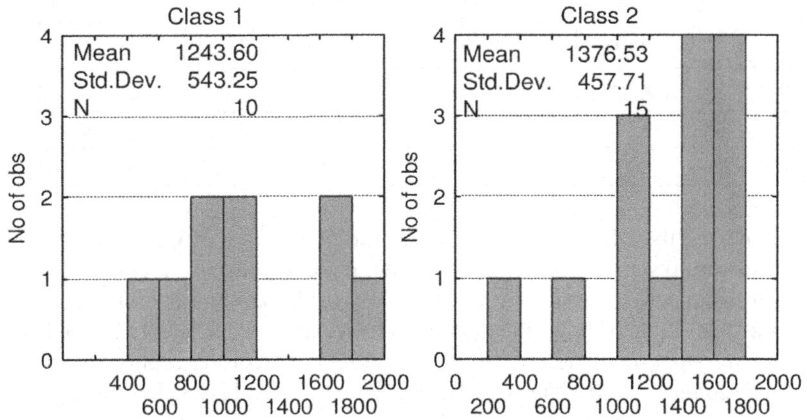

Figure 7: Histogram of the IMP Scores

Figure 7 shows the histograms and descriptive statistics for the two classes. Indeed, all participants outperform the (28, 35) benchmark policy. Nevertheless, there would be still room for improvement. When comparing the mean total costs to an ideal ordering policy, class one participants could have achieved 1,548 € instead of a mean of 2,612 €; in class two, minimal total costs could have been 1,566 € instead of a mean value of 2,099 €.[4] One can conclude that the performance of the participants in the SFM task is better than the rather poor results in the SFT test indicate. However, almost all participants could have performed better. Only the top performers come close to the outcome of an ideal inventory management policy.

[4] The ideal ordering pattern was determined using the actual demand sequence and optimizing the 25 decisions on the order quantity separately using again Vensim's Powell optimizer. The grid search was restarted more than 100 million times. The participants, however, could have achieved those results only by mere chance; even if they had correctly anticipated demand, it would have been impossible for them to find the optimal solution in the short time span available. Therefore those ideal results were not used as benchmarks.

5 Testing the Link between SFT- and SFM-Performance

The hypothesis that was stated above links the understanding of how flows accumulate in stocks to the performance in managing a stock and flow system. By using the observation settings outlined in the previous chapters, this hypothesis is operationalised as follows:

The better people do in the SFT tasks, that is, the higher their score, the better they perform in the inventory management game, which means the higher their IMP measure (= SFM performance).

Statistically, this hypothesis can be tested by determining the correlation coefficient for the SFT and IMP measures. As both measures are not normally distributed, the nonparametric Spearman Rank Order Correlation Coefficient is calculated.[5] The results for groups one and two separately as well as the whole data set are shown in Table 5. As is obvious from the table, no acceptable p-level can be found. Therefore, the hypothesis has to be considered as rejected.

Table 5: Spearman Rank Order Correlations for SFT and IMP Total Costs

	Group	Valid N	Spearman R	t(N – 2)	p-level
SFT & IMP	1 & 2	25	–0.2080	–1.0201	0.3183
SFT & IMP	1	10	–0.5031	–1.6466	0.1382
SFT & IMP	2	15	0.0615	0.2221	0.8277

For group one and the whole data set, even negative (although insignificant) correlations are calculated. This would stand for the exact opposite of the hypothesised relation. As this test outcome is rather unexpected, it might be worthwhile to additionally look at the detailed cost performance measures. Table 6 shows the Spearman Correlation Coefficients for SFT performance and IMP ordering, stock-out, and inventory costs. Again, with one exception, no significant correlations can be found. And the one significant correlation expresses that the higher the partic-

Table 6: Spearman Rank Order Correlations for SFT Performance and IMP Detailed Costs

	Group	Valid N	Spearman R	t(N – 2)	p-level
SFT & IMP Ordering Cost	1 & 2	25	0.1966	0.9617	0.3462
SFT & IMP Stock Out Costs	1& 2	25	–0.2005	–0.9816	0.3365
SFT & IMP Inventory Costs	1 & 2	25	–0.3307	–1.6805	0.1064
SFT & IMP Ordering Cost	1	10	0.3469	1.0461	0.3261
SFT & IMP Stock Out Costs	1	10	–0.6894	–2.6915	0.0274
SFT & IMP Inventory Costs	1	10	–0.4260	–1.3316	0.2197
SFT & IMP Ordering Cost	2	15	–0.0577	–0.2083	0.8382
SFT & IMP Stock Out Costs	2	15	0.1701	0.6222	0.5445
SFT & IMP Inventory Costs	2	15	–0.2496	–0.9292	0.3697

[5] Missing data are pair-wise deleted.

ipants' SFT ability was, the worse was their IMP measured by stock-out costs. Once more, this contradicts the hypothesis stated above.

The rather unexpected results of the correlation analysis raise the question why the widely claimed causal relationship between SFT and SFM performance was not found. This could, of course, be attributed to the fact that the sample size in this preliminary study was very small. The number of 25 valid observations is clearly below the N achieved in other studies. However, the scatter plot shown in Figure 8 suggests extending the number of observations in future research and investigating further influencing factors and developing a more complex causal model.

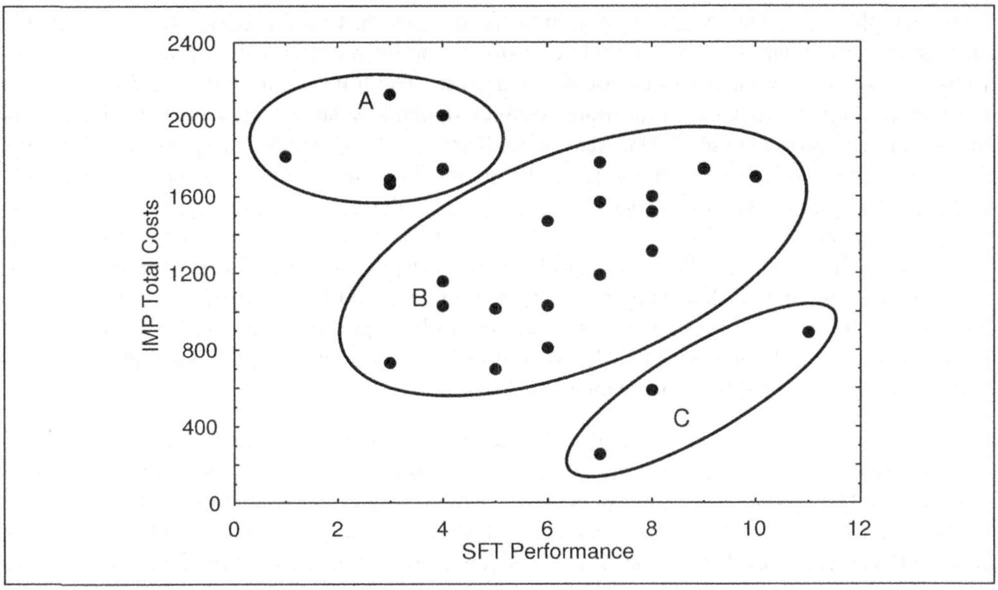

Figure 8: Scatter Plot Visualising the Relation between SFT Performance and IMP Total Costs

At first glance, the spatial distribution of the data points confirms the non-significant, yet slightly negative correlation between SFT and IMP performance. However, after a while, three clusters emerge. I am grateful to Prof. Dr. Olaf Stotz for his valuable comments. Cluster A contains a set of seven data points belonging to participants with rather poor results in the SFT test and extremely good results in the SFM task. The B cluster covers the majority of cases. In this cluster, at least visually, the hypothesised positive correlation between SFT and IMP performance holds. The third cluster, entitled "C" cluster, encompasses only three participants. They are characterized by rather good results in the SFT test combined with poor results in the inventory management game. Again, the hypothesised correlation seems to hold, yet the extremely low number of three cases does not indicate high resilience. Obviously, the reliability and robustness of these results are limited by the rather low number of in total 25 cases.

The three clusters that can be identified in the scatter plot in Figure 8 could indicate that the stated monocausal relationship between SFT and SFM performance is too simple and not appropriate. A more complex causal model with further moderating and directly influencing factors might be needed. In the following section, a first attempt is made to introduce some findings and ideas from psychological research on decision making performance in dynamically complex environments.

6 Towards a More Complex Explanatory Model for Inventory Management Performance

Stock and flow management, as operationalised in the game used in this study, is not a dynamically complex task. The inventory system to be managed has no feedback, no non-linearities, and no internal dynamics. It is a simple one stock, one inflow, and one outflow system with a four-week delay between order placement and delivery. Contrary to this, dynamic decision making research focuses usually on far more complex dynamic systems, such as an air traffic control system (Ackerman et al., 1993; Ackerman, Kanfer, & Goff, 1995), a city (Dörner, Kreuzig, & Reither, 1994), or a high tech company (Wittmann & Hattrup, 2004). For these dynamically complex tasks, elaborate and corroborated theories exist that relate intelligence to decision making performance. Especially Ackerman's (1996) PPIK theory has been bolstered by many empirical studies (see, e.g., Wittmann et al., 2004). Despite the much lower complexity of the inventory management task used in this study, building on the PPIK theory as theoretical framework for an advanced follow-up investigation could be a promising approach. Therefore, the PPIK theory is briefly introduced within the following paragraphs, and a more elaborate causal explanation model of SFM performance is suggested.

The first 'P' of PPIK stands for intelligence-as-process, which encompasses reasoning, memory-span (also short-term or working memory), perceptual speed, and spatial rotation (Ackerman, 1996). The second 'P' denotes personality, which is described to include first openness (or similarly defined traits, such as Intellectence or Culture) and second typical intellectual engagement (TIE) (Ackerman, 1996). The 'I' in PPIK represents interests, specifically realistic, investigative, and artistic interests. Finally, the 'K' stands for intelligence-as-knowledge, about which Ackerman (1996) remarks that it has to be seen as contextual.

Based upon Ackerman's PPIK theory outlined above, Figure 9 illustrates an advanced causal model for predicting SFM performance (SFMP). SFT ability, as measured by using the rain water tank task, the bank branch task, and the budget deficit task, could be seen as one component of intelligence-as-knowledge required to support the inventory management game. Of course, other knowledge aspects might be necessary for a satisfactory explanation of SFMP. Therefore, one could try to measure the general economic knowledge, as, for example, Wittmann and Hattrup (2004) did in their study, as well as specific inventory management knowledge. For the constructs intelligence-as-process, interests, and personality well-tried instruments are available. Intelligenc-as-process could, for example, be assessed using the BIS test (Jäger, Süß, & Beauducel, 1997); for the measurement of personality, the revised NEO personality inventory (Costa & McCrae, 1992) could be used in combination with the inventory developed by Goff & Ackerman (1992). Finally, to measure interests, one could, for example, employ the ACT's Interest Inventory (UNIACT). Besides the inventory management game other SFM tasks could be used to asses SFMP; for example, a SFM task with a more continuous character and less (or no) stochastic elements could provide an alternative measure for SFMP.

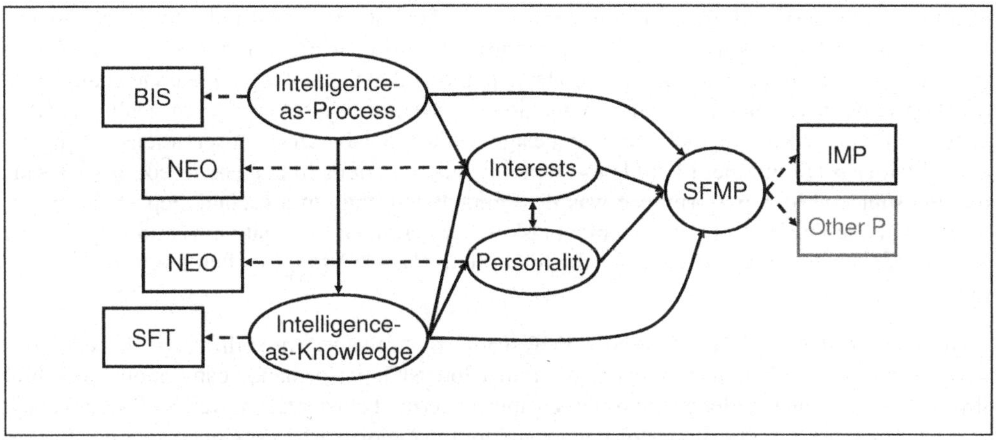

Figure 9: An Advanced Model for Prediction of IMP Based on the PPIK Theory

The gains from using established psychological tests could be threefold: First, one could expect to find the clustering factor or factors, which causes the pattern in Figure 8; second, one could investigate how strong SFT ability relates to SFM performance in direct comparison to a selection of other factors already proven to be significant; third; one could build on a vast body of psychological research and learn from it. However, the major disadvantage was that the time exposure of the subjects, which had to be observed in the various tests, would be enormous – approximately four hours.

To reduce the test load for the student subjects, a broad range of factors related to the model depicted in Figure 9 could be assessed in a second pilot study using already existing databases of demographic and study performance data. Where those objective sources are not available, self-assessment questionnaires could help to identify factors with considerable impact. For example, if a university administers an admission test, components measuring intelligence-as-process are often included; these results, although often determined at an earlier point in time, could be used as preliminary indicators. Additionally, grades on various knowledge domains could be analyzed and checked for relevance. Finally, university databases contain a broad range of socio-demographic data, which could be queried to find clustering factors. By doing this, the enormous range of influencing factors on SFMP, which could be derived from the PPIK theory, can hopefully be condensed.

7 Discussion, Limitations and Conclusions

Initiated and influenced by prior research on stock and flow thinking capabilities, this study focused on the issue whether poor SFT performance, that is, bad understanding of accumulation, indeed predicts poor performance in a dynamic SFM problem. The hypothesis that this causal link does exist can be derived from discussions by, for example, Cronin et al. (2009), Sterman (2002), or Booth Sweeney & Sterman (2000). Those studies, however, primarily attempt to measure SFT performance and try to provide explanations for the poor results – for example, the widespread use of a simple correlation heuristic (Cronin et al., 2009). No attempt is made to test the hypothesised relation empirically. Specifically, this research aims at contributing to narrowing that research gap. The hypothesis that the better people understand stocks and flows, the better they perform in managing an inventory system was empirically tested by setting up a non-experimental research design with two laboratory observations. Using the indeed rather small number of students attending an Operations Management course as a sample, the subjects' SFT performance was determined first, and, in a second step, their success level in a dynamic inventory management task was ascertained. A negative, yet non-significant, Spearman Correlation Coefficient for the total group (N = 25) suggests that the hypothesis has to be rejected.

However, further analysis of the SFT IMP scatter plot revealed three different clusters. For a small group of seven subjects (cluster A), rather low SFT performance came along with high IMP scores; an even smaller group of three subjects, termed cluster C, showed SFT scores above average, yet substandard IMP performance; and for the majority of 15 subjects, assigned to cluster B, average SFT performance was associated with average IMP performance. This clustering can be seen as an indication of the existence of other factors, which were not controlled in the pilot study. If a causal or moderating impact of another factor had been hypothesized and this factor had been controlled for, it is likely that a positive correlation between SFT and IMP performance could have been found. At least the visual impression suggests a strong positive correlation between SFT and IMP performance within clusters B and C. Although no direct evidence for a positive link between SFT understanding and IMP performance can be derived from the pilot study, its outcome is conducive to further research. The results strongly suggest searching for other relevant factors, which cause the clustering and therefore mask a positive correlation within each cluster.

As primarily psychological research (e.g., Ackerman et al., 1993; Wittmann et al., 2004) has already tried to predict dynamic decision making performance using various intelligence constructs, the search for the other factors could benefit from their findings. Therefore, it is suggested to employ Ackerman's established PPIK theory as a framework guiding the development of more complex causal models explaining SFM performance. The main contribution of this pilot study can indeed be seen in providing valuable information supporting an advanced research design for a follow-up study. While one major limitation of this study is indeed the low number of cases (N = 25), simply increasing the sample size without advancing the causal model probably will not yield better results. Future research should try to control a broad range of other factors presumably influencing or moderating the subject's success in the SFM task. As a consequence, the need may arise to add more observations to the non-experimental laboratory research design.

The pilot study, however, does not give rise to a fundamental alteration of the design. The inventory used for measuring the SFT performance seems to be appropriate. The poor understanding of accumulation found by others (Cronin et al., 2009; Kainz et al., 2002; Ossimitz, 2002; Sterman, 2002) could be confirmed. Although the inventory game was not used in prior research to determine SFM ability, no obvious shortcomings were detected while conducting the study and analysing its outcomes. It was rather easy to conduct and produced sufficiently strewing performance measures. While one might argue that the stochastic nature of the task adds another unwanted source of disturbance, a stochastic demand pattern seems to be the only way to provide for the formation of multiple groups without running the risk that information about demand is spread among the groups. Stochastic demand also allows to replicate the game, for example, to determine learning. Yet, for a follow-up study, the participants' stochastical knowledge could be measured, too.

This research engaged in a first attempt to determine the contribution of SFT ability to predict decision making performance in IM. Further research should help to build and test a more elaborate explanatory model. A better understanding is needed how SFT ability fits in the psychological intelligence construct and contributes to dynamic decision making performance. Based on such a theory, improved methods could be developed to, firstly, educate all of us to reach higher levels of performance in stock and flow problems and, secondly, to select the best people for the most demanding stock and flow management tasks.

References

2008a: "Out of stock" tops list of shoppers' pet hates. In-Store: 6–6.

2008b: Retailers running risk of abandoned shopping trolleys. In-Store: 7–7.

Ackerman, P. L. (1996): A theory of adult intellectual development: Process, personality, interests, and knowledge. *Intelligence* 22(2): 227–257.

Ackerman, P. L. and M. Goff (1994): Typical Intellectual Engagement and Personality: Reply to Rocklin (1994). *Journal of Educational Psychology* 86(1): 150–153.

Ackerman, P. L. and E. D. Heggestad (1997): Intelligence, Personality, and Interests: Evidence for Overlapping Traits. *Psychological Bulletin* 121(2): 219–245.

Ackerman, P. L. and R. Kanfer (1993): Integrating Laboratory and Field Study for Improving Selection: Development of a Battery for Predicting Air Traffic Controller Success. *Journal of Applied Psychology* 78(3): 413–432.

Ackerman, P. L., R. Kanfer and M. Goff (1995): Cognitive and Noncognitive Determinants and Consequences of Complex Skill Acquisition. *Journal of Experimental Psychology: Applied* 1(4): 270–304.

Barlas, Y. and M. G. Özevin (2004): Analysis of stock management gaming experiments and alternative ordering formulations. *Systems Research and Behavioral Science* 21(4): 439–470.

Bloomfield, R. J., F. Gino and S. Kulp (2007): *Behavioral Causes of the Bullwhip Effect in a Single Echelon: SSRN.*

Booth Sweeney, L. and J. D. Sterman (2000): Bathtub Dynamics: Initial Results of a Systems Thinking Inventory. *System Dynamics Review* 16(4): 249–294.

Brehmer, B. (1995): Dynamic decision making: human control of complex systems. *Acta Psychologica* 81: 211–241.

Camerer, C. F. and R. M. Hogarth (1999): The Effects of Financial Incentives in Experiments: A Review and Capital-Labor-Production Framework. *Journal of Risk and Uncertainty* 19(1–3): 7–42.

Costa, P. T. and R. R. McCrae (1992): *Revised NEO Personality Inventory (NEO PI-R) and NEO Five-Factor Inventory (NEO-FFI)*. Odessa: Psychological Assessment Resources.

Cronin, M. and C. Gonzalez (2007): Understanding the building blocks of system dynamics. *System Dynamics Review* 23(1): 1–17.

Cronin, M. A., C. Gonzalez and J. D. Sterman (2009): Why don't well-educated adults understand accumulation? A challenge to researchers, educators, and citizens. *Organizational Behavior and Human Decision Processes* 108(1): 116–130.

Croson, R. and K. Donohue (2003): Impact of POS Data Sharing on Supply Chain Management: An Experimental Study. *Production and Operations Management* 12(1): 1–11.

Croson, R. and K. Donohue (2006): Behavioral Causes of the Bullwhip Effect and the Observed Value of Inventory Information. *Management Science* 52(3): 323–336.

Davern, M. J., R. Mantena and E. A. Stohr (2008): Diagnosing decision quality. *Decision Support Systems* 45(1): 123–139.

Diehl, E. and J. D. Sterman (1995): Effects of feedback complexity on dynamic decision making. *Organizational Behavior and Human Decision Processes* 62(2): 198–215.

Dörner, D. (1996): *The logic of failure. Strategic thinking for complex situations*. New York: Metropolitan Books.

Dörner, D., H. W. Kreuzig and F. Reither (1994): *Lohhausen. Vom Umgang mit Unbestimmtheit und Komplexität* (Unveränd. Nachdr. der Ausg. von 1983/mit einem Beitrag von Dietrich Dörner Zwölf Jahre danach: Lohhausen im Rückblick. ed.). Bern et al.: Huber.

Foster, L. (2004): *Excess inventory stalls Sears performance*, Financial Times.

Goff, M. and P. L. Ackerman (1992): Personality-Intelligence Relations: Assessment of Typical Intellectual Engagement. *Journal of Educational Psychology* 84(4): 537–552.

Hansell, S. (2008): *The iPhone Shortage*, The New York Times.

Hastie, R. and R. M. Dawes (2001): *Rational choice in an uncertain world. The psychology of judgement and decision making*. Thousand Oaks, CA; London: Sage Publications.

Jäger, A. O., H.-M. Süß and A. Beauducel (1997): *Berliner Intelligenzstruktur-Test. BIS-Test.* Form 4. Göttingen et al.: Hogrefe.

Kahneman, D. and A. Tversky (1972): Subjective probability: A judgment of representativeness. *Cognitive Psychology* 3(3): 430–454.

Kainz, D. and G. Ossimitz (2002): *Can Students Learn Stock-Flow-Thinking? An Empirical Investigation*. Paper presented at the 20th International Conference of the System Dynamics Society, Palermo, Italy.

Keren, G. and W. B. d. Bruin (2003): On the Assessment of Decision Quality: Considerations Regarding Utility, Conflict and Accountability. In: Hardman, D. and L. Macchi (eds.): *Thinking: Psychological Perspectives on Reasoning, Judgment and Decision Making*, 347–363.

Kleinmuntz, D. N. (1985): Cognitive Heuristics and Feedback in a Dynamic Decision Environment. *Management Science* 31(6): 680–702.

Milne, R. (2005): *Bosch in move to put pump problems behind it,* Financial Times.

Ossimitz, G. (2002): *Stock-flow-thinking and reading stock-flow-related graphs: An emperical investigation in dynamic thinking abilities*. Paper presented at the 20th International Conference of the System Dynamics Society, Palermo, Italy.

Pala, O. and J. A. M. Vennix (2005): Effect of system dynamics education on systems thinking inventory task performance. *System Dynamics Review* 21(2): 147–172.

Reichert, U. and D. Dörner (1988): Heurismen beim Umgang mit einem „einfachen“ dynamischen System. *Sprache und Kognition* 7(1): 12–24.

Renshaw, J. R. and A. Heuston (1957): *The Game Monopologs*, RAND Research Memorandum.

Senge, P. M. (1990): *The fifth discipline. The art and practice of the learning organization*. New York: Doubleday.

Sterman, J. D. (1989a): Misperceptions of feedback in dynamic decision making. *Organizational Behavior and Human Decision Processes* 43(3): 301–335.

Sterman, J. D. (1989b): Modeling managerial behavior: Misperceptions of feedback in a dynamic decision making experiment. *Management Science* 35(3): 321–339.

Sterman, J. D. and L. Booth Sweeney (2002): Cloudy skies: Assessing public understanding of global warming. *System Dynamics Review* 18(2): 207–240.

Sterman, J. D. and L. Booth Sweeney (2007): Understanding public complacency about climate change: Adults' mental models of climate change violate conservation of matter. *Climatic Change* 80(3–4): 213–238.

Süß, H.-M. (1996): *Intelligenz, Wissen und Problemlösen. Kognitive Voraussetzungen für erfolgreiches Handeln bei computersimulierten Problemen*. Göttingen et al.: Hogrefe.

Trochim, W. M. K. and J. P. Donnelly (2007): *The Research Methods Knowledge Base* (3. ed.): Atomic Dog Publishing.

Wittmann, W. W. and K. Hattrup (2004): The relationship between performance in dynamic systems and intelligence. *Systems Research and Behavioral Science* 21(4): 393–409.

On Reproduction, Replication, and Validation in Economic Sciences and System Dynamics

Rainer Schwarz and Peter Maybaum

Brandenburg University of Technology at Cottbus
Department of Mechanical, Electrical and Industrial Engineering

Abstract

We argue that replication is the basis for the success of empirical sciences. In the paper, the concept of replication is differentiated from reproduction, verification and validation. We review replication research in the social sciences and show that replications are rarely conducted in system dynamics. Finally we add to the replication fund of system dynamics and discuss results of a particular replication study, addressing Lyneis' company model.

Keywords: Reproduction, Replication, System Dynamics, Verification, Validation

1 Introduction

In the beginning, economic sciences were a spin-off of philosophical reasoning. In the 19th century, they started to imitate physics using the mathematical method. Based on the empirical and theoretical achievements, physics reached the status of a model for scientific reasoning. Until now, physics has been the main object of study for the methodology of science (Popper, Kuhn and others). However, the application of mathematics to empirical systems is only one foundation for the success of physics as a science. Two other equally important fundamentals for that success are, first, the establishment of sophisticated measurement systems and units and, second, a precise documentation of experimental settings as the basis for an exact reproduction (repetition or replication) of any experiment. If somebody claims to have discovered cold fusion, he has to present a detailed description of the experiment, the equations, and the software, i.e. all elements needed to reproduce the same effect or behaviour. Every laboratory in the world will hurry to repeat that effect: to check if there really is cold fusion under those circumstances – or confusion.

From this perspective, the evolution of physics can be seen as a continuous repetition, refinement, and modification of experiments, going hand in hand with the refinement of measurement units, mathematical methods, models, and theories that describe or explain physical systems and allow the prediction of hitherto unknown physical effects. Trying to reproduce the results of other scientists is a common method of validation and scientific progress in other empirical sciences as well. The German saying can be re-stated as follows: repetition is the mother of physics and other empirical sciences.

In this work, it is argued that the role of reproduction of findings for scientific progress is underestimated in the economic sciences and in the field of System Dynamics. The argument is presented in two parts. The first part looks at the state of the art of replication research in the economic sciences and at validation concepts in System Dynamics. The following section introduces five relevant concepts: verification, falsification, reproduction, replication, and validation. In section 3, we look at the state of the art of replication research, mainly in the economic sciences. Obstacles to replication are considered in section 4. Section 5 contains information about the replication policy of some journals in the economic and social sciences and the System Dynamics Review. A short survey about the concepts of validation in the System Dynamics literature completes the first part of the article. In the second part, we summarize some results of our replication of Lyneis' (1988) dynamic firm model.

2 Basic Concepts

2.1 Verification and Falsification

"Verification" (from Latin, veritas, meaning truth) has different meanings in the English language. First, the word is used as a synonym for checking. Second, it is the proof that a sentence or statement is true. In many cases experimentation, practical application, or empirical observation render the sentence to be true. We follow the usage in Popper's (1959, 32pp.) context of deductive testing of scientific theories. The conclusions from the system are checked in experiments or practical applications. If they are accepted, they are verified. Otherwise, they are falsified. For Popper (1959, 44) "... *objectivity* of scientific statements lies in the fact that they can be *inter-subjectively tested*".[1] We need "such rules as will ensure the testability of scientific statements, which is to say, their falsifiability" (Popper, 1959, 49). Of course, a scientific statement is not objectively true or false because of such a possibility but only if it has been tested in many observations (or replications of the original experiment, model run, etc.) by other researchers. Verification of a statement is the result of the inter-subjective verification process of checking and proofing.

Popper (1959, 32 pp., 251) argues that there is an asymmetry between verification and falsification of scientific theories. "Theories are not verifiable but they can be 'corroborated'." The verification of a conclusion from the theory renders the theory temporarily correct. It only supports the corroboration of the theory. In Popper's understanding, theories are never "true". In contrast, the falsification of a conclusion from the theory results in the final falsification of the theory. The same logic applies to the falsification of mathematical models of real systems.

In checking deductive scientific theories or deductions from a mathematical model, we compare the concurrence of two kinds of statements about real effects. One statement results from a chain of deductions within the theory (or from a model run). It predicts an effect that has or has not been observed in reality. The other statement is received through experiments producing the effect, or through direct observations of the effect. Physical theories have predicted ether in the universe, gravitation waves, the planet Uranus, the element hafnium, dark mat-

[1] For him it is a "... methodological rule ... that only such statements may be introduced in science as are inter-subjectively testable ..." (Popper, 1959, 56).

ter, and other real effects or objects. Hafnium and the planet Uranus have been observed; therefore, the conclusions from these theories have been verified. The corresponding theories have been corroborated. The ether theory has been rejected. The search for dark matter is still ongoing.

In contrast to the theory of science, "verification" in engineering means quality control: checking that a product meets a standard or the specification requirements. In software engineering, verification is "the process of evaluating software to determine whether the products of a given development phase satisfy the conditions imposed at the start of that phase [IEEE-STD-610]". The verification concept in modelling and computer simulation is quite the opposite to that in physics and the methodology of science (which in itself is mostly a generalization of the history and methodology of physics). Oberkampf et al. (2002, 2) assert: "In verification, the relationship of the simulation to the real world is not an issue". A physicist would not claim that cold fusion has been verified if he had not conducted his research in the real world.

2.2 Reproduction and Replication

Reproduction can be seen as the precondition for verification. Popper (1959, 45) remarks that we don't take our own observations seriously in a scientific way if we did not **test** them **by repeated observations or experiments** until we are convinced that they are reproducible and can therefore be tested in an inter-subjective way. He writes: "Indeed the scientifically significant *physical effect* may be defined as that which can be regularly reproduced by anyone who carries out the appropriate experiment in the way prescribed". The experimental arrangement has to be produced and reproduced in order to repeat the physical effect. However, reproduction of an experiment is never precise (Popper, 1959, 207). The concept of reproduction is connected to the idea of variation or mutation. This concept of reproduction is reformulated today by the term "replication".[2]

2.3 Replication

This term has no unique definition. Blalock (1961, 343) was among the first to introduce this word. As Popper, he is concerned with the repetition of experiments. He sees "two purposes of replication":

1. "To vary experimental conditions in order to isolate the effects of disturbing influences", and
2. "To obtain more accurate measurement".

Today, replication literature distinguishes between two main types of replication:[3]

- Investigation of whether the findings of a past study are reproducible (whether the application of the same methods to the same data achieves the same result); and
- Application of the same methods to different objects, subjects, population, or regions.

[2] Lucas (2003, 248) writes "Reproducible findings are findings that are repeated under identical conditions, and this is what is usually meant by replication research. Will the study, repeated again in the same conditions, produce the same findings?" This author is one of the few that reflect Popper.

[3] See King (1995, 451); Herrnson (1995, 452); Tsang and Kwan (1999, 766–768).

The first type of replication is also called "duplication", "confirmation", "verification", "reanalysis", "retest replication", or "exact replication". The second is called "empirical generalization" or "replication".[4] In replication literature, one can find more detailed proposals of replication types. For example, Tsang and Kwan (1999, 766–768) also include in their typology the use of different measurement procedures and methods.

2.4 Validation

As in verification, the concurrence of two kinds of statements is also tested in validation. Commonly understood, validation denotes the establishment or assessment of legitimacy, i.e. the test to see if something corresponds to a norm. We speak of a valid ticket, a valid credit card, a valid contract. A valid argument should correspond to the norms of formal logic; it should not be based on logical contradictions. Similarly, software without bugs or a model that is internally consistent can be said to be valid.[5] However, authors from the modelling and simulation community used to say that such software is verified. They use "validation" as a synonym for "verification", namely, the comparison of simulation results with experimental data.[6] The engineering concept of validation is different, too. Validation checks that a product satisfies the intended use or customer. IEEE-Standard-610 defines validation as "the process of evaluating software during or at the end of the development process to determine whether it satisfies specified requirements."

This short overview of the terms verification, falsification, reproduction, replication, and validation can be summarized as follows. In the methodology of science, these terms are centred on the establishment of truth for scientific statements, their verification. A logical set of such statements – be it a theory or a mathematical model – can, because of the modus tollens, never be verified. However, such a set should produce at least one statement that can be falsified. In physics, these are predictions that can be tested by empirical observations, or deductions that are not in agreement with new or old observations of real effects. This agreement can be established only by repeated, reproduced or replicated observations respectively experiments conducted by independent researchers. A statement is valid if it is in agreement with a verified scientific statement, i.e. with truth. In a much weaker sense, validation also means that a theory, a mathematical model, or a software package, is in agreement with logic, does not contain logical contradictions, bugs, or so on. This understanding of validation is not necessarily scientific. Astrological software and computer games are valid in this sense, too.[7] In scientific literature, we find the term "validation" with three meanings: comparison of a statement with observations of the real world (verification), usefulness of a product for a purpose or a customer, and internal consistency of a model.

[4] For a good example of the second type see the replication of the Aston study reported by Child (1972). The replication confirmed some results of the original study and modified others.

[5] See Oreskes et al. (1994, 642).

[6] Barlas and Carpenter (1990, 164), Oberkampf et al. (2002, 2).

[7] Authors in the modelling community will call such a computer program "verified" if its "internal consistency" is established (see Barlas and Carpenter 1990, 164; Pala et al., 1999, 16; Oberkampf et al. 2002, 2).

Long before Popper, Alfred Marshall already studied the physical method as being relevant for the method of economics: the "... physical sciences ... aim at exactness. That is they all aim at precipitating the results of a multitude of observations into provisional statements, which are sufficiently definite to be brought under test by other observations of nature. These statements, when first put forth, seldom claim a high authority. But after they have been tested by many independent observations and especially after they have been applied successfully in the prediction of coming events, or of results of new experiments, they graduate as laws... their progress depends on the multitudinous co-operation of armies of workers."[8]

In the next few sections we will see that replications (reproductions or repetitions) of scientific statements, i.e. "many independent observations" by other researchers are still rather rare in the economic sciences and in System Dynamics.

3 Empirical Findings in Replication Literature

From Popper to the modern methodological literature, the importance of replication is stressed. King (1995, 444) writes: "As virtually every good methodology text explains the *only way to understand and evaluate an empirical analysis fully is to know the exact process by which the data were generated and the analysis produced*. Without adequate documentation, scholars often have trouble replicating their *own* results months later." Hubbard et al. (1998, 244) use strong words: "Unreplicated research findings, even those that are highly statistically significant, are only speculative in nature (Hubbard and Armstrong, 1994) and 'virtually meaningless and useless' in themselves (Lindsay and Ehrenberg, 1993: 219)." However, reproduction and replication of the results of other authors is mostly an exception in the economic and social sciences. These sciences mainly tried to adopt from physics the use of the mathematical method.

A new development in replication research started in 1982, when the Journal of Money, Credit and Banking adopted an explicit replication policy. In a corresponding research project, authors of empirical articles were asked to provide programs and data used in their articles.[9] In the first group, 62 authors of empirical papers published since 1980 were approached. Of them, 42 responded, and only 22 submitted data sets and programs. Only one data set posed no problems for replication. The second group covered 92 authors from 1982–1984, whose articles were either accepted or under review. 3 data sets within the group of accepted papers allowed a replication and 24 had problems. 18 authors under review did not submit data upon request, 23 data sets were useless for replication, and only 4 were complete.[10] All in all, 14 data sets were found to be complete enough to allow an attempt at replication. Dewald et al. (1986) report about their detailed replication of 9 empirical articles. "We replicated the results of two articles in their entirety ... We reproduced exactly almost all the results of V. Vance Roley (1983) and obtained qualitatively similar results for John Merric (1983)."[11]

[8] Marshall (1938, 30, 31).

[9] See Dewald et al. (1986).

[10] Dewald et al. (1986, 591, 592).

[11] Dewald et al. (1986, 593, 594).

We summarize this project as follows: of the 154 empirical papers, only 14 (or 9 percent) provided an opportunity for confirmation by the scientific community, and only 2 could be confirmed fully – 1 directly and 1 in a qualitative way.

Hubbard and Vetter (1996) found, in their content analysis of published replication research in 18 leading business journals during the time period from 1970 to 1991 in accounting, economics, finance, management, and marketing, that "… such research typically constitutes less than 10% of published empirical work in the accounting, economics, and finance areas, and 5% or less in the management and marketing fields. Further, when such work is undertaken the results usually conflict with existing findings …". This is consistent with the findings of other authors.[12] These authors summarize as a result, that "… published replication and extension research is uncommon in business disciplines."

Hubbard et al. (1998, 244) remark, "… The vast majority of empirical articles in these areas consist of uncorroborated 'single-shot' studies. More disturbingly, in the few instances where extensions are undertaken, they often conflict with, or at best partially support, the original findings … This suggests that the knowledge bases in these fields rest on shaky ground." Of 701 empirical articles in strategic management journals, only 5.3 percent were replications with extensions. From the period 1976–85 to the period 1986–95, no increase in the frequency of published replication research was found.[13]

Replication can have flaws when the software is not available or badly documented. Econometric results can be software-dependent. Different econometric software can lead to different results in replication attempts. Software packages are never perfect. It is well known that bugs in software are corrected in subsequent versions of the software. McCullough and Vinod (1999) presented several cases of serious numerical discrepancies between econometric packages. Also, the data and program archives collected by some journals and other institutions in the last two decades contain erroneous or incomplete entries. An investigation of the data and program archive collected by the Journal of Money, Credit and Banking could replicate results from only 14 of the 69 entries in the data archive.[14]

In recent years, the article "Why Most Published Research Findings Are False" has provoked a lively discussion. Ioannidis' (2005) argument was based on previous replication attempts of articles in the field of medicine (regarding clinical trials, traditional epidemiological studies, modern molecular research, and others). He writes, "There is increasing concern that in modern research, false findings may be the majority or even the vast majority of published research claims. … Research findings are defined here as any relationship reaching formal statistical significance."[15] In another paper he states, "Even the most influential clinical research published in the top journals may often be refuted".[16] His arguments are mostly based on sophisticated statistical problems that are debated in statistical literature.

[12] Hubbard et al. (1998, 244).

[13] Hubbard et al. (1998, 247, 248).

[14] McCullough et al. (2006, 1105).

[15] Ioannidis (2005, 0696).

[16] Ioannidis (2005b, 740); in this source are more references to the evidence, see also Ioannidis and Lau (1999).

4 Obstacles to Replication

Replication is the expression of that doubt on which science is based. The result of a replication study often renders at least some results of another author incorrect, or else it does not confirm them. Replication produces a situation of cognitive dissonance; therefore all statements of the theory of cognitive dissonance apply. "In addition, replications may be interpreted as reflecting a lack of trust in another scientist's integrity and ability, as a critique of the scientist's findings, or as a personal dispute between researchers."[17] A critic is often not welcome and sometimes suppressed. But there are not only cognitive or mental problems.

The observed empirical situation of replication in economic and other social and medical sciences is, in an important way, grounded in the reward structure within scientific communities. Vital career and strong financial interests resist a lively replication culture. Dewald et al. (1986, 587, 601) comment on the reward structure in this way: "Scientific and professional laurels are not awarded for replicating another scientist's findings. ... In fact, little benefit accrues to authors by providing programs and data, and little reward accrues to researchers conducting replication studies unless they can show that a major scientist has committed either fraud or a significant error in his research. This situation is not unique to economics ..." It is reinforced by the policy of many journals that prefer original work and interpret a replication as an act of intellectual mediocrity. (See also next section.)

Changing this situation is not as simple as it may seem. The problem is not only in "providing programs and data" in a well documented way. In many cases, the researcher did spend a lot of time and other resources in collecting large and complex data sets, as well as in the development and in the modification of computer programs. A replication standard requires, in addition, a perfect documentation of the software and the data set which can often be quiet tiresome work. After this much effort, the product must be given away for free. This can reduce the incentive for individual investigators to collect complex sets of data. This may also be the reason that authors often provide erroneous data sets and bad or useless documentation, which do not allow a replication.

Scientists may also suffer from confirmation bias, and selectively present data which is favourable to their preconceptions. They may then have an incentive to document their work poorly, in order to prevent others from replicating it.[18] Sterman (1991, 159) observes: "Failure to replicate may arise because published results do not include the raw data or because descriptions of methods and models are too vague. Limitations on article length and lack of incentives to replicate someone else's work have often resulted in wholly inadequate documentation."

Added to all this is the fact that, with a replication, important financial interests can be at stake. Krimsky et al. (1998) found that 15% of the authors in their sample of 1,105 university authors from Massachusetts institutions had a financial interest relevant to one of their publications. Nowadays equations are patented as financial innovations and simple words like "Eva", "Stage gate" and many others are claimed as property rights in the business science. Articles

[17] Dewald et al. (1986, 587).

[18] Sterman (2002, 521).

with these words strengthen the interests connected to such equations or words, and a replication article bears a financial threat if it cannot fully duplicate the original. Even more money can be at stake when an article in the field of biomedical research has been falsified through replication.

5 Replication Policy of Journals in the Economic Sciences and in System Dynamics

Genuine scientists have always supported the importance of criticism for the development of a scientific field. However, this support is very limited if it refers to the editorial policy of empirical papers in economic journals. As far as we can see, Ragnar Frisch (1933) started to change this situation when, as editor, he formulated the following policy in the first issue of Econometrica: "In statistical and other numerical work presented in Econometrica the original raw data will, as a rule, be published, unless their volume is excessive. This is important in order to stimulate criticism, control, and further studies."[19]

A new step was taken when, in 1982, the Journal of Money, Credit and Banking adopted an explicit replication policy, requesting from authors the programs and data used in their articles and making these programs and data available to other researchers upon request. However, in 1983, the subsequent editor of the JMCB abandoned the practice of requesting data from authors.[20] Not until 1996 were authors once again asked to provide "the data and programs used in generating the reported results."[21]

Beginning with the 1990s, a new epoch in the replication policy of journals in economic sciences can be attributed to the American Economic Review, the leading journal of the American Economic Association: "It is the policy of the *American Economic Review* to publish papers only if the data used in the analysis are clearly and precisely documented and are readily available to any researcher for purposes of replication. Authors of accepted papers that contain empirical work, simulations, or experimental work must provide to the *Review*, prior to publication, the data, programs, and other details of the computations sufficient to permit replication. These will be posted on the *AER* Web site."[22]

Among American journals with a replication policy, McCullough et al. (2006, 1095) differentiate between "journals that have 'policies' requiring authors to make their data and code available upon request (e.g., Labour Economics, International Journal of Industrial Organization, Journal of Human Resources) and journals that have data and code archives (e.g., this journal (Journal of Money, Credit and Banking), Macroeconomic Dynamics, and Fed. Res. St. Louis Review)".

---

[19] Frisch (1933, 3).

[20] According to McCullough and Vinod (1999, 661).

[21] See McCullough et al. (2006).

[22] On http://www.aeaweb.org/aer/data_availability_policy.html a detailed list of replication requirements for authors can be found.

As early as 1991, Sterman formulated the policy of the System Dynamics Review (SDR) in complete agreement with the concepts outlined in section 2: "A hallmark of the scientific method is the requirement that independent investigators be able to replicate experimental results. ... The policy of the System Dynamics Review is to require all model-based analysis to be supported by full and complete documentation."[23] However, nowadays this ability of "independent investigators" is restricted by a money barrier: "Readers requesting documentation and paying costs of preparation and handling should be able to obtain from authors documented model listings and parameter values supporting published results."[24] It seems a bit strange that the reader should pay for replicating the findings of an author and for proving them true or correct. The AER has shifted this money burden to the authors' submission fee.

In German-speaking countries, a replication policy similar to that of the American Economic Review and other journals mentioned above cannot be detected in business economics. All of the leading journals of business economics (Betriebswirtschaftslehre), namely: Zeitschrift für Betriebswirtschaft (ZfB), Zeitschrift für betriebswirtschaftliche Forschung (Zfbf) or Schmalenbach Business Review, Journal für Betriebswirtschaft, Die Unternehmung and Die Betriebswirtschaft, don't require the data, model listings, program codes, and documentation needed to reproduce the results of published empirical articles. This is also the case for specialized management journals like Zeitschrift für Controlling & Management.

A missing replication policy seems to be the case for the majority of journals in the field of economics worldwide. Until now, only a minority of American economic journals has been leading the way in the development of the field towards the reproduction and replication standards of physics, chemistry and some other successful empirical sciences. McCullough et al. (2006, 1095) summarize the situation as follows: "Consequently, each economics journal can be said to operate in one of two distinct markets: the market for reproducible results, and the market for irreproducible results."

Finally, we will note that Political Science has also arrived in the 1990s with a high replication standard. The Public Affairs Video Archive at Purdue University and the Inter-University Consortium for Political and Social Research at the University of Michigan collect information about the process by which data was collected, coded, analyzed, and reported.[25]

Beginning in 1994, the American Journal of Political Science and the journal Political Analysis require footnotes about replication data sets to be included with all articles. The British Journal of Political Science and the Policy Studies Journal have adopted similar policies.

6 Validation in the System Dynamics Community

For many years, the interest in model validation in the SD community has been stronger than the interest in replication, as judged by the number of articles published in SDR and elsewhere. But the understanding of validation differs widely. The three connotations mentioned above can

[23] Sterman (1991, 159).

[24] See System Dynamics Review, Guidelines for authors.

[25] See King (1995, 446) for details.

be found: comparison of a statement with observations of the real world (verification), usefulness of a product for a purpose or a customer, and internal consistency of a model:

- "Validity, as an abstract concept divorced from purpose, has no useful meaning." (Forrester 1961, 116)
- Validation is "… the process by which we establish sufficient confidence in a model to be prepared to use it for some particular purpose." Coyle (1977)[26]
- Validation means "… the process of establishing confidence in the soundness and usefulness of a model with respect to its purpose." (Forrester and Senge 1980)
- "Model validation is a gradual process of building confidence in the usefulness of a model." (Barlas and Carpenter 1990, 157)
- "Validity of a system dynamics model primarily means validity of its internal structure …. Direct structure tests assess the validity of the model structure, by direct comparison with knowledge about real system structure." (Barlas 1996, 188,189)
- Validity of a model being defined as "well-suited to its purpose and soundly constructed … The model should do the same things as the real system *and for the same reasons*." (Coyle 1996, Coyle and Exelby 2000, 33)
- "Validation: Checking whether the model (formal or conceptual) is an accurate, good enough representation of reality; checking the correspondence with the real system." (Pala, Vennix and Kleijnen 1999, 16)[27]
- "The behaviour of the model must be like that of the real system and changes to the model's structure, parameters and policies must produce changed behaviour which is plausible and explicable." (Coyle and Exelby 2000, 35, 36)
- "Today, more and more social scientists recognize the impossibility of validation." (Sterman, 2002, 521)

In chapter 21 of his book "Business Dynamics", Sterman (2000) seems to have dropped the concept "validation" of models: "In fact, validation and verification of models is impossible".[28] This statement is similar to Popper's statements about theory. Sterman's argument takes note of the results and debates within the philosophy of science, especially regarding falsification. Consequently, he renames the validation tests developed by the SD community into "tests to uncover flaws and improve models"[29] or "model testing".[30] At the same time, he combines the philosophy of science with positions in the SD community. He retains the need to create useful models and the "gradual process" of validation. The latter is reinterpreted as a process of learning and social communication. Sterman's approach focuses "… on creating models that are useful, on the process of testing, on the ongoing comparison of the model against all data of all types, and on the continual iteration between experiments with the virtual world of the model and experiments in the real world."[31] And, where Popper underlines the need to reproduce the

[26] Citation after Coyle and Exelby (2000, 28).

[27] The authors use this definition together with "Verification: Checking the internal consistency of the computer program" (Pala et al., 1999, p. 16).

[28] See Sterman (2000, 846) and Sterman (2002).

[29] See Sterman (2000, 858).

[30] See Sterman (2002, 521).

[31] See Sterman (2002, 521).

physical effect, Sterman, in the same spirit, presses for replication (see Business Dynamics, Chapter 21, 855pp.):" You should not accept any result generated by a model you can't replicate."[32]

We agree with Sterman's (2002, 522) assessment of replication within the system dynamics community: "We must insist on the highest standards of documentation. Models must be fully replicable and available for critical review. … We must open the modelling process to the widest range of people we can, including our critics. … Unfortunately, all too often testing is inadequate, documentation is incomplete, important critics and stakeholders are excluded, and assessment is never undertaken. Worse, model testing is often designed to "prove" the model is "right" and model tests are presented as evidence designed to promote client acceptance. We are continually pressured by our clients, our students, our colleagues, and our own egos to slip out of the role of questioner and learner into the role of expert and teacher. … Taking the perspective that we are selling a "product" to the client is antithetical to a genuine inquiry process. Such an approach is designed to deflect criticism and promote the status and authority of the modeller. Instead, it makes learning difficult and ultimately erodes the impact of the model and the credibility of the modeller – and of all modellers."

Our screening of the word "replication" in the System Dynamics Review archive resulted in just one replication article: Kampman (1991) replicated the dynamic model of an anthropological-ecological theory. He reports "serious technical errors" in this model that did not change the results. In this sense the model is a valid interpretation of the theory. The theory itself was neither confirmed nor falsified, but was taken by Kampman as a given.

Despite the possibility of getting the documentation of some models on the enterprise level, replication, reproduction or repetition of such models is hard to find in a field that was founded as "Industrial Dynamics" more than 50 years ago. On the enterprise level, repetition is used in system dynamics almost exclusively for that part of industrial dynamics which is embedded in the beer game – the inventory system. Structure and behaviour have been repeated by different members of the SD community over many years. In the following section we will extend the number of replication studies in system dynamics by our contribution.

7 Replication of a Dynamic Firm Model

With the purpose of deepening the understanding of the evolution of a firm among students of management, we were looking for a system dynamics model that fulfilled the following requirements:

1. It represents the economic theory of the firm.
2. It contains the most important variables, which are empirically known to influence the success of an elementary firm.
3. Equations and output behaviour represent observed empirical relationships.
4. Simulation runs allow for the understanding of the implications of typical growth strategies.

[32] See Sterman (2000, 858); section 21.3.3 of his book "Business Dynamics" is devoted to replication and considers important results of the replication literature.

Compared to other model descriptions of business dynamics, Lyneis (1988) gives many prerequisites needed for an attempt to replicate his model. He defines variables and presents equations, some assumptions and interpretations, the computer program of the final model, and time behaviours of variables which can be used in the work of other members of the scientific community. Equations, data, and program listings can also be found in certain other books concerned with business dynamics.[33]

We use Lyneis' equations but a different software (POWERSIM, whereas Lyneis used DYNAMO) in our replication effort. His book develops the following building blocks for a company model: the two-stage inventory system (ch. 4, 5), connected with the parts supplier sector (ch. 6), the labour sector (ch. 7), a market interaction sector (ch. 8), the accounting sector (ch. 9, 10), the capital equipment sector (ch. 11) connected with financial resources (ch. 12) and professional resources (ch. 13). As we have shown elsewhere[34], the equations in these chapters don't fit into a comprehensive company model because the production rate is defined in a different way. In the two-stage inventory system, the production rate (PR) is influenced by information about the customer order rate (COR), work in process (WIP), and finished inventory (FI). In chapter 5, the production rate is determined by the desired production rate (DPR, incorporating the former influences on PR), and the effect of parts inventory level (EPILPR). Within the labour sector, the influence structure on PR changes. The potential output from labour (POL) determines the production rate, together with EPILPR. DPR now has an indirect influence, mediated mainly by labour (L) and overtime (OT). In chapter 8 (company-market interaction), DPR is the only factor determining PR directly, i.e. without the influences of labour and labour productivity. In chapter 12, PR influences UO (unfilled orders). In the market sector, the opposite holds true.

Also, because of the following reasons, we could not replicate connections between some blocks of the model as described in the different chapters. Chapter 10 does not present a separate building block but rather a table function for the effect of financial pressure (EFDPR) on desired production rate (DPR) and parts order rate (POR).There are no hints at a connection to other blocks. The effects of the labour sector are based on the assumption that capital equipment (CE) does not constrain production. The building block of capacity expansion takes such effects into account. The financial needs for capacity expansion are considered in chapter 12. Here there are no variables or equations which could be connected to other blocks or be interpreted in the context of the company model. Chapter 13 (professional resources) exercises an impact only on the market share (MS). Therefore this block is very loosely coupled with the variables determining the evolution of the firm, not to mention the measurement problems of that impact.

The accounting sector of the book is not suited for management education. In accounting literature and practice, fixed costs are those costs that one has to bear even when there is no output. Lyneis defines fixed costs as a fixed percentage of the average dollar value of sales. Therefore they are variable costs depending on output (sales).

---

33 See the comparision with the models of the firm proposed by Zahn (1971), Coyle (1996) and Wolstenholme in Schöneborn (2004).

34 Schwarz and Maybaum (2000).

For all of these reasons, the chapters of the book cannot be interpreted as building blocks of a company model. We interpret them as a didactical introduction to the final company model. In other words, Lyneis traces the dynamics of some parts of the company in different building blocks. Their dynamics is explained by different variables, which are defined by different equations. These equations are not integrated into one comprehensive model. However, a final company model is presented by Lyneis in the 27 pages of appendix C and D of his book. They contain the equation listing of the company model as a DYNAMO program. We were able to replicate these equations with POWERSIM.

Before presenting these results, we will describe the main result of our replication of the detailed model structure of Lyneis' two-stage inventory system and the corresponding equations (from chapter 4 of his book). The time behaviour of key variables in our POWERSIM-simulation[35] is shown in Figure 1 (see p. 320). One can find only minor differences from the result of Lyneis (Fig. 4.2 in his book). This means that the core building block of the company model proposed by Lyneis can be replicated. Investigation of the differences needs further research. One of the possible reasons can be the differences in the software used: DYNAMO versus POWERSIM. It is well known that even different standard econometric software packages present "serious numerical discrepancies" for identical data sets.[36] In our replication, the numerical discrepancies are not serious. It is our opinion that a model is better corroborated if it runs with nearly the same results on different software.

We could also replicate the equations of Lyneis' final model in POWERSIM.[37] The equations of the model blocks in the 27 pages of the final company model[38] look very different compared to the equations in the book. The replication confirms that the final model is internally consistent and runs smoothly in POWERSIM. However, the simulation runs with the final model resulted in time behaviour for important economic variables that is not characteristic for viable companies in economic reality. Some start-up conditions and assumptions for the modelled company in the list of equations also don't represent empirical findings in business economics.

The firm produces only one type of product, which does not change over 5 years. In the beginning, the firm employs 400 people. One person is producing, on one unit of capital equipment (machine), one unit of product per day. Market demand does not change over 5 years. 40 units are needed in the market. Market share is 10% in the beginning, so 4 units per day are shipped. At the start, customer order rate (COR) is also 4 units per day, but increases to 28 units per day in the end. The hidden assumption is that only other suppliers go bankrupt. Production and shipment rate (SR) is 400 units on the first day; shipment rate breaks down to 4 units/day and increases then to 28 units/day approaching equilibrium with COR (Fig. 2, see p. 321).

[35] The equations are shown in Schwarz and Maybaum (2000), source on the web.

[36] See McCullough and Vinod (1999).

[37] Our translation of the DYNAMO program into POWERSIM can be seen in appendixes II and III in Schwarz and Maybaum (2000). Lyneis' comment in his program suggests that the final model is only intended for use in chapter 13 of the book.

[38] See Lyneis (1988, appendix C and D).

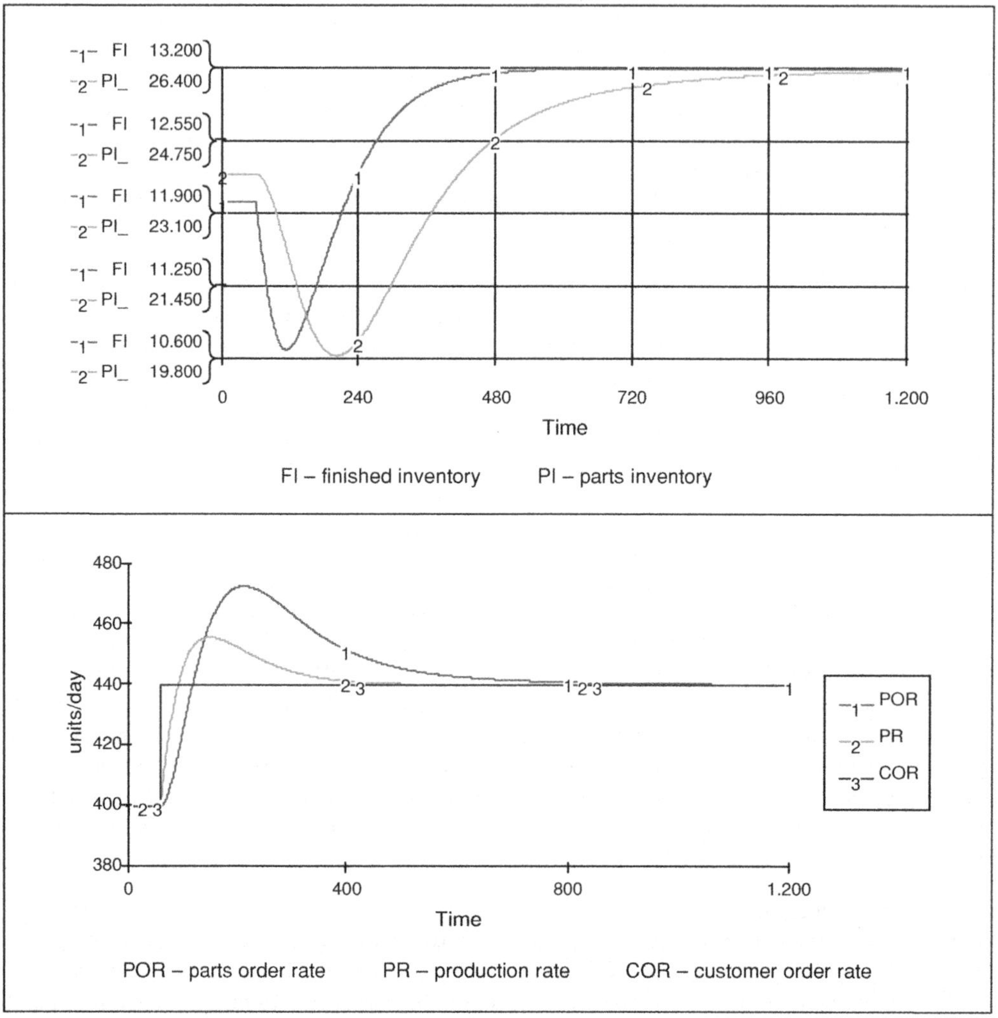

Figure 1: Behaviour of POR, PR and COR in the Two-Stage Inventory System

In the finished inventory (FI), the firm has 12000 units at its start-up. It is astonishing why it produces at all. If it ships 4 units per day according to customer order rate (COR), it has enough inventories for many years – without any need to produce. In light of this starting condition, the behaviour in Figure 2 is very understandable: production rate is zero within the first 400 days. The production started afterwards has the ultimate result of a much greater inventory of final products (FI): 20000 units after 5 years (Fig. 3). The company accrues only loss and no profit (Fig. 4, see p. 322). Such production makes no economic sense. At the same time, the logic of an economist is satisfied: it is no wonder that this firm starts with 400 workers and ends with 32. But we would not call it business dynamics.

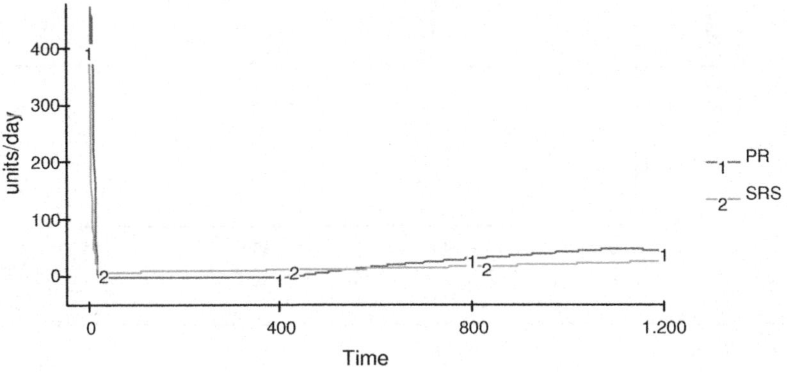

Figure 2: Time Behaviour of Production Rate (PR) and Shipment Rate from Stock (SRS)

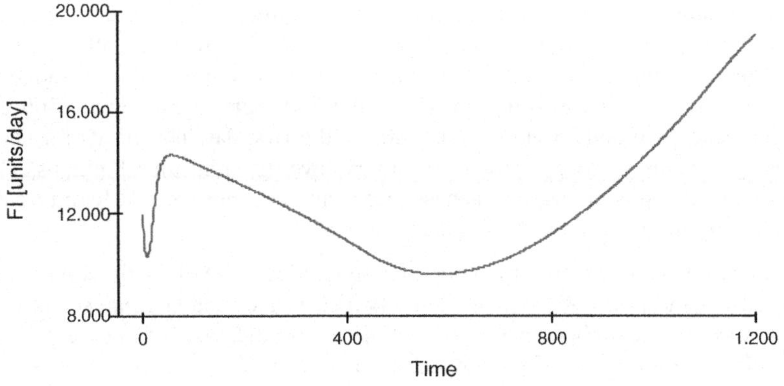

Figure 3: Time Behaviour of Finished Inventory (FI)

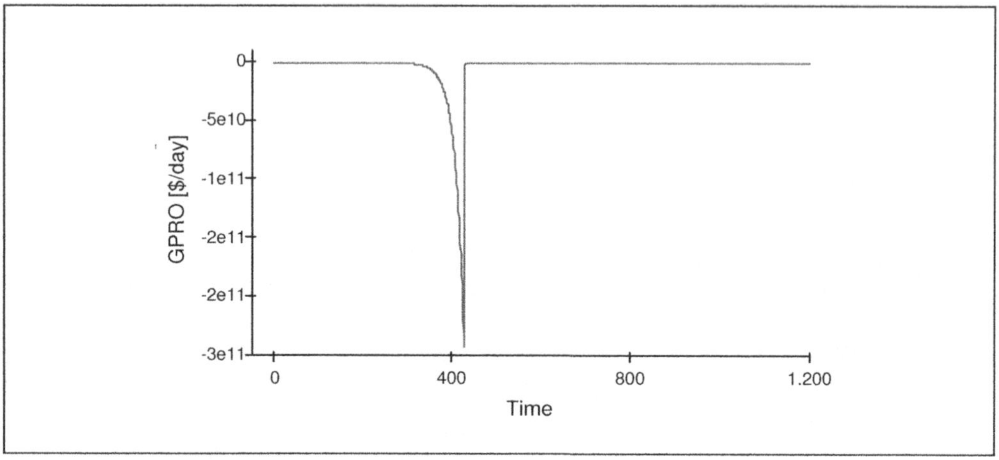

Figure 4: Time Behaviour of Gross Profits (GPRO)

8 Discussion and Final Remarks

Lyneis has produced a sufficiently rich model description for our attempt to bridge the gap between SD and the business economics literature. We have presented only first results of our attempt to replicate this model. For one building block, it could be demonstrated that the model structure produces the same time behaviour with quite different SD-software. This is not trivial considering the differences in numerical results different software packages produce.

But the different building blocks in the book are not integrated into one complex company model. The complex company model of Lyneis exists only in the form of an equation listing in a DYNAMO program. A replication of that program in POWERSIM is possible. One possible cause for the unstable – and in the understanding of economics and accounting unusual – results can be seen in the initial conditions of that dynamic system. But there are other reasons as well. One critical sector seems to be capital equipment. For an economist, it is a strange vision that in a company of 400 people, working on 400 of the 500 units of equipment, 500 units of the machinery are discarded and 75 units are bought on the first day. This needs further investigation. Inventory dynamics and equipment dynamics have different time horizons. The discrete step expansion of equipment has, in business praxis and accounting, a different treatment than the relatively continuous movement of material and parts.

As a conclusion from our search for a complex dynamic model of a firm compatible with the theory of the firm and Betriebswirtschaftslehre (which is a special German scientific approach to systemize the empirical phenomena of viable firms on the basis of microeconomic theory) we see the following interesting directions for further scientific research:

1. Investigation of all explicit and implicit model assumptions in the context of the theory and typical praxis of the firm.
2. More systematic investigation of the initial conditions of the Lyneis model comparing them with the typical conditions of a start-up firm and the initial data of a typical firm at the beginning of a usual year.

3. Simulation experiments with realistic initial data and the final Lyneis model.
4. Development of a reduced company model with the following requirements:
   - the core variables should have a clear definition, which is the same in all building blocks of the model; and this definition must have an interpretation which is compatible with similar definitions in economic theory (or praxis);
   - the essential dynamical structures of a typical firm should be captured; and
   - the time behaviour of the reduced model should be compatible with the empirical results of the business economics literature.
5. Development of a capital equipment model on the basis of economic theory, capturing the discrete nature of company expansion and producing time behaviours similar to empirical time series.

The debates between Popper, Kuhn, Lakatos and Feyerabend did end with a mood of "anything goes" or "abandoning method". In the philosophy of science, the debate goes on and does not give us a solid foundation in methodology.[39] Despite all discussions between philosophers, there is no doubt regarding the main point of our contribution. A scientific statement is objective if it has been verified (or validated). However, if it was the deduction from a theory or the result of an experiment with a model, neither a theory nor a model can be verified or validated. This follows from the modus tollens. In order to verify a scientific result, one needs to be able to replicate (or reproduce) it. There should be inter-subjective testing and critique of scientific results – by the "multitudinous co-operation of armies of workers" (in Marshall's words).

However, replication research is seldom undertaken in the economic sciences and in system dynamics. Since the study of Dewald et al. (1986), progress is moving slowly. There is still much to be done in order to match the replication standards of physics.

Acknowledgements

The authors thank anonymous reviewers, Robert Schwarz, Marthe Klöcking and Anya Cornell for their suggestions that helped to improve this text.

References

Barlas, Y. (1989): Multiple Tests for Validation of System Dynamics Type of Simulation Models. *European Journal of Operational Research* 42: 59–87.

Barlas, Y. (1996): Formal aspects of model validity and validation in system dynamics. *System Dynamics Review* 12(3): 183–210.

Barlas, Y. and S. Carpenter (1990): Philosophical roots of model validation: two paradigms. *System Dynamics Review* 6(2): 148–166.

Blalock, Jr., H. M. (1961): Theory, Measurement, and Replication in the Social Sciences. *The American Journal of Sociology* 66(4): 342–347.

Child, J. (1972): Organization Structure and Strategies of Control: A Replication of the Aston Study. *Administrative Science Quarterly* 17(2): 163–177.

[39] Preston (1994, 317) argues that Popper's "... account of epistemology and methodology is extensively confused".

Coyle R. G. (1977): *Management System Dynamics*. Chichester: Wiley.

Coyle, R. G. (1996): *System Dynamics Modelling. A Practical Approach*. London: Chapman & Hall.

Coyle, G. and D. Exelby (2000): The validation of commercial system dynamics models. *System Dynamics Review* 16(1): 27–41.

Dewald, W. G., J. G. Thursby and R. G. Anderson (1986): Replication in Empirical Economics: The Journal of Money, Credit and Banking Project. *The American Economic Review* 76(4): 587–603.

Forrester, J. W. and P. M. Senge (1980): Tests for Building Confidence in System Dynamics Models. In: Legasto, A. A., J. W. Forrester and J. M. Lyneis (eds.): *System Dynamics*, New York, NY: North-Holland, 209–228.

Frisch, R. (1993): Editorial. *Econometrica* 8 (January).

Herrnson, P. S. (1995): Replication, Verification, Secondary Analysis, and Data Collection in Political Science. *PS: Political Science and Politics* 28(3): 452 ff.

Hubbard, R., D. E. Vetter and E. L. Little (1998): Replication in Strategic Management: Scientific Testing for Validity, Generalizability, and Usefulness. *Strategic Management Journal* 19(3): 243–254.

Hubbard, R. and D. E. Vetter (1996): An empirical comparison of published replication research in accounting, economics, finance, management, and marketing. Drake University, USA Central Michigan University, USA, in: *Journal of Business Research* 35, Issue 2, February 1996: 153–164, Abstract available online: http://www.sciencedirect.com/science/article/B6V7S-3VV68XR-S/2/993cb1031b94043b268279 13e102b65b, 19 February 2009.

Ioannidis, J. P. A and J. Lau (1999): State of the Evidence: Current Status and Prospects of Meta-Analysis in Infectious Diseases. *Clinical Infectious Diseases* 29(5): 1178–1185.

Ioannidis, J. P. A. (2005): Why Most Published Research Findings Are False. *PLoS Medicine* 2(8).

Ioannidis, J. P. A. (2005b): Molecular Bias. *European Journal of Epidemiology* 20(9): 739–745.

Kampmann, C. (1991): Replication and revision of a classic system dynamics model: critique of "Population Control Mechanisms in a Primitive Agricultural Society". *System Dynamics Review* 7(2): 159–198.

King, G. (1995): Replication, Replication. *PS: Political Science and Politics* 28(3): 444–452.

Kuhn, T. S. (1970): *The Structure of Scientific Revolutions* (2. ed.). Chicago: University of Chicago Press.

Krimsky, S., L. S. Rothenberg, P. Stott, and G. Kyle (1998): Scientific Journals and Their Authors' Financial Interests: A Pilot Study. *Psychotherapy and Psychosomatics* 67(4–5).

Lakatos, I. (1970): History of Science and Its Rational Reconstructions, in: *PSA: Proceedings of the Biennial Meeting of the Philosophy of Science Association* 1970: 91–136, published by: The University of Chicago Press on behalf of the Philosophy of Science Association.

Lane, D. C. (1995): The Folding Star: A comparative reframing and extension of validity concepts in system dynamics, in: *Proceedings of the International System Dynamics Conference*, Tokyo, Japan, Vol. 1: 111–130, source on the web: http://www.systemdynamics.org/conferences/1995/proceed/index.htm, 27.1.2009.

La Sorte, M. A. (1972): Replication as a Verification Technique in Survey Research: A Paradigm. *The Sociological Quarterly* 13(2): 218–227.

Laudan, L. (1986): Methodology's Prospects, in: *PSA: Proceedings of the Biennial Meeting of the Philosophy of Science Association* 1986, Volume Two: Symposia and Invited Papers (1986): 347–354, Published by: The University of Chicago Press on behalf of the Philosophy of Science Association.

Lucas, J. W. (2003): Theory-Testing, Generalization, and the Problem of External Validity. *Sociological Theory* 21(3): 236–253.

Lyneis, M. J. (1988): *Corporate Planning and Policy Design*. Cambridge: Pugh-Roberts Association Inc.

Marshall, A. (1938): *Principles of Economics* (8. ed.). Macmillan and Co., London.

Matthes, B. und R. Schwarz (1983): *Dialogsystem der Reproduktion DDR. Zur quantitativen Analyse von Reproduktionskreisläufen und für volkswirtschaftliche Vorausberechnungen*. Manuskriptdruck, Hochschule für Ökonomie, Zentralinstitut für Sozialistische Wirtschaftsführung, Berlin.

McCullough, B. D. and H. D. Vinod (1999): The Numerical Reliability of Econometric Software. *The Journal of Economic Literature*: 633–665.

McCullough, B. D., K. A. McGeary and T. D. Harrison (2006): Lessons from the JMCB Archive. *Journal of Money, Credit, and Banking* 38(4).

Oreskes, N., K. Shrader-Frechette and K. Belitz (1994): Verification, Validation, and Confirmation of Numerical Models in the Earth Sciences. *Science*, New Series 263(5147): 641–646.

Oberkampf, W. L., T. G. Tucano and C. Hirsch (2002): *Verification, Validitation and Predictive Capability in Computational Engineering and Physics*, paper for the Foundation for Verification and Validitation in the 21th Century Workshop, October 22–23, 2002, Johns Hopkins University, source on the web: www.usacm.org/vnvcsm/PDF_Documents/Oberkampf-Trucano-Hirsch.pdf, 27. 1. 2009

Pala, Ö., J. A. M. Vennix and J. P. C. Kleijnen (1999): Validation in Soft Or, Hard Or and System Dynamics: a Critical Comparison and Contribution to the Debate, source: http://www.systemdynamics.org/conferences/1999/PAPERS/PARA199.PDF, 27. 1. 2009.

Popper, K. R. (1959): *The Logic of Scientific Discovery*. London: Hutchinson (deutsch: Logik der Forschung, J. C. B. Mohr, Tübingen (1969)).

Preston, J. (1994): Methodology, Epistemology and Conventions: Popper's Bad Start, in: *PSA: Proceedings of the Biennial Meeting of the Philosophy of Science Association* 1994, Volume One: Contributed Papers: 314–322, Published by: The University of Chicago Press on behalf of the Philosophy of Science Association.

POWERSIM AS (1996): *Powersim 2.5 Reference Manual*. Sterling: Colorcraft of Virginia.

Repenning, N. P. and J. D. Sterman (1994): *Unanticipated Side Effects of Successful Quality Programs: Technical Documentation*, System Dynamics Group Working Paper D-4999, Cambridge, MA, System Dynamics Group, MIT.

Richardson, G. P. (1996): Problems for the future of system dynamics. *System Dynamics Review* 12(2).

Schöneborn, F. und R. Schwarz (2002): *An elementary dynamic model of a small start-up firm*, paper for the 20th International Conference of the System Dynamics Society, Palermo, Italy, 28. 07.–01. 08. 2002.

Schöneborn, F. (2004): *Strategisches Controlling mit System Dynamics*. Heidelberg: Physica-Verlag.

Schwarz, R. and P. Maybaum (2000): *Is it possible to reproduce the Lyneis-Model?*, paper for the 18th International Conference of the System Dynamics Society, Bergen, Norway, 06. 08.–10. 08. 2000; source on the web: http://www.systemdynamics.org/conferences/2000/PDFs/, file schwarz3, 27. 1. 2009

Sterman, J. D. (1991): *Preface to Kampmann*.

Sterman, J. D. (2002): *Business Dynamics*, Chapter 21.

Sterman, J. D. (2002): All models are wrong: reflections on becoming a systems scientist. *System Dynamics Review* 18(4): 501–531.

Tsang, E. W. K. and K.-M. Kwan (1999): Replication and Theory Development in Organizational Science: A Critical Realist Perspective. *The Academy of Management Review* 24(4): 759–780.

Zahn, E. (1971): *Das Wachstum industrieller Unternehmen*. Wiesbaden: Gabler.

What Does the Arrow Mean?
Observations on System Dynamics Mapping and the Potential for Experimentation with Other Methods

David C. Lane and Elke Husemann

London School of Economics and Political Science

Abstract

Increasingly, maps developed in the field of system dynamics (SD) are combined with other mapping techniques. This has produced successful results; occasionally such experiments have ended in disappointment. Certain similarities between a variety of mapping techniques encourage experimentation. At the same time, these very similarities sometimes confuse clients and students with respect to the distinct differences between the methods supported by the various techniques. Confusion as to the purpose of a certain type of map relates to confusion about the use of mapping tools, down to individual symbols: what does the arrow mean in one map or another? This paper therefore attempts to explore the specific contribution that SD mapping can make and the potential usefulness of combining it with elements from other fields. The paper considers views from within the field of SD on the purpose of maps, their strengths and limitations. It shows how the prime purpose of maps within SD is the elucidation of the link between structure and behaviour but that the usage of maps with this purpose has changed since the field's beginning. The paper also explores a sample of other mapping techniques in their contexts, their distinctive nature as well as the similarities with SD mapping. The conclusion is that a complementarist attitude built on a clear acknowledgement of the distinct prime purpose of each approach and the distinct contribution that each tool was crafted to make offers many creative possibilities.

Keywords: Causal maps, simulation modelling, causal mechanisms, soft systems methodology, cognitive maps, influence diagrams, problem structuring methods, complementarism, mixing methods

1 Introduction

1.1 On System Dynamics and OR/MS

Recently there has been a considerable increase in linkages between system dynamics (SD) and the broader world of OR/MS. As part of this development, SD increasingly features as a topic at OR conferences in Europe and North America; the British Operational Research Society has an 'SD+' special interest group, the aim of which is to increase activities involving system dynamics and other OR/MS approaches; late in 2008 the German OR Society and the German chapter of the international Systems Dynamics Society organised a special joint event; and Jay W. Forrester has been inducted into the 'Operational Research Hall of Fame' (Lane, 2006), a group of only 23 individuals deemed by the International Federation of OR Societies to have laid the foundations of OR/MS (Rand, 2006).

This is not the place for a detailed analysis of the meaning of this development, its causes and its longer terms consequences for system dynamics. Here, then, are just a few remarks. First, system dynamics was created in part in response to Forrester's turning away from operational research (as it then was) because he felt that the approach dealt with only "isolated company problems" and so could not make a significant contribution to management (Forrester, 1958, p. 38; 1968d). This resulted in a "parting of the ways" when it came to OR/MS and system dynamics, as described further elsewhere (Lane, 1994). Thus the increase in linkages in recent years is worth noting. Second, there are various plausible causes of this: the perceived commonality of the ideas of system dynamics and those of OR/MS; the shared interest in group model building approaches; or the interest in experimenting with a wider range of tools, all may increase an understanding of what other fields can contribute.[1] Third and last, the longer term consequences for system dynamics are unclear. There are obvious advantages in having system dynamics widely used amongst managers (Senge, 1990), or even having it located as a standard systems, or OR/MS tool that any management scientist might consider using to solve a practical problem (c.f. Homer, 2007). At the same time, there are consequences which, alongside the potential benefits, bear the risk of diminishing the specific contribution that system dynamics can make (Machuca, 1992; Lane, 1998; Größler, 2004b; Forrester, 2007). This paper takes as its starting point one aspect of the broader development: changes in the use of system dynamics mapping tools.

1.2 Common Interests and Distinct Strengths

While system dynamicists and OR/MS practitioners (re)discover areas of overlapping interests and put their discoveries to good use, there is also, on occasion, confusion about the intended purpose of various tools and disappointment about the results. This extends to clients and students. The latter especially sometimes struggle when trying to assess one method against others. This can arise from a certain elision of the styles, a blurring of focus when it comes to the purpose of each mapping tool. System dynamics-based mapping is sometimes used in a manner arguably not consistent with the ideas of system dynamics. One example might be the use of 'causal loop diagrams', or CLDs, in a manner akin to the purpose of cognitive maps. In such instances the main attention seems to be on the variables and the linkages, with little apparent interest in behaviour over time, or in how changes in structure might produce different behaviours. To make no use of this potential would indeed overlook the greatest strength of system dynamics mapping: the concentration on the relationship between causal mechanisms and the behaviour of systems over time. Disappointment can also result if system dynamics mapping is used in situations the very nature of which does not seem suited to the strengths of system dynamics. For example, we have seen CLDs being criticised because they are poor at representing specific decisions. This is said – quite correctly – to arise because the variable names in CLDs are formulated in a way which aims to capture a flow of processes rather than an individual event or incident. That is indeed how one is recommended to formulate CLDs.[2] It is true that CLDs are not particularly good at supporting discussions about an event or a decision. Nor are they the most obvious tool to use to probe certain types of conflict situations. A screwdriver is indeed a poor tool for driving a nail into a plank – but it has its uses.

[1] For indicative references see Flood & Jackson (1991), Richardson et al. (1994), Pidd (1996), Mingers & Gill (1997), Lane & Oliva (1998) and Jackson (2000; 2003).

[2] See, for example: Goodman (1974), Richardson & Pugh (1981) and Roberts et al. (1983).

However, there have been successful attempts at both combining the use of different mapping tools and engaging with the visible similarities in mapping between different methods. Some examples are touched upon below.

This paper attempts to explore the specific contribution that SD mapping can make. The intent is to consider how maps might be used in new ways and still unfold their full advantage: the ability to deal with dynamic phenomena. The hope is that the use of mapping tools in new combinations will go on to produce good results.

The paper proceeds as follows. In Section 2 system dynamics maps are considered from an internal perspective: the paper draws, as it were, a line around system dynamics and reviews the aspirations within the field for maps and mapping, including the relationship with simulation models. Section 3 moves outside SD: it briefly explores the distinctive nature of some other approaches and their mapping techniques and touches on the similarities or otherwise with SD. The paper closes with some comments on the range of uses for SD-based maps and on where the best opportunities may lie for exploring common interests with other methods.

2 An Internal Perspective: System Dynamics Mapping

The mapping techniques that have emerged from SD have been developed as part of the aims and assumptions of that approach. This section therefore looks at these in order to offer a clear statement of what mapping is used for amongst system dynamicists. The first subsection concentrates on mapping. Because simulation modelling is a key element of SD and SD mapping should be seen in its relation to simulation modelling, this is considered in the following subsection.

2.1 The Purpose, Form and Benefits of CLDs

The Purpose of Maps in System Dynamics

The core ideas of SD are encapsulated in what has become the foundation story of the approach; based on Forrester's experiences in the mid-1950s. He had worked on servo-mechanism devices, an aircraft training simulator, the world's first digital computer and the information system designed to defend the airspace over North America (Forrester, 1992; Lane, 2006). Shortly after his appointment at the newly created Sloan School of Management at MIT, Forrester examined the case of an electronic components manufacturer which had been experiencing sustained and highly disruptive oscillations in inventory levels and workforce numbers. Attempts to reduce the oscillations had failed and the preferred explanation was that 'noise' was being imported into the company from the external environment. Using a modelling approach drawn from his servo-mechanism training Forrester rapidly concluded that this explanation was incorrect. His modelling indicated that the collection of feedback loops brought into existence as managers tried to steer the company towards its desired inventory levels and headcounts was actually amplifying the oscillations. As well as offering this explanation, the modelling suggested ways of changing the policies embedded in the structure of the system so that the oscillations could be calmed (Forrester, 1956, 1958; 1961a).

The story exemplifies the central idea of SD: 'structure influences behaviour'. That is, that by looking at the interconnection of flows of information and resources – the causal mechanisms –

it is possible to gain a plausible and compelling account of why a system behaves as it does over time, and why it might behave otherwise if the mechanisms were altered. Social systems, it is said, may usefully be viewed in terms of causal mechanisms which make up collections of reinforcing and balancing feedback loops; the interaction of those loops generates system behaviour.

In SD various forms of maps exist. A non-exhaustive list might include: causal loop diagrams, stock/flow diagrams, counter-intuitive system archetypes, subsystem diagrams, policy structure diagrams, and strategic architecture maps. Generally, the purpose that all of these forms share, though perhaps to different degrees and with different emphases, is to enable a process of inquiry based on the 'structure influences behaviour' idea. Such maps are used to elicit, communicate, test, debate and understand ideas about causal mechanisms. The emergence of these different forms and the uses to which they have been and are put has been considered elsewhere (Morecroft, 1982; Paich, 1985; Lane & Smart, 1996; Schaffernicht, 2007; Lane, 2008). To examine further the purpose of these maps the concentration is on causal loop diagrams, or CLDs. However, a second form of mapping, stock/flow diagrams, is also briefly treated in the subsection examining maps and their relation to simulation models.

On Causal Loop Diagrams

Arguably the simplest and almost certainly the most widely used form of mapping employed by system dynamicists, causal loop diagrams – CLDs hereafter – have their roots in the wish to explain the dominant feedback structure of a simulation model. Their usage spread with their inclusion in a number of textbooks (see listing in Note 2). An example is shown in Figure 1.

In the system structure part of the diagram variable names are couched in terms which allow users to imagine their taking on different values at different times. The arrow collapses an enormous span of scientific philosophy and methodology concerning causality into a symbol which is best read as 'influences the value of'.[3] CLDs are deceptively simple in form but can be a highly effective vehicle for the ideas of SD. They fulfil a number of functions. In simple terms they indicate influence and therefore constitute a bold and unambiguous hypothesis, a means of constructing a formal theory of a social system (Lane, 2000; Lane & Schwaninger, 2008). They can be used to reveal long chains of consequence, serving as an aid to thinking which generally experiences cognitive difficulty in considering more than a few related concepts (Miller, 1956; Sterman, 1994). They encourage the consideration of 'side-effects' – better thought of as effects additional to those most readily thought of. Their contribution here is to record effects of first interest in a safe and tangible manner, so freeing users to explore other consequences safe in the knowledge that their 'main effect' has not been removed from consideration.

Finally, they portray feedback effects. This is important for two reasons. First, as they are cycles of influence, feedback loops are particularly hard to describe in terms of text. A problem frequently experienced by learners is 'where to start the loop'. In a CLD the question is dis-

[3] This seemingly simple symbol is laden with sophisticated meaning and ideas. For example, Riggs & Inoue (1975) discuss the ideas of modern systems analysis from an OR/MS perspective and argue that some of these originate in Aristotle's understanding of causality. Roberts et al. (1983) give a detailed account of the range of meanings that system dynamicists employ within the ubiquitous causality arrow. The different graphical possibilities are explored in the chapter 'Links and Causal Arrows: Ambiguity in Action' in Tufte (2006).

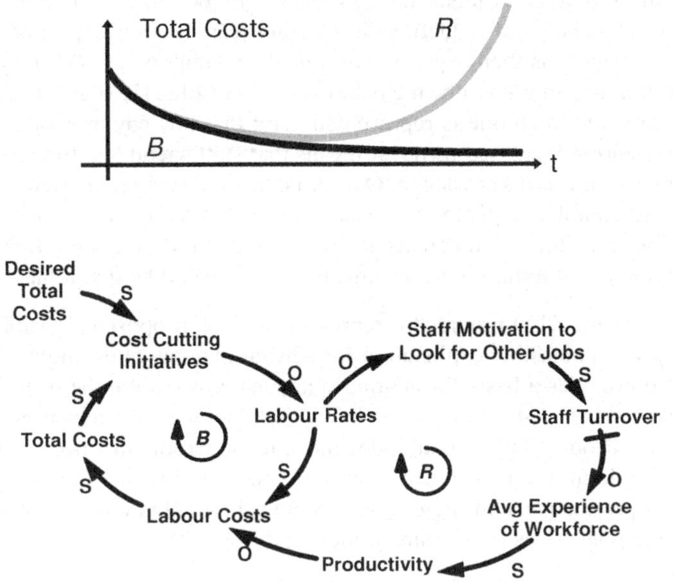

Figure 1: A CLD representation of some of Pfeffer's ideas on the dynamic consequences of attempting to control costs by reducing hourly pay rates. If the balancing mechanism is the only one present, or if it dominates, then the declining, goal-seeking behaviour over time results (black). If the reinforcing effect is present and, in time, dominates this main effect, then unlimited growth would result (grey). Note that the s/o convention for indicating link polarity has been used. Adapted from Lane and Husemann (2008b).

solved; the diagram itself indicates that any variable could be a suitable point of entry but that the essential unit of analysis is the whole loop (c.f. Richardson & Pugh, 1981). In this context, a description using words is more difficult. Whilst linkages, even long ones and alternative ones, can be described using text, damage is done to a feedback loop when it must be broken at some arbitrary point due to the linear nature of text. A CLD reminds the user of the nature of the situation under examination. The second reason is that feedback loops are the units that create behaviour over time. The isolated reinforcing loop creates exponential behaviour. The isolated balancing loop results in equilibration. Combinations of loops, playing out over time give rise to a wide range of dynamic behaviours. Careful, rigorous thinking allows behaviour over time to be sketched in a manner which is consistent with – or does its best to be consistent with – the hypothesised mechanisms in the system structure.

Figure 1 is an example of how CLDs may help to clearly and concisely represent ideas on the structure of a situation. It is based on Pfeffer's thoughts on the possible consequences of trying to hold down company costs by implementing a reduction in hourly pay rates for workers, the 'main effect' of interest (Pfeffer, 2007). He uses words to put forward a rigorous argument, which includes empirical data on labour costs from different industries. His argument can be represented and then explored – by way of a CLD – in terms of system structure and resulting dynamic behaviour. The aspiration to reduce costs implies the existence of some preferred level of total costs. This and other variables have influences in the same 's' direction or in the opposite 'o' direction. The choice of reductions in pay rates can be seen as part of a balancing loop and the desired behaviour is then expressed as a goal-seeking one of declining costs. However, according to Pfeffer, this might not be the behaviour that results. He suggests a number of 'side-effect' mechanisms, of which one is represented here: that low pay motivates staff to look for other jobs. The resulting increased turnover means that staff spend less time in the organisation and so amass a lower level of knowledge. Over time this reduces productivity, that is, increases the time needed to complete a given task. The result is that the main effect is overwhelmed by the operation of what is illustrated here as an unexpected reinforcing loop. In principle, without further intervention or saturating mechanisms, the effect would be that total costs rise.

What benefit does the CLD provide? It represents a set of proposed plausible influences in a concise way. It gives a plausible explanation for why cutting pay rates might work – and why it might not. It also provides a basis for action. In any actual situation the influences will have a real though unknown strength. The CLD shows that useful performance measures might be 'Staff Turnover' or 'Productivity'; should they move in the wrong directions, this might indicate that the reinforcing loop in this instance is strong. This would render the new pay policy fruitless, even counter productive, and suggest its withdrawal. Should they not alter appreciably then the balancing loop may act as the dominant loop in the system.

The most important point to make here is that the defining purpose of CLDs is to offer a framework for exploring the link between structure and behaviour. CLDs are used to gain insight into the structural source of behaviour. They may give an indication of the performance measures in a system, the most effective policy levers and perhaps even the direction in which those levers are best shifted to indicate a desired effect.

Central to this, however, is the requirement that behaviour over time is included. This cannot be guaranteed because, "no diagramming method offers any assurance that users will apply to themselves the self-disciplining step of trying to link ideas about structure as captured in diagrams with logically consistent ideas of the behaviour" (Lane, 2008, p. 17). Beyond this, the concentration purely on mechanism without consideration of the expected behaviour is one occasionally observed use of SD mapping which tends to confuse. Strictly within the assumptions of SD, it is an error to use CLDs without considering behaviour over time. Therefore, such use will not bring out the advantages and insights that CLDs are intended to produce, insights that relate to the core ideas of SD. It is, naturally, conceivable that other, different benefits are sought and found by other users. Such are the advantages of experimentation. However, where such use ends in disappointment or leads to unfavourable assumptions on the usefulness of SD mapping tools compared with those of neighbouring fields, two points cannot be stressed enough: that, as with most tools, these generally unfold their greatest strength when used as designed, and that this strength lies in supporting the exploration and explanation of puzzling dynamic phenomena.

2.2 Maps and Simulation Modelling

Tremendously useful as CLDs are in explaining and exploring situations, they have their limitations even in terms of SD itself. These have mainly to do with the difficulties in deducing actual behaviour once the representation of systems moves beyond a few simple loops – and it frequently does. Stock/flow diagrams (SFDs) are said to overcome some of these limitations, though they in turn lack some of the attractions offered by CLDs. Neither kind of map offers the full benefits of another SD tool: simulation modelling. This goes to the origins of SD and is of the greatest importance inside SD. Therefore, when considering the usefulness of SD mapping tools inside or outside the field, it should be remembered how they relate to simulation modelling and that what SD has to offer goes beyond its mapping tools.

The ability that simulation has to take a set of assumptions about a social system and rigorously deduce the implied behaviour over time is a central idea in SD (Forrester, 1960; 1961a; 1968c). Forrester asserts that social systems can behave in a counter-intuitive way; there is empirical observation to support this (Sterman, 2006). He conceived of the idea that such systems might plausibly be modelled as containing non-linear relationships between variables, delayed influences, and linkages which correspond to accumulation into (or draining out of) state variables. However, according to Forrester, when following up on this idea, then, very simple situations aside, one rapidly arrives at sets of assumptions the consequences of which, as they move forward in time, cannot be determined by the un-aided human mind. Simulation modelling is designed to overcome this problem. The move towards simulation modelling requires the discipline of a completely specified description (in algebraic and numerical terms) which can be 'run' on a computer. Such models can provide insights beyond those that can be derived from qualitative maps.

An illustration of these points can be made using an example of an 'adoption-diffusion model'; a class of systems that has been studied extensively by Peter Milling (e.g. Milling, 1974, 1986, 1996, 1999, 2002).

Consider a simple model for the rate at which the population of a certain geographical area is persuaded to see a cinema film (based on Lane & Husemann, 2004). This situation is represented in Figure 2 (see p. 334), first as a CLD and then as an SFD. Advertising creates interest in the film before it has even appeared in cinemas. When viewing becomes possible, interested people go to see the film and are then able to talk about it. This word-of-mouth process can create further interest amongst the population. However, films are transitory social products, with few individuals talking about them in an enduring way; most people move on, talking about a newer film or another experience completely. So how do you deduce the behaviour which the mapped out structures would produce over time?

First, consider what can be done with the different kinds of map. CLDs have all the advantages of their, sometimes deceptively, self-explanatory and easy to use elements (which is of course what makes them attractive for all manner of uses and experiments). And they can give a good overview. SFDs require a little more engagement with their symbols and way of construction. With regard to the limitations of CLDs, SFDs can provide more of the information required.[4] This is because CLDs do not present all effects. Non-linear relationships and delays are not well represented. However, traditionally, attention has fallen most heavily on their not representing the flows associated with stocks (Richardson, 1986). Emerging from the diagrams

[4] Indeed, there is a body of work that attempts algorithmically to convert one type of map into the other, see Burns (1977), Burns et al. (1979) and Ramos (1983).

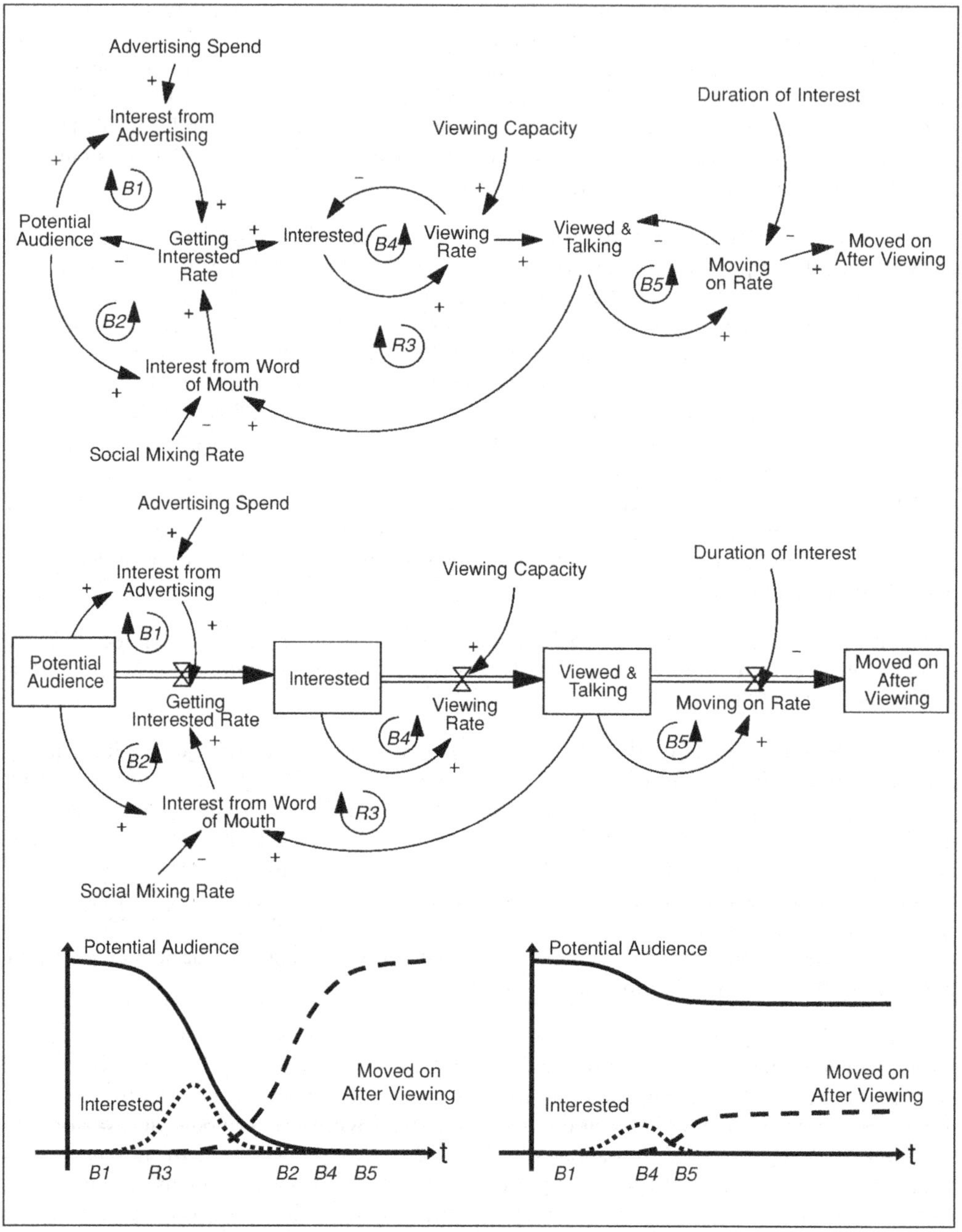

Figure 2: A simple model of the dynamics of film-going, represented as a CLD (top) and an SFD (middle). Note that the ± convention for indicating link polarity has been used. The bottom of the figure shows two sets of behaviour modes that this system might generate; the dominant loops in each case are shown on the horizontal axis. Adapted from Lane and Husemann (2004).

originally developed by Forrester (1961a; 1961b), SFDs do show such effects.[5] The SFD in Figure 2 represents the idea that whilst the value of the 'Viewing Rate' can, at any instant be determined if the value of those 'Interested' and the 'Viewing Capacity' are known, this is not true of the stock 'Interested'. Instead, values of the 'Getting Interested Rate' accumulate into this stock, and values of the 'Viewing Rate' drain from it. The value of the stock at any time is therefore determined from its initial value and the integral of the inflow minus the outflow. The ability of SFDs to elucidate very different types of causal links (and so reveal the state variables in a system) is the most visually significant aspect of these maps though there are other advantages that follow (Lane, 2008). For example, the CLD shows the 'Viewing Rate' as having two effects, one on each of its neighbouring stocks. This can be misleading if one is exploring ways of changing structure, perhaps by severing one of these two apparent links. In the SFD the effect of this variable is shown as a single entity, a flow subtracting from the left hand stock and adding to the right hand one, two aspects of what is a single process.

The SFD may contain more information. Nevertheless, when it comes to inferring behaviour, there is still a gap between what either map can provide and what a simulation model can reveal. Looking at a map alone, many kinds of behaviour can be inferred. To illustrate this point, here are just two kinds of behaviour, telling two very different stories. Both stories share the same frame of epidemiological references, since the structure of the model is similar to the standard SIR model of epidemiology (Murray, 1989).[6] The behaviour in each is very different.

Story A may be viewed as an epidemic (see Figure 2, left hand side). Loop B1 starts things off and then the film produces very good word-of-mouth and loop R3 dominates the system. Eventually, in rapid succession, loops B2, B4 and B5 dominate simply because no potential audience remains, all those who were interested have seen the film, and these have subsequently moved off to discuss something else. Many of the potential audience have seen the film.

Story B may be viewed as a case of herd immunity (Fine, 1993). Again, loop B1 dominates at first but the film produces poor word-of-mouth. Loop R3 is weak and the stock of those talking about the film drains faster than it refills, loops B4 and B5 rapidly dominate. Few people have seen the film.

The point is that both stories are entirely plausible. Either of the two behaviours could result; the different loops of the system could dominate in the way described. The maps of system structure are quite consistent with the sketches of behaviour over time – both sets of behaviour. There is simply no way of determining what the system structure will actually produce, the maps provide no answer. This is the key point about behavioural inferences from maps: when

[5] An example in which the distinction between stocks and flows is central to understanding the structure of the system is healthcare. See Lane & Husemann (2008a).

[6] In this case the susceptibles are the 'Potential Audience', the infectives are 'Viewed and Talking' and the removed class are the stock 'Moved on After Viewing'. This structure may also be compared with econometric models of new technology adoption (Stoneman, 2002). However, econometric models tend to exclude the capacitated nature of the adoption rate, limited as it is physically by the availability of capacity. Lane & Husemann (2004) discuss the difference. Milling (e.g. Milling, 1996; and Milling & Maier, 1996) and also Homer (1987) show examples of more realistic models of technology adoption and diffusion.

they are possible, they may be ambiguous. Richmond goes further: "using causal-loop diagrams to make inferences about behaviour is a treacherous business" (1994, p. 144). Neither can SFDs completely avoid this problem; it applies to all forms of qualitative inference.[7]

A map, then, may be quite adequate; indeed, it may be a significant advance on previous thinking. It may provide all that is required. However, its descriptive power will be limited. In terms of SD, the answers to questions such as in the example above are often best sought through the means of a simulation model where the complex interplay of non-linearities, delays and accumulations can be simulated and the full range of possible behaviours more rigorously deduced (Sterman, 1988; 2000).

In summary, both the limitations and huge advantages of SD mapping tools arise within the context of the specific aspirations formulated for SD. This might be remembered when considering how best to use them inside and outside SD. This section has also considered what system dynamicists seek to do with their maps: their purpose is to aid the exploration of the relationship between the structure of social systems and the behaviour over time that that structure generates. This is the most important aim of SD, and maps derived from that field give good results when they are used with that aim kept in mind.

3 Some Other Mapping Techniques

In this section we step outside the field of SD and turn towards a sample of other mapping techniques used in OR/MS. The treatment here does not aim to be definitive by any means. The interest is in the similarities in mapping and what these mean when it comes to mixing and combining methods. The idea is to look briefly at some of the general aims and key concepts of a field and at the associated form and use of mapping before considering how these might relate to SD.

3.1 Soft Systems Methodology

Developed primarily by Peter Checkland, the purpose of 'SSM' is to contribute to the organisation of purposeful human activities by taking into account a range of subjective interpretations of the world adopted by people to give meaning to their actions (Checkland, 1981; 2006). The central concept is that of the 'W', or 'Weltanschauung', a word that might be rendered as: a view of the world through which all that is observed and experienced is interpreted, its significance understood. Activities are considered using a range of Ws, some central to an apparent aim, some used as provocative alternatives. A number of linguistic and mapping devices are used to bring systems ideas to bear. The activities developed in these are then considered in order to support debate on what should or should not be done.

[7] The balance between qualitative mapping and quantitative simulation modelling is often discussed by system dynamicists. For example, a forceful argument has been put forward about the additional time needed to move from a CLD to a model and whether this can be justified in terms of the extra insight generated (Coyle, 2000). In response, the perils of maps and the effectiveness of models have been reasserted (Homer & Oliva, 2001).

Two types of mapping are seen in SSM. 'Rich picture diagramming' encourages an almost unstructured expressing of different Ws and has little in common with SD mapping. However, 'conceptual models' have a role and form that is of interest. For each W used, a conceptual model represents the activities that need to be engaged with if the required aims are to be met. Thus, staff in a service organisation might create one conceptual model for the W that customers should be dealt with politely, accurately and efficiently and, in order to provoke alternative thinking, another for the W that customers should have encounters with an organisation which are irritating and fruitless. An example is shown in Figure 3.

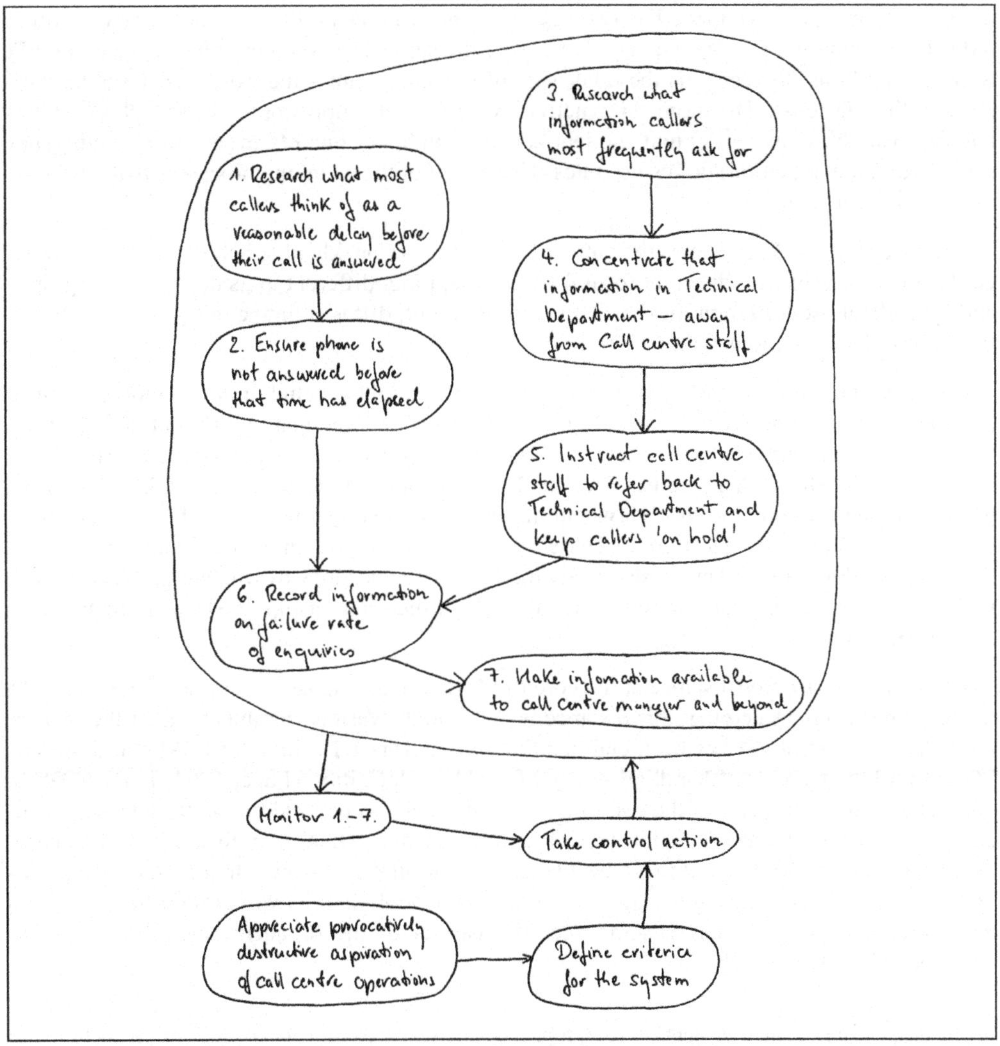

Figure 3: Example of a simple conceptual model from SSM. This provocative example shows some of the activities required of a call centre if it is to avoid providing callers with fast and useful information which might lead to a sale.

The diagram shows the obvious point of comparison – and potential confusion – between conceptual models and SD maps. Though conventionally hand-drawn, they do look a little like CLDs: there are words connected by arrows; and certainly some concept of feedback is employed in the way that the monitoring of activities is represented. Looks, however, are deceptive. Conceptual models are "logical machines" (Tsouvalis & Checkland, 1996). There is no specific interest in either dynamics or causal mechanisms. They represent the steps necessary to make manifest in the world a set of systemic ideas about how best to organise a human activity. This is clearly stated in the following: "An arrow from activity x (say, 'obtain raw material') to activity y ('convert raw material to product') shows that y is *contingent upon* x" (Checkland, 1989, p. 89, italics in original). The two key differences are clear. First, the arrows can at times indicate a requirement, a dependency. This is not the same as a continuing influence in a CLD. Second – and this difference is the other side of the same coin – the words used are not variables in the SD sense. The monitoring activities might well imply continuous feedback effects but the 'variables' in conceptual models can also indicate one-off events (the contingency described in the quotation) or yes/no states. These are not the changing processes that CLDs are required to represent.

The success of SSM indicates the value of such maps (Checkland & Scholes, 1990). However, it is clear that this is a different form from SD mapping, different in its detailed iconography and syntactical use, different in what it aims to represent, different in the over-arching perspective on problem situations that it embodies.

The attention paid in SSM to discrete events alone might preclude much reciprocal use of SSM and SD mapping tools, especially given Forrester's advice that one should not be drawn into representing "knowledge of the discreteness of various decisions and actions" (Forrester, 1961a, p. 453). Although a case has been made for the opposite view (Coyle, 1985), Forrester's general advice is applied to the overwhelming majority of situations dealt with in SD. However, there is still an open question, discussed in the field, whether, in a small number of cases, there is a need to include key events in SD models.[8] The questions of whether and how to deal with discrete events in maps are ones that also affect the relationship of SD with the methods considered below.

The social constructivist stance at the core of SSM can also make it seem rather far from SD, though it has been argued that this distance is overstated.[9] Various combinations of the two are possible. For example, it has been claimed that the interpretivist thrust of SSM could provide SD with a broader way of handling issues of problem definition (Lane, 1994; Lane & Oliva, 1998), and that a synthesis of the two might also allow SD to be used to specify questions concerning different courses of action and their consequences (Lane & Oliva, 1998). Indeed, it should always be remembered that Checkland's aspiration for SSM was that it would be a general inquiry process. Hence the suggestion in his 1981 book that SD work might flow out of an SSM study and might address some specific aspects of the broader issues that SSM has unearthed (Checkland, 1981).

[8] For example, project management deals with phenomena relating to this point, such as the inclusion of activity dependencies which require the completion of one activity before another can begin (Ford & Sterman, 1998).

[9] See further in section 4.2 and note 13.

3.2 Cognitive Mapping

Developed by Colin Eden and colleagues, these maps can be seen as an element of an evolving series of approaches which aim to deal with complex problems and aid strategic thinking. They draw heavily on ideas from cognitive psychology (Eden et al., 1979; Eden et al., 1983; Eden, 1989; 2004; Bryson et al., 2004). The approach was first called SODA – strategic options development and analysis – and the term ‘Journey Making’ is also used (c.f. Eden & Ackermann, 1998). These approaches aim to be very broadly applicable, treating both the qualitative and quantitative elements of a situation. Importance is attached to both the content of any analytical work done and the process used with participants. Participants’ interpretation of events and the meaning that they impart to situations is of prime interest. All are based on ‘personal construct theory’ (Kelly, 1955). They proceed by helping to elicit individual and shared mental constructs with the aim of assisting an organisation in coming to a greater understanding of its strategic options, to agree a way forward and to create commitment to a chosen course of action.

Various forms of mapping are used but the focus for the purpose here is on cognitive mapping.[10] Cognitive mapping is a language to express personal constructs in order to display the meaning ascribed to a concept by discussing and representing how it relates to other concepts. Cognitive maps are used as facilitative devices. They are drawn during individual interviews and/or projected onto a screen to record and assist a group discussion. Software packages exist to support this; two examples are COPE and Decision Explorer (White & Palocsay, 1999). Specific issues may emerge from part of a map which lead to the application of other OR/MS approaches. A simple example of a map is shown in Figure 4 (see p. 340).

When comparing cognitive maps with CLDs, again, similarities are already visible on the surface: digraphs formed of word strings connected by arrows, and the occasional negative link polarity marker. Additionally, recent versions of software-enabled cognitive maps have attempted to deal with circular connections by treating them as feedback loops. Some differences are also readily apparent e.g. the use of rectangles or ovals around some variables. Closer examination reveals deeper differences. Cognitive maps consist of concepts which are frequently (though not always) conceptualised as an idea and its antithesis, the two are then connected by an ellipsis. The use of these bi-polar pairs as concepts is very different from variable conceptualisation in SD. It takes a very particular view of how humans construct shared descriptions. Those concepts can include statements about options (i.e. available courses of action), constraints, goals and pitfalls to avoid, as well as events and decisions. It follows from this that the connecting arrows are used in a manner different from SD maps: “Arrows (links) illustrate chains of argument and, therefore, through providing detail in terms of the material linking in (options/explanations, etc.) and linking out (consequences/ramifications) of the statement more insight into what is meant is revealed” (Ackermann & Eden, 2004, p. 128). What is clear is that although a cognitive map may illustrate a line of logical argument, or a piece of means-ends argumentation, the constituent concepts cannot necessarily be thought of as evolving through time – because there is no specific interest in such questions. In terms of its aspiration to ‘make

[10] Note that today the term ‘cognitive map’ is increasingly used only for representations of an individual’s ideas, representation of shared thinking with the aim of choosing amongst options being referred to as ‘causal maps’ (Eden & Ackermann, 1992; Montibeller & Belton, 2006).

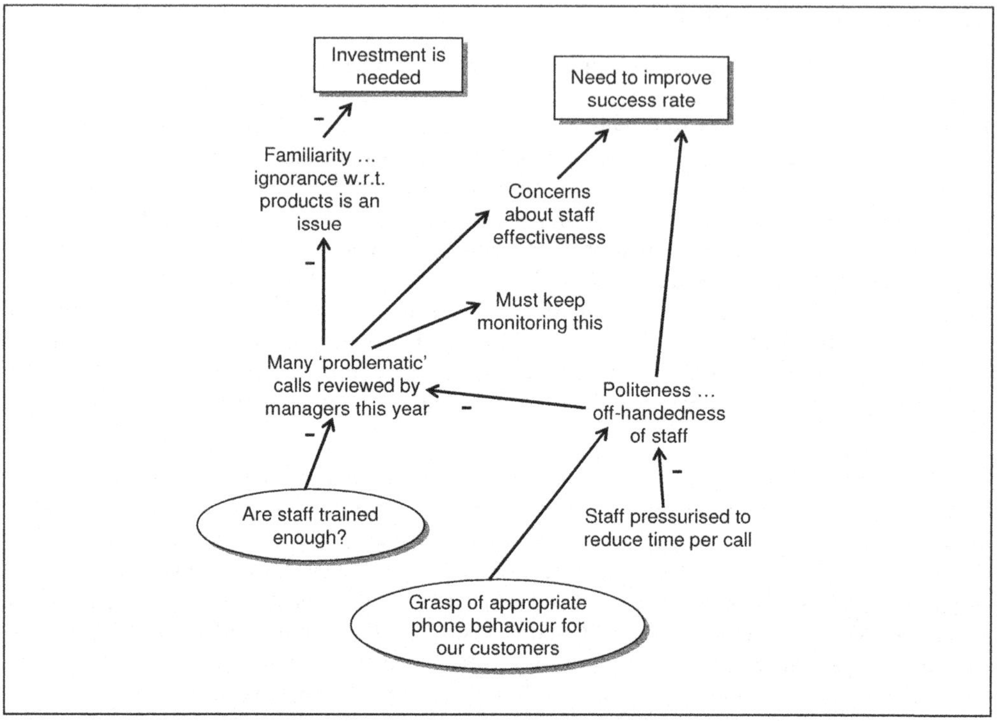

Figure 4: A simple cognitive map relating to a call centre. The map includes concepts relating to the number of problem calls observed, possible reasons for this (within ovals) and options for taking action (within rectangles).

sense', the net of the broader approaches within which cognitive mapping is employed is cast wider than in SD. To system dynamicists the breadth of cognitive mapping is arguably purchased at the cost of depth; their analytical potential in terms of representing causal mechanisms that form the basis of dynamic behaviour is extremely limited. Simply put, because cognitive maps are not designed to bring to life time evolutionary behaviour, they generally do not represent the sort of causal theories that system dynamicists aspire to create. Their concentration is on events and decisions rather than processes and structures.

Yet cognitive mapping can be immensely powerful when used in the manner for which its tools have been so carefully created. In turn, the potential of SD was recognised by Eden, Jones and Sims as early as 1983, when it was observed that SD might be used to address some of the issues identified by a cognitive map (Eden et al., 1983). There have been a number of studies, for which SODA-like approaches which include cognitive mapping have generated SD modelling work and have then assisted in the interpretation of that work (Williams et al., 1995; Ackermann et al., 1997). Furthermore, Howick, Ackermann and Andersen have shown how one may move from cognitive maps towards CLDs and thereby transport knowledge elicited from clients in the shape of event-based thinking into a process-based thinking approach (Howick et al., 2006).

3.3 Influence Diagrams

Emerging from decision theory and the decision analysis field, influence diagrams are a generalised version of Bayesian networks. Such networks represent a set of possible events and how their probabilities depend on the occurrence of other events in the network. Influence diagrams add to this the representation of decision points, flowing out of which one sees the choices available to a decision maker. Emerging from decision theory, influence diagrams are used to represent visually situations which involve one or more decisions which have to be made in a context of uncertain outcomes (Howard, 1966; Raiffa, 1968; Howard & Matheson, 1984; Watson & Buede, 1987; French, 1988).

In simple terms influence diagrams are directed graphs. Decision nodes (rectangles or diamonds) represent any decisions that must be made; the arrows out of them indicate the alternatives to choose from. Event nodes (circles or ovals) indicate situations in which there is uncertainty about what will occur, making it necessary to portray the range of outcomes and the probabilities associated with each; the outward arrows indicate the possible situations that could arise. An example is shown in Figure 5. Such visual representations have been used to clarify a very wide range of complex decision problems and conditionalities, including in the legal sphere (e.g. Edwards, 1991). However, influence diagrams can also be used to find the best (in a normative sense) set of decisions to take. By applying the criterion of maximum expected utility it is possible to 'solve' the diagram, that is, formulate a set of instructions which specifies what alternatives a decision maker should follow in any of the situations that might occur.

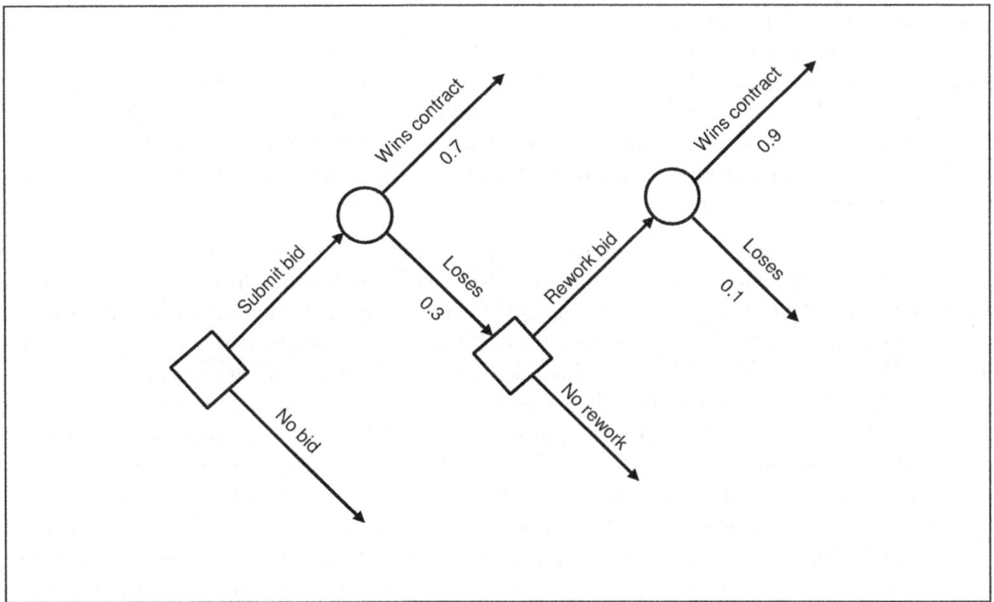

Figure 5: Influence diagram for a company trying to decide whether to bid for a contract which it might win and also whether it might rework its bid after an initial rejection. Note that a full version would also include information about costs and benefits relating to decisions, events and final outcomes.

The words and arrows in influence diagrams are based on different ideas than the similar symbols in, say, CLDs. Arrows in influence diagrams represent a number of ideas – which is why the arrows themselves are labelled and not merely with simple link polarities. When arrows connect into a decision node they are information arcs and indicate that there is an outcome for the node at the tail of the arrow, be it a decision node or an event node. However, when arrows pass into an event node they are conditional arcs, indicating that the outcome of the event is probabilistically conditioned (in a Bayesian sense) on the outcomes of the nodes on the tails. Moreover, there is a key sense in which only one of the numerous arrows emerging from any node is actually present in a given situation, representing which specific event has occurred or decision been made. In SD links may at different times have strong or weak effects on behaviour but this is a very different thing. Therefore, whilst there are some similarities, this is obviously a very different usage of arrow symbols than that in SD. The same can be said when comparing the nodes in influence diagrams with SD variables, whether these are all represented in the same way (CLDs) or whether stocks and flows are distinguished (SFDs).

No further iconographical exegesis is required since these differences are only a manifestation of the fundamental difference in interest between SD and decision analysis. First, the probabilistic aspect of influence diagramming (and Bayesian belief nets) is simply not a central concern for SD which focuses on how quite deterministic systems can create extremely complex behaviour which defeats intuition (Forrester, 1970). Second, the same point relates also to the representation of decisions as nodes. The focus in SD is on policies, by which is meant the relationships in a social system that convert streams of input (information) into streams of output (decisions). Certainly one discusses the point in models at which decision making is occurring – and it is central to SD that knowledge of decision making is available when building the model (Forrester, 1961a, Chapter 10). But Forrester was clear that the concern of SD was the entire assembly of stocks, material flows, information links, and decisions (emerging from policy functions, probably embedded in rates), and the behaviour over time that the resulting closed feedback loops in the system created (see also Forrester, 1958; 1968a). When two approaches have such different aims there seems little purpose in trying to make the tool of one do the specific job required in another.

Instead, there are some broader connections to be made based on some overlapping areas of interest between decision theory and SD as methods. Their tools might then be used to complement each other. As to those common interests, for example, decision points in SD models are informed by behavioural decision theory ideas (Sterman, 2000) and multiple attribute utility theory can assess model outputs (Gardiner & Ford, 1980; Reagan-Cirincione et al., 1991).[11] However, the most significant link is the broader idea that decision modelling can be used interactively with management teams to bring to situations some analytical content and an element of procedural rationality (Simon, 1976). In the 'decision conferencing' school of decision analysis great importance is attached to the value of visual modelling, of facilitating a group in the articulation of their thinking, of using an iterative process, and of providing a model that is what is required by the group in question at a particular point in time (Phillips, 1984; 1990). All of this could be said about group modelling processes with SD as the central analytical approach. Such similarities led to an argument for improved communication between these (then) relative-

[11] The work of Brans offers an extensive exploration of this idea (e.g. Brans et al., 1998; Macharis et al., 1998).

ly distinct approaches to 'group decision support' (Lane, 1994). As it happened, this was not a lone opinion since a fully developed engagement was already in train and appeared shortly after (Vennix, 1996). Vennix also stressed the more general conclusion: since the advantages of using visual aids in the form of maps had been discovered in several fields, insights gained in one might well prove useful to (and save work in) another.

4 Closing Remarks

Different mapping techniques have distinctly different underlying assumptions as well as similarities both at the surface and, in some places, at deeper levels. Where the similarities hide the differences, this can lead to confusion. At the same time, the situation offers tempting opportunities for experiments with combinations. Having looked at maps inside SD and sampled a few other techniques, what comments can be offered?

4.1 On Using Maps in System Dynamics

In re-asserting the specific contribution of mapping in SD it is important to emphasise that the view on maps in SD has not been static. Equally, the use of maps has changed considerably. One example concerns CLDs (Keys, 1988). When these initially appeared they had an explanatory purpose (e.g. Forrester, 1968b):[12] a situation would be conceptualised and formulated using SFDs and a computer language, then that model would be used to find the different modes of behaviour and dominant loops; one or more CLDs would be used to summarise the structural source of the behaviours. But this 'expository mode' led within a few years to a 'conceptualisation mode', in which CLDs were used as a loose tool for conceptualising feedback effects prior to identifying stocks and formulating a model (Lane, 2008). Today CLDs are used in both modes or in a combined mode, in which they are used first for conceptualisation and later also for exposition. CLDs are also used independently of simulation models to diagnose behavioural puzzles in complex systems. It might be noted that the latter kind of experimentation – taking place solely inside SD – was already criticised from within as having moved away from one of the field's key assumptions (Forrester, 1994).

Generally, mapping in SD is an active area of debate and development. For example, Cavana and Mares (2004) have explored representations of the rationale for a given policy by combining CLDs and 'critical thinking' (used here to mean logical reasoning), and chapter 5 of Morecroft (2007) describes the changing ways in which various mapping techniques can be incorporated into an SD study.

Part of this changing usage is related to a loosening up of ideas about what different SD maps might best be used for. For example, there is a frequent interpretation that qualitative maps (primarily CLDs, less often SFDs) are appropriate for 'soft' situations, whilst quantitative models

[12] This is not the first usage of CLDs, simply one of the best, and best known examples. One of Forrester's PhD students, F. Helmut Weymar, introduced CLDs in 1960 as a teaching and communication device (Roberts, 2007). Something similar can be seen in the research on corporate growth in Forrester and Packer (1962), and Jarmain (1963) uses similar maps. See Lane (2008) for a detailed account of the provenance of CLDs.

indicate a 'hard' orientation. This is not necessarily so. Simulation modelling, though obviously requiring more assumptions, can still be used in a structured, albeit speculative and provisional, manner with issues involving many soft factors – hence the notion of 'exploratory or impressionistic models', or 'conceptual simulation models' (respectively Homer, 1996; Größler, 2004a). Equally, John Morecroft, who trained originally as a physicist, has pointed out in conversation that "a CLD can be hard", that is, it can be used to represent a set of ideas that would normally be the object of interest for the natural sciences. The soft/hard dichotomy cannot provide a basis for easy decisions on the appropriate use of mapping or simulation modelling in SD.

So, SD mapping is not static and it is perhaps more flexible in its applicability than previously thought. However, none of this alters the fact that all SD mapping techniques serve a prime concern: the wish to explain how behaviour over time comes about, how behaviour is linked to structure and what interventions might work to alter that behaviour.

4.2 Creating a Complementarist Platform

Experiments with features from neighbouring fields offer great opportunities. Besides SD and the three others briefly presented here, there are many more to explore. Within OR/MS, for example, in project management critical path analysis makes standard use of PERT charts to represent dependencies between different parcels of work to be done and the durations of those parcels, whilst activity cycle diagrams are used in discrete event simulation to illustrate queues and processes in systems. Similarly, mapping techniques can be found in other fields, including information systems development and production engineering. Moreover, there are more tools than mapping tools.

Those fields briefly looked at in this paper have shared strengths: for example, their tools provide a combination of process and content benefits; in cognitive science terms they are used in a way which effectively increases working memory (Klein, 1994). Even though, as described here, each field is based on a distinctive understanding of particular 'problems' in the world, this is itself an advantage: problems do not arise in neat boxes and so it is frequently necessary to use a combination of techniques – to 'just model through' (c.f. Pidd, 1999).

It may be a matter for regret that it has taken so long for SD tools to be included in a larger kit. To some extent this relates to the underlying social theoretic ideas of different approaches. Many mapping techniques derived from the 'problem structuring methods' school are soft, in part because they adopt a social-constructivist, or interpretivist view of the social phenomena being studied. In contrast, the central concern in SD with system structure is seen by some to be a hard stance, involving an almost naïve realism, positivism and a functionalist view of social reality (Jackson & Keys, 1984; Mingers, 2003). However, from Forrester's earliest writings and their focus on mental models onwards, SD has never been that limited. Simulation models can themselves play an iterative role in shaping social reality (Bowen, 1994; Lane, 2000) and it has been argued that SD is best seen as having an implicit integrative stance, seeing social structure and human agency as interacting.[13] So tools from SD can be part of the OR/MS toolbox, to be

[13] See Lane (1994; 1999) for the proposal that SD has always contained an implicit interpretivist element. For the arguments in favour of viewing that element as part of an integrated agency/structure grounding: (Lane, 2000; 2001) and (Lane & Husemann, 2008b).

drawn into the mix and combined as seems appropriate. And system dynamicists themselves may find something useful to them in that same large toolbox.

The starting point of this paper was changes in the uses of system dynamics mapping and the question as to the potential opportunities. It closes with the hope that the exploration of surface similarities will encourage and not prevent the further exploration of links at all levels. As the examples above seek to demonstrate: both the changed usage of tools and the combination of tools offer opportunities; sometimes it may be more promising to engage at another level: to work on joint projects or to build on insights gained in another field.

Certainly, experimentation always risks disappointment. However, some of this can be avoided if it is acknowledged from the beginning that, despite similarities, all approaches are not the same. This would avoid criticism of an approach and of its tools for not doing what they were never designed to do. In the case of SD, maps are indeed 'limited' by their focus on the link between structure and behaviour. But one might just as well say that they are 'defined' by that focus, that they derive their analytical purchase from it. It is always worth recalling one of Mike Jackson's favourite remarks; "All systems approaches are very restrictive".[14]

Conversely, a complementarist attitude built on a clear acknowledgement of the distinct prime purpose of each approach and the distinct contribution that each tool was crafted to make offers many creative possibilities.

References

Ackermann, F. and C. Eden (2004): Using Causal Mapping – individual and group, traditional and new. In: Pidd, M. (ed.): *Systems Modelling: Theory and practice*, Chichester: Wiley, 127–145.

Ackermann, F., C. Eden and T. Williams (1997): Modeling for Litigation: Mixing qualitative and quantitative approaches. *Interfaces* 27(2): 48–65.

Bowen, M. G. (1994): System Dynamics, Determinism and Choice: Toward a reconsideration of the image of "system man". *Sys. Dyn. Rev.* 10(1): 87–90.

Brans, J. P., C. Macharis, P. L. Kunsch, A. Chevalier and M. Schwaninger (1998): Combining Multicriteria Decision Aid and System Dynamics for the Control of Socio-economic Processes: An iterative real-time procedure. *Eur. J. Opl. Res.* 109(2): 428–441.

Bryson, J. M., F. Ackermann, C. Eden and C. B. Finn (2004): *Visible Thinking: Unlocking causal mapping for practical business results*. London: Wiley.

Burns, J. R. (1977): Converting Signed Digraphs to Forrester Schematics and Converting Forrester Schematics to Differential Equations. *IEEE Transactions on Systems, Man and Cybernetics* smc-7(10): 695–707.

Burns, J. R., O. M. Ulgen and H. W. Beights (1979): An Algorithm for Converting Signed Digraphs to Forrester Schematics. *IEEE Transactions on Systems, Man and Cybernetics* smc-9(3): 115–124.

Cavana, R. Y. and E. D. Mares (2004): Integrating Critical Thinking and Systems Thinking. *Sys. Dyn. Rev.* 20(3): 223–235.

[14] Jackson has described how this is derived from a comment by C W Churchman at the end of his book *The Systems Approach* (1968): ''The systems approach goes on to discovering that every world view is terribly restricted". Jackson comments: "Churchman understood the quote to be self-referential, so that the systems approach itself was also restricted and had to be exposed to its enemies, etc. etc." (Jackson, 2008, *pers. com.*)

Checkland, P. and J. Poulter (2006): *Learning for Action: A Short Definitive Account of Soft Systems Methodology and its use for Practitioners, Teachers and Students*. Chichester: John Wiley.

Checkland, P. B. (1981): *Systems Thinking, Systems Practice*. Chichester: Wiley.

Checkland, P. B. (1989): Chapter 4 Soft Systems Methodology. In: Rosenhead, J. (ed.): *Rational Analysis for a Problematic World: problem structuring methods for complexity, uncertainty and conflict*, Chichester: J. Wiley, 71–100.

Checkland, P. B. and J. Scholes (1990): *Soft Systems Methodology in Action*. Chichester: Wiley.

Churchman, C. W. (1968): *The Systems Approach*. New York: Delacorte Press.

Coyle, R. G. (1985): Representing Discrete Events in System Dynamics Models: a theoretical application to modelling coal production. *J. Opl. Res. Soc.* 36(4): 307–318.

Coyle, R. G. (2000): Qualitative and Quantitative Modelling in System Dynamics: Some research questions. *Sys. Dyn. Rev.* 16(3): 225–244.

Eden, C. (1989): Using cognitive mapping for strategic options development and analysis (SODA). In: Rosenhead, J. (ed.): *Rational Analysis for a Problematic World: problem structuring methods for complexity, uncertainty and conflict*, Chichester: Wiley, 21–42.

Eden, C. (2004): Analyzing cognitive maps to help structure issues or problems. *Eur. J. Opl. Res.* 159: 673–686.

Eden, C. and F. Ackermann (1992): The analysis of causal maps. *Journal of Management Studies* 29(3): 309–324.

Eden, C. and F. Ackermann (1998): *Making Strategy: The journey of strategic management*. London: Sage.

Eden, C., S. Jones and D. Sims (1983): *Messing About In Problems*. Oxford: Pergamon Press.

Eden, C., S. Jones, D. Sims and H. Gunton (1979): Images into models: the subjective world of the policy maker. *Futures* (February): 56–62.

Edwards, W. (1991): Influence Diagrams, Bayesian Imperialism, and the *Collins* Case: An appeal to reason. *Cardozo Law Review* 13(2–3): 1025–1074.

Fine, P. E. M. (1993): Herd Immunity: History, theory, practice. *Epidemiologic Reviews* 15(2): 265–302.

Flood, R. L. and M. C. Jackson (1991): *Creative Problem Solving: Total Systems Intervention*. Chichester: Wiley.

Ford, D. and J. D. Sterman (1998): Expert Knowledge Elicitation for Improving Mental and Formal Models. *Sys. Dyn. Rev.* 14(4): 309–340.

Forrester, J. W. (1956): Dynamic Models of Economic Systems and Industrial Organizations (2003 republication of a 'Note to the Faculty Research Seminar. November 5, 1956' and MIT 'D-memo' zero). *Sys. Dyn. Rev.* 19(4): 331–345.

Forrester, J. W. (1958): Industrial Dynamics: A major breakthrough for decision makers. *HBR* 36(4): 37–66.

Forrester, J. W. (1960): The Impact of Feedback Control Concepts on the Management Sciences. In: *Collected Papers of Jay W. Forrester (1975 collection).* Cambridge, MA: Wright-Allen Press, 45–60.

Forrester, J. W. (1961a): *Industrial Dynamics*. Cambridge, MA: MIT Press.

Forrester, J. W. (1961b): Standard Symbols for Industrial Dynamics Flow Diagrams. *MIT D-memo* 41-1: 1–6.

Forrester, J. W. (1968a): Industrial Dynamics – A response to Ansoff and Slevin. *Mgmt. Sci.* 14(9): 601–618.

Forrester, J. W. (1968b): Market growth as influenced by capital investment. *Industrial Management Review (now the Sloan Management Review)* 9(2): 83–105.

Forrester, J. W. (1968c): *Principles of Systems*. Cambridge, MA: MIT Press.

Forrester, J. W. (1968d): Industrial Dynamics – After the first decade. *Mgmt. Sci.* 14(7): 398–415.

Forrester, J. W. (1970): Counterintuitive behaviour of social systems. In: *Collected Papers of Jay W. Forrester (1975 collection).* Cambridge, MA: Wright-Allen Press, 211–244.

Forrester, J. W. (1992): From the Ranch to System Dynamics. In: Bedeian, A. G. (ed.): *Management Laureates: A collection of autobiographical essays (vol. 1)*, Greenwich CT: JAI Press, 335–370.

Forrester, J. W. (1994): System Dynamics, Systems Thinking, And Soft OR. *Sys. Dyn. Rev.* 10(2–3): 245–256.

Forrester, J. W. (2007): System Dynamics – The next fifty years. *Sys. Dyn. Rev.* 23(2–3): 359–370.

Forrester, J. W. and D. W. Packer (1962): A Model For The Study of Corporate Growth. *MIT D-memo* 151-1: 1–128.

French, S. (1988): *Decision Theory*. Chichester: Ellis Horwood Limited.

Gardiner, P. C. and A. Ford (1980): Which policy run is best, and who says so? In: Legasto, A. A., Forrester, J. W. and J. M. Lyneis (eds.): *System Dynamics. TIMS Studies in the management sciences Vol. 14.* Oxford: North-Holland, 241–257.

Goodman, M. R. (1974): *Study Notes in System Dynamics*. Cambridge, MA: MIT Press.

Größler, A. (2004a): Quantification Makes Sense Even When Empirical Data Is Limited: A model of the Bhopal crisis. In: Kennedy, M. and G. W. Winch (eds.): *Proceedings of the 2004 International System Dynamics Conference (Oxford, England)*. Albany, NY: System Dynamics Society (CD based).

Größler, A. (2004b): Don't Let History Repeat Itself – Methodological issues concerning the use of simulators in teaching and experimentation. *Sys. Dyn. Rev.* 20(3): 263–274.

Homer, J. B. (1987): A Diffusion Model with Application to Evolving Medical Technologies. *Technological Forecasting and Social Change* 31(3): 197–218.

Homer, J. B. (1996): Why we iterate: scientific modelling in theory and practice. *Sys. Dyn. Rev.* 12(1): 1–19.

Homer, J. B. (2007): Reply to Jay Forrester's "System dynamics – the next fifty years". *Sys. Dyn. Rev.* 23(4): 465–267.

Homer, J. B. and R. Oliva (2001): Maps and Models in System Dynamics: A Response to Coyle. *Sys. Dyn. Rev.* 17(4): 347–355.

Howard, R. A. (1966): Decision Analysis: Applied decision theory. In: Herty, D. B. and J. Melese (eds.): *Proceedings of the fourth International Conference on Operational Methods*, New York: Wiley-Interscience, 55–71.

Howard, R. A. and J. E. Matheson (1984): Influence Diagrams. In: Howard, R. A. and J. E. Matheson (eds.): *Readings on the Principles and Applications of Decision Analysis, Vol. II*, Menlo Park CA: Strategic Decisions Group, 719–762.

Howick, S., F. Ackermann and D. Andersen (2006): Linking Event Thinking with Structural Thinking: Methods to improve client value in projects. *Sys. Dyn. Rev.* 22(2): 113–140.

Jackson, M. C. (2000): *Systems Approaches To Management*. New York: Kluwer/Plenum.

Jackson, M. C. (2003): *Systems Thinking: Creative holism for managers*. Chichester: Wiley.

Jackson, M. C. and P. Keys (1984): Towards a system of system methodologies. *J. Opl. Res. Soc.* 35(6): 473–486.

Jarmain, W. E. (ed.) (1963): *Problems in Industrial Dynamics*. Cambridge, MA: MIT Press.

Kelly, G. A. (1955): *The Psychology of Personal Constructs*. London: Weidenfeld and Nicholson.

Keys, P. (1988): System Dynamics: A methodological perspective. *Trans. Inst. Measurement & Control* 10(4): 218–224.

Klein, J. H. (1994): Cognitive Process and Operational Research: A human information processing perspective. *J. Opl. Res. Soc.* 45(8): 855–866.

Lane, D. C. (1994): With A Little Help From Our Friends: How system dynamics and 'soft' OR can learn from each other. *Sys. Dyn. Rev.* 10(2–3): 101–134.

Lane, D. C. (1998): Can We Have Confidence In Generic Structures? *J. Opl. Res. Soc.* 49(9): 936–947.

Lane, D. C. (1999): Social Theory and System Dynamics Practice. *Eur. J. Opl. Res.* 113(3): 501–527.

Lane, D. C. (2000): Should System Dynamics Be Described As A 'Hard' Or 'Deterministic' Systems Approach? *Syst. Res. & Beh. Sci.* 17(1): 3–22.

Lane, D. C. (2001): Rerum cognoscere causas: Part II – Opportunities generated by the agency/structure debate and suggestions for clarifying the social theoretic position of system dynamics. *Sys. Dyn. Rev.* 17(4): 293–309.

Lane, D. C. (2006): IFORS' Operational Research Hall of Fame – Jay Wright Forrester. *Int. Trans. OR* 13(5): 483–492.

Lane, D. C. (2008): The Emergence and Use of Diagramming in System Dynamics: A critical account. *Syst. Res. & Beh. Sci.* 25(1): 3–23.

Lane, D. C. and C. Smart (1996): Reinterpreting 'generic structure': evolution, application and limitations of a concept. *Sys. Dyn. Rev.* 12(2): 87–120.

Lane, D. C. and R. Oliva (1998): The Greater Whole: Towards a synthesis of system dynamics and soft systems methodology. *Eur. J. Opl. Res.* 107(1): 214–235.

Lane, D. C. and E. Husemann (2004): Movie Marketing Strategy Formation with System Dynamics: Towards a multidisciplinary adoption/diffusion theory of cinema-going. In: Maier, F (ed.): *Komplexität und Dynamik als Herausforderung für das Management: Festschrift zum 60. Geburtstag von Peter Milling*. Wiesbaden: Deutscher Universitäts-Verlag, 179–222.

Lane, D. C. and M. Schwaninger (eds.) (2008): *Theory Building with System Dynamics (Selected papers from the third European system dynamics workshop, University of St. Gallen, Switzerland)*. Special Edition of the international journal *Systems Research and Behavioral Science* 25(4).

Lane, D. C. and E. Husemann (2008a): System Dynamics Mapping of Acute Patient Flows. *J. Opl. Res. Soc.* 59(2): 213–224.

Lane, D. C. and E. Husemann (2008b): Steering without Circe: Attending to reinforcing loops in social systems. *Sys. Dyn. Rev.* 24(1): 37–61.

Macharis, C., J.-P. Brans and B. Mareschal (1998): The GDSS Promethee Procedure. *J. Dec. Sys.* 7(3): 283–307.

Machuca, J. A. D. (1992): Are we losing one of the best features of system dynamics? *Sys. Dyn. Rev.* 8(2): 175–177.

Miller, G. A. (1956): The Magical Number Seven, Plus Or Minus Two: Some limits on our capacity for processing information. *Psychological Review* 63(1): 81–97.

Milling, P. M. (1974): *Der technische Fortschritt beim Produktionsprozeß – Ein dynamisches Modell für innovative Industrieunternehmen*, Wiesbaden: Gabler.

Milling, P. M. (1986): Diffusionstheorie und Innovationsmanagement. In: Zahn, E. (ed.): *Technologie- und Innovationsmanagement*, Berlin: Duncker & Humblot, 49–70.

Milling, P. M. (1996): Modeling Innovation Processes For Decision Support And Management Simulation. *Sys. Dyn. Rev.* 12(3): 211–234.

Milling, P. M. (1999): System Dynamics at Mannheim University. *J. Opl. Res. Soc.* 50(4): 309–310.

Milling, P. M. (2002): Understanding and Managing Innovation Processes (Jay Wright Forrester Prize 2001 Lecture). *Sys. Dyn. Rev.* 18(1): 73–86.

Milling, P. M. and F. Maier (1996): *Invention, Innovation und Diffusion: Eine Simulationsanalyse des Managements neuer Produkte*. Berlin: Duncker & Humblot.

Mingers, J. (2003): A Classification of the Philosophical Assumptions of Management Science Methods. *J. Opl. Res. Soc.* 54(6): 559–570.

Mingers, J. and A. Gill (eds.) (1997): *Multimethodology: The theory and practice of combining management science methodologies*. Chichester: John Wiley & Sons.

Montibeller, G. and V. Belton (2006): Causal maps and the evaluation of decision options – a review. In: Franco, A., D. Shaw and M. Westcombe (eds.): *Problem Structuring Methods (Special Edition of the Journal of the Operational Research Society)* 57(7): 779–791.

Morecroft, J. D. W. (1982): A critical review of diagramming tools for conceptualising feedback system models. *Dynamica* 8(1): 20–29.

Morecroft, J. D. W. (2007): *Strategic Modelling and Business Dynamics: A feedback systems approach.* Chichester: John Wiley.

Murray, J. D. (1989): *Mathematical Biology*. Berlin: Springer-Verlag.

Paich, M. (1985): Generic Structures. *Sys. Dyn. Rev.* 1(1): 126–132.

Pfeffer, J. (2007): *What Were They Thinking? Unconventional wisdom about management.* Boston, MA: HBS.

Phillips, L. D. (1984): A Theory of Requisite Decision Models. *Acta Psych.* 56(1): 29–48.

Phillips, L. D. (1990): Decision analysis for group decision support. In: Eden, C. and J. Radford (eds.): *Tackling Strategic Problems: The Role of Group Decision Support.*

Pidd, M. (1996): *Tools For Thinking: Modelling in management science.* Chichester: John Wiley.

Pidd, M. (1999): Just Modeling Through: A Rough Guide to Modeling. *Interfaces* 29(2): 118–132.

Raiffa, H. (1968): *Decision Analysis: Introductory lectures on choices under uncertainty.* Reading, MA: Addison-Wesley.

Ramos, J. M. (1983): Some Modifications to the Burns Algorithm. *IEEE Transactions on Systems, Man and Cybernetics* smc-13(1): 108–110.

Rand, G. (2006): IFORS' Operational Research Hall of Fame. *Int. Trans. OR* 13(6): 583–584.

Reagan-Cirincione, P., S. Schuman, G. P. Richardson and S. A. Dorf (1991): Decision Modelling: Tools for strategic thinking. *Interfaces* 21(6): 52–65.

Richardson, G. P. (1986): Problems with casual-loop diagrams (originally published in 1976). *Sys. Dyn. Rev.* 2(2): 158–170.

Richardson, G. P. and A. L. Pugh (1981): *Introduction to System Dynamics Modelling with DYNAMO (republished edition).* Cambridge, MA: Productivity.

Richardson, G. P., E. F. Wolstenholme and J. D. W. Morecroft (eds.) (1994): Systems Thinkers, Systems Thinking. *System Dynamics Review 10(2–3).*

Richmond, B. (1994): Systems Thinking/System Dynamics: Let's just get on with it. *Sys. Dyn. Rev.* 10(2–3): 135–157.

Riggs, J. L. and M. S. Inoue (1975): *Introduction to Operations Research and Management Science: A general systems approach.* New York: McGraw-Hill.

Roberts, E. B. (2007): Making System Dynamics Useful: A personal memoir. *Sys. Dyn. Rev.* 22(2–3): 119–136.

Roberts, N., D. F. Andersen, R. Deal, M. Garet and W. Shaffer (1983): *Introduction to Computer Simulation: A System Dynamics Approach.* Reading, MA: Addison Wesley.

Schaffernicht, M. (2007): Causality and diagrams for system dynamics. *Paper presented at the 2007 International System Dynamics Conference (Boston, USA).* Program Chairs: John Sterman and Rogelio Oliva.

Senge, P. M. (1990): *The Fifth Discipline: The art and practice of the learning organization.* New York: Doubleday/Currency.

Simon, H. (1976): From Substantive To Proceedural Rationality. In: Latsis, S. J. (ed.): *Method And Appraisal In Economics,* Cambridge: CUP, 129–148.

Sterman, J. D. (1988): A skeptic's guide to computer models. In: Grant, L. (ed.): *Foresight and National Decisions*, Lanham, MD: University Press of America, 133–169.

Sterman, J. D. (1994): Learning In And About Complex Systems. *Sys. Dyn. Rev.* 10(2–3): 291–330.

Sterman, J. D. (2000): *Business Dynamics: Systems thinking and modeling for a complex world.* New York: Irwin/McGraw-Hill.

Sterman, J. D. (2006): Learning from Evidence in a Complex World. *American Journal of Public Health* 96(3): 505–514.

Stoneman, P. (2002): *The Economics of Technological Diffusion*. Oxford: Blackwell.

Tsouvalis, C. and P. B. Checkland (1996): Reflecting on SSM: the dividing line between 'real world' and 'systems thinking world'. *Syst. Res.* 13(1): 35–45.

Tufte, E. R. (2006): *Beautiful Evidence*. Cheshire, CT: Graphics Press.

Vennix, J. A. M. (1996): *Group Model-building: Facilitating team learning using system dynamics*. Chichester: Wiley.

Watson, S. R. and D. M. Buede (1987): *Decision Synthesis: the principles and practise of decision analysis*. Cambridge: Cambridge University Press.

White, M. M. and S. W. Palocsay (1999): Decision Explorer (Software Review). *OR/MS Today* (October): 62–64.

Williams, T., C. Eden, F. Ackermann and A. Tait (1995): The effects of design changes and delays on project costs. *J. Opl. Res. Soc.* 46(7): 809–818.

Made in the USA
Las Vegas, NV
13 November 2024

11635937R00201